People
as
Partners

People as Partners

---

second edition

Jacqueline P. Wiseman
University of California—San Diego

CANFIELD PRESS • San Francisco
A Department of Harper & Row Publishers, Inc.
New York • Hagerstown • London

Cover Design: Jaren Dahlstrom

For information address Harper & Row, Publishers, Inc.,
10 East 53rd St., New York, N.Y. 10022.

Library of Congress Cataloging in Publication Data

Wiseman, Jacqueline P.   comp.
    People as partners.

    Includes bibliographical references.
    1. Family life education—Addresses, essays, lectures.
I. Title.
HQ10.W57 1977   301.42   77-2008
ISBN 0-06-389425-4

77 78 79   10 9 8 7 6 5 4 3 2 1

Contents

6   Problems and Crises

Life being what it is, people do not live "happily ever after" when they decide to live together. They will encounter problems as well as good fortune. A test of the relationship is how the partners react to the problems.

7   The Family as a Locus for Personal Development

Unlike other social institutions, the family is built on close, primary relationships and life-time affiliation in many cases. With such permanency and emotional importance, the family has a great effect on the personal development of all its members.

8   The Family in Later Portions of the Life Cycle   304

The family as a unit has its own life cycle, just as individuals do. As parents become older and children become adults, the dynamics of family relationships change.

9   Continuing Pressures for Change in the Family   346

The stage is being set today for the family of tomorrow. Many factors will affect the form of the family, its viability, and even its emotional content and the relationships of its members.

10   Societal Reactions and Policy Intervention to Changing Family Forms

Preface to the Second Edition

The study of the family is one of the fastest changing fields of research in the social sciences today. During the past decade, it has gone from a somewhat stolid but respectable sub-area to the leading edges of sociological and psychological investigation. Research topics reflect a vibrant, alive, questioning stance toward the shibboleths about family at all stages of the life cycle.

The first edition of *People as Partners* was published at a time when the family was beginning to be challenged by some because of the way in which it set boundaries on the expression of basic emotions. The necessity for formal marriage vows, for traditional sex roles for husbands and wives, and even having children were questioned. It appeared that individual development and rewarding life styles were taking precedence over the holistic family welfare.

Now, nearly a decade later, while new patterns of marriage and family living are still emerging, some old patterns have been reaffirmed. The family remains an integrating and sheltering force in society despite numerous modifying forces for change. As an institution, it remains the locus of the most vital and dynamic human emotions—love, hate, self-sacrifice, sadness, happiness, sexual desire, and security, to name but a few.

Today, most of the general issues raised in the first edition remain important, but they have developed into somewhat different and certainly more complex forms. A brief chapter by chapter comparison of the two editions will give some indication of these subtle shifts. For example, in Chapter 1, *The Status of the Family in Society,* the emergence of a changing climate was observed. In the second edition, the forces for change have become an accepted fact of social life, calling upon us to understand the many reasons for these pressures to remodel the family in greater depth. On the other hand, the first edition caveat that there existed a historical case for a potential reversion to traditional family forms after periods of experimentations is reaffirmed.

In Chapter 2, *The Partner-Selection Process,* the second edition finds both researchers and social beings have become somewhat more sophisticated about the mechanics of this phenomenon than they were a decade before. Thus, the personal, racial, religious, and social class characteristics people look for in potential partners is of less interest than the strategic aspects of selection and the disparity of tactical position between the sexes. Living together without legal sanction was noted as a new phenomenon in the first edition. Now it is an accepted part of today's partner-selection process on a fairly widespread basis. People now want to know more about the various outcomes of this practice.

The second edition changes in Chapter 3, *Sex Partners and Sex Problems,* continue to reflect the interest and concern about male and female sexuality as a part of the general interest in techniques sparked by the sexual revolution, but in a far broader sense. Whereas, the first edition presented findings of sex research bearing on the physiological and psychological aspects of sexual techniques, the second recognizes the complex interpersonal concerns that have emerged as a result of the new sexually permissive atmosphere. The sexual revolution may have dispelled some of the initial fears, shames, or hesitancies traditionally surrounding intercourse, but, at the same time, it has proved devoid of an ethos by which people can understand their partner and cope with the emotional aspects of an act that has many more possible meanings than were ascribed to it formerly.

In Chapter 4, *Partner Arrangements in Role Responsibilities and the Division of Labor,* the first and the second editions present an interesting juxtaposition of views. The initial articles offer discussions of the different traditional roles and responsibilities in marriage for each spouse. The discussion of the "working wife" emphasized the importance of a woman handling an outside career so as not to slight the wife-mother role. Today, with working couples on the increase, the second edition reflects growing awareness of the absence of parity between the spouses in task division based on traditional sex roles. Discussion of the relationship of employed women and men to each other as spouses, and to society as a whole, reflects the growing awareness that certain rigid patterns of marital interaction can create particularly frustrating existences, especially for women. Additionally, we have become increasingly aware of the variety in role enactment which can give marriage relationships quite different ambiences.

The first edition Chapter 5, *Children as Junior Partners,* called attention to the very real adjustment problems of new parents, and to the traditional tasks of the family in the socialization of children. The second edition reflects more recent awareness of the ambiguous position the father occupies in the family, growing doubts by some about the cost-satisfaction ratio of raising children, and the continued existence of the phenomenon of the sixties, the communal parenthood, with particular emphasis on the contrast in child-rearing practices with the traditional.

Some of the crises mentioned in the first edition Chapter 6, *Problems and Crises,* are now discussed elsewhere in the book. Extramarital affairs and divorce have become more than personal problems—they are pressures for change in family form. Widowhood is covered in a new section on middle and later portions of the life cycle. Retained in this section of the second edition are crises which can occur *despite* alterations in family form and where coping is necessary and adjustments must be made. These include the development of incompatibility and discontent with one's mate and one's marriage, the serious illness of a family member, and unemployment of a family member. The articles discuss the response of traditional families. How alternative forms will react is still an important question to be answered.

Chapter 7, *The Family as a Locus for Personal Development,* is new, reflecting the continuing ethos of individualism, the desire for family relationships that do not stifle personal development or limit personal expression. This problem was touched on tangentially in the first edition in an article that discussed how spouses can remain exciting to each other (and themselves). Today, there is a growing awareness of what the marital relationship could be and what it often deteriorates to being. Current sex role expectations have resulted in women being shortchanged more often in marriage than men, although husbands are not without problems. Both spouses can benefit from growth allowed beyond sex role expectations.

The addition of Chapter 8, *The Family in Later Portions of the Life Cycle,* represents a growing awareness of the importance of understanding the middle years and old age if there is to be a complete picture of the marriage relationship. The problems that middle-aged and older couples face are different in quality and quantity than those which were faced by young marrieds. Children become adults and sometimes almost completely sever the family cord, the economic situation of the family may change sharply, or a spouse will die, all of which will result in emotional upheavals and the necessity for new personal adjustments.

Chapter 9, *Continuing Pressures for Change in the Family,* includes discussions of the interplay between population characteristics and age of marriage, proportion remaining unmarried, number of children, length of parenthood, and household composition. These facts are vital to understanding the larger picture of family change in the United States. The black family is also discussed with particular attention to its different history as this accounts for its current culture and form. Pressures for more personal freedom within marriage have been a catalyst for the commune movement. Today, we know more about the variety of relationships in this approach to the family than we did in its earlier years.

There was no policy chapter in the first edition. Chapter 10, *Societal Reactions and Policy Intervention,* is a recognition of the growing importance of the need to review public policy and even attempt to modify societal reaction to people who dare to be different.

Chapter 11, *Summing Up—What Form for the Family in the Future?* reflects the current debate as to whether the family as we know it will survive all the pressures for change, and the losses and/or gains to both individuals and society if it should not. The final article suggests the possibility of a return to traditional marriage, with some important modifications reflecting the desire for reform that has been expressed by the dissident voices of the past decade.

No longer are radical reformists so certain they are right. They have encountered too many problems to be able to maintain this stance. Likewise, traditionalists have been forced to see some of the disservices marriage and family can do to individuals. Now that ideological dogma is being discarded in both directions, study of the family should be more intellectually challenging and yield more practical information than ever before.

JACQUELINE P. WISEMAN
University of California—San Diego

Introduction

These are exciting but confusing times for people to become partners. The family is in a state of transition. Old norms are being challenged and new norms are being fostered; a battle is raging. The emphasis on individual development, pleasure, and satisfaction rather than the good of the family group appears at an all-time high. No clear-cut expectations of standard family relationships currently exist.

The family is seen by many as filled with flaws—unhealthy for adults, children, and other living things. Yet the very nature of humans is to desire not only the contact with social groups, but also to need close interaction with one special group. Thus, as one form of the family appears to be cast aside, other forms are being created to fill the void.

These new social structures, founded for certain purposes or to redress assumed wrongs, have almost always developed in unintentional directions as well as in the manner planned. Thus participants in experimental family forms created in the best of faith, for the purpose of providing more freedom, self-actualization, or for whatever goal, may find themselves faced with another set of problems growing out of their very attempt to handle the flaws of the earlier family structure!

For instance, we find that when college dormitories become coeducational and loosely chaperoned if at all, male and female students spend more time together in informal dormitory living, but date or go out together less than when they lived in separate quarters, because of the "incest taboo" (i.e., fear of continuing to see the person after an always-possible breakup). Heterosexual cohabitation of college students does solve some problems of getting to know a possible marriage partner better and in a freer atmosphere before taking a legal step, but many cohabiters experience problems not unlike those found in the early part of any marriage and thus the arrangement is not completely predictive as to how the partnership will take shape over the years.

Sex is another problematic area. It seems almost impossible to free sexual relations from their burden of strong social control and inhibiting guilt or shame. Persons espousing sexual freedom of one kind or another actually find they must develop many inhibiting rules for each new approach they create. The advent of technically sophisticated methods of contraception has not abolished unwanted pregnancies, because it has failed to change traditional romantic notions about intercourse.

Love is probably the most potent force of all in partner formation, because being loved helps us love ourselves and, in turn, loving ourselves makes us able to love others. Yet love creates its share of paradoxes. Persons in love are assumed to want the very best for their loved ones. However, avowed lovers may exploit each other. Men, while loving their wives, may try to force them into a role that is stultifying to their continued mental growth. Children, on whom parents lavish a great deal of love, often return very little when they grow up. Marriages that are conceived in love and exciting companionship can gradually diminish into a dull partnership over the years that is brightened only by illicit affairs.

One of the strengths of the family has been its ability to help its members when trouble strikes. However, there is now some evidence that this function may be unsuited to the free-flowing individualistically oriented family structures currently being invented by persons to overcome some of the faults of the family. Governmental welfare services may be more urgently needed for antiestablishment families than for their traditional counterparts.

Despite the numerous contradictions in the family form of today, there are many positive developments. The high-powered game playing and status striving that were important parts of what was once called *dating* are somewhat less prominent portions of the partner selection process today, although some strategic aspects still exist. Women's sexuality, so long a mystery, is finally being understood and women no longer have to fake orgasms. Increasing numbers of wives are entering the labor force, thereby improving the life-style of their families and their own self-development at the same time (if they are able to get into some sort of a satisfactory and creative career). They will also make more exciting mates for their husbands. Women are also becoming aware that they need not be the only persons in the family responsible for the housework and child rearing. They are asking for—and often receiving—equal assistance from their husbands. Many of these men, in turn, are discovering that they enjoy certain aspects of what they had formerly considered a "woman's world," and further, they are glad to shed some of the demands of the traditional masculine role. Studies also show that many spouses actually enjoy their older years together when the children have left home.

Whole groups of people are demanding, and gradually receiving, equal status and civil rights with those in power. The Woman's Liberation Movement, the Gay Liberation Movement, and the Gray Panthers (elderly people) are just some of the groups refusing to play out the stereotyped roles that they once accepted.

What does all this mean to the family? In this decade, the possibilities are wide open. Individuals are both creating and reacting to new elements in the culture and social structure. From the big demographic, legislative, and social service picture on down to communes, swinging groups, cohabiting couples, marrieds, and single-parent families, there are pressures both for continued change and a return to tradition. By the next edition of *People as Partners,* some resolutions may be discernible! But there are none now. We may be puzzled and insecure, but one thing we cannot complain about: The family is not a dull topic!

1

The Status of the Family in Society

The family has been called a *universal institution,* inasmuch as some form of it has been found in all societies. In Western industrialized countries, the family has evolved to a form referred to by sociologists as the *traditional monogamous nuclear family,* consisting of a father (the head of the household), a mother, and their children, living separately from, and no longer responsible to, their own aging parents. Included in society's expectations for such a family is a division of labor in which the male works outside the home and supports the family while the female is a full-time housewife and mother handling most of the matters concerned with socialization of the children. Sexual fidelity between mates is the ideal norm, although it is recognized that the male might have discreet sexual excursions if not satisfied by one partner. Because of the father's economic importance to the family, his needs and wishes are considered to take precedence over other members. Marriage is considered a life-time contract and, while divorces are granted, a divorced status is a somewhat stigmatized one.

As all of us are aware, this traditional family system has been the subject of criticism for some time. Its detractors claim that standard sex roles and division of labor among family members are stunting the growth potential of involved individuals in various ways. Expectations of sexual fidelity are thought to be unnecessary restrictions on an enjoyable activity, and to be a violation of personal freedom. Children are not necessarily considered a desirable addition to the family, nor is the nuclear family considered the best locus for their socialization. Thus one hears cries for a change for the good of all concerned.

This chapter contains a discussion of both sides of this debate on family form—what has been, what is, and what should be. What actually *will* be, however, is anyone's guess. The social forces buttressing the traditional family are still strong and vital; alternative approaches, while stridently advocated, are as yet without the structural reinforcements and experience needed for success. A burst of radical experimentation may be followed by conservative reaction.

3

A gradual slipping back to traditional ways of pairing and family life-styles may occur. History, however, never quite repeats itself. The forces for change will aid in the dissemination of some new norms of male-female behavior that, in all probability, will be melded with the more acceptable norms of the past, so that the results might be more accurately labeled a sort of cyclical *progressive evolution*.

The Family as an Element in the Social Structure

William J. Goode

Down through the ages, in all societies, the family has demonstrated its amazing tenacity. In human group life, the family is the pivotal mechanism—both affecting and being affected by society. Because it socializes the young and continues to exert control and influence far beyond the early years, the family is a major mediating influence between society and the individual. Governmental awareness of this power of the family is evidenced by the amount of control the government attempts to exert over family matters. Revolutionaries and utopians often seek to reduce or terminate the power of the family. Usually, however, they find that even among their most loyal compatriots the family bond is not easily overcome. Even when apparently eradicated or on an obvious decline, the family has shown amazing power of resilience; news of its death and/or disintegration must be considered greatly exaggerated.

In all known societies, almost everyone lives his life enmeshed in a network of family rights and obligations called role relations. A person is made aware of his role relations through a long period of socialization during his childhood, a process in which he learns how others in his family expect him to behave, and in which he himself comes to feel this is both the right and the desirable way to act. Some, however, find their obligations a burden, or do not care to take advantage of their rights. This wide range of behavior leads to one of the commonest themes of conversation found in all societies—just what the duties of a given child or parent, husband or wife, cousin or uncle ought to be, and then, whether he *has* done his duty. This type of discussion is especially common in societies undergoing industrialization, where arguments are frequent concerning the duties of women.

From William J. Goode, ed., *The Family* © 1964. (Englewood Cliffs, N.J.: Prentice-Hall, 1964), pp. 1–3, 4–6. Reprinted by permission of Prentice-Hall, Inc.

The intense emotional meaning of family relations for almost all members of a society has been observable throughout man's history. Philosophers and social analysts have noted that society is a structure made up of *families,* and that the peculiarities of a given society can be described by outlining its family relations. The earliest moral and ethical writings suggest that a society loses its strength if people fail in their family obligations. Confucius thought, for example, that happiness and prosperity would prevail in the society if only everyone would behave "correctly" as a family member—which primarily meant that no one should fail in his filial obligations. The relationship between a ruler and his subjects, then, was parallel to that of a father and his children. Similarly, much of the early Hebrew writing, in Exodus, Deuteronomy, Ecclesiastes, Psalms, and Proverbs, is devoted to the importance of obeying family rules. In India, too, the earliest codified literature (the *Rig-Veda,* about the last half of the 2nd millenium B.C., and the Law of Manu, about the beginning of the Christian Era) devote great attention to the family.

From time to time, imaginative social analysts or philosophers have sketched out plans for societies that *might* be created—utopias—in which new definitions of family roles are presented as solutions to traditional social problems. Plato's *Republic* is illustrative of this approach. He was probably the first to urge the creation of a society in which all people, men and women alike, would have an equal opportunity to develop their talents to the utmost, and to achieve a position in society solely through merit. Since family relations in all known societies prevent a selection based solely on individual worth, in Plato's utopia the tie between parents and children would play no part, because no one would know who was his own child or parent. Conception would take place at the same times each year at certain hymeneal festivities. Children born out of season would be eliminated (along with those born defective); all children would be taken from their parents at birth, and reared under challenging conditions by specially designated people. Similarly, experimental or utopian communities, like Oneida, the Shakers, and the Mormons in this country, insisted that changes in family relations were necessary to achieve their goals.

Included among the aims of many revolutions since the French Revolution of 1789 has been a profound alteration in family relations. Since World War II, the leaders of all countries undergoing industrialization have introduced new laws, well ahead of public opinion, intended to create family patterns that would be more in conformity with the demands of urban and industrial life.

All these facts, by demonstrating that philosophers, reformers, and religions, as well as secular leaders, have throughout history been at least implicitly aware of the importance of family patterns as a central element in the social structure, also suggest that the social analyst must understand family behavior in order to understand social processes generally.

The strategic significance of the family is to be found in its *mediating* function in the larger society. It links the *individual* to the larger social structure.

A society will not survive unless its many needs are met, such as the production and distribution of food, protection of the young and old, the sick and the pregnant, conformity to the law, the socialization of the young, and so on. Only if *individuals* are motivated to serve the needs of the society will it be able to survive. The formal agencies of social control (such as the police) are not enough to do more than force the extreme deviant to conform. Socialization makes most of us wish to conform, but throughout each day we are often tempted to deviate. Thus both the internal controls and the formal authorities are insufficient. What is needed is a set of social forces that responds to the individual whenever he does well or poorly, supporting his internal controls as well as the controls of the formal agencies. The family, by surrounding the individual through much of his social life, can furnish that set of forces.

The family then, is made up of individuals, but it is also part of the larger social network. Thus we are all under the constant supervision of our kin, who feel free to criticize, suggest, order, cajole, praise, or threaten, so that we will carry out our role obligations. Even in the most industrialized and urban of societies, where it is sometimes supposed that people lead rootless and anonymous lives, most people are in frequent interaction with other family members. Men who have achieved high position usually find that even as adults they still respond to their parents' criticisms, are still angered or hurt by a brother's scorn.

Thus it is *through the family* that the society is able to elicit from the *individual* his necessary contribution. The family, in turn, can continue to exist only if it is supported by the larger society. If the society as a larger social system furnishes the family, as a smaller social system, the conditions necessary for its survival, these two types of systems must be interrelated in many important ways.

· · · ·

The Family as a Unique Institution

A brief consideration of certain peculiarities of the family as an element of the social structure will suggest how better theory and a fruitful general approach are needed in this area.

The family is the only social institution other than religion which is *formally* developed in all societies. Indeed, the term "social structure" in anthropology is often used to mean the family and kinship structure. By contrast, some have argued that in certain societies legal systems do not exist because there is no formally organized legislative body or judiciary. Of course, it is possible to abstract from concrete behavior the legal *aspects* of action, or the economic aspects, or the political dynamics, even when there are no explicitly labeled agencies formally in control of these areas in the society. However, the kinship statuses and their responsibilities are the object of both formal and informal attention in societies at a high or a low technological level.

Family duties are the *direct* role responsibility of everyone in the society, with rare exceptions. Almost everyone is both born into a family and founds one of his own. Each person is kinsman to many. Many people, on the other hand, may escape the religious duties which others take for granted, or the political burdens of the society. Almost no family role responsibilities can be delegated to others, as more specialized obligations can be in a work situation.

Participation in family activities has a further interesting quality, that though it is not backed by the formal punishments supporting many other kinds of obligations, almost everyone takes part nonetheless. We must, for example, engage in economic or productive acts, or face the alternative of starving. We must enter the army, pay taxes, and appear before courts, or face physical penalties and force. However, no such penalties face the individual who does not wish to marry, or refuses to talk with his father or brother. Nevertheless, so pervasive and recurrent are the social pressures, and so intertwined with indirect or direct rewards and punishments, that almost everyone either conforms, or claims to conform, to family demands.

Next, as suggested earlier, the family is the fundamental *instrumental* foundation of the larger social structure, in that all other institutions depend on its contributions. The role behavior that is learned within the family becomes the model or prototype for role behavior required in other segments of the society. The content of the socialization process is the cultural traditions of the society; by passing them on to the next generation the family acts as a conduit or transmission belt by which the culture is kept alive.

Next, each individual's total range of behavior, how he budgets his time and energies, is more easily visible to the family than to outsiders. Family members can evaluate how the individual is allocating his time and money in various of his role activities. Consequently, the family acts as a source of pressure on him to adjust—to work harder and play less, or go to church less and study his school lessons more. In all these ways, the family is an instrument or agent of the larger society; its failure to perform adequately means that the goals of the larger society may not be attained effectively.

A further striking characteristic of the family is that its major functions are separable from one another, but in fact are not separated in any known family system. The family contributes these services to the society: reproduction of the young, physical maintenance of family members, social placement of the child, socialization, and social control. Clearly, all these activities could be separated. The mother could send her child to be fed in a neighborhood mess hall, and of course some harassed mothers do send their children to buy lunch in a local snack bar. Those who give birth to a child need not socialize the child. They might send the child to specialists, and indeed specialists do take more responsibility for this task as the child grows older. Parents might, as some eugenicists have suggested, be selected for their breeding qualities, but these might not include any great talent for training the young. Status-placement might be accomplished by random drawing of lots, by IQ tests or periodic examinations in physical and intellectual skills, or by polls of popularity, without regard to an individual's parents, those who socialized or fed him, or others who controlled his daily behavior.

Separations of this kind have been suggested from time to time, and a few hesitant attempts have been made here and there in the world to put them into operation. However, three conclusions relevant to this kind of division can be made. (1) In all known societies, the *ideal* (with certain qualifications to be noted) is that the family be entrusted with all these functions. (2) When one or more family tasks are entrusted to another agency by a revolutionary or utopian society, the change can be made only with the support of much ideological fervor, and sometimes political pressure as well. (3) These instances are also characterized by a gradual return to the more traditional type of family. In both the Israeli *kibbutzim* and the Russian experiments in relieving parents of child care, the ideal of completely communal living was urged, in which husband and wife were to have only a personal and emotional tie and not be bound to each other by constraint. The children were to see their parents at regular intervals but to look to their nursery attendants and mother-surrogates for affection and direction during work hours. Each individual was to contribute his best skills to the cooperative unit without regard to family ties or sex status (i.e., there would be few or no "female" or "male" tasks). That ideal was maintained for a while, but behavior has gradually dropped away from the ideal. The only other country in which the pattern has been attempted on a large scale is China. Whether the Chinese commune will retreat from its high ambitions remains to be seen, but chances are good that it will follow the path of the *kibbutz* and the Russian *kolkhoz*.

Various factors contribute to such a deviation from the ideal, but the two most important sets of pressures cannot easily be separated from each other. First is the problem, also noted by Plato, that individuals who develop their own attitudes and behaviors in the usual Western (i.e., European and European-based) family system do not adjust to the problems of the communal "family." The second is the likelihood that when the family is radically changed, the various relations between it and the larger society are changed, so that new strains are created, demanding new kinds of adjustments on the part of the individuals in the society. Perhaps the planners must develop somewhat different agencies, or a different blueprint, to transform the family.

Concretely, some of the factors reported as "causing" a deviation from the ideal of family living are the following. Some successful or ambitious men and women wish to break away from group control, and leave to establish their lives elsewhere. There, of course, they do not attempt to develop a communal pattern of family living. Parents do try to help their own children secure advantages over other children, where this is possible. Parents not only feel unhappy at not being with their children often enough (notice that youngsters need not "be home for meals"!), but perhaps some feel the husband-wife relationship itself is somewhat empty because children do not occupy in it their

9

usually central place. Husband and wife usually desire more intimacy than is granted under communal arrangements. Finally, the financial costs of taking care of children outside the family are rather high.

These comments have nothing to do with "capitalism" in its current political and economic argument with "communism." It merely describes the historical fact that though various experiments in separating the major functions of the family from one another have been conducted, none simply evolved slowly from a previously existing family system; and the two modern important instances represent a retreat from the ideals of a previous generation. It is possible that some functions can be more easily separated than others; or that some family systems might lend themselves to a separation of functions more easily than others. Nevertheless, we have to begin with the data available now. Even cautiously interpreted, they suggest that the family is a rather stable institution.

The Fragmented Family

Robert Thamm

The opening reading has established the power and tenacity of a social institution such as the traditional family imbedded as it is in the social system. Thamm here discusses the flaws of the traditional institution. As the family evolved from the three-generational extended structure to the two-generational nuclear form, its members gained more freedom, but lost some security. Reduced size for the monogamous family means less flexibility in selection of role models and more possessive dependence of children and parents on each other. Standard sex role assumptions, so integral to this type of family, rob each member of his or her complete potential. Instead the individual is socialized to develop in stereotypical fashion. These narrowly defined roles tend to erect a barrier preventing one sex from empathizing with and understanding the other. Combined with monogamy, this can mean that sexual expression becomes a tedious routine.

> *The family may neither vanish nor enter upon a new Golden Age. It may— and this is far more likely—break up, shatter, only to come together again in weird and novel ways.*
>
> *—Alvin Toffler*
> Future Shock

Compared with our modern nuclear family, our traditional extended family was generally more supportive. The early American family, for example, was dominated and controlled by the father, and women were expected, primarily for economic reasons, to have several children. The early family as a group was composed of husband and wife, numerous children, children's children, and dependent relatives. Spinsters and widows were in great demand for their competence in household management, and adult male relatives were assets because of their ability to work the land and contribute to the family income. Many families, usually related, lived close to one another and shared the responsibilities for providing economic and psychological aid to other family members. Children typically had several adults of each sex with whom they could closely identify.

As the children developed strong emotional ties to relatives other than their biological parents, their dependencies for economic as well as psychological rewards became more dispersed. Because of this diffused involvement, children in the early American family could tap several sources of gratification. In the event that one or both of their parents left the family setting, were deceased, or even temporarily rejected them, the children had easy access to other adults who were willing to care for them and assume the roles of their parents. Because of the larger size of the family clan, a great deal of security for the children was built into the structure itself.

Although this kind of family provided for economic and psychological security in the rearing of children, in other respects it was quite restrictive. Occupational choices were extremely limited, roles were rigidly defined, and strong punishments were handed out to those who dared to innovate. Social mobility, both up and down in the class structure and from one position to another at the same social level, was curtailed in the former by an inflexible caste or status structure and in the latter by custom and tradition. Membership in a family was usually determined along blood lines and by marriages planned and controlled by family elders.

The authoritarian traditional family was usually headed by a strong patriarch. There was little respect for women and children who were relegated to lower status positions. The presence of a rigid hierarchy of family positions with privileged persons filling the top ranks was apparent in most traditional societies. An excessive demand on conformity, order, and obedience was reflected in the symbolism and the seriousness of the family rituals. Many people seemed to be property or possessions of someone else (for example, slaves, concubines, child labor, subservient wives) and people functioned according to highly restrictive roles and values. There was little or no opportunity for rebellion or change.

Our traditional family, then, had some characteristics which contributed to increasing need-satisfaction and some which did not. The extended structure provided the opportunity for children as well as adults to develop a larger number of deep and more meaningful relationships within the family itself. This could have led to a greater amount of economic and psychological security if it weren't for the many accompanying restrictions, taboos, and authoritarian impositions. There was little question of the identity of each member, for few if any alternatives were available and expected behavior was rigidly constructed. These limitations, because they were largely predetermined, failed to take individual differences into account. Individuals, for example, could not select their own mates nor the number of mates. They could not easily move from one community to another without greatly disrupting the course of family living. Rather than encouraging people to go into positions which corresponded to their own traits, capacities, and interests, these capacities and interests were made to fit roles dictated by age, sex, and social class of parents.

Frustrations and discontent arising from the failure of our traditional family to adapt to individual needs laid the groundwork for its eventual breakdown. In addition, the Industrial Revolution, bringing the deterioration of an agrarian economy, gave impetus to a growing technology. Because of better forms of communication and transportation, family and individual mobility became more prominent and acceptable. The migration from a small, highly personal, and integrated family situation to a more impersonal, bureaucratic, and urban environment had the effect of fragmenting the relatively stable and secure extended structure.

Two conclusions can be drawn from examining these changes in family structure.

1. Children and adults in the *traditional structure* had a greater amount of psychological security due to the larger number of people who served as dependable sources of emotional and affective gratification, but they had a great deal of frustration due to the rigid system's failure to allow for the expression of individual differences.

2. Children and adults in the *nuclear structure* have much less psychological security and fewer emotional resources, due to the small size of the unit, but have increased mobility, flexibility, and freedom to make choices, due to increased structuring for individual differences.

Our nuclear family evolved favorably in all respects except in the area of providing increased security and emotional benefits for its members. Although the fragmentation of the extended form, because of its psychologically threatening implications, should be considered an undesirable trend, the breakdown of traditional authoritarian structures which occurs in the nuclear type can be seen as a more positive development.

One could, for example, point to many liberating effects which this change has brought about. It has liberated creative activities from the bondage of familistic servitude and opened up the personality market for freer unfolding of talent, aptitude, and individualistic choice. In short, one must not lose sight of the general principle that any change brings about a host of reactions. Some may be judged functional and some dysfunctional.[1]

Today, the most traditional extended family structure and norms have almost completely disappeared. Our primary socializing agency, the extended family, failed to adapt to a modern, growing, industrialized world. From the shattered extended family, a residual, smaller, and more mobile nuclear structure emerged. The general characteristics of this newer family contrast sharply with the traditional type. Blood relatives are located throughout a wider geographic area and children must rely more upon parents than other relatives for economic and psychological support. These conditions as well as the smaller size of the unit and the detached and depersonalized surroundings of urban life, result in a lesser sense of family security.

In other respects, the nuclear family offers us an increasing amount of flexibility, mobility, and emancipation from the traditional family's rigid and discrimatory practices. Choice of occupation is a function of interest and capacities, rather than being ascribed. Because of the breakdown of the rigid caste system, the possibility of upward social mobility increases, allowing for greater variation in the selection of roles. Younger members of the traditional family migrate to larger urban centers, breaking down the authority of the family elders and providing themselves with the opportunity to select their own mates and govern their own family units. A more recent trend emancipating women from narrow household and child-rearing duties, as well as from male domination, allows them wider choices in deciding occupation and general life style. The relaxing of the traditional structure thus enables family members who were most discriminated against to rebel and to search for new identities.

However, alternative institutions which center around more egalitarian values are not readily available. Because of this, an increasing number of single and divorced people who are in some way involved in a personal crisis are desperately searching for a new way of life but have no place to go, no institution to identify with, and no hope of enjoying any kind of family living. Their alienation and despair suggest the grave necessity for experimenting with and institutionalizing new life styles and family forms.

．　．　．　．

SIZE OF THE FAMILY

One of the major changes that has been taking place in our family is the gradual decrease in the number of members constituting a unit. The average size of the U.S. household decreased from 5.5 per unit in 1850 to 3.14 in 1971.[2] As a result of this decrease, our family seems to be moving toward more and more isolation residentially and economically; with this fragmentation it is becoming less able to meet the more generalized traditional functions. The family now focuses on socialization and the exchange of emotional support and affection. The small size of our nuclear family and its isolation thus have ramifications on the socialization process of children and their emotional security. Parent-child tensions are increased, leading to a greater possibility of dissolution. As the family unit becomes smaller, the chances for parental error increase. "Each child becomes more crucial."[3]

Somewhat contrary to these notions are findings suggesting that smaller families are less authoritarian, and that there is more parental affection toward children and vice versa and thus less parental stress.[4] Perhaps the crucial factor is the ratio of children to parent figures in the family unit. Maybe larger families with larger numbers of adults than children will show the most favorable dispositions and gratifications on the part of the members. Such a family might be more representative of the general population in terms of age distribution. If there are about two or three adults for each child in society, perhaps this ratio could be maintained in larger families not based upon kinship. Our chil-

14

dren would have several parental models to relate to in contrast to the situation in large middle-class families where many children in the unit are confined to one or two parent relationships. Tension and competition for affection could be lessened allowing for greater integration in the family.

Parents also use children to satisfy their own needs, sometimes more than they use themselves to satisfy the children's needs. They "hang on" their children their own unrealized potential and see not the child but the projected image of the person they themselves would like to be. The loving parents clothe their children with a great deal of themselves and cling to the children possessively. The fewer the number of children they have, the more intense the desire to retain their property. In a more extended family or in the family with a larger number of children, this need on the part of the parents to possess their children might be decreased or at least diffused.

Because of the possessive demands which many of us impose upon our children, there is an increased tension which occurs in the life cycle of the family as the children reach maturity and begin to break the parental ties. This tension is aggravated by the extreme dependence on the parents encouraged in the small nuclear family. The lack of continuity, as family members grow up and move into adult roles, is a weakness in the nuclear structure. The move involves breaking off old ties and creating a new family unit which is stable largely to the extent to which the new marriage is stable. The probability of this stability resulting is rather dismal as seen later in a review of the trends in divorce rates.

Children's emotional identification and dependency upon one adult male and one adult female are also limiting factors in our modern family. In our extended family, young boys and girls could choose models from among a number of visible adult relatives and could derive an image of what he or she wanted to be. But in the nuclear family such choice is limited, particularly if one parent is not easily observable. As a consequence, children of nuclear families seek models in their peer groups and adults outside of the family setting. Generally, these models lead to conflicts in loyalties, value systems, and time commitments.

* * * *

SEX-ROLE DIFFERENCES

It is an understatement that the role of the adult male in the marriage and family institutions has been traditionally different from that of the adult female. Men were socially independent, complete individuals. Women, confined to reproductive and domestic roles, were never considered equal to men, those producers whose existence was justified by the work they did. The expectations of the husband-father in the nuclear structure are still highly differentiated from those of the wife-mother.

* * * *

15

Self-Alienation

Expectations in the family generally require, among other things, that men be more rational, independent, aggressive, self-confident, innovative, realistic, and competitive than women. Women are expected to be more emotional, dependent, passive, self-conscious, conventional, idealistic, and compassionate than men. By not allowing each sex to display the characteristics attributed to the opposite sex, half of these personality traits are suppressed. Males, for example, may feel inadequate if they fail to control their emotions, become dependent upon females in some way, or are not interested in competitive activities. Females, on the other hand, may feel some negative social pressures if they become too intellectual, respond aggressively, or become economically independent. Thus, each sex must hold back half of its potentials so as to fit into the prevailing structure.

* * * *

Sex-role differences thus restrict us from expressing half of our humanity. The sex-role structure in the family is ineffective in that it leads to self-alienation, projection, restrictions in expressing certain behaviors and emotions, mate idealizations, possessiveness, and jealousy.

Cross-Sex Empathy

Because males and females have been socialized into such different kinds of roles, they have become different kinds of people with different kinds of behaviors, attitudes, and feelings. A common complaint among husbands and wives is that their spouses do not understand them. This might be attributed to the differences in the way they were raised. These differences make it more difficult for them to put themselves symbolically in the place of their mates and to feel and think as their mates feel and think. If being able to empathize with one's spouse is an important part of understanding, and understanding and empathy between men and women are desirable, then perhaps the perpetuation of differences in the roles of males and females in the modern family should be halted.

* * * *

Intimacy. Sex-role differences are imposed upon us rather early in life. During adolescence the norms in dating groups emphasize sexual antagonism and exploitation, since males and females gain prestige in peer groups in directly opposite ways: the male by maximizing physical contact and minimizing expenses, the female by minimizing the former and maximizing the latter. Intimacy is minimized if each partner, even during physical contact, is keeping an account with regard to these dating norms.

These opposing norms then create social distance between males and females at an early age, and it is no surprise that this distance, antagonism, and exploitation later carry over into the family setting. Thus, the nuclear family is not functioning to the extent to which it curtails an early, more open and frank interchange between the sexes leading to the development of intimacy. Sex-role distinctions learned by the young do not contribute to that end.

Sexuality and Sex-Roles

If sex-role differences lead to antagonism and a lack of intimacy, it would seem to follow that in situations in which these differences are magnified, problems in heterosexuality would be more common. In a cross-cultural study of marital sexuality, Lee Rainwater concluded that in societies with separation in the roles of husbands and wives, the couple will not develop a close sexual relationship, and the wife will not find sexual relations with her husband sexually gratifying.[5] Although the evidence is limited, sex-role distinctions seem to detract from satisfying sexual relationships.

• • • •

ROLE OF THE FEMALE

The problems inherent in the role of the female are of no recent origin. It is a part of the long-standing Christian tradition.

Unto the women [God] said, I will greatly multiply thy sorrow and thy conception; in sorrow thou shalt bring forth children; and thy desire shall be to thy husband, and he shall rule over thee.

—Genesis 3:16

And, as ruling husbands, men have imposed the duties which they found less desirable upon their wives. And their wives, as good Christian wives, have learned their roles well and have even thought these duties were honorable and fulfilling. But only when women decided to question the role structure of the "sacred" family were they able to see, in an objective sense, the inequality, the oppression, and the exploitation built into the traditional female role.

In the traditional role, women are not given the opportunity to grow to their full capacities and to retain their human individuality. They have been bought off by men to be content with washing diapers, cleaning house, buying groceries, and the like. Their reward is economic security; the cost, in many cases, is sexual and emotional gratification for their husbands.

Perhaps it is not an exaggeration to call the state of the housewife a sickness. Betty Friedan asks if the house of the American suburban wife is in reality a comfortable concentration camp. She suggests that they have adjusted to their biological role and have become dependent, passive, childlike; they have given up their adult status to live at a lower human level. The work they do is simple, endless, monotonous, and unrewarding.[6]

The increasing isolation of the nuclear family is best exemplified in the housewife role, for the male is out of the house all day and therefore can be neither overlord nor companion.

With the father absent, radio and television provide the mother with a watery substitute for adult companionship. A young colleague told me recently that his wife leaves the radio on all day merely to hear the sound of a grown-up voice. The continual chatter of little children can be profoundly irritating, even to a naturally affectionate person. The absence of servants from nearly all American middle class households brings the wife face to face with the brutalizing features of motherhood and housework. If she had the mentality of a peasant, she might be able to cope with them more easily.[7]

But this isolation, leading to emotional and intellectual poverty, is not universal. In societies in which the domestic role works, the housewife is part of a large extended family or a close-knit village community or both. Both the small size of the nuclear family and its isolated nature contribute to the restrictions imposed upon the average housewife. But what happens to her under these kinds of conditions?

Many women attempt to escape the monotony and boredom of their daily existence. Perhaps TV soap operas provide the greatest escape for the American housewife. The afternoon "soaps" foster an ideology based upon female passivity, ineptness, and subservience, even for women of the highest professional status. They are raped, divorced, abandoned, misunderstood, given drugs, attacked by mysterious diseases and go mad, and have more brain tumors and die more than the males do. The TV commercials follow the same pattern, showing women inside of the home involved in household tasks 43 percent of the time, as adjuncts to men 38 percent of the time, and 17 percent of the time as sex objects. The plots in these series may make the housewife feel safe and secure but may make these same viewers dissatisfied with their own dull lives. When she turns off the TV, looks into the mirror, and greets her husband, the comparison is not pleasant.[8] Thus, women use the mass media, the soap operas, the love magazines, and the gossip they can conjure up in coffee sessions with neighbors as mechanisms for creating fantasies. In these fantasies, they live as they would like to live, but they live vicariously, not in the real world. Their escape from reality only points out the possibility of a more severe problem: a total reliance upon fantasies for satisfying needs frustrated by the family system. The possibility of schizophrenia, or even worse, suicide, looms over them.

Others may try to recreate themselves through their children. They may project so much of themselves onto their daughter or son that they find the child's presence indispensable. The "adjusted" American mother, in this context, maintains the needs of her child leaving little time for other things. This she sees as evidence of her conscientiousness. She insists that a child needs her full attention and that she loves her baby so much she is glad to devote her life to her child. The latter is true enough. The result may well be a continuous destructive interference with the life of the child and an inevitable emptiness in her own.

If she cannot find fulfillment through her children, she may turn to material things. Since she *does* nothing, she seeks self-fulfillment in what she *has.* If these material possessions become her *raison d'être,* she could spend her days endlessly polishing and cleaning them, always being prepared to display them proudly to whoever might pass by. She eventually loses sight of *who she is,* for all of her rewards come as a result of *what she has.*

When fantasy, vicarious living, and materialism have failed, she still has two realistic alternatives, neither of which contributes to the maintenance of the old family. Either a job or an affair may serve as a release from domesticity.

Another problem which faces the woman in the family is her role in the completion of the child-rearing functions. Increasingly, child rearing is concentrated into a substantially shorter period of time than before. As of the most recent information, women are on the average likely to bear their last child at the age of 30 or 31. Thus, partly by living longer in a better state of health and partly by reducing the time span of their primary attention to motherhood, women are freed for other functions. There is a vacuum between the ages of 40 or 45 until death, an average of about 30 years. I already noted the increased suicide rate of women over 40. This would suggest a deterioration of their psychological well-being, to say the least. A study of Vassar graduates who were 20 or 25 years out of college showed that for the most part they were adjusted as suburban housewives, conscientious mothers, and were active in their communities. It was also found, however, that upon graduation they did not continue to grow mentally, emotionally, or personally, and after 20 years, those with the most psychological problems were the most traditionally feminine.[9]

The role of the housewife thus seems detrimental to the growth and development of middle-aged women. It defines their function as child rearing but fails to provide a meaningful alternative function once the children are reared. It is almost impossible for elderly women to participate in a child-rearing role later in life, given the present evolution of the family.

The housewife role, in summary, limits the aspirations which most women have of reaching their full potential. They are commonly exploited and forced to become parasites. In their traditional role, they fail to grow mentally, emotionally, and personally; in the more isolated family setting, they are left with fantasy, materialism, possessiveness of their children, and a feeling of emptiness in their later years. The fate of the married woman, as expressed by Simone de Beauvoir, is one of becoming "a gilded mediocrity lacking ambition and passion, of aimless days indefinitely repeated, of living a life that slips away gently toward death without questioning its purpose."[10] The prognosis is more positive. Women's roles are beginning to become more optional and diversified. As the possibilities for new wife and mother roles increase, there might emerge a more egalitarian sex role structure in the family of the future.

ROLE OF THE MALE

The male's role in the family perhaps is more appealing than the female's. He initially marries to obtain anchorage which satisfies his sexual-emotional needs and provides him with a sense of belonging and of self-esteem. He desires to confine his wife and children to the home for ready access to his gratifications, but not to be himself confined. He is bored by repetition, and seeks novelty, opposition, risks, and friends outside the marriage unit.

But the absence of the father from the family setting in many situations places a good deal of stress on the stability of the marriage and upon the father-child relationship. The successful maintenance of the family unit is partially a function of the extent to which the father is present. When occupational and military obligations call him away for long periods of time, family continuity is disrupted. The children lose the one adult male model with whom they can identify and the wife is left without the one male companion the institution allows her. During this period, the wife has to assume some responsibility for the children that would normally belong to the husband. When the father returns, the roles must be redistributed and the lines of authority reestablished. In a research project during World War II, Reuben Hill discovered that it was not always easy for the couple to "pick up where they left off" when the father returned from the armed forces. An unpublished study was made of blue-collar construction workers who had to work out of town. Almost all of these men agreed such jobs posed real problems for them and their families.[11]

An additional problem is that the family is not designed for a mobile father. The needs which the family supplies to the father are also commonly frustrated during his departure. He is expected to remain faithful and lonely until the time he can be reunited with his family. If his commitment to his wife is exercised, he endures his frustration. When this happens, the family system can be seen as reinforcing sexual-emotional masochism on the part of the wife as well as the husband. If the commitment is not abided by, extramarital relationships may lead to deceit at least, or at most, to dissolution of the marriage.

The stability of the family is also contingent upon the sexual compatibility of the couple. Family stress is more likely to occur if the husband is not a satisfactory lover or becomes involved with another woman. Men are expected to be faithful to their wives or leave the home and marry "the other woman." What all of this means is that if anything happens to the marriage, the male may find himself separated from his children, in spite of his honest desires to be a good father.

The closeness between the father and his children is dependent upon a close relationship between the man and his wife. Family norms place strong emotional pressures upon the father as he is torn away from his children due to an incompatible marriage. The increased mobility of the father, due to occupational or military obligations, as well as the expectation that he leave the family setting in case of an incompatible marriage, both contribute to a weakening of the father-child relationship and the loss of the only adult male model for male children. Kingsley Davis argued that the weak link in the family group is this father-child bond. He maintained that there is no necessary association and no easy means of identification between the two as between the mother and child.[12] The weak bond between father and child may be attributed to the trend which gives the father more freedom and mobility and more access to additional sexual involvements.

Our family has thus failed to evolve in a direction which would allow for this increased mobility and still provide a basis for family stability, strong bonds between adult males and children, and an adult male role model. It also fails to provide for continuous sexual-emotional gratification for separated parents whether the separation be one day or a divorce.

SEXUALITY NORMS

Our old nuclear family has a monogamous structure. The couple enact a contract wherein they explicitly agree that other intimate relationships with the same or the other sex shall cease and each partner shall be the sole source of comfort and gratification for the other. Within these norms exists an assumption that it is only possible to love one mate. We as spouses are expected to meet each of our partner's sexual and emotional demands and in effect come to accept the equation of our mate satisfying our needs with the needs themselves. So long as our spouse is ever-present to satisfy frustrated needs (which doesn't happen), there is no problem. Even if habitual behaviors are not effective, we have difficulty recognizing this fact or altering our behaviors. What I am suggesting is that norms which provide for only one source of gratification, as does monogamy, are not adequate. They provide no alternative means of sexual-emotional satisfaction. In specifying our mate as the sole means of meeting these needs, such norms prevent continuous gratification and frequently lead to neurosis.[13] Part of this neurosis can be attributed to the more or less total mutual dependency that the members of the couple develop for each other, which in turn may lead in monogamy to monotony, restrictiveness, the demise of romantic love, and other evils.

Perhaps one of these "evils" is the degeneration of sexual desire for the spouse and the increase in vicarious fantasy. An example of this is

the case of a woman of twenty-five who could attain a slight orgasm with her husband if she imagined a powerful older man was taking her by force. Thus the wife imagines that she is being raped, that her husband is not himself but an *other*. The husband enjoys the same dream; in his wife he is possessing the legs of some dancer he has seen on the stage, the bosom of a pin-up girl whose picture he has looked at, a memory, an image. Or he may fancy his wife desired, possessed, violated, which is a way of restoring her lost alterity.[14]

If it were possible to get an open response from married couples of long standing, some vicarious sexual imagery as described above might be more the rule than the exception.

One manifestation of vicarious living is a structured over-dependency on our spouse, a need for his or her constant presence and acceptance. This need is often mistaken for love. The intense pleasures produced while being with that one person who is allowed to give such gratifications can be more objectively defined as a dependent attachment rather than a loving commitment. These attachments are possessive and lack the essential characteristics of genuine love—devotion, understanding, and extreme satisfaction in the individuality of the partner.

The effect of all of this is a mechanical, depersonalized interaction between the two people who seem to be controlling and threatening each other, or in the less extreme cases, compromising themselves to maintain the dependency contract. Sexual pleasure and exploration are degraded to a form of "joint masturbation." If they continue to make love to one another, it is in a sense of shame and guilt, for they are aware of their extramarital desires. For this reason the frequency of lovemaking may decrease over the duration of the marriage. For sexual release, each member of the couple may resort to increased independent masturbation in secret. A friend of mine, for example, told me that he masturbated more when he was married than at other times. During his marriage he hesitated to inform his wife of his self-gratification for fear of reprisal. Because of the mechanistic, routine and somewhat frustrating manner in which he related sexually to his wife, he preferred to fantasize, at his convenience and need, that he was having sexual intercourse with his wife's best friend, to whom he was very attracted, and thereby satisfy himself. Many couples, however, cannot admit this kind of repression to themselves, least of all to each other. So they live the vicarious life regarding each other only as a tool for the satisfaction of their needs.

Another problem arises because monogamous norms restrict sexual activity to our spouses. When gratification is not sufficient on the part of one of the couple, frustration results. If this need cannot be satisfied in some manner consistent with the conjugal norms, aggression directed to our mates or to others may develop. Restrictions on sexual expression, far from neutralizing aggression, tend to arouse it, just as the frustration-aggression hypothesis suggests. Sexuality norms function in the monogamous situation when both members are equally demanding of sexual gratification and when monotony and a lack of desire for variety prevail. Not very many couples are able to meet these conditions. Differences in demand for frequency of sexual intercourse and a real desire for a variety of sexual partners (repressed in most couples) places a heavy stress on the monogamous bond.

There is frequent resort to divorce, but within the pretension of monogamy, promiscuous petting outside of marriage, adultery, prostitution, and various other forms of nonmonogamous sex relations are quite prevalent. Our monogamy is honored more often in theory than in practice. A. C. Kinsey found that by age 55, for example, one out of two American men engaged in extramarital sex. These figures are conservative because they are so outdated. In a recent study comparing the prevalence of extramarital relations to Kinsey's findings 25 years ago, it was found that young husbands are only a little more likely, but young wives are much more likely, to engage in extramarital sexual activity today. Twenty-four percent of wives and 32 percent of husbands under 25 had done so. Virginia Satir elaborates by pointing out that many people engage in either extramarital affairs or some kind of polygamy (mate-swapping or consecutive marriages).[15]

Monogamy is talk for friends and relatives; polygamy is the reality of our guarded behavior and our subjective feelings and desires. In maintaining the monogamy myth, we have perpetuated the sacredness of the marriage institution and have discouraged experimentation with possibly more rewarding family models. In maintaining the monogamy myth, we have also reinforced a norm that has partly led us to become jealous, possessive, guilt-ridden, self-repressive bundles of anxiety, full of fear and frustration. In confining our mates, we have helped destroy ourselves. The norms which govern this kind of activity surely must be ineffective in part, if not in their totality.

• • • •

Notes

[1] Hans Sebald, *Adolescence: A Sociological Analysis* (New York: Appleton-Century-Crofts, 1968), p. 51.

[2] U.S. Bureau of the Census, *Statistical Abstract of the United States, 1972* (Washington, D.C.: Government Printing Office, 1972), p. 39.

[3] E. E. LeMasters, *Parents in Modern America* (Homewood, Ill.: Dorsey Press, 1970), p. 4.

[4] F. Ivan Nye, John Carlson, and Gerald Garrett, "Family Size, Interaction, Affect and Stress," *Journal of Marriage and the Family* 32, no. 2 (May 1970): 216–225.

[5] Lee Rainwater, "Marital Sexuality in Four Cultures of Poverty," *Journal of Marriage and the Family* 26, no. 4 (November 1964): 466.

[6] Betty Friedan, *The Feminine Mystique* (New York: Dell Publishing, 1963), p. 296.

[7] Barrington Moore Jr., "Thoughts on the Future of the Family," in *Identity and Anxiety,* eds. Maurice Stein et al. (New York: The Free Press, 1960), p. 395.

[8] Nora Scott Kinzer, "Soapy Sin in the Afternoon," *Psychology Today,* August 1973, p. 48.

[9] Mervin B. Freedman, "Studies of College Alumni," in *The American College,* ed. Sanford Nevitt (New York: Wiley, 1962), p. 878.

[10] De Beauvoir, *Second Sex,* p. 422; also, F. Ivan Nye and Feliz Bernardo, *The Family, Its Structure and Interaction* (New York: Macmillan, 1973), pp. 255–260.

[11] Reuben Hill, *Families Under Stress* (New York: Harper and Brothers, 1949). For unpublished study, see LeMasters, *Parents,* p. 143.

[12] Kingley Davis, *Human Society* (New York: Macmillan, 1949), p. 400.

[13] Putney and Putney, *Adjusted American,* p. 13.

[14] De Beauvoir, *Second Sex,* p. 421.

[15] A. C. Kinsey et al., *Sexual Behavior in the Human Male* (Philadelphia and London: W. B. Saunders Co., 1948), p. 259 and pp. 585–588; for the more recent study, see Morton Hunt, "Sexual Behavior in the 1970s," *Playboy,* October 1973, p. 88; Virginia Satir, "Marriage as a Human-Actualizing Contract," in *The Family in Search of a Future,* ed. H. A. Otto (New York: Appleton-Century-Crofts, 1970), pp. 62–63.

2

The Partner Selection Process

Family membership comes about in two ways—a person may be born or adopted into a family (family of orientation) or may start his or her own family (family of procreation). In the first approach, the new member usually has no choice; but in the second, selection is consciously made. How this pairing is handled in a society where the family of orientation no longer has the power to manage such matters is of sociological interest as well as personal concern to people currently tackling the matter.

Early studies of mate selection focused almost exclusively on the similarity or complementarity of traits, background characteristics, and interests of each person in an engaged pair. "Happiness" or "success" in marriage was often predicted on these bases. Now, sociologists are beginning to realize what people involved in finding partners have always known instinctively—that there is more to this enterprise than merely locating someone of similar interests and background to whom you can relate. There are strategies, there are hidden norms, there is impression management, and there is still trial and error—with women more prone to making mistakes about selection of a partner than men. Both sexes, however, base decisions that will have a lifetime impact on less than adequate information. This may be even more true today because despite more freedom of association on an intimate level, norms of partner selection and attraction are in great flux and one of the assets of tradition—predictability—is lost. For most partners, there is no clear-cut guidance for action, but a blend of many approaches that can produce unexpected behaviors, often seeming contradictory and puzzling to participants. The emotional involvement of love may further cloud any attempts at objectivity.

Knowledge and Power in Bargaining for a Marriage Partner

Philip M. Marcus

The traditional boy-meets-girl, boy-falls-in-love-with-girl, boy-marries-girl approach to pairing (note who is active and who is passive!) is analyzed here in market theory terms, which, in many ways, are quite appropriate. Although choice of mate is more crucial to the woman than the man, because his success in a job will probably determine her lifestyle, it is the male who has more adequate clues on which to make this important (and perhaps lifetime) decision. The potential wife has little idea as to how well her husband-to-be will do in an occupation. He, on the other hand, can tell how she will act in the expressive sphere of the home more easily—behavior that will affect his life with her. This is because a woman can show her homemaking abilities and her willingness to defer to the man's judgment (desirable traits in the traditional wife) before marriage, while a man cannot easily exhibit his career potential. He caters to her before they are married, but she is often unaware just how much she is to cater to him after the marriage. Once in the marriage, the wife's value peaks early, while the husband's value increases steadily, until he may view his wife as a liability. This quid-pro-quo approach to the marital relationship, while seemingly cold in nature, illustrates rather cogently why mutual interests and similar backgrounds may be the basis for initial attraction but may not be sufficient to sustain the equal interest of both partners in the marriage over time.

At present, a female's choice of mate lingers as one of her crucial decisions because virtually an entire life style hinges upon the husband's occupation and resources given to him. And yet, as important as this decision remains, a female receives relatively little training in selecting and obtaining a husband. The peer group, selecting its role models primarily from the popular arts, formulates

From Philip M. Marcus, "Courtship as Knowledge and Bargaining Power." Reprinted by permission of the author.

and governs the implementation of norms that affect a female's behavior.[1] The family establishes only the basic parameters or boundaries; a father's occupation provides material resources that place the girl in a general network of male and female social relationsips, but she selects among many sets of symbols that attract boys. Because mothers have been socialized at different times and places, they can only offer broad behavioral guidelines, and many of the symbols once considered valuable as exchange commodities with males, no longer attract. Indeed, an attractive adolescent girl may inadvertently threaten her mother psychically, as glamor symbols have different meanings over the life cycle.[2]

Generally, adolescent girls become somewhat alienated from the adult society while in the process of selecting and obtaining a husband. Requiring great visibility, their clothing fashions become exaggerated and a unique slang and language develops. Adults often punish their behavior with males when affective commodities appear too freely given and not bargained prudently.[3]

If young girls receive relatively little assistance from their parents, and rely increasingly on peers, they will become concerned with paying debts to friends rather than family, and will have little incentive to obey parental directives.[4]

In the process of selecting a mate, a female maximizes her opportunity to partake fully in the American value system. While many of the specific sets of symbols used, e.g., dress, vocabulary, charm, reflect the overall socio-economic level of her father, the young female still employs a greater degree of individuality and competitive tactics than usually considered appropriate for the traditional woman's role. Inadvertently, the educational system trains the female to compete, and very successfully, with males and other females. But with the exception of courtship, females use these adaptive skills hesitantly and sparingly. Either females play a relatively submissive role, or cloak their aggressiveness into devious and socially acceptable channels.[5]

Males, in striking contrast to females, receive direct and exclusive training for an occupation. Successful job performance will supposedly win rewards of money, prestige and, indirectly, a desirable wife. Therefore, the male must focus upon and learn the tasks one performs as an adult, and the formal educational system, controlled by adults, precisely delineates the steps toward success. Ironically, success in the male role induces one to act out, think creatively and independently, while the education system constrains and directs these adult virtues. Females, less rewarded by the occupational structure, find themselves thrust onto peers for support and less upon the educational opportunities. Thus, females receive less adult control and little inculcation of the values of independence and autonomy; indeed, with less adult supervision, the society enjoins females to internalize docile and compliant behavior.

At the point when one actually decides to select a specific mate, the male possesses better predictors of his future wife's behavior than the female has about her husband. Here again the occupational system, and the training attendant upon it, mitigates against the female. Usually in his early 20's, no one expects the male to have arrived at the apex of a career. In most cases, with schooling incomplete, or while serving on a first job, the male continues to acquire additional knowledge and experience for later social mobility. The ultimate position of the male, then, remains unknown, and the female selects one whose potential appears adequately satisfactory. Obviously, a female does possess many clues, such as the male's performance in school, his father's occupation and the career to which he aspires. However, one cannot confuse clues with evidence. If she tries to ascertain some measure of the male's potential, strong norms requiring marriage based on love mediate against careful status estimation and assessment.[6] Ironically, a female's parents often become those who most strongly suggest that the male's status potential receive close scrutiny and consideration. However, since the female has consistently rejected much of her parents' guidance while dating, she cannot accept and utilize this advice when selecting her mate.

At this point in their relationship, the male possesses relatively strong evidence when assessing the female. Should he encounter difficulties, he can observe whether or not his intended spouse offers supportive and sympathetic behavior. During sex activities that accompany dating, males can asertain the degree that females give or withhold symbols of social-emotional support (e.g., caresses, kisses) and the amount of bargaining necessary to receive them. Courtship provides males with an opportunity to trade companionship, manifestations of interest and the provision of entertainments, for expressive behavior. Status as an exchange commodity remains a potential that the female does not and cannot consider because the male also uses expressive behavior in exchange. The female evaluates, then, her own resources and the ability to bargain effectively, and assumes she can use these skills when the male finally obtains additional instrumental commodities. To some extent, then, both partners focus their analysis of exchange behavior upon the female's commodities. As we shall see, the male's commodities change while those of the female remain relatively stable.

EARLY MARRIAGE

During the first few years of marriage, aside from those couples patently mis-mated, romantic overtones of courtship decreasingly becloud the relationship. Expectations, vague and general at marriage, now require bargaining for specification in the unwritten marital exchange contract. During this time, a male's instrumental status remains vague and potential, while a female begins rewarding immediately in expressive behavior. The female's costs start to mount as her profits remain relatively small; she must still calculate on the future. Conversely, the male debt rises as the value of his return rises above his investment.[7]

Females often take a job in order to reduce the financial burden on the male, thereby increasing their investment in the male's future potential to reward. Young females often work in a relatively depreciated and minor capacity, lower than their training and ability would predict or dictate: they hold subordinate positions with little responsibility. Because they consider the job temporary, advancement and personal satisfactions from it become relatively unimportant: pregnancy or a husband's transfer will induce the wife to leave the job. Indeed, the lack of gratification from the job, being normatively determined, makes it easier to move if necessary.

If the female acquires and utilizes some of the traditional male commodities at first, the early period of marriage finds the male utilizing expressive symbols to a greater extent than he will in later years. His attentiveness and emotional demands all flatter the female. Then, too, he often provides assistance in the upkeep of the house. However, as the advancements on the job continue, he increases his investments at work and decreases social-emotional or expressive inputs into the family.

Gouldner has suggested that indebtedness may stabilize a system when one must accumulate resources to repay the debt.[8] This may partially explain why, during the early years of marriage, the male continues to invest heavily in his work, and make adjustments to new communities and social relationships. He repays his debt to his wife with a relatively steady increase of rewards obtained in the form of raises, promotions, and other symbols of social advancements. Society recognizes the male's contribution to the family enterprise, i.e., he is a good provider.

But social relationships on the job affect the husband-wife exchanges. Anxieties created may be reduced partially by peer interaction, and decrease the male's dependence on the female for social-emotional support; he has alternatives to sources for these commodities. The female finds it relatively difficult to help with male job anxieties when she is removed from the specific circumstances, and lacks adequate training to administer therapy. A further complication is that male job anxieties may portend social failure, thereby threatening the female's investment in her husband. Thus, his job tensions contribute to her anxieties, decreasing her ability to provide expressive commodities.

The female, on the other hand, provides the marriage with few tangible and measurable commodities. She consumes the bulk of the male's earnings, and, at best, virtuously becomes a good manager who tries never to over-extend the family resources. She initially resists social pressures to conceive a child until the male can absorb the entire financial responsibility. In contrast to the male, then, female inputs rapidly decline, thereby decreasing male profit. Hence, his satisfaction in early marriage is lower than the female's, whose disillusionment accumulates at a continual but accelerating rate.[9]

When the female leaves her job and becomes a full-time homemaker, she confronts a new set of demands for which she received little preparation. Certainly, no formal education has trained the female for her household tasks. Schools generally focus upon symbolic manipulation and, inadvertently, depreciate manual tasks in the home. If the female has machinery to assist her, e.g., prepared foods and cleaning appliances, the value of her output decreases further.[10] Whereas a formerly held job had prescribed duties, structured and integrated with other persons, the female now finds herself confronted by a series of tasks whose performance is interrupted by the demands of others as well as by her own inclinations. Peer interaction cannot reduce anxieties created by the lack of structure or inadequate training because the female's own home or apartment isolates her from others. Initiating interaction requires social skills, entails possible rejection, or acknowledges inferiority.[11] The costs of peer interaction compare unfavorably for the female who has moved from job holder to homemaker when contrasted to those relatively structured social exchanges at work, e.g., coffee breaks, lunch contacts, or car pools.

The advent of the first child tends to complicate the exchanges between the two marital partners. First of all, the appearance of the child increases the social value of the family by performing a replacement function. Then, too, Slater has speculated that the *first* child prevents social regression by the married couple, i.e., the child is entrusted to the parents only under the close supervision and guidance of social representatives, such as doctors and teachers.[12] This supervision imposes demands upon the family to comply with norms; failure to do so brings about sanctions for the couple.

Pregnancy forces a renegotiation of a family's exchange rates. Producing a child increases the social value of the female more than the male. The child, even unborn, becomes to the male a competitor for the female's expressive output. In order to prevent his own profit loss, and bargain more effectively, the male must increase the set of rewards he gives the female. He may work harder to insure the security of his job, his social prestige and other exchange commodities. The norms also compel a male to decrease the price of his commodities and lower his demands for expressive outputs. For some women, pregnancy becomes a state of legitimated semi-invalidism, a dependency whereby output is sharply curtailed.[13]

Producing a child increases some rewards for the female, and lowers some costs, but others mount. The actual handling and caring for the child adds manual labor, a depreciated activity. The female's education has not provided her with techniques for child care and they must be learned rapidly from some social representative, i.e., a relative, a doctor, a written authority.[14] Society's emphasis upon proper child care, coupled with vague prescriptions and the absence of specified duties, and the female's lack of training, all increase costs by creating anxiety. The relative isolation of the female in her own home decreases the possibility of anxiety reduction through social interaction with peers, forcing her to rely even more heavily on the social representatives. The more the intrusion of social representatives, the more manifest the female's ineptitude, the lower the value of her output. At present, nursery and formal schooling for children constitute but another link in a chain of depreciations of the female's output value. Child abuse, whose occurrence appears across all social classes, may be but one consequence of the frustratingly low return on the female investment.[15]

THE MIDDLE YEARS OF MARRIAGE

For convenience, we consider the middle years of marriage as commencing with the partners at age 35.[16] Actually, depending upon the male's occupation, a family will attain the situation we describe slightly earlier or later; however, the 35–40 year old group will certainly experience changes in their marital relationships.

We have noted that at this point in the mariage, males provide potentially high status for the female in exchange for social-emotional support. The male promise, however, is impossible to attain fully because no clearly defined upper limits exist, i.e., no criteria for the acquisition of success. At approximately age 35, the male reaches an occupational asymptote and begins to reformulate his expectations. The major job commitments ahve been made and the possibilities for increased status have been set. While minor changes continue to emerge, e.g., raises in pay and position, they will not radically alter the family position and its relationships within a community. The 35 year old junior execu-

29

tive who falters on his way to the top may begin to seek alternative sources of job satisfaction.

At this time, the female also experiences reformulation of expectations. In the marriage, she has invested social-emotional support with the expectation that increased status from her husband will result. However, the return she has received has not met her expectations; the costs have continued to mount. In order to increase her profit, the female seeks to modify her bargaining power with the male, thereby increasing her rewards.

Of the available female behavioral alternatives, a withdrawal from the relationship appears most obvious, but this precludes the possibility of reclaiming the husband's debt. Divorce is also costly when the female has children who require care and her own job market skills have decreased. Those skills she possessed have lain fallow for approximately a decade, and new techniques in her specialty have emerged that require additional training; she often lacks confidence in interpersonal skills with men which may have deteriorated because she interacted primarily with children and other non-working women. Punitive norms often make many working mothers feel they neglect or partially hinder their children's development.[17]

Some women extend their participation in community affairs and voluntary associations. Activity in voluntary associations undoubtedly provides some rewards, but the larger society that does not fully comprehend work performed without pay, minimizes such service.[18] The prestige that women bring to the family through their contacts in voluntary associations remains secondary and subordinate to the male's occupational position.

The male at this time will seek sets of reward alternatives to rectify the inequality of marital exchanges. He depreciates the rewards from marriage, claiming unfulfilled expectations and disenchantment with the mate.[19] The experience of a sense of debt becomes a feeling of guilt and inadequacy because of the inability to compensate. Withdrawing from the partner partially relieves the feeling of guilt as it lowers the value of another's commodities as rewards. Hostility toward the person who arouses a sense of inadequacy and guilt also devalues the worth of the other's rewards.

Males increase participation in community affairs and voluntary associations as alternative sources of rewards. For example, rates of voting increase for persons over the age of 35, as does participation in community organizations.[20] Kinsey reports that educated males decrease the use of marital intercourse as a source of sexual outlet at about this age.[21] The male can use his bargaining power with younger women in the community, such attachments providing the fantasy of making him appear young once again, without limit and ready to start on his endless pursuit of success.[22]

NOTES

[1]Talcott Parsons, "Age and Sex in the Social Structure of the United States" in *Essays in Sociological Theory* (Glencoe, Illinois: The Free Press, 1954), pp. 92–93.
[2]Below we shall argue that adolescent girls use glamor symbols to attract boys, but middle age women use them to compensate for low rewards in marriage.

[3]Divorcees and widows face the same problems because they act as threats to married women in the communities.

[4]Relative to the male, the female adolescent is more dependent upon the family. The concern here is to emphasize the low utility of the girl's family, the lack of guidance from adults, the value of the adolescent peer group to supplant the adult world.

[5]Mirra Komarovsky, "Cultural Contradictions and Sex Roles, " *American Journal of Sociology* 52 (September 1946), pp. 184–189.

[6]William J. Goode, "The Theoretical Importance of Love," *American Sociological Review* 24 (February 1959), pp . 38–47.

[7]"Distributive justice may, of course, fall in the other direction, to the man's advantage rather than to his disadvantage, and then he may feel guilty rather than angry; he has done better for himself than he ought to have done. But he is less apt to make a prominent display of his guilt than of his anger. Indeed a man in this happy situation is apt to find arguments convincing to himself that the exchange is really not to his advantage at all." Homans, *op. cit.*, pp. 75–76.

[8]Alvin W. Gouldner, "The Norm of Reciprocity," *American Sociological Review* 25 (April 1960), p. 175.

[9]Boyd C. Rollins and Harold Feldman, "Marital Satisfaction Over the Family Life Cycle," *Journal of Marriage and Family Living* 32 (February 1970), p. 25. The reader should remember that we are only discussing the early years of marriage at this point.

[10]The increased use of machinery in the home does not decrease manual labor for the female; it merely raises the expectations and standards she tries to meet.

[11]Blau, *op. cit.*, p. 98.

[12]Philip E. Slater, "On Social Regression," *American Sociological Review* 25 (June 1963), p. 356.

[13]The frequency of morning sickness early in the pregnancy, a dramatic symbol, proclaims the renegotiation of exchange rates.

[14]In this connection, an interesting study would be the specification of family relationships and infant feeding. Breast-feeding increases the costs of the child to the female but may increase her claims for limited output to the male, e.g., she has interrupted sleep. Bottle feeding, if performed partially by the male, deprives the new mother of some of her bargaining power. An important contribution, consistent with our analysis, of husband-wife relationships during the early years of marriage and child rearing can be found in Alice S. Rossi, "Transition to Parenthood," *Journal of Marriage and The Family* (February 1968), pp. 26–39.

[15]The proper preparation of food, formally a valued female output, decreased in value with improved technology. Automobiles enable one to reach a restaurant easily and prepared foods, stored at home under refrigeration, compete very effectively with the completely home cooked meal. The value of the wife's cooking lies no longer in the taste of food, but in the symbol of the effort itself. As a trivial example, advertisers have learned their products sell better if the woman can say she "made it." For this reason eggs and milk are frequently left out of preparing baking mixes. A comprehensive, role-oriented description of housewives can be found in Helena Z. Topata, *Occupation: Housewife* (New York: Oxford University Press, 1971).

[16]Those researchers who utilize life cycle stages would call the period we are to describe late Stage IV, early Stage V.

[17]Partial withdrawal from the relationship, a very unstable state, entails high psychic and social costs with almost random rewards. For example, sexual liaisons are usually temporary excursions. Parsons discusses at some length reasons why the glamor role is relatively unrewarding to the married female. Parsons, *op. cit.*, p. 99.

[18]Most well rewarded charitable work, controlled by males, has become professionalized.

[19]Rollins and Feldman report marital satisfaction is lowest in Stage IV and rises only slightly in Stage V. Rollins and Feldman, *op. cit.*, p. 25. See also Peter C. Pineo,

"Disenchantment in the Later Years of Marriage," *Marriage and Family Living* 23 (February 1961), pp. 3–11.

[20]Seymour Martin Lipset, *Political Man* (Garden City, New York: Anchor Books, Doubleday and Company, 1963), p. 189.

[21]A. C. Kinsey *et al.*, "Social Level and Sexual Outlet," in R. Bendix and S. M. Lipset, (eds.) *Class, Status, and Power* (Glencoe, Illinois: The Free Press, 1953), p. 306.

[22]Adultery for the female, relatively more costly than for the male, receives more severe negative sanctions when detected. Also, female social interaction is relatively limited, providing few desirable contacts; she must make greater effort than the male and her bargaining power is low compared to younger females. In adultery, males may fantasize their rewarding youth, obtaining flattery when in contact with a younger female; but women engaged in extra-marital affairs almost invariably form liaisons with older men. These liaisons may provide temporary titillations, but impede the construction of rewarding fantasy when youth symbols are not present.

Unmarried Heterosexual Cohabitation on the University Campus

Eleanor Dorsey Macklin

One alternative to the "dating game" that helps to eliminate guesswork as to what a person will be like to actually live with (discussed by Marcus in the previous reading) is what is referred to as heterosexual cohabitation. *Presently, in varying degrees all over the country, young men and women are living together without benefit of a marriage license or a long-term commitment. This approach to pairing is a growing phenomenon among college students as well as among young adults outside the college environment. Little is known as yet whether such premarital living arrangements will eventually result in happier marriages, or, alternatively, in happier persons able to change partners when the costs of the liaison to them, as years go by, outweigh the benefits. One of the findings of this study is that almost all of the students interviewed stated that heterosexual cohabitation was a beneficial learning experience. Most also said they would never marry without living with the person first.*

Research like Macklin's gives the impression, however, that today's young men and women are a much more sophisticated group than their parents were at the same age, and that they are managing to get together more openly without hesitancy, embarrassment, or uncertainty about where they stand with their partner. Further, when cohabiting pairs break up, it is implied that this is done with finesse and equanimity. Yet, according to the brief discussion from the Los Angeles Times (which follows Macklin's research), college youths suffer the same agonies of pairing that their parents did when dating. There apparently is no easy path to mutual attraction and a meaningful relationship between two persons.

Eleanor D. Macklin, Ph.D., is Visiting Assistant Professor, Department of Psychology, State University College, Oswego, New York.

The author is indebted to Frank H. Sadowski and the students who worked under his direction to help develop and administer the questionnaire, and to Wendy Jennis and Denise Meyer who also helped to analyze the results.

This is an abridged version of a paper which was published in *The Social Psychology of Sex*, Jacqueline Wiseman, ed., (Harper & Row, Publishers, Inc., New York, 1970).

During the latter part of the sixties, observers of the campus scene became aware that a new dimension was being added to the traditional courtship pattern. No longer did the student couple part at midnight—he to walk alone back to his room, she to scurry into the dorm just as the housemother closed the door. Instead, with increasing frequency and openness, student couples, at various stages of commitment, were spending the night together, not just once a week or on weekends, but often quite steadily.

The public was first made aware of this trend toward "living together unmarried" through publicity given the case of a Barnard coed who, in 1968, was found to be living off-campus with a male friend (*Time*, 1968). But it was given few objective facts with which to assess the new phenomenon. Most of the information was available only through the popular press, which at that point had to rely on interviews with a few selected couples, or with professionals who were willing to venture personal opinions based on their own living experience or on their contact with clinical samples. How many students were "living together," who they were, the nature of the living arrangements, how they felt about one another, or what effect the experience had on them—no one really knew, for the research had not yet been done.

Research to date has been hampered by many problems, among them, the lack of any standard operational definition of cohabitation, the difficulty of obtaining adequate samples, the lack of agreement regarding the criteria to be used in evaluating the cohabitation experience, the need to develop appropriate scales and methods of measuring relevant variables (e.g., commitment, quality of relationship, personal growth), and the amount of time and money required to do the necessary longitudinal research.

The first research efforts involved structured interviews with small numbers of cohabiting couples, usually living in communities surrounding the college campus and located through informal friendship networks, door-to-door inquiry or requests in class or local newspapers. Some of these sought to describe the characteristics of the cohabiting relationship, and the persons involved, by studying only the cohabiting couple (e.g., Clatworthy, 1973; Danziger and Greenwald, 1973; Kieffer, 1972). Others matched the cohabiting couples to married, going-together or engaged couples for purposes of comparison (e.g., Johnson, 1968; Lyness, 1972; Storm, 1973).

These efforts were soon joined by surveys designed to measure the attitudes and cohabitation experience of larger portions of the student population and to compare persons who had ever cohabited with persons who had not. Initially these were given to students enrolled in courses to which the surveyor had easy access (e.g., Lautenschlager, 1972; Macklin, 1972; Shuttlesworth and Thorman, 1973) or were distributed among as many individual students as could be persuaded to participate (e.g., Arafat and Yorburg, 1973). But increasingly the effort has been made to survey representative samples of the undergraduate population (e.g., Cole, in progress; Henze and Hudson, 1973; Peterman, Ridley and Anderson, 1973, 1974). The research reported here will be of the latter type and reports a study done in April, 1972, at Cornell University, a 16,000 student coeducational (11,000 men, 5,000 women) institution in upstate New York.

From the 11,500 undergraduates (7,500 males, 4,000 females) a stratified sample of 400 was selected: 100 male sophomores, 100 female sophomores, 100 male seniors, and 100 female seniors. Each was mailed a letter asking that they come at specified times to fill out a 32-page questionnaire on non-marital heterosexual cohabitation. Of the 400 students, 75 percent completed usable questionnaires (69 male sophomores, 79 female sophomores, 69 male seniors, 82 female seniors). Of the 101 who did not complete the questionnaire, 33 were never located, 17 refused to participate (largely because of time), 36 agreed to participate but did not do so, and 15 were in fact juniors or graduate students who had been inaccurately classified in the computer files. Fourteen of the 299 respondents were married (seven of whom had cohabited prior to marriage). The respondents appeared representative of the larger student population, in that the proportion of respondents from each of the colleges within the University closely approximated the actual enrollment proportions.

• • • •

DEFINITION OF COHABITATION

Numerous terms have been used by writers to refer to persons of the opposite sex sharing a common bedroom while unmarried. Among these are: living together, two-stage marriage, companionate marriage, unmarried college liaisons ("unmalias"), non-married units, and "the arrangement." In the public press, writers often use far less neutral terms. Which term one uses is often indicative of one's philosophical orientation to the phenomenon (e.g., "shacking up" as opposed to "consensual cohabitation") and reflects whether one is primarily thinking about a temporary arrangement, a testing-out of a possible marriage relationship, or an alternative to marriage (e.g., "unmarried liaison" vs. "trial marriage" vs. "unmarried marrieds"). The amount of time the couple needs to have spent together before they are considered to be cohabiting may also differ from study to study. In some instances, the definition has been entirely unspecified, as when the questionnaire item reads: "Have you ever lived with someone of the opposite sex without being legally married?" These differences in definition have led to much confusion in the research findings to date.

In the Cornell research, the following definition was used: To have shared a bedroom and/or bed with someone of the opposite sex (to whom one was not married) for four or more nights a week for three or more consecutive months. (A cohabitant, in this study, is therefore anyone who has ever experienced, or is currently experiencing, such a relationship.) It must be clearly understood that according to this definition, cohabitation does not include overnight relationships of a lesser duration (e.g., a stable "weekender" relationship which may have continued for three or more months, or an intense seven-night-a-week relationship which has not lasted three months). Nor does it include homosexual cohabitation relationships which clearly deserve as much attention and study in their own right. The value of focusing on the physical sharing of the bedroom, rather than on the nature of the involvement of the couple, is that it allows one to examine the full range of possible cohabitation relationships, including the non-sexually involved coed roommates as well as the couple who lives together because of an intense emotional commitment.

35

As can be seen from Table 1, cohabitation is relatively common on the Cornell campus. When one combines sophomores and seniors, men and women, almost one-third of the respondents (20 percent males, 40 percent females) indicated having had a cohabitation experience. By April of their senior year, 54 percent of the women and 27 percent of the men had experienced, at some point in time, such a relationship. Of the 92 persons in the present sample who had ever cohabited, 76 had had only one such relationship, 14 had had two, one three and one four. (This does not mean, of course, that they had not experienced other overnight relationships of a briefer nature.)

TABLE 1
PERCENTAGE OF CORNELL RESPONDENTS WHO HAVE EVER EXPERIENCED A COHABITATION RELATIONSHIP

	SOPHOMORES		SENIORS		
	Men	Women	Men	Women	Total
	(N: 69)	(N: 79)	(N: 69)	(N: 82)	(N: 299)
Cohabitants (4+ nights a week for 3+ months)	13%	27%	27%	54%	31%
Some non-marital overnight relationship but no cohabitation	43	51	40	37	42
No non-marital overnight relationship	44	22	33	10	27

The fact that more women than men had experienced cohabitation fits with other data gathered on their degree of sexual experience. In every category of sexual activity, with the exception of the "one-night affair involving intercourse, did not date person again," women outnumbered men. For instance, 82 percent of all women respondents and 74 percent of the men were non-virgins, 59 percent of the unmarried women and 43 percent of the unmarried men had experienced intercourse in the past month (however, none of these were in "one night affair" situations, thus cautioning one not to view these students as "promiscuous").

It is also interesting to note in Table 1 that only 10 percent (8) of the senior women had not had a non-marital overnight relationship of some sort. When one realizes that three of these eight women are married seniors who are simply indicating that they did not have an overnight relationship before they were married, the number becomes even smaller. This group, rather than the non-virgin woman or the unmarried cohabitant, has now become the new minority, and one does well to ask what are the circumstances surrounding these women which have caused them to postpone this kind of involvement for so long in face of such evident counterpressures.

• • • •

ATTITUDES

Students at Cornell and at a small midwestern college (Cole₁) were asked, "What kind of relationship do you feel should prevail before college-aged students cohabit?" and "What kind of relationship needs to prevail before *you* could feel comfortable cohabiting?" It is apparent from Table 2 that the great majority approve of cohabitation outside of marriage. Moreover, most feel no need for any commitment to a long-term relationship prior to cohabitation, although they do prefer a strong affectionate monogamous relationship with the person. (There was no significant difference between men and women, and relatively little difference between the two institutions, except that a higher percentage at the midwestern institution felt persons should be at least tentatively engaged before living together.)

When Cornell respondents were asked to estimate what proportion of the students at the University would cohabit at some time before graduation, the mean estimate was 30 percent. When asked how many of their close friends had experienced cohabitation, only 13 percent said "none," 11 percent said "most or all of them," and the remainder ranged between. When asked what policy the University should take with regard to students staying together overnight, 98 percent checked, "Whether or not a couple spends the night together should be entirely their own decision, as long as the feelings of others are considered." The remaining two percent indicated that students should not be allowed to stay together overnight in the dormitory, but what they did elsewhere was their own business.

When non-cohabitants were given a list of seventeen possible reasons why they had not cohabited, and were asked to check the most important reason, only 7 percent of the 192 non-cohabitants checked, "I consider cohabitation morally wrong outside marriage." The two most common reasons checked were "have not yet found someone with whom I'd like to stay for four or more nights a week" (20 percent) and "geographic distance from partner" (25 percent). It would appear that lack of opportunity, rather than disapproval of cohabitation, was seen as the major deterring factor by many people.

It seems clear that the great majority of Cornell undergraduates view cohabitation as an acceptable, to-be-expected, life style for the college-aged individual, that many feel they would be comfortable engaging in cohabitation, and that many of those who haven't would cohabit if they could. Not one Cornell student checked as his reason for not cohabiting, "It would be morally unacceptable to peers or to the local community." Of those who had cohabited, 90 percent indicated that they had experienced no disapproval from other students, and when persons had experienced disapproval, it was generally because their friends disapproved of their particular partner. Over 90 percent indicated that

TABLE 2
KIND OF RELATIONSHIP WHICH UNDERGRADUATE STUDENTS FEEL SHOULD EXIST BEFORE COHABITING WITH SOMEONE OF THE OPPOSITE SEX

| | CORNELL | | COLE₁ |
| | Others* | Self* | Others |
	(N:299)	(N:299)	(N:190)
Should be married	5%	6%	2%
Should be formally engaged	1	2	10
Should be tentatively engaged (contemplating marriage)	6	13	16
Should have strong affectionate relationship; not dating others ("going steady")	45	50	42
Should have strong affectionate relationship; could also be dating others	13	9	13
Should be friends	10	12	7
No relationship need exist (e.g., can be assigned roommate; together because of mutual attraction or convenience)	19	7	10
Other	1	1	—

*Others: relationship that should prevail before college-aged students cohabit
*Self: relationship that needs to prevail before respondent can feel comfortable cohabiting

they had experienced no problem with disapproval from landlords or from other aspects of the local community, and 99 percent indicated no problem with disapproval from college administration or other staff. It is obvious that the local norms at Cornell either disregard or provide a supportive environment for living together, and it is accepted by many as a natural course of events. These findings are consistent with what information is available from other campuses, although the strength of acceptance varies somewhat from locale to locale.

DESCRIPTION OF THE COHABITATION EXPERIENCE

A wide variety of types of cohabitation experiences has been revealed: among them, living with an opposite sex roommate in a co-op (with no sexual involvement and with both roommates having other romantic attachments); living with an opposite sex roommate, but having a romantic involvement with a third, same-sex, roommate; sharing a dormitory or fraternity room alone as a couple or with a roommate; or sharing a room with another cohabiting couple. However, the most commonly reported pattern was for the girl to move into the boy's room in an apartment or house which he was sharing with several other males (one of whom might also have a girl living in). Almost sixty percent of the Cornell cohabiting couples had lived together in an apartment shared with others. About 20 percent had shared a dorm room, and almost 10 percent had lived in a fraternity. Only 15 percent had ever lived *alone* as a couple in an off-campus setting. Seniors were more likely to live in apartments, while the dormitory cohabitors were more likely to be sophomores. These data seem consistent with those reported at campuses with housing patterns similar to Cornell.

In the majority of cases, living quarters had not been obtained initially with living together in mind (although students often try to have a single room in order to allow privacy for any potential entertaining). Living arrangements were not usually jointly arranged until the second year of a relationship. However, even then, couples were hesitant to arrange for a single joint living situation, and planning simply involved ensuring that the potential apartment-mates were willing to have one's partner share the premises.

At least three-quarters of the Cornell cohabitants maintained two residences (the male's official residence and the female's official residence), rather than having a single shared residence. When Cornell cohabitants were asked why they chose to maintain two residences, 50 percent or more checked the following reasons: desire to prevent confrontation with parents, to ensure opportunity for privacy, to maintain relationship with friends, and to have a place to live if the relationship did not go well. Two-thirds of those living away from their official residence returned each day to that residence, with the major reasons being to get mail and messages (90 percent), to change clothes and get belongings, and to visit roommates and friends.

There was a wide range in amount of time spent together. In almost half of the relationships, the Cornell couple spent seven nights a week together. (In the remaining half, the girl returned to her own room one or two nights a week in order to allow each some time alone with his friends or because of an early morning schedule conflict.) Most couples ate the majority of their meals together, although occasionally dinner was eaten separately because of the inconvenience involved in having an extra person at dinner or because her parents had already paid for her meals on campus and funds were tight. There was practically no instance of total pooling of finances in these relationships, although the couple normally shared food and entertainment expenses. Usually the girl paid her way and maintained her own separate finances, either because the couple could not afford otherwise or as a matter of principle. When chores were involved, the couple generally did them together (e.g., shopping or laundry), although there was a tendency for the girl to assume responsibility for cooking and cleaning. There was a wide range in the degree to which they shared activities (e.g., classes, study, or hobbies) or spent time with others. The tendency was to share the majority of activities, to have many mutual friends, and to spend much of their time with others as opposed to time only with one another.

Ninety-seven percent of the Cornell cohabitations were full sexual relationships. However, 8 percent of the sexually active cohabitants had lived together three or more months before having intercourse (and many of the non-cohabitants had had less extensive overnight relationships in which there was not a full sexual relationship). It is obvious, that, contrary to much older-generation opinion, spending the night together, even in the same bed, need not imply intercourse. As sleeping together becomes more commonplace and a more customary part of the early dating relationship, sexual involvement may develop more quickly, but probably goes through the same stages as in the more traditional "non-sleeping together" dating relationship. To say a couple slept together can no longer be necessarily interpreted as a nice way of saying they "had sex."

Why Students Live Together

There are three aspects to the question of why students are now living together: the circumstances existing at the particular institution, the broader societal reasons, and the personal motivations of the specific students.

Changes in dormitory regulations and the slow demise of *in loco parentis* have greatly facilitated the development of the new pattern. If one goes back to earlier issues of the Cornell campus newspaper (*Cornell Daily Sun,* 1962, 1963, 1964), one notes that in 1962, a graduate student was indefinitely suspended from the University for living with a woman in his apartment, and in 1964, a male student was reprimanded for staying overnight at a local hotel with a non-University female. Sexual morality was considered a legitimate concern of the University faculty and "overnight unchaperoned mixed company" was considered by the Faculty Council on Student Conduct to be a violation of sexual morality. (*Cornell Daily Sun,* 1962, 2)

Today, Cornell students are free to live in much the same way that non-students who are living and working in the outside world are free to live: they are likely to be residing in a structure which also houses persons of the opposite sex (many of the dorms are now coed, with men and women segregated by floors, wings or suites, although there is experimentation with men and women living on the same corridor); they are free to elect to live off campus; and they may entertain someone of the opposite sex in their room at any time during the 24-hour day. Official policy still prohibits "continuous residence" with someone of the opposite sex in the dormitory setting, but no effort is made to police this. Similar changes have been occurring at universities across the country.

These changes in curfew and dormitory policy must be seen as a reflection of broader social changes: a change in the status of women which makes it difficult to justify different regulations for men and women, youth's increasing demand that they no longer be treated as children, a questioning of the rigid sexual mores which have traditionally governed people's lives, a greater willingness to grant individuals the right to select their own life style, and the increasing availability of contraception and abortion services.

When Cornell students were asked in pre-survey interviews to nypothesize why cohabitation has become more common and more open, they mentioned youth's search for meaningful relations with others and the consequent rejection of the superficial "dating game"; the loneliness of a large university and the emotional satisfaction that comes from having someone to sleep with who

40

cares about you; the widespread questioning of the institution of marriage and the desire to try out a relationship before there is any, if ever any, consideration of permanency; the desire on the part of many to postpone commitment until there is some certainty that individual growth will be compatible with growth of the relationship; the fact that young people mature earlier and yet must wait so long until marriage is feasible; and the fact that the university community provides both sanction and feasibility for such a relationship to develop. Given peer group support, ample opportunity, a human need to love and be loved, and a disposition to question the traditional way, it seems only natural that couples should wish to live together if they enjoy being together. One might almost better ask: why do couples choose *not* to live together?

When Cornell students were asked to check the most important reason for why they chose to live with someone, about 70 percent checked "emotional attachment to each other—i.e., love, desire to be together." When asked to indicate the second most important reason: one-quarter checked "security and companionship," with the remainder divided among "enjoyment—thought it would be fun to live with someone of the opposite sex" and "it was more practical and convenient to live together." On occasion, curiosity about what it would be like to live with the opposite sex was involved, and sometimes "to test out the relationship" was checked, but cohabitation was rarely a purposeful act.

In fact, living together was seldom the result of a considered decision, at least initially. Most relationships involved a gradual (and sometimes not so gradual) drifting into sleeping more and more frequently with each other— only 25 percent indicated that they had discussed whether to live together before starting to do so. The general pattern was to stay over one night; in several weeks, if all was going well, to stay for the weekend, in another few weeks to add a week night, in another few weeks, a second week night, and so forth. In half of the relationships which became cohabitations, the couple had begun staying together four or more nights a week by the end of three months of dating. If and when a decision with conscious deliberation was made, it was usually precipitated by some external force (e.g., need to make plans for the summer or next fall, graduation, unexpected pregnancy, or a necessary housing or room change). Until this time, there was only a mutual, often unspoken, recognition of the desire to be together—a natural progression of the relationship.

NATURE OF THE RELATIONSHIP

Most of the Cornell cohabitation relationships involved a strong, affectionate relationship at the time they started living together, with the majority of them exclusive, monogamous relationships (see Table 3). In the old days, we would have said these couples were "going steady," but that term is no longer popular. When asked to indicate degree of commitment to the relationship at the time they started living together four or more nights a week, only 10 percent indicated that future marriage to the partner was definitely planned. Most cohabitants held either a "let's see" attitude ("test the relationship and stay together as long as mutually satisfying"—46 percent) or "planned to do all they could to develop a lasting relationship, but future marriage was not definite" (31 per-

41

cent). Only 10 percent indicated that initially the cohabitation was seen as a temporary experience with no intent to continue it (it is possible that many such relationships dissolve before reaching three months).

This raises some question about the label "unmarried marrieds" which has often been applied in the popular literature to unmarried cohabitation. Most of the undergraduate couples do not consider themselves married in any sense of the word. In fact, they had rarely considered marriage as a viable alternative to their present cohabitation. When Cornell cohabitants were asked if they had considered the possibility of getting married instead of living together, over three-quarters said "no," the most common reasons being they did not feel personally ready for marriage or were not ready to commit themselves to that particular person. Marriage might be seen as a possibility for the future (only 12 percent of the "no" group said they questioned the institution of marriage), but the distant future. Of those cohabitants who indicated that they *had* considered marriage instead of simply living together, the majority chose cohabitation either because it was impractical to marry at this time or they did not feel personally ready for marriage.

TABLE 3

NATURE OF RELATIONSHIP EXISTING AT INITIATION OF
MOST RECENT CORNELL COHABITATION (N: 92)

Formally engaged	2%
Tentatively engaged (contemplating marriage)	10
Strong affectionate relationship; not dating others	58
Strong affectionate relationship; also dating others	25
Friends	4
Other	1

PROBLEMS ENCOUNTERED

Respondents were asked to indicate the degree to which they had experienced problems in the following five areas: emotional, parental, sexual, living-situation related, and community reaction.

The major emotional problem for Cornell cohabitants was a tendency to become overinvolved, and to feel a subsequent loss of identity, lack of opportunity to participate in other activities or be with friends, and an over-dependency on the relationship (62 percent of the respondents indicated some problem in this area). Closely related problems were jealousy of partner's involvement in other relationships or activities, or of his past relationships (57 percent rated this as a problem area), and a feeling of being trapped in the relationship (49 percent indicated some problem with this). One is tempted to hypothesize that how one deals with the problem of overdependency and subsequent jealousy and feeling of entrapment may well be one of the major issues facing cohabiting couples. As in marriage, achieving security without giving up the freedom to be oneself, and growing together while leaving enough space so that the individuals may also grow, may well be central to success in the relationship.

It is important to note that more than two-thirds of the Cornell cohabitants indicated no feeling of guilt, with less guilt experienced as the relationship progressed. In the pre-survey interviews, it seemed that when guilt was present, it was usually related to having to conceal the relationship from parents, or it occurred in those instances when the respondent knew from the beginning that the relationship could not last.

A major problem area was parents. Almost 50 percent of the Cornell cohabitants indicated that parents had caused "some" or "many" problems for the relationship. Sixty percent checked that they had experienced "sorrow at not being able to discuss or share the relationship with their parents," and 48 percent indicated that fear their parents would discover and object to the relationship had created a problem. Because of fear of disapproval or unpleasant repercussions, almost 80 percent indicated that they had tried at some point to conceal the relationship from their parents (30 percent said they tried to hide the relationship "all the time")—by not telling them the whole story, by distorting the truth, and by developing often elaborate schemes to prevent discovery.

One-third of the Cornell cohabitants indicated that their parents definitely did not know about the cohabitation at the time it occurred, a third indicated that their parents definitely did know, and one-third were unsure. Females were three times as likely as males to indicate that their parents did not know about the cohabitation (35 percent of sophomore and 43 percent of the senior female cohabitants said their parents did not know; 11 percent of the sophomore and 17 percent of the senior male cohabitants). Most of those students who indicated that their parents did know, had told them themselves. About half of the respondents' parents who knew of the relationship at the time it occurred had apparently accepted it; about 30 percent of those who knew had strongly disapproved and tried to interfere with the cohabitation. Of those whose parents did not definitely know of the cohabitation, 60 percent predicted that their parents would disapprove.

● ● ● ●

Sexual problems were common but not serious, and sound very much like the sexual problems traditionally associated with the young married couple. The problems checked most frequently were differing periods or degree of sexual interest (71 percent), fear of pregnancy (62 percent), and problems with lack of orgasm (62 percent). However, although many indicated some problem in these areas, the degree of problem was generally very low. It is probably indicative that 96 percent rated their relationship as sexually satisfying. Practically all used contraception (with the majority using the pill), and almost three-quarters had started contraception before or at the time of first intercourse in the cohabitation.

Problems related to the living situation were also relatively common. Lack of adequate space was the most frequent problem, with lack of privacy, friction with apartment mates, and lack of sufficient funds mentioned about equally often. As mentioned above, there was practically no problem experienced as a result of the external community, i.e., landlords, local employers, school administration, neighbors, or contemporaries.

When one looked at the weightings given the above problems, it became clear that in most cases, the problem, even when existant, was not serious. (Most problems received a mean weighting of 2 or 3 on a 1–5 scale of difficulty.) By far the most difficult problems were those presented by parents—in particular, parental objections to the partner and parental discovery of and objection to the cohabitation—and by pregnancy when it occurred. (Nine of the 92 cohabitants had experienced a pregnancy). There is no way of knowing from this analysis whether the problems experienced by cohabitors are any more serious or any more destructive (or growth-producing) than are those experienced by young persons involved in other love relationships characteristic of this age period.

Cornell cohabitants were also asked to evaluate the effect of the cohabitation experience on five academic areas: time to study, motivation to study, capacity to concentrate, amount of studying, and course grades. In general, there was a strong feeling that the cohabitation had had a neutral effect on academics (about 50 percent indicated "no effect," with the remainder split rather evenly between negative and positive effects), with the following exceptions: effect on time to study and amount of studying was rated as more negative than positive; effect on motivation to study and on course grades was rated as more positive, with the strongest positive effect reported by the senior men.

BENEFITS

It is important that the reader not be led by the above discussion to see the problems as outweighing the values of such relationships. When Cornell cohabitants were asked to evaluate their cohabitation, indicating the degree to which it was successful, pleasurable, and maturing: 78 percent indicated that it was successful or very successful (10 percent unsuccessful); 93 percent rated it pleasurable or very pleasurable (1 percent unpleasurable); and 91 percent rated it as maturing or very maturing (no one rated it as not at all maturing). When asked to check which of the following best described their cohabitation experience: 74 percent said "maturing and pleasant"; 18 percent, "maturing but painful"; 4 percent, "pleasant but not particularly maturing"; 1 percent, "rather neutral experience"; and 0 percent, "detrimental experience."

Cornell cohabitants were asked to rate the effect of the cohabitation experience on a number of specific personal growth areas (e.g., self-confidence, emotional maturity, ability to understand and relate to others, insight into the opposite sex, etc.). In all areas, 80 percent or more indicated that the experience had had a positive effect (and where it was not positive, it tended to be neutral), with the strongest positive effects being on "understanding what is involved in a relationship" (96 percent), and on "insight into self" (94 percent). Although one may argue that "cognitive dissonance" theory could account for these positive self-evaluations, this is not apparent when one interviews these young persons.

When asked how they now felt about cohabitation as an experience, over three-quarters of the Cornell cohabitants stated that they would never marry without living with the person first. No one said that they would never again cohabit outside of marriage, and with the exception of one person who was "unsure," all indicated that they would recommend the experience to others.

· · · ·

In reviewing all available data, one is repeatedly impressed by the very strong positive attitudes toward cohabitation which are held by those who have experienced it. The main message which one consistently gets from cohabitants is all the many ways in which the experience served to foster their own personal growth and maturity. While hesitant to say what others should do, they appear to feel that the move toward college cohabitation can only be seen as a healthy trend.

CURRENT STATE OF THE RELATIONSHIP

At the time of this study, about 5 percent of the Cornell cohabitation relationships had ended in marriage, 25 percent were at a stage of tentative or formal engagement, 50 percent were still on-going but as yet uncommitted relationships (however, a number of these were no longer living together due to geographic separation, desire for more freedom, or pressure from parents), and 20 percent of the relationships had dissolved. This strong evidence of relationship stability, coupled with the fact that about three-quarters had only experienced one such relationship to date, indicates that those living-together relationships which last for the initial three-month period tend to be relatively durable, at least during one's college career. These data are very consistent with data from elsewhere, if the definition of cohabitation is held constant. Although we have traditionally held durability of a love relationship as a desirable thing in this society, one must at least raise the research question of whether it is at this stage of development.

It is interesting to note that the above figures are very similar to the divorce statistics for first marriages in this country (about 20 percent of all first marriages have tended to end in divorce). This fact has caused some to question whether these cohabitation relationships might essentially be serving as first marriages, even though the couple may not view them as such at the time. Since the argument is often made that many divorces occur because the individual married the wrong person for the wrong reason at the wrong time, it could be that cohabitation, by postponing the decision to marry, may in fact weed out these "wrong decision" marriages, and as a result lower the official divorce rate. However, this must remain pure speculation at this point.

CONCLUDING COMMENTS

1. It is clear that cohabitation has become an increasingly common aspect of campus courtship, and one would predict that the trend will continue. Prevalence of cohabitation clearly varies with the opportunity for cohabitation. It is

more frequent at institutions which permit off-campus housing, 24-hour visitation and coed dormitories, and where there are large numbers of the opposite sex. (Whether it also varies with geographic region is not yet clear, for comparable institutions within different regions have not yet been studied using similar measures.) Where these conditions exist, it is not surprising to find between 25 and 35 percent of the undergraduates indicating having had a living-together experience of some variety. Even on campuses where there is not high prevalence, there is high acceptance of cohabitation, with many indicating that if the opportunity were available, they would participate.

2. As cohabitation becomes increasingly accepted, it becomes more difficult to isolate those variables which differentiate cohabitants from non-cohabitants. At institutions where large proportions of the student population experience such a relationship, the cohabiting student appears in many ways to be very similar to other students. Persons reporting cohabitation experience hold somewhat more liberal religious and personal values, and may well possess interpersonal competences which facilitate the development of such a relationship. However, to what extent these differences are due to the experience itself is not clear.

3. Although the phenomenon of unmarried persons living together is obviously not a new one, either in this society or others (Berger, 1971), it has certainly not been a common phenomenon among unmarried middle class youth in the United States until quite recently. Some pass it off by saying that it is merely a more open expression of what students have been doing sexually on the sly for years, but this suggests a very narrow interpretation of the present situation. The pattern which is currently evolving appears to be primarily concerned with total relationships, and only incidentally with the sexual aspects, which are assumed to grow as the relationship grows. Cohabitation at the undergraduate level appears to be characterized by strong dyadic, relatively monogamous relationships with much commitment to relationship, strong emotional involvement, and extensive sharing of all phases of daily life. It is this concern with getting to know another as a whole person and the emphasis on sharing as openly and as completely as possible with that person, which is probably the major new dimension being added to the old courtship pattern.

4. Cohabitation as now practiced on the college campus does not appear to be either a "trial marriage" or an alternative to marriage. Trial marriage tends to imply a level of commitment usually associated with the engagement portion of the courtship continuum, which is not characteristic of most of the campus relationships studied. These students did not, in general, see themselves as consciously testing or even contemplating a potential marriage, at least not initially. Instead, in most cases, living together seems to be a natural component of a strong, affectionate "dating" relationship—a living out of "going steady"— which may grow in time to become something more, but which in the meantime is to be enjoyed and experienced because it is pleasurable in and of itself.

5. What effect college cohabitation will have on the individuals involved and on society at large is not clear at this time. The great majority of students who have cohabited indicate that it was a positive and growth-producing experience for them. However, there are many questions which are as yet unanswered. For example, would objective assessment indicate the same growth which has been reported by the participants? What are the factors which lead to a positive

cohabitation experience (e.g., are there minimal levels of socio-emotional maturity, interpersonal competence, intra-couple consensus, parental and peer support which must be present)? Are these factors any different from those necessary for the success of any intense dyadic relationship? Does involvement in a cohabitation relationship during the college years interfere in any way with the personal development of the participants? Does it perhaps retard autonomy and identity development, or might it instead provide a base of emotional security and a degree of living experience which facilitates this development? Does cohabitation with its emotional commitment and heavy time involvement allow a student less opportunity to explore other relationships and hence, freeze the young person into a relationship too early? Or was this just as likely to happen in the old "going steady" relationship where the couple parted at midnight?

Although at present, cohabitation primarily affects premarital behavior and the majority of cohabitants indicate an eventual desire to marry, will it in time lead to changes in our marriage patterns, and if so, what effect will this have on later generations? It does not appear at the moment that campus cohabitation will greatly affect the marriage rate in this country (although it may delay the age at which persons officially enter marriage), but we do not know what effect it will have on the marriage relationship itself. Will the increased opportunity for self-knowledge and the increased experience that comes from living intimately with another lead to more "fully functioning" persons and more successful later relationships? (And by what criteria shall we measure success?) Or will cohabitation teach persons to withhold commitment and to become more concerned with their own happiness and less with the well-being of a relationship? Will cohabitation help to break down the sex-role stereotyping associated with traditional marriage, or are cohabitation relationships merely mirrors of traditional male/female relations? If cohabitation does in fact encourage persons to practice equal sharing of responsibility and dividing of time between individual growth and relationship growth, does this carry over into later marriage, or does somehow the fact of marriage bury all this? To what extent is cohabitation a courtship pattern limited to the college campus, or is it also increasingly practiced by those youth who are not in college?

Longitudinal research, and studies on non-college populations, will be necessary before we can have answers to the above questions. On the other hand, perhaps cohabitation is so quickly winning an established place within our courtship patterns that to study its advantages and disadvantages is merely an intellectual exercise. Perhaps it would be more to the point to spend the same research time and effort to explore how persons might by helped to maximize the opportunity for growth afforded by this life style, and to seek ways to help persons develop the understandings and competences needed to relate effectively in any intimate living relationship, married or unmarried.

6. There appears to be a great need to help society adjust to the evolving courtship patterns. The popular press continues to suggest that cohabitation is antithetical to all that is healthy or moral (e.g., Adams, 1973; Lobsenz, 1973; Safire, 1973), and yet the research data do not appear to document this conclusion. One of the most dramatic findings of the Cornell study was the great gap which students believe exists between their attitudes and those of their parents, and the degree to which students seek to hide this part of their lives from their

parents. It is important to investigate the extent to which this gap—in attitude and in awareness—does indeed exist, and to see what can be done to help the two generations deal more constructively with the changes.

Colleges and universities also have the responsibility of facing up to the changes in living patterns which are occurring on their campuses and of dealing with these realistically. For too long the tendency has been to "sweep the matter under the rug" and to maintain publicly that "university policy does not approve unmarried cohabitation." Increasingly students are pressing to have hetero-sexual cohabitation an official option within on-campus housing and graduate couples who compose much of the resident hall staff are asking to be hired unmarried. College staff must become aware of the courtship patterns existing on their particular campuses, be honest with themselves and the public about this, and provide the necessary support services for a sexually active population. To do so, however, will often require a lot of soul searching, open dialogue, and courage.

• • • •

The legal problems caused by increasing cohabitation are only beginning to be explored. (There is, for instance, the well known case of the young woman whose auto insurance was revoked because she was found to be living with someone unmarried.) It is not yet known what protections are or should be made available to persons who are involved in this life style. Bank officials find themselves having to counsel parents as they wrestle with setting up trust funds for offspring whose cohabiting behavior they cannot approve, or having to oversee trust accounts for students whose cohabitation behavior they do not themselves approve. Ministers who have long been expected to uphold the sanctity of marriage and the principle of abstinence are being called upon to re-evaluate the traditional position of the church and to see if indeed the teach-ings are as clearcut with regard to these issues as had been once supposed. Secondary schools must recognize the kind of personal choices which students will be asked to make as soon as they reach the university campus (if not before), and reassess whether they are adequately preparing youth to make wise choices. The area of public life touched by the new patterns are broad indeed. The challenge for all of us is to acknowledge that these changes are in fact happen-ing, and to be willing to entertain the hypothesis that they may in fact be an improvement on the traditional patterns.

BIBLIOGRAPHY

Adams, James R. "Casualties of the Sexual Revolution." *Wall Street Journal,* October 1, October 9, and October 15, 1973.

Ald, Roy. *Sex Off Campus.* New York: Grosset and Dunlap, 1969.

Arafat, Ibithaj and Betty Yorburg. "On Living Together Without Marriage." *Journal of Sex Research,* May, 1973, pp. 997–1006.

Berger, Miriam E. "Trial Marriage: Harnessing the Trend Constructively." *The Family Coordinator,* 1971, 20, 38–43.

Berger, Miriam. *Trial Marriage Follow-Up.* (Write to author at 140-70 Burden Crescent, Jamacia, New York 11435). Unpublished manuscript, 1974.

Bloch, Donald. "Unwed Couples: Do They Live Happily Ever After?" *Redbook,* April, 1969, pp. 90+.

Clatworthy, Nancy M. "Couples in Quasi-Marriage." In: Nona Glazer-Malbin (ed.), *Old Family/New Family: Interpersonal Relationships.* New York: Van Nostrand, in press.

Coffin, Patricia. "Young Unmarrieds: Theresa Pommett and Charles Walsh, College Grads Living Together." *Look,* January 26, 1971, pp. 634+.

Cole, Charles L. *Emerging Dating and Intimacy Requirements at a Midwestern University: A Study of Cohabitation and Other Alternative Courtship Forms.* Denison University, Granville, Ohio (in progress).

Cornell Daily Sun. October 9, 1962; October 8, 1963; March 6, 1964.

Danziger, Carl and Mathew Greenwald. *Alternatives: A Look at Unmarried Couples and Communes.* Research Services, Institute of Life Insurance, 277 Park Ave., New York, New York 10017, 1973.

Davids, Leo. "North American Marriage: 1990." *The Futurist,* October, 1971, pp. 190–194.

Edwards, Maxine P. *College Students' Perceptions of Experimental Life Styles.* Master's thesis: Oklahoma State University, Oklahoma City, Oklahoma, 1972.

Garza, Joseph. *Living Together and the Double Funnel Theory of Courtship.* Paper delivered at Fourth Annual Sociological Research Symposium, Virginia Commonwealth University, Richmond, Virginia, February 28–March 2, 1974. (Paper available from author at Georgia State University, Atlanta, Georgia).

Gavin, Mary C. *The Living-Together Phenomenon.* Master's thesis: Washington State University, Pullman, Washington, 1973.

Grant, A. "No Rings Attached: A Look at Premarital Marriage on Campus." *Mademoiselle,* April, 1968, 66, pp. 208+.

Hennon, Charles B. *Open-Systems Theory and the Analysis of Non-Marital Cohabitation.* West Virginia University, Morgantown, West Virginia. Unpublished manuscript, 1974.

Henze, Lura F. and John W. Hudson. *Personal and Family Characteristics of Non-Cohabiting and Cohabiting College Students.* Arizona State University, Tempe, Arizona. Unpublished manuscript, 1973.

Hickrod, Lucy Jen Huang. *Religious Background of College Students and Attitudes Toward Living Together Before Marriage.* Illinois State University, Normal, Illinois. Unpublished manuscript, 1972.

Hudson, John W. and Lura F. Henze. "A Note on Cohabitation." *The Family Coordinator,* October, 1973, p. 495.

Jackson, Tom and Jan Jackson. *Living Together: A Guide for Unmarried Couples.* (Write to authors at Wayne County Community College, Goldsboro, North Carolina). Unpublished manuscript.

Johnson, Michael P. "Commitment: A Conceptual Structure and Empirical Application." *Sociological Quarterly,* Summer, 1973, 14, 395–406.

Johnson, Michael P. *Courtship and Commitment: A Study of Cohabitation on a University Campus.* Master's thesis. University of Iowa, Iowa City, 1968.

Kalmbach, Carla. *Replication Study of Heterosexual Cohabitation Among Unmarried College Students: Cornell University vs. Central Michigan University.* (Write to author at Michigan State University, East Lansing, Michigan.) Unpublished manuscript, 1973.

Karlen, Arno. "The Unmarried Marrieds on Campus." *New York Times Magazine,* January 26, 1969, pp. 29+.

Keller, James and James Croake. Paper on cohabitation presented at annual meeting of Southwestern Council on Family Relations, Blacksburg, Virginia, 1973.

Kieffer, Carolynne M. *Consensual Cohabitation: A Descriptive Study of the Relationships and Sociocultural Characteristics of Eighty Couples in Settings of Two Florida Universities.* Master's thesis: Florida State University, Tallahassee, Florida, 1972.

Kopecky, Gini. "Unmarried, But Living Together." *Ladies Home Journal,* July, 1972, pp. 66+.

Lautenschlager, Sheryl Y. *A Descriptive Study of Consensual Union Among College Students.* Master's thesis: California State University at Northridge, 1972.

LeHecka, Charlotte. *Premarital Dyadic Formation in Germany and the United States: A Cross-National Comparison.* Master's thesis: University of Georgia, Athens, Georgia (in progress).

LeShan, Eda J. *Mates and Roommates: New Styles in Young Marriages.* Public Affairs Pamphlets, No. 468, 1971.

Lewis, Robert A. "The Dyadic Formation Inventory: An Instrument for Measuring Heterosexual Couple Formation." *International Journal of Sociology of the Family,* September, 1973.

Lewis, Robert A. *Measurement of Premarital Dyadic Formation.* Paper presented to National Council on Family Relations, Portland, Oregon, 1972. Available from author, Pennsylvania State University, University Park, Pennsylvania.

Liddick, Betty. "Practicing Marriage Without a License." In: George Roleder (ed.), *Marriage Means Encounter.* Dubuque, Iowa: William C. Brown, 1973.

Life. "Coed Dorms: An Intimate Campus Revolution." November 20, 1970, pp. 32+.

Lindsey, Ben B. "The Companionate Marriage." *Redbook,* October, 1926; March, 1927.

Lobsenz, Norman N. "Marriage vs. Living Together." *Modern Bride,* April/May, 1973, pp. 124+.

Lobsenz, Norman N. "Living Together: A New Fangled Tango or an Old-Fashioned Waltz?" *Redbook Magazine,* June, 1974, 86+.

Lyness, Judith L. *Aspects of Long-Term Effects of Non-marital Cohabitation.* Purdue University at Fort Wayne, Indiana. Unpublished manuscript, 1974.

Lyness, Judith L., Milton E. Lipetz, and Keith E. Davis, "Living Together: An Alternative to Marriage." *Journal of Marriage and the Family,* May, 1972, 34, pp. 305–311.

Macklin, Eleanor D. "Heterosexual Cohabitation Among Unmarried College Students." *The Family Coordinator,* October, 1972, pp. 463–472.

Macklin, Eleanor D., ed. *Cohabitation Research Newsletter.* Issue #1, October, 1972; Issue #2, April, 1973; Issue #3, October, 1973; Issue #4, June, 1974.

Maxa, Rudy. "Living Together: The Aftermath." *The Washington Post (Potomac),* April 14, 1974, pp. 14+.

McWhirter, William A. "The Arrangement at College." *Life,* May 31, 1968, 56+.

Mead, Margaret. "A Continuing Dialogue on Marriage: Why Just Living Together Won't Work." *Redbook,* April, 1968, 130, pp. 44+.

Mead, Margaret. "Marriage in Two Steps." *Redbook,* July, 1966, 127, pp. 48+.

Montgomery, Jason P. *Towards an Understanding of Cohabitation.* Ph.D. thesis: University of Massachusetts, Amherst, Massachusetts, 1972.

Montgomery, Jason P. *Commitment and Cohabitation Cohesion.* Paper presented at National Council of Family Relations, Toronto, October, 1973. (Available from author at University of Edmonton, Edmonton, Canada.)

Mosher, Joan. *Correlates of Attraction to the New Alternatives in Marriage.* Ph.D. thesis: University of Connecticut, Storrs, Connecticut, 1974.

Newsweek. "Unstructured Relationships: Students Living Together." July 4, 1966, 78.

Peterman, Dan J., Carl A. Ridley, and Scott M. Anderson. *A Comparison of Background, Personal, and Interpersonal Characteristics of Cohabiting and Non-Cohabiting College Students.* Pennsylvania State University, University Park, Pennsylvania, 1973. (mimeo)

Peterman, Dan J., Carl A. Ridley, and Scott M. Anderson. "A Comparison of Cohabiting and Non-Cohabiting College Students," *Journal of Marriage and the Family,* Vol. 36, May, 1974, pp. 344–354.

Reuben, David. "Alternatives to Marriage." *McCall's,* February, 1972, 38+.

Rollin, Betty. "New Hang-up for Parents: Coed Living." *Look,* September 23, 1969, 22+.

Rosenblatt, Paul D. and Linda G. Stevenson. *Territoriality and Privacy in Married and Unmarried Cohabiting Couples.* University of Minnesota, St. Paul, Minnesota. Unpublished manuscript, 1973.

Russell, Bertrand. "On Marriage." In: Arlene S. and Jerome H. Skolnick (eds.), *Family in Transition.* Boston: Little, Brown and Co., 1971, 283–286.

Safire, William. "On Cohabitation." *New York Times,* September 24, 1973, 31M.

Schrag, Peter. "Posse at Generation Gap: Implications of the Linda LeClair Affair." *Saturday Review,* May 18, 1968, 81.

Sheehy, Gail. "Living Together: The Stories of Four Young Couples Who Risk the Strains of Non-marriage and Why." *Glamour,* February 1, 1969, 136+.

Shuttlesworth, Guy and George Thorman. *Living Together Unmarried Relationships.* University of Texas, Austin, Texas. Unpublished manuscript, 1973.

Silverman, Ira. *Unmarried Students Who Lived Together: A Comparison of Two Campuses.* University of South Florida, Tampa, Florida. Unpublished manuscript, 1974.

Smith, Joan. "The Arrangement: As Acceptable as Going Steady." *Wisconsin State Journal,* Section 7, April 27, 1969, 1+.

Smith, Patrick B. and Ko Kimmel. "Student-Parent Reactions of Off-Campus Cohabitation." *Journal of College Student Personnel,* May, 1970, 188–193.

Storm, Virginia. *Contemporary Cohabitation and the Dating-Marital Continuum.* Master's thesis: University of Georgia, Athens, Georgia, 1973.

Thorman, George. *Cohabitation: A Report on Thirty Living-Together Couples at a Texas University.* University of Texas, Austin, Texas. Unpublished manuscript, 1973.

Thorman, George. "Cohabitation: A Report on the Married-Unmarried Life Style." *The Futurist,* December, 1973, pp. 250–254.

Time. "Linda, The Light Housekeeper." April 26, 1968, 51.

Trost, Jan. *Various Forms of Cohabitation and Their Relation to Psychical and Social Criteria of Adaptation.* Paper presented at Third International Stress Symposium, Stockholm, May, 1972. Paper available from author at Uppsala Universitet, Uppsala, Sweden.

Trost, Jan. *Married and Unmarried Cohabitation: The Case of Sweden with Some Comparisons.* Paper to be presented at the Eighth World Congress of Sociology, Committee on Family Research, Toronto, August 18–24, 1974 (mimeo).

Wells, Theodora and Lee S. Christie. "Living Together: An Alternative to Marriage." *The Futurist,* April, 1970, 4, 50–51.

Whitehurst, Robert N. *Living Together Unmarried: Some Trends and Speculations.* University of Windsor, Windsor, Ontario. Unpublished manuscript, 1973.

Whitehurst, Robert N. *The Unmalias on Campus.* Presented at NCFR Annual Meeting, 1969. Unpublished manuscript.

Whitehurst, Robert N. *The Double Standard and Male Dominance in Non-Marital Living Arrangements: A Preliminary Statement.* Paper presented at the American Orthopsychiatric Association Meeting, New York, 1969. Unpublished manuscript.

What Sex Revolution?
Harvard's Face Is Crimson

Judith Martin

In an article that asks, "Is there sex after Harvard?" the Harvard Independent, a student newspaper, indicates that there certainly isn't much during.

A Radcliffe senior is quoted as moaning, "I've learned that men here often
mistake friendliness for a sexual invitation. I'm careful not to flirt with anyone,
and I'll rarely risk going to visit a guy I know from the dining hall."

A Harvard senior whines, "If you invite a woman out a few times and she
goes but never calls you, what does that mean?"

Another Radcliffe senior sighs that coeducational living quarters are "relaxed to the point where nobody went out at all. The upshot was that I had
no sexual or emotional ties at all."

Another Harvard senior complains that "Harvard's a difficult place to gain
such experience (with women). The lack of defined dating forms has unquestionably made things more difficult for someone like me."

And so on. "You become defensive and try to turn off your emotions."
"There are always people around here, so many casual friends, that you don't
really need to make any deep relationships." There is little "interpersonal
contact, because too many people feel they'd rather be safe than sorry." It's
difficult to have male acquaintances who are more than dining hall companions.
"If I dropped in to see a male friend whom I knew from the dining hall, I'm
afraid he would assume I was trying to pick him up."

Now, where have you heard this sort of drivel before? At college, right?
At your coffee shop or other dateless Saturday night refuges, back in the old
uptight '50s or worse.

So what does it mean, pouring out of the privileged little mouths of mid-'70s
undergraduates? Brace yourself, this is more horrifying than anything any
middle-aged parent could have dreamed of.

It means that two decades of struggle have gone for nothing. Somebody had
to invent the Pill, it had to be marketed, generations of students had to agitate

From Judith Martin, "Harvard's Face Is Crimson," *The Los Angeles Times*, "View,"
part IV, Oct. 14, 1976. Reprinted by permission of *The Washington Post*.

to have it distributed at college dispensaries; age-old parental laws had to be fought and conquered; even older sexual and social customs had to be discussed to death before they could be buried; and living patterns, many of them with their own substantial endowments from alumni, had to be done away with, before those children could enjoy the healthy, freedoms hardly imagined by their elders.

And now they're telling us they can't get any action?

That seems to be the complaint. They can't meet anybody to date, because they're all living together in such a friendly, brother-and-sister way. They can't spend comfortable evenings together anyway, because there is no established dating pattern, such as dinner-movie-drink-kiss. They can't fall in love because they don't want to get involved. And they can't get any because—what was it they said?

To a rule-paralyzed adult, this is very scary. Here we all were, happy and secure in the thought that all those kids were having all that fun, and what were they really up to behind our backs?

For one thing, one Harvard senior swears, they are "not going all the way." For another, they are taking advantage of the living arrangements to spend the night with their whatever-you-call-thems, without "really doing anything." Some have even been known to say that they are "saving themselves."

And that's not the worst, either. As the Harvard Independent article explains, "Individuals will worry for hours over their relationships here, tease out old memories, shake them and hold them to the light to see where things went wrong. They wonder why people who are so very articulate in the classroom are so afraid to speak to each other about personal feelings. Women ask whether they can be a feminist without putting off men, or whether they should be interested in men who dislike their politics. People try to affix blame for relationships that failed. Seniors about to graduate think ruefully of the people they might have liked to know better and wonder why they never found the courage to be a bit forward. And finally, people wonder how much being at Harvard has affected the nature of their social lives?"

My God, that's what *we* were doing. And we could do it and still all get back in our own rooms by curfew time.

A Research Note on Male-Female Differentials in the Experience of Heterosexual Love

Eugene J. Kanin, Karen R. Davidson, and Sonia R. Scheck

In the foregoing readings, love—defined as a heightened state of interpersonal attraction—is mentioned, yet does not play an important role in the analysis of partner selection. Sex differences in susceptibility to falling in love, in particular, have not been analyzed. Research reported on here reinforces an earlier discussion. Marcus (Reading 3) suggests that women's strongest bargaining positions (but not necessarily the best information on which to base a decision) are obtained during courtship, since men fall in love more easily than women. At the same time, women love more deeply and longer than men. This emotional difference is strategically detrimental to women in later power relationships, inasmuch as it is the partner least in love who has the greatest control over the situation. The fact that men find it easier to fall out of love than do women compounds the possibility that the husband has less to lose by leaving his wife than a wife has by leaving her husband.

INTRODUCTION

This study focuses on sex differences in love experience. Although there is a paucity of data on male-female differences in love behavior, the existing literature suggests differential response patterns. More specifically there ap-

From Eugene J. Kanin, Karen R. Davidson, and Sonia R. Scheck, "A Research Note on Male-Female Differentials in the Experience of Heterosexual Love," *The Journal of Sex Research* 6:1 (February 1970): 64–72. Reprinted by permission of the publisher.

pears to be some convergence of evidence suggestive of males being more romantic than females. Kephart (1966) reports that approximately twice as many males as females indicate it was very easy to become attracted to persons of the opposite sex. Burgess and Wallin (1953) and others (Combs and Kenkel, 1966) found that males rather than females were more apt to show interest in their partners at the time of their initial encounter. There is also evidence that males score higher than females on romanticism scales (Hobart, 1958). Hawkins (1962), studying love relationships of college students, found that males were significantly more likely to recognize love earlier than females.

It is curious then, leaving aside for the moment possible explanations for such a differential, that we do entertain a popular stereotype—culturally fostered and perpetuated in the entertainment media—of the female as the more romantic being. She is readily portrayed as impulsive and somewhat foolish in the affairs of the heart. The male, on the other hand is pictured as the relatively sensible and sober party. We propose to present evidence suggesting that the sex ascription of the label "more romantic" is probably a fruitless and unwarranted exercise. Either the male or female can be the recipient of the "more romantic" label, depending upon which criterion is employed for assessing romanticism.

METHOD

A schedule designed to investigate varied aspects of heterosexual love was distributed, anonymously completed, and received from 778 students in 48 varied classes in a large midwestern state university. A few brief and general remarks concerning the nature of the study preceded each administration of the schedule. Cooperation was excellent. Although the voluntary character of the study was stressed, no one refused. Eighty (10.2 percent) schedules were defined as incomplete and an additional 19 (2.5 percent) were discarded because the respondents had never been in love. The remaining 679 cases, 250 males and 429 females, constitute the data for this study.

One methodological aspect of this investigation warrants comment. The data obtained on love behavior reported here focuses on a single love experience for each respondent—either an affair which was then in progress or, if the respondent was not in love at the time of the administration of the schedule, an affair which had terminated since college entrance. The respondents, then simply had to focus on one love experience rather than to generalize or abstract from all prior love experiences. This method further has the virtue of largely restricting experiences to those that occurred among relatively mature young people. These reported heterosexual experiences do not necessarily reflect the most intense emotional experiences, nor perhaps even the typical experiences of their lives. Rather it permits the analysis of the current or last love involvement of 679 university students.

As with all investigations in this area of human behavior, definitional problems loom large. As a precaution against the redefinition of the love experience once it has terminated, these respondents were only requested information concerning their "most recent love affair (even though now you may call it infatuation)." The episodes these respondents reported then, were at the time, if they were terminated when the schedule was administrated, considered to be love involvements. By and large, these love involvements represented advanced pair involvement. Approximately two-thirds of both males and females reported their involvement to be at the regular-steady date stage or at some more advanced level of intimacy.

RESULTS

The research schedule contained several items aimed at determining whether love proneness tended to be sex linked. Love proneness here simply refers to the rapidity with which one becomes aware of love for the other. Regardless of the measure utilized, males consistently appear to develop love feelings earlier in the relationship than females. An inquiry as to where in the dating-courtship history of the pair love for the other was recognized, found approximately 40 percent of the males and 29 percent of the females reporting the superficial stages of pair intimacy ranging from first date to occasional date ($X^2 = 7.26$; $P < .01$). Employing the number of pair encounters necessary to precipitate love for the partner further illustrates this sex differential. It was found that 27 percent of the males but only 15 percent of the females reported recognizing love for the other within the span of the first four dates. At the other extreme, approximately 43 percent of the females and 30 percent of the males failed to recognize love until after twenty or more dates ($X^2 = 18.88$; $P < .001$). These data support Hawkins' earlier findings that males tend to fall in love more readily than females.

Although these males tend to recognize love earlier, it does not follow that this more rapid involvement extends back to the initial encounter, i.e., love at first sight, either in incidence or frequency. Love at first sight appears to be an equally probable experience for both sexes, being reported by slightly less than one-third of our respondents.

Turning now to the love experience per se, we find that once in love the stereotypic romantic reactions are more apt to be associated with the females. Prior to the construction of the schedule, university students were requested to describe what they experienced when they were in love—that is, the emotional components of love. These obtained reactions, largely in accord with the elements comprising romantic love, easily lent themselves to the construction of eight items, and these were presented in the schedule on a five-point Likert-type scale. (For purposes of analysis the five scale categories "None, Slight, Moderate, Strong and Very Strong" were collapsed into Slight, Moderate, and Strong. Only in the case of the item "General Feeling of Well Being" this procedure was not followed since it was the only item where a sizeable sex differential existed at the Very Strong category.) The respondents then, were asked to indicate the degree to which these reactions were experienced in this one love involvement. Opportunity for write-ins was provided but all offerings were readily subsumed under the existing eight items. An examination of Table 1 shows that in the case of the four items that demonstrate a significant sex differential, the female is more apt to indicate the item as strongly present in the love affair reported in the schedule. In one other, "Feeling giddy and carefree," although not reaching the .05 level, shows a response pattern biased in favor of females.

TABLE 1
INTENSITY OF LOVE REACTIONS OF MALES AND FEMALES (PERCENT)

	Male (N = 250)	Female (N = 429)	Total (N = 679)	
Floating on a cloud				
Slight	45.2	36.3	39.6	P <.05
Moderate	30.8	31.2	31.1	P <.05
Strong	24.0	32.4	29.3	
Wanted to run, jump, scream				
Slight	64.0	45.2	52.1	
Moderate	20.4	28.4	25.2	P <.001
Strong	15.6	26.3	22.4	
Trouble concentrating				
Slight	47.2	31.2	37.1	
Moderate	23.2	27.0	25.6	P <.001
Strong	29.6	41.7	37.2	
Felt giddy and carefree				
Slight	57.6	48.7	52.0	
Moderate	26.0	29.4	28.1	P <.10
Strong	16.4	21.9	19.9	
General feeling of well being				
Slight	8.8	5.6	6.8	
Moderate	18.4	12.4	14.6	P <.001
Strong	43.2	36.4	38.9	
Very Strong	29.6	45.7	39.7	
Nervous before dates				
Slight	58.8	54.4	56.1	
Moderate	19.6	24.0	22.4	N.S.
Strong	21.6	21.5	21.5	
Physical sensations: cold hands, butterflies in stomach, tingling spine, etc.				
Slight	59.6	56.6	57.7	
Moderate	22.0	22.8	22.5	N.S.
Strong	18.4	20.5	19.8	
Insomnia				
Slight	68.0	69.4	68.9	
Moderate	22.0	17.2	19.0	N.S.
Strong	10.0	13.3	12.1	

It is interesting to observe that with the possible exception of one item, "Wanted to run, jump, scream," there does not appear to be any evidence suggesting uniquely sex-linked reactions. That is, although the female may be prone to stronger reactions, the items in general maintain the same hierarchical order for both sexes. While "General feeling of well being" and "Trouble concentrating" are the most popular reactions for both males and females, the least favored reaction, insomnia, is equally shunned by both sexes. The comparative infrequency with which insomnia is associated with love experience is somewhat curious since it is probably one of the most celebrated symptoms in popular lore.

Recognizing the possible influence of age on the distribution of these romantic reactions, an analysis was conducted holding age constant. Although no statistically significant differences were found, there appeared a slight tendency for older males to indicate strong reactions less frequently while females generally maintained the same pattern in all age groups.

The evidence thus far suggests that it is the female rather than the male who is more apt to experience the traditional romantic emotions of love—the euphoria of love. Our data further suggest that idealization is also a sexually differentiated phenomenon that is more likely to characterize the female love experience. Eight items were employed in an effort to assess whether extremely favorable perceptions of the loved companion and the love relationship with that companion tend to be sex linked. Five of the items, taken from the Burgess and Wallin investigation (1953), concern the personality traits of moodiness, quick temperedness, stubbornness, irritability, and selfishness. The ratings of the companion were made on a four-point scale ranging from "considerably" to "not at all." The three other items were concerned with rating the relationship and aspects of the relationship. For purposes of analysis (Table 2) the responses to these idealization items were telescoped so that the most extreme response was contrasted to all other responses, i.e., those scale points indicating something less than the most extreme favorable response.

Contrasting the males and females on these items revealed only three to be statistically significant, all distinguishing the female as the idealizing party. She was found to be less apt to view her companion as moody and stubborn, and more apt to assess her interests as being very similar to the male's. The remaining items failed to uncover any sex differences.

TABLE 2
COMPANION-RELATIONSHIP ASSESSMENTS MADE BY "EXTREMELY IN LOVE" MALES AND FEMALES

	MALE	FEMALE	
Partner not moody	27.9	72.4	P < .001
Partner not quick tempered	37.2	60.4	P < .001
Partner not stubborn	15.2	89.8	P < .001
Partner not irritable	46.8	57.8	P < .05
Partner not selfish	58.2	51.3	N.S.
Interests very similar to partner	48.1	60.7	P < .02
I could not have a better relationship with another	64.3	76.8	P < .01
Partner's personality couldn't be better	38.6	27.6	P < .05

In reconsidering the phenomenon of idealization, it would seem that the mere contrasting of males and females who indicate they are "in love" is too crude a method since it completely ignores variations in love intensity. The basic function of idealization is to render more perfect that to which one becomes emotionally committed. Emotional commitment, of course, can be expressed as a degree of love involvement. In addition there is also evidence that the conduct of the female in a pair relationship is heavily dependent upon the degree of affect she experiences in that relationship. Our data substantiate the foregoing comments and convey support for considering love intensity as crucial in determining certain aspects of love conduct. The respondents were provided with the opportunity to select from four statements the one which best described how they felt about their partners when they were most in love. These descriptive statements which were geared to measure intensity were: 1. Extremely in love (can't think of possibly loving any more intensely); 2. Very much in love; 3. In love; 4. Somewhat or mildly in love. In analysis it became apparent that the first and second items and the third and fourth items should be telescoped since they elicited comparable responses. These will be referred to as "extremely in love" and "mildly in love," respectively.

When a contrast is made of the sexes who fall in the "mildly in love" category, the same three items that significantly distinguished the males and the females of the entire sample were found to still retain this ability. However, an analysis of the "extremely in love" respondents provides us with a considerably more pervasive and convincing picture of the female as the sex more apt to idealize. Inspection of Table 2 shows that she favorably assesses her love partner and the relationship on six of the eight items. One item completely fails to distinguish the males from the females and another finds the male responses more favorable than the females. It may seem paradoxical that females can more favorably assess males on four of five personality traits and yet it is the males who indicate that their partner's personality couldn't be better. It may be that there are sex-linked personality preferences that obfuscate these findings. Females, for example, may rate the male more favorably on the given traits but it may well be that there are other significant personality facets which we have not considered here. Regardless, these data continue to affirm the previous findings that, although males may initially demonstrate romantic tendencies, it is the female, once in love, who still behaves in accordance with our popular romantic stereotype.

DISCUSSION

In view of the components comprising romantic love, there is evidence from these limited data that ascribing "more romantic" to one sex is a questionable practice. Both sexes are "more romantic" if consideration is given to differential criteria of romanticism. If by "more romantic" we refer to the speed of involvement and commitment, then the male appears to be more deserving of that label. If, on the other hand, we mean the experiencing of the emotional dimension of romantic love, then the female qualifies as candidate for "more romantic." It appears, however, that the female demonstrates her "more romantic" behavior in a somewhat more judicious and rational fashion. She chooses and commits herself more slowly than the male but, once in love, she engages more extravagantly in the euphoric and idealizational dimensions of loving.

From a social psychological perspective the foregoing findings make sense. Certainly heterosexual involvements, premarital and marital, constitute a more encompassing and significant area of activity for the female. For her the entire process undoubtedly connotes a greater investment of self and involves a payment of a greater price. In premarriage alone, the awareness of possible sexual exploitation and its more dramatic status consequences could readily lead her to be the more calculated and rational creature in the initial stages of courtship. The implications of pair involvement for the male are not such as to render him as cautious and circumspect. Perhaps this contributes to his ability to score "more romantic" on romanticism scales. It also appears that the aggressor role of the male in dating and courtship would be relevant to this discussion. Being more attracted to physical qualities—qualities that are readily assessable early in pair involvement—and more responsive to visual stimuli, plus the fact that he is the one who initially precipitates the encounter, would make it reasonable that he should recognize love earlier than the female. This, however, does not preclude the possibility that some females may be experiencing comparable emotions at the same time but are selectively employing a more cautious vocabulary. Males may feel free to label their new emotional state as love, whereas females may merely be "snowed."

The female's more pronounced ability to idealize and experience the euphoria of love may be the consequence of two factors. First, it is quite apparent that she is subjected to a highly romanticized anticipatory socialization for love and marriage that begins in early childhood. Secondly, the status and role consequences of marriage for females make the selection of a love object a more crucial experience. The comparatively more encompassing and significant nature of love for the female can create something of an urgency that she choose well. She may very well be the pair member who is socially more coerced to view her choice favorably and to recognize signs that validate her choice as proper.

SUMMARY

Selected aspects of the experience of being in love were studied in 250 males and 429 females. The findings suggest that males tend to recognize love feelings earlier in the history of the pair relationship than females. However, once love feelings are recognized, the female is more apt to experience the romantic response of euphoria. She is further more prone to idealization of the love object, but only at the more intense levels of loving. It is suggested that the ascription of "more romantic" to one sex is probably an unprofitable exercise since different criteria of romanticism permit either sex to be the recipient of the label.

REFERENCES

Burgess, E. W., and Wallin, P., *Engagement and Marriage*. Philadelphia: J. B. Lippincott and Company, 1953.

Combs, R. H., and Kenkel, W. F. "Sex Differences in Dating Aspirations and Satisfaction with Computer-Selected Partners." *Journal of Marriage and the Family, 28:* 62–66, 1966.

Hawkins, J., *A Sociopsychological Investigation of Heterosexual Response*. Master's Thesis. Purdue University, 1962.

Hobart, C. W., "The Incidence of Romanticism During Courtship." *Social Forces, 36:* 362–367, 1958.

Kephart, W. M., *The Family, Society, and the Individual*. Boston: Houghton Mifflin Company, 1966.

3

Sex Partners and
Sex Problems

Sexual intercourse is an intrinsic part of pairing and marriage. Sexual interaction is challenging to analyze because of the complex interplay of its many facets—physiological, psychological, and sociological. For instance, intercourse can be termed "successful" or "unsuccessful," depending in part on achievement of pleasure and orgasm of both partners. Ability to reach orgasm and aid one's partner to do so can be affected by knowledge of the sexuality of the partner and the technical aspects of intercourse. An additional factor may be the quality of relationship at the time of intercourse or the meaning each person assigns to intercourse in general and to his or her partner in particular. For instance, when one person suggests to another that he or she desires sexual relations, the request can mean anything from sheer interest in physical release to deep love. Then, each partner must decide what the act means not only to himself or herself, but to the significant other as well. Then both must decide if they can accept this definition. Unfortunately, much of this analysis goes on after the fact, rather than before the decision.

In addition to the immediate meaning of intercourse or its aftereffects as people review it, coitus can have far-reaching consequences—pregnancy and the birth of a child. Thus the issues of contraception, abortion, and/or parenthood are really part of intercourse decisions. If indulgence in sexual relations was actually exploitation of one partner by the other, or merely a show of affection between friends, then pregnancy is most unwelcome, and may result in a decision for abortion. On the other hand, if both partners have a stable relationship that includes long-term love and commitment, conception can be an occasion of great joy.

Although the readings that follow may seem particularly meaningful to persons just beginning their sexual careers, they are equally important to married couples or persons in other types of stable unions as years go by. Wives and husbands can often use help in their sexual techniques. Men, particularly, need to learn how women best achieve orgasm, inasmuch as the nonorgasmic woman is no longer a scientific mystery (see Reading 6). The meaning of intercourse within marriage can change over the years also, and husbands and wives have demonstrated that they can be as careless about contraception as their unmarried counterparts, even while not desiring to increase their family.

The Myth of the Vaginal Orgasm

Anne Koedt

The Women's Liberation Movement has challenged many so-called "sexist" practices and beliefs in American society today. Perhaps the most threatening attack, so far as men have been concerned, is of alleged male exploitation during intercourse. Koedt's essay charges that female "frigidity" is actually the result of male selfishness and ignorance of female sexuality. She argues that the locus of the orgasm for women is the clitoris, not the vagina, and that the male superior position (male on top of female) gives only the male satisfaction unless he is aware of the female's needs. Findings by Masters and Johnson suggest that Koedt is right.

GENERAL STATEMENT

Whenever female orgasm is discussed, a false distinction is made between the vaginal and the clitoral orgasm. Frigidity has generally been defined by men as the failure of women to have vaginal orgasms. Actually, the vagina is not a highly sensitive area and is not physiologically constructed to achieve orgasm. The clitoris is the sensitive area and is the female equivalent of the penis. I think this explains a great many things. First, the so-called frigidity rate among women is phenomenal. Usually we are told that it is our hang-up if we don't have an orgasm, and most women accept this analysis. But men are hung-up too, and they have orgasms, so I think we must look for the causes elsewhere.

What actually happens is this: there is only one area for sexual climax although there are many areas for sexual arousal—the clitoris. All orgasms are extensions of sensations from this area. Since the clitoris is usually not directly stimulated in the conventional sexual positions, we are left "frigid." The only other kind of stimulation is purely psychological, the kind of orgasm achieved through fetishes or thinking about someone. But this kind of orgasm is *not* caused by friction with the vagina and therefore cannot be considered a vaginal orgasm. Rather, it is a psychologically caused orgasm which manifests itself physically in the clitoris. Of the orgasms that are caused by physical contact with the clitoris, there may be many degrees of intensity—some more localized and some which are more diffuse and sensitive. The physical organ which causes them, however, is the clitoris.

All this leads to some interesting questions about conventional sex and our role in it. Men have orgasms essentially by friction with the vagina, not the clitoris, which is external and not able to cause friction the way penetration does. Women have thus been defined sexually in terms of what pleases men; our own biology has not been properly analyzed. Instead, we are fed the myth of the liberated woman and her vaginal orgasm, an orgasm which in fact does not exist.

What we must do is redefine our sexuality. We must discard the "normal" concept of sex and create new guidelines which take into account mutual sexual enjoyment. While the ideal of mutual enjoyment is acknowledged in marriage manuals, it is not followed to its logical conclusion. We must begin to demand that if a certain sexual position now defined as "standard" is not mutually conducive to orgasm, then it should no longer be defined as standard. New techniques must be used or devised which transform our current sexual exploitation.

FREUD—A FATHER OF THE VAGINAL ORGASM

Freud contended that the clitoral orgasm was adolescent, and that upon puberty, when women began having intercourse with men, women should transfer the center of orgasm to the vagina. The vagina, it was assumed, was able to produce a parallel, but more mature, orgasm than the clitoris. Much work was done to elaborate on this theory, but not much was done to challenge the basic assumptions.

To fully appreciate this incredible invention, perhaps Freud's general attitude about women must first be realized. Mary Ellman (*Thinking About Women*) said it this way:

> Everything in Freud's patronizing and fearful attitude toward women follows from their lack of a penis, but it is only in his essay "The Psychology of Women" that Freud makes explicit . . . the deprecations of women which are implicit in his work. He then describes women as intellectually less able and prescribes for them the abandonment of the life of the mind, which will interfere with their sexual function. When the psychoanalyzed patient is a male, the analyst sets himself the task of developing the man's capacities, but with women patients, the job is to resign them to the limits of their sexuality. As Mr. Rieff puts it: for Freud, "analysis cannot encourage in women new energies for success and achievement, but only teach them the lesson of rational resignation."

Once having laid down the law about our sexuality, Freud, not so strangely, discovered a tremendous problem of frigidity in women. (Frigidity defined as failure to achieve a vaginally caused and experienced orgasm.) His cure was that a woman who was frigid needed psychiatric care. She was suffering from failure to mentally adjust to her "natural" role as a woman. Frank S. Caprio, a contemporary follower of these ideas:

> . . . Whenever a woman is incapable of achieving an orgasm via coitus, provided her husband is an adequate partner, and prefers clitoral stimulation to any other form of sexual activity, she can be regarded as suffering from frigidity and requires psychiatric assistance *(The Sexually Adequate Female).*

The explanation given was that women were envious of men—"renunciation of womanhood." Thus is was diagnosed as an anti-male phenomenon.

It is important to emphasize that Freud didn't base this theory upon a study of the woman's anatomy, but rather upon his assumptions of woman as an inferior appendage to the man, and her consequent social and psychological role. In their attempts to deal with the ensuing problem of mass frigidity, Freudians created elaborate mental gymnastics. Marie Bonaparte, in *Female Sexuality* (Grove Press, p. 148), goes so far as to suggest surgery to help women back on their rightful path. Having discovered a strange connection between the non-frigid woman and the location of the clitoris near the vagina,

> It then occurred to men that where, in certain women, this gap was excessive, and the clitoridal fixation obdurate, a clitoridal-vaginal reconciliation might be effected by surgical means, which would then benefit the normal erotic function. Professor Halban, of Vienna, as much biologist as surgeon, became interested in the problem and worked out a simple operative technique. In this, the suspensory ligament of the clitoris was severed and the clitoris secured to the underlying structures, thus fixing it in a lower position, with eventual reduction of the labia minora.

But the severest damage was not in the area of surgery, where Freudians absurdly ran around trying to change the anatomy to fit their basic assumptions. The worst damage was done to the mental health of women who either suffered silently with self-blame or flocked to the psychiatrists, looking desperately for the hidden and terrible repression that kept them from their vaginal destiny.

LACK OF EVIDENCE?

One can perhaps at first claim that these areas are unknown and unexplored areas, but upon closer examination this is certainly not true today, but was not even true in the past. For example, men have known that women suffered from frigidity often during intercourse. So the problem was there. Also, there is much specific evidence. Men knew that the clitoris was and is the essential organ for masturbation, whether in children or adult women. So obviously women made it clear where *they* thought their sexuality was located. Men also seemed suspiciously aware of the clitoral powers during "foreplay" when they want to arouse women and produce the necessary lubrication for penetration. Foreplay is a concept created for male purposes, but works to the disadvantage of woman since as soon as she is aroused the male changes to vaginal stimulation and leaves her both aroused and unsatisfied.

It has also been known that women need no anesthesia inside the vagina during surgery, thus pointing to the fact that the vagina is in fact not a highly sensitive area.

Today, with anatomy and Kinsey and Masters and Johnson, to mention just a few sources, there is *no* ignorance on the subject. There are, however, social reasons why this knowledge has not been accepted. We are living in a male power structure which does not want change in the area of women.

ANATOMICAL EVIDENCE

Rather than starting with what women *ought* to feel, it would seem logical to start out with what the anatomical facts are regarding the clitoris and vagina.

The Clitoris

A small equivalent of the penis, except for the fact that the urethra does not go through it as in the man's penis. Its erection is similar to the male erection, and the head of the clitoris has the same type of structure and function as the head of the penis. G. Lombard Kelly, in *Sexual Feeling in Married Men and Women,* p. 35 (Pocket Books), says:

> The head of the clitoris is also composed of erectile tissue, and it possesses a very sensitive epithelium or surface covering, supplied with special nerve endings called genital corpuscles, which are peculiarly adapted for sensory stimulation that under proper mental conditions terminates in the sexual orgasm. No other part of the female generative tract has such corpuscles.

The clitoris has no other function than that of sexual pleasure.

The Vagina

Its functions are related to the reproductive function. Principally, (1) menstruation, (2) receive penis, (3) hold semen, and (4) birth passage. The interior of the vagina, which according to the defenders of the vaginally caused orgasm is the center and producer of the orgasm, is:

> ... like nearly all other internal body structures, poorly supplied with end organs of touch. The internal entodermal origin of the lining of the vagina makes it similar in this respect to the rectum and other parts of the digestive tract (Kinsey, *Sexual Behavior in the Human Female,* p. 580).

The degree of insensitivity inside the vagina is so high that "Among the women who were tested in our gynecologic sample, less than 14% were at all conscious that they had been touched" (Kinsey, p. 580).

Even the importance of the vagina as an *erotic* center (as opposed to center for orgasm) has been found to be minor.

Other Areas

Labia minora and the vestibule of the vagina. These two sensitive areas may trigger off a clitoral orgasm. Because they can be effectively stimulated during 'normal' coitus, though infrequent, this kind of stimulation is incorrectly thought to be vaginal orgasm. However, it is important to distinguish between areas which can stimulate the clitoris, but are incapable of producing the orgasm themselves, and the clitoris:

> Regardless of what means of excitation is used to bring the individual to the state of sexual climax, the sensation is perceived by the genital corpuscles and is localized where they are situated: in the head of the clitoris or penis (Kelly p. 49).

Psychologically Stimulated Orgasm

Aside from the above mentioned direct and indirect stimulations of the clitoris, there is a third way an orgasm may be triggered. This is through mental (cortical) stimulation, where the imagination stimulates the brain, which in turn stimulates the genital corpuscles of the glans to set off an orgasm.

WOMEN WHO SAY THEY HAVE VAGINAL ORGASMS

Confusion

Because of the lack of knowledge of their own anatomy, some women accept the idea that an orgasm felt during 'normal' intercourse was vaginally caused. This confusion is caused by a combination of 2 factors. One, failing to locate the center of the orgasm, and two, by a desire to fit her experience to the male defined idea of sexual normalcy. Considering that women know little about their anatomy, it is easy to be confused.

Deception

The vast majority of women who claim vaginal orgasm to their men are faking it to, as Ti-Grace Atkinson says, "get the job." In a new best-selling Danish book, *I Accuse* (my own transl.), Mette Ejlersen specifically deals with this common problem, which she calls the "sex comedy."

This comedy is caused by many reasons. First of all, the man brings a great deal of pressure to bear on the woman, because he considers his ability as a lover at stake. So as not to offend his ego, the woman will comply with the prescribed role and go through simulated ecstacy. In some of the Danish women mentioned, women who were left frigid were turned off on sex, and pretended vaginal orgasm to hurry up the sex act. Others admitted that they had faked vaginal orgasm to catch a man; in one case, to get him to leave his first wife, who admitted being vaginally frigid. The woman pretended that she was "normal," which greatly pleased the man. Later she was forced to fake orgasm, as she obviously couldn't tell him to stimulate her clitorally.

Many more were simply afraid to establish their right to equal enjoyment, seeing the sexual act as being primarily for the man's benefit, and any pleasure that the woman got as an added extra.

Another woman, with just enough ego to reject the man's idea that she needed psychiatric care, refused to admit her frigidity. She wouldn't accept self-blame, but she didn't know how to solve the problem, not knowing the physiological facts about herself. So she was left in a peculiar limbo.

Perhaps one of the most infuriating and damaging results of this whole charade has been that women who were perfectly healthy sexually were taught that they were not. So aside from being sexually deprived, these women were told to blame themselves when there was none. Looking for a cure to a problem that has none, can lead women on an endless path of self-hatred and insecurity. For she is told by her analyst that not even her one role allowed in a male society—the role of *Women*—is she successful in. She is put on the defensive, with phony data as evidence against her, that she better try to be even more feminine, think more feminine, and reject her envy of men. That is, shuffle even harder, baby.

WHY MEN MAINTAIN THE MYTH

Sexual Penetration Is Preferred

The best stimulant for the penis is the woman's vagina. It supplies the necessary friction and lubrication. From a strictly technical point of view this position offers the best physiological condition, even though the man may try other positions for variation.

"The Invisible Woman"

One of the elements of male chauvinism is the refusal or inability to see women as total, separate human beings. Rather than this approach, men have chosen to define women only in terms of how they benefited men's lives. Sexually, a woman was not seen as an individual wanting to share equally in the sexual act, any more than she was seen as a person with independent desires when she did anything else in society. Thus, it was easy to make up what was convenient about women; for on top of that, society was so controlled that women were not organized to even form a vocal opposition to the male experts.

Penis as the Epitome of Masculinity

Men define their lives greatly in terms of masculinity. It is a universal ego builder, whereas racism, for example, is connected with particular areas of racial mixture. Masculinity is defined culturally by what is the most non-female. The essence of chauvinism is not the practical, economic comfortable services women supply. It is the psychological superiority. This negative kind of definition of self, rather than a positive definition based upon one's own achievements and development of one's potentials, has of course chained the victim and the oppressor both. But *by far* the most brutalized of the two is the victim.

The analogy is racism, where the white racist compensates his feeling of unworthiness by creating an image of the black man (this is primarily a male struggle) which is inferior to him. Because of his power in a white male power structure, the white man can socially enforce this mythical division.

To the extent that men try to prove male superiority through physiological differentiation, masculinity depends on being the *most* muscular, the most hairy, the deepest voice, and the biggest penis. Women, on the other hand, are approved of (i.e., called feminine) if they are weak, petite, shave their legs, have high soft voices, and no penis.

Since the clitoris is almost identical to the penis, one finds a great deal of evidence of men in various societies trying to either ignore the clitoris and emphasize the vagina, *or,* as in many places in the Mideast, actually performing clitoridectomy (Bonaparte, p. 151). Freud saw this ancient and still practiced custom as a way of further "feminizing" the female by removing this cardinal vestige of her masculinity (Bonaparte, p. 151). It should be noted also that a big clitoris is considered ugly and "masculine." Some cultures pour chemicals on the clitoris to make it shrivel up into proper size.

It seems clear to me that men in fact fear the clitoris as a threat to their masculinity.

Sexually Expendable Male

Men fear that they will become sexually expendable if the clitoral organ is substituted for the vaginal as the basic pleasure for women. Actually this has a great deal of validity if one considers *only* the anatomy. The position of the penis inside the vagina, while perfect for reproduction, does not usually stimulate an orgasm in women because the clitoris is not usually located there, but rather externally and higher up. Women must thus rely upon indirect stimulations in this "normal" position.

Lesbian sexuality, in rubbing one clitoris against the other, could make an excellent case, based on anatomical data, for the extinction of the male organ. Albert Ellis makes a statement something to the effect that a man without a penis can make a woman an excellent lover.

Considering that the vagina is very desirable from a man's point of view, purely on physical grounds, one begins to see the dilemma for men. And it forces us to discard many "physical" arguments explaining why women go to bed with men. What is left, it seems to me, are psychological reasons why women select men at the exclusion of other women.

Control of Women

One reason given why men cut the clitoris off women in the Mideastern countries is that it will keep the women from straying. Removing the sexual organ capable of orgasm, it must be assumed that her sexual drive will diminish. Considering how much men look upon their women as property, we should begin to consider a great deal more why it is not in the men's interest to have women totally free sexually. The double standard, as practiced for example in Latin America, is set up to keep the women bound as property, while men are free to have affairs as they wish.

Lesbianism

Aside from the strictly anatomical reasons why women might seek women lovers, there is a great fear on men's part that women will seek the company of other women on a full human basis. The establishment of clitoral orgasm as fact would threaten the heterosexual *institution*. The oppressor always fears the unity of the oppressed, and the escape of women from the psychological hold men now maintain. Rather than imagining a future free relationship between individuals, men tend to react with paranoid fears of revenge on the part of women.

REFERENCES

Kinsey, Alfred C., *Sexual Behavior in the Human Female,* Pocket Books, 1953.
Bonaparte, Marie, *Female Sexuality,* Grove Press, 1956.
Ellis, Albert, *Sex Without Guilt,* Grove Press, 1965.
Kelly, G. Lombard, *Sexual Feelings in Married Men and Women,* Pocket Books, 1961.
Ejlersen, Mette, *I Accuse (Jeg Anglager),* Chr. Erichsens Forlag (Danish), 1969.

The Language of Sexual Behavior

Viktor Gecas and Roger Libby

Sexual intercourse is more than a physical act. It has a rather wide range of social and psychological meanings. Sex partners may, in fact, each see the meaning of their relationship quite differently. In early Judeo-Christian teachings, sex was seen as a necessary evil, to be indulged in for the purpose of procreation only. Naturally, it was to occur only within marriage. As years went by, sexual intercourse began to be viewed as a manifestation of love between two people. Even more recently, sociologists have observed and reported on exploitative sex and sex for pleasure, although it is probable that there have been exploiters and pleasure seekers since the dawn of humanity. Gecas and Libby refer to these belief systems as "scripts," because they set off an entire chain of events, the tone and direction of which depends on the original meaning of the sex act to participants. The personal (and sociologically interesting) problem for participants is not so much what they themselves believe about a relationship that includes sexual intercourse, but what they assume their partner thinks about it. The area becomes highly problematic when each partner has different expectations as to the meaning of the relationship to the other or when one partner shifts to another meaning. It might prove interesting to focus research on how the meaning of sexual intercourse changes over time, both within marriage and outside it.

The perception of sexual behavior as symbolic communication is most directly evident in the writings of Simon and Gagnon, who introduce the concept of social script and unequivocally state that "All human sexual experience is

Viktor Gecas is Associate Professor in the Department of Rural Sociology, Washington State University, Pullman, Wash. 99163. Roger W. Libby is Visiting Associate Professor of Human Development, and Research Director at the Institute for Family Research, Syracuse University, Syracuse, N.Y. 13210.

From Viktor Gecas and Roger Libby, "Sexual Behavior as Symbolic Interaction," *The Journal of Sex Research*, Vol. 12 (February 1976): 33–49. Reprinted by permission of the publisher and authors.

scripted behavior. Without the proper elements of a script that defines the situation, names the actors, and plots the behavior, little is likely to happen" (1968: 175). This overstates the case, since some sexual behavior is spontaneous, exploratory, and non-normative. However, in general their point is well taken. They define *script* as follows:

> Our use of the term *script* with reference to the sexual has two major dimensions. One deals with the external, the interpersonal—the script as the organization of mutually shared conventions that allows two or more actors to participate in a complex act involving mutual dependence. The second deals with the internal, the intra-psychic, the motivational elements that produce arousal or at least a commitment to the activity (Gagnon and Simon, 1973, p. 20).

This conception of sexual experience is very similar to the views of social life offered by Goffman (1959), Stone (1962), Burke (1962), Lyman and Scott (1970) and others of what has come to be called the dramaturgical school of symbolic interactionism. Here the organizing metaphor for social life is the theater and the emphasis is on such elements of interaction as "staging," "acting parts," "taking roles," and "presenting selves" in front of various "audiences," etc. Scripts are normative clusters which specify the parameters for lines of action in given social contexts. With regard to sexual behavior, they tell us how to behave sexually.

These scripts are usually located in broader meaning and value systems rooted to various institutions and processes in society, such as, courtship, marriage, family, and religion. In contemporary American society there are at least four identifiable and coherent philosophies or codes regarding sexual behavior: the traditional-religious, romantic, recreational, and utilitarian-predatory. The traditional-religious philosophy views sexual activity outside marriage as sinful, particularly for women. It requires virginity for unmarried women and demands fidelity for both partners. The meaning of sexual activity is derived from its procreative function, although its connection with affection is recognized.

The prevalence and influence of this philosophy of sexual restraint and restriction to the marital bond is undoubtedly decreasing, although there is even doubt over the degree to which it was followed in the past. Nevertheless, to the extent that we still view sexual behavior in traditionally moral terms, consider sexual transgressions as sinful, and feel guilty when we engage in these, we are reflecting the influence of the traditional religious code.

The romantic philosophy has tended to temper the influence of the traditional-religious code. The romantic code emphasizes the value of being in love. Love is a prerequisite to sexual relations. It justifies sexual intercourse, and sexual intercourse strengthens the bond between the lovers. Without love, coitus is considered bestial and/or meaningless. Marriage is the preferred context for the expression of love and sexuality but sexual intimacy outside marriage is justified on the grounds of love.

This sexual orientation has been held most prominently by our urban middle classes. It has also been a major theme in mass media such as movies, novels, fiction magazines, and even commercial advertising. The kind of script for sexual interaction that emanates from the romantic code identifies the eligible interactants (those in love with each other), the necessary emotional state (love expressed in uncontrollable passion), the appropriate rhetoric (romantic), and the situational conditions (as close to the spontaneous expression of affection as possible). Women are socialized into this sexual code more than are men in our society, which often presents problems in heterosexual relations.

The recreational philosophy ignores or de-emphasizes both the institutional implications of sex and the values of romantic love. This orientation is the one most clearly associated with the "sexual revolution" in this country—the liberalization of sexual constraints. The recreational philosophy is concerned with sex primarily as a pleasurable activity. It should not be limited to marriage and love is not a necessary precondition for engaging in sexual interaction. Sex is fun. It is a source of pleasure for oneself and a means of giving pleasure to others, and this is justification enough for engaging in it.

This philosophy is more and more frequently appearing in the mass media. It is most clearly reflected in various men's magazines, such as *Playboy,* and is even becoming evident in some women's magazines. For example, *Playgirl* has recently emerged as a takeoff on *Playboy* with the aim of catering to the "prurient interests" of women. Its typical "foldout-of-the-month" is a nude male.

The scripts associated with this philosophy stress the actions and vocabularies which emphasize enjoyment, playfulness, self-abandonment, and, to an increasing extent, technique. This has resulted in a curious paradox: as sex becomes freed from the constraints of religion and romance, as enjoyment becomes its primary requirement and justification, greater emphasis is placed on the mechanics of sexual intercourse, and the individual comes to be evaluated primarily on his technical competence in this sphere. This places a considerable burden on the individual to perform well, increasing his level of self-consciousness and control over his actions (the opposite of abandonment), and decreasing his level of enjoyment. In short, for some operating from this philosophy the character of sexual experience has changed from play (cf. Foote, 1955) to work (cf. Lewis and Brissett, 1967). The proliferation of sex manuals which stress technique is an indication of this trend. The recurrent pitch of these sex manuals, as Lewis and Brissett (1967) point out, is that sex should not be taken lightly and its enjoyment cannot be taken for granted—one must *work* at it in order to be successful.

In some ways this view is similar to the fourth philosophy, the utilitarian predatory view. This orientation views sex as a means to some other end. It can be *used* to gain money (as in prostitution), or power (as in certain types of heterosexual bargaining), or prestige (status in one's peer group). For these reasons, the activity may not even be pleasurable. But even when there is pleasure in sex the real payoff comes from (non-sexual) sources. An example of this kind of normative system can be found in the subcultures of various adolescent males who "keep score" and gain status in their peer groups for their sexual prowess. The concept of "machismo" in Latin cultures has some of the values placed on sexual prowess associated with manliness (cf. Rainwater, 1964; and Lewis, 1959). From another angle, the more militant feminists also tend to view sexual relations in power rather than pleasure terms (cf. Kate Millet, 1970).

The scripts emanating from this philosophy often involve elements of misrepresentation, especially with regard to motives. The working strategy is often to present a "line" and create a situation that is convincing to the other in the interaction and which will produce the desired outcome. The important skills in this effort involve being, in Goffman's terms, a good impression manager: one who can create the situation to his own advantage.

It is clear that the relative influence of these philosophies is changing and that new meanings for sexual interaction are appearing. For example, a recent emergent which is gaining popularity is a variant of the recreational philosophy. Lever and Schwartz (1971) call it "friendly sex," and describe it as recreational sex with affection. Its central features are (1) the self-conscious advocacy of a single standard of sexual behavior applicable to both men and women, (2) the location of sexual interaction in the context of casual but warm interpersonal relations, and (3) the tendency to extend this orientation into marriage so that marriage does not constitute sexual exclusivity for either spouse. This philosophy, getting much of its coherence and impetus from the "hippie subculture" of the sixties, is finding contemporary expression in such works as Rimmer's *The Harrad Experiment* (1966) and Rogers' *Becoming Partners: Marriage and Its Alternatives* (1972).

This description of various sexual philosophies is not meant to be inclusive or extensive. Rather, the point is to indicate the range of meanings associated with sexual activity and to consider their implications for social scripts.

Another element which is relevant to the outcome of sexual interaction is the degree of *awareness* the actors have of the relevant scripts in the situation. Glaser and Strauss (1964) used the concept of "awareness context" to refer to the extent of knowledge that the actors have about one another's identities or conditions. It is not uncommon for people engaged in sexual interaction to enter into the relationship with different scripts. For example, the male may be operating from a script which views sex as a recreational activity while the female may have a romantic script in mind. Skipper and Nass (1966) in their study of the dating patterns of student nurses and college men found that the nurses had a different script and therefore different motives for dating (primarily romantic and courtship) than the men, who were more interested in the nurses as an "easy score." Similarly, Bernard (1972), in commenting on the contemporary American marriage scene, states that there is a "marriage for the man and a marriage for the woman." That is, the meaning of marriage differs for men and women.

The degree of awareness each participant has of the other's script, especially the motives associated with the script, makes a good deal of difference for the course of the relationship. In general, we can say that the person who has the greater knowledge or awareness of the scripts involved in the interaction has the greater control over the course of the interaction. This of course assumes that knowledge of the other actor is useful in negotiating one's own actions in that relationship.

Along with the different scripts brought into an interaction by the different persons involved, a person may hold a number of competing scripts springing from commitment to different reference groups and value positions. This may contribute to a sense of anxiety, ambivalence, or immobility as he deliberates, for example, whether he should follow the religious script developed in his family of orientation or the recreational script of his peer group. Over the course of a lifetime a person may go through a number of different scripts as the various stages of life give him various perspectives on sex.

The social script is a useful concept through which we can organize a number of other concepts of symbolic interactionism and apply them to the sexual domain—concepts such as identities, lines of action, vocabularies of motive, and definitions of the situation. The social script enables a sexual interaction to take place because it provides persons with a program or strategy of action along with reasons for engaging in the activity.

The Costs of Contraception

Kristin Luker

The recent advancement in contraceptive methods has made planned parenthood available to everyone. Yet, with abortion legalized, the persons who come to the abortion clinics are often women who could have taken proper precautions to prevent conception. Why don't they? Gecas and Libby (Reading 7) talk about five scripts that give meaning to intercourse. Luker's research indicates that any script has a network of behavior norms, many of which militate against the use of contraceptives. Esthetics and morality are intertwined in such a way as to result in a spoiled moment if the woman has not contracepted in advance, or in a spoiled identity for a woman if she is unmarried, yet contracepts on a regular basis. Even if married, the romance of the moment may seem too fragile, the intensity of feelings too insistent, to permit the pause of a few minutes in which to insert a diaphragm. Yet the pressures for spontaneity, which presumably aid the pleasure of the moment, can have a serious consequence—pregnancy. Thus sex starts as a scripted act between two people and becomes a causal agent in the linkage of three. The very act of preserving one's image in intimacy can result in the casting of a larger shadow on the woman's reputation.

One of the most unexpected aspects of recent fertility history in the United States has been the high rate of legal induced abortions. While it is true that abortion has certainly been one of the oldest and most widespread forms of fertility control, there were many reasons to assume, prior to the recent liberalization of abortion laws which culminated in the Supreme Court decisions, that abortion would never be very frequent or very popular in the United States. Prior to the Supreme Court decisions, abortion had been illegal for almost a hundred years, and until recently, the legal taboo was matched with a normative one: most Americans disapproved of abortion except to save the life of the mother. Perhaps most importantly, those countries which have had very

Adapted by permission from Kristin Luker, *Taking Chances: Abortion and the Decision Not to Contracept*, (Berkeley: University of California Press, 1975). Copyright © 1975 by Regents of the University of California; reprinted by permission of the University of California Press.

high rates of legal (and illegal) induced abortion have also been those countries where for historical, religious, or economic reasons, contraceptive devices have been relatively unavailable. It has generally been assumed that in a contraceptively sophisticated society like the United States, people, given the choice, would prefer to prevent rather than interrupt pregnancies.

There is increasing evidence that this is not necessarily the case. The sheer numbers of legal induced abortions (over 700,000 in 1975) suggest that these abortions cannot be accounted for only by "method failures." In addition, many practitioners report incidences of repeat abortions in populations which are known to have been given contraceptive follow-up after their first abortion. Finally, calculations on age specific pregnancy rates seem to point to this conclusion as well.

What accounts for the high rate of induced abortion in a society like the United States? In order to begin to answer this question, an exploratory study was undertaken on a series of women seeking abortion at a Planned-Parenthood affiliate. The medical records of the first five hundred women were analyzed, and sixty women were interviewed in an intensive, semi-structured way and verbatim accounts were taken. A preliminary analysis of the medical records suggested that a majority of the women seeking abortion in this clinic were "contraceptive risk takers"—that is, women who had successfully used effective contraception in the past, but who used either sporadic contraception or no contraception prior to the pregnancy which was being terminated. 75% of these women had used some form of contraception in the past, (not including douching, rhythm, and withdrawal) and 50% had been prior pill takers.

At least part of the problem of induced abortion in the United States, then, is what makes people contraceptive risk takers? i.e., what makes people with earlier histories of effective contraception choose not to use those contraceptives to prevent a pregnancy which subsequently ends in an induced abortion?

Usually it is assumed that women with unwanted pregnancies have gotten pregnant because of either "contraceptive ignorance" where they are not able to have access to contraceptives which would prevent the pregnancy, or because of psychic conflict which inhibits them from using the contraceptive effectively. In this study, however, it is clear from the statistics cited above that these women could not be considered contraceptively ignorant, since most of them had successfully used contraception in the past. While it is harder to determine if these women were psychically conflicted, we suggest that an exclusively intrapsychic theory of contraceptive risk taking is not adequate to explain the very large number of contraceptive risk takers in this population.

An alternative explanation for contraceptive risk taking suggests that the use of contraception is a social act, not merely a technological one, and that using contraception brings with it a series of social and cultural meanings. For better or worse, intercourse and the reproduction of human beings is an activity subjected to a high degree of social control. Whether it is argued that social control of sexual activity stems from a need to keep women in circulation so as to promote other forms of social cooperation (Lévi-Strauss), or for basic libidinal reasons (Freud), or because any society must control sexual activity as a component of the reproduction of the species (Davis), it is clear that sex is a social act surrounded by a multitude of taboos and sanctions.[1] Contraception, which is directly related to sexual activity (as in the chemical and mechanical methods of birth control) or indirectly related (as in the use of the pill or the IUD) therefore carries with it many of the same social taboos and meanings as intercourse itself, and like intercourse itself, these meanings are emotionally charged.

Within this study, women cited a number of socially defined "costs" that came with using contraception; these costs made it more rational at times to choose not to use contraception, even though the unwanted pregnancy, when it occurred, was more "costly" socially than using contraception would have been. (It should be noted that risk-taking women are not alone in this desire to postpone immediate costs even when the penalty for such postponement is higher long-term costs. A National Safety Council study suggests that two-thirds of the cars on the road today have safety related defects which owners postpone repairing because of the cost of repairs, although the resulting accident should it occur will inevitably be more expensive. The principle is the same.)

Women interviewed in this study listed four such "costs" of using contraception, given the social and cultural meaning attached to it: that using contraception means acknowledging intercourse, that contraception means planning intercourse, that continuing contraception over time means that a woman is sexually available, and that contraception means that sex is planned and is not therefore spontaneous.

Costs of Acknowledging Intercourse

Acknowledgement can be to oneself or to others. Of all the costs cited by women in this study, acknowledging intercourse to oneself was named least frequently. Technically, of course, all acknowledging of costs calls for some degree of acknowledging to oneself, privately, that intercourse is occurring. The cost of this acknowledgement, however, was evidenced by women who said that contraception is "unnatural." This implies a belief that sex is "natural" but that rational planning for it in terms of contraception is not. Also, it is traditionally the woman who has held the decision-making power over whether or not intercourse should occur. Thus it is possible for a woman to acknowledge only minimally that she is having intercourse, because without artificial contraception love-making is more "pure" and has only a nominal connection with sex. To reverse this statement in terms of costs, the use of contraception would compel the acknowledgement that intercourse is occurring to this person, *just as it does to everyone else*. The degree of planning and foresight that contraception demands can make a desirably warm and intimate emotional experience appear impersonally "cold-blooded" and hence costly:

I: How did he feel about using rhythm?

R: We were being puritanical because we didn't want to use artificial things.

I: Artificial?

R: Just a chemical effect on your body or having something inserted in you. The collusion of the male partner in this strategy is also evident. As one male respondent said:

R: It seems kind of phoney to use contraception. It doesn't seem natural or the right way.

More significant for most women, the decision to obtain contraception acknowledges to others whose opinions count that sex is occurring, and the cost of this can be very high. Whether the "significant other" is the sex partner, parents, or some abstract moral judge (as, for example, the Catholic Church), the woman is reluctant to take steps which might notify them that she is participating in sexual behavior which she has reason to suppose they will disapprove. This splitting off of the action from the acknowledgement of the action—the belief that it is one thing to have intercourse and another to admit such intercourse openly—is not unique to people breaking sexual taboos. Since by their standards they are deviant, in order to be contraceptively protected they would have to be openly deviant. Few deviants, or pseudo-deviants such as these women (premarital intercourse is far from statistically deviant), are willing to risk the costs of *public* deviance, no matter what the benefits. This is particularly true in the case of contraception, when the benefits are ambiguous. In avoiding contraception, the woman is protecting herself from a present cost (the censure of significant others) at the expense of a future cost (the possible occurrence of a pregnancy):

    I: You said that you had used the pill previously and had run out. Where did you get the pills the first time?

    R: A family planning clinic in Southwest City.

    I: Why didn't you get the prescription refilled?

    R: Because of my father. . . . We live in a small town, and the medical and dental people are very close, and I couldn't go to another doctor without his finding out and I think it would hurt him.

The focus on the present to the exclusion of the possible future also acts as a leveler between the heavier but future costs of an unwanted pregnancy, should it occur, and the lesser but more immediate costs surrounding the acknowledging. As one male respondent said:

    I: Why did you not use the pill?

    R: (Male) We were worried about the financial hassles involved in getting the pill.

    I: But isn't an abortion more expensive than using the pills?

    R: (Male) Yeah, but it took us six and a half months to need an abortion. And we didn't think we were going to need an abortion, anyway.

The fact that this couple was a married couple, and hence not risking an illegitimate pregnancy, brings to light another important aspect of the acknowledging process, the role of internalized norms. Perhaps the most frequently cited "significant other" in this study was the Catholic Church. (Catholics made up approximately one-third of the clientele of the Abortion Clinic, and they represent about one-third of the total population of the greater Northern California metropolitan area where the study was made.[2]) Church dogma presents the normative standard that the only acceptable intercourse is for procreation and not for personal pleasure. By this standard, both married and unmarried Catholics can have "deviant" sexual intercourse. There was a noticeable tendency in this population for Catholic respondents to conform to and reject the Church's teachings at the same time, in a "zero sum" game fashion: to engage in deviant intercourse but not to compound that "sin" by using contraception, which is both a deviant act by Church standards and an acknowledgement that premeditation precedes the sin:

    I: Did you think you might get pregnant not using contraception?

    R: I thought so, I mean, I knew there was a possibility. But there was this problem of my religious background. If you are familiar with the Catholic

Church it is against the Church to use contraception or to have premarital sex, and I was always brought up in a strict Catholic home. It was always "do this, don't do that." Just using a contraceptive seems like you're planning.

Thus, the individual has to answer for only one deviance at a time: deviant intercourse, but not deviant intercourse plus prohibited contraception. That a later, costlier deviance—an induced abortion—was the outcome for all the risk-takers in this study, Catholic and non-Catholic alike, only demonstrates once again the tendency to focus on present and obvious costs rather than on future and ambiguous costs.

The concurrent accepting and rejecting of normative standards (specifically those of the Catholic Church) tends to produce either erratic behavior patterns or erratic belief systems in the same individual. What this appears to represent is a desire to conform to an ideology when feasible, but in a context where feasibility is constantly being redefined over time. Incompatible goals and beliefs are exhibited in the following interview statement, where one "significant other," the mother, supports the ideological position of a second "significant other," the Church, and the respondent rejects both as unreasonable but refrains from using contraception herself:

I: Why didn't you use more effective contraception?

R: I always thought about it, but never did anything about it. I used to think about the pill, but my sister used it, she's married now and stuff, and my mother used to tell me she'd die. That it would wreck you up. She's really Catholic. But it seems as if most of my friends are on it.

The conflicting pressures faced by this respondent include her perception that her sister has "gotten away with" contraception with no side effects, her perception that predictions of death are unreasonable, an implied normative demand on the part of the mother, and a competing normative structure presented by her peers, most of whom are perceived as taking the pill. When buffeted by such conflicting demands and pressures, it is not surprising that respondents often postpone any action whatsoever, or engage in erratic contraceptive behavior.

COSTS OF PLANNING CONTRACEPTION

Structurally, as first discussed, this means that contraception forces a woman to define herself as a person who is sexually active. Planning specifically suggests not only that a woman has been sexually active once, but that she intends to be so again. A woman who plans is actively anticipating intercourse: in the terminology of the women interviewed, she is "looking to have sex." A woman who is "looking to have sex," then, is a woman who must take initiative, view herself as sexually aggressive, and abandon the traditional role of female passivity. Thus the costs of planning can be very high. As an example, one woman who was interviewed had a hard time saying openly that she had had intercourse, much less planned to have it again, despite a relationship of fairly long duration with one man:

I: Did you ever think about getting pregnant?

R: Sometimes I thought about it, but I didn't really pay too much attention, because we weren't really into . . . we were goofing around . . . in an intimate . . .

I: Could you clarify that?

R: We started in on one thing and then we would go on to another thing and finally we would have intercourse. We never said, "Well, we're going to do it today." It just happened.

The pretense that it always "just happened" (in this case almost every night for over a year) is one way of escaping the social definition of being a person who is sexually active by choice.

A woman who plans intercourse is also socially defined as an experienced woman: virgins and "innocents" do not use contraceptives. A woman may refuse to plan contraception to avoid a social (and male) definition of being a "woman who's been around."

I: How did you decide not to contracept this time?

R: Actually sex for me wasn't steady and it was really with only one or two people I knew. It's been a year leading up to when I got pregnant that I slept with anyone.

A woman who is "too active" sexually loses status. One woman in the study, for example, said that women who are too active are contemptuously referred to by both men and women in her circle as "rabbits." One way to avoid this definition is to have each and every sexual encounter be unanticipated, and hence free from the stigma of being continuous:

I: Did you think about what might happen if you didn't use contraception?

R: Yeah, I thought about it to a certain extent, but I thought it could never happen to me. It wasn't something I'd planned for. If I'd planned to have intercourse every night—you know what I'm trying to say.

COSTS OF CONTINUING CONTRACEPTION

Just as a woman beginning her sexual career may find it costly to acknowledge herself as a fully sexual person who expects to have sexual intercourse and plans for it, the woman who has been successfully contracepting within a relationship must acknowledge to herself that she intends to remain sexually available if she continues contraception after the end of that relationship. This appears to be the reason why so many women have "relation-specific" contraceptive patterns. They use contraception effectively with one male friend (or husband) but discontinue contraception when the relationship ends. The following pattern is typical of women who experience this group of costs:

I: According to the information on the fact sheet, you said you used pills with your first boy friend, and stopped when you broke up with him. Why didn't you use contraception with this boy friend?

R: In this first place, this guy I was going out with, I thought I wouldn't need to . . . I had already decided to go away. If I had gotten pills I would have had to wait.

I: Did you think of using any other contraception that you wouldn't have to wait for?

R: Not at the time.

I: Did you think you could get away without using contraception?

R: Yes.

Again the pattern of not expecting intercourse is displayed, but unlike women who had never had regular intercourse (and thus have some grounds for not expecting sex), women in this group typically had extensive contraceptive experience in one or more long-term relationships, and gave reasons like this:

I: What made you go off the pills?

R: About the time I started the pills we started not getting along and I came up here to live and they didn't agree with my body so I gave them up.

Or this:

I: What made you choose rhythm after you went off the pill?

R: I didn't have regularized sex.

Two things make it costly to continue contraception after a relationship ends. First, to continue contraception implies that one expects intercourse with a new partner, and this flies in the face of a strong taboo; sex is to be expected only within a relationship of some duration and commitment:

I: Why did you go off the pill?

R: At the time I broke up, I had no reason to continue and then, well, my first guy, I was engaged with, Larry, when we broke up, there was no logical reason to continue, so I didn't. I have nothing against sex, but I feel that there has to be a mutual feeling, that you have to be very much in love. It's my way of giving everything I have to someone.

This statement exposes a second belief that makes continued contraception costly. If sex is defined as "giving everything I have to someone," to continue contraception would be to acknowledge an expectation of readily meeting another person to whom one could "give everything," which would cheapen both oneself and the gift. Experiencing this conflict between romantic values and pragmatism is a heavy cost for many women. Continuing contraception beyond the confines of one relationship forces a woman to acknowledge that she is always sexually available—a "sexual service station" as one woman bitterly expressed it. Both men and women share in this assumption, so that a woman who continues to take the pill or who keeps her IUD in place is by social definition frankly admitting that she is available. Not only is this an unpleasant acknowledgement for a woman to make about herself, but it loses her an important bargaining position. If she is frankly expecting sex, as evidenced by her continued use of contraception, she need not be courted on the same terms as a woman whose sexual availability is more ambiguous. For many women, the loss of this bargaining position outweighs all the benefits of contraception.

COSTS TO SPONTANEITY

Finally, the use of contraception can kill feelings of spontaneity. One part of the sexual ideology surrounding intercourse is that it must be romantic, an

act of impulse infused with passion and noble feelings. Introducing contraceptives (except the pill and the IUD) into this act can seem dishearteningly
"mechanical":

I: Did you consider using foam or condoms?

R: I did, I bought some, and I didn't even open it. It just seems like a hassle.
I don't know, it's just my damn carelessness. But I bought the foam and
never used it. It's hard to jump out of bed, it just ruins the whole mood.

The mechanics of any type of contraception remind people that while engaging
in a romantic act, or looking forward to it, they are also engaged in the down-
to-earth process of preventing a pregnancy. In addition, the particular methods
of contraception used by the Clinic population (and many other women) have
undesirable effects on pleasure or aesthetics:

I: What did you think about using contraceptive foam?

R: Well, the foam is such a bitch to use. Especially for him because it just
gets all over the place.

I: How did you decide not to use your diaphragm?

R: God, I used to get so turned off putting it inside me, so I tried to get him
to help do it, like they say in those marriage manuals and it just turned
us *both* off.

The use of contraception obviously demands that women feel at ease with
themselves, their bodies, and their lovers, and also be able to accept some of
the less romantic aspects of bodily functions. A great deal of motivation sustained over time is needed to continue accepting and carrying through the
contraceptive act under these conditions.

Sometimes, the costs to romantic spontaneity alone are enough to make
women skip the use of contraception "just this once," even though in the long
run "just this once" tends to end in pregnancy. A powerful demonstration of
exactly how high these costs can be, and how important the corresponding
benefits can seem, may be found in the following statement (by a woman in
her middle thirties with two children, which reminds us that costs to spontaneity
are not restricted to the young and unmarried):

I: How did you get pregnant this time?

R: The children had left for the weekend with their grandparents, so we
could be alone together. We'd gone out to dinner and we'd enjoyed ourselves very much. Our backyard ends and all we have is National Park.
We're very isolated. My husband was feeling very amorous, and when
we pulled up in our driveway he went to the trunk of the car and pulled
out an Army blanket, and proceeded to take me by the hand, over the
fence into the National Park. And to the edge of the bluffs overlooking
the river, a forty-foot drop into the West River. It was beautiful, the moon
was just reflecting off the water and he spread out the Army blanket and
what came next was that I was pregnant. He was so cool. I'm so in love
with that guy. Here I am married to him for six years and I'm more in
love with him than ever.

I: So you used nothing?

R: No Delfin cream, no nothing. One night. But it was worth it. It cost us
three hundred dollars, but it was worth it.

In summary, the larger social and cultural meanings that society assigns to
sexuality can often make the use of contraception seem costly in the short run.
When using a contraceptive socially proclaims the user to be a sexually active

woman, a "cold-blooded" planner, a hard-eyed realist with no romance in her soul, and a woman who is perhaps too sexually active to be a "lady," it is not surprising that women often prefer to avoid contraception rather than run the risk of having to deal with these unpleasant "social halos."

NOTES

[1] For these three theories regarding the origin of social control of sexual activity, see: Claude Lévi-Strauss, *Structural Anthropology* (Garden City, New York: Anchor Books, 1967), p. 60; Sigmund Freud, *Civilization and its Discontents* (New York: W.W. Norton and Company, 1961), pp. 49–53; and Kingsley Davis and Judith Blake, "Social Structure and Fertility: An Analytic Framework," *Economic Development and Cultural Change*, Vol. 14 (April 1956), pp. 211–235.

[2] These data are from the Catholic Social Services and the Catholic *Voice,* who supplied both the *numbers* of nominal Catholics in the area and the *percentage*. When 1970 Census data became available, the percentages given us by these sources were rechecked by independently computing them with fresh population figures as the denominator. (The Census Bureau does not now do surveys on religion, and has not done so since one *Current Population Report* survey in 1958. The author is indebted to Laura Tow for investigative and computational aid for this data.)

4

Partnership Arrangements in Role Responsibilities and the Division of Labor

---

Marriage or some permanent living arrangement is sometimes seen as the culmination of a relationship. So-called love stories usually feature people who meet, grow increasingly fond of each other, overcome tribulation, and eventually marry—presumably to live happily ever after. Yet the *details* of marital living are often ignored, despite the fact that while the partner selection process may take anywhere from a few days to a few years, marriage can be for life. The complex nature of living in families presents a never-ending parade of problems, solutions, relationships, expectations, satisfactions, and dissatisfactions.

A good deal of family life can be broken down into tasks and responsibilities. When two people live together, they must develop understandings as to how these myriad duties of daily life are to be handled. Who does what? Time was when this question was settled by traditional role relationships—the men worked outside the home, earned the living; the women stayed home, kept house, cooked, and raised the children. These automatic expectations are now being questioned. For both partners, the day can become an unremitting daily grind, depriving them of opportunities to do other things they would like to do and that would enhance the self-development of each. Can these duties and responsibilities be arranged so as to spread undesirable tasks more equitably, thus imposing on no one and favoring no one either? What is the quality of life for the family when both the husband and the wife work? How do they relate to each other when the traditional division of labor is replaced by more equalitarian arrangements?

More important than task assignment (but related to it to some extent), are the overall relationships that develop among family members. When individuals form a partnership, two families are joined to the new couple. Each spouse's parents become the other spouse's in-laws. While, unlike Eastern cultures, it is not the norm for three generations to live together, young couples are not totally cut off from their in-laws, and the relationships developed through their interaction can be quite important to the success of the new partnership—as the advice columns of newspapers testify.

Additionally, although couples in love appear to go through a stage where their relationships are so similar that poets, songwriters, novelists, and playwrights can herald them in almost identical and recognizable terms down through the ages, the more complex relationships that develop between husbands and wives in the years that follow the wedding ceremony may take many distinctively different paths.

Roles of Family Members

Theodore B. Johannis, Jr.

In the opening article of this book, Goode says that people living in families have reciprocal role obligations. He does not, however, elaborate as to the content of these responsibilities nor how they are divided among family members. Johannis investigated family participation in three spheres of family life—economic activity, household tasks, and child care. From his results, shown in table form, we are reminded that a great deal of family living is composed of mundane activities that are divided in certain patterned ways among family members. The grounds for this division of labor at the time this study was done appear to be based in great part on what has been traditionally considered to be man's or woman's work.

PARTICIPATION IN FAMILY ECONOMIC ACTIVITY

One of the topics seldom discussed in the texts used in functional courses on marriage and the family is the division of responsibility within the family, especially in the area of economic activity. Data describing the participation by fathers and mothers and their teen-age offspring in such activity are presented below.

The data were supplied by 1,027 high school sophomores living in non-broken white families in Tampa, Florida in the spring of 1953. The median age of the fathers was 43.7 years, of the mothers 39.6 years and of respondents 15.1 years. The fathers and mothers had been married a median of 19.0 years and had a median of 2.2 children of whom a median of 1.9 were still living at home. The median education of fathers was 9.1 years, of mothers 8.9 years.

From Theodore B. Johannis, "Roles of Family Members," in *Family Mobility in Our Dynamic Society,* ed., Iowa State University Center for Agricultural Economic Development (Ames, Iowa: Iowa State University Press, 1965), pp. 69–79. Reprinted by permission of Iowa State University Press. Appreciation is due the E. C. Brown Trust and the Graduate School of the University of Oregon for financial assistance in the data analysis phase of this study.

One-half of the fathers and one-half of the mothers who worked were in "blue-collar" and service occupations. Seven out of ten fathers and mothers had been reared in the southeastern section of the United States.

TABLE 1

PERCENT OF FATHERS, MOTHERS, AND TEEN-AGE SONS AND DAUGHTERS PARTICIPATING IN SELECTED FAMILY ECONOMIC ACTIVITY*

(A Study of 1,027 Nonbroken White Families)

	Family Member				
Activity	A Shared Activity (Percent)	Father (Percent)	Mother (Percent)	Teen-age Son (Percent)	Teen-age Daughter (Percent)
Selects large household equipment	61.9	68.7	90.2	5.0	6.8
Shops for furniture and furnishings	61.3	62.3	93.5	4.6	13.7
Shops for groceries	55.1	42.5	84.1	32.0	37.4
Plans family's savings	47.2	68.8	73.2	3.0	2.1
Shops for family's clothes	46.4	29.3	95.6	30.1	44.3
Provides for family's new car	46.4	91.3	46.5	10.8	15.0
Provides children's spending money	45.7	77.3	56.1	21.4	4.6
Pays bills	39.7	76.8	58.2	7.4	7.6
Earns money for family	38.3	97.9	32.8	15.7	2.2
Range High	61.9	97.9	95.6	32.0	44.3
Low	38.3	29.3	32.8	3.0	2.1

*These items are listed in rank order according to the percentage of the families in which the activity was shared, i.e., usually participated in by two or more members of the family.

TABLE 2

PERCENT OF FATHERS, MOTHERS, AND TEEN-AGE SONS AND
DAUGHTERS PARTICIPATING IN SELECTED HOUSEHOLD TASKS*
(A study of 1,027 Nonbroken White Families)

Activity	A Shared Activity (Percent)	Father (Percent)	Mother (Percent)	Teen-age Son (Percent)	Teen-age Daughter (Percent)
Picks up and puts away clothes	60.2	18.1	82.0	38.5	78.0
Makes beds	50.0	3.5	75.3	28.8	72.9
Takes care of yard	49.4	49.5	24.4	79.8	31.9
Cleans and dusts	48.6	5.3	71.7	12.8	74.3
Does main meal's dishes	46.4	5.8	51.6	27.0	76.9
Does ironing	44.7	1.9	69.3	6.5	67.0
Locks up at night	36.7	63.4	40.7	45.7	28.2
Clears table for main meal	36.1	4.7	49.2	28.6	72.2
Sets table for main meal	32.5	3.5	50.1	23.3	75.5
Fixes broken things	29.1	77.5	9.2	51.6	4.1
Sets breakfast table	29.1	9.4	74.2	13.4	39.8
Takes care of garbage and trash	28.8	27.5	25.1	66.0	33.3
Does family wash	28.4	4.9	75.8	5.5	30.8
Gets main meal	27.3	7.8	86.6	9.4	33.1
Does breakfast dishes	22.7	4.1	70.8	10.1	34.4
Clears breakfast table	23.1	6.0	70.0	16.4	38.8
Gets breakfast	22.4	13.4	87.7	12.6	26.6
Mends family's clothes	20.4	3.2	88.8	2.8	27.5
Range High	60.2	77.5	88.8	79.8	78.0
Low	20.4	1.9	9.2	2.8	4.1

*These items are listed in rank order according to the percentage of the families in which the activity was shared, i.e., usually participated in by two or more members of the family.

TABLE 3
PERCENT OF FATHERS, MOTHERS, AND TEEN-AGE SONS AND DAUGHTERS PARTICIPATING IN SELECTED CHILD CARE AND CONTROL ACTIVITY
(A study of 1,027 Nonbroken White Families)

Activity	A Shared Activity (Percent)	Father (Percent)	Mother (Percent)	Teen-age Son (Percent)	Teen-age Daughter (Percent)
	Family Member				
Teaches children right from wrong and correct behavior	75.5	77.4	92.2	7.8	8.0
Sees children have fun	68.2	66.0	80.7	23.4	22.6
Teaches children facts and skills	65.4	75.5	76.9	13.7	11.4
Punishes children for doing wrong	60.7	76.0	77.4	2.1	3.2
Helps children choose what they will do after finishing school	56.1	61.6	65.5	18.7	19.5
Sees children come in on time at night	53.5	69.0	73.8	7.0	3.0
Sees children have good table manners	51.2	47.8	86.0	11.2	18.3
Helps children with schoolwork	45.3	42.9	56.6	25.1	30.9
Sees children do homework	40.8	43.1	69.5	13.4	18.5
Sees children go to bed on time	40.6	45.7	71.9	11.3	13.5
Cares for children when sick	39.3	34.7	95.6	3.2	8.2
Sees children get to school or work on time	28.9	26.8	75.6	19.1	21.7
Sees children eat right foods	24.9	19.7	84.9	12.3	14.7
Sees children get up in morning on time	22.5	23.8	72.5	14.2	20.2
Sees children wear right clothes	19.8	5.6	66.4	25.1	35.4
Sees children get dressed	19.7	5.6	60.8	25.6	39.2
Range High	75.5	77.4	95.6	25.6	39.2
Low	19.7	5.6	56.6	2.1	3.0

*These items are listed in rank order according to the percentage of the families in which the activity was shared, i.e., usually participated in by two or more members of the family.

I Want a Wife

Judy Syfers

The traditional role of wife contains an implied status difference between spouses. The husband's comfort, schedule, career, friends, and wishes take precedence. Even more important, the wife's role is so structured that, to fulfill it properly, she is of great and constant service to him—a live-in servant and companion. It is she who handles the many routine details listed in the previous reading. As women have begun to have career and other self-fulfilling aspirations, they have found a need to eliminate or drastically prune traditional wifely responsibilities. They also have discovered they could use some of the help traditionally provided by a wife. In this essay, Syfers puts the case cogently—we could all use a wife!

I belong to that classification of people known as wives. I am A Wife. And, not altogether incidentally, I am a mother.

Not too long ago a male friend of mine appeared on the scene fresh from a recent divorce. He had one child, who is, of course, with his ex-wife. He is obviously looking for another wife. As I thought about him while I was ironing one evening, it suddenly occurred to me that I, too, would like to have a wife. Why do I want a wife?

I would like to go back to school so that I can become economically independent, support myself, and, if need be, support those dependent upon me. I want a wife who will work and send me to school. And while I am going to school I want a wife to keep track of the children's doctor and dentist appointments. And to keep track of mine, too. I want a wife to make sure my children eat properly and are kept clean. I want a wife who will wash the children's clothes and keep them mended. I want a wife who is a good nurturant attendant to my children, who arranges for their schooling, makes sure that they have an adequate social life with their peers, takes them to the park, the zoo, etc. I want a wife who takes care of the children when they are sick, a wife who

Judy Syfers is married and has two children. To accompany this article, she wanted us to make the following statement: Ms. Syfers wishes to stress that "the problems of an American wife stem from the fact that we live in a society which is structured in such a way as to profit only a few at the expense of the many. As long as we women tolerate such a capitalist system, all but a privileged few of us must necessarily be exploited as workers and as wives."

From Judy Syfers, "Why I Want a Wife," *The First Ms. Reader* (New York: Warner Paperback Library, 1973) pp. 23–25. Copyright © 1971 by Judy Syfers. Reprinted by permission of the author.

arranges to be around when the children need special care, because, of course, I cannot miss classes at school. My wife must arrange to lose time at work and not lose the job. It may mean a small cut in my wife's income from time to time, but I guess I can tolerate that. Needless to say, my wife will arrange and pay for the care of the children while my wife is working.

I want a wife who will take care of *my* physical needs. I want a wife who will keep my house clean. A wife who will pick up after me. I want a wife who will keep my clothes clean, ironed, mended, replaced when need be, and who will see to it that my personal things are kept in their proper place so that I can find what I need the minute I need it. I want a wife who cooks the meals, a wife who is a *good* cook. I want a wife who will plan the menus, do the necessary grocery shopping, prepare the meals, serve them pleasantly, and then do the cleaning up while I do my studying. I want a wife who will care for me when I am sick and sympathize with my pain and loss of time from school. I want a wife to go along when our family takes a vacation so that someone can continue to care for me and my children when I need a rest and change of scene.

I want a wife who will not bother me with rambling complaints about a wife's duties. But I want a wife who will listen to me when I feel the need to explain a rather difficult point I have come across in my course of studies. And I want a wife who will type my papers for me when I have written them.

I want a wife who will take care of the details of my social life. When my wife and I are invited out by my friends, I want a wife who will take care of the baby-sitting arrangements. When I meet people at school that I like and want to entertain, I want a wife who will have the house clean, will prepare a special meal, serve it to me and my friends, and not interrupt when I talk about the things that interest me and my friends. I want a wife who will have arranged that the children are fed and ready for bed before my guests arrive so that the children do not bother us. I want a wife who takes care of the needs of my guests so that they feel comfortable, who makes sure that they have an ashtray, that they are passed the hors d'oeuvres, that they are offered a second helping of the food, that their wine glasses are replenished when necessary, that their coffee is served to them as they like it.

And I want a wife who knows that sometimes I need a night out by myself.

I want a wife who is sensitive to my sexual needs, a wife who makes love passionately and eagerly when I feel like it, a wife who makes sure that I am satisfied. And, of course, I want a wife who will not demand sexual attention when I am not in the mood for it. I want a wife who assumes the complete responsibility for birth control, because I do not want more children. I want a wife who will remain sexually faithful to me so that I do not have to clutter up my intellectual life with jealousies. And I want a wife who understands that *my* sexual needs may entail more than strict adherence to monogamy. I must, after all, be able to relate to people as fully as possible.

If, by chance, I find another person more suitable as a wife than the wife I already have, I want the liberty to replace my present wife with another one. Naturally, I will expect a fresh, new life; my wife will take the children and be solely responsible for them so that I am left free.

When I am through with school and have a job, I want my wife to quit working and remain at home so that my wife can more fully and completely take care of a wife's duties.

My God, who *wouldn't* want a wife?·

Dual-Career Families: Problems They Face; How They Manage; What They Gain

Rhona and Robert Rapaport

It has been argued persuasively in the foregoing selections that it is to the wife's benefit for the traditional division of labor by sex role to be modified or abolished. It may ultimately benefit the husband as well. But how do some alternative approaches work? And what are the psychic costs? As the Rapaports point out, there are myriad decisions and arrangements necessary to make a dual-career family work smoothly. Should the husband and wife try to find jobs with the same work hours, so they are home at the same time, or different hours, in order to take turns "covering" the home? Should one spouse have a secure job to allow the other to take financial risks for possible higher gain? How should domestic duties and child care be handled and apportioned fairly? What can be done by hired help (and is it possible to hire someone who will do things as well as a family member would)? There is a great deal of evidence in this study and others that hired help has its limitations. Women, more than men, take up the slack, retaining both the career and homemaker role, trying to be a sort of superwoman, working sixteen hours a day. Even couples who arrange these home labor problems to their own satisfaction find themselves the target of disapproving peers. Career women with a family are especially likely to bear the brunt of this criticism of their "unnatural" way of life. Dual-career couples have to offer sympathetic reinforcement to each other, as well as locate like-minded friends.

There is also some evidence that each spouse fears the worst for himself or herself and the marital relationship in these situations. Unless each partner can overcome these fears, he or she may forego the personal gains that are possible for all family members from this increasingly popular life-style.

Adapted from Rhona and Robert Rapaport, *Dual-Career Families* (London: Penguin Books, 1971). Reprinted by permission of the authors.

Introduction

The dual-career family is a structural type emerging as an important option for a future in which both men and women will have increased education and training and in which family life is likely to remain a fundamental institution fulfilling essential social and psychological functions. The analysis of the life experience of the dual-career families presented indicates a number of elements in complex interplay. There seem to be many paradoxical elements, the resolution of which is essential in sustaining this pattern.

The dual-career pattern provides major sources of satisfaction while at the same time creating burdens. Each couple operates at a high level of strain but they have all chosen this as their style of life; and when contemplating other patterns they usually reject them as less satisfactory for themselves as individuals and as families.

The individuals in dual-career families are singularly determined and purposeful and yet they seem to have evolved their patterns through a series of almost accidental events and choices. They have ended up with patterns reflecting their flexibility and their general determination rather than a specific preconceived goal.

• • • •

Occupations—Flexibility for at Least One Spouse

The families presented were selected to show the different occupational careers of the wives, so this source of variation is manifest in the materials. The more individual "entrepreneurial" way of organizing one's occupation provides greater flexibility to the individual but also entails greater risk. The woman who is a salaried employee of a large organization, who is in a more "bureaucratic" work setting, must conform to the norms of the organization (and these may be relatively rigid or relatively flexible) but she gains in the security of a known income which has advantages in planning and domestic organization, children's schooling and so on. The husband may see either work context as advantageous, assuming that he supports the general idea of his wife having a career. If she has a career within an organizational structure, he may feel that he can take greater risks in his own work, or at least that his economic responsibilities towards her and his family are being shared. Alternatively, he may opt for the more secure occupational situation for himself, encouraging entrepreneurial activity by his wife as a way of engaging as a family in the excitement of risk taking, but covering the hazards at the same time.

The Kileys have more overlap in domestic activities than the Harrises, who show only moderate overlap in this sphere as well as in work. In the Jarrets there is a lower degree of overlap in this particular sphere, which is unusual in its characteristics, but there is nevertheless a sharing of interest in that Mr. Jarret has had theatre as a hobby all his life and this is her work. Mrs. Jarret has had a strong respect for aesthetic and socially significant activities, and this is his work. Their actual involvement in one another's work problems, however, is that of sympathetic listeners rather than active participants.

The Kileys have the greatest degree of shared division of labor at home with Mr. Kiley doing more around the house, usually together with his wife, than any of the other husbands. The Bensons are perhaps a close second, partly because of the physical presence of the work activities in the household. The Neals also share a good deal while the Jarrets and Harrises maintain a more conventional division of labor between husband and wife. In all cases this issue is eased by the provision of domestic helpers, who take on many of the less desired aspects of domestic work, freeing the two heads of the family for the activities they choose—usually cooking (which remains primarily the wife's domain) and gardening (which may be either and is often joint).

. . . .

WIDE VARIATIONS IN CHILD CARE ARRANGEMENTS

Child care is an area where the variations are marked not only in terms of general philosophy of child-rearing but more particularly in relation to the conception held of the child's role in family life. In some of the families, the child has been protected from involvement in the chore aspects of family living. In the Jarret family, for example, the son's involvement in domestic chores came only when he became interested in electrical wiring as a hobby. In the Kileys and Neals by contrast, the children have had definite roles within the family and the expectation has been that they will help with what has to be done. In the Benson family it is assumed that the children will be relatively independent, and they are not assigned specific tasks.

It is probably true to say that in all of the families—whether the children actively participate and carry responsibility for family chores or not, there is an emphasis on enhancing the children's independence and competence. None of the dual-career families show the pattern sometimes found among families of their income level of having their children waited on, serviced and chauffeured around. Delight is expressed by the parents when the children show mastery and aspire to a high level of accomplishment, whether in one of the parents' fields of interest or not. The emphasis on high standards and excellence at what one does is very marked. It should be noted that this is not an emphasis on "going higher" but on doing whatever one does as well as possible. This emphasis is independent of the sex of the child. In no case among the dual-career families was there a stereotyped conventional orientation to sex roles. Where a daughter may favor a more conventional role this has not been discouraged but tends to be regarded as a personal choice.

STRAINS

The families studied have shown a good many elements both of strain and satisfaction associated with the pattern of life they have evolved. Similar strains and gains might be found in more conventional types of families. On the basis of broad experience with families of different kinds, which serves as a kind of control, it is possible at least tentatively to pick out some of the strains and gains that do seem highly associated with the dual-career family. We have isolated five dilemmas which in their nature set up strains. They are dilemmas because of the choice element. The dual-career family, once chosen, entails particular strains; and sustaining the pattern means sustaining the strains.

Each family varies in the extent to which each of the dilemmas is problematic but the five selected dilemmas are common to all the couples and always entail some degree of strain. They are:

1. Overload
2. Environmental sanction
3. Personal identity and self esteem
4. Social network dilemmas
5. Dilemmas of multiple role-cycling

Overload

Sheer overloading is something that each of the families experienced, though they differed in the ways they handled it. Not having the wife at home to do the conventional "back-up" work of domestic care or supervision, child care, social arrangements and so on, this work had either to be redistributed or neglected. Redistribution through the use of various domestic helpers is widespread, though rarely completely satisfactory. For one thing the caliber of help is not satisfactory for people with the level of standards shown by the dual-career families. For another thing, the intrusion into family privacy of the help personnel is often experienced as an additional strain, particularly where there are adolescent au pair girls who are acting out their own family rebellion problems on their temporary family substitutes.

In varying degree, the husband or the wife or both take up the slack to accomplish the tasks necessary for running the household at the standard they require. The actual pattern depends on the individuals and their situations. Doing so, however, usually involves a considerable strain because each sustains a demanding occupational role and needs support. Sometimes standards are deliberately lowered for the maintenance of the household, sometimes the children are pressed into helping roles. The latter tactic tends to be seen as a constructive socialization policy as well as an expedient in the overload situation.

97

For the most part the additional load is simply absorbed, adding to the physical strains and diminishing the amount of free time which one often does not recognize as existing but which is present in most families' time budgets to allocate variously according to need. Most of the dual-career couples have to plan deliberately to create this kind of free time, even if only to be lazy or without immediate purpose. Sometimes they do it by having a weekend cottage retreat, as with the Bensons and the Jarrets; sometimes they make a point of *not* taking work home or of taking up a family hobby such as boating (Kileys). This kind of leisure is deliberately arranged in dual-career families rather than being 'there' as a matter of course, and families that do not work at creating and conserving it find that their 'work' at home and outside can consume all of their time and leave very little for other pleasures.

Environmental Sanctions

Sex Role Problems. Times have changed in terms of the pervasiveness of negative sanctions in relation to married women working. The mass media and the more diffuse expressions of sentiment in this respect are, if anything, swinging in the direction of slightly disparaging the idea of women (particularly highly qualified women) being only housewives. On the other hand, continuous work at a highly demanding occupation and full participation on a competitive basis with men is another matter. The difficulties encountered at work are one thing, where women have to be particularly good and particularly careful (as in the experience of other minority groups in society) lest their deficiencies be reacted to stereotypically and chalked up to the expected shortcomings of their sex rather than (as with men and with dominant groups generally) an individual matter. While these aspects of environmental strain are present, they are known and accepted by women pursuing careers as part of what they must face if they wish to succeed; and there is a clear and definite tendency for this sort of strain arising from traditional sex-stereotypes to diminish. In part the improvement is due to the demonstration that blanket stereotypes are false in individual cases; partly it is due to the changing conception of work roles, 'de-masculinizing' them to some extent. The idea that work is physically arduous, dirty, ruthless and cut-throat may be partly true; but, aside from the fact that some women can participate in this on men's own terms, it is also clear that work nowadays is more a matter of intelligence, judgement, human relations and the manipulation of refined skills, all of which are attributes of both men and women.

Handing the Judgements of Others. The area of environmental disapproval that is less clearly manageable and less clearly changing to a more supportive situation has to do with child-rearing. If a family chooses not to have children, they not only face their own feelings of unfulfillment as human beings as a possible hazard, but they may be considered odd by people generally, or at best unfortunate. If they choose to have children, as most families do, they are expected to provide conventional care, i.e., with the mother staying at home and exercising her "natural maternal" instincts. Unless this is done, it is often assumed that irreparable harm may be done to the child, and this may at a later stage affect society through the development within it of a 'psychopathic' member, affectionless, dependent or aggressive. A good deal of information and misinformation from the writings of psychiatrists and pediatricians has come into popular usage through the mass media, and is applied indiscriminately to particular cases. Sometimes this indiscriminate application of a little knowledge is fuelled by envy. Women who have given up their own aspirations to take on the conventional housewife role may express their resentment at others who seem to be managing an alternative pattern by lashing out at them critically in social situations. They may indicate that they consider the dual-career wives to be bad mothers, bad wives, and perhaps bad and selfish individuals.

A balanced view of the matter would suggest that while extreme cases of maternal deprivation such as those experienced in wartime or under conditions of institutionalization in backward and old-fashioned care institutions contribute to pathological outcomes, the situation of a mother continuing to work has to be assessed in individual terms. If the mother is not particularly maternal she may not be doing her infant the best possible service by being confined to her home with it. This is particularly true if her main aspirations are in the world of work and she has the problem of frustration to cope with in addition to her own disinclination towards "mothering." The infant may be a scapegoat in such a situation, which as any clinician's casebooks will support, may produce greater problems than if good partial mother-surrogate care were arranged. This is an extreme case. Most of the dual-career mothers show considerable maternal wishes together with considerable interest in the occupational sphere. The challenge for them is how to distribute the care in such a way as to allow enough highly involved "mothering" (by the actual mother *and* father) to take place along with filling the long hours of more routine care with competent ancillary people. Couples of the type studied here have gone to great lengths to assure that their help is reliable, stable and in harmony with their own outlook. In addition, in many cases of dual-career families, the husband's greater participation in domestic life has led to an increase in the children's exposure to their father than usual in conventional families and this may serve to correct an unfortunate imbalance in the conventional child-care and socialization situation in our culture.

An element that makes the child-care area more problematic than the sex-role stereotype problems at work is that, unlike the work situation, it is unclear in the child-care situation where the pattern is going or how it will be dealt with. While there have been a number of developments in child-care nurseries, housing facilities and industrial crèches which are known to many of the couples studied, they have not had institutional resources of these kinds available to them. The child care supplemental pattern is at a much earlier stage in its evolution than are the work role patterns.

Mechanisms of Coping. One way of handling negative environmental sanctions is to avoid them by not associating with people known to be critical. Some insulation from others results automatically from the overload which leaves little extra energy available for casual sociability. In addition, the pressures of many career-demands are so great as to make it important to some people to have relative quiet and seclusion for their off-work periods. The Jarrets represent this pattern. Another way of handling it, perhaps best seen in the Kileys, is to treat it humorously. 'Most of the people around here think we're a bit mad' kind of attitude. The Bensons seem to have worked out a public dual personality so that they are considered part of the interesting scene in the world of art and architecture—a sort of professional Siamese twins—expected always to

99

appear and perform together. As Mr Benson observed on this: 'Wouldn't you be irritated if you invited Richard Burton to a party and he showed without Elizabeth Taylor?' In still other cases there has been insistence that they be accepted as they are, different but worthy; but it has almost always been experienced as an uphill struggle against popular opinion and attitude. All of the couples developed friendships which supported them by providing positive sanctions and limited legitimation for what they were doing. Most wished that the positive sanctions were more diffuse and the legitimation felt on a more widespread basis.

Personal Identity and Self-Esteem

Self-doubts, Guilts. Most of the dual-career couples studied experienced dilemmas of personal identity and self-esteem more or less autonomously of environmental sanctions. Issues as to whether the wife was being a good wife and mother, or more fundamentally a "good human being" when she chose to pursue her career involvements, and whether the husband was sacrificing his "manliness" in altering his domestic life to take on more of a participative role were widespread.

The sources of this internal doubt and anxiety are clear enough. The individuals in the study were socialized in terms of norms and values of thirty years ago and more. While there was enough of an egalitarian ethos at the time most of them were growing up to make it possible for girls as well as boys to develop high career aspirations, the pattern was not fully worked through. Textbooks, cautionary tales, folklore, aphorisms, role models and much of the detailed warp and woof of culture was still woven in the old pattern. Even now, sex role stereotypes are very pervasive in educational materials and family practices. Boys have been and still are in many schools considered "normally" interested in machines and in money, in fame and power, status and authority, while girls "normally" are taken to be interested in beauty and the arts, and in human relations and care functions. In fact, boys and girls have mixtures of these attributes, and particular boys and girls have individual mixtures which may vary from the stereotypes without implying pathology. Variance from the stereotyped sex-role interests and activities, e.g. girls showing technological aptitudes and aspirations, tended in the past to arouse negative reactions. This inevitably led to these internal doubts and ambivalences persisting into adult life, giving rise to guilt, anxiety and tensions of various kinds. At work, the individual may hesitate to press herself at a crucial point, and thus may be considered lacking in drive; at home, the individual may react in various ways, for example, by being overindulgent to a child because of feeling guilty about being out at work.

Feelings of concern, guilt, ambivalence and so on may take different forms in familiar relationships. A wife's defensiveness about following her chosen career line may make her particularly sensitive to criticism or it may exacerbate periods of self-doubt and depression. The husband may make great personal and career sacrifices to help achieve the dual-career structure for its value to both parties, but he may show irritation or resentment at having modified his own personal identity in order to incorporate a successful wife into his pattern, sometimes in place of a more successful self. Most families develop what we have termed a "tension line" which is set up more or less unconsciously between the pair and recognized as a point beyond which each will not be pushed. Compromises are worked out within the framework of this tension line.

While it has sometimes been asserted on the basis of clinical case literature that these difficulties undermine the intimate side of the marital relationship, we have no evidence that problems arising in this sphere are greater in dual-career families than in any range of complicated people with busy lives. Indeed, if anything there is some suggestion—still to be explored in more systematic research—that families of this kind are particularly good at working through problems that confront them. When these problems happen to arise in their intimate lives, they may handle these too with more communication and more purposeful decision-making than many other families.

Intra-family Solidarity as a Coping Mechanism. The management of personal and interpersonal problems in the marital relationship is not only a matter of being purposeful and rational. Some couples manage by taking special care to provide the more affectionate components of the relationship—to deal with the sensitivities of their partners in a rather fundamental way, so as to balance the other's self esteem at points recognized to be vulnerable. Mr. Benson, for example, emphasizes that criticism is important in any partnership if the work is to be maintained at a high standard, but where the partnership is a marital one as well and the partner may be vulnerable to the more general meanings of criticism from one's spouse, the criticism given in work matters must be done "with love."

Another way of managing these issues—more prevalent where husbands and wives are not work partners as well—is seen in the Kileys and Jarrets, where a very sharp segregation is made between work and home roles. When Mrs. Jarret comes home she becomes "cook" and "my husband's wife." When Mrs. Kiley leaves the office she attempts to hang up with her white lab coat her authoritarian mode of relating to people at work, and become a warm and sympathetic wife and mother.

•   •   •   •

Dilemmas of Multiple Role Cycling

In each of the major spheres of life people are engaged in a set of role involvements which make different demands at different stages of the cycle. When one enters a marriage, for example, the demands of family life are less, particularly for the wife, before children arrive. Similarly for work. When one enters an occupational role, particularly the career-type of occupation which involves a developmental sequence of roles, there are differences according to stage. Here the most demanding stages tend to be early on, when one is establishing oneself. Later, when a stable pattern is developed, a plateau may be reached from which functioning in work roles may be taxing but somewhat stabilized.

When one is dealing with the conventional form of family–work relationships, the family cycling may dovetail well with the work cycling in that many couples marry at the stage of the husband's entering into a regular occupational role. The high demands on him in his own establishment phases are supported by the relative non-turbulence in the family scene. Even if children arrive some-time during the occupational establishment phase, the fact that the conventional wife remains at home attending to their care tends to take the pressure off the husband where economic problems are minimal.

In dual-career families there is a wide range of variation. A common feature, however, is that the patterns differ importantly from the conventional one of the establishment phase of the husband's career coinciding with the wife bear-ing children. In most of the dual-career families in this study, occupational establishment for both husband and wife preceded child-bearing. In the Kileys' case, Mrs. Kiley's occupational establishment preceded that of her husband, and she supported his preparatory and early establishment phases through her own occupational activity. This was assisted by his willingness to provide sup-port on the domestic front. This pattern, while unusual for people of their background and circumstances, is less unusual among contemporary students. Marriage nowadays is earlier and there is widespread recognition that different opportunities for stipends, training, occupational entry and so on will make for different timetables between the marital partners.

The Bensons show another pattern, where they were jointly establishing their occupational situation and their family life at the same time. In this in-stance the incorporation of their office into their home provided the key struc-tural arrangement making it feasible. They dealt with the dilemmas arising from high demands for both members in both spheres by overlapping the two as much as possible, allowing the children to "be around" in the office and the office to intrude into the home setting.

The couples in this particular study tended to establish themselves occupa-tionally prior to having children; they then had their children in a compressed period and the wives tended to interrupt their work minimally. By this time the couples had usually achieved a sufficient level of income so that they could support the domestic service side of the dual-career family's pattern. To some extent an occupational plateau was reached by most of the women before having children in terms of either position within an organization, reputation or clientele.

For young couples, new patterns of role-cycling may emerge. Child-bearing may take place earlier and there may be a return to work at an earlier point in the occupational cycle. As will be discussed in the next chapter this will de-pend to some extent on how society deals with such issues as providing oppor-tunity for mature student training and occupational re-entry.

GAINS

Financial Factors

Aside from the intrinsic gratifications that many couples have found in the sheer experience of mastering the numerous dilemmas in the way of making a dual-career family work well against many difficulties, there are a number of gains in the end product.

The financial gains are more important than are frequently acknowledged. Very often in writing about working women, the observation is made that highly-qualified women tend to work out of intrinsic interest while those with lower qualifications tend to work more for the money. Be this as it may, the financial return is an important element in the career development picture from several angles. First, the families emphasized how important it is for dual-career families to have a relatively high income, because they have relatively high standards for domestic living, child-care, clothing and transportation and so on. To pay out the extra that is involved in all this, their income must be relatively high, particularly as help is more costly and tax benefits do not encourage the pattern. Many of the couples also indicated that the overloads experienced made it important to provide for leisure and holidays which may be relatively costly because of the need on such occasions to be looked after so that the marital pair can regenerate their energies. They work so hard in between that they often feel that they "deserve" to be pampered a bit on holidays, which eats still further into the increase in family income that the extra worker provides.

In some of the families it is agreed that it is preferable to have both partners working somewhat less than "flat out" rather than the husband, in order to get the highest possible income, giving himself so much to "the rat race" that they sacrifice some of the family life that they might enjoy together. The Kileys expressed this sort of attitude.

Also present in some families is the issue of financial security against possible disasters. The accumulation of savings, independent pension rights, and so on are of some importance. The Harrises felt this way.

Some of the women in the study experienced early economic deprivation and are very much aware that this factor has been important in driving them towards a goal of economic security. By the time they were successful enough in their careers to have come to the attention of the study, they were sophisticated and secure enough to give less emphasis to this as a personal need than as a wish to give their children more security than they had had themselves. The husbands tend to support this, and in fact often obtain direct gratification from their wives' earning ability.

Personal Gains for the Wife

However, while money as such is more important than is sometimes recognized, it is by no means the most important element for the dual-career families studied. The crucial element for most of the families is something that can be subsumed under the general category of "self-expression." Mrs. Benson would feel incomplete unless she were creating something—if not in architecture, then in creative art or writing; Mrs. Harris would not feel fulfilled unless she were achieving recognition as a designer and producing tangible products of her work; Mrs. Kiley feels that if she had to turn all of her managerial energies into the family she would be impossible to live with, and Mrs. Jarret expresses a related idea when she says that even if she did not have her professional work (which is unthinkable) she would not want to be the sort of woman who confined her energies to her home and child. Mrs. Neal, while protesting to some extent about the degree to which she is involved in her career, feels in her work major satisfactions of ideas and decisions. When she says that she would like to be able to work less, she means a thirty-hour week, which may become something like full time for many professions before long.

All of the women in this sample have as part of their personal identities a sub-identity associated with a professional work role. Many indicated that if the satisfactions from work were to be removed, they would experience a major loss. Though the particular jobs they do may represent compromises with their original idealized conceptions, in every case they are realizing in major degrees what they really want to do and feel is worth doing as human beings, making full use of their capacities.

Personal Gains for the Husband

The gains for their husbands are also more complex than is often recognized in writings about women and their careers. It is often observed that a husband who has a wife getting satisfactions from work has a happier wife; this may be true but not in a simplistic sense. The gains that most dual-career families derive from having the wife at work are part of a cluster of reactions to it. As well as satisfactions, the wives also experience strains, anxieties, conflicts, guilt and sheer exhaustion which may contribute to the difficulties in the marital relationship as well as to its enrichment. As has been indicated above, many of the husbands' involvement in their wives' careers derived from an interest which they as individuals have felt but have not realized in their own work. Mr. Harris's interest in his wife's public recognition and her entrepreneurial risk-taking activities reflects elements of his own wishes which he has to mute in order to press other elements of his aspirations. Mr. Jarret's interest and sympathy with his wife's problems as a dramatic director express some of his own earlier interest in the theatre and keep that interest alive. Mr. Kiley's interest in his wife's scientific work reflects his own earlier unfulfilled interest in research, from which he himself diverged. Though he has succeeded in another line of endeavour, the scientific interest is both alive and helpful to him. Mr. Neal and particularly Mr. Benson participate even more directly in the interests and problems of their wives. While these involvements may not persist through the entire life cycle of the marriage, they seem to be crucial in the establishment phase when the dual-career structure is being crystallized; and, as more than one dual-career husband has commented, 'Once they've tasted the dual-career pattern, it's difficult to settle for anything else.' This is untenable as a total generalization as is seen from the relatively large proportion of career-oriented wives who show the interrupted work pattern; but it would seem to be a tendency.

Gains for the Children

Finally, there are gains reported for the children in dual-career families. So much has been written to emphasize the deprivations that such children may experience—based mostly on institutional or traumatic experiences quite unlike those provided by professional women going to work—that some corrective statements are needed. A review of the research which has been done so far indicates that the case for damage to children as a direct consequence of mothers' working is unproven. Our data suggest that while there are indeed problems raised by mothers having careers, the kinds of competent individuals who are in dual-career families tend to make arrangements for child-care which compare favorably with what would have occurred had the mothers stayed at home. The parents report advantages deriving from the situation, e.g. that the children in the dual-career families show independence and resourcefulness. Helping with family tasks is seen as giving the children a sense not only of independence and competence but also of social worth. They contribute to the overall family needs and this legitimates their right to have a share in the family goods. Another perquisite of being in such families is a certain sense of "special" merit, deriving from mother's work role. Often the children in these families show pride in their parents' accomplishments. This may take the form of tangible benefits—like Mrs. Harris designing the school uniform for her daughter's school; or Mrs. Kiley sending along bacteriological cultures for the science master to use. More often it takes the form of special interest and knowledge in the family that arouses in the child a feeling of competence and involvement in the wide range of interests that both parents have. The fact that both parents have interests allows a greater range of role models for children of both sexes, and this enlarges the area of occupational life and experience they can know at close hand.

Of course all these things can have pathological manifestations. Leaving children to be resourceful can fail and arouse greater-than-ever dependency; guilt over this may lead the parent towards overprotectiveness and the child may become unusually demanding. Poor or unstable staff may confuse the child and give it additional problems. Successful parents can be a burden for a child as well as a help. Multiple role models can confuse as well as clarify. The crucial points are likely to be how the situations are managed and what social pressures and sanctions are operating. However, these things occur in ordinary conventional families as well as in dual-career families, and our impression is that the positive benefits of the latter have been under-valued generally. The potential damages are real enough but may be exaggerated as specific to this type of situation. Furthermore, just as mental health interventions are possible to attempt to head off and work with the pathologies of conventional family structures, the same is true for dual-career families. Neurotic difficulties, confused identification, loneliness and disturbance seem to be products much more of bad management of child-care and sexual disapproval of variant patterns than of a particular family structure. The families studied differed in their talents in this regard, but the same individuals would not be likely to produce more psychologically healthy children if they sacrificed their own wishes and needs so as to operate the conventional family structure. In the next chapter we shall consider some of the issues raised by this study of dual-career families and what practical measures may be taken in a society to facilitate this pattern if it is seen to be of value by some of its citizens.

• • • •

105

SUMMARY

The dual-career families of today are, in a sense, pioneers for families of tomorrow. They had no role models or exemplars on whose patterns they could develop their own styles of life. Indeed, in most instances they had to struggle against the existing patterns in society to cut out for themselves viable niches in a social fabric that was woven with quite other designs for living in mind. To achieve their positions, they worked creatively, often under considerable tension and conflict. In so doing they had to overcome a number of obstacles, and the adaptive qualities that have won through in this process are a peculiar combination of determination and flexibility, not always available to most people. It is not as though they started off with a pre-conceived plan and worked relentlessly to implement it. On the contrary, for most the pattern that they evolved came into being through a series of happenings which make sense in retrospect. It was the unusual couple that knew what they were going to do and aimed purposefully towards it.

How to Write Your Own Marriage Contract

Susan Edmiston

If marriage is analyzed as though it were like any other job or occupation re-quiring the acceptance of certain responsibilities and the development of particular skills, it seems almost inconceivable that persons accept what can be a lifetime position without prior investigation into what, in the business world, is called the job description. *Yet this is a common occurrence in marriage where the division of family tasks is never clearly settled in advance and in detail. Rather, husbands and wives enter these positions with role expectations (rights and responsibilities) of themselves and each other, usually based on how their parents managed their household. What happens if one or both partners do not agree on who should do what? Or what if one partner tires of the role expectations of the other? A promise to love, honor, and cherish hardly covers the matter. The advent of the Women's Movement highlighted these problems and revitalized a somewhat disused concept of family law—the marriage contract. In reading possible inclusions, notice the tremendous range of marital matters that have customarily been left to chance, or more likely to tradition.*

First we thought marriage was when Prince Charming came and took you away with him. Then we thought that marriage was orange blossoms and Alençon lace and silver patterns. Then we thought that marriage—at least—was when you couldn't face signing the lease on the new apartment in two different names. But most of us never even suspected the truth. Nobody ever so much as mentioned that what marriage is, at its very heart and essence, is a contract. When you say "I do," what you are doing it not, as you thought, vowing your eternal love, but rather subscribing to a whole system of rights, obligations and

Susan Edmiston is a writer, editor, columnist and contributor to many national magazines. She is now at work on a book, "A Literary Guide to New York."

responsibilities that may very well be anathema to your most cherished beliefs.

Worst of all, you never even get to read the contract—to say nothing of the fine print. If you did, you probably wouldn't agree to it. Marriage, as it exists today, is a peculiarly vague, and yet inflexible, arrangement of institutionalized inequality which goes only one step beyond the English common-law concept of husband and wife as one, and, as the saying goes, "that 'one' is the husband." We have progressed from the notion of wife as legal nonentity to the notion of wife as dependent and inferior.

In recent years, many people have taken to writing their own marriage ceremonies in a desperate attempt to make the institution more relevant to their own lives. But ceremonies, they are finding, do not reach the heart of the matter. So some couples are now taking the logical next step of drawing up their own contracts. These agreements may delineate any of the financial or personal aspects of the marriage relationship—from who pays which bills to who uses what birth control. Though many of their provisions may not be legally binding, at the very least they can help us to examine the often inchoate assumptions underlying our relationships, help us come to honest and equitable terms with one another, and provide guidelines for making our marriages what we truly want them to be.

Before their first child was born, Alix Kates Shulman and her husband had an egalitarian, partnership marriage. Alix worked full time as an editor in New York, and both shared the chores involved in maintaining their small household. After two children, however, the couple found that they had automatically fallen into the traditional sex roles: he went out and worked all day to support his family; she stayed home and worked from 6 a.m. to 9 p.m. taking care of children and housework. Unthinkingly, they had agreed not only to the legalities of marriage but to the social contract as well.

After six years at home—six years of chronic dissatisfaction—Alix became involved in the Women's Liberation movement and realized that it might be possible to change the contract under which she and her husband lived. The arrangement they worked out, basically a division of household duties and child care, rejected "the notion that the work which brings in more money is more valuable. The ability to earn . . . money is a privilege which must not be compounded by enabling the larger earner to buy out of his/her duties."

Sitting down and writing out a contract may seem a cold and formal way of working out an intimate relationship, but often it is the only way of coping with the ghosts of 2,000 years of tradition lurking in our definitions of marriage. After three years, Alix had written six books, and both Shulmans found their agreement a way of life rather than a document to be followed legalistically.

No less an antagonist than Norman Mailer has attacked the Shulmans' contract. After describing it in *The Prisoner of Sex,* he writes (in his characteristic third person): "No, he would not be married to such a woman. If he were obliged to have a roommate he would pick a man. . . . He could love a woman and she might even sprain her back before a hundred sinks of dishes in a month, but he would not be happy to help her if his work should suffer, no, not unless her work were as valuable as his own." Mailer's comment makes the issues clear: under the old contract the work of child-rearing and housekeeping is assumed to be less important than the work a man does—specifically, here, the career of self-aggrandizement Mailer has cut out for himself—and a wife, unless able to prove otherwise, must do the housework.

The Shulmans' contract renegotiates husband's and wife's roles as far as the care of children and home are concerned. Psychologists Barbara and Myron Koltuv took their agreement one step further.

"We agreed in the beginning that since I didn't care a bit about the house, he would do a lot of cleaning and I would do a lot of cooking," says Barbara. "He does a lot of the shopping, too, because he likes to buy things and I don't. Whenever either of us feels 'I'm doing all the drudge work and you're not doing anything,' we switch jobs. Gradually we've eliminated a lot of stuff neither of us wanted to do. In the early days, we'd cook dinner for people because we didn't feel it was hospitable to ask them to go out, but now we often go out instead.

"In the beginning we literally opened up separate bank accounts. We split our savings and checking accounts. At the time he made a third more money than I did. I deferred to him all the time, even though it was only a third. I felt that if he didn't spend so much money on the eight dozen book clubs he belongs to, I would only have to work about two hours a day. He said I wasn't realistic, that I didn't know how much we had and was being tight.

"Each of us paid the bills alternate months. I thought this was the only way to prove to him I could handle money. After six months, when I figured out how much I was spending and how much of his money I was using, I decided to take on more patients to expand my practice. I found I was spending as much on cabs as he was on book clubs. Since that time we haven't had a single argument about money."

When the Koltuvs' child was born, they reopened negotiations. "We decided to split the care of our daughter between us equally. We knew there were certain hours we'd both be working so we found a woman to take care of her during these hours. Then I had the mornings and he had the evenings. The person whose time it was had to make all the decisions—whether she could have Pepsi-Cola, whether she could visit a friend, and so forth.

"The hardest thing was being willing to give up control. What we call responsibility is often control, power, being the boss. When I was really able to recognize that my husband's relationship with Hannah is his and mine is mine, everything was all right. He's going to do it differently but he's going to do it all right. We've been teaching her all along that different people are different."

Agreements to disagree with the common marriage mores are nothing new. They have their roots in a fine old tradition that probably began with Mary Wollstonecraft, that first feminist of us all, who in 1792 wrote *A Vindication of the Rights of Women*. Though Mary and her husband, English essayist and political theorist William Godwin, submitted to marriage, it was on their own terms. Godwin took an apartment about twenty doors from the couple's house to which he "repaired" every morning. A letter of the time describes this arrangement: "In order to give the connection as little as possible the appearance of such a vulgar and debasing tie as matrimony, the parties have established separate establishments, and the husband only visits his mistress like a lover when each is dressed, rooms in order, etc." The couple agreed that it was wrong for husband and wife to have to be together whenever they went out into "mixed society" and therefore, as Godwin writes, "rather sought occasions of deviating from, than of complying with, this rule."

The principle of separate quarters, which recently cropped up again in reports of a contract between Jacqueline Kennedy and Aristotle Onassis, also appears in the agreement birth-control pioneer Margaret Sanger signed with her husband, J. Noah H. Slee. Their contract stated that they would have separate homes and, later, separate quarters within the same house. Neither was to have the slightest influence over the business affairs of the other, and, when both were busy, communications were to be exchanged through their secretaries. They also agreed that Margaret Sanger would continue to use her own name. (Sanger, in fact, was the name of her first husband, but she had already made it a famous one.)

The ultimate feminist contract, however, was the one Lucy Stone and Henry Blackwell wrote when they married in 1855. Their agreement is a concise catalogue of the legal inequities of marriage in America at that time:

"While we acknowledge our mutual affection by publicly assuming the relationship of husband and wife," they wrote, "we deem it a duty to declare that this act on our part implies no sanction of, nor promise of voluntary obedience to, such of the present laws of marriage as refuse to recognize the wife as an independent, rational being, while they confer upon the husband an injurious and unnatural superiority." The contract went on to protest especially against the laws which gave the husband custody of the wife's person, the sole ownership of her personal property and the use of her real estate, the absolute right to the product of her industry and the exclusive control and guardianship of the couple's children. Finally, they protested against "the whole system by which 'the legal existence of the wife is suspended during marriage' so that, in most States, she neither has a legal part in the choice of her residence, nor can she make a will, nor sue or be sued in her own name, nor inherit property."

While it is obvious that we have made some progress since Lucy Stone's day, in many ways we are still living under the heritage of the kind of laws she deplored. The American institution of marriage derives from English common law, which developed a peculiar concept, unknown on the Continent, called the "unity of spouses." As Blackstone put it, "By marriage, the husband and wife are one person in law; that is, the very being or legal existence of the woman is suspended during marriage, or at least is incorporated or consolidated into that of the husband."

Beginning in 1839, one version or another of what was called the Married Women's Property Act was passed in each state of the Union, correcting some of the gross injustices of marriage. Most of these laws granted married women the right to contract, to sue and be sued without joining their husbands, to manage and control the property they brought with them to marriage, to engage in gainful employment and retain the earnings derived from it. Like a case of bad genes, however, the fiction of the unity of the spouses has never quite gone away. Husband and wife today are like Siamese twins: although largely separate persons under the law, they are still joined together in one spot or another. In one state, the wife's ability to contract may still be impaired; in another, she may not have full freedom to use her maiden name; in a third, she may not be considered capable of conspiracy with her husband.

These vestiges of the unity of spouses, however, are not the only ways in which marriage treats man and woman unequally, for we have evolved a different—but still unequal—concept of marriage. Today we regard husband as head of household and wife as housewife; husband as supporter and wife as dependent; husband as authority and wife as faithful helpmeet. This concept of marriage has not been *created* by the law but is an expression of culturally shared values which are *reflected* in the law. It is the conventional notion of marriage consciously embraced or unthinkingly held by many, if not most, Americans.

What's wrong with it? The responsibility of support is commonly thought to favor women at the expense of men; I leave it for men to document how this notion injures them and will only deal here with the disabilities from a woman's point of view. Like all commonly held notions, the idea of marriage as a relationship between supporter and dependent is so much a part of our very atmosphere that it is hard to see it objectively. (To counter this difficulty, many women's groups are suggesting that people wishing to get a marriage license should have to take a test on the laws, as they do to get a driver's license.) Basically, the bargain in today's unwritten marriage contract is that the husband gets the right to the wife's services in return for supporting her. Whereas under common law the husband had "the absolute right to the product of the wife's industry," today the husband has only the absolute right to the product of the wife's industry *within the home*. "The wife's services and society are so essential a part of what the law considers the husband entitled to as part of the marriage," says Harriet Pilpel in *Your Marriage and the Law*, "that it will not recognize any agreement between the spouses which provides that the husband is to pay for such services or society."

The concept of the husband as supporter and wife as dependent underlies all the current legal inequalities of married women. To cite some specific examples:

Property. In common-law property states—like New York—husband and wife each exercise full control of what they own before, or acquire during, the marriage. But the woman who works only inside the home never has a chance to acquire property of her own, and therefore may never have any legitimate interest in, or control of, the family assets. (The only way she can acquire property is by gift, which makes her subject to her husband's patronage.) As John Gay said in *The Beggar's Opera*, "The comfortable estate of widowhood is the only hope that keeps up a wife's spirits." Her situation is improved by her husband's death; in every common-law property state, each spouse has a non-barrable interest in the estate of the other. However, this sometimes adds up to very little. For instance, in New Jersey, a wife only has "dower rights"; if her husband dies, she is entitled to one-third of the income from his real property. If the couple lived in an apartment and didn't own any real estate, the law guarantees her nothing.

Even in six of the eight community-property states where the spouses share equally in the property acquired during the marriage, the husband is given management control. Thus a woman may earn as much as her husband and have no say in how her money is spent. In the two exceptions, Washington and Texas, husband and wife have separate control of the property each acquires. Even this arrangement leaves the non-earning spouse without any control of the purse strings.

Name. In many states the law deprives the wife of full freedom to use her own name: in Illinois in 1965 when a woman sought the right to vote although she had not registered under her married name, the Appellate Court said she couldn't. In a recent case, a three-judge Federal court upheld the Alabama law requiring a woman to assume her husband's surname upon marriage by ruling that a married woman does not have a right to have her driver's license issued in her maiden name. In Michigan, if a man changes his last name his wife must also change hers; she may not contest the change, although the couple's minor children over the age of sixteen may do so.

Domicile. Domicile is a technical term sometimes defined as a "place where a person has a settled connection for certain legal purposes." (You can live in one place and be domiciled in another.) Domicile affects various legal rights and obligations, including where a person may vote, hold public office, serve on juries, receive welfare, qualify for tuition advantages at state educational institutions, be liable for taxes, have his or her estate administered, and file for divorce. In general, a wife's domicile automatically follows that of her husband and she has no choice in the matter. (NOW members have been challenging this law in North Carolina.)

The husband, generally, also has had the right to decide where he and his wife live, although recently he has been required to make a reasonable decision taking her wishes into account. The burden of proving she is reasonable, however, still rests with the wife.

To some women the loss of these rights may seem a small price to pay for support. In fact, the arrangement works out differently depending on economic

---

THE ONASSIS MARRIAGE CONTRACT

According to Christian Kafarakis, former chief steward on Aristotle Onassis' yacht, the marriage contract between Onassis and Jacqueline Bouvier Kennedy contains 170 clauses, covering every possible detail of their marital life.

There have been charges and countercharges, proofs and refutations flying ever since the contract was printed in *The People,* a Sunday newspaper in England. Does the contract exist? Was it created by an ex-steward with great legal imagination? Was Christian Kafarakis even a steward?

Truth or hoax, the document works more to support the current system of wife-as-prostitute than to equalize men and women. But it does spur our imaginations to greater possibilities of contract-making.

Separate bedrooms are stipulated, according to Mr. Kafarakis, for instance. He feels this may explain why Jackie O. has her own house on the island of Skorpios and stays in her Fifth Avenue apartment rather than in Onassis' floor-through at the Hotel Pierre.

So that Mrs. Onassis may be "sheltered from want," the Greek millionaire is supposed to have contracted for $600,000 a year in maintenance.

More, according to Mr. Kafarakis:

"If Onassis should ever part from Jackie, he will have to give her a sum of nearly £ 4.2 million [$9.6 million] for every year of their marriage.

"If she leaves him, her payoff will be a lump sum in the neighborhood of £ 7.5 million [$18 million], which is a highly desirable neighborhood. That is, if the parting comes before five years.

"If she sticks it out longer, she will receive, in addition to the £ 7.5 million, an alimony of £ 75,000 a year for ten years.

"If Onassis dies while they are still married, she will inherit the staggering sum of £ 42 million [$100 million]."

class. The higher up the ladder her husband is, the better a woman is supported and the fewer services she gives in return. For the many millions of women who work outside the home, on the other hand, the bargain is not a terribly good one: in reality all they earn for the services they give their husbands is the responsibility of working outside the home as well as in it to help their families survive. These women learn another price they pay for the illusion of support— the low salaries they receive compared with men's are ironically justified by the argument that the "men have families to feed." This is not the fault of husbands but of an economy structured on the unpaid services of women.

But the heaviest price those women who accept the role of dependent pay is a psychological one. Economic dependency is in itself corrupting, as can be seen in the rawest form in country-and-Western songs of the "I-know-he's-being-untrue-but-I-never-confront-him-with-it-because-if-he-left-me-who-would-support-the-children" variety. And economic dependency breeds other kinds of dependency. The woman who has no established legal right in the family income fares better or worse depending on how well she pleases the head of the household. In the attempt to please she may surrender her own tastes, her own opinions, her own thoughts. If she habitually defers to or depends on her husband's decisions she will eventually find herself incapable of making her own.

The solution is not that wives should never work in the home or that husbands should not share their incomes with them. The solution is that we must begin to recognize that the work wives do belongs to them, not their husbands, and should be accorded a legitimate value. If wives make the contribution of full partners in their marriages, they should receive the rights of partners—not only, like slaves, the right to be housed, clothed and fed, or in other words, supported. This is hardly a new idea: in 1963 the Report of the President's Commission on the Status of Women recommended that "during marriage each spouse should have a legally defined right in the earnings of the other, in the real personal property acquired through these earnings, and in their management."

There is, however, hope of progress. Although the Uniform Marriage and Divorce Act drafted by the National Conference of Commissioners on Uniform State Laws has not yet been adopted anywhere (Colorado has adopted the divorce portion of the law), it embraces some of the principles of marriage as partnership. It would make irremediable breakdown of the marriage the only ground for divorce, institute a division of property based on the assumption that husband and wife have contributed equally to the marriage, and determine custody according to the best interests of the child without the traditional bias in favor of the mother.

Should the Equal Rights Amendment be passed, it may require that most of the inequalities in the marriage relationship be abolished. According to an analysis published in *The Yale Law Journal,* the amendment would give women the freedom to use any name they wish, given them the same independent choice of domicile that married men have now, invalidate laws vesting management of community property in the husband alone, and prohibit enforcement of sex-based definitions of conjugal function. "Courts would not be able to assume for any purpose that women had a legal obligation to do housework, or provide affection and companionship, or to be available for sexual relations, unless men owed their wives exactly the same duties. Similarly, men could not be assigned the duty to provide financial support simply because of their sex." Even should the amendment pass, however, it would take years of action in the courts to implement it. Meanwhile, perhaps the best we can do is to say with Lucy Stone and Henry Blackwell that while we wish to acknowledge our mutual affection by publicly assuming the relationship of husband and wife, we do not promise obedience to laws that discriminate against us. And perhaps, by writing our own contracts we can modify the effect of those laws.

The problem with a husband and wife sitting down together and drafting a legal contract incorporating their beliefs concerning marriage is that the state immediately horns its way into the act. Marriage, contrary to popular belief, is more *ménage à trois* than *folie à deux*. It is a contract to which the state is a third party, and though you and your spouse may be in perfect accord, there are certain things the state will not tolerate. Most of these things are against what is known as public policy. Under public policy, according to Harriet Pilpel, "the courts, in many states, will not enforce any agreement which attempts to free the husband from the duty of support to the wife. . . . Nor will the courts uphold any agreement which attempts to limit or eliminate the personal or conjugal rights of marriage as distinguished from property rights. An agreement that the parties will not live together after marriage is void. So is an agreement not to engage in sexual intercourse or not to have children. One court has even held that it is against public policy for an engaged couple to agree that they will live in whatever place the wife chooses. Under the law, said the court, that is the "husband's prerogative and he cannot relinquish it." Public policy also forbids contracts which anticipate divorce in any way. Agreements defining what will happen if a couple divorces or the conditions under which they will divorce are seen as facilitating the dissolution of marriages.

There are certain contracts, called ante-nuptial agreements, that the state clearly permits us to make. These contracts, according to Judith Boies, a matrimonial and estate lawyer with the New York law firm Paul, Weiss, Rifkind, Wharton & Garrison, may concern property owned before marriage, property acquired after marriage by gift or inheritance, and property right in each other's estates. A wife cannot waive support, but she can waive interest in her husband's estate.

Some lawyers believe that people should be able to make whatever marriage contracts they like with one another. "Why should marriage be any different from any other contract?" asks constitutional lawyer Kristin Booth Glen, who teaches a course in women's rights at New York University Law School. She believes that the state's intervention in people's marriages may be in violation of Article I, Section 10, of the United States Constitution, which says that the states are forbidden to pass laws "impairing the obligation of contracts." Other lawyers feel that we don't really know which of the contracts we might wish to make concerning marriage would be enforceable. "There will have to be some litigation first," says Kathleen Carlsson, a lawyer for the Lucy Stone League. "In the light of the new feminist atmosphere, the decisions rendered today might not be the same as those rendered twenty years ago."

Judith Boies concurs with this view and feels that couples should begin right now to make whatever contracts suit their needs. If both spouses are wage-earners, they should contract how money and expenses will be divided. If they decide to have any joint bank accounts, they should sign a written agreement defining in what proportions the money in the account belongs to them. Then

THE UTOPIAN MARRIAGE CONTRACT

1. The wife's right to use her maiden name or any other name she chooses.
2. What surname the children will have: husband's, wife's, a hyphenated combination, a neutral name or the name the children choose when they reach a certain age.
3. Birth control: Whether or not, what kind and who uses it. (One couple—the wife can't use the Pill—splits the responsibility 50-50. Half the time she uses a diaphragm, half he uses a condom.)
4. Whether or not to have children, or to adopt them, and if so how many.
5. How the children will be brought up.
6. Where the couple will live: Will the husband be willing to move if the wife gets a job offer she wants to take? Separate bedrooms? Separate apartments?
7. How child care and housework will be divided: The spouse who earns less should not be penalized for the inequities of the economic world by having to do a larger share.
8. What financial arrangement will the couple embrace? If husband and wife are both wage-earners, there are three basic possibilities:

   a) Husband and wife pool their income, pay expenses and divide any surplus. (This was Leonard and Virginia Woolf's arrangement. At the end of the year, after payment of expenses, they divided the surplus between them equally so each had what they called a personal "hoard.")

   b) Husband and wife pay shares of expenses proportional to their incomes. Each keeps whatever he or she has left.

   c) Husband and wife each pays 50 percent of expenses. Each keeps what he or she has left.

   If husband earns significantly more than wife, the couple might consider a) that the disparity is a result of sexist discrimination in employment and there should perhaps be some kind of "home reparations program" to offset this inequity, and b) whether the couple really has an equal partnership if one has greater economic strength, and therefore possibly greater power psychologically, in the relationship.
9. Sexual rights and freedoms. Although any arrangement other than monogamy would clearly be against public policy, in practice some people make arrangements such as having Tuesdays off from one another.
10. The husband might give his consent to abortion in advance.   —S.E.

if one party cleans out the account—a frequent if unfortunate prelude to divorce—the contract would establish how they had intended to share the property.

Wives often assume—erroneously—that everything their husbands own belongs to them. In the common-law property states, property belongs to the person whose name it is in. When property is jointly owned, half presumably belongs to each spouse. However, this presumption is rebuttable. The husband can claim, for instance, that he and his wife only have a joint account so she can buy groceries.

The second kind of agreement couples might make is one in which the husband agrees to pay the wife a certain amount for domestic services. If there is no money to pay her, the debt accrues from year to year. When money becomes available, the wife would have first claim on it.

A third kind of financial contract could be made between husband and wife when one spouse puts the other through medical school or any other kind of education or training. The wife could agree to provide the husband with so much money per year to be paid back at a certain rate in subsequent years. This contract has a good chance of being enforceable, since even the tax laws recognize that spouses make loans to one another.

"All these financial contracts have a reasonably good chance of standing up in court," says Judith Boies. The one with the least chance is the one providing payment for household services. Since the financial contracts are more likely to be valid than those affecting personal aspects of the marriage, they should be made separately.

Judith Boies believes that, ideally, the personal contracts should also be valid. "The state shouldn't even marry people; it should just favor every contract that makes adequate provision for wife and children." The areas that might be covered in a comprehensive, total, utopian contract might include the wife's right to use the name she chooses, the children's names, division of housework and child care, finances, birth control, whether or not to have children and how many, the upbringing of the children, living arrangements, sexual rights and freedoms, and anything else of importance to the individual couple.

Since the marriage relationship is not a static one, any contract should permit the couple to solve their problems on a continuing basis. It should be amendable, revisable or renewable. One possibility is to draw up the first contract for a short period of time, and renegotiate later.

Although current policy clearly makes any agreement concerning it invalid, our utopian contract might also cover divorce. After all, the court in California's Contra Costa County now permits couples to write their own divorce agreements and receive their decrees by mail.

At this point, many readers are probably thinking, "Why get married at all, why not just draw up a contract that covers all contingencies?" Again, the state got there first. Such an agreement would be considered a contract for the purpose of "meretricious relations," or in other words an illicit sexual relationship, and therefore would be invalid.

Other readers are probably thinking, "But we love each other, so why should we have a contract?" As Barbara Koltuv says, "Part of the reason for thinking out a contract is to find out what your problems are; it forces you to take charge of your life. Once you have the contract, you don't have to refer back to it. The process is what's important."

Whether these contracts are legally enforceable or not, just drawing them up may be of great service to many couples. What we are really doing in thrashing out a contract is finding out where we stand on issues, clearing up all the murky, unexamined areas of conflict, and unflinchingly facing up to our differences.

THE SHULMANS' MARRIAGE AGREEMENT

I. Principles.

We reject the notion that the work which brings in more money is more valuable. The ability to earn money is a privilege which must not be compounded by enabling the larger earner to buy out of his/her duties and put the burden on the partner who earns less or on another person hired from outside.

We believe that each partner has an equal right to his/her own time, work, values, choices. As long as all duties are performed, each of us may use his/her extra time any way he/she chooses. If he/she wants to use it making money, fine. If he/she wants to spend it with spouse, fine.

As parents we believe we must share all responsibility for taking care of our children and home—and not only the work but also the responsibility. At least during the first year of this agreement, *sharing responsibility* shall mean dividing the *jobs* and dividing the *time.*

II. Job Breakdown and Schedule

(A) Children

1. Mornings: Waking children; getting their clothes out; making their lunches; seeing that they have notes, homework, money, bus passes, books; brushing their hair; giving them breakfast (making coffee for us). Every other week each parent does all.

2. Transportation: Getting children to and from lessons, doctors, dentists (including making appointments), friends' houses, etc. Parts occurring between 3 and 6 p.m. fall to wife. She must be compensated by extra work from husband. Husband does weekend transportation and pickups after 6.

3. Help: Helping with homework, personal questions; explaining things. Parts occurring between 3 and 6 p.m. fall to wife. After 6 p.m. husband does Tuesday, Thursday and Sunday; wife does Monday, Wednesday and Saturday. Friday is free for whoever has done extra work during the week.

4. Nighttime (after 6 p.m.): Getting children to take baths, brush their teeth, put away their toys and clothes, go to bed; reading with them; tucking them in and having nighttime talks; handling if they awake at night. Husband does Tuesday, Thursday and Sunday. Wife does Monday, Wednesday and Saturday. Friday split according to who has done extra work.

5. Baby sitters: Baby sitters must be called by the parent the sitter is to replace. If no sitter turns up, that parent must stay home.

6. Sick care: Calling doctors; checking symptoms; getting prescriptions filled; remembering to give medicine; taking days off to stay home with sick child, providing special activities. This must still be worked out equally, since now wife seems to do it all. In any case, wife must be compensated (see 10 below).

7. Weekends: all usual child care, plus special activities (beach, park, zoo). Split equally. Husband is free all Saturday, wife is free all Sunday.

(B) Housework

8. Cooking: Breakfasts during the week are divided equally; husband does all weekend breakfasts (including shopping for them and dishes). Wife does all dinners except Sunday nights. Husband does Sunday dinner and any other dinners on his nights of responsibility if wife isn't home. Whoever invites guests does shopping, cooking and dishes; if both invite them, split work.

9. Shopping: Food for all meals, housewares, clothing and supplies for children. Divide by convenience. Generally, wife does daily food shopping; husband does special shopping.

10. Cleaning: Husband does dishes Tuesday, Thursday and Sunday. Wife does Monday, Wednesday and Saturday. Friday is split according to who has done extra work during the week. Husband does all the house-cleaning in exchange for wife's extra child care (3 to 6 daily) and sick care.

11. Laundry: Home laundry, making beds, dry cleaning (take and pick up). Wife does home laundry. Husband does dry-cleaning delivery and pick-up. Wife strips beds, husband remakes them.

In-Laws, Pro and Con

Evelyn M. Duvall

One of the major adjustments the married pair must make is that of arriving at workable role relationships with in-laws (with the possible exception of those couples who live great distances from them). This may pose some aggravating problems, for the family of procreation is usually loath to forsake all control over its children even though they are grown and married. In addition, each married partner runs the danger of becoming a relative by marriage to someone of whom he cannot approve or for whom he has no feelings of warmth. The saying, "You cannot choose your relatives, but thank God, you can choose your friends," no doubt stems from these sentiments. Yet the married pair themselves will someday be in-laws. Perhaps a better adjustment can be achieved if they perceive the universal problems of in-law relationships as developed by Duvall's timeless study.

MOTHER-IN-LAW IS THE MOST DIFFICULT

Mother-in-law heads the list of difficult in-laws by a wide margin. Of the 992 having in-law difficulties of any kind (the total of 1,337 minus 345 having "no problems"), one out of every two (49.5%; 491) mentions mother-in-law as most difficult.

More than one-third of the total 1,337 men and women, 491 (36.8%) named mother-in-law their most difficult in-law. These mother-in-law mentions were not evenly distributed among the groups. Individual groups mentioning mother-in-law as most troublesome ranged from 11.9% to 76.5%.

Nine out of ten complaints about mothers-in-law came from women (1,227 specific complaints; 89.6%); while men list only 142 (10.4%) specific com-

From Evelyn M. Duvall, *In-Laws, Pro and Con* (New York: Association Press, 1954), pp. 117, 221, 244–245, 260–261, 286–290, 328–330. Reprinted by permission of Association Press.

119

plaints against their mothers-in-law out of a total of 1,369 from the entire group (Table 1). These data do not support the popular notion that it is the man who professes the greater difficulty with his mother-in-law. These data

TABLE 1
MOTHER-IN-LAW DIFFICULTIES REPORTED BY 491 PERSONS

WHAT MOTHER-IN-LAW DOES THAT MAKES HER MOST DIFFICULT IN-LAW	SPECIFIC CRITICISM NAMED	
	NUMBER	PERCENT
1. Meddles, interferes, dominates, intrudes on our privacy, etc.	383	28.0
2. Is possessive, demanding, overprotective, forces attention, etc.	193	14.1
3. Nags, criticizes, complains, finds fault, ridicules, etc.	150	10.9
4. Ignores us, is indifferent, uninterested, not helpful, aloof, does not accept me/us, not close, unsociable, etc.	99	7.2
5. Clings, is irresponsible, immature, childish, dependent, has no life of her own, no interests beyond us, undependable, etc.	93	6.8
6. Disagrees on traditions, has different standards, is old-fashioned, resists change, is intolerant of our ways, has nothing in common with us	84	6.2
7. Is thoughtless, inconsiderate, selfish, unappreciative, etc.	76	5.6
8. Takes sides, plays favorites, shows partiality, spoils and pampers my husband, plays one family against the other, etc.	72	5.3
9. Abuses hospitality, comes without invitation, overstays visits, lives with us more than necessary, does not reciprocate, etc.	58	4.2
10. Is self-righteous, superior, always right, egotistical, smug, boastful, lords it over me/us, brags, knows all the answers	41	3.0
11. Talks too much, asks useless questions, doesn't listen, is full of idle chatter, gushes, doesn't try to understand	39	2.8
12. Tattles, gossips, misrepresents facts, exaggerates, lies, is dishonest, insincere, deceitful, etc.	34	2.5
13. Is jealous, rivalrous, envious, covets what we have, etc.	33	2.4
14. Does not do own job well, is not a good mother, neglects her family, is extravagant, doesn't take care of her home, etc.	12	0.9
15. Drinks, gambles	2	0.1
Total	1,369	100.0

show that it is the woman who feels the mother-in-law problem more often. In this respect our findings corroborate Paul Wallin's[1] report that among those couples in the Burgess-Wallin sample, more wives (17.1%) than husbands (8.3%) dislike their mothers-in-law.

In general, younger women mentioned mother-in-law most difficult significantly more frequently than did older women.

. . . .

Sister-in-Law Is a Real Problem

Sister-in-law is the Number Two hazard among in-laws. She comes second to mother-in-law in number of complaints and in the experience of most people. In several respects sister-in-law outdistances mother-in-law in troublesomeness.

Sister-in-law is a center of strain in other cultures too. Margaret Mead[2] reports that in the Admiralty Islands the sister-in-law relationship is one of strain and opposition. The wife enters the husband's family as a stranger and hostility ensues between her and his sisters, who until then have given him female companionship. Among the Manus, Mead reports that the wife is obligated to care for her sister-in-law during pregnancy and childbirth; and that this is a troublesome, annoying, and nonreciprocal discharge of duty. Generally, among these peoples, sisters-in-law are institutionally opposed to each other.

Here in the United States it is generally expected that mother-in-law is most troublesome. The stereotyped hostility-humor and avoidance are directed exclusively toward her. Sister-in-law, however, is *not* the butt of in-law jokes. Nor is she generally assumed to be particularly troublesome. Yet, she is mentioned as being difficult significantly more frequently than any other in-law except the mother-in-law.

Out of 2,611 criticisms directed at in-laws, 701 (26.8%) are those attributed to sisters-in-law.

. . . .

The roster of things sister-in-law does that make life difficult for her relatives by marriage is found in Table 2. These are the things reported by the 272 men and women who in their experience have found sister-in-law most difficult of in-laws. These 272 persons represent 27.4% of the 992 men and women who report that they have trouble with their in-laws (1,337 minus 345 persons with no in-law problems).

Brother-in-Law Is Not So Bad

People do not often find brothers-in-law difficult to get along with. Out of the 1,337 men and women who participated in the group interview phase of

121

TABLE 2
SISTER-IN-LAW DIFFICULTIES REPORTED BY 272 PERSONS

WHAT SISTER-IN-LAW DOES THAT MAKES HER MOST DIFFICULT	SPECIFIC CRITICISM NAMED	
	NUMBER	PERCENT
1. Meddles, interferes, dominates, intrudes on privacy, etc.	130	18.5
2. Ignores us, is indifferent, uninterested, unsociable, aloof, etc.	72	10.3
3. Is thoughtless, inconsiderate, selfish, unappreciative, etc.	72	10.3
4. Nags, criticizes, complains, finds fault, ridicules, etc.	69	9.8
5. Clings, is immature, irresponsible, childish, dependent, etc.	49	7.0
6. Is jealous, rivalrous, envious, covets what we have, etc.	48	6.9
7. Tattles, gossips, exaggerates, lies, is deceitful, insincere, etc.	47	6.7
8. Is self-righteous, always right, egotistical, smug, bragging, etc.	39	5.6
9. Is not a good mother, neglects her family, is extravagant, etc.	37	5.2
10. Disagrees on traditions, has different standards, uncongenial	36	5.1
11. Is possessive, demanding, overprotective, forces attention, etc.	33	4.7
12. Talks too much, asks useless questions, doesn't listen, etc.	28	4.0
13. Takes sides, plays favorites, shows partiality, pampers, spoils	18	2.6
14. Abuses hospitality, comes without invitation, overstays visits	18	2.6
15. Drinks, gambles, is unconventional, unfaithful, etc.	5	0.7
Total	701	100.0

this study, 72 (5.4%) report brother-in-law as their most difficult in-law. Of the 2,611 things that in-laws do that make life difficult, 186 (7.2%) are attributed to brothers-in-law. In both the number of times he is named the most difficult in-law and in the number of criticisms made of him, brother-in-law ranks third of all relatives by marriage, being significantly less difficult than either sister-in-law or mother-in-law. He outranks father-in-law by but a fraction of one percent (0.4%) in both criticisms and persons reporting. Men and women both mention brother-in-law as most difficult in proportions equivalent to their numbers in the sample.

The problems people report having with their brothers-in-law appear in rank order in Table 3.

In several ways difficulties with brothers-in-law are different from those that people report they have with their mothers-in-law, fathers-in-law, and sisters-in-law.

SOME FATHERS-IN-LAW ARE TROUBLESOME

When 1,337 men and women name their most difficult in-law relationship, only 52 mention father-in-law (1.5%). Of the 2,611 things that are specifically mentioned as making in-law relationships difficult, 179 (6.8%) are attributed to fathers-in-law. This is significantly fewer than criticisms of mothers-in-law. Specific criticisms of father-in-law rank as shown in Table 4.

TABLE 3
BROTHER-IN-LAW DIFFICULTIES REPORTED BY 72 PERSONS

WHAT BROTHER-IN-LAW DOES THAT MAKES HIM MOST DIFFICULT IN-LAW	SPECIFIC CRITICISM NAMED	
	NUMBER	PERCENT
1. Incompetency—does not do own job well	27	14.5
2. Immaturity—is childish, irresponsible, dependent, etc.	24	12.9
3. Thoughtlessness—is selfish, unappreciative, etc.	23	12.4
4. Indifference—is uninterested, not close, non-accepting, etc.	18	9.7
5. Self-righteousness—is superior, egotistical, boastful, etc.	17	9.1
6. Interference—is meddling, dominating, etc.	16	8.6
7. Criticalness—nags, complains, finds fault, etc.	14	7.5
8. Uncongeniality—different standards, intolerant, old-fashioned	12	6.5
9. Misrepresentation—gossips, tattles, exaggerates, etc.	8	4.3
10. Unconventionality—drinks, gambles, etc.	8	4.3
11. Possessiveness—is demanding, overprotective, forces attention	5	2.7
12. Rivalrousness—is jealous, envious, covetous, etc.	5	2.7
13. Partiality—takes sides, plays favorites, spoils, pampers, etc.	3	1.6
14. Intrusion—comes without invitation, abuses hospitality, etc.	3	1.6
15. Talkativeness—asks useless questions, chatters, etc.	3	1.6
Total	186	100.0

TABLE 4

FATHER-IN-LAW DIFFICULTIES REPORTED BY 52 PERSONS

WHAT FATHER-IN-LAW DOES THAT MAKES HIM THE MOST DIFFICULT IN-LAW	SPECIFIC CRITICISM NAMED	
	NUMBER	PERCENT
1. Meddles, interferes, dominates, intrudes on our privacy, etc.	31	17.3
2. Nags, criticizes, complains, finds fault, ridicules, etc.	26	14.5
3. Resists change, disagrees on traditions, uncongenial, etc.	21	11.7
4. Ignores us, is indifferent, uninterested, aloof, not close, etc.	17	9.5
5. Is possessive, demanding, overprotective, forces attention, etc.	13	7.3
6. Is self-righteous, superior, always right, smug, bragging, etc.	13	7.3
7. Talks too much, asks useless questions, doesn't listen, etc.	13	7.3
8. Is thoughtless, inconsiderate, selfish, unappreciative, etc.	11	6.1
9. Is irresponsible, immature, childish, dependent, no life of own	8	4.5
10. Drinks, gambles, is unconventional, etc.	8	4.5
11. Does not do his own job well, incompetent, lazy, etc.	7	3.9
12. Takes sides, plays favorites, shows partiality, pampers the children, plays one of us against the other, etc.	5	2.8
13. Abuses hospitality, comes without invitation, overstays visits	4	2.2
14. Tattles, gossips, exaggerates, lies, is insincere	2	1.1
15. Is jealous, rivalrous, envious, covets what we have, etc.	0	0.0
Total	179	100.0

Some interesting differences are apparent in the rank order of criticisms of father-in-law as compared with that of mother-in-law (Tables 4 and 1 respectively). Possessiveness, which ranks second for mother-in-law, ranks fifth for father-in-law. Immaturity, which ranks fifth for mother-in-law, ranks ninth for father-in-law. Pampering, which ranks eighth for mother-in-law, ranks twelfth for father-in-law. Intrusion, ranking ninth for mother-in-law, ranks thirteenth for father-in-law. Thus, in four characteristics mother-in-law offends perceptibility more frequently than does father-in-law; possessiveness, immaturity, pampering, and intrusion.

On the other hand, where uncongeniality ranks sixth for mother-in-law, it appears in third place for father-in-law. Where self-righteousness ranks tenth for mother-in-law, it ranks sixth for father-in-law. Where talkativeness ranks eleventh for mother-in-law, it comes in seventh place for father-in-law. Where unconventionality as seen in drinking, gambling, etc., ranks last at fifteenth place for mother-in-law, it ranks tenth for father-in-law. Incompetence in terms of not doing one's own job well ranks fourteenth for mother-in-law and eleventh for father-in-law. So, five criticisms rank considerably higher for father-in-law than mother-in-law; uncongeniality, self-righteousness, talkativeness, unconventionality, and incompetence.

·   ·   ·   ·

WHY SOME PEOPLE HAVE NO PROBLEMS WITH THEIR IN-LAWS

Some people have no trouble getting along with their in-laws. They tell us in no uncertain terms that they have no problems with their relatives by marriage. How they do it and what the factors are that lead to family harmony give us many leads on how to be better in-laws.

"They accept me," is the primary reason for accord among in-laws given nearly one out of five times (18.6%). When this top-ranking category is merged with other responses of similar attitude, the factor of acceptance looms imposingly large, as we see in Table 5.

LET THE REST OF THE WORLD GO BY (SUMMARY)

"With someone like you," so the popular song goes, "a pal good and true, I'd like to leave it all behind, and go and find, some place that's known to God alone—just a spot to call our own. We'll find perfect peace, where joys never cease—out there beneath the kindly sky. We'll build a sweet little nest, somewhere in the West—and let the rest of the world go by."

This might well be the theme song of those who would escape the intrusion of the world. It is close to the heart of the in-law situation; for what these young lovers are saying is, "Let's give ourselves a chance to settle down and make our own home, far from the possibilities of intruding in-laws, meddling relatives, and the family responsibilities, loyalties, and conditionings that both of us have."

Everybody is "in-laws" when you are married. The big task of marriage is to develop the mutual loyalty that makes *Our* family come before either *Yours* or *Mine*.

Some in-law problems have their bases in the family history or the early development of the man or the woman, which, carrying over into marriage, may make that person vulnerable to certain types of in-law problems, or "allergic" to in-laws.

TABLE 5
REASON FOR NO PROBLEMS WITH IN-LAWS
REPORTED BY 345 PERSONS

WHY IN-LAWS ARE "NO PROBLEM"	SPECIFIC CRITICISM REPORTED	
	NUMBER	PERCENT
1. They accept me; they are friendly, helpful, close	139	18.6
2. They do not meddle, interfere, or butt into my life	112	14.9
3. They are thoughtful, kind, considerate, generous	88	11.8
4. They are too far away; we rarely see them; haven't met	88	11.8
5. No reason given for "No problem" report	54	7.2
6. No in-laws: I married an orphan, etc.	43	5.8
7. Determination to adjust: we respect each other's rights; we work things out as they come up; etc.	38	5.1
8. They are mature, have outside interests, are independent	36	4.8
9. They love me; we have mutual affection and trust; they back me when I need it; etc.	33	4.4
10. We are congenial, have similar interests and standards; they fit in, are tolerant of our differences; etc.	33	4.4
11. They come only when invited, do not overstay visits, are always welcome, do not abuse hospitality, etc.	29	3.9
12. They understand me, listen to me, are understanding people	25	3.3
13. They are not critical, do not get impatient with me, etc.	18	2.4
14. They are not demanding or possessive; let us be free; etc.	9	1.2
15. They do not act superior, nor make me feel inferior, etc.	3	0.4
Total	748	100.0

Any member of either family who threatens the autonomy of the couple or delays the independence of the pair is in danger of being a difficult in-law. So we find aunts-in-law, grandparents-in-law, nieces-in-law, cousins-in-law, as well as closer relatives by marriage being reported as troublesome. Criticisms of these other in-laws follow the same general pattern as those for all in-laws.

Apparent in the constellations of complaints about in-laws is the mother-in-law syndrome of meddlesomeness, possessiveness, and nagging; the complaint of distance, including mentions of thoughtlessness and indifference; the sibling syndrome of self-righteousness, incompetency, playing favorites, gossiping, and jealousy; and the father-in-law syndrome of ineffectuality, unconventionality, talkativeness, and incompetence.

Women more than men are involved in in-law problems, possibly because of the role assignment to the women of the family of close interpersonal and intrafamily relationships. Older family members are criticized more frequently than are younger for two apparent reasons: (1) the emancipatory thrust of youth that makes them more critical of older family members than vice versa; and (2) the traditional taboo on discussing family matters outside the family that restrains more older than younger persons.

NOTES

[1] Paul Wallin, "Sex Differences in Attitudes to In-Laws." *American Journal of Sociology*, March, 1954, pp. 466–469.
[2] Margaret Mead, *Kinship in the Admiralty Islands.* New York: Anthropological Papers of the American Museum of Natural History, 1934, p. 305.

Five Types of Marriage

John F. Cuber and Peggy B. Harroff

The sex role orientation or general division of labor between two spouses is but one facet of the marital relationship. Perhaps more basic is the emotional content or general ambience of the relationship. Cuber and Harroff asked respondents who had been married at least ten years or more to describe their marriages in their own words. From these descriptions, five different styles of relationships emerged, all with their own form of stability (since none of the couples were even contemplating divorce). There are couples whose relationship is characterized by continuous fights, big and small. There are couples who once found each other exciting, but who now turn their energies to their children and see their partner primarily as a good parent. Another group of couples, who married carefully if not ecstatically, have cultivated a marriage of convenience that does not interfere with other interests. There are couples who glory in each other's company, while still leading very separate identities. Finally, some couples are so bound to each other by love and interest that they almost cease to have separate identities. A sociologically interesting question is how these marriage types develop over time. It is also worth mentioning that this research was conducted before the hippie commune movement, the sexual freedom movement, and the Women's Liberation Movement. Have new emotional and interactional types developed as a result of marriages within these new ideologies?

The qualitative aspects of enduring marital relationships vary enormously. The variations described to us were by no means random or clearly individualized, however. Five distinct life styles showed up repeatedly and the pairs within each of them were remarkably similar in the ways in which they lived together, found sexual expression, reared children, and made their way in the outside world.

The following classification is based on the interview materials of those people whose marriages had already lasted ten years or more and who said that they had never seriously considered divorce or separation. While 360 of the men and women had been married ten or more years to the same spouse, exclusion of those who reported that they had considered divorce reduced the number to 211. The discussion in this chapter is, then, based on 211 interviews: 107 men and 104 women.

The descriptions which our interviewees gave us took into account how they had behaved and also how they felt about their actions past and present. Examination of the important features of their lives revealed five recurring configurations of male-female life, each with a central theme—some prominent distinguishing psychological feature which gave each type its singularity. It is these preeminent characteristics which suggested the names for the relationship: the *Conflict-Habituated,* the *Devitalized,* the *Passive-Congenial,* the *Vital,* and the *Total.*

THE CONFLICT-HABITUATED

We begin with the conflict-habituated not because it is the most prevalent, but because the overt behavior patterns in it are so readily observed and because it presents some arresting contradictions. In this association there is much tension and conflict—although it is largely controlled. At worst, there is some private quarreling, nagging, and "throwing up the past" of which members of the immediate family, and more rarely close friends and relatives, have some awareness. At best, the couple is discreet and polite, genteel about it in the company of others—but after a few drinks at the cocktail party the verbal barbs begin to fly. The intermittent conflict is rarely concealed from the children, though we were often assured otherwise. "Oh, they're at it again—but they always are," says the high-school son. There is private acknowledgment by both husband and wife as a rule that incompatibility is pervasive, that conflict is ever-potential, and that an atmosphere of tension permeates the togetherness.

An illustrative case concerns a physician of fifty, married for twenty-five years to the same woman, with two college-graduate children promisingly established in their own professions.

You know, it's funny; we have fought from the time we were in high school together. As I look back at it, I can't remember specific quarrels; it's more like a running guerrilla fight with intermediate periods, sometimes quite long, of pretty good fun and some damn good sex. In fact, if it hadn't been for the sex, we wouldn't have been married so quickly. Well, anyway, this has been going on ever since. . . . It's hard to know what it is we fight about most of the time. You name it and we'll fight about it. It's sometimes something I've said that she remembers differently, sometimes a decision— like what kind of car to buy or what to give the kids for Christmas. With regard to politics, and religion, and morals—oh, boy! You know, outside of the welfare of the kids—and that's just abstract—we don't really agree about anything. . . . At different times we take opposite sides—not deliberately; it just comes out that way.

Now these fights get pretty damned colorful. You called them arguments a little while ago—I have to correct you—they're brawls. There's never a bit of physical violence—at least not directed to each other—but the verbal gunfire gets pretty thick. Why, we've said things to each other that neither of us would think of saying in the hearing of anybody else. . . .

Of course we don't settle any of the issues. It's sort of a matter of principle *not* to. Because somebody would have to give in then and lose face for the next encounter. . . .

When I tell you this in this way, I feel a little foolish about it. I wouldn't tolerate such a condition in any other relationship in my life—and yet here I do and always have. . . .

No—we never have considered divorce or separation or anything so clear-cut. I realize that other people do, and I can't say that it has never occurred to either of us, but we've never considered it seriously.

A number of times there has been a crisis, like the time I was in the automobile accident, and the time she almost died in childbirth, and then I guess we really showed that we do care about each other. But as soon as the crisis is over, it's business as usual.

There is a subtle valence in these conflict-habituated relationships. It is easily missed in casual observation. So central is the necessity for channeling conflict and bridling hostility that these considerations come to preoccupy much of the interaction. Some psychiatrists have gone so far as to suggest that it is precisely the deep need to do psychological battle with one another which constitutes the cohesive factor insuring continuity of the marriage. Possibly so. But even from a surface point of view, the overt and manifest fact of habituated attention to handling tension, keeping it chained, and concealing it, is clearly seen as a dominant life force. And it can, and does for some, last for a whole lifetime.

THE DEVITALIZED

The key to the devitalized mode is the clear discrepancy between middle-aged reality and the earlier years. These people usually characterized themselves as having been "deeply in love" during the early years, as having spent a great deal of time together, having enjoyed sex, and most importantly of all, having had a close identification with one another. The present picture, with some variation from case to case, is in clear contrast—little time is spent together, sexual relationships are far less satisfying qualitatively or quantitatively, and interests and activities are not shared, at least not in the deeper and meaningful way they once were. Most of their time together now is "duty time"—entertaining together, planning and sharing activities with children, and participating in various kinds of required community responsibilities. They do as a rule retain, in addition to a genuine and mutual interest in the welfare of their children, a shared attention to their joint property and the husband's career. But even in the latter case the interest is contrasting. Despite a common dependency on his success and the benefits which flow therefrom, there is typically very little sharing of the intrinsic aspects of career—simply an acknowledgment of their mutual dependency on the fruits.

Two rather distinct subtypes of the devitalized take shape by the middle years. The following reflections of two housewives in their late forties illustrate both the common and the distinguishing features:

Judging by the way it was when we were first married—say the first five years or so—things are pretty matter-of-fact now—even dull. They're dull between us, I mean. The children are a lot of fun, keep us pretty busy, and there are lots of outside things—you know, like Little League and the P.T.A. and the Swim Club, and even the company parties aren't always so bad. But I mean where Bob and I are concerned—if you followed us around, you'd wonder why we ever got *married*. We take each other for granted. We laugh at the same things sometimes, but we don't really laugh together—the way we used to. But, as he said to me the other night—with one or two under the belt, I think—"You know, you're still a little fun now and then." . . .

Now, I don't say this to complain, not in the least. There's a cycle to life. There are things you do in high school. And different things you do in college. Then you're a young adult. And then you're middle-aged. That's where we are now. . . . I'll admit that I do yearn for the old days when sex was a big thing and going out was fun and I hung on to every thing he said about his work and his ideas as if they were coming from a genius or something. But then you get the children and other responsibilities. I have the home and Bob has a tremendous burden of responsibility at the office. . . . He's completely responsible for setting up the new branch now. . . . You have to adjust to these things and we both try to gracefully. . . . Anniversaries though do sometimes remind you kind of hard. . . .

The other kind of hindsight from a woman in a devitalized relationship is much less accepting and quiescent:

I know I'm fighting it. I ought to accept that it has to be like this, but I don't like it, and I'd do almost anything to bring back the exciting way of living we had at first. Most of my friends think I'm some kind of a sentimental romantic or something—they tell me to act my age—but I do know some people—not very darn many—who are our age and even older, who still have the same kind of excitement about them and each other that we had when we were all in college. I've seen some of them at parties and other places—the way they look at each other, the little touches as they go by. One couple has grandchildren and you'd think they were honeymooners. I don't think it's just sex either—I think they are just part of each other's lives—and then when I think of us and the numb way we sort of stagger through the weekly routine, I could scream. And I've even thought of doing some pretty desperate things to try to build some joy and excitement into my life. I've given up on Phil. He's too content with his balance sheets and the kids' report cards and the new house we're going to build next year. He keeps saying he has everything in life that any man could want. What do you *do*?

131

Regardless of the gracefulness of the acceptance, or the lack thereof, the common plight prevails: on the subjective, emotional dimension, the relationship has become a void. The original zest is gone. There is typically little overt tension or conflict, but the interplay between the pair has become apathetic, lifeless. No serious threat to the continuity of the marriage is generally acknowledged, however. It is intended, usually by both, that it continue indefinitely despite its numbness. Continuity and relative freedom from open conflict are fostered in part because of the comforts of the "habit cage." Continuity is further insured by the absence of any engaging alternative, "all things considered." It is also reinforced, sometimes rather decisively, by legal and ecclesiastical requirements and expectations. These people quickly explain that "there are other things in life" which are worthy of sustained human effort.

This kind of relationship is exceedingly common. Persons in this circumstance frequently make comparisons with other pairs they know, many of whom are similar to themselves. This fosters the comforting judgment that "marriage is like this—except for a few oddballs or pretenders who claim otherwise."

While these relationships lack visible vitality, the participants assure us that there is "something there." There are occasional periods of sharing at least something—if only memory. Even formalities can have meanings. Anniversaries can be celebrated, if a little grimly, for what they once commemorated. As one man said, "Tomorrow we are celebrating the anniversary of our anniversary." Even clearly substandard sexual expression is said by some to be better than nothing, or better than a clandestine substitute. A "good man" or a "good mother for the kids" may "with a little affection and occasional attention now and then, get you by." Many believe that the devitalized mode is the appropriate mode in which a man and woman should be content to live in the middle years and later.

THE PASSIVE-CONGENIAL

The passive-congenial mode has a great deal in common with the devitalized, the essential difference being that the passivity which pervades the association has been there from the start. The devitalized have a more exciting set of memories; the passive-congenials give little evidence that they had ever hoped for anything much different from what they are currently experiencing.

There is therefore little suggestion of disillusionment or compulsion to make believe to anyone. Existing modes of association are comfortably adequate—no stronger words fit the facts as they related them to us. There is little conflict, although some admit that they tiptoe rather gingerly over and around a residue of subtle resentments and frustrations. In their better moods they remind themselves (and each other) that "there are many common interests" which they both enjoy. "We both like classical music." "We agree completely on religious and political matters." "We both love the country and our quaint exurban neighbors." "We are both lawyers."

The wife of a prominent attorney, who has been living in the passive-congenial mode for thirty years, put her description this way:

We have both always tried to be calm and sensible about major life decisions, to think things out thoroughly and in perspective. Len and I knew each other since high school but didn't start to date until college. When he asked me to marry him, I took a long time to decide whether he was the right man for me and I went into his family background, because I wasn't just marrying him; I was choosing a father for my children. We decided together not to get married until he was established, so that we would not have to live in dingy little apartments like some of our friends who got married right out of college. This prudence has stood us in good stead too. Life has moved ahead for us with remarkable orderliness and we are deeply grateful for the foresight we had. . . .

When the children were little, we scheduled time together with them, although since they're grown, the demands of the office are getting pretty heavy. Len brings home a bulging briefcase almost every night and more often than not the light is still on in his study after I retire. But we've got a lot to show for his devoted effort. . . .

I don't like all this discussion about sex—even in the better magazines. I hope your study will help to put it in its proper perspective. I expected to perform sex in marriage, but both before and since, I'm willing to admit that it's a much overrated activity. Now and then, perhaps it's better. I am fortunate, I guess, because my husband has never been demanding about it, before marriage or since. It's just not that important to either of us. . . .

My time is very full these days, with the chairmanship of the Cancer Drive, and the Executive Board of the (state) P.T.A. I feel a little funny about that with my children already grown, but there are the grandchildren coming along. And besides so many of my friends are in the organizations, and it's so much like a home-coming.

People make their way into the passive-congenial mode by two quite different routes—by default and by intention. Perhaps in most instances they arrive at this way of living and feeling by drift. There is so little which they have cared about deeply in each other that a passive relationship is sufficient to express it all. In other instances the passive-congenial mode is a deliberately intended arrangement for two people whose interests and creative energies are directed elsewhere than toward the pairing—into careers, or in the case of women, into children or community activities. They say they know this and want it this way. These people simply do not wish to invest their total emotional involvement and creative effort in the male-female relationship.

The passive-congenial life style fits societal needs quite well also, and this is an important consideration. The man of practical affairs, in business, government service, or the professions—quite obviously needs "to have things peaceful at home" and to have a minimum of distraction as he pursues his important work. He may feel both love and gratitude toward the wife who fits this mode.

A strong case was made for the passive congenial by a dedicated physician:

I don't know why everyone seems to make so much about men and women and marriage. Of course, I'm married and if anything happened to my wife, I'd get married again. I think it's the proper way to live. It's convenient, orderly, and solves a lot of problems. But there are other things in life. I

133

spent nearly ten years preparing for the practice of my profession. The biggest thing to me is the practice of that profession, to be of assistance to my patients and their families. I spend twelve hours a day at it. And I'll bet if you talked with my wife, you wouldn't get any of that "trapped housewife" stuff from her either. Now that the children are grown, she finds a lot of useful and necessary work to do in this community. She works as hard as I do.

The passive-congenial mode facilitates the achievement of other goals too. It enables people who desire a considerable amount of personal independence and freedom to realize it with a minimum of inconvenience from or to the spouse. And it certainly spares the participants in it from the need to give a great deal of personal attention to "adjusting to the spouse's needs." The passive-congenial ménage is thus a mood as well as a mode.

Our descriptions of the devitalized and the passive-congenials have been similar because these two modes are much alike in their overt characteristics. The participants' evaluations of their *present situations* are likewise largely the same—the accent on "other things," the emphasis on civic and professional responsibilities, the importance of property, children, and reputation. The essential difference lies in their diverse histories and often in their feelings of contentment with their current lives. The passive-congenials had from the start a life pattern and a set of expectations essentially consistent with what they are now experiencing. When the devitalized reflect, however, when they juxtapose history against present reality, they often see the barren gullies in their lives left by the erosions of earlier satisfactions. Some of the devitalized are resentful and disillusioned; . . . others, calling themselves "mature about it," have emerged with reasonable acceptance of their existing devitalized modes. Still others are clearly ambivalent, "I wish life would be more exciting, but I should have known it couldn't last. In a way, it's calm and quiet and reassuring this way, but there are times when I get very ill at ease—sometimes downright mad. Does it *have* to be like this?"

The passive-congenials do not find it necessary to speculate in this fashion. Their anticipations were realistic and perhaps even causative of their current marital situation. In any event, their passivity is not jarred when teased by memory.

THE VITAL

In extreme contrast to the three foregoing is the vital relationship. The vital pair can easily be overlooked as they move through their worlds of work, recreation, and family activities. They do the same things, publicly at least; and when talking for public consumption say the same things—they are proud of their homes, love their children, gripe about their jobs, while being quite proud of their career accomplishments. But when the close, intimate, confidential, empathic look is taken, the essence of the vital relationship becomes clear: the mates are intensely bound together psychologically in important life matters.

Their sharing and their togetherness is genuine. It provides the life essence for both man and woman.

> The things we do together aren't fun intrinsically—the ecstasy comes from being *together in the doing*. Take her out of the picture and I wouldn't give a damn for the boat, the lake, or any of the fun that goes on out there.

The presence of the mate is indispensable to the feelings of satisfaction which the activity provides. The activities shared by the vital pairs may involve almost anything: hobbies, careers, community service. Anything—so long as it is closely shared.

It is hard to escape the word *vitality*—exciting mutuality of feelings and participation together in important life segments. The clue that the relationship is vital (rather than merely expressing the joint activity) derives from the feeing that it is important. An activity is flat and uninteresting if the spouse is not a part of it.

Other valued things are readily sacrificed in order to enhance life within the vital relationship.

> I cheerfully, and that's putting it mildly, passed up two good promotions because one of them would have required some traveling and the other would have taken evening and weekend time—and that's when Pat and I *live*. The hours with her (after twenty-two years of marriage) are what I live for. You should meet her. . . .

People in the vital relationship for the most part know that they are a minority and that their life styles are incomprehensible to most of their associates.

> Most of our friends think we moved out to the country for the kids; well—the kids *are* crazy about it, but the fact of the matter is, we moved out for ourselves—just to get away from all the annoyances and interferences of other people—our friends actually. We like this kind of life—where we can have almost all of our time together. . . . We've been married for over twenty years and the most enjoyable thing either of us does—well, outside of the intimate things—is to sit and talk by the hour. That's why we built that imposing fireplace—and the hi-fi here in the corner. . . . Now that Ed is getting older, that twenty-seven-mile drive morning and night from the office is a real burden, but he does it cheerfully so we can have our long uninterrupted hours together. . . . The children respect this too. They don't invade our privacy any more than they can help—the same as we vacate the living room when Ellen brings in a date, she tries not to intrude on us. . . . Being the specialized kind of lawyer he is, I can't share much in his work, but that doesn't bother either of us. The *big* part of our lives is completely mutual. . . .

Her husband's testimony validated hers. And we talked to dozens of other couples like them, too. They find their central satisfaction in the life they live with and through each other. It consumes their interest and dominates their thoughts and actions. All else is subordinate and secondary.

This does not mean that people in vital relationships lose their separate identities, that they may not upon occasion be rivalrous or competitive with one another, or that conflict may not occur. They differ fundamentally from the conflict-habituated, however, in that when conflict does occur, it results from matters that are important to them, such as which college a daughter or son is to attend; it is devoid of the trivial "who said what first and when" and "I can't forget when you. . . ." A further difference is that people to whom the relationship is vital tend to settle disagreements quickly and seek to avoid conflict, whereas the conflict-habituated look forward to conflict and appear to operate by a tacit rule that no conflict is ever to be truly terminated and that the spouse must never be considered right. The two kinds of conflict are thus radically different. To confuse them is to miss an important differentiation.

THE TOTAL

The total relationship is like the vital relationship with the important addition that it is more multifaceted. The points of vital meshing are more numerous—in some cases all of the important life foci are vitally shared. In one such marriage the husband is an internationally known scientist. For thirty years his wife has been his "friend, mistress, and partner." He still goes home at noon whenever possible, at considerable inconvenience, to have a quiet lunch and spend a conversational hour or so with his wife. They refer to these conversations as "our little seminars." They feel comfortable with each other and with their four grown children. The children (now in their late twenties) say that they enjoy visits with their parents as much as they do with friends of their own age.

There is practically no pretense between persons in the total relationship or between them and the world outside. There are few areas of tension, because the items of difference which have arisen over the years have been settled as they arose. There often *were* serious differences of opinion but they were handled, sometimes by compromise, sometimes by one or the other yielding; but these outcomes were of secondary importance because the primary consideration was not who was right or who was wrong, only how the problem could be resolved without tarnishing the relationship. When faced with differences, they can and do dispose of the difficulties without losing their feeling of unity or their sense of vitality and centrality of their relationship. This is the mainspring.

The various parts of the total relationship are reinforcing, as we learned from this consulting engineer who is frequently sent abroad by his corporation.

She keeps my files and scrapbooks up to date. . . . I invariably take her with me to conferences around the world. Her femininity, easy charm and wit are invaluable assets to me. I know it's conventional to say that a man's wife is responsible for his success and I also know that it's often not true. But in my case I gladly acknowledge that it's not only true, but she's indispensable to me. But she'd go along with me even if there was nothing for her to do because we just enjoy each other's company—deeply. You know, the best part of a vacation is not *what* we do, but that we do it together. We plan it and reminisce about it and weave it into our work and other play all the time.

The wife's account is substantially the same except that her testimony demonstrates more clearly the genuineness of her "help."

It seems to me that Bert exaggerates my help. It's not so much that I only want to help him; it's more that I want to do those things anyway. We do them together, even though we may not be in each other's presence at the time. I don't really know what I do for him and what I do for me.

This kind of relationship is rare, in marriage or out, but it does exist and can endure. We occasionally found relationships so total that all aspects of life were mutually shared and enthusiastically participated in. It is as if neither spouse has, or has had, a truly private existence.

The customary purpose of a classification such as this one is to facilitate understanding of similarities and differences among the cases classified. In this instance enduring marriage is the common condition. The differentiating features are the dissimilar forces which make for the integration of the pair within each of the types. It is not necessarily the purpose of a classification to make possible a clear-cut sorting of all cases into one or another of the designated categories. All cannot be so precisely pigeonholed; there often are borderline cases. Furthermore, two observers with equal access to the facts may sometimes disagree on which side of the line an unclear case should be placed. If the classification is a useful one, however, placement should *as a rule* be clear and relatively easy. The ease is only relative because making an accurate classification of a given relationship requires the possession of amounts and kinds of information which one rarely has about persons other than himself. Superficial knowledge of public or professional behavior is not enough. And even in his own case, one may, for reasons of ego, find it difficult to be totally forthright.

A further caution. The typology concerns relationships, not personalities. A clearly vital person may be living in a passive-congenial or devitalized relationship and expressing his vitality in some other aspect of his life—career being an important preoccupation for many. Or, possibly either or both of the spouses may have a vital relationship—sometimes extending over many years—with someone of the opposite sex outside of the marriage.

Nor are the five types to be interpreted as *degrees* of marital happiness or adjustment. Persons in all five are currently adjusted and most say that they are content, if not happy. Rather, the five types represent *different kinds of adjustment* and *different conceptions of marriage*. This is an important concept which must be emphasized if one is to understand the personal meanings which these people attach to the conditions of their marital experience.

Neither are the five types necessarily stages in a cycle of initial bliss and later disillusionment. Many pairings started in the passive-congenial stage;

in fact, quite often people intentionally enter into a marriage for the acknowledged purpose of living this kind of relationship. To many the simple amenities of the "habit cage" are not disillusionments or even disappointments, but rather are sensible life expectations which provide an altogether comfortable and rational way of having a "home base" for their lives. And many of the conflict-habituated told of courtship histories essentially like their marriages.

While each of these types tends to persist, there *may* be movement from one type to another as circumstances and life perspectives change. This movement may go in any direction from any point, and a given couple may change categories more than once. Such changes are relatively *in*frequent however, and the important point is that relationship types tend to persist over relatively long periods.

The fundamental nature of these contexts may be illustrated by examining the impact of some common conditions on persons of each type.

Infidelity, for example, occurs in most of the five types, the total relationship being the exception. But it occurs for quite different reasons. In the conflict-habituated it seems frequently to be only another outlet for hostility. The call girl and the woman picked up in a bar are more than just available women; they are symbols of resentment of the wife. This is not always so, but reported to us often enough to be worth noting. Infidelity among the passive-congenial, on the other hand, is typically in line with the stereotype of the middle-aged man who "strays out of sheer boredom with the uneventful, deadly prose" of his private life. And the devitalized man or woman frequently is trying for an hour or a year to recapture the lost mood. But the vital are sometimes adulterous too; some are simply emancipated—almost bohemian. To some of them sexual aggrandizement is an accepted fact of life. Frequently the infidelity is condoned by the partner and in some instances even provides an indirect (through empathy) kind of gratification. The act of infidelity in such cases is not construed as disloyalty or as a threat to continuity, but rather as a kind of basic human right which the loved one ought to be permitted to have—and which the other perhaps wants also for himself.

Divorce and separation are found in all five of the types, but the reasons, when viewed realistically and outside of the simplitudes of legalistic and ecclesiastical fiction, are highly individual and highly variable. For example, a couple may move from a vital relationship to divorce because for them the alternative of a devitalized relationship is unendurable. They can conceive of marriage only as a vital, meaningful, fulfilling, and preoccupying interaction. The "disvitality" of any other marriage form is abhorrent to them and takes on "the hypocrisy of living a public lie." We have accounts of marriages which were unquestionably vital or total for a period of years but which were dissolved. In some respects relationships of this type are more readily disrupted, because these people have become adjusted to such a rich and deep sharing that evidences of breach, which a person in another type of marriage might consider quite normal, become unbearable.

I know a lot of close friendships occur between men and women married to someone else, and that they're not always adulterous. But I know Betts—and anyway, I personally believe they eventually do become so, but I can't be sure about that. Anyway, when Betty found her self-expression was furthered by longer and longer meetings and conversations with Joe, and I detected little insincerities, not serious at first, you understand, creeping into the things we did together, it was like the little leak in the great dike. It didn't take very long. We weren't melodramatic about it, but it was soon clear to both of us that we were no longer the kind of pair we once were, so why pretend. The whole thing can go to hell fast—and after almost twenty years!

Husbands in other types of relationships would probably not even have detected any disloyalty on the part of this wife. And even if they had, they would tend to conclude that "you don't break up a home just because she has a passing interest in some glamorous writer."

The divorce which occurs in the passive-congenial marriage follows a different sequence. One of the couple, typically a person capable of more vitality in his or her married life than the existing relationship provides, comes into contact with a person with whom he gradually (or suddenly) unfolds a new dimension to adult living. What he had considered to be a rational and sensible and "adult" relationship can suddenly appear in contrast to be stultifying, shallow, and an altogether disheartening way to live out the remaining years. He is left with "no conceivable alternative but to move out." Typically, he does not do so impulsively or without a more or less stubborn attempt to stifle his "romanticism" and listen to well-documented advice to the effect that he should act maturely and "leave the romantic yearning to the kids for whom it is intended." Very often he is convinced and turns his back on his "new hope"—but not always.

Whether examining marriages for the satisfactions and fulfillments they have brought or for the frustrations and pain, the overriding influence of life style—or as we have here called it, relationship type—is of the essence. Such a viewpoint helps the observer, and probably the participant, to understand some of the apparent enigmas about men and women in marriage—why infidelities destroy some marriages and not others; why conflict plays so large a role for some couples and is so negligible for others; why some seemingly well-suited and harmoniously adjusted spouses seek divorce while others with provocations galore remain solidly together; why affections, sexual expression, recreation, almost everything observable about men and women is so radically different from pair to pair. All of these are not merely different objectively; they are perceived differently by the pairs, are differently reacted to, and differently attended to.

If nothing else, this chapter has demonstrated that realistic understanding of marital relationships requires use of concepts which are carefully based on perceptive factual knowledge. Unfortunately, the language by which relationships between men and women are conventionally expressed tends to lead toward serious and pervasive deceptions which in turn encourage erroneous inferences. Thus, we tend to assume that enduring marriage is somehow synonymous with happy marriage or at least with something comfortably called adjustment. The deception springs from lumping together such dissimilar modes of thought and action as the conflict-habituated, the passive-congenial, and the vital. To know that a marriage has endured, or for that matter has been dissolved, tells one close to nothing about the kinds of experiences, fulfillments, and frustrations which have made up the lives of the people involved. Even to know, for example, that infidelity has occurred, without knowledge of circumstances, feelings, and other essences, results in an illusion of knowledge which masks far more than it describes.

To understand a given marriage, let alone what is called "marriage in general," is realistically possible only in terms of particular sets of experiences, meanings, hopes, and intentions. This chapter has described in broad outline five manifest and recurring configurations among the Significant Americans.

5

Children as Junior Partners

Down through the centuries to the present day, there have been many myths about the place of children in the family and the techniques and goals of child rearing. Today, about all that is known for certain is that we really do not know a great deal about this topic.

Where it was once thought that children were just miniature adults, there is fairly general acceptance of the fact that they are immature not only in stature, but also in emotional development, knowledge, and the ability to make wise decisions in their own behalf. Formerly it was also thought that motherhood was a state that came naturally to women; yet we are becoming increasingly aware that they must *learn* how to nurture and that the manner in which motherhood is expressed will vary with each woman. Where once it was thought that fathers took a certain distant pride in their progeny, we are beginning to realize how uncomfortable they are about never getting close to their children in the same way that a mother does. Where we once assumed that parents were almost totally responsible for the way in which their children eventually matured, we now wonder how much influence they have. Where it was once hoped that children provided a special bond that might hold an otherwise unhappy marriage together, it is now learned that their presence is just as likely to create unhappiness between spouses as ameliorate it. Where once it was expected that children would love, honor, and obey their parents, as well as be a comfort to them in their old age, we are discovering that even this adage is not a dependable predictor of the future relationships of parent and child.

Yet despite all these uncertainties, the family remains the crucible of socialization for the child, and if the many innovative forms of pairing begin to dominate the family scene, children are going to receive their socialization in some very non-traditional family arrangements. Communes, one-parent families, living with step-siblings, and alternating between residence of mothers and fathers may become more a norm than an exception as years go by. As a result, we may learn more about the nature of children and their socialization as they adapt to family situations that are new and different from those previously studied.

Transition to Parenthood

Alice S. Rossi

Does parenthood just "come naturally" to the average wife and husband? Rossi thinks not, and suggests, in fact, that in American society parenthood is more demanding and abrupt in transition than either marriage or occupation adjustment. Furthermore, less preparation is available for it than for other roles. Thus, parenthood is not an ordinary turn of events, but rather has many unique features that can trigger a crisis in the marriage.

The impending arrival of a child and its birth is only one point of crisis. Parenthood has a career, as do most roles. There are problems of the parent-child relationship as both pass through various ages and stages. There is the crisis of disengagement from the active parent role when children are grown. Variations in satisfaction with parenthood deserve more research attention, rather than being taken for granted.

THE PROBLEM

The central concern in this sociological analysis of parenthood will be with two closely related questions. (1) What is involved in the transition to parenthood: what must be learned and what readjustments of other role commitments must take place in order to move smoothly through the transition from a childless married state to parenthood? (2) What is the effect of parenthood

From Alice S. Rossi, "Transition to Parenthood," *Journal of Marriage and the Family,* February, 1968, pp. 26–39. Copyright © 1968 by The National Council on Family Relations. Reprinted by permission. Paper presented to the American Orthopsychiatric Association, Washington, D.C., March 22, 1967. Grateful acknowledgment is made to the National Institutes of Health, sponsor of my work under a Research Career Development Award, and to my friend and former colleague Bernice Neugarten, at the University of Chicago, whose support and stimulation were critical in supplementing my sociological training with the human development perspective.

on the adult: in what ways do parents, and in particular mothers, change as a result of their parental experiences?

To get a firmer conceptual handle on the problem, I shall first specify the stages in the development of the parental role and then explore several of the most salient features of the parental role by comparing it with the two other major social roles—the marital and work role. Throughout the discussion, special attention will be given to the social changes that have taken place during the past few decades which facilitate or complicate the transition to and the experience of parenthood among young American adults.

FROM CHILD TO PARENT: AN EXAMPLE

What is unique about this perspective on parenthood is the focus on the adult parent rather than the child. Until quite recent years, concern in the behavioral sciences with the parent-child relationship has been confined almost exclusively to the child. Whether a psychological study such as Ferreira's on the influence of the pregnant woman's attitude to maternity upon postnatal behavior of the neonate,[1] Sears and Maccoby's survey of child-rearing practices,[2] or Brody's detailed observations of mothering,[3] the long tradition of studies of maternal deprivation[4] and more recently of maternal employment,[5] the child has been the center of attention. The design of such research has assumed that, if enough were known about what parents were like and what they in fact did in rearing their children, much of the variation among children could be accounted for.[6]

The very different order of questions which emerge when the parent replaces the child as the primary focus of analytic attention can best be shown with an illustration. Let us take, as our example, the point Benedek makes that the child's needs for mothering is *absolute* while the need of an adult woman to mother is *relative*.[7] From a concern for the child, this discrepancy in need leads to an analysis of the impact on the child of separation from the mother or inadequacy of mothering. Family systems that provide numerous adults to care for the young child can make up for this discrepancy in need between mother and child, which may be why ethnographic accounts give little evidence of postpartum depression following childbirth in simpler societies. Yet our family system of isolated households, increasingly distant from kinswomen to assist in mothering, requires that new mothers shoulder total responsibility for the infant precisely for that stage of the child's life when his need for mothering is far in excess of the mother's need for the child.

From the perspective of the mother, the question has therefore become: what does maternity deprive her of? Are the intrinsic gratifications of maternity sufficient to compensate for shelving or reducing a woman's involvement in non-family interests and social roles? The literature on maternal deprivation cannot answer such questions, because the concept, even in the careful specification Yarrow has given it,[8] has never meant anything but the effect on the child of various kinds of insufficient mothering. Yet what has been seen as a failure or inadequacy of individual women may in fact be a failure of the so-

143

ciety to provide institutionalized substitutes for the extended kin to assist in the care of infants and young children. It may be that the role requirements of maternity in the American family system extract too high a price of deprivation for young adult women reared with highly diversified interests and social expectations concerning adult life. Here, as at several points in the course of this paper, familiar problems take on a new and suggestive research dimension when the focus is on the parent rather than the child.

BACKGROUND

Since it is a relatively recent development to focus on the parent side of the parent-child relationship, some preliminary attention to the emergence of this focus on parenthood is in order. Several developments in the behavioral sciences paved the way to this perspective. Of perhaps most importance have been the development of ego psychology and the problem of adaptation of Murray[9] and Hartmann,[10] the interpersonal focus of Sullivan's psychoanalytic theories,[11] and the life cycle approach to identity of Erikson.[12] These have been fundamental to the growth of the human development perspective: that personality is not a stable given but a constantly changing phenomenon, that the individual changes along the life line as he lives through critical life experiences. The transition to parenthood, or the impact of parenthood upon the adult, is part of the heightened contemporary interest in adult socialization.

A second and related development has been the growing concern of behavioral scientists with crossing levels of analysis to adequately comprehend social and individual phenomena and to build theories appropriate to a complex social system. In the past, social anthropologists focused as purely on the level of prescriptive normative variables as psychologists had concentrated on intrapsychic processes at the individual level or sociologists on social-structural and institutional variables. These are adequate, perhaps, when societies are in a stable state of equilibrium and the social sciences were at early stages of conceptual development, but they become inadequate when the societies we study are undergoing rapid social change and we have an increasing amount of individual and subgroup variance to account for.

Psychology and anthropology were the first to join theoretical forces in their concern for the connections between culture and personality. The question of how culture is transmitted across the generations and finds its manifestations in the personality structure and social roles of the individual has brought renewed research attention to the primary institutions of the family and the schools, which provide the intermediary contexts through which culture is transmitted and built into personality structure.

It is no longer possible for a psychologist or a therapist to neglect the social environment of the individual subject or patient, nor is the "family" they are concerned with any longer confined to the family of origin, for current theory and therapy view the adult individual in the context of his current family of procreation. So too it is no longer possible for the sociologist to focus exclusively on the current family relationships of the individual. The incorporation of psychoanalytic theory into the informal, if not the formal, training of the sociologist has led to an increasing concern for the quality of relationships in the family of origin as determinants of the adult attitudes, values, and behavior which the sociologist studies.

Quite another tradition of research has led to the formulation of "normal crises of parenthood." "Crisis" research began with the studies of individuals undergoing traumatic experiences, such as that by Tyhurst on natural catastrophes,[13] Caplan on parental reponses to premature births,[14] Lindemann on grief and bereavement,[15] and Janis on surgery.[16] In these studies attention was on differential response to stress—how and why individuals vary in the ease with which they coped with the stressful experience and achieved some reintegration. Sociological interest has been piqued as these studies were built upon by Rhona and Robert Rapoport's research on the honeymoon and the engagement as normal crises in the role transitions to marriage and their theoretical attempt to build a conceptual bridge between family and occupational research from a "transition task" perspective.[17] LeMasters, Dyer, and Hobbs have each conducted studies of parenthood precisely as a crisis or disruptive event in family life.[18]

I think, however, that the time is now ripe to drop the concept of "normal crises" and to speak directly, instead, of the transition to and impact of parenthood. There is an uncomfortable incongruity in speaking of any crisis as normal. If the transition is achieved and if a successful reintegration of personality or social roles occurs, then crisis is a misnomer. To confine attention to "normal crises" suggests, even if it is not logically implied, successful outcome, thus excluding from our analysis the deviant instances in which failure occurs.

Sociologists have been just as prone as psychologists to dichotomize normality and pathology. We have had one set of theories to deal with deviance, social problems, and conflict and quite another set in theoretical analyses of a normal system—whether a family or a society. In the latter case our theories seldom include categories to cover deviance, strain, dysfunction, or failure. Thus, Parsons and Bales' systems find "task-leaders" oriented to problem solution, but not instrumental leaders attempting to undercut or destroy the goal of the group, and "sociometric stars" who play a positive integrative function in cementing ties among group members, but not negatively expressive persons with hostile aims of reducing or destroying such intragroup ties.[19]

Parsons' analysis of the experience of parenthood as a step in maturation and personality growth does not allow for negative outcome. In this view either parents show little or no positive impact upon themselves of their parental role experiences, or they show a new level of maturity. Yet many women, whose interests and values made a congenial combination of wifehood and work role, may find that the addition of maternal responsibilities has the consequence of a fundamental and undesired change in both their relationships to their husbands and their involvements outside the family. Still other women, who might have kept a precarious hold on adequate functioning as adults had they *not* become parents, suffer severe retrogression with pregnancy and childbearing, because the reactivation of older unresolved conflicts with their own mothers is not favorably resolved but in fact leads to personality deterioration[20] and the transmission of pathology to their children.[21]

Where cultural pressure is very great to assume a particular adult role, as it is for American women to bear and rear children, latent desire and psychological readiness for parenthood may often be at odds with manifest desire and actual ability to perform adequately as parents. Clinicians and therapists are aware, as perhaps many sociologists are not, that failure, hostility, and destructiveness are as much a part of the family system and the relationships among family members as success, love, and solidarity are.[22]

A conceptual system which can deal with both successful and unsuccessful role transitions, or positive and negative impact of parenthood upon adult men and women, is thus more powerful than one built to handle success but not failure or vice versa. For these reasons I have concluded that it is misleading and restrictive to perpetuate the use of the concept of "normal crisis." A more fruitful point of departure is to build upon the stage-task concepts of Erikson, viewing parenthood as a developmental stage, as Benedek[23] and Hill[24] have done, a perspective carried into the research of Raush, Goodrich, and Campbell[25] and of Rhona and Robert Rapoport[26] on adaptation to the early years of marriage and that of Cohen, Fearing *et al.*[27] on the adjustments involved in pregnancy.

ROLE CYCLE STAGES

A discussion of the impact of parenthood upon the parent will be assisted by two analytic devices. One is to follow a comparative approach, by asking in what basic structural ways the parental role differs from other primary adult roles. The marital and occupational roles will be used for this comparison. A second device is to specify the phases in the development of a social role. If the total life span may be said to have a cycle, each stage with its unique tasks, then by analogy a role may be said to have a cycle and each stage in that role cycle, to have its unique tasks and problems of adjustment. Four broad stages of a role cycle may be specified:

Anticipatory Stage

All major adult roles have a long history of anticipatory training for them, since parental and school socialization of children is dedicated precisely to this task of producing the kind of competent adult valued by the culture. For our present purposes, however, a narrower conception of the anticipatory stage is preferable: the engagement period in the case of the marital role, pregnancy in the case of the parental role, and the last stages of highly vocationally oriented schooling or on-the-job apprenticeship in the case of an occupational role.

Honeymoon Stage

This is the time period immediately following the full assumption of the adult role. The inception of this stage is more easily defined than its termination. In the case of the marital role, the honeymoon stage extends from the marriage ceremony itself through the literal honeymoon and on through an unspecified and individually varying period of time. Raush[28] has caught this stage of the marital role in his description of the "psychic honeymoon": that extended postmarital period when, through close intimacy and joint activity, the couple can explore each other's capacities and limitations. I shall arbitrarily consider the onset of pregnancy as marking the end of the honeymoon stage of the marital role. This stage of the parental role may involve an equivalent psychic honeymoon, that post-childbirth period during which, through intimacy and prolonged contact, an attachment between parent and child is laid down. There is a crucial difference, however, from the marital role in this stage. A woman knows her husband as a unique real person when she enters the honeymoon stage of marriage. A good deal of preparatory adjustment on a firm reality-base is possible during the engagement period which is not possible in the equivalent pregnancy period. Fantasy is not corrected by the reality of a specific individual child until the birth of the child. The "quickening" is psychologically of special significance to women precisely because it marks the first evidence of a real baby rather than a purely fantasized one. On this basis alone there is greater interpersonal adjustment and learning during the honeymoon stage of the parental role than of the marital role.

Plateau Stage

This is the protracted middle period of a role cycle during which the role is fully exercised. Depending on the specific problem under analysis, one would obviously subdivide this large plateau stage further. For my present purposes it is not necessary to do so, since my focus is on the earlier anticipatory and honeymoon stages of the parental role and the overall impact of parenthood on adults.

Disengagement-Termination Stage

This period immediately precedes and includes the actual termination of the role. Marriage ends with the death of the spouse or, just as definitively, with separation and divorce. A unique characteristic of parental role termination is the fact that it is not clearly marked by any specific act but is an attenuated process of termination with little cultural prescription about when the authority and obligations of a parent end. Many parents, however, experience the marriage of the child as a psychological termination of the active parental role.

UNIQUE FEATURES OF PARENTAL ROLE

With this role cycle suggestion as a broader framework, we can narrow our focus to what are the unique and most salient features of the parental role.

In doing so, special attention will be given to two further questions: (1) the impact of social changes over the past few decades in facilitating or complicating the transition to and experience of parenthood and (2) the new interpretations or new research suggested by the focus on the parent rather than the child.

Cultural Pressure to Assume the Role

On the level of cultural values, men have no freedom of choice where work is concerned: They must work to secure their status as adult men. The equivalent for women has been maternity. There is considerable pressure upon the growing girl and young woman to consider maternity necessary for a woman's fulfillment as an individual and to secure her status as an adult.[29]

This is not to say there are no fluctuations over time in the intensity of the cultural pressure to parenthood. During the depression years of the 1930s, there was more widespread awareness of the economic hardships parenthood can entail, and many demographic experts believe there was a great increase in illegal abortions during those years. Bird has discussed the dread with which a suspected pregnancy was viewed by many American women in the 1930s.[30] Quite a different set of pressures were at work during the 1950s, when the general societal tendency was toward withdrawal from active engagement with the issues of the larger society and a turning in to the gratifications of the private sphere of home and family life. Important in the background were the general affluence of the period and the expanded room and ease of child rearing that go with suburban living. For the past five years, there has been a drop in the birth rate in general, fourth and high-order births in particular. During this same period there has been increased concern and debate about women's participation in politics and work, with more women now returning to work rather than conceiving the third or fourth child.[31]

Inception of the Parental Role

The decision to marry and the choice of a mate are voluntary acts of individuals in our family system. Engagements are therefore consciously considered, freely entered, and freely terminated if increased familiarity decreases, rather than increases, intimacy and commitment to the choice. The inception of a pregnancy, unlike the engagement, is not always a voluntary decision, for it may be the unintended consequence of a sexual act that was recreative in intent rather than procreative. Secondly, and again unlike the engagement, the termination of a pregnancy is not socially sanctioned, as shown by current resistance to abortion-law reform.

The implication of this difference is a much higher probability of unwanted pregnancies than of unwanted marriages in our family system. Coupled with the ample clinical evidence of parental rejection and sometimes cruelty to children, it is all the more surprising that there has not been more consistent research attention to the problem of *parental satisfaction,* as there has for long

148

been on *marital satisfaction* or *work satisfaction*. Only the extreme iceberg tip of the parental satisfaction continuum is clearly demarcated and researched, as in the growing concern with "battered babies." Cultural and psychological resistance to the image of a non-nurturant woman may afflict social scientists as well as the American public.

The timing of a first pregnancy is critical to the manner in which parental responsibilities are joined to the marital relationship. The single most important change over the past few decades is extensive and efficient contraceptive usage, since this has meant, for a growing proportion of new marriages, the possibility of and increasing preference for some postponement of childbearing after marriage. When pregnancy was likely to follow shortly after marriage, the major transition point in a woman's life was marriage itself. *This transition point is increasingly the first pregnancy rather than marriage.* It is accepted and increasingly expected that women will work after marriage, while household furnishings are acquired and spouses complete their advanced training or gain a foothold in their work.[32] This provides an early marriage period in which the fact of a wife's employment presses for a greater egalitarian relationship between husband and wife in decision-making, commonality of experience, and sharing of household responsibilities.

The balance between individual autonomy and couple mutuality that develops during the honeymoon stage of such a marriage may be important in establishing a pattern that will later affect the quality of the parent-child relationship and the extent of sex-role segregation of duties between the parents. It is only in the context of a growing egalitarian base to the marital relationship that one could find, as Gavron has,[33] a tendency for parents to establish some barriers between themselves and their children, a marital defense against the institution of parenthood as she describes it. This may eventually replace the typical coalition in more traditional families of mother and children against husband-father. Parenthood will continue for some time to impose a degree of temporary segregation of primary responsibilities between husband and wife, but, when this takes place in the context of a previously established egalitarian relationship between the husband and wife, such role segregation may become blurred, with greater recognition of the wife's need for autonomy and the husband's role in the routines of home and child rearing.[34]

There is one further significant social change that has important implications for the changed relationship between husband and wife: the increasing departure from an old pattern of role-inception phasing in which the young person first completed his schooling, then established himself in the world of work, then married and began his family. Marriage and parenthood are increasingly taking place *before* the schooling of the husband, and often of the wife, has been completed.[35] An important reason for this trend lies in the fact that, during the same decades in which the average age of physical-sexual maturation has dropped, the average amount of education which young people obtain has been on the increase. Particularly for the college and graduate or professional school population, family roles are often assumed before the degrees needed to enter careers have been obtained.

Just how long it now takes young people to complete their higher education has been investigated only recently in several longitudinal studies of college-graduate cohorts.[36] College is far less uniformly a four-year period than high school is. A full third of the college freshmen in one study had been out of

149

high school a year or more before entering college.[37] In a large sample of college graduates in 1961, one in five were over 25 years of age at graduation.[38] Thus, financial difficulties, military service, change of career plans, and marriage itself all tend to create interruptions in the college attendance of a significant proportion of college graduates. At the graduate and professional school level, this is even more marked: the mean age of men receiving the doctorate, for example, is 32, and of women, 36.[39] It is the exception rather than the rule for men and women who seek graduate degrees to go directly from college to graduate school and remain there until they secure their degrees.[40]

The major implication of this change is that more men and women are achieving full adult status in family roles while they are still less than fully adult in status terms in the occupational system. Graduate students are, increasingly, men and women with full family responsibilities. Within the family many more husbands and fathers are still students, often quite dependent on the earnings of their wives to see them through their advanced training.[41] No matter what the couple's desires and preferences are, this fact alone presses for more egalitarian relations between husband and wife, just as the adult family status of graduate students presses for more egalitarian relations between students and faculty.

Irrevocability

If marriages do not work out, there is now widespread acceptance of divorce and remarriage as a solution. The same point applies to the work world: we are free to leave an unsatisfactory job and seek another. But once a pregnancy occurs, there is little possibility of undoing the commitment to parenthood implicit in conception except in the rare instance of placing children for adoption. We can have ex-spouses and ex-jobs but no ex-children. This being so, it is scarcely surprising to find marked differences between the relationship of a parent and one child and the relationship of the same parent with another child. If the culture does not permit pregnancy termination, the equivalent to giving up a child is psychological withdrawal on the part of the parent.

This taps an important area in which a focus on the parent rather than the child may contribute a new interpretive dimension to an old problem: the long history of interest, in the social sciences, in differences among children associated with their sex-birth-order position in their sibling set. Research has largely been based on data gathered about and/or from the children, and interpretations make inferences back to the "probable" quality of the child's relation to a parent and how a parent might differ in relating to a first-born compared to a last-born child. The relevant research, directed at the parents (mothers in particular), remains to be done, but at least a few examples can be suggested of the different order of interpretation that flows from a focus on the parent.

Some birth-order research stresses the influence of sibs upon other sibs, as in Koch's finding that second-born boys with an older sister are more feminine than second-born boys with an older brother.[42] A similar sib-influence interpretation is offered in the major common finding of birth-order correlates, that sociability is greater among last-borns[43] and achievement among first-borns.[44] It has been suggested that last-borns use social skills to increase acceptance by their older sibs or are more peer-oriented because they receive less adult stimulation from parents. The tendency of first-borns to greater achievement has been interpreted in a corollary way, as a reflection of early assumption of responsibility for younger sibs, greater adult stimulation during the time the oldest was the only child in the family,[45] and the greater significance of the first-born for the larger kinship network of the family.[46]

Sociologists have shown increasing interest in structural family variables in recent years, a primary variable being family size. From Bossard's descriptive work on the large family[47] to more methodologically sophisticated work such as that by Rosen,[48] Elder and Bowerman,[49] Boocock,[50] and Nisbet,[51] the question posed is: what is the effect of growing up in a small family, compared with a large family, that is attributable to this group-size variable? Unfortunately, the theoretical point of departure for sociologists' expectations of the effect of the family-size variables is the Durkheim-Simmel tradition of the differential effect of group size or population density upon members or inhabitants.[52] In the case of the family, however, this overlooks the very important fact that family size is determined by the key figures *within* the group, i.e, the parents. To find that children in small families differ from children in large families is not simply due to the impact of group size upon individual members but to the very different involvement of the parents with the children and to relations between the parents themselves in small versus large families.

An important clue to a new interpretation can be gained by examining family size from the perspective of parental motivation toward having children. A small family is small for one of two primary reasons: either the parents wanted a small family and achieved their desired size or they wanted a large family but were not able to attain it. In either case, there is a low probability of unwanted children. Indeed, in the latter eventuality they may take particularly great interest in the children they do have. Small families are therefore most likely to contain parents with a strong and positive orientation to each of the children they have. A large family, by contrast, is large either because the parents achieved the size they desired or because they have more children than they in fact wanted. Large families therefore have a higher probability than small families of including unwanted and unloved children. Consistent with this are Nye's finding that adolescents in small families have better relations with their parents than those in large families[53] and Sears and Maccoby's finding that mothers of large families are more restrictive toward their children than mothers of small families.[54]

This also means that last-born children are more likely to be unwanted than first- or middle-born children, particularly in large families. This is consistent with what is known of abortion patterns among married women, who typically resort to abortion only when they have achieved the number of children they want or feel they can afford to have. Only a small proportion of women faced with such unwanted pregnancies actually resort to abortion. *This suggests the possibility that the last-born child's reliance on social skills may be his device for securing the attention and loving involvement of a parent less positively predisposed to him than to his older siblings.*

In developing this interpretation, rather extreme cases have been stressed. Closer to the normal range, of families in which even the last-born child was desired and planned for, there is still another element which may contribute to the greater sociability of the last-born child. Most parents are themselves aware of the greater ease with which they face the care of a third fragile new-born than the first; clearly, parental skills and confidence are greater with last-born children than with first-born children. But this does not mean that the attitude of the parent is more positive toward the care of the third child than the first. There is no necessary correlation between skills in an area and enjoyment of that area. Searls[55] found that older homemakers are *more* skill-ful in domestic tasks but experience *less* enjoyment of them than young home-makers, pointing to a declining euphoria for a particular role with the passage of time. In the same way, older people rate their marriages as "very happy" less often than younger people do.[56] It is perhaps culturally and psychologically more difficult to face the possibility that women may find less enjoyment of the maternal role with the passage of time, though women themselves know the difference between the romantic expectation concerning child care and the incorporation of the first baby into the household and the more realistic ex-pectation and sharper assessment of their own abilities to do an adequate job of mothering as they face a third confinement. Last-born children may experience not only less verbal stimulation from their parents than first-born children but also less prompt and enthusiastic response to their demands—from feeding and diaper-change as infants to requests for stories read at three or a college education at eighteen—simply because the parents experience less intense gratification from the parent role with the third child than they did with the first. The child's response to this might well be to cultivate winning, pleasing manners in early childhood that blossom as charm and sociability in later life, showing both a greater need to be loved and greater pressure to seek approval.

One last point may be appropriately developed at this juncture. Mention was made earlier that for many women the personal outcome of experience in the parent role is not a higher level of maturation but the negative outcome of a depressed sense of self-worth, if not actual personality deterioration. There is considerable evidence that this is more prevalent than we recognize. On a qualitative level, a close reading of the portrait of the working-class wife in Rainwater,[57] Newsom,[58] Komarovsky,[59] Gavron,[60] or Zweig[61] gives little suggestion that maternity has provided these women with opportunities for personal growth and development. So too, Cohen[62] notes with some surprise that in her sample of middle-class educated couples, as in Pavenstadt's study of lower-income women in Boston, there were more emotional difficulty and lower levels of maturation among multiparous women than primiparous women. On a more extensive sample basis, in Gurin's survey of Americans viewing their mental health,[63] as in Bradburn's reports on happiness,[64] single men are less happy and less active than single women, but among the married respondents the women are unhappier, have more problems, feel inadequate as parents, have a more negative and passive outlook on life, and show a more negative self-image. All of these characteristics increase with age among mar-ried women but show no relationship to age among men. While it may be true, as Gurin argues, that women are more introspective and hence more attuned to the psychological facets of experience than men are, this point does not ac-count for the fact that the things which the women report are all on the nega-tive side; few are on the positive side, indicative of euphoric sensitivity and pleasure. The possibility must be faced, and at some point researched, that women lose ground in personal development and self-esteem during the early and middle years of adulthood, whereas men gain ground in these respects during the same years. The retention of a high level of self-esteem may depend upon the adequacy of earlier preparation for major adult roles: men's training adequately prepares them for their primary adult roles in the occupational system, as it does for those women who opt to participate significantly in the work world. Training in the qualities and skills needed for family roles in contemporary society may be inadequate for both sexes, but the lowering of self-esteem occurs only among women because their primary adult roles are within the family system.

Preparation for Parenthood

Four factors may be given special attention on the question of what preparation American couples bring to parenthood.

Paucity of preparation. Our educational system is dedicated to the cognitive development of the young, and our primary teaching approach is the pragmatic one of learning by doing. How much one knows and how well he can apply what he knows are the standards by which the child is judged in school, as the employee is judged at work. The child can learn by doing in such subjects as science, mathematics, art work, or shop, but not in the subjects most relevant to successful family life: sex, home maintenance, child care, interpersonal competence, and empathy. If the home is deficient in training in these areas, the child is left with no preparation for a major segment of his adult life. A doctor facing his first patient in private practice has treated numerous patients under close supervision during his internship, but probably a majority of American mothers approach maternity with no previous child-care experience beyond sporadic baby sitting, perhaps a course in child psychology, or occasional care of younger siblings.

Limited learning during pregnancy. A second important point makes adjustment to parenthood potentially more stressful than marital adjustment. This is the lack of any realistic training for parenthood during the anticipatory stage of pregnancy. By contrast, during the engagement period preceding marriage, an individual has opportunities to develop the skills and make the adjustments which ease the transition to marriage. Through discussions of values and life goals, through sexual experimentation, shared social experiences as an engaged couple with friends and relatives, and planning and furnishing an apartment, the engaged couple can make considerable progress in developing mutuality in advance of the marriage itself.[65] No such headstart is possible in the case of pregnancy. What preparation exists is confined to reading, consultation with friends and parents, discussions between husband and wife, and a minor nesting phase in which a place and the equipment for a baby are prepared in the household.[66]

Abruptness of transition. Thirdly, the birth of a child is not followed by any gradual taking on of responsibility, as in the case of a professional work role. It is as if the woman shifted from a graduate student to a full professor with little intervening apprenticeship experience of slowly increasing responsibility. The new mother starts out immediately on 24-hour duty, with responsibility for a fragile and mysterious infant totally dependent on her care.

If marital adjustment is more difficult for very young brides than more mature ones,[67] adjustment to motherhood may be even more difficult. A woman can adapt a passive dependence on a husband and still have a successful marriage, but a young mother with strong dependency needs is in for difficulty in maternal adjustment, because the role precludes such dependency. This situation was well described in Cohen's study[68] in a case of a young wife with a background of co-ed popularity and a passive dependent relationship to her admired and admiring husband, who collapsed into restricted incapacity when faced with the responsibilities of maintaining a home and caring for a child.

Lack of guidelines to successful parenthood. If the central task of parenthood is the rearing of children to become the kind of competent adults valued by the society, then an important question facing any parent is what he or she specifically can do to create such a competent adult. This is where the parent is left with few or no guidelines from the expert. Parents can readily inform themselves concerning the young infant's nutritional, clothing, and medical needs and follow the general prescription that a child needs loving physical contact and emotional support. Such advice may be sufficient to produce a healthy, happy, and well-adjusted preschooler, but adult competency is quite another matter.

In fact, the adults who do "succeed" in American society show a complex of characteristics as children that current experts in child-care would evaluate as "poor" to "bad." Biographies of leading authors and artists, as well as the more rigorous research inquiries of creativity among architects[69] or scientists,[70] do not portray childhoods with characteristics currently endorsed by mental health and child-care authorities. Indeed, there is often a predominance of tension in childhood family relations and traumatic loss rather than loving parental support, intense channeling of energy in one area of interest rather than an all-round profile of diverse interests, and social withdrawal and preference for loner activities rather than gregarious sociability. Thus, the stress in current child-rearing advice on a high level of loving support but a low level of discipline or restriction on the behavior of the child—the "developmental" family type as Duvall calls it[71]—is a profile consistent with the focus on mental health, sociability, and adjustment. Yet the combination of both high support and high authority on the part of parents is most strongly related to the child's sense of responsibility, leadership quality, and achievement level, as found in Bronfenbrenner's studies[72] and that of Mussen and Distler.[73]

Brim points out[74] that we are a long way from being able to say just what parent role prescriptions have what effect on the adult characteristics of the child. We know even less about how such parental prescriptions should be changed to adapt to changed conceptions of competency in adulthood. In such an ambiguous context, the great interest parents take in school reports on their children or the pediatrician's assessment of the child's developmental progress should be seen as among the few indices parents have of how well *they* are doing as parents.

[1]Antonio J. Ferreira, "The Pregnant Woman's Emotional Attitude and its Reflection on the Newborn," *American Journal of Orthopsychiatry,* 30 (1960), pp. 553–561.

[2]Robert Sears, E. Maccoby, and H. Levin, *Patterns of Child-Rearing,* Evanston, Illinois: Row, Peterson, 1957.

[3]Sylvia Brody, *Patterns of Mothering: Maternal Influences During Infancy,* New York: International Universities Press, 1956.

[4]Leon J. Yarrow, "Maternal Deprivation: Toward an Empirical and Conceptual Re-evaluation," *Psychological Bulletin,* 58:6 (1961), pp. 459–490.

[5]F. Ivan Nye and L. W. Hoffman, *The Employed Mother in America,* Chicago: Rand McNally, 1963; Alice S. Rossi, "Equality Between the Sexes: An Immodest Proposal," *Daedalus,* 93:2 (1964), pp. 607–652.

[6]The younger the child, the more was this the accepted view. It is only in recent years that research has paid any attention to the initiating role of the infant in the development of his attachment to maternal and other adult figures, as in Ainsworth's research which showed that infants become attached to the mother, not solely because she is instrumental in satisfying their primary visceral drives, but through a chain of behavioral interchange between the infant and the mother, thus supporting Bowlby's rejection of the secondary drive theory of the infant's ties to his mother. Mary D. Ainsworth, "Patterns of Attachment Behavior Shown By the Infant in Interaction with His Mother," *Merrill-Palmer Quarterly,* 10:1 (1964), pp. 51–58; John Bowlby, "The Nature of the Child's Tie to His Mother," *International Journal of Psychoanalysis,* 39 (1958), pp. 1–34.

[7]Therese Benedek, "Parenthood as a Developmental Phase," *Journal of American Psychoanalytic Association,* 7:8 (1959), pp. 389–417.

[8]Yarrow, *op. cit.*

[9]Henry A. Murray, *Explorations in Personality,* New York: Oxford University Press, 1938.

[10]Heinz Hartmann, *Ego Psychology and the Problem of Adaptation,* New York: International Universities Press, Inc., 1958.

[11]Patrick Mullahy (ed.), *The Contributions of Harry Stack Sullivan,* New York: Hermitage House, 1952.

[12]E. Erikson, "Identity and the Life Cycle: Selected Papers," *Psychological Issues,* 1 (1959), pp. 1–171.

[13]J.Tyhurst, "Individual Reactions to Community Disaster," *American Journal of Psychiatry,* 107 (1951), pp. 764–769.

[14]G. Caplan, "Patterns of Parental Response to the Crisis of Premature Birth: A Preliminary Approach to Modifying the Mental Health Outcome," *Psychiatry,* 23 (1960), pp. 365–374.

[15]E. Lindemann, "Symptomatology and Management of Acute Grief," *American Journal of Psychiatry,* 101 (1944), pp. 141–148.

[16]Irving Janis, *Psychological Stress,* New York: John Wiley, 1958.

[17]Rhona Rapoport, "Normal Crises, Family Structure and Mental Health," *Family Process,* 2:1 (1963), pp. 68–80; Rhona Rapoport and Robert Rapoport, "New Light on the Honeymoon," *Human Relations,* 17:1 (1964), pp. 33–56; Rhona Rapoport, "The Transition from Engagement to Marriage," *Acta Sociologica,* 8, facs, 1–2 (1964), pp. 36–55; and Robert Rapoport and Rhona Rapoport, "Work and Family in Contemporary Society," *American Sociological Review,* 30:3 (1965), pp. 381–394.

[18]E. E. LeMasters, "Parenthood as Crisis," *Marriage and Family Living,* 19 (1957), pp. 352–355; Everett D. Dyer, "Parenthood as Crisis: A Re-Study," *Marriage and Family Living,* 25 (1963), pp. 196–201; and Daniel F. Hobbs, Jr., "Parenthood as Crisis: A Third Study," *Journal of Marriage and the Family,* 27:3 (1963), pp. 367–372. LeMasters and Dyer both report the first experience of parenthood involves

extensive to severe crises in the lives of their young parent respondents. Hobbs' study does not show first parenthood to be a crisis experience, but this may be due to the fact that his couples have very young (seven-week-old) first babies and are therefore still experiencing the euphoric honeymoon stage of parenthood.

[19]Parsons' theoretical analysis of the family system builds directly on Bales' research on small groups. The latter are typically comprised of volunteers willing to attempt the single task put to the group. This positive orientation is most apt to yield the empirical discovery of "sociometric stars" and "task leaders," least apt to sensitize the researcher or theorist to the effect of hostile nonacceptance of the group task. Talcott Parsons and R. F. Bales, *Family, Socialization and Interaction Process,* New York: The Free Press, a division of the Macmillan Co., 1955.

Yet the same limited definition of the key variables is found in the important attempts by Straus to develop the theory that every social system, as every personality, requires a circumplex model with two independent axes of authority and support. His discussion and examples indicate a variable definition with limited range: support is defined as High (+) or Low (−), but "low" covers both the absence of high support and the presence of negative support; there is love or neutrality in this system, but not hate. Applied to actual families, this groups destructive mothers with low-supportive mothers, much as the non-authoritarian pole on the Authoritarian Personality Scale includes both mere non-authoritarians and vigorously anti-authoritarian personalities. Murray A. Straus, "Power and Support Structure of the Family in Relation to Socialization," *Journal of Marriage and the Family,* 26:3 (1964), pp. 318–326.

[20]Mabel Blake Cohen, "Personal Identity and Sexual Identity," *Psychiatry,* 29:1 (1966), pp. 1–14; Joseph C. Rheingold, *The Fear of Being a Woman: A Theory of Maternal Destructiveness,* New York: Grune and Stratton, 1964.

[21]Theodore Lidz, S. Fleck, and A. Cornelison, *Schizophrenia and the Family,* New York: International Universities Press, Inc., 1965; Rheingold, *op. cit.*

[22]Cf. the long review of studies Rheingold covers in his book on maternal destructiveness, *op. cit.*

[23]Benedek, *op. cit.*

[24]Reuben Hill and D. A. Hansen, "The Identification of a Conceptual Framework Utilized in Family Study," *Marriage and Family Living,* 22 (1960), pp. 299–311.

[25]Harold L. Raush, W. Goodrich, and J. D. Campbell, "Adaptation to the First Years of Marriage," *Psychiatry,* 26:4 (1963), pp. 368–380.

[26]Rapoport, *op. cit.*

[27]Cohen, *op. cit.*

[28]Raush *et al., op. cit.*

[29]The greater the cultural pressure to assume a given adult social role, the greater will be the tendency for individual negative feelings toward that role to be expressed covertly. Men may complain about a given job but not about working per se, and hence their work dissatisfactions are often displaced to the non-work sphere, as psychosomatic complaints or irritation and dominance at home. An equivalent displacement for women of the ambivalence many may feel toward maternity is to dissatisfactions with the homemaker role.

[30]Caroline Bird, *The Invisible Scar,* New York: David McKay Company, 1966.

[31]When it is realized that a mean family size of 3.5 would double the population in 40 years, while a mean of 2.5 would yield a stable population in the same period, the social importance of withholding praise for procreative prowess is clear. At the same time, a drop in the birth rate may reduce the number of unwanted babies born, for such a drop would mean more efficient contraceptive usage and a closer correspondence between desired and attained family size.

[32]James A. Davis, *Stipends and Spouses: The Finances of American Arts and Sciences Graduate Students,* Chicago: University of Chicago Press, 1962.

[33]Hannah Gavron, *The Captive Wife,* London: Routledge & Kegan Paul, 1966.

[34]The recent increase in natural childbirth, prenatal courses for expectant fathers, and greater participation of men during childbirth and postnatal care of the infant may therefore be a *consequence* of greater sharing between husband and wife when both work and jointly maintain their new households during the early months of marriage. Indeed, natural childbirth builds directly on this shifted base to the marital relationship. Goshen-Gottstein has found in an Israeli sample that women with a "traditional" orientation to marriage far exceed women with a "modern" orientation to marriage in menstrual difficulty, dislike of sexual intercourse, and pregnancy disorders and complaints such as vomiting. She argues that traditional women demand and expect little from their husbands and become demanding and narcissistic by means of their children, as shown in pregnancy by an over-exaggeration of symptoms and attention-seeking. Esther R. Goshen-Gottstein, *Marriage and First Pregnancy: Cultural Influences on Attitudes of Israeli Women,* London: Tavistock Publications, 1966. A prolonged psychic honeymoon uncomplicated by an early pregnancy, and with the new acceptance of married women's employment, may help to cement the egalitarian relationship in the marriage and reduce both the tendency to pregnancy difficulties and the need for a narcissistic focus on the children. Such a background is fruitful ground for sympathy toward and acceptance of the natural childbirth ideology.

[35]James A. Davis, *Stipends and Spouses: The Finances of American Arts and Sciences Graduate Students, op. cit.;* James A. Davis, *Great Aspirations,* Chicago: Aldine Publishing Company, 1964; Eli Ginsberg, *Life Styles of Educated Women,* New York: Columbia University Press, 1966; Ginsberg, *Educated American Women: Self Portraits,* New York: Columbia University Press, 1967; National Science Foundation, *Two Years After the College Degree—Work and Further Study Patterns,* Washington, D.C.: Government Printing Office, NSF 63-26, 1963.

[36]Davis, *Great Aspirations, op. cit.;* Laure Sharp, "Graduate Study and Its Relation to Careers: The Experience of a Recent Cohort of College Graduates," *Journal of Human Resources,* 1:2 (1966), pp. 41–58.

[37]James D. Cowhig and C. Nam, "Educational Status, College Plans and Occupational Status of Farm and Nonfarm Youths," U.S. Bureau of the Census Series ERS (P-27), No. 30, 1961.

[38]Davis, *Great Aspirations, op. cit.*

[39]Lindsey R. Harmon, *Profiles of Ph.D.'s in the Sciences: Summary Report on Follow-up of Doctorate Cohorts, 1935–1960,* Washington, D.C.: National Research Council, Publication 1293, 1965.

[40]Sharp, *op. cit.*

[41]Davis, *Stipends and Spouses, The Finances of American Arts and Sciences Graduate Students, op. cit.*

[42]Orville G. Brim, "Family Structure and Sex-Role Learning by Children," *Sociometry,* 21 (1958), pp. 1–16; H. L. Koch, "Sissiness and Tomboyishness in Relation to Sibling Characteristics," *Journal of Genetic Psychology,* 88 (1956), pp. 231–244.

[43]Charles MacArthur, "Personalities of First and Second Children," *Psychiatry,* 19 (1956), pp. 47–54; S. Schachter, "Birth Order and Sociometric Choice," *Journal of Abnormal and Social Psychology,* 68 (1964), pp. 453–456.

[44]Irving Harris, *The Promised Seed,* New York: The Free Press, a Division of the Macmilllan Co., 1964; Bernard Rosen, "Family Structure and Achievement Motivation," *American Sociological Review,* 26 (1961), pp. 574–585; Alice S. Rossi, "Naming Children in Middle-Class Families," *American Sociological Review,* 30:4 (1965), pp. 499–513; Stanley Schachter, "Birth Order, Eminence and Higher Education," *American Sociological Review,* 28 (1963), pp. 757–768.

[45]Harris, *op. cit.*

[46]Rossi, "Naming Children in Middle-Class Families," *op. cit.*

[47]James H. Bossard, *Parent and Child*, Philadelphia; University of Pennsylvania Press, 1953; James H. Bossard and E. Boll, *The Large Family System*, Philadelphia: University of Pennsylvania, 1956.

[48]Rosen, *op. cit.*

[49]Glen H. J. Elder and C. Bowerman, "Family Structure and Child-Rearing Patterns: The Effect of Family Size and Sex Composition on Child-Rearing Practices," *American Sociological Review*, 28 (1963), pp. 891–905.

[50]Sarane S. Boocock, "Toward a Sociology of Learning: A Selective Review of Existing Research," *Sociology of Education*, 39:1 (1966), pp. 1–45.

[51]John Nisbet, "Family Environment and Intelligence," *in Education, Economy and Society*, ed. by Halsey *et al.*, New York: The Free Press, a division of the Macmillan Company, 1961.

[52]Thus Rosen writes: "Considering the sociologist's traditional and continuing concern with group size as an independent variable (from Simmel and Durkheim to the recent experimental studies of small groups), there have been surprisingly few studies of the influence of group size upon the nature of interaction in the family," *op. cit.*, p. 576.

[53]Ivan Nye, "Adolescent-Parent Adjustment: Age, Sex, Sibling, Number, Broken Homes, and Employed Mothers as Variables," *Marriage and Family Living*, 14 (1952), pp. 327–332.

[54]Sears *et al., op. cit.*

[55]Laura G. Searls, "Leisure Role Emphasis of College Graduate Homemakers," *Journal of Marriage and the Family*, 28:1 (1966), pp. 77–82.

[56]Norman Bradburn and D. Caplovitz, *Reports on Happiness*, Chicago: Aldine Publishing, 1965.

[57]Lee Rainwater, R. Coleman, and G. Handel, *Workingman's Wife*, New York: Oceana Publications, 1959.

[58]John Newsom and E. Newsom, *Infant Care in an Urban Community*, New York: International Universities Press, 1963.

[59]Mirra Komarovsky, *Blue Collar Marriage*, New York: Random House, 1962.

[60]Gavron, *op. cit.*

[61]Ferdinand Zweig, *Woman's Life and Labor*, London: Camelot Press, 1952.

[62]Cohen, *op. cit.*

[63]Gerald Gurin, J. Veroff, and S. Feld, *Americans View Their Mental Health*, New York: Basic Books, Monograph Series No. 4, Joint Commission on Mental Illness and Health, 1960.

[64]Bradburn and Caplovitz, *op. cit.*

[65]Rapoport, "The Transition from Engagement to Marriage," *op. cit;* Raush *et al., op. cit.*

[66]During the period when marriage was the critical transition in the adult woman's life rather than pregnancy, a good deal of anticipatory "nesting" behavior took place from the time of conception. Now more women work through a considerable portion of the first pregnancy, and such nesting behavior as exists may be confined to a few shopping expeditions or baby showers, thus adding to the abruptness of the transition and the difficulty of adjustment following the birth of a first child.

[67]Lee G. Burchinal, "Adolescent Role Deprivation and High School Marriage," *Marriage and Family Living*, 21 (1959), pp. 378–384; Floyd M. Martinson, "Ego Deficiency as a Factor in Marriage," *American Sociological Review*, 22 (1955), pp. 161–164; J. Joel Moss and Ruby Gingles, "The Relationship of Personality to the Incidence of Early Marriage," *Marriage and Family Living*, 21 (1959), pp. 373–377.

[68]Cohen, *op. cit.*

[69]Donald W. MacKinnon, "Creativity and Images of the Self," in *The Study of Lives*, ed. by Robert W. White, New York: Atherton Press, 1963.

[70]Anne Roe, *A Psychological Study of Eminent Biologists, Psychological Monographs*, 65:14

(1951), 68 pages; Anne Roe, "A Psychological Study of Physical Scientists," *Genetic Psychology Monographs*, 43 (1951), pp. 121–239; Anne Roe, "Crucial Life Experiences in the Development of Scientists," in *Talent and Education*, ed. by E. P. Torrance, Minneapolis: University of Minnesota Press, 1960.

[71]Evelyn M. Duvall, "Conceptions of Parenthood," *American Journal of Sociology*, 52 (1946), pp. 193–203.

[72]Urie Bronfenbrenner, "Some Familial Antecedents of Responsibility and Leadership in Adolescents," in *Studies in Leadership*, ed. by L. Petrullo and B. Bass, New York: Holt, Rinehart, and Winston, 1960.

[73]Paul Mussen and L. Distler, "Masculinity, Identification and Father-Son Relationships," *Journal of Abnormal and Social Psychology*, 59 (1959), pp. 350–356.

[74]Orville G. Brim, "The Parent-Child Relation as a Social System: I. Parent and Child Roles," *Child Development*, 28:3 (1957), pp. 343–364.

The Paradox of the Contemporary American Father

Myron Brenton

Although the disjunctions in the socialization of women to motherhood may be fairly obvious, they are much more insidious in the case of the father A major clue to the way fatherhood is viewed may be noted by comparing how men are portrayed in the media if they are single (as adventurers and lovers) as compared to husbands and fathers (as good-natured buffoons and well-meaning squares). The traditional role of mother is at least well-defined, has few contradictions, and is honored in society. Not so the role of father. So much and, at the same time, so little is expected of him that he hardly knows how to act with his children. Further, his traditional role burdens him with the responsibility of monetary support, while at the same time denying him a totally sympathetic and empathic relationship with his children. Often, he is not at home enough to get to know his children. And he has the added burden of the masculinity myths, which make a close relationship with the children almost contrary to his nature. Most child socialization is abdicated to mothers, although being a biological mother and "mothering" (nurturing) a child are not synonymous. Men could learn to mother just as women must, if the culture provided early socializing experience and the right cues. If this were done, the father's relationship with his children could be close without the phony "good pal" approach to sons or authoritarian patriarch stance with daughters.

Fathers Are Parents, Too, *by Dr. O. Spurgeon English*
"The Vanishing American Father," McCalls Magazine
"What Ever Happened to Daddy?" *a chapter in* Suburbia's Coddled Kids, *by Peter Wyden*
Has Anybody Seen My Father? *by Harrison Kinney*
"Putting Down Father," The New York Times Magazine—*partial list of critical literature about the contemporary American father.*

From Myron Brenton, "The Paradox of the Contemporary American Father," *The American Male* (New York: Coward, McCann & Georghegan, 1966), pp. 133–158. Copyright © 1966 by Myron Brenton. Reprinted by permission of Coward McCann & Geoghegan, Inc.

"It's easier to make money than it is to be a good father. If you're willing to put in the hours, willing to stick your nose to the grindstone, you can really bring in the greenbacks. This applies to every strata of society. I think that for many fathers making money is something tangible, something that can be shown immediately, at the end of the week. 'I made this much money, and it shows what a man I am.' Now, to be a good father, what are the tangible rewards? For many people the rewards come much later, when the kids are grown up and out on their own. Then, too, the family is a risky proposition in terms of rewards and self-enhancement. The kids might not turn out well—while on the job you get paid."—Dr. Paul Vahanian, in a conversation with the author.

EVERY DAY IS MOTHER'S DAY

Comparisons between men and women on which sex has it rougher in this world are both onerous and pointless. Yet it is fair to say that in at least one area men face far more difficult problems than women. I refer specifically to the parental role.

It is no easier, of course, to be a mother than a father. The important difference is that while the mothering role has remained essentially the same throughout the ages, the father's role has been changing radically. The mother has always nurtured her children, exercised discipline over them, and involved herself deeply in their socialization, in seeing to it that they grow up more or less adjusted to the requirements of society.

The role of the contemporary American father, however, is inconsistent with the patterns of the past. Since he works outside the home and often has to travel a considerable distance to get to his place of employment and back again, today's father has little opportunity to be with his children or even to make his presence felt by them. The trend to the equality of the sexes is rapidly doing away with the external scaffolding of authority that used to structure him in the past. The shrinking of the wider family unit to its nuclear base focuses the spotlight of paternal responsibility directly on him, and this responsibility has enlarged in inverse ratio to his authority. In other words, his duties have expanded while his rights have diminished. Today's father no longer teaches his children his craft, as he did in rural America. He no longer apprentices them to others. He no longer controls their education, nor does he even have the illusion of doing so. He has little, if anything, to say about their marriages. On the other hand, he's expected to exhibit a wide range of fatherly responses. He's supposed to support his youngsters financially, as always; support them all the way through college and even graduate school, if possible; be firm with them but understanding; involve himself in their problems; help his wife care for them physically; baby-sit with them occasionally; discipline them effectively, but be a pal to them as well; present an authoritative masculine figure that his girls will admire and his boys will emulate; act as friend of and wise counselor to his brood; be warm and affectionate with them; and be their link to the wider community.

Countless books, magazine articles, speeches by child-care specialists, parent-training manuals, and pronouncements by psychologists tell him of these re-

161

sponsibilities and make him feel guilty—or, more likely, spur his wife on to make him feel guilty—about not meeting them adequately. Advice and criticism have been coming in thickly and heavily for the past decade or so. It seems that there's little he does or *can* do right. If he moves his family from city to suburb, he's placing them in a "manless" environment. If he concentrates on being a pal to his son, he's evading his role as authority figure. If he has a nurturing bent, some of the psychiatrists call him a motherly father. If he doesn't do any nurturing to speak of, he's accused of distancing himself from his children. If he's the sole disciplinarian, he takes on, in his youngsters' eyes, the image of an ogre. If he doesn't discipline them sufficiently, he's a weak father. If he's well off and gives his children all the material advantages he didn't have, he's spoiling them, leaving them unprepared for life's hard knocks. If he's well off but doesn't spoil them the way other fathers in the community do their boys and girls, he gains the reputation of a latter-day Scrooge. If his work keeps him away during the week and he tries to compensate by spending extra time with his children on weekends, by doing special things with them, this is also wrong. He's told either that he's making himself into a goody-goody figure with them, while his wife has all the dirty work of really bringing them up, or that he'll eventually come to resent the concentrated time he spends with them because he'd rather be out playing golf. And, repeatedly, the accusing voices tell him that he has given up his rightful place as head of his family, as guide and mentor to his children.

If the advice is contradictory at times, and the criticism more so, it is in part due to the fact that the experts themselves have widely divergent opinions on the proper role of the father. So does the society in general. In fact, American society is somewhat schizoid in its attitude toward fatherhood. This is the result of another one of the innumerable ironies springing out of the patriarchal system. The Victorian mother might have shouldered most of the responsibility for the children's care and upbringing, but she gained in turn a powerful form of compensation: She was glorified. She was idealized. Her virtues were praised to the skies, and of faults she was deemed to have none. To an extent we have inherited this glorification of the mother. True, vituperation is often hurled at the possessive, castrating, domineering Mom that Philip Wylie first thrust into the spotlight some twenty years ago, and currently there are attempts by some neofeminist writers to downgrade the mother's importance. But theirs isn't a winning battle. The "cult of motherhood," as Wylie aptly described it, is still fairly potent. In fact, when sociologist Helena Lopata at Roosevelt University in Chicago asked more than 600 urban and suburban wives what a woman's most important roles are, in order of importance, the great majority of the ladies voted first for "mother." ("Wife" came in second; "homemaker," third.)

As for fatherhood, there is no cult. Nobody votes the father's role as the most important in a man's life (although it's highly questionable whether either sex should consider the parental role the most important in its life). Despite all the demands that contemporary society makes on the father, despite all the expectations it has regarding his performance, fatherhood in America is accorded little respect.

An anonymous saying goes, "God could not be everywhere, and so he made mothers." In a nation in which Mother's Day not only is a yearly ritual but also generates $1,500,000,000 worth of business, such an aphorism is devoutly

162

believed. From the mother-child mysticism stem such clichés as "Nobody knows a child the way its mother does" and "A boy's best friend is his mother." There's some truth to them, of course. Why shouldn't there be, if Pop hasn't been around much and traits like sympathy and understanding are labeled feminine?

Orthodox psychoanalysis, which has had such a pervasive influence on American culture, tends to elevate the emotional response between mother and child to impossibly lofty heights—heights to which no mere father could aspire. Consider Dr. Marynia Farnham's declaration: "The special genius of women has always been that of nurture, for which man has no talent whatsoever."[1] Consider Dr. Erich Fromm's phenomenally successful analysis of love, *The Art of Loving,* which states, "Mother's love is bliss, is peace, it need not be acquired, it need not be deserved. . . . It is for this altruistic, unselfish character that motherly love has been considered the highest kind of love, and the most sacred of all emotional bonds."[2] Consider Dr. Ashley Montagu's pronouncement in another work that has garnered a huge readership over the years, *The Natural Superiority of Women:* "The sensitive relationships which exist between mother and child belong to a unique order of humanity, an order in which the male may participate as a child, but from which he increasingly departs as he leaves childhood behind."[3]

Even the nation's child custody laws prove how potent the cult of motherhood still is. In almost every state both the law and court practice give the mother a clear and almost insurmountable advantage in divorce cases in which there's a battle between mother and father over custody of the children. Unless it can be shown that she's a distinct hazard to the health or welfare of her offspring—something very difficult to do—most courts in most states award full custody rights to the mother under the blanket assumption that a child needs to be with its mother. It is the case even when the father is just as willing and just as competent to raise the children as she is. In some courts it is the case even when the mother is obviously the less desirable parent from the standpoint of both morals and competence. It could be argued that men want it this way, that it precludes saddling them with the physical responsibility for the offspring. This may have been true at one time, but the frequency of child-custody battles shows that at least for some fathers times have changed. (Both lay people and legal authorities in some states are trying to correct the situation. Attempting to effect legal reforms in his state, for instance, an Ohio jurist, Judge Roy C. Scott, has observed that "a man's status in divorce cases and domestic problems is not an enviable one" and that "the father in many cases is just as well equipped to have custody since he, too, can hire a baby sitter.")[4]

It should be possible to acknowledge the vital role of love and nurture that a mother plays without giving it the inflated stress that borders on caricature, without making the father's role seem peripheral and inconsequential by comparison. But this has not been happening. Not surprisingly, the *Thesaurus of Quotations* lists thirty-one "apt thoughts" and "felicitous expressions" for motherhood and a scant ten for fatherhood, the most felicitous of the sparse lot being the proverb "It's a wise child that knows its own father." Not surprisingly, either, psychiatrists and sociologists complain about the dearth of solid data on fatherhood, pointing out that the behavioral sciences have concentrated primarily on motherhood. Even the mass media, grown so critical of the American father, make their own intriguing commentary on the condition of fatherhood today merely by the way they present this criticism. The majority of articles pointing out what's wrong with the contemporary father appear in the women's magazines, which most men don't read. Speeches on the subject are frequently given by women—and to an audience of women. In 1965 a series of television programs on the problems facing the American male, including those concerning his role as parent, took place on a mid-morning show whose viewing audience is composed primarily of housewives. The ludicrous conclusion one could come to is that fatherhood is somehow feminine!

A goodly portion of the professional literature that exists on fatherhood suggests that the best father is the one who has relatively tenuous emotional ties with his young ones. When the child is in infancy, according to this view-point, the father's primary role is to protect and support (both psychologically and financially) the new mother. As the child grows older, it's permissible for him to show love, provided that this love is exclusively conditional—that is, strictly earned, given as a reward for good behavior or accomplishment. Woe to the father's image if he diapers the baby, feeds the child, or displays in any way the kind of warmth we have come to associate with motherliness. His image, many psychiatrists still insist, will turn motherly. It goes without saying that in such patriarchal eyes the father who has a nurturing bent, who enjoys help-ing take care of the little ones, who doesn't withdraw love from his children even when he exercises discipline, and who gets considerable emotional gratifi-cation out of their love for him is somewhat lacking in masculinity—and will create unmasculine sons.

As psychoanalyst Irene M. Josselyn is frank to admit, a great deal of psycho-logical literature "tends to minimize the significance of any possible psychological response specifically called fatherliness." Pointing to a definite psychological existence of fatherliness, she includes among its elements the child as a nar-cissistic extension of the father, as proof of the father's manliness, as rival, and as an object of "tender love." Dr. Josselyn adds, "Unfortunately, when this emotion acts as a cohesive force in men, it is too often considered evidence of the repressed femininity of the man."[5]

The very term "tender love" within the context of fatherhood still sounds somewhat strange, so seldom is it used. It is not that the contemporary father fails to display warmth and affection to his children. By and large he does, at least when they are young. We have come a long way from the nineteenth-century aloofness, when a studied coolness was the mode between father and child. Today there are warmth, laughter, and spontaneous affection. Today some fathers delight in sharing with mothers in the care of even very young infants.

Still lacking is a really basic awareness that a father can enjoy, wholly as a man, the give-and-take of psychic nurturing that we tend to associate primarily with mothers. Actually, the father who permits this give-and-take to occur finds his own scope widening as a result. As Dr. Milton R. Sapirstein has pointed out, this kind of participation allows the father to resolve his own "residual dependencies," affords him an opportunity for "fulfilling his creative drives," and helps him to open up emotionally, for "many a father has learned to be a healthy emotional human being only through contact with his children."[6] Despite scattered insights such as these, there is still little real intellectual crys-tallization of father love.

Furthermore, the most recent sociological studies on the subject show that the boys who see their fathers giving warm positive affection, as well as providing discipline, are more likely to identify with them than the boys who don't. Hence, those are the boys least likely to have problems with their masculine identity.[7] Important as these findings are (and they're beginning to be publicized), it certainly seems as important to stress the joys of fatherhood—the emotional rewards it provides for the father—as to stress the duties and obligations the paternal role imposes on him. Too often the emphasis is on what the father must do, with little or nothing said about what he can receive. Then, too, unless he's profoundly involved with his children on an emotional level, today's father is apt to have ambivalent feelings about them, for unlike youngsters in a rural setting, they constitute economic liabilities, and he must work all the harder to provide for them than he would otherwise. If the involvement isn't there, he's likely to feel, if a bit guiltily, "Is it all really worth it?" Here, then, is another reason for stressing the fact that fatherhood is potentially a two-way street, that it provides rewards, as well as imposes obligations.

THE DAGWOOD BUMSTEAD SYNDROME

"What about the father? As far as his biological role is concerned, he might as well be treated as a drone. His task is to impregnate the female and then to disappear," wrote the great anthropologist Bronislaw Malinowski. The contemporary American father isn't being looked on as a drone, of course, but the atmosphere surrounding him is oddly jeering or contemptuous. So lacking in essential dignity has Dad become (except on Father's Day, when his presence makes a healthy impact on the gross national product) that he's tailor-made for the sneer approach. Whatever his shortcomings and however much he may have fooled himself about his power, the patriarchal father of 50 or 100 years ago at least didn't have to sit by and watch the mass media amuse themselves at his expense. Nor, one suspects, would he have permitted such a thing to happen.

For one thing, he wasn't exposed to the denigrating magazine cartoons prevalent during the past several decades. *Playboy*'s "Love, Death and the Hubby Image" surveyed the cartoon scene as it reflects the contemporary father image and found the American male lampooned in dozens of cartoons in magazines like *The New Yorker, Look,* and *Good Housekeeping.* Author William Iversen concluded that "examples of such down-with-Daddy husband razzing are so numerous that it would take no more than a few minutes to fully document a charge of pictorial sadism, verbal castration or symbolic patricide."[8]

One of the favorite techniques, both in cartoons and in articles, seems to be the portrayal of Dad as something other than human, the anthropomorphic insult. Needless to say, the image is never flattering. The June, 1965, issue of *Family Circle* is a case in point. It carries an article entitled "How to Get More Mileage out of Daddy," which compares the family man to the family jalopy. The blurb entices the housewife reader as follows: "Like a station wagon that isn't paid for, a daddy needs constant loving maintenance to keep him in good working order. Remember—appreciation helps cut down depreciation."[9] The advice in the body of the text is just as patronizing, just as condescending. Yet, on reflection, the piece leaves one with the impression that likening father to a car may not be such a bad idea after all, at least not if the intent is to convey subliminally the idea that mother is fairly well ensconced in the driver's seat.

Comic strips do their considerable share to make Pop the butt of the joke. Whereas most of the unmarried comic-strip heroes are adventurers, swashbucklers, and romantics, with virility oozing out of every pore, the married ones with few exceptions are good-natured buffoons. A Temple University professor has described the typical male comic-strip character as "a Dagwood Bumstead, a well-meaning idiot who is constantly outwitted by his children, his wife, and even his dog."[10]

Television provides another practically endless stream of verbal and visual insults that yesteryear's father was lucky enough to do without. Some of the commercials take such deadly aim that it's difficult to believe the sponsors aren't deliberately trying to offend at least the male segment of the viewing audience. A detergent commercial, for instance, shows two married men doing their families' wash in the basement laundry. There is nothing wrong with men throwing the wash into the machine but there's everything wrong with deliberately caricaturing them as gushing-housewife types, men who clearly ape their mates. A commercial sponsored by a salt company shows two men discussing the relative merits of various brands of salt. Again, there is nothing wrong with this—except for the fact that the two men are portrayed as simpering mother-attached caricatures of the American male. Columnist William S. White commented, in discussing the male who's so consistently denigrated by television commercials:

> For him, the apogee of enchantment, the very mountaintop of bliss, is attained when, happy, happy moment, he is able to show that his wife approves his choice of deodorant, and even uses the same one herself. This for him is the highest measure of their togetherness; he is, after all, something of a fellow, is he not?[11]

Nor is the viewing time *between* commercials often more uplifting to the male. This is clearly apparent in television's tiresome parade of situation comedy shows, another insult that yesteryear's father was lucky enough to do without. In most of these shows, Father can be classified as the village imbecile. When he tries to fix a faucet, he winds up with a flooded basement (either his bride or a husky repairman comes to the rescue). When he attempts to fend for himself, he nearly sets the whole house afire, trying to cook a meal. Bring a beautiful sexpot into his orbit—usually a teacher he is all set to give hell to because she has been picking on Junior—and he degenerates into a drooling adolescent.

The sad-sack state of the contemporary television father is summed up in the ending of one of the *Danny Thomas* shows. Pointing to a plate of hors d'oeuvres, a housewife asks, "What's that ridiculous-looking thing?"

Without thinking, the other woman points to her own husband. "That's Charlie," she answers.

Maybe in time the men of the nation will tire of such emasculation and will let the offending parties know their feelings in no uncertain terms. Until it happens, though, the mass media's mass castration will proceed apace, and the contemporary American father will be ever more emphatically confirmed as a vestigial figure.

THE BIOLOGICAL MYTH

The father's status as a vestigial figure and the mother's much greater prestige derive from some popular and, in part, debatable interpretations of biology. These interpretations are based on one unquestionable fact: The father impregnates, but the mother conceives. She's the one who has the fundamental biological connection with the child. Fatherhood, it has been emphasized by Margaret Mead and others, is a "social invention" learned "somewhere at the dawn of history"—society's way of providing protection for mother and child. Some behavioral scientists—Dr. Josselyn for one—challenge the view that, as she put it, "the role of fatherhood is a psychologically foreign one, artificially imposed by the culture for the survival of the race."[12] Nevertheless, the fact remains that in any popular comparison between the roles of mothering and fathering, the latter—being far less based on biological ties—seems relatively unimportant.

One may ask whether the mothering role does indeed find its wellspring entirely in conception and parturition or whether learning plays a more significant part than is popularly granted. Is woman born with a full array of maternal feelings which grow and mature in conjunction with her physical maturation? Or do these feelings take on shape and form during the process of enculturation? As with all other aspects of the biology versus culture dilemma, there's no simple answer. "It simply is not possible to dissociate the two aspects of mothering—biological and social," Dr. Nathan W. Ackerman has observed. Referring to studies which have attempted to measure the existence of a maternal instinct in women, Dr. Ackerman has noted that the results do not lend themselves to definite conclusions:

> The constitutional factors influencing mothering are difficult to estimate in and of themselves, insofar as their manifestations can never be observed in pure form; their influence can only be inferred because their effects are always clothed in socially structured patterns.[13]

The fact that she *can* become a mother may give a woman *some* inborn psychological tendency toward motherhood and maternal response. It's this tendency—if it exists at all, and many authorities are inclined to doubt it—that's so often exaggerated and idealized, so often paralleled with the much more clearly delineated mothering instincts found in the animal world. A woman is not a salmon, struggling bravely upstream finally to deposit her eggs and then, spent, to die. A woman is not a rhesus macaque that gives birth approximately 50 percent of her life. A woman is, as Morton M. Hunt as pointed out in his balanced exploration of the subject, a human being and is therefore "born almost completely unequipped with rigidly patterned instincts." Although she has "powerful amorphous drives toward food, comfort, sex, and so on," she nevertheless has no "inborn, predetermined mechanisms which automatically come into play to satisfy those drives."[14]

She isn't *automatically* a mother, with all the subtleties and complexities of attitude and action the word implies. All these she learns from her culture, absorbing its particular ways of motherliness. The learning process doesn't begin the moment that the rabbit test shows positive; it doesn't begin when the pubertal breasts first ripen and the menstrual flow initially starts. It begins, as the result of countless cultural clues, much farther back, from infancy on. As Hunt observed, a human mother, unlike an animal mother, must *"learn how to be kind and loving, and how to want and to care for a child."*

Here, then, is a crucial point to consider in this exploration of fatherhood: When we view the maternal role in the context of a learning process, the dichotomy between it and the paternal role becomes far less striking. *Both* mothers and fathers are—and must be—culturally prepared for their child-rearing functions. The differences between motherhood and fatherhood become even less striking when we consider the relative ease with which women can suppress their mothering tendencies—can, in effect, learn *not* to want children or at least not a sizable number of them. The alacrity with which women latch on to each new advance in contraceptives specifically designed for them—like the famous pill—shows that the maternal drive (if there is any such thing) isn't so powerful that nonmaternal wishes can't supersede it.

MISSING: THE CONCEPT OF FATHERHOOD

Seen in the light of learned maternal behavior, American males are on the whole woefully shortchanged when it comes to learning and being encouraged to learn their paternal roles. Preparation for motherhood is, as we have seen, a cumulative experience. It starts in very early childhood and is progressively reinforced until the girl actually becomes a mother. By comparison, men are clearly disadvantaged in their preparation for fatherhood. Since their potential for the paternal role isn't structured by a biological framework, boys ought to be made especially cognizant of the multifarious parental responses they'll be called on to exhibit one day. Instead, they see—in their own homes—that fatherhood either assumes narrow dimensions or is more or less irrelevant. They don't get the feel of fatherhood the way a girl gets it for motherhood. The result is that, as psychoanalyst Bruno Bettelheim has said, "Only very occasionally, for boys, is fatherhood added like an afterthought as part of their self-image as mature men."[15]

No wonder fatherhood so often and so quickly bores a man. No wonder a research study into what preadolescent (eight-to-eleven-year-old) boys consider the appropriate images for themselves and for girls shows enormous differences in orientation. These boys think girls must stay close to home; keep clean; play more quietly and gently than boys; are prone to cry when scared or hurt; and are afraid to venture to hazardous places like rooftops and empty lots. Girls play with dolls; fuss over babies; talk about clothes; need to learn cooking, sewing and child-care—but it's much less important for them than for boys to learn such things as spelling and arithmetic.[16]

The fact that the girls would become mothers someday was implicit throughout. Contrast this with the way that the same boys viewed their own roles. Only in the most indirect fashion did they acknowledge their own potentialities for fatherhood—and then only in terms of the breadwinning (protective) role. Boys "have to be able to fight in case a bully comes along; they have to be athletic; they have to be able to run fast; they must be able to play rough games; they need to know how to play many games—curb-ball, baseball, basketball, football; they need to be smart; they need to be able to take care of themselves." They should also know all of the things girls don't know—how to climb, make a fire, carry things. Furthermore, "they should have more ability than girls; they need to know how to stay out of trouble; they need to know arithmetic and spelling more than girls do."[17]

One wonders how a boy building up a mosaic of stereotypes like these (suitably laced with male chauvinism) will grow into a man able to handle the various paternal challenges, big and little, that come along to test his mettle as a father and a male. How, for instance, will the father handle the first major crisis—the birth of his first child? Unprepared for the new demands that will be made on them, lacking readiness for the new roles they'll be called on to play, many fathers face the prospect of parenthood with real foreboding and genuine feelings of inadequacy. The insecurity such a man feels is heightened by the fact that he's suddenly shoved out of the favored position in the family as his wife necessarily identifies much more closely with the needs of the new baby than with his. He may then withdraw psychically or become a submissive, loving, but easily manipulated third party to the symbiotic mother-child dyad.

How, being relatively unprepared for the fathering role, will he handle the close attachment that his young sons are likely to develop for their mothers? Freud postulated the existence of an Oedipus complex, stating that each boy, from the ages of (roughly) three to seven, passes through a difficult phase in which he views his father as a rival for his mother's affections. In Freud's terms, it's the crucial phase in the formulation of the boy's masculine identity. There's considerable skepticism among a portion of the psychological community about the reality of the Oedipus complex as an innate phenomenon. Anthropological data deny its existence in many other cultures. But there can be no doubt that in our society a triangle situation often does develop between the boy, the mother who gives him so much attention and provides for so many of his needs, and the father. Frequently the father considers himself—or is made to consider himself—extraneous to this close relationship between the two others and withdraws even further from the fathering role. Alternatively, he meets the boy's hostility and moodiness toward him with his own hostility and moodiness. Either way, a lack of balance is created in the family. The boy misses a male figure whom he can respect and identify with and who will help him grow out of this phase.

• • • •

To an extent, of course, a mother sensitive to the situation can compensate for a father who absents himself physically or psychically. She can maintain his identity in the home, his presence and importance, as it were, by the way she refers to him in front of the children when he isn't there. But if she herself feels cheated by his absence—as is sooner or later likely to happen—the tensions that build up aren't going to predispose her to refer to him affirmatively. On the contrary, consciously or unconsciously, she's apt in time to denigrate him and tear down his image.

How will the unprepared father handle the feelings of rivalry likely to come when his son is a teen-ager anxious to display his own burgeoning masculinity? The boy may be a source of pride—but also a threat. By his very presence he tells the father, "Your strength can't go on forever. I'm here to challenge you." Some competition may be inevitable, and on the boy's part it may be a healthy aspect of growing up. If the father feels inadequate as a parent or as a male, he's likely to show ambivalence: urging the youngster to do well, but trying to crush his ego at the same time. Many fathers are "thrown" by a son's first request for the use of the family car or for a bigger allowance for dating purposes or by other manifestations of approaching manhood. The Crestwood Heights study of suburbia showed fathers becoming pals with their sons as a "cultural ideal" because the community's "concept of time makes ageing and the looming prospect of the termination of the career a very real threat to the man; the prospect can be softened by playing down the actual gap in years between father and son."[18]

How will the man who has little concept of the fathering role handle his relationship to his daughter—a relationship presenting its own delicate problems? To his daughter, the father represents, so to speak, the first man in her life. He's largely responsible for the way she forms her general attitude toward men. If he is fearful of women and shows it either by retreating into passivity, by using brutal authoritarianism, or by insisting that the females in his family adhere to rigidly patriarchal patterns, she soon senses it. It doesn't take her long to discover that—directly or via the manipulative approach—her mother is the real, the only, strength in the family. Her images of masculinity and feminity, of the male-female relationship, develop accordingly.

• • • •

How is the father going to handle the most difficult and crucial job—that of giving his children the materials they need to fashion a coherent, mature, meaningful set of personal values for themselves? How is he going to provide them with the guidelines that will help them recognize the differences between freedom and license, assertiveness and anarchy, self-worth and self-seeking? This is the crux of the matter, the area of his paternal functioning in which his failure to exercise sufficient authority and initiative shows the most blatantly deleterious results. That he *is* failing is hardly surprising. History has given him a powerful nudge in that direction, but there's more to it than this. When the pace was slower, life's changes less kaleidoscopic, and the pressures for success and for security less intense than they are now, a man had the *mental* leisure to acquire, assimilate, and pass on—or have his wife pass on—meaningful values. He was also supported by the fact that his range of choices was fewer and his life—both on inner and outer levels—more clearly delineated. He knew much better who he was and what he was, so it became much easier for him to offer his identity to his family. Caught in compulsive, contradictory patterns, the contemporary father is hard put to define himself and his own values, much less convey them without confusion to his offspring.

A goodly number of American fathers follow one or the other of two courses of action: (1) They leave the guidance and decision-making aspects of fathering pretty much to their wives, or (2) they involve themselves, but narrowly—concentrating on instilling the achievement motive in their youngsters. Let us consider the probable results of the two courses.

The Children Take Over

Without the old supports she used to have, eager in many instances to assume *less*, rather than *more*, responsibility in the home, the wife is ill equipped to be the sole family authority. She nags her husband, understandably enough, to do more in this area. Reluctantly, he leaves the home workshop—which he set up in part to isolate himself from too much family involvement—and mouths the standard verities to his children. But unless he practices what he preaches, reciting a kind of Boy Scout Promise has little effect, and what the children swiftly grasp is not the verities but his own bewilderment. Increasingly, the wife goes elsewhere for help. She devours reams of material on child rearing. She becomes unspontaneous, afraid to act on her own initiative with her children. She relies more and more on outside sources—such as teachers, counselors, and even babysitters—to assist her in playing the mother-father role. The obvious result is that the children tend to look less and less inside the family for the structuring they used to get there. Dr. Otto O. von Mering put it this way at a meeting of the Family Service Association of America:

> The maze of youth clubs and councils, recreation centers, and agencies, presided over by child specialists, and the widespread collective membership in streetcorner and schoolyard societies have encouraged children to adhere prematurely to extra-familial values and norms of behavior. Together with and reinforced by the welter of merchandise and pulp literature, movies, and television presentations with the youth brand stamped on them, they have all too often provided the only form of "supervision" and the only standards by which today's children are asked to live.[19]

In effect, the sequence of events goes like this: the parents feel inadequate to assume authority in the home and evade that responsibility; this creates a kind of power vacuum; as in any vacuum, somebody steps in, and in this case it's the children themselves; since the young people have taken over the stronger role, the parents now count on them for a sense of direction; the mass media, the advertisers, and the manufacturers feed the situation and capitalize on it by aiming their sales guns with ever-increasing fervor at the burgeoning youth market; the youngsters themselves gain an ever-increasing sense of power; and, presto, you have a child-centered culture.

All this makes it apparent that the marketplace is an integral part of the phenomenon. While some of the experts still debate whether husbands or wives have the greater consumer-purchasing influence, the youngsters themselves are stepping in to take command. B. S. Durant, president of the giant RCA Sales Corporation, stated publicly that although American youth was doing "a $24 billion business above the surface, we estimate that their total buying influence extends to four times this amount." Referring to a handsome increase in the sale of portable phonographs, Durant added that teen-agers are no longer content with $20 models; instead, "they seem to be persuading their parents to buy them our $150 models."[20]

The spectacle of father depending on mother depending on the children themselves to say how they'll be brought up and how much to spend on consumer items is dismaying to behold. The youngsters are pushed to make decisions they simply aren't equipped to make; the accent is on instant gratification; the emphasis in the parent-child relationship comes to be rather more on materialism than on essential communication. Frequently, teen-agers seem to know more about their fathers' money than they do about its source. Dr. William A. Schonfeld, past president of the American Society of Adolescent Psychiatry says, "Many modern youngsters can't even describe accurately what Father does between 8:10 when his train leaves and 6:20 when it brings him back."[21]

It may be said that in America the young have always led the way, their elders (particularly among immigrant groups) looking to them for help in assimilating to the American way of life. It may also be said that in the face of industrialization and urbanization some loss of parental authority is unavoidable. This is true, but the point is that the pendulum has swung too far. In recent years the reliance and concentration on—and the exploitation of—the young have become intense enough to create a peer-group culture so potent that now even many parents who *want* to assume authority have a hard time bucking it. Some of the more thoughtful parents among my interviewees were sincerely troubled by the situation. Many of the experts I talked with were also troubled. Typical of them was Dr. Gertrude Hengerer. Acknowledging that in some students today there is a growing social awareness, she nevertheless stated:

I'm worried that we're not geared at this time in our nation to teach responsibility as early as people ought to have it. Children are being pushed out much earlier without the protections they used to have. I'm very much concerned about our creating an irresponsible, immature, undisciplined people. Here we see many, many more impulsive young persons. This is the trend.

When inexperienced youngsters look for guidance to other inexperienced youngsters, when children don't even know what their fathers do for a living, this trend is hardly astonishing. The peer-group culture is admittedly difficult for parents to compete against at this late stage, but the less communication there is between them and their offspring, the more difficult it becomes. A father cannot control his children's education these days, but he can discuss with them some of his business problems; can possibly bring them to his place of employment from time to time; can take them to political meetings, government offices, and the like; and can give them closer contact with what Dr. Paul Popenoe calls "the serious side of the family's undertakings" by providing them with an understanding of leases, installment contracts, insurance policies, and the family's budget. Few fathers take the trouble to engender this kind of communication. It is, of course, easier to be a pal.

A number of psychiatrists contacted while this book was being researched saw in the current lack of paternal authority the root not only of immaturity but also of male passivity and of a disinclination in the contemporary American male to take risks. The indulgent father who exhibits no meaningful authority, they said, thereby engenders more terror in his sons than even a really harsh father could. Dr. Ralph Greenson explained this seeming paradox:

> A strict father is a very tough father to deal with. But no father is far worse, because then the child's fantasies have free play and it creates another father who is so frightening that he's much more terrifying than the really harsh father could be. A child's instincts are far more primitive and destructive than an adult's behavior. If you don't have a father who corrects your notions about your fantasies, you will create a much worse father by yourself.

For some time, probably as a reaction to the authoritarian Victorian concepts of fatherhood, the experts have thought that children who were given a great deal of freedom and permissiveness would grow up to be psychologically healthier. But the opposite is occurring. When no limits are set, no rules established and no punishment meted out, a child becomes frightened of all authority because he has no experience within the family to cope with it and grow with it. Such a child projects his own fearful instincts onto this blank surface, as it were—or becomes so instinct-ridden and impulse-ridden that he cannot set up any controls for himself. According to Dr. Greenson, males who have had very good-natured and easygoing fathers—fathers who never contended with them, never fought with them—often become quite terrified of violence. The terror originates in "projections of their own violence which were never corrected by the realities of father."

THE SUCCESS MOTIVE

Many American fathers today—particularly in the middle and upper-middle classes—pride themselves on the fact that they're not being too good-natured, too easygoing. They're sure that they display authority. So they do, but it's on narrow and erratic terms, for the men involved are the ones for whom masculinity is very strongly tied up with the success motive and for whom status becomes the validation of success. They know that you can no longer get anywhere in life without a college degree (although they may not realize that such men as they have created this closed-shop intellectual system), so they push their sons to get good grades in school. They push very hard, as though grades were all that mattered, and the compulsiveness with which they insist on the high marks, the good schools, the right classes, and the proper fraternities (if possible) bespeaks more than an interest in readying their offspring for the rigors of the world. Some of these fathers have "made it" themselves and want their sons to do as well or better; many others haven't been notably successful but at least want to take credit for producing offspring that are.

Mothers, too, abide by the success motive. At the Family Service Association of Palo Alto and Los Altos, California, I was told that frequently this pushing "is the parents' only common area of agreement. To get Johnny up, up the ladder." At the Family Service Agency of Marin County, California, a caseworker said, "I've never seen anything like it as a syndrome in the San Francisco peninsula and in Marin County. You push them in school, haul them to horseback-riding lessons, to music lessons, to tennis lessons. . . . The kids have got to accomplish."

On the East Coast, but surveying the national scene, Dr. Dan W. Dodson, director of the Center for Human Relations and Community Studies at New York University, put the pushing syndrome into perspective: "The thing which is bringing status today is whether the children are leading their classes in making grades in school. Whether they are academically curious or not is of small consequence; the grades represent goals of status rather than goals of growth or achievement." Dr. Dodson told me of suburban parents who give their children trips to Florida and winter vacations if they attain high grades— a form of academic payola.

The competitive pressure to get the boys into college is, according to many observers, fantastic; the pressure to get them into graduate school is becoming increasingly so. Whether a young man is college or graduate-school material is irrelevant; the important thing is to be admitted, to obtain the degree. Once again the competition is of a distorted kind; the goal is not individual excellence but making the top grades in class or, at the very least, manipulating things to get by.[22] One perceptive lad, victim of the status-competition game remarked:

> I've always had the feeling that I was an employee of my parents. I was supposed to be something—like their car or their house—that they could point to with pride.[23]

From any standpoint and for both sons and fathers this exaggerated emphasis on competition and status, on the externals, is a loser's game. If the lad is docile and good and true, if he makes the top grades, if he gets into the finest schools, if he always does better in comparison with others in his peer group, and if this represents his meaning as a person, his success pleases himself and his parents and his community. It gives him a sense of accomplishment. But it also engenders grave problems in identity, and the sense of accomplishment remains curiously ephemeral. He can never really be himself, a person with a core, someone who believes in something. The problem is that he has been highly conditioned to associate success with approval (love). To succeed— first at school, later at work—means to be loved. Success being transitory and love being necessary, he becomes the proverbial man on a treadmill, the compulsive one who can never relax and stop running.

Referring to "yardstick rearing"—the continuous comparison of one's child to others—the Episcopal minister Gibson Winters notes that such a child "comes to see himself only as a doer—a performer" as he becomes an adult.

> He is a bundle of performances which can be called forth by the right signals. . . . A person's insides shrivel in this atmosphere. . . . He becomes

174

increasingly worried about failure. Every failure is a tragedy, because one belongs only if one succeeds. One must not fail. One has to succeed, because this is who we are—those who succeed. Successful jobs have always depended on effective work. This is nothing new. What is new to our way of life is the feeling that we can only belong as long as we succeed.[24]

So the lad who tries like hell but just can't measure up to his parents' expectations faces a real inner struggle when, say, he winds up at Podunk U. instead of at Princeton. He'll find it tough to get rid of the guilty feeling that gnaws at his psyche—that he has let Dad down. He'll find it even tougher still to rid himself of the gnawing suspicion about himself—that he really doesn't measure up as a man.

It's less than a surprise that the compulsive approach to competition—this radical shift of emphasis from the joy of learning to the quest for a high mark on the report card, which is being pushed by the school, as well as by parents and peer groups—is occurring at a time when the rate of cheating, nervous breakdowns, random violence, normless Beat rebelliousness, and even suicide soars among middle-class youths.

The father in such a case is, of course, painfully aware that he has somehow failed in the father-son relationship—failed, that is, as a man. It may be the first time he really, consciously, associates fatherhood with masculinity.

NOTES

[1] Quoted by Sapirstein, *op. cit.*, p. 191.

[2] Erich Fromm, *The Art of Loving* (New York: Harper & Bros., 1956), pp. 39, 50.

[3] Ashley Montagu, *The Natural Superiority of Women* (New York: The Macmillan Co., 1952), p. 142.

[4] Quoted by Don Oakley, New York *World-Telegram* (June 25, 1964). Lest it be thought Judge Scott is biased in favor of men, he has also championed the rights of women —particularly mothers—in Ohio.

[5] Irene M. Josselyn, "Cultural Forces, Motherliness and Fatherliness," *American Journal of Orthopsychiatry* (April, 1956). The traditional view holds that the father should be the sole disciplinarian and the sole provider of conditional love, because it's his exclusive job to instill conscience. Thus, Fromm states (*op. cit.*, p. 43) that "Father's love should be guided by principles and expectations," and although he insists that the father ought to be "patient and tolerant," rather than "threatening and authoritarian," the effect is nevertheless a distancing and lack of spontaneity between father and child.

[6] Sapirstein, *op. cit.*, p. 176.

[7] Donald E. Payne and Paul H. Mussen, "Parent Child Relations and Father Identification Among Adolescent Boys," *The Journal of Abnormal and Social Psychology* (May, 1956). Also, Paul Mussen and Luther Distler, "Masculinity, Identification and Father-Son Relationships," *The Journal of Abnormal and Social Psychology* (November, 1959). Also, Charlotte Himber, "So He Hates Baseball," *The New York Times Magazine* (August 29, 1965).

[8] William Iversen, "Love, Death and the Hubby Image," *Playboy* (September, 1963).

[9]A. M. Greenwood, "How to Get More Mileage out of Daddy," *Family Circle* (June, 1965).

[10]Jhan and June Robbins, "Why Young Husbands Feel Trapped," *Redbook* (March, 1962).

[11]William S. White, New York *Journal-American* (April 12, 1965).

[12]Josselyn, *op. cit.*

[13]Nathan W. Ackerman, *The Psychodynamics of Family Life* (New York: Basic Books, Inc., 1958), p. 172.

[14]Hunt, *Her Infinite Variety,* p. 170.

[15]Bruno Bettelheim, "The Problem of Generations," *Daedalus* (Winter, 1962).

[16]Hartley, "Sex Role Pressures and the Socialization of the Male Child," *op. cit.*

[17]*Ibid.*

[18]Seeley, Simm, and Loosley, *op. cit.,* p. 201.

[19]Otto O. von Mering, "Forms of Fathering in Relation to Mother-Child Pairs," *The Significance of the Father* (New York: Family Serivce Association of America, 1959), p. 7.

[20]*Newsweek* (November 30, 1964).

[21]Quoted by Phyllis Battelle, New York *Journal-American* (March 25, 1965).

[22]Hillel Black, *They Shall Not Pass* (New York: William Morrow & Co., 1963), p. 23. Also, John Keats, *The Sheepskin Psychosis* (New York: J. B. Lippincott Co., 1965).

[23]Quoted by Joseph Lelyveld, "The Paradoxical Case of the Affluent Delinquent," *The New York Times Magazine* (October 4, 1964).

[24]Gibson Winter, *Love and Conflict* (New York: Doubleday & Co., 1958), p. 73.

Structural Problems
of the One-Parent Family

Paul Glasser and
Elizabeth Navarre

The attention of sociologists has been focused on the presumed isolation of the nuclear family (composed of mother, father, and children, but no in-laws, in the same household). However, little research effort has been expended on the more serious isolation and accompanying problems of the one-parent family. Such families are usually headed by women and have grave economic difficulties. The lone parent must handle all the tasks of running the family, even in a crisis. The demands are so great (when combined with making a living) that some tasks must be short-changed or ignored altogether. The areas of communications, family power structure, and affectional relationships are often the ones that become strained when one parent attempts to maintain the family alone.

Recent concern about the problems of people who are poor has led to renewed interest in the source of such difficulties. While these are manifold and complexly related to each other, emphasis has been placed upon the opportunity structure and the socialization process found among lower socio-economic groups. Relatively little attention has been paid to family structure, which serves as an important intervening variable between these two considerations. This seems to be a significant omission in view of the major change in the structure of family life in the United States during this century,

From Paul Glasser and Elizabeth Navarre, "Structural Problems of the One-Parent Family," *Journal of Social Issues,* January, 1965, pp. 98–109. Reprinted by permission of The Society for the Psychological Study of Social Issues. The conceptualization in this paper grew out of work on Project D-16, "Demonstration of Social Group Work With Parents," financed by a grant from the Children's Bureau, Welfare Administration, Department of Health, Education and Welfare. The authors are indebted to Professor Edwin Thomas for his suggestions.

and the large number of one-parent families classified as poor. The consequences of the latter structural arrangements for family members, parents and children, and for society, is the focus of this paper.

One-parent families are far more apt to be poor than other families. This is true for one-fourth of those headed by a woman. Chilman and Sussman summarize that data in the following way:

> About ten percent of the children in the United States are living with only one parent, usually the mother. Nonwhite children are much more likely to live in such circumstances, with one-third of them living in one-parent families. Two-and-a-quarter million families in the United States today are composed of a mother and her children. They represent only one-twelfth of all families with children but make up more than a fourth of all that are classed as poor. . . .
>
> Despite the resulting economic disadvantages, among both white and nonwhite families there is a growing number headed only by a mother. By 1960 the total was 7½ per cent of all families with own children rather than the 6 per cent of ten years earlier. By March 1962 the mother-child families represented 8½ per cent of all families with own children (4, p. 393).

When these demographic findings are seen in the context of the relative isolation of the nuclear family in the United States today, the structural consequences of the one-parent group take on added meaning. It may be seen as the culmination of the effective kin group.

> This "isolation" is manifested in the fact that members of the nuclear family, consisting of parents and their still dependent children, ordinarily occupy a separate dwelling not shared with members of the family of orientation. . . . It is, of course, not uncommon to find a (member of the family of orientation) residing with the family, but this is both statistically secondary, and it is clearly not felt to be the "normal arrangement" (9, p. 10).

While families maintain social contact with grown children and with siblings, lines of responsibility outside of the nuclear group are neither clear nor binding, and obligations among extended kin are often seen as limited and weak. Even when affectional ties among extended family members are strong, their spatial mobility in contemporary society isolates the nuclear group geographically, and increases the difficulty of giving aid in personal service among them (2, 6).

Associated with the weakening of the extended kinship structure has been the loss of some social functions of the family and the lessened import of others. Nonetheless, reproduction, physical maintenance, placement or status, and socialization are still considered significant social functions of the modern American family although they often have to be buttressed by other institutions in the community. At the same time, however, the personal functions of the family including affection, security, guidance and sexual gratification have been heightened and highlighted (3, 9). These functions are closely and complexly related to each other but can serve as foci for analysis of the consequences of family structure. In the one-parent family neither reproduction nor sexual gratification can be carried out within the confines of the nuclear group itself. But more importantly, the other personal and social functions are drastically affected also, and it is to these that this paper will give its attention. A few of the implications for social policy and practice will be mentioned at the end.

While it is recognized that all individuals have some contact with others outside the nuclear group, for purposes of analytic clarity this paper will confine itself to a discussion of the relationships among nuclear family members primarily. Two factors will be the foci of much of the content. The age difference between parent and children is central to the analysis. Although it is understood that children vary with age in the degree of independence from their parents, the nature of their dependence will be emphasized throughout. The sex of the parent and the sex of the children is the second variable. Cultural definitions of appropriate behavior for men and women and for girls and boys vary from place to place and are in the process of change, but nonetheless this factor cannot be ignored. Since the largest majority of one-parent families are headed by a woman, greater attention will be given to the mother-son and mother-daughter relationships in the absence of the father.

Structural Characteristics of One-Parent Families and Their Consequences

Task Structure

The large majority of tasks for which a family is responsible devolve upon the parents. Providing for the physical, emotional, and social needs of all the family members is a full-time job for two adults. If these tasks are to be performed by the nuclear group during the absence or incapacity of one of its adult members, the crucial factor is the availability of another member with sufficient maturity, competence, and time to perform them. The two-parent family has sufficient flexibility to adapt to such a crisis. Although there is considerable specialization in the traditional sex roles concerning these tasks, there is little evidence that such specialization is inherent in the sex roles. It is, in fact, expected that one parent will substitute if the other parent is incapacitated and, in our essentially servantless society, such acquired tasks are given full social approval. However, in the one-parent family such flexibility is much less possible, and the permanent loss of the remaining parent generally dissolves the nuclear group.

Even if the remaining parent is able to function adequately, it is unlikely that one person can take over all parental tasks on a long-term basis. Financial support, child care, and household maintenance are concrete tasks involving temporal and spatial relationships, and in one form or another they account for a large proportion of the waking life of two adult family members. A permanent adjustment then must involve a reduction in the tasks performed and/or a reduction in the adequacy of performance, or external assistance.

In addition to limitations on the time and energy available to the solitary parent for the performance of tasks, there are social limitations on the extent to which both the male and the female tasks may be fulfilled by a member of one sex. If the remaining parent be male, it is possible for him to continue to perform his major role as breadwinner and to hire a woman to keep house and, at least, to care for the children's physical needs. If, however, the solitary parent be a female, as is the more usual case, the woman must take on the male role of breadwinner, unless society or the absent husband provides financial support in the form of insurance, pensions, welfare payments, etc. This is a major reversal in cultural roles and, in addition, usually consumes the mother's time and energy away from the home for many hours during the day. There is little time or energy left to perform the tasks normally performed by the female in the household and she, too, must hire a female substitute at considerable cost. The effect of this reversal of the sex role model in the socialization of children has been a matter of some concern, but the emphasis has been upon the male child who lacked a male role model rather than upon the effect of the reversal of the female role model for children of both sexes. In both cases, the probability seems great that some tasks will be neglected, particularly those of the traditionally female specialization.

The wish to accomplish concrete household tasks in the most efficient manner in terms of time and energy expenditure may lead to less involvement of children in these tasks and the concomitant loss of peripheral benefits that are extremely important to the socialization process and/or to family cohesion. Some tasks may be almost completely avoided, especially those which are not immediately obvious to the local community, such as the provision of emotional support and attention to children. A third possibility is to overload children, particularly adolescents, with such tasks. These may be greater than the child is ready to assume, or tasks inappropriate for the child of a particular sex to perform regularly.

Females are often lacking in skills and experience in the economic world, and frequently receive less pay and lower status jobs than men with similar skills. The probability of lower income and lower occupational status for the female headed household are likely to lower the family's social position in a society, which bases social status primarily upon these variables. If the family perceives a great enough distance between its former level and that achieved by the single parent, it is possible that the family as a whole may become more or less anomic, with serious consequences in the socialization process of the children and in the remaining parent's perception of personal adequacy.

Communication Structure

Parents serve as the channels of communication with the adult world in two ways; first, as transmitters of the cultural value system which has previously been internalized by the parents; and secondly, as the child's contact with and representative in the adult world. Except for very young children, the parents are not the sole means of communication, but for a large part of the socialization process, the child sees the adult world through the eyes and by the experience of his parents, and even his own experiences are limited to those which can be provided for him within whatever social opportunities are open to his parents. More importantly, to the extent that the child's identity is integrated with that of the family, he is likely to see himself not only as his parents see him but also as the world sees his parents.

Since sex differences have been assumed in the ways men and women see the world and differences can be substantiated in the ways that the world sees men and women, the child can have a relatively undistorted channel of communication only if both parents are present. Therefore, whatever the interests, values, and opinions of the remaining parent, the loss of a parent of one sex produces a structural distortion in the communications between the child and the adult world and, since such communication is a factor in the development of the self-image, of social skills, and of an image of the total society, the totality of the child's possible development is also distorted.

The type and quality of experiences available even to adults tend to be regulated according to sex. In the two-parent family not only is the child provided with more varied experiences, but the parent of either sex has, through the spouse, some communication with the experiences typical of the opposite sex. Thus, the housewife is likely to have some idea of what is going on in the business or sports worlds even if she has no interest in them. The solitary parent is not likely to be apprised of such information and is handicapped to the extent that it may be necessary for decision making. The female who has taken on the breadwinner role may be cut off from the sources of information pertinent to the female role as she misses out on neighborhood gossip about the symptoms of the latest virus prevalent among the children, events being planned, the best places to shop, etc.

Finally, the solitary parent is likely to be limited in the social ties that are normal channels of communication. Most social occasions for adults tend to be planned for couples and the lone parent is often excluded or refuses because of the discomfort of being a fifth wheel. Her responsibilities to home and children tend to never be completed and provide additional reasons for refusing invitations. Lone women are particularly vulnerable to community sanctions and must be cautious in their social relationships lest their own standing and that of the family be lowered. Finally, the possible drop in social status previously discussed may isolate the family from its own peer group and place them among a group with which they can not or will not communicate freely.

Power Structure

Bales and Borgatta (1) have pointed out that the diad has unique properties and certainly a uniquely simple power structure. In terms of authority from which the children are more or less excluded by age and social norms, the one-parent family establishes a diadic relationship, between the parent and each child. Society places full responsibility in the parental role, and, therefore, the parent becomes the only power figure in the one-parent family. Consequently, the adult in any given situation is either for or against the child. Some experience of playing one adult against the other, as long as it is not carried to extremes, is probably valuable in developing social skills and in developing a view of authority as tolerable and even manipulable within reason, rather than absolute and possibly tyrannical. In the one-parent family the child is more likely to see authority as personal rather than consensual, and this in itself removes some of the legitimation of the power of parents as the representatives of society.

Even if benevolent, the absolutism of the power figure in the one-parent family, where there can be no experience of democratic decision making between equals in power, may increase the difficulty of the adolescent and the young adult in achieving independence from the family, and that of the parent in allowing and encouraging such development. Further, the adult, the power, the authority figure, is always of one sex, whether that sex be the same sex as the child or the opposite. However, in contemporary society where decision making is the responsibility of both sexes, the child who has identified authority too closely with either sex may have a difficult adjustment. The situation also has consequences for the parent, for when the supportive reinforcement or the balancing mediation which comes with the sharing of authority for decision making is absent, there may be a greater tendency to frequent changes in the decisions made, inconsistency, or rigidity.

Affectional Structure

The personal functions of the family in providing for the emotional needs of its members have been increasingly emphasized. There is ample evidence that children require love and security in order to develop in a healthy manner. Although there is nearly as much substantiation for the emotional needs of parents, these are less frequently emphasized. Adults must have love and security in order to maintain emotional stability under the stresses of life and in order to meet the emotional demands made upon them by their children. In addition to providing the positive emotional needs of its members, the family has the further function of providing a safe outlet for negative feelings as well. Buttressed by the underlying security of family affection, the dissatisfactions and frustrations of life may be expressed without the negative consequences attendant upon their expression in other contexts. Even within the family, however, the expressions of such basic emotions cannot go unchecked. The needs of one member or one sub-group may dominate to the point that the requirements of others are not fulfilled, or are not met in a manner acceptable to society. To some extent this danger exists in any group, but it is particularly strong in a group where emotional relationships are intensive. Traditionally, the danger is reduced by regulating the context, manner, and occasion of the expression of such needs.

Family structure is an important element both in the provision and the regulation of emotional needs. The increasing isolation of the nuclear family focuses these needs on the nuclear group by weakening ties with the larger kin group. Thus, both generations and both sexes are forced into a more intensive relationship; yet the marital relationship itself is increasingly unsupported by legal or social norms and is increasingly dependent upon affectional ties alone for its solidity. Such intense relationships are increased within the one-parent family, and possibly reach their culmination in the family consisting of one parent and one child.

In a two-person group the loss of one person destroys the group. The structure, therefore, creates pressure for greater attention to group maintenance through the expression of affection and the denial of negative feelings, and in turn may restrict problem-solving efforts. In a sense, the one-parent family is in this position even if there are several children because the loss of the remaining parent effectively breaks up the group. The children have neither the ability nor the social power to maintain the group's independence. Therefore, the one-parent family structure exerts at least some pressure in this direction.

However, where there is more than one child there is some mitigation of the pattern, though this in itself may have some disadvantages. In a group of three or more there are greater possibilities for emotional outlet for those not in an authority role. Unfortunately, there are also greater possibilities that one member may become the scapegoat as other members combine against him. In spite of the power relationships, it is even possible that the solitary parent will become the scapegoat if the children combine against her. This problem is greatest in the three-person family as three of the five possible

Sub-Group Choices Among Groups of Varying Sizes*

FIGURE 1: THE FOUR-PERSON GROUP

1. A, B, C, D	5. B, C, D	9. B, D
2. A, B, C	6. A, B	10. A, D
3. A, B, D	7. C, D	11. B, C
4. A, C, D	8. A, C	12. All persons independent; no sub-group

FIGURE 2: THE THREE-PERSON GROUP

1. A, B, C	3. A, B	5. All persons independent; no sub-group
2. B, C	4. A, C	

FIGURE 3: THE TWO-PERSON GROUP

1. A, B	2. Both persons independent; no sub-group

*Persons designated by letter.

183

sub-groups reject one member (Figure 2). The problem is also present in the four-person family, although the possible sub-groups in which the family combines against one member has dropped to four out of twelve (Figure 1). The relation of group structure to emotional constriction has been clearly expressed by Slater:

> The disadvantages of the smaller groups are not verbalized by members, but can only be inferred from their behavior. It appears that group members are too tense, passive, tactful, and constrained, to work together in a manner which is altogether satisfying to them. *Their fear of alienating one another seems to prevent them from expressing their ideas freely.* (Emphasis is ours.)
>
> These findings suggest that maximal group satisfaction is achieved when the group is large enough so that the members feel able to express positive and negative feelings freely, and to make aggressive efforts toward problem solving even at the risk of antagonizing each other, yet small enough so that some regard will be shown for the feelings and needs of others; large enough so that the loss of a member could be tolerated, but small enough so that such a loss could not be altogether ignored (11, p. 138).

Interpersonal relationships between parents and children in the area of emotional needs are not entirely reciprocal because of age and power differences in the family. Parents provide children with love, emotional support, and an outlet for negative feelings. However, while the love of a child is gratifying to the adult in some ways, it cannot be considered as supporting; rather it is demanding in the responsibilities it places upon the loved one. Support may be received only from one who is seen as equal or greater in power and discrimination. Nor can the child serve as a socially acceptable outlet for negative emotions to the extent that another adult can, for the child's emotional and physical dependency upon the adult makes him more vulnerable to possible damage from this source. The solitary parent in the one-parent family is structurally deprived of a significant element in the meeting of his own emotional needs. To this must be added the psychological and physical frustrations of the loss of the means for sexual gratification. In some situations involving divorce or desertion, the damage to the self-image of the remaining parent may intensify the very needs for support and reassurance which can no longer be met within the family structure.

The regulation of emotional demands of family members is similar in many ways to the regulation of the behavior of family members discussed under power structure. As there was the possibility that authority might be too closely identified with only one sex in the one-parent family, there is the similar danger that the source of love and affection may be seen as absolute and/or as vested in only one sex. Having only one source of love and security, both physical and emotional, is more likely to produce greater anxiety about its loss in the child, and may make the child's necessary withdrawal from the family with growing maturity more difficult for both parent and child. Again, as in the power structure, the identification of the source of love with only one sex is likely to cause a difficult adjustment to adult life, particularly if the original source of love was of the same sex as the child, for our society's expectations are that the source of love for an adult must lie with the opposite sex.

One of the most important regulatory devices for the emotional needs of the group is the presence and influence of members who serve to deter or limit demands which would be harmful to group members or to group cohesion, and to prevent the intensification of the influence of any one individual by balancing it with the influence of others. Parental figures will tend to have greater influence in acting as a deterrent or balance to the needs and demands of other family members because of their greater power and maturity. The loss of one parent removes a large portion of the structural balance and intensifies the influence of the remaining parent upon the children, while possibly limiting the ability of this parent to withstand demands made upon her by the children. There is also a tendency for any family member to transfer to one or more of the remaining members the demands formerly filled by the absent person (8). There would seem to be a danger in the one-parent family that:

1. The demands of the sole parent for the fulfillment of individual and emotional needs normally met within the marital relationship may prove intolerable and damaging to the children, who are unable to give emotional support or to absorb negative feelings from this source,

or:

2. The combined needs of the children may be intolerable to the emotionally unsupported solitary parent. Since the emotional requirements of children are very likely to take the form of demands for physical attention or personal service, the remaining parent may be subject to physical as well as emotional exhaustion from this source.

When emotional needs are not met within the family, there may be important consequences for the socialization of the children and for the personal adjustment of all family members. Further, fulfillment of such needs may be sought in the larger community by illegitimate means. The children may exhibit emotional problems in school or in their relations with their play group. A parent may be unable to control her own emotions and anxieties sufficiently to function adequately in society. When there are no means for the satisfaction of these demands they may well prove destructive, not only to the family group and its individual members, but to society as well.

The consequences of the problems discussed above may be minimized or magnified by the personal resources or inadequacies of the family members, and particularly the solitary parent in this situation. But, the problems are structural elements of the situation, and must be faced on this level if they are to be solved.

IMPLICATIONS FOR SOCIAL POLICY AND PRACTICE

The Introduction describes the growth of the number of one-parent families during the last generation. Chilman and Sussman go on to describe the financial plight of many of these families.

The public program of aid to families with dependent children (AFDC) that is most applicable to this group currently makes payments on behalf of children in nearly a million families. Three out of every four of these families have no father in the home. Less than half of the families that are estimated to be in need receive payments under the program and, "...with the low financial standards for aid to dependent children prevailing in many states, dependence on the program for support is in itself likely to put the family in low-income status.... The average monthly payment per family as reported in a study late in 1961 was only $112....

"The overall poverty of the recipient families is suggested by the fact that, according to the standards set up in their own states, half of them are still in financial need even with their assistance payment" (4, p. 394; 10).

There is increasing evidence that both the one-parent family structure and poverty are being transmitted from one generation to the next.

"A recently released study of cases assisted by aid to families with dependent children shows that, for a nationwide sample of such families whose cases were closed early in 1961" more than 40 per cent of the mothers and/or fathers were raised in homes where some form of assistance had been received at some time. "Nearly half of these cases had received aid to families with dependent children. This estimated proportion that received some type of aid is more than four times the almost 10 per cent estimated for the total United States population..." (4, p. 395; 10).

If poverty and one-parent family structure tend to go together, providing increases in financial assistance alone may not be sufficient to help parents and children in the present and future generation to become financially independent of welfare funds. Under the 1962 Amendments to the Social Security Act states are now receiving additional funds to provide rehabilitation services to welfare families, and these programs have begun. Creative use of such funds to overcome some of the consequences of one-parent family structure is a possibility, but as yet the authors know of no services that have explicitly taken this direction.

A few suggestions may serve to illustrate how existing or new services might deal with the consequences of one-parent family structure:

1. Recognition of the need of the mother without a husband at home for emotional support and social outlets could lead to a variety of services. Recreation and problem-focused groups for women in this situation, which would provide some opportunities for socially sanctioned heterosexual relationships, might go a long way in helping these parents and their children.

2. Special efforts to provide male figures to which both girls and boys can relate may have utility. This can be done in day-care centers, settlement house agencies, schools, and through the inclusion of girls in programs like the Big Brothers. It would be particularly useful for children in one-parent families to see the ways in which adults of each sex deal with each other in these situations, and at an early age.

3. Subsidization of child care and housekeeping services for parents with children too young or unsuitable for day-care services would provide greater freedom for solitary mothers to work outside the home. Training persons as homemakers and making them responsible to an agency or a professional organization would reduce the anxiety of the working parent, and provide greater insurance to both the parent and society that this important job would be done well.

More fundamental to the prevention of poverty and the problems of one-parent family status may be programs aimed at averting family dissolution through divorce, separation and desertion, particularly among lower socio-economic groups. Few public programs have addressed themselves to this problem, and there is now a good deal of evidence that the private family agencies which provide counseling services have disenfranchised themselves from the poor (5). The need to involve other institutional components in the community, such as the educational, economic and political systems, is obvious but beyond the scope of discussion in this paper (7). Increasing the number of stable and enduring marriages in the community so as to prevent the consequences of one-parent family structure may be a first line of defense, and more closely related to treating the causes rather than the effects of poverty for a large number of people who are poor.

SUMMARY

One-parent families constitute more than a fourth of that group classified as poor, and are growing in number. Family structure is seen as a variable intervening between the opportunity system and the socialization process. The task, communication, power and affectional structure within the nuclear group are influenced by the absence of one parent, and the family's ability to fulfill its social and personal functions may be adversely affected. Some of the consequences of this deviant family structure seem related to both the evolvement of low socio-economic status and its continuation from one generation to the next. Solutions must take account of this social situational problem.

REFERENCES

1. Bales, R. F. and Borgatta, E. F. "Size of Group as a Factor in the Interaction Profile." In Hare, Borgatta and Bales (Eds.), *Small Groups*. New York: Knopf, 1955.
2. Bell, W. and Boat, M. D. Urban neighborhoods and informal social relations. *Amer. J. Soc.*, 1957, 43, 391–398.
3. Bernard, J. *American Family Behavior*. New York: Harper, 1942.
4. Chilman, C. and Sussman, M. Poverty in the United States. *J. Marriage and the Family*, 1964, 26, 391–395.

5. Cloward, R. A. and Epstein, I. Private social welfare's disengagement from the poor: the case of family adjustment agencies. Mimeographed, April 1964.
6. Litwak, E. Geographic mobility and extended family cohesion. *Amer. Soc. Rev.,* 1960, 25, 385–394.
7. Lutz, W. A. Marital incompatibility. In Cohen, N. E. (Ed.), *Social Work and Social Problems.* New York: National Association of Social Workers, 1964.
8. Mittleman, B. Analysis of reciprocal neurotic patterns in family relationships. In V. Eisenstein (Ed.), *Neurotic Interaction in Marriage.* New York: Basic Books, 1956.
9. Parsons, T. and Bales, R. F. *Family Socialization and Interaction Processes.* Glencoe, Illinois: The Free Press, 1954.
10. *Poverty in the United States.* Committee on Education and Labor, House of Representatives, 88th Congress, Second Session, April 1964. U.S. Government Printing Office, Washington, D. C.
11. Slater, P. E. Contrasting correlates of group size, *Sociometry,* 1958, 6, 129–139.

Personality Development—
The Special Task of the Family

Glenn R. Hawkes

Regardless of the original lack of commitment to, or training for, the roles of parenthood, male and female members of a marital partnership are responsible for the care and socialization of their children. What methods do families use to socialize their children and what effect do these methods have on the personality development of the child? Research has not yet established a clearcut cause-effect relationship between method and result. Hawkes attempts to look at the larger context of the home atmosphere and general parental attitude where some interesting guiding principles on child rearing emerge. The family's effectiveness in working with the child in the areas of internalization of discipline, development of life goals, dealing with aggression and competition, and sex role development is discussed from this broadened perspective.

American institutions are organized to give the basic role of personality development to the family. In our highly complex society some other social institutions may take on part of the job of supplementing the family in its critical task. In the examination of personality development in a dynamic society it is necessary that we look at the importance of the family in personality formation, examine where our knowledge has led us and attempt the development of theories which will aid us with further research.

Sigmund Freud's study of the neurotic personality threw light on the importance of infantile and childhood experiences in the shaping of adult behavior. His theoretical and methodological contributions represented a revolutionary appraisal of man's emotions and intellect which highlighted first

From Glenn R. Hawkes, "Personality Development—The Special Task of the Family," in *Family Mobility in Our Dynamic Society*, ed., Iowa State University Center for Agricultural Economic Development (Ames, Iowa: Iowa State University Press, 1965), pp. 114–30. Reprinted by permission of Iowa State University Press.

the developmental process and second the impact of early interactions on this process. It is to Freud and his disciples that we owe the impetus for the intensive study of parent-child relationships and the recognition that these relationships are central to the understanding of personality formation.

It is significant to note that the insights into early experiences arose out of therapeutic experiences with neurotic adults. The attempt to overcome these unfortunate early experiences gave rise to psychoanalysis as a mode of psychiatric treatment. The first insights, following the development of the Freudian theory, came through case studies. Case study is implicit in the psychoanalytical process; its aim is to learn everything relevant about one person's behavior and motivations as well as the origins of his motivations and his capacities for growth. The analyst must deal with the totality of a specific personality as it exists today with the historical context in which it grew and failed to blossom. The case study approach, fruitful in therapy, has never lent itself to the rigorous test of modern science. Conclusions drawn from one, two or a dozen cases do not provide the fodder for conclusive statistical tests.

Sociologists must have a word for the reactionary forces which led to the ascendency of John B. Watson following the temporary rejection of Freud and his followers. Watson's philosophy of the child in the family gave rise to this statement:

> There is a sensible way of treating children. Let your behavior always be objective and kindly, firm. Never hug and kiss them; never let them sit on your lap. If you must, kiss them once on the forehead when they say goodnight. Shake hands with them in the morning.[1]

Regardless of the allegiance of any one group, Freudian or behaviorist, the following statement from the Scope and Methods of the Family Service Agency expresses well the beliefs of either group:

> The quality of family relationships has profound effects, both positive and negative, on the emotional development and the social adjustment of all members of the family. Positive experiences within a family provide the foundation for satisfactory personality development from birth to maturity.[2]

Man in his attempts at new social orders has evolved groups other than the family for the socialization process. The Oneida Community (see page 345 of this book), the Hitler Youth and the Israeli Kibbutz (see page 358 of this book) are all examples of different and at least theoretically sound ways of rearing children. In each case, however, adaptations of the original have always swung back toward the basic primary family group. The future may hold a more appropriate group, but it seems not to have been found as yet. In spite of other changes taking place within the family this primary task of developing personality remains a critical charge to the family group.

This function consists of conditioning the young to the norms and patterns of the civilization in which the family is found. Moreover those groups— schools, churches, social agencies and so forth—which work with the young all state a part of their philosophy of programming as the strengthening of family life by "helping" families rather than superseding them.

Even though society takes many risks in allowing nearly all natural parents the right to rear their own children, this assurance runs through our laws and mores. Indeed one is on shaky ground in supporting this view as always the "best" way. There must be other basic reasons why society returns after each experimentation to the basic family group as the purveyor of culture to the young.

PARENTHOOD AS A VALUE

No doubt we view parenthood as a value. In spite of or because of religious belief in life after death, children can be viewed as a representation of immortality. They constitute a link between the parent and the future. Children are our "own flesh and blood" and they represent our reach into the future. In a very real sense children also help us retain our touch with the past. Seeing our own growth patterns repeated in them we are likely to recall nostalgically our days as youngsters. The paradox of this view is the realization that children may make us seem older because they symbolize our own aging process.

We become ego involved in the successes and failures of our children. They represent the products of our psychological recipes. Through their successes and failures we evaluate our ability to rear in a sound or unsound fashion. With rising technology there is less opportunity for the direct viewing of our accomplishments. The business deal has taken the place of the newly plowed field. A TV dinner substitutes for the home-cooked meal. A "number" painting replaces the original patchwork quilt as a mark of accomplishment. It is not surprising, therefore, to hear mothers and fathers compare the date of the first word, the Little League batting average and the report cards of their offspring. Children, more and more, become the symbols of status. They represent the concrete proof of our effectiveness.

Moreover, caring for and about children symbolizes, for many, the highest form of service to mankind. Here lies the opportunity to assist the less able, the smaller member of our society. To serve mankind is suggested as a mark of maturity. What better way to prove to ourselves and others that we are able to delay the satisfactions of our own needs and to help those who are less able to match their wits against the rigors of society and nature?

I wonder, furthermore, if one strong reason for the preservation of the primary family as the vehicle for the transmission of culture is the realization that children represent concrete or real property in our cultural eyes. Each child is the product of a pregnancy individually carried and born. Even though the psychiatrist George Preston[3] reminds us that successful parents lose their children and retain their property we still speak of children as "ours" or "mine." No matter how highly noble we may be, we do not give up our property without much suffering. In fact one reason for our mobility is the opportunity it seems to offer for the increase of property.

Granted, then, the role of the family as the primary external force in the personality development of the young, what are the effects of this parent-child relationship? How do certain parental practices contribute to or detract from healthy personality development? What is the nature of interaction which promises the greatest return for all of society? What types of attitudes and values should society encourage in order to be assured that manpower is conserved? What should be the nature of the educational process to insure increasing capability as the demands of the culture increase? In short, what has research told us is the most effective way to get the job done? And what can we expect from future research?

SPECIFIC PARENTAL PRACTICES

Much research energy over the past two or three decades has been expended in an effort to specify the effects of specific parental practices on the development of the child. Many of these practices have been scrutinized because of Freudian statements to the effect that they will lead to maldevelopment. Such practices as breast feeding, late weaning, severe toilet training, and spanking have been researched. The significance of these early parental practices has been repeatedly emphasized in the analytic literature and psychoanalytical clinical practice. Moreover, parent educators have been strongly influenced by "specific practice" theory. An examination of literature available to parents reflects the deep inroads such ideas have held.

Harold Orlansky[4] made an exhaustive analysis of the research literature up to 1946. He found that researchers had failed to produce a definitive answer to the question of the relation between specific practices with infants and character or personality development. His review provided also a critical look at the inadequate research that had been attempted up to that date. Any student of child development had to develop a more cautious attitude regarding some favorite assumptions about cause and effect and personality development.

Sewell, Mussen and Harris,[5] writing in the *American Sociological Review* in 1955, found that the intervening nine years had not changed the situation markedly. As a matter of fact some of their analyses showed that in some cases where a cause and effect was postulated, the effect was opposite to that postulated!

Such analyses would seem to leave us a choice of conclusions. We can conclude that there is no relationship between specific practices, or we can conclude that the dynamic interaction between child and parent is such that specific practices get lost in the total complex of relationships. Another choice open to us is to assume that a relationship does exist but that present theoretical and methodological problems are so complex we have not yet found a way to cut to the heart of the matter. Evidence from clinical practice seems to suggest that specific practices become overshadowed by their setting. Evidence is mounting that such an approach will help us find the answers we seek. The researcher, however, is left with a most difficult field of investigation.

Martin[6] has suggested that the problem is one of theory and method. Too long we have followed the scientific methods laid down by the physical scientists. He advances the notion that we need to re-think the development of theory. Cause and effect hypotheses, as they are traditionally formulated, might not be at all appropriate with such complex problems as personality formation and parent-child relationships. Again the researcher is left with a very small measure of comfort. His education and training have not equipped him with the skills needed for this grossly different approach.

Parenthood in the Larger Setting

Patterns of Child Rearing, the report of a study by Sears, Maccoby and Levin,[7] attempted to take a look at the larger scene. Their study involved much more than specific practice as related to specific effect. They got at the over-all feelings of mothers. With the extensive interview technique they discussed with their subjects motherhood, womanliness, wifehood and related subjects. Following the interviews the data were analyzed into seven key factors which seemed to cluster and organize. Of these key factors the "warmth" of the mother was found to be the most pervasive of influences. That is to say, severity of a specific practice such as toilet training was much less critical than the attitude of the mother toward body function and mess. If mothers rejected their role as woman and wife they also tended to reject their role as mother and nurturance provider. Attitudes tended to cluster and be pervasive, spilling over into relationships with the young. For that matter these attitudes cropped up in feeling about men and husbands also.

Viewing the over-all effects of punishment rather than a specific punishment as related to a specific mis-act on the part of the child led Sears, Maccoby and Levin to conclude:

> ...the amount and use of punishment that we measured was essentially a measure of a personality quality of the mothers. Punitiveness, in contrast with rewardingness, was a quite ineffectual quality for a mother to inject into her child training. The evidence for this conclusion is overwhelming. The unhappy effects of punishment have run like a dismal thread through our findings. Mothers who punished toilet accidents severely ended up with bed-wetting children. Mothers who punished dependency to get rid of it had more dependent children than mothers who did not punish. Mothers who punished aggressive behavior severely had more aggressive children than mothers who punished lightly. They also had more dependent children. Harsh physical punishment was associated with high childhood aggressiveness and with the development of feeding problems.
>
> Our evaluation of punishment is that it is ineffectual over the long term as a technique for eliminating the kind of behavior toward which it is directed.

The conclusions regarding permissiveness, when viewed in the larger context, were much less decisive. Permissive attitudes with aggression encourages the child to express himself in an aggressive fashion. On the other hand permissiveness was associated with a low frequency of feeding and toilet problems. More research needs to be done to unravel this complex attitude and its net effect upon the child being reared.

In a series of studies performed by Hattwick[8] in which the behavior of children was rated and related to factors in the home, confirmation was found of the associations between parent behavior and child personality patterns which were noted also in case studies of the children. Relationships were found between parental overattentiveness and infantile withdrawing behavior and dependency. Furthermore, inadequate parental attention led to aggressive behavior in children. When the home background was growth oriented, good social adjustment tended to result.

At Minnesota, Radke[9] investigated the relationships between parental discipline and authority and children's behavior and attitudes. She concluded that variations in the behavior of children are related to variations in home discipline and atmosphere. Even where these changes are slight she found a marked effect in her child subjects.

In attempting to find why certain children were well adjusted, Langdon and Stout[10] studied the home atmosphere of their subjects. No specific practice could be isolated with extensive analysis. As a matter of fact they found great variance in the practices in the homes. The pervading quality found, regardless of specific practice, was the acceptance of the child by his parents. He was viewed and then treated as a unique person with characteristics innately his. Again the larger look led to some conclusions that are useful in understanding the over-all effect of the parent-child relationship. It is also significant to note that socioeconomic class, occupation of parent, number of siblings and level of aspiration of parent were not found to be significant factors in the development of the well-adjusted child.

Nationwide attention has been focused on the study by the Gluecks.[11] They found in their study of 500 delinquent and 500 nondelinquent boys that five factors in the relationship of the boy to his parents which probably operated prior to school entrance could be evaluated and summated to produce a score that would be indicative of probable future delinquency. While our concern is not necessarily with delinquency we are concerned with parental attitudes and practices which seem to predispose to certain types of behavior on the part of offspring. The five factors found were: (1) discipline of the boy by the father, (2) supervision of the boy by the mother, (3) affection of the mother, (4) affection of the father and (5) cohesiveness of the family.

The potential for trouble was found in boys who were characteristically exposed to overstrict or erratic discipline by the father. (The term overstrict, I realize, is ambiguous. The Gluecks are not very helpful in this regard. One gets the picture of justice meted out in the letter of the law and not with the spirit. I can only presume that this is what overstrict means.) The boys were given "unsuitable" supervision by the mother. (One wonders about the meaning of unsuitable.) Indifference and/or hostility was shown on the part of both parents. There was much evidence that the collection of people called the family, in these cases, was not an integrated group. That is to say there were many signs that consensus of goals, values and ideas had not taken place.

The Gluecks used the "chance of becoming" approach. They found an element of predictability but it was not sufficient that one could postulate absolute cause and effect. Their work does constitute an important step in the direction of understanding the larger setting in which child growth takes place. Furthermore, the focus on parental attitudes as shapers of personality adds mounting evidence of the necessity of understanding such attitudes before we can understand more of the dynamics of personality adjustment as it proceeds within the family.

The Fels Research Institute[12] was an early leader in conducting research on the atmosphere of the home. Clusters of behavior were found to represent major dimensions of parental behavior. Warmth, for example, emerged in both clinical and statistical analyses. This cluster was found to be made up of acceptance, direction of criticism (approval-disapproval), affectionateness, rapport, child-centeredness, and intensity of contact.

Two other key clusters helped to define the general climate of the home— objectivity of the parents' attitudes toward the child and parental control. The summation of these clusters could help to give one a picture of the nature of the home and family as a child-rearing center. And yet, the clusters did not lend themselves to integration. Again, there is the logical conclusion that behavior must be seen in the larger setting in order to understand the dynamics of development. The job of the researcher is complicated.

Another complicating, but fascinating, pattern found by the Fels Research group related to the democratic home. Democracy was found to exist on a continuum from warm and spontaneous to cold and intellectual. Where democracy existed the child was given opportunity to explore, question and test reality. Children from such homes were found to be in favored positions in the peer groups although they were often aggressive and bossy. They were in favored positions because they made their aggressiveness and bossiness work. They also rated high on activities demanding intelligence, curiosity, originality and constructiveness. Democracy as a factor had impact on behavior of the offspring. But it had a varying effectiveness because, as pointed out earlier, democracy was found to be an attitudinal approach to living which could be warm and spontaneous or it could be cold, calculating and noninterfering. There is some evidence,[13] incidentally, that this latter type of democratic home may help to produce the scholar who can pursue an intellectual problem with the type of candid objectivity often needed.

The studies at Fels were some of the first attempts to study the complex family interrelationships related to personality development of the child. Their method of direct observation has been used more and more as investigators have come to grips with the sheer necessity of understanding personality development as a factor of the social context of the family. Ackerman,[14] Hawkes,[15] Pease and Hawkes[16] and Parsons and Bales[17] have all pointed out the necessity of direct observation as a method of understanding personality development. As Ackerman states:

> It is essential to view the dominant modes of behavior in the growing child as being shaped by the total psychosocial configuration of the family rather than by the child-parent relationship in isolation. What is implied here is the need to define parental role functioning and child-parent interaction in broader context of the psychosocial pattern of the family as a whole.

This direct observation of family interaction presents some very difficult problems to the researcher. He must find ways to minimize his effect on the interaction he wishes to observe. The complexity of the interaction is such that it is almost impossible to comprehend and analyze the total interaction process without destroying what it really means. Furthermore, he must find ways to control his perceptions so that his own attitudes, biases and mental sets do not delude him into observing only that which has relevance to him. Research in this type of methodology is moving forward. The very complexity of the method means that a breakthrough may be slow in coming.

Observation without a focus is not very meaningful. Theory of inter-relationships must keep pace with research in methodology. In fact, it is safe to say that the problems may be researched concurrently. In any event, the complex family setting in which personality development forges ahead must be studied along with the sheer dynamics of personality formation. More will be said concerning theory later in the chapter.

A perusal of journals, conferences and conventions concerning themselves with children and families leads one to the conclusion that there are fewer areas of greater concern than those related to personality formation of children within the modern mobile American family. Whether the mobility be vertical or horizontal these processes merit the attention of producers and consumers of research. Winch[18] describes them as follows: (1) internalization of discipline or development of conscience, (2) development of goals or the ego-ideal, (3) lasting effects of parental control or identification and possibly (4) sex-role development.

INTERNALIZATION OF DISCIPLINE

"Social man's most necessary nuisance"[19]—conscience—has its roots in the family. The newborn is ushered into the world with all kinds of needs which demand immediate gratification. When he is hungry, he demands food. When he needs to eliminate, he eliminates. When he wants freedom of movement or relief from pain his cries connote little patience with delay. The controls which ultimately come to govern his behavior are all controls from without. They differ from conscience controls in a major way: conscience controls come from within the individual. The process of socialization is to transform outer controls to inner controls. This process is called internalization.

Three things exemplify the internalization of controls: resistance to temptation, feelings of guilt, and attaining of "good." Feelings of guilt occur when resistance to temptation has not been successful. In the more complete conscience, feelings of guilt occur when good has not been accomplished. The ultimate goal for maturity is to develop adequate conscience in children. Conscience can be too strong and it can be too weak. Early in the school years we often see manifestations of impossible ideals children have set up for themselves and for other people. When these ideals are not attained we witness guilt feelings, often of a severe nature. Many of the most severe problems in therapy are produced by too much guilt.

There are, no doubt, gross cultural and class differences in conscience. Allison Davis[20] points out that the middle class contains vastly more future rewards for present self-denial than does the subculture of the lower class. It is consistent with these differences in rewards that middle-class morality should emphasize thrift, saving, prolonged professional and vocational training and mobility for opportunity rather than immediate gratification.

The subtle ways in which cultural standards and values are imparted within the family group poses real problems for families. A study by Harris[21] and associates typifies this process. Three thousand children between the ages of 10 and 16, from a variety of towns and cities, participated. The study aimed to link home duties with an attitude of responsibility. Results of the testing did not support the hypothesis that the number of home duties assumed by the child bore a substantial relation to his sense of responsibility. Nor was there any evidence that the relationship existed with older children who had more years of family training. There appeared to be a connection, however, between the sense of responsibility in children and the type of activities in which the parents participated. The subtle influence of action seemed to override any verbal exhortations that were not backed by modeling in the adult members of the family.

In our modern mobile society with its complex problems of interaction and interrelatedness we are faced with some sobering societal deliberations. Can society tolerate the family as the cradle of conscience development? If we focus on problems of racial equality and race relations it becomes apparent that attitudes are deep-rooted and fostered early in the life of the child. Clinical evidence makes it abundantly clear that such attitudes are highly resistant to erosion. In many cases intensive therapy yields little in an attitudinal change. As we understand more about the process of internalization will it be necessary for society to develop some other institution to supplement the family in this area in order to foster the attitudes which society deems necessary to evolve?

One cannot assume that later experiences and peer associates do not have their impact. Yet the potency of the early experience is apparent. With an increasingly pluralistic society evolving primarily because of mobility, the problem takes on keener proportions.

If we take a look at the effect of religious institutions on moral and/or conscience standards we find that relatively few studies have been done. Those which have been done, however, point to the minimal effect of church attendance on honesty, cooperativeness and resistance to delinquency. With home attitude supplementation in this area society still has not found the way to re-enforce those conscience ideas which it deems vital.

DEVELOPMENT OF GOALS

The development of goals or the inculcation in the child of an ego-ideal is an important part of parental function in personality development. Research by Havighurst, Robinson and Dorr[22] points out that the child, after suffering disenchantment with parents, moves to other adults in the surroundings for goal setting. In a strong kin family society this type of goal setting could occur with adult kin, and the larger families' "way of life" would be perpetuated. In a highly mobile society the absence of kin means a reaching out for other adults to furnish ideal images. This may lead to an enrichment by breeding diversity into a society, but it may also introduce discordant factors. In a recent book about adolescent society the Hechingers[23] point out the problems for adolescents who select as their ego-ideals other teen-agers. They maintain this reduces the urge to maturity in adolescent citizens. On the other hand, Moss and Gingles[24] and Burchinal[25] found that low parental aspirations was a factor related to the early marriage of adolescents. Possibly finding ego-ideals in other than their immediate family could have raised the level of aspiration of the adolescents. A higher level of aspiration might forestall many of the problems in adolescent marriages.

Differences between expectations of males and females, while undergoing radical change, still is a confusing element in the setting of goals. Komarovsky[26] and Wallin[27] report that girls and women suffer emotionally from uncertainty as to which goals and values are appropriate and expected of them. Miller and Swanson[28] report further confusion, not necessarily due to sex differences, but because of possible basic orientation shifts of the family from entrepreneurial to bureaucratic. It is to be anticipated that mobility may produce further changes in more families as technology and bureaucracy become factors in making families move both vertically and horizontally.

Mass communication may further complicate the problem of goal setting. Impressionable children exposed to a wide range of goals never before possible may be tempted or forced to select goals highly inappropriate to their primary family group.

LASTING EFFECTS OF PARENTAL CONTROL

One approach to understanding the lasting effects of parents or the socialization impact is to view it as a process in which the child learns what is expected of him because of his age, sex and social class. Related to this is the permanency of this learning. In American culture some of the most marked expectations concern the expression of aggression in competition and achievement. Middle-class parents instruct their small boys that it is not fitting to "pick" fights, particularly with someone smaller or with a girl. On the other hand, to fail to defend oneself or one's honor is to fail. The child must, therefore, learn the difference between these two situations.

In the lower class, there is little or no cultural pressure to avoid physical contact. It may, in fact, be encouraged. Both boys and girls are expected to protect themselves with strong action.

Competitive achievement may be defined as a close ally to aggression. In middle-class families this type of action is encouraged. As a matter of fact, middle-class families seem to seek out ways for their children to compete— Little League, Scouts, 4-H and so forth. Research by Douvan[29] contributes evidence that middle-class adolescents differ from lower-class adolescents in valuing achievement for its own sake. In this study subjects established a level of performance on being rewarded: middle-class subjects tended to carry on at a high level of performance when the reward was withdrawn; lower-class subjects did not.

The lasting effects of such teachings seem to show up in the different ways in which conflicts are resolved at the adult level. Labor union members protect their rights with strikes which sometimes lead to violence. Professional groups tend to resort to debate, influencing of public opinion and, in the main, avoid a show of physical force. In a fluid class society one would expect blending of these two diverse approaches. Recently teachers in Utah and New York threatened strikes, but the strikes did not materialize. The labor unions are accused of being less vigorous than formerly. Does this mean they are moving toward middle class? With vertical mobility the effects may be less lasting than in a rigid society. In this same vein of questioning one must look and be amazed at the ability of the southern Negro to persist in nonviolence when his early learnings must have prepared him for aggressive action. It is clear that there is some persistence, but it is equally clear that change is taking place. The more subtle impact of vertical mobility must tax the resources of families in knowing what approach to use in dealing with aggression.

Sex-Role Development

In most cultures, sex-role development or sex-typing begins early in life. These differences extend far beyond anatomical characteristics but begin with them. Sex-role development refers to the identification the individual makes regarding his biological, sociological, and psychological self in the maleness-femaleness dimension. This identification comes about through his relationships with those of the same and the opposite sex.

In the family, boys find it natural and rewarding to pattern themselves after their fathers, and father is pleased to note this emulation of his qualities, attitudes and masculinity. The mother who loves the father finds such patterning acceptable in her son. Explorations, both conscious and unconscious, of being like mother convince the boy that this is not his proper or approved role. He goes back to his identification with his father. In the healthy family the same picture holds true for the girl.

Where there is parental disharmony the situation is different. When chronic antagonism exists between the parents, the boy finds that if he identifies with his father he loses his mother's love ar.d approval. If he then tries to be like his mother, he incurs his father's anger besides risking the general disapproval connected with being a "sissy."

Many investigators have found that problems related to improper sex-role development precede the school-age period. They seem to have their roots in less than adequate functioning of one or both parents. With the confusion that exists today as to proper role, freedom of role decisions and other vital questions, it is readily apparent that some maladjustment should be present. In a society where vertical mobility may be assisted by the female assuming parts of the role traditionally held only by males we can expect children to be caught in the backwash. This will continue to occur until we have learned to institutionalize the changes that are taking place in our societal practice.

Theory of Personality Development

Earlier in this chapter it was indicated that there would be a discussion of personality formation which seemed to lend itself to creative research and more particularly to the role of the family in this personality formation. Abraham H. Maslow, using well the theories of the past, has developed a concept or theory of motive hierarchy leading toward self-actualization which clearly defines many enlightened functions the family has and can play in personality formation.

According to Maslow[30] all an individual's capacities and energy are always mobilized in the interest of any strong motivational need. And although behavior is usually determined by multiple needs, only in its absence does a motivational need bcome an important determinant of behavior. Food, for example, would be a poor schoolwork incentive, because most children's hunger needs are taken care of by an almost automatic schedule of eating. Teacher approval is better, because the need for this boost to one's self-esteem is more constantly active. Further, according to Maslow, motives are hierarchically arranged; only as more basic motives are satisfied (at least minimally) do motives higher in the hierarchy become potent behavior determinants. But when motives lower in the hierarchy are satisfied, then automatically, because of the inherent nature of man, motives higher in the hierarchy motivate activity and effort. Motivational needs higher in the hierarchy keep man continuously striving as lower needs are satisfied. The hierarchical order is as follows:

1. Physiological needs, such as hunger, thirst, activity, rest.

2. Safety needs, security, and release from anxiety aroused by threats of various kinds.
3. Love needs, including love, affection, acceptance, and a feeling of belonging.
4. Esteem needs, including both self-esteem from mastery and confidence in one's worth, adequacy, and capacities, and esteem from social approval.
5. Need for self-actualization through creative self-expression in personal and social achievements; need to feel free to act, to satisfy one's curiosity, and to understand one's world.

The emergence of this fifth level of motivation, however, depends upon the prior satisfaction of the lower-order needs. A child who is hungry, insecure or unloved, whose confidence has been undermined, or who feels disapproved would not be expected to reach this fifth level. What better environment could be constructed than a family to provide for the first four needs? Within this *small* group with its adults he can be fed, clothed and sheltered, loved and encouraged to grow. Physical health and protection nearly always precede constructive and creative work. There is much reason to believe that if lower-level needs are met mobility can be handled by children with greater ease.

When all a child's lower-level needs are satisfied, he would not need to be pressed into constructive and creative study and work. In such activity for such a child, the opportunity for self-actualization in expression of talents and interests offers its intrinsic, high reward. According to Maslow's theory, a child is not driven or pressed to constructive effort; his energies for such effort from lower-order needs are released!

As Maslow states:

> From Freud we learned that the past exists now in the person. Now we must learn, from growth theory and self-actualization theory that the future also now exists in the person in the form of ideals, hopes, duties, tasks, plans, goals, unrealized potentials, mission, fate, destiny, etc. One for whom no future exists is reduced to the concrete, to hopelessness, to emptiness. For him, time must be endlessly "filled." Striving, the usual organizer of most activity, when lost, leaves the person unorganized and unintegrated. Mobility and striving seem to be very much related.
>
> Of course, being in a state of Being needs no future, because it is already *there*. Then Becoming ceases for the moment and its promissory notes are cashed in the form of the ultimate rewards, i.e., the peak experiences, in which time disappears and hopes are fulfilled.[31]

Adaptation of research efforts to this theory gives us a framework of insights into how the family succeeds or fails in its task of developing personality in the child. For adequate parenting some measure of self-actualizing must have occurred for parents. If we view children as *becoming* we would assess their development in the hierarchical order. Possibly one task is to assure ourselves that investigators are operating at the self-actualizing level. If not, we can hardly expect creativity from their efforts.

Undoubtedly the future will give us further refinement of Maslow's theory, or it may be even supplanted. In any event our task is to lend all of our creative resources to the task of determining how best we can grow the "best" children in a dynamic and mobile society.

NOTES

[1] John B. Watson, *Psychological Care of Infants and Children*, W. W. Norton, New York, 1928, pp. 81–82.

[2] Family Service Association of America, "Scope and Methods of the Family Service Agency," New York, 1953.

[3] George Preston, *The Substance of Mental Health*, Rinehart and Co., New York, 1946.

[4] Harold Orlansky, "Infant Care and Personality," *Psychological Bulletin*, 46:1–48, 1949.

[5] W. H. Sewell, P. H. Mussen and C. W. Harris. "Relationships Among Child Training Practices," *Amer. Soc. Rev.*, 20:137–48, 1955.

[6] W. E. Martin, "Rediscovering the Mind of the Child: A Significant Trend in Research in Child Development," *Merrill-Palmer Quarterly*, 6:67–76, 1959–60.

[7] R. S. Sears, E. E. Maccoby and H. Levin. *Patterns of Child Rearing*, Row, Peterson and Co., Evanston, Ill., 1947, p. 484.

[8] B. W. Hattwick, "Interrelations Between the Preschool Child's Behavior and Certain Factors in the Home," *Child Development*, 7:200–26, 1936.

    B. W. Hattwick and M. Stowell, "The Relation of Parental Over-Attentiveness to Children's Work Habits and Social Adjustments in Kindergarten and the First Six Grades of School," *Jour. of Educational Research*, 30:169–76, 1936–37.

[9] M. J. Radke, "The Relation of Parental Authority to Children's Behavior and Attitudes," University of Minnesota Institute of Child Welfare Monograph Series, No. 22, 1946.

[10] G. Langdon and I. W. Stout, *The Discipline of Well-Adjusted Children*, John Day, New York, 1952.

[11] S. Glueck and E. Glueck, *Unraveling Juvenile Delinquency*, Harvard University Press, Cambridge, Mass., 1950.

[12] A. L. Baldwin, J. Kalhorn and F. H. Breese, "The Appraisal of Parent Behavior," Psych. Monographs, Vol. 63, No. 4, 1949.

[13] Frank Barron, *Creativity and Psychological Health*, D. Van Nostrand Co., Princeton, N.J., 1963.

[14] N. W. Ackerman, "An Orientation to Psychiatric Research on the Family," *Marriage and Family Living*, 19:68–74, 1957.

[15] G. R. Hawkes, "The Child in the Family," *Marriage and Family Living*, 19:46–51, 1957.

[16] D. Pease and G. R. Hawkes, "Direct Study of Child-Parent Interactions," *Journal of Orthopsychiatry*, Vol. 30, No. 3, July, 1960.

[17] T. Parsons and R. F. Bales, *Family Socialization and Interaction Process*, Free Press, Glencoe, Ill., 1955.

[18] Robert F. Winch, *The Modern Family*, revised ed., Holt, Rinehart and Winston, New York, 1963.

[19] R. R. Sears, "The Growth of Conscience," in I. Iscoe and H. W. Stevenson, eds., *Personality Development in Children,* University of Texas Press. Austin, 1960.

[20] Allison Davis, "American Status System and the Socialization of the Child," *Amer. Soc. Rev.,* 6:345–54, 1941.

[21] D. G. Harris, K. G. Clark, A. M. Rose and F. Valasek, "The Relationship of Children's Home Duties to an Attitude of Responsibility," *Child Development,* 25:21–28, 1954.

[22] R. J. Havighurst, Myra Robinson and Mildred Dorr, "The Development of the Ideal Self in Childhood and Adolescence," *Jour. of Educational Research,* 40:241–57, 1946.

[23] Grace Hechinger and Fred Hechinger, "Teen-Age Tyranny," William Morrow and Co., New York, 1963.

[24] J. J. Moss and R. J. Gingles, "The Relationship of Personality to the Incidence of Early Marriage," *Marriage and Family Living,* 21:373–77, 1959.

[25] L. G. Burchinal, "Adolescent Role Deprivation and High School Age Marriage," *Marriage and Family Living,* 21:378–84, 1959.

[26] M. Komarovsky, "Cultural Contradictions and Sex Roles," *Amer. Jour. of Sociology,* 52:189, 1946.

[27] Paul Wallin, "Cutural Contradictions and Sex Roles: A Repeat Study," *Amer. Soc. Rev.,* 15:288–93, 1950.

[28] D. R. Miller and G. E. Swanson, *The Changing American Parent,* John Wiley & Sons, New York, 1958.

[29] Elizabeth Douvan, "Social Status and Success Strivings," *Jour. of Abnormal and Social Psychology,* 52:219–23, 1956.

[30] A. H. Maslow, "A Theory of Human Motivation," *Psychological Review,* 50:370–96, 1943.

A. H. Maslow, *Toward a Psychology of Being,* D. Van Nostrand Co., Princeton, N.J., 1962.

[31] *Ibid.,* pp. 199–200.

Child Rearing in Communes*

Bennett Berger, Bruce Hackett,
and R. Mervyn Millar**

The socialization of children—how they are taught to act and the means by which this is accomplished—can, if carefully observed and skillfully analyzed, tell a great deal about the social group of which the child is a part. After all, the child is being raised, or treated, or instructed in such a way as to fit him or her into that group. Alternatively, to understand socialization of children in a specific group, one should understand the norms and values of the group. The child-rearing process in hippie communal families is a good illustration of the sociological connection between parent and community norms. Berger et al. discuss in some detail the different organizing principles of these communes, and the manner in which communards view their children and themselves as parents. The hippie communards Berger studied believe in the essential equality of all individuals and children are no exception. Thus, they are given almost equal freedom and responsibility. Parents do not necessarily see themselves as persons responsible to "raise" or "produce" children. The mother perceives herself as still a "kid" and thus views her child differently from mothers who see themselves as adults. The father often sees himself as essentially a free agent who just happened to sire a child essentially belonging to the mother. As a result, he may not stay around long enough even to see his child begin walking.

*Abstracted by the Guest Editor with permission of the authors from a report to the National Institute of Mental Health, Child Rearing Practices of the Communal Family.

**Bennett M. Berger, Ph.D., is Professor of Sociology, Department of Sociology, University of California at Davis 95616. Bruce Hackett is Associate Professor of Sociology, University of California at Davis. R. Mervyn Millar is Research Assistant with the project on Child-Rearing Practices of the Communal Family.

From Bennett M. Berger, Bruce M. Hackett, and Mervyn Millar, "Child-Rearing Practices in the Communal Family," in Hans Peter Dreitzel (ed)., *Family, Marriage and the Struggle of the Sexes*, (New York: The Macmillan Company, 1972) pp. 271–300. Reprinted by permission of the authors.

INTRODUCTION

Although the major mandate of our study was child rearing in hip communes, we discovered very early in our participant-observation that we could not begin to understand the lives of commune children without close attention to the social structure of family life in communes and to the culture (beliefs, religions, ideologies) which envelops the lives of children in them. Our report, then, is concerned not only with the specific character of child-child and child-adult interaction in communal families but with communal life in general, which constitutes the familial and other environmental settings in which and through which the lives of children are made meaningful. In addition to the child-rearing data *per se,* therefore, we are reporting other data under the structural headings which bear most directly upon the viability of the communal setting, and, therefore, upon the role of children. Primary among these are the basic economic arrangements of communal life, the structure of nuclear family units and the character of male-female relations in them, the problems of leadership, authority, and decision-making, recruitment, and ideology.

TWO BASIC DISTINCTIONS

In our initial attempts to make sense of our findings thus far, we have found it useful to make distinctions between urban and rural communes, and between what we call "creedal" and "non-creedal" communes.

We have found the urban-rural distinction useful because urban communes are easier to start—if not to sustain; all it takes is a rented house and a group of willing people. Because they are easier to start, urban communes tend to have a more fluid membership; it is sometimes difficult to tell who is a member, who is a visitor, and who is a crasher. Around the college, university, and bohemian districts of the San Francisco Bay area, group living is not a very deviant choice for young people, many of whom are poor and in the early stages of breaking away from their parental families. This suggests that urban communes represent a less thorough commitment to serious communal experiment than rural communes because choosing to live in an urban commune is not so profoundly consequential a choice; it does not necessarily involve isolation from and inaccessibility to one's former milieu, a radical change in the structure of one's daily life, and engagement in unfamiliar forms of work which may require the development of new skills which present a deep challenge to one's very identity.

It is for reasons like these that we believe that rural communes represent a relatively more advanced stage, a purer form of the "New Age" movement than urban communes do. It is for this reason, too, that a recurrent topic of discussion in urban communes is whether to get some land and move to the country, while rural communes almost never talk about collectively moving back to the city—although individual communards of course do.

The distinction between creedal and non-creedal communes is more complex. Creedal communes are those organized around a systematic or otherwise formally elaborated doctrine or creed to which members are either required

205

or eventually expected to adhere: communes of "Jesus Freaks," or ashrams devoted to the teachings of an Indian saint, or crusading communes devoted to the eccentric visions of a self-proclaimed Messiah. Creedal communes often have sacred books or other written documents which are regarded as the repository of the groups affiliated with a religious leader or movement whose following includes more than a single commune. Some creedal communes, however, do not have constitutive documents or sacred books, but in these communes there are usually one or two central figures whose oral command of doctrine (the ability to "lay down a good rap"), backed by a physical or psychological authority, serves as an embodiment of collective beliefs.

Although in non-creedal communes there is no formal repository of ideology or collective beliefs, there does tend to be a taken-for-granted set of beliefs which is assumed to be widely known and shared by the members, even though constitutional precepts or other written documents are absent. But the distinction between creedal and non-creedal communes is not ideologically hard and fast because there is often very little difference in the content of what they believe, and it is this fact, among others, which gives to communes, regardless of whether or not they are creedal, the character of a movement.

Although much of the hip-communal value system or ideology transcends the distinction between creedal and non-creedal communes, the distinction is important for several reasons. For one thing, creedal communes almost by their very nature tend to have a firmer structure of authority (and are occasionally extremely authoritarian) because one of the things a formal creed does is make explicit the rules of conduct which adherents are expected to observe. Rules against drug use, for example, are almost exclusive to creedal communes. Particularly where the creed is a religious or quasi-religious doctrine, there is frequently a holy man or his chief disciple(s) at hand in whom ultimate authority resides. Members of creedal communes seem on the whole somewhat younger than members of non-creedal communes perhaps because their more tender years make them more susceptible to grand cosmologies and charismatic leaders. Because creedal communes are sometimes missionary (while non-creedal ones are rarely or never so) their membership tends to be more open so that at any given time there are likely to be several members or incipient members who, fresh from the street or responding to the missionary appeal, do not actually know each other or the older members very well. Non-creedal communes, on the other hand, tend to rely on friendship networks as sources of membership, so that members of non-creedal communes tend to know each other very well. Indeed, non-creedal communes may be said in general to rely upon the history of friendship as a source of solidarity which creedal communes try to find in their commitment to doctrine.

WHAT COMMUNARDS BELIEVE

There now exist in the literature of the hip-communal subculture several more or less adequate attempts to summarize the values, beliefs, and ideology of this movement (Fred Davis, Bennett Berger, Nathan Adler, Philip Slater, Theodore Roszak, Kenneth Keniston and Charles Reich), and our own findings have not produced reasons for major argument with them. It should suffice in this summary report to affirm that the ideology is a genuinely "contra-cultural" (Milton Yinger) or culturally revolutionary one, though not thereby directly threatening in a political sense to established interests, in that its major tenets represent an almost systematic reaction against or disaffirmation of the culture taken for granted by most middle class Americans of the middle generation.

Thus, they prefer candid, total, effusive, and unrestrained expression of feeling, joy and sensuality, as well as anger and hostility, to the careful, guarded, modulated balances, and instrumental (or manipulative) modes of personal relatedness; "upfrontness" is for them a term of high praise. They want to possess and consume as little as they need rather than as much as they can be induced to want. They affirm the present, the immediate, the NOW, over careful future planning and anticipated future gratification. They value the "natural" for nature is benign—particularly for rural communards—for ex-ample in nudity, organic foods, organic architecture, etc., over the civilized, the synthetic, the contrived. They prefer the colorful and the romantic to the classical, the sober, and the orderly. Their sensibility is given to impulse and spontaneity rather than calculations and structure. Although they have and recognize leaders, their modes of relationship to each other affirm brotherhood and egalitarianism rather than hierarchy. They prefer the primitive to the sophisticated, transcendent ecstasy to order and security. They prefer invoking mystical and magical forces to scientific ones. Their impulse is to share as much of their lives as they can with the community of their brothers and sisters, some-times even beyond the point where it threatens those areas of privacy and reserve to which many communards are still at least partially attached. They want to share a mutually dependent communal fate without the obligatory constraints of social bonds; indeed, they depend upon the affirmation by their brothers and sisters of the value of personal expressiveness to enable each of them to exercise an unbounded freedom to do his thing; to engage, above all, in a spiritual search for personal meaning, for health and happiness, for self and selflessness, for transcendence and godhood.

Like any other value system, moreover, the hip communal one is replete with logical contradictions and discontinuities between theory and practice. Freedom and communal solidarity can and do cause conflicts, and the balance between privacy and communal sharing is a recurrent problem in several of the communes we have observed. Despite the emphasis on spontaneity and impulse, the apples have to be picked when ripe, the goats have to be milked regularly, the meals have to be cooked and the dishes washed. Despite the benignity of nature, something has to be done about the flies in the kitchen and the mice in the cupboard. Despite egalitarianism, some communards are deferred to more than others; despite the emphasis on the present and the immediate, wood has to be laid up for the winter, crops put in for the growing season, and money set aside for the rent or the mortgage and the taxes; despite transcendent ecstasy, the communards have to be discreet about acid or peyote freak-outs in town. And they wear clothes when alien eyes will be offended by their nudity.

Like other value systems, finally, the hip-communal versions may be re-garded as an adaptive response to circumstances rather than a transcendence of them. Perhaps the best things in life *are* free, but that is certainly more convenient for poor people to believe than for rich people; perhaps urban-industrial society will sink into oblivion under the weight of its garbage, its pollution, its racial conflicts, and its individual loneliness and personal estrangement, but that is certainly more convenient for down-home country folk to believe, secure in their possession of the primitive skills it will take to survive the apocalypse, than it is for the urban professional—who may not be able to change a light bulb—to believe. Most people try to make moral capital out of the resources available to them—including not only communards but social scientists.

Nevertheless, communal ideology is important because it has serious consequences, as will be made evident below, for the rearing of children and for most other common concerns, for it affects everything from the nursery rhymes (". . . this little piggy had yogurt . . .") which are sung to children, to the very conception of what children are: autonomous human beings, equal to adults.

RECRUITMENT

Commune recruitment comes by and large from the pool of middle class youth in the larger society. Friendship networks in the youth culture, whose members already have some commitment to many of the ideas in the hip belief system, are the major source of new members for communes. In urban, non-creedal communes, it is usually a matter of deciding to share living arrangements with a group of friends or of moving into one previously established by other friends. Given this prior knowledge of many of the people and the ideas they share, as well as the mutual economic interest young, poor people have in sharing their resources for food and housing, such conflicts that arise are only rarely concerned with major ideological matters, except when interpersonal hostilities are escalated into a moral confrontation (for example, when the suggestion of one member that a Shell No-Pest strip be hung in the kitchen was met with accusations that he was in favor of poisoning nature), or when an occasional major upheaval (for example, a drug bust) provokes a search for blame.

Creedal communes, on the other hand, are usually founded by an individual and a few of his disciples, although they may often expand in terms of friendship networks, such as non-creedal ones. While the sources of recruitment are similar, actual induction into creedal communes often has a more formal or ceremonial character, sometimes because the required ideological credentials are more explicit (e.g., abstention from drugs, acceptance of Christ, etc.) and sometimes because they are more at variance, possibly to an extreme extent, with the ideas that even an alienated youth is ready to believe.

In creedal communes, then, there may be books, lectures, encounter groups, initiations, and other rituals that a prospective member may be required to go through in order to achieve one or another stage of membership on his way to fully accredited status. In noncreedal communes, on the other hand, recruitment is much less formalized. In urban places, where turnover tends to be rapid, a new member or couple is likely to be accepted when a room becomes available if he or they are merely friends of friends, and if the prospective member is particularly attractive or compatible, room may be made for him or her. Because turnover tends to be less rapid in rural, non-creedal communes and because family solidarity tends, therefore, to be stronger, new members are accepted much less easily. Members may be privileged to invite a guest, usually a friend, for a limited period who, if the others like him, may be asked to stay longer and eventually, if he wishes, be considered for membership at a commune meeting. In non-creedal communes, then, the difference between a transient, guest, extended visitor, probationary member, and member is sometimes difficult to tell; with the exception of fully accredited members, the transitions are gradual.

In our analysis of recruitment to communes, we are currently exploring two interpretive perspectives, one of them, we believe, quite unusual. The first is whether communal development, particularly in its rural manifestations, can be understood as continuous with long-existing social trends; for example, the exodus from the cities, the suburbanization of the past 25 years (of which the parents of communards were presumably a part) which expressed at least partly the ideology of "togetherness" much publicized in the late 1940s and 50s: the suburban family, warm and secure in its domestic enclave full of plenty. Other existing social trends include the increasing diffusion of the encounter movement in middle-class circles, the development of homogeneous communities, represented by retirement communities and apartment developments renting exclusively to young "swingles," groups which come together on the basis of common problems they have by virtue of age or some other status attribute which they can solve collectively but not singly. In this perspective, communes are not nearly so radical a phenomenon as they are commonly thought to be.

The other perspective, of course, is that communes represent a radically discontinuous social trend which is best understood from the standpoint of deviance theory. In support of the first perspective is the fact that joining most communes does not involve a conversion experience for most members; it is the outcome of an individual's confrontation of available alternatives and situational contingencies, and from that perspective is no more deviant—though statistically less likely—than entrance into business or the professions. In support of the second perspective is the radical divergence in ideology, world view, and personal conduct from those sanctioned by law and custom in the nation represented by Richard Nixon.

There is obvious sense in the latter perspective, but we think that there is much that can be done with the former perspective. There is a sense in which the more serious rural communards, despite their apparently total rejection of middle class industrial styles of life, may be said to be conservative in the sense that this term is sometimes applied to rural or small town folk who resist the technological incursions of modernity. Concerned primarily with the creation and sustenance of a relatively self-contained community composed of people they regard as kinsmen, tribesmen, clansmen, they are sometimes distrustful of strangers, intolerant of threats to their solidarity, and suspicious of unfamiliar vibrations. We intend to explore these matters more fully by using our interview data to make inferences about the extent to which the communal phenomenon represents a more or less reluctant and *ad hoc* adaptation for youth without more attractive alternatives, and the extent to which it is a pioneering attempt to recreate or restore some of the lost but nostalgically still-yearned-for rural virtues on a postindustrial basis.

A distinctive normative feature of communal life is the desire for economic independence or self-sufficiency. Rural communes, especially of the non-creedal variety, emphasize agricultural life, and take self-sufficiency ideally to mean that they consume only that which is produced on the land—including not only food, but the making of clothing and shelter from available raw materials. None of the communes we observed have achieved such self-sufficiency, but they often interpret this in developmental terms: It reflects the newness of the commune, the priority of survival, and remains an aim to be achieved at an indefinite future time.

For the present, "unearned" income is crucial to the majority of communes, rural and urban, which we have studied. Welfare is a major source of income on which many communes we have seen, particularly rural ones, depend, a fact which serves to enhance the attractiveness of unattached mothers and their babies in much the same way that in the working class districts of industrializing England, eighteenth and early nineteenth century mothers with several illegitimate children were regarded as desirable wives because the children were significant more as breadwinners than as mouths to feed. "Crazy" people with disability income from the state are also a not uncommon phenomenon in communal settings.

The Department of Agriculture's surplus food program is also an important source of sustenance, particularly in rural places. Although we have been to more than one delicious communal dinner in which the bartered-for freshly caught red snapper was swimming in surplus butter, surplus food distribution is itself too little institutionalized to allow for real dependence on it. More important as another source of income is a category we call "windfalls," which include occasional inheritances, birthday checks from parents or grandparents, or other unsolicited gifts from relatives and benefactors (communards tend to come from relatively prosperous backgrounds and the communal movement has occasionally enlisted the support of wealthy benefactors). We suspect that this source of income may be more important than it may appear at first glance.

Agriculture in rural communes tends to be limited to a well organized and sometimes extensive garden growing a wide variety of vegetables, and the cultivation of some fruit trees. Animal husbandry, limited mainly to chickens for eggs and goats for milk, is not highly developed, perhaps because it would require levels of technology and rational social organization which would threaten the valued looseness of communal life at the present time. An expenditure of $10 per month per person for food not provided by the land seems at this writing to be an accurate estimate; $40 per month per person is about the median contribution to the communal treasury expected of each member but this is an expectation rather than a fact. Some who can afford it pay more, and those who have no personal sources of income may be supported by the group so long as it is economically feasible and they are valued members in other respects. Communal families also occasionally discuss at meetings whether members should contribute all of their income regardless of what it is, but at one meeting we attended this proposal caused a great deal of controversy and a bitter remark by one member that he would contribute all his income if it were a real family, by which he did not mean a blood family but a more "together" one.

Much non-grown food is procured through trade rather than purchase; barter arrangements are valued for social as well as economic reasons, and there is typically considerable exchange of vegetables and goat's milk for fish, wool, grain, hardware, and similar commodities. "Gathering" is also a widespread source of food supply in the rural communes we have studied—as in the extensive picking of the rich supply of a variety of wild berries along the northern California coast during what one communard, quoting Yeats, referred to as "the season of mists and mellow fruitfulness."

Scavenging is likewise important, although perhaps not primarily as a matter of practical economics. A skilled picker-over of the county dump in one commune and a cook in another who can obtain and utilize the produce discarded when supermarket vegetable displays are arranged are highly valued people, and ingenious methods for recycling a variety of materials find frequent appreciation, though for what seem more aesthetic and political reasons than economic ones. Indeed, the motif of survival is an important one in the hip setting, and almost anything that contributes to it in what is regarded as a hostile social environment is cause for satisfaction, although this motif is more prevalent among hippies who live in loose-knit communities than those in relatively well established communes. In either case, however, there exists considerable concern for the development of what could be termed a non-growth economic system.

Whereas most rural communes, particularly of the non-creedal variety, see to their economic needs through subsistence farming, barter, welfare, and windfalls, some rural communes and most urban ones, in addition to the latter two, have other sources of income. In a model urban commune, for example, some members are likely at any given time to be employed in a relatively straight job; small time drug-dealing provides some income in one urban commune we studied closely, and probably in others. But in addition to these, several communes and near communes, urban and rural, are organized around collective enterprises which are both ideologically respectable and remunerative as well, such as rock bands, "free schools," automobile repair, underground newspapers, and other institutions of the hip community.

It is important to note that the relationships developed from these enterprises have sometimes served as the basis upon which communes are formed, in which communion itself rather than the economic enterprise, becomes the central focus.

Moreover, some urban and rural communes have well-developed cottage industries which provide a major source of income. Although there are exceptions, there seems to be some tendency for these communes to be creedal, to adhere to an elaborate system of religious doctrine. The firmer authority structure of these communes may contribute the essential element that makes industry possible, namely, a commitment to a relatively regularized and impersonal devotion to duty. And the enterprises themselves, e.g., a restaurant or an incense factory, bind the members together, require relatively continuous work on behalf of the group, limit outside contacts which may undermine loyalty to the commune, and result in a clearly collective monetary income.

It is also true that the nature of the work associated with industry is accepted at best only ambivalently in the hip world. The avowed and repeatedly voiced ideal is to undertake only those tasks which are intrinsically and not merely instrumentally valued, to eliminate the distinction between work and play, to make work a holy and a personal concern. This is easier to accomplish in rural, agricultural communes where we have encountered quite explicit attempts to tailor the *pace* of work to what is regarded as an "organic" model. Work should be slow, periodic, integrated and not separated from other spheres of life such as courtship, play, "visiting," and even philosophical reflection; not, that is to say "alienated."

One consequence of this morality is to actually enlarge the individual's contribution to collective welfare, precisely because it is viewed as self-serving rather than coerced. In the cottage industries of creedal communes, on the other hand, it is only a strong ideology of service that stands between an individual's labors and his sense of doing alienated work.

One of the most potentially important consequences of this approach to work is its application to the status of children. One rural creedal commune has recently been extensively debating a proposal to have children over the age of six join adults in doing the work of the farm and another urban creedal commune has actually organized the children around their own cottage industry. The stated rationale for this is that it will both enhance the independence of children and promote the desired integration of work and play. There is a sense in which communards, having rejected middle-class models of maturity, are faced with having to rethink the definitions of childhood, adulthood, and the relations between them. And there is more than a suggestion that this rethinking involves a rejection of the idea of children as incompetent dependents with a special psychology needing special protections and nurturings. Like the big "kids" who are their parents, communal children seem to be just smaller kids, less skilled, less experienced, and only perhaps less wise.

CHILDREN

The birth of a child, particularly in a rural commune and especially if the birth is "natural" as many of them are, is often the occasion of a collective celebration of great significance. In the case of the earliest first generation communards, the event can have a virtually constitutional meaning, symbolizing the collective property as a home to its occupants, and the occupants themselves as members of a single family. Natural childbirth is additionally constitutional in the degree to which its clear cut contrast with the studied impersonality of the hospital setting gives palpable reality to the communards' rejection of those technologies which are seen as depersonalizing of life in general.

In partial contrast, however, to the solidarity-affirming nature of birth ceremonies, communal children tend to be viewed as rather independent, self-contained persons, although they participate, to be sure, in the higher cosmic unities (for example, in the widespread belief and slogan that "we are all One"). This is of special interest because the ways in which adults conceptualize and thus act toward children vary historically and between social groups, and the hippie theory of children is in some respects distinctive.

212

In viewing the history of how children are conceptualized by adults, social scientists have thus far emphasized the differences between preindustrial, agricultural, or sometimes lower-class views on the one side, and industrial or middle-class views on the other. In the former view, the status of children is seen as essentially ascribed at birth and rooted in the kinship system. In this view, children are seen as simply small or inadequate versions of their parents, totally subject to traditional or otherwise arbitrary parental authority. The modern industrial middle-class view, by contrast, tends to treat the child as a distinctive social category: children have their own special psychology, their own special needs, patterned processes of growth often elaborated into ideas about developmental states which may postpone advent to "full" adulthood well into a person's twenties and sometimes still later. The task of parents and other socializers in this view is to raise the child according to scientifically elaborated principles of proper child management, a process which in many middle-class families results in the differentiation of family roles in a way that transforms a woman-with-child into a full-time child raiser.

The view that we found prevalent in the hip-communal settings studied fits neither of these models with precision. Young people are regarded as independent of the family but not as members of an autonomous category of children; instead, their status is likely to be ascribed as that of person, a development which can be understood as part of an equalitarian ethos, and as complementary to parallel developments in the status of females from women (or even mothers) to people, and in the status of men from being characterized in invidious status terms to being characterized as above all a human being.

As a practical matter, however, children are not simply independent, autonomous individuals. Age makes an important and understandable difference. Infants and "knee babies" are almost universally in the charge of their mothers who have primary responsibility for their care. Communards, particularly rural ones, frequently discuss the possibility of communalizing even infants, as in the notion of placing infants at an available breast rather than an exclusively parental one but this proposal seems as yet to be too radical. We have, however, made several observations of what could be called communal child care; for example, collective feeding, bathings, etc.

Children aged two to four or slightly older frequently belong to the commune in a stronger sense than infants and knee babies because they are less dependent upon continuous supervision although even with children of this age the conventional pattern of sharing their care is largely limited to the group of mothers-with-children. This is not to say that young children do not get a lot of fathering; they do. Fathers hold the children often, feed them, cuddle them, and may be attentive in other respects. This depends upon the personal predispositions of the men involved. There are not strong norms apparent which require the attentiveness of fathers.

For children older than four or five, the responsibilities of either parents or the other adult communards may be much attenuated. All children are viewed as intrinsically worthy of love and respect but not necessarily of attention. As they grow out of primitive physical dependence upon the care of adults, they are treated and tend to behave as just another member of the extended family, including being offered and taking an occasional hit on a joint of marijuana as it is passed around the family circle. When problems arise, children are particularly susceptible to being labeled and understood astrologically as cosmic wards, with their own karma or fate and their own problems that they must work out themselves. They are expected to use first names in referring to their parents and other adults (the children themselves have names like Cloud, Forest, Blue Jay, River, Sweet Pea, etc.), are seen as the equal of adults (they fall quickly and easily into use of the hip vernacular), and are in more than a few instances drawn into doing adult work. In one setting the children have, with adult approval, established their own separate residences.

The extent to which a child belongs to its parents or to the extended communal family is more often due to sequential development occurring as the child grows older than to a variation in types of communes. Insofar as there exists a role for adults in facilitating the development of children, the role is essentially exemplary (charismatic) rather than paternalistic and authoritarian (traditional), or didactic and hortatory (rational). In spite of this limitation which learning-through-imitation-of-adults places on the belief that children must work out their own fate, attempts are seriously made by adults to allow children to grow naturally, to be autonomous and free. But the single most important belief governing the relation between children and adults is that the experiences had by children not be fateful or self-implicating for adults, that adults cannot be legitimately characterized in terms of what they do with or to their children—in rather clear contrast to both preindustrial and middle-class views in which the behavior of children reflects upon their parents who are in some sense responsible for it.

In saying this, some important cautions are in order. First, the great majority of the children we have observed are six or under and there are numerous communes that are only now beginning to recognize a schooling problem, and it may be that in time a distinctive child psychology and set of child management practices will emerge. There may also be important sex differences in the ways adults relate to children; communal ideologies tend to be elaborated by men, and the men are clearly the most mobile sex (from time to time women express some wishes that men would spend more time with the children), and therefore most likely to seek freedom from parental responsibilities—a freedom that is itself legitimated in part by the view of children as autonomous.

The women share this view, also, and benefit from its application. One young mother, harried with the care of her two-year-old, said, "What I wanted was a baby; but a kid, that's something else." That is to say, having babies is good because it is natural, organic, earthy, and beautiful, and besides which babies represent human potential unspoiled by the corrupting influence of repressive institutions. But "raising" a child involves obligations to which they have not committed themselves in the sense that many middle-class mothers who regard their lives as settled and their futures as a working out of what is already implicitly present (home, husband, and children), devote themselves to the full-time job of child rearing. As we have noted, however, hippies, including communal mothers, tend to regard themselves as kids, their lives as unsettled, their futures uncertain, and are generally unwilling to sacrifice their own personal questings for meaning, identity, transcendence, etc. to full-time devotion to child rearing. It is in this context that the hippie theory of children seems most relevant.

Communards generally tell us that communes are good for the children, one of the meanings many of their own parents almost certainly gave to their suburban communities. The setting itself may be said to possess medicinal qualities. In this respect there may be an important continuity between the generations, although communards frequently report their own childhoods were frustrating experiences of little autonomy and little opportunity to develop real skills. In relatively isolated and sometimes bucolic rural communes, it is possible to grant children much autonomy without much risk of waywardness, and children do, in fact, enjoy some of what are probably the real benefits of an inadvertent rather than a compulsory education.

Everything we have said about the children of the communes occurs in the context of hippie relationships and family structures, and it is important to understand these, not only because they are the most palpably real aspect of the research scene but because they contain the seeds of the potential futures of the commune movement.

The most important single feature of hip relationships is their fragility. We mean by this not that many of the relationships don't last; quite the contrary. In several of our more stable communes couples have been "together" as long as the commune has existed (two to three years), and sometimes longer. We mean, rather, that there tend to be few if any cultural constraints or structural underpinnings to sustain relationships when and if they become tension-ridden or otherwise unsatisfying. The uncertainty of futures hovers over hip relationships like a probation officer, reminding the parties of the necessary tentativeness of their commitments to each other.

Very few nuclear units, for example, are legally married; neither the men nor the women have the kinds of jobs that bind them to a community; in other respects their investments in the environmental locale or its institutions are minimal. Like many of their parents (whom theorists have suggested have been highly mobile—a hypothesis which we will test in our interviewing), they move around a great deal, getting into and out of "intimate" relations rather quickly through such techniques as spontaneous "encounter" and other forms of "up-frontness." And above and beyond these, there is a very heavy emphasis on "present orientation"—a refusal to *count on* futures as a continuation of present arrangements—and a diffuse desire to remain "kids" themselves in the sense of unencumberedness, a freedom *from* the social ties that constrain one toward instrumental action.

Yet despite the fact of (and the attitudinal adjustment to) the fragility of relationships, there are romantic images also superimposed. Although the fragility of old man–old lady relationships is a fact, communards of all sorts are generally reluctant to believe in a future of serial monogamy. Many communards, particularly the women, hope for an ideal lover or a permanent mate but tend to have not much real expectation that it will happen. Instead, compensatory satisfactions are found in the *image* of the communal family and household, always full of people, where a group of brothers and sisters, friends as kin, spend all or most of their time with each other, working, playing, loving, rapping, "hanging out"—where wedding bells, far from breaking up the old gang, are themselves so rare that they are occasions for regional celebrations of solidarity when they do ring out.

Where it exists, it is the fact of communal solidarity which functions as the strongest support for fragile relations among couples. For when the communal scene is a wholesome and attractive one, as it sometimes is, couples whose relationship is very unstable may elect to stay together in order to share those benefits rather than threaten them by breaking up.

But in spite of the fragility of relationships in a system which defines futures as uncertain and in an ideology emphasizing spontaneity and freedom, heterosexual couples are the backbone of most communes, urban or rural, creedal or not. They seem more stable and dependable as members than single people do, if only because their search for partners is ended, even if that ending is temporary. The temporary character of the relationships is more pronounced in urban communes, both, we believe, because the very presence of couples in rural comunes is itself generally evidence of more stable commitment, and because of the higher probability in urban scenes of meeting another man or woman who is ready and willing to enter into a close relationship at little more than a moment's notice.

When a couple has a child, their mobility is reduced somewhat, of course, even when the child is the product of a previous union of either the female or male. But only "somewhat," because of the importance of what we call the "splitting" phenomenon, particularly as it applies to men. We mentioned previously that children (especially very young ones) "belong" to their mothers, and that norms *requiring* paternal solicitude for children are largely absent. What this means is that fathers are "free"—at the very least free to split whenever they are so moved. Since they are not "legally" fathers (even if they biologically are) they have no claims on the child, and since there is generally a strong communal norm *against* invoking the legal constraints of straight society (i.e., calling the police), fathers have no obligation to the child that anyone is willing to enforce. Moreover, no norm takes priority over the individual's (particularly the male's) search for himself, or meaning, or transcendence, and if this search requires father's wandering elsewhere "for a while," there is nothing to prevent it.

One consequence of this family pattern is the frequency of woman-with-child (and without old man) in many of the communes we have studied—although this occurs as often as a result of the woman-with-child arriving on the commune scene that way as it does as a result of her partner "splitting." A situation like this does not typically last a long time in any commune we have studied, although it was present in almost all of them. Even when the women involved say they prefer celibacy, there is some doubt that they actually do. One afternoon in a tepee, three young women (without men) with infants on the breast agreed that they welcomed a respite from men, what with their bodies devoted almost full time to the nursing of infants. Within a week, two of them had new old men and the third had gone back to her old one. Celibacy or near celibacy occurs only in those creedal communes whose doctrines define sexual activity as impure or as a drain on one's physical and spiritual resources for transcendence.

But although celibacy is rare and although couple relations are fragile, this should not be taken to mean that sex is either promiscuous or disordered. At any given time, monogamous coupling is the norm in all the communes we studied closely; in this respect hippies tend to be more traditional than the "swingers" and wife-swappers one reads about in the middle class. Although there are communes whose creed requires group marriage (in the sense that all the adults are regarded as married to all the others, and expected to have sexual relations with each other), we have not studied any of these at first hand. But even in communes where coupling is the norm, there seems to be evidence of a natural drift toward group marriage—although it may still be ideologically

216

disavowed. For one thing, when couples break up in rural communes, it is as likely as not that each will remain on the land; and this occurs frequently in urban communes too. Without a drift toward group marriage, situations like this could and do cause great communal tensions which threaten the survival of the group. Whereas, on the other hand, a not uncommon feature of communes is a situation in which over a long period of time, many of the adults have had sexual relations with each other at one or another point between the lapses of "permanent" coupling. Under these conditions, group marriage can seem like a "natural" emergence rather than unnaturally "forced" by a creed—a natural emergence which, by gradually being made an item of affirmed faith, can conceivably solve some of the problems and ease some of the tensions generated by the fragility of couple relations and the break-ups which are a predictable result of them. Broken-up couples may still "love" each other as kin, under these conditions—even if they find themselves incapable of permanently sharing the same tent, cabin, or bed, an incapacity more likely to be explained astrologically than any other way. (Astrology is used to explain "problems" with respect to children and intimate relations between couples.)*

But the widespread presence of women-with-children as nuclear units in the communes is not merely an artifact of the splitting of men or an expression of the belief of hip parents in the unwisdom of staying together "for the sake of the child." The readiness of hip women to bear the child even of a "one-night stand" is supported by social structures which indicate its "logic." Unlike middle-class women, for example, a hippie female's social status does not depend upon her old man's occupation; she doesn't need him for that. The state is a much better provider than most men who are available to her. Having a baby, moreover, helps solve an identity problem by giving her something to do. An infant to care for provides more meaning and security in her life than most men could. And in addition, these women are often very accpetable to communes as new members. They are likely to be seen as potentially less disruptive to ongoing commune life than a single man; they are likely to be seen as more dependable and stable than a single man; and these women provide a fairly stable source of communal income through the welfare payments that most of them receive. From the point of view of the hip mothers, commune living is a logical choice; it solves some of the problems of loneliness—there are always others around; it provides plenty of opportunities for interaction with men—even if they aren't always immediately "available"; instead of having to go out to be picked up, a hip mother can rely on a fairly large number of male visitors passing through the commune, with whom she may establish a liaison. And if she does want to go out, there are usually other members of the family present to look after her child, and other males to act as surrogate fathers.

If these descriptions sound as if they bear some similarity to working-class or lower-class patterns in extended-kin groups, the similarity is not inadvertent,

---

*We think, indeed, that there is a close relationship between the commune movement, on the one hand, and the complex of stirrings in the middle class which includes the encounter movement, swingers, sensitivity training, and the incipient gestures toward group marriage represented by "wife-swapping." Each represents an attempt to cope with similar problems (e.g., alienation, existential discontents with the prospects or the realities of middle-class life) by groups of people differently situated in the life-career cycle: the communards being mainly college dropouts in their twenties, the others being mainly married couples in their thirties or forties with children and already well into their professional careers with which they may have become disenchanted.

although the correspondence is far from perfect. Communal life tends to be very dense, although most communes do have clearly marked areas of privacy. Most communes of all kinds are typically divided into public or communal areas and private areas. In rural communes, there is usually a communal house where people cook, eat, and engage in other collective activities such as meetings, musicales, entertainment of visitors, and so on. In addition there may be a library, sewing rooms, room for spare clothing, and other needs for whose satisfactions collective solutions are made. But rural communes tend to discourage "living" (i.e., sleeping) in the communal house, except when the commune is crowded with visitors, guests, or new prospective members. Sleeping quarters are private, and one of the first expressive commitments of a new member in a rural commune is building his own house (containing usually a single room)—a tepee, an A frame, a dome, a shack or lean-to—out of available local materials, and ideally out of sight of the nearest other private dwelling.

In urban communes, the kitchen and living room-dining room generally serve as communal areas, whereas the bedrooms are private and "belong to" the couples who sleep in them. Privacy, of course, is more difficult to sustain in urban communes than in rural ones, even though knocking on closed or almost closed bedroom doors before entering is an item of communal good manners.

In urban and rural communes, children tend to sleep in the same room as their parents (or mother), although if space is available older children may sleep in a room of their own or, as in one rural commune, in a separate house. Although a typical item of commune architecture is the use of sleeping lofts both to increase privacy and to make use of unused space above the head but below the roof, children are regularly exposed to sexual activities—as is true in any community where people cannot afford a lot of space. But the less than perfect privacy for sexual and excretory functions—particularly when the commune is crowded with visitors or crashers—although sometimes a source of tension, is not typically a major problem because of the latent communal belief in most places that no normal and honorable functions *need* to be hidden from public view. The high value of upfrontness, the commonness of nudity, the glass on bathroom or outhouse doors (or no doors at all) and the general belief that people are and should be perfectly transparent to each other is not always enough to overcome years of training in shyness, modesty, etc., regarding sexual and excretory functions, but it generally is enough to at least constrain people to regard their remaining shynesses as hang-ups which they should try to overcome in the name of communal sharing of as much as can conceivably be shared.

Nevertheless, even under crowded conditions, communards develop ways of creating private spaces for the activities, such as sex, for which they still require privacy. Thus tapestries will often be tacked up between one mattress and the next or music will constantly be coming from a radio or record player to cover sounds of love-making or private conversations. People sometimes forgo sexual activity when conditions are crowded, but we have also seen strong compensatory satisfactions taken from the simple fact of a lot of people just sleeping together.

In the report for 1970 we mentioned that the women's liberation movement would probably not approve of the position of women in most communes. Although this is still largely true, it requires some explication. The fact is that in most communes of all types women tend to do traditional women's work: most of the cooking and cleaning (they are more concerned with tidiness than most men), and, in the rural communes, much of the traditional female farm roles in addition. But it is also true that women share in the general ethos of equalitarianism of most communes. With the exception of those religious communes which have an explicitly "sexist" creed, women can be found doing any but the most physically arduous labors, and in several communes we have studied closely, women do play important leadership roles. But on the whole they are less ideologically forceful than men, and express themselves with generally less authority—although we have encountered important exceptions to this tendency.

Concern over the status of women is more common in urban communes than rural ones (this is true in general of political matters), and female liberation has been a heavy topic of conversation in two urban communes we have studied (along with the male liberation which female liberation is said to bring in its wake). And in one of these communes, there is a distinctly "funky" working-class atmosphere, combining a lot of roughhouse play (ass- and crotch-grabbing, mock-rape, etc.) by both the men and the women, with a fairly equal sexual division of labor.

• • • •

The High Cost of Childhood

Esquire Magazine

Discussion of the war between the generations focuses on the structural reasons parents fear and repress their children, as well as why the children rebel against their well-meaning parents. The disappointment each generation has in the other is apparently inevitable. New data about this phenomenon consist of two important items: (1) a youth culture has evolved that seems highly resistant to responsible adult parenthood (see Berger et al., Reading 19); (2) in addition to the fact that children have lost usefulness as a family asset with advancing industrialization, their value as a source of companionship, an amusement, and an emotional outlet has also declined to the point where many would-be parents think twice about taking on the child-rearing burden after they look at the balance sheet. A hardhearted study of the estimated cost of raising a child, presented below, although perhaps a bit on the luxurious side, for the most part is quite realistic. Even though a child in the family is paid for on a twenty-one-year installment plan, today some would-be parents are asking themselves in just what other more satisfactory ways they might use their time and money. They have every reason to believe (if they examine their relationship to their own parents) that the "product" on which they will have to lavish all this money and care often turns out to be ungrateful, rebellious, and of little help or comfort in old age.

The following tables represent Esquire's estimate of the price of raising one good-to-superior-quality child in a major city from the moment of conception through a suitable graduate education. Not every child, of course, will be so deserving as to require *all* the expenditures that appear here; nor will every parent be able to afford them. But as privileged people living in a prosperous country, we'd all want our kids to have at least the advantages we did, plus a little bit thrown in, right? As for the figures themselves, naturally most of them are guesses. The authority of guesses is hard to estimate with accuracy; the food costs, for example, are based on estimates of the United States Department of Agriculture, which is perhaps prone to err in the direction of optimism. In any case, since the numbers make no allowance whatsoever for inflation, it's safe to believe that in the long run the actual price of raising a child will be more, not less, than the sufficiently astonishing sums shown here.

Conception to Age One	BOY	GIRL
Obstetrician (may run from as little as $450 to $1,000 or more, depending on complications and doctor's rent district)	800	
Hospital (5 days @ $100 per day)	500	
Delivery	100	
Nursery ($40 per day for five days)	200	
Circumcision		60
Baby wardrobe	125	
Nursery furnishing, including room refinishing	450	
Feeding equipment	40	
Miscellaneous (including vitamins, diaper service, any number of things that might happen)	100	
Maternity wardrobe	400	
Medical care (nine trips to the pediatrician @ $20, plus one fifty-dollar emergency)	230	
Food (U.S.D.A. "liberal" allowance for 1973, adjusted five dollars a month upward to account for price rises since then)	400	
Housing (baby needs an extra room; in choice urban spots that will add $100 a month to the rent)	1,200	
Clothing (U.S.D.A. calculates replacement on layette at $1.80 a week)	94	
Practical nurse (two weeks @ $175 a week)	350	
Toys (including exercisers and perception-stimulators to hang from crib; also books on how to raise baby, for amusement of parents)	200	
Silver spoon	13	
Baby's nest egg (beginning savings account)	100	
Photographing baby professionally	100	
Total to date	**5,462**	**5,402**

Babyhood (ages one through five: five years)		BOY	GIRL
Food (U.S.D.A. figures, plus $5 a month again)	3,000		
Housing ($1,200 × 5)	6,000		
Furnishing and decorating kid's room	300		
Clothing ($250 a year for the first two years, $300 a year thereafter)	1,400		
Medical care (three checkups a year for the first two years @ $25, two a year thereafter, plus five visits when something seems to be wrong)	425		
Dentist (once a year, $25 each trip)	125		
Nursery school and kindergarten from ages three to five Tuition ($1,350 a year)	4,050		
Transportation ($60 a month, nine months, three years)	1,620		
Toys (including birthday and Christmas presents and books)	1,000		
Baby-sitting (one night a week @ $15, based on a rate of $2.25 an hour plus cab fare)	3,900		
Organized play school for ages four and five (twice a week, including transportation but not cost of entrance to an admission-paid activity such as bowling)	900		
Two special birthday parties ($150 each)	300		
Vacations (live-in baby-sitter, $24 a day for three weeks each year while parents go to Caribbean)	2,520		
Subtotal		**25,540**	**25,540**
Total to date		**31,002**	**30,942**

Childhood (ages six through eleven: six years)		BOY	GIRL
Food (U.S.D.A. figures, adjusted, minus two months' summer camp)		4,332	4,260
Housing	7,200		
Redo child's room at age nine (new bed, desk, chair, bureau, rug, decorating)	500		
Clothing (Community Council of Greater New York allows $215 a year for "modified intermediate moderate income." But if that's all you have, you can't afford a kid at all. Therefore, your kid's annual clothing cost is $400)	2,400		
Medical care (two checkups and one special visit a year @ $25)	450		
Tonsillectomy	450		
Dentist (twice a year @ $25)	300		
Private school (disregard if you live in a sufficiently lavish suburb) Tuition, grades one through six	12,500		
School bus ($60 a month for nine months)	3,240		
Lab and craft supplies, etc., for six years	1,580		
Toys, games and goodies (a flexible figure in any case, but better allow, say, $250 a year)	1,500		
Special extra-lavish toy (electric-train set or furnished dollhouse)		125	125
Supervised play school, continued through age eight	1,350		
Allowance (one dollar a week through age eight, $2.50 a week thereafter)	546		
Piano lessons (once a week starting at age eight, with three months off each summer; $35 a month)	1,260		
Piano for above	1,500		
Dancing lessons for little girl (once a week, starting at age nine; $120 a year)			360
Dance equipment (shoes, etc.)			100

Figure skating for little girl, also starting at age nine		
One group lesson a week @ $4 for 28 weeks each year, plus three private lessons a year @ $8		408
Ice time (two hours twice a week, $5 per session for 28 weeks)		840
Equipment (three pairs of skates, $100 each, plus outfits)		525
Little League ice hockey for boy (including equipment, instruction, ice time and league membership; $250 a year beginning at age nine)	750	
Football for boy (equipment)	100	
Summer camp from ages eight to eleven ($1,000 a year)	4,000	
Extra "off-campus" camp trip ($100 each year)	400	
Movies (twice a month @ $2.50, plus 50 cents worth of candy each time)	432	
Circus and Ice Follies (one $5 ticket for each event once a year, plus $1.50 for souvenirs)	78	
Spectator sports (one each baseball, football, basketball and ice-hockey game a year, plus hot dogs, Cokes, programs)	180	
Baby-sitting (continued)	4,200	
Family dog		
Purchase price	200	
Shots and yearly veterinary fees ($75 a year)	450	
Dog food ($250 a year for large dog)	1,500	
Three special birthday parties (with catering and decorations, $350 each)	1,050	
Hired clowns, $50 each party	150	
Haircuts		
Girl, twice-yearly cut and style @ $5		60
Boy, eight times a year @ $1.25 (non-union barber)	60	
Vacations (as before)	3,024	
Subtotal	**55,807**	**56,938**
Total to date	**86,809**	**87,880**

Adolescence (ages twelve through seventeen: six years)		BOY	GIRL
Food		5,814	4,932
Housing	7,200		
Clothing		2,400	3,000
Private school (continued)			
Tuition	14,500		
Transportation (using pass for travel on city buses, 50 cents a month)	27		
Extras	1,900		
Medical expenses (as before, but special visits only every second year)	375		
One major injury (broken leg or equivalent)	500		
Dentist (three times a year; all teeth now permanent)	450		
Orthodontia	2,000		
Nose job (girl only; $1,000 for surgery plus three nights in hospital)			1,300
Summer camp through age fifteen (four more years)	4,000		
One special trip each year	400		
Toys, games and goodies	1,500		
Ten-speed bicycle	100		
Electric guitar		110	
Amplifier		200	
Lessons (twenty-five @ $5)		125	
Piano lessons (girl continues for four more years; boy does not)			1,260
Kid takes up skiing (skis $100, boots $60, bindings $50, poles $15)	225		
Teen-age ski vacation every other year @ $200	600		
Movies	432		
Spectator sports for boy as before; girl still doesn't care		180	
Special events (ballet, opera, concert or similar; twice a year @ $7.50)	90		

Kid starts using telephone, but makes only two calls a day and keeps them short ($.071 each, $54.50 a year)	327	
Room refurnished and decorated for teen-ager	500	
Allowance		
Twelve through fifteen, $5 a week	1,040	
Sixteen through seventeen, $10 a week	1,040	
Stereo phonograph	250	
Records (one a month for six years @ $3.89)	280	
Camera (serviceable 35 mm.)	100	
Film and developing (one roll a month @ $4)	288	
Dog (continued)		
Shots and vet, $75 a year	450	
Food	1,500	
Color TV for kid's room	350	
Haircuts (cost is now the same for either; six times a year @ $3.50)	126	
Watch (cheap)	25	
Kid is now old enough to travel alone around town (that's $3 a week for cabs, minus ten weeks for summer camp and other occasional layoffs; and six subway trips a week, 35 cents each)	1,285	
Cosmetics, starting at thirteen (*Seventeen* magazine estimate)		230
One big party (for Bar Mitzvah, Sweet Sixteen or whatever, catered and so on)	2,000	
Vacations (parents stop going to Caribbean, take summer vacations to correspond with summer camp; but at sixteen, kid goes on supervised group trip to Europe, $1,500 plus $200 spending money)	1,700	
Subtotal	54,389	56,282
Total to date	141,198	144,162

College (ages eighteen through twenty-one: four years)		BOY	GIRL
Food (at home four months a year)		1,274	1,064
Housing (extra room is now under-used, but there's no way to do without it)	4,800		
Clothing ($700 a year for girls, $550 for boys)		2,200	2,800
School (Harvard or equivalent) Tuition ($3,200 for four years)	12,800		
Room ($905 a year)	3,620		
Board ($920 a year)	3,680		
Other expenses (estimated) $600 a year	2,400		
Allowance ($65 a month, but applies only to the four months a year that kid is not at Harvard)	1,040		
Travel between home and school (by air, four times a year, once to come and go at beginning and end of school year, plus Thanksgiving, Christmas and Easter; fare is $49 round trip to New York, other cities extra)	784		
One Summer tour of Europe Air fare	629		
Expenses ($15 a day for 60 days)	900		
Sixty-day Student-Railpass	150		
One spring vacation to Mexico (air fare $329, plus $10 a day for ten days)	429		
Local winter skiing after first-semester exams ($200 a year)	800		
New and better ski equipment (skis $200, boots $150, poles $15, bindings $50)	415		
Medical care (now provided by Harvard; still, allow one visit a year to private physician @ $25)	100		
Dentist (four times a year @ $25; kid is now in early stages of periodontal disease, thanks to careless cleaning during orthodontia)	400		
Dermatologist or gynecologist, choose at least one. One annual visit @ $30	120		

	BOY	GIRL
Abortion		350
Psychiatrist for two years (twice weekly for eight months @ $35 an hour)	4,800	
Car (not even fancy) Insurance for car (at youthful-driver rates, $460 a year for boys, $350 for girls)	1,840	1,400
Pot bust (for more than one quarter of an ounce in New York or the equivalent penalty in other states; legal fees)	1,500	
Portable typewriter	70	
Luggage	200	
Wedding (only happens once; if twice, beyond parents' liability; if you are merely the parents of the groom, you need pay only the honeymoon and one party)	1,500	10,000
Dog, still alive, vet, etc.	300	
Food for dog, still alive, still $250 a year, but dies at the end of this period	1,000	
Subtotal	**47,751**	**56,551**
Total to date	**188,941**	**200,691**
Graduate School (ages twenty-two through, in the hypothetical case, twenty-five—three more years)	**BOY**	**GIRL**

By this stage, your offspring should be able to find a part-time job or full-time wife/husband to meet the elementary costs of living—which will, of course, be much lower now that he/she is in charge of finding the money. Still, you wouldn't want to interrupt a promising and lucrative career in the larval stage; therefore you are willing to stand still for the basic fixed costs of, in this example, three years of Harvard Law School. Medical school costs much more; in the School of Arts and Sciences, however, a teaching fellowship can lower the cost considerably.

Harvard Law, three years' tuition	7,200	
Medical fee ($155 for each of three years)	465	
Books and supplies (estimated)	600	
Room and board ($1,940 a year)	5,820	
Subtotal	**14,085**	
Total Direct Costs		
Conception through graduate school:	203,026	214,776

Just in case you think that's all there is to it . . .

Now you know what your child is going to cost; you're going to need insurance to pay for it in case you're not around. To start with, suppose you're twenty-five when baby is born. A five-year renewal and convertible term policy for $200,000 is what you need, and at your age that's $4.30 per thousand, or	860
Four more years at the same rate	3,440
When child reaches five, start new terms: the new policy is for $190,000 at $4.40 per thousand, which over five years adds up to	4,180
When child is ten, father is thirty-five; insurance is $5 per thousand and now you need about $140,000 worth	3,500
The next rate change comes when child is fifteen, you're forty; your requirement is about $87,000 and the rate is $6.60; five years of that makes	2,871
Things calm down a little when the kid reaches twenty; you now need only about $30,000 more, but at forty-five the rate is $9 a thousand, or $270 a year for the next five years	1,350

Total cost of insurance for twenty-five years	**$16,201**
If that's not enough, consider that mother's probably going to lose about fifteen years of possible employment until the child is old enough to take care of himself during the working day. The 1969 Commission on Population Growth and the American Future figures the maximum lost "opportunity costs" of a non-working mother at $6,762 a year. If that's what your wife is worth, in fifteen years it adds up to	**$101,430**

6

Problems and Crises

Many stories featuring the relationship between men and women end with marriage and pledges of love. Certainly, the chances of happiness in life are substantially enhanced by a compatible partner with whom one has mutual feelings of love and respect. Yet these factors alone are not enough to stave off the inevitable problems of living that develop over the years. Awareness of this truth is built into the marriage vows—"for better or for worse, in sickness and in health, till death do you part."

People in love can become unhappy with their partner's behavior, and love may cool while longing for a more satisfactory intimate relationship increases. Illness, alcoholism, or drug addiction can strike any family member. We know of our own recent national experience that the most skilled and earnest workers can become unemployed as a result of drastic economic upheavals. A spouse or other family member may die. One major function of the family is to try to cushion these problems as they occur, aiding the member most involved to overcome them, if possible. Problems in the family are times of suffering for all members and are also times when each one may be called on to be unselfish and to comfort and support the other.

This section touches on but a few of the problems that can plague a marriage; but they are not endemic to marriages. They happen to individuals too, and people without families may find it very difficult to cope alone. People in alternative life-styles that do not include long-term commitment of members may find some crises cause termination of the relationship. It is in such cases that social services are most needed.

Marital Problems, Help-Seeking, and Emotional Orientation as Revealed in Help-Request Letters

James E. DeBurger

For what kinds of marital problems do people seek professional help? Who is more likely to seek such help—the husband or the wife? What differences can be discerned in the types of problems that concern the husband and wife and in their emotional orientation to them? DeBurger attempts to answer some of these questions by analyzing the letters people write to marriage counselors. Again, it will not surprise readers of this volume that the major complaints are to be found in the areas of affectional and sexual relations. Personality problems are also mentioned quite frequently. However, husbands and wives differ as to the details of the same general problem, as well as in their emotional reaction to it. (For the beginning student, the technical details of this article may be ignored. It is the general content that is important.)

$\mathbf{A}$ student perusing the literature on marital problems may find some recent research based on clinical, mass-communications, and survey data which delineates the characteristics of persons engaged in the process of seeking help for such problems.[1] However, sparse indeed are published reports based on systematic analysis of "natural" data voluntarily provided by persons in the initial phases of dealing with their marital problems.[2] The question, "Who

From James DeBurger, "Marital Problems, Help-Seeking, and Emotional Orientation as Revealed in Help-Request Letters," *Journal of Marriage and the Family,* November, 1967, pp. 712–21. Copyright © 1967 by The National Council on Family Relations. Reprinted by permission.

seeks marriage counseling?" probably cannot be answered adequately from records kept by clinics or counselors. For, as marriage counselors well know, there is a phenomenal rate of attrition in the referral process. It would seem that more empirically derived knowledge is needed about persons in the very first stages of "help-seeking"; information of this kind might be useful in comparing those who are actually counseled with the much larger population of those who have indicated "need" for counseling or for purposes of validating generalizations about marital problems based on client populations. Such knowledge might also contribute to the less practical but basic task of testing hypotheses about relations between familial social structure and family problems, sex differences in potential for marital conflict, etc.

This article briefly summarizes selected findings of a study which focused on verbal materials produced by persons who were in the first stages of seeking professional help for their marital problems. In one recent ten-year period (1950-1959), the national office of the American Association of Marriage Counselors received 15,430 letters. Of this number, 93 percent (14,323) were "help-request" letters wherein the correspondent sought referral and/or other guidance in connection with his marital troubles. The research discussed here concentrated on these help-request letters. At least two previously published studies dealt with letters received by "lovelorn" or advice columnists.[3] The writer is not aware, however, of any systematic, large-scale study of help-request letters which included correspondents of both sexes and in which all correspondents were explicitly seeking help for marital problems.

METHOD AND PROCEDURES

As might be expected, there was much variation in the content of the 14,323 help-request letters; some were sparse on details while others were relatively profuse. The documents ranged in length from one to 15 pages, each represented one marriage, and each contained a request for referral and/or other help. From this overall collection, 1,412 letters were selected for intensive analysis. To qualify for inclusion in this subgroup, each document had to contain (1) a specification of the problem for which help was sought, (2) basic information regarding geographic source and residence, and (3) information pertaining to at least two aspects of the reported marital problem (e.g. duration of the problem, number of persons involved, etc.). Letters in this subgroup were therefore of greater length and comparatively richer in detail than the other documents. The summary of findings presented here is based on data from the subgroup of 1,412 letters. For all items in which comparisons between the overall collection (14,323) and subgroup (1,412) were possible, no statistically significant differences were found. For example, the proportion of males to females in the subgroup (18 percent males, 82 percent females) was almost identical to the proportions observed in the overall collection of letters.

For fuller discussion of the larger project on which this article is based, the reader is referred to the original work.[4]

The content analysis of the letters was formulated so that optimum information might be derived in regard to: (1) the demographic characteristics of the correspondents, (2) the kinds of problems they revealed, (3) their patterns of help-seeking, and (4) their emotional orientation regarding their problems and the related help-seeking. Empirical questions suggested by prior research were formulated so that the coding procedure would yield the four kinds of data enumerated above. For each case, a total of 75 content items was recorded on a code sheet from which an IBM card record was then prepared. The reliability of coding was checked by two measures applied to a ten-percent sample of the documents. The first of these consisted of a "test-retest" measure of the investigator's consistency in coding; for this, the percentage of agreement in coding of all data on two separate occasions was 91 percent. The second check involved a measure of inter-analyst agreement, using two trained coders; for this, the percentages of agreement ranged from 75 to 93 percent for independent codings on the same set of documents.[5]

Prior research bearing on sex differences in marital problems suggested the feasibility of comparing husbands and wives on each set of findings produced by the content analysis.[6] In comparing husbands and wives as groups, a frequency criterion was used (e.g., proportionate differences in the appearance of a particular theme in the letters). The basic methodological assumption was that the writing of a help-request letter represented a verbal opportunity for the correspondent to relate various aspects of his marital trouble. Variations in occurrence of particular content items might therefore be explainable under theoretically based expectations of sex differentials. The Chi-square statistic was used for testing the significance of group differences in the proportions indicating various content items; a probability level of .05 was used for determining significance.

Summary of Findings

Description of the Correspondents

Results of preliminary sorting for the content analysis showed that 82 percent (1,160) of the help-request letters were written by wives. A similar predominance of females in voluntary problem-disclosure and initial help-seeking has been observed in other research.[7] Each case was categorized as either "blue-collar" or "white-collar" social class. In 676 cases, this classification was based on occupational information revealed by the correspondent; for the remainder, the social class situation of the correspondent was estimated by a technique based upon the verbal quality of the communication, stationery quality, and the mode of writing. This technique has been previously employed in several content analyses.[8] White-collar classification was assigned to 61 percent of the cases, and 39 percent were categorized as blue-collar social class.[9]

Various other descriptive characteristics may be summarized.

(1) *Residence.* All correspondents were United States residents. Using Census Bureau listings of urbanized areas and urban place,[10] 97 percent of the correspondents were classified as urban and 3 percent as rural. There was a rank-order correlation coefficient of .95 between the proportion of letters from each region and the number of married couples in each region as reported by the United States Census. Differences in sex representation by regions were not statistically significant.

(2) *Race and religion.* Information regarding their race was seldom explicitly revealed by the correspondents; only four non-white cases were identified in the preliminary coding, and these were not included in the subgroup of 1,412. It was assumed that all marriages represented by the help-requests were white. On the basis of information from 14 percent of the correspondents, 90 percent were Protestant.

(3) *Age.* Information regarding age was revealed by 979 of the correspondents. Most correspondents (60 percent of the wives, 70 percent of the husbands) were under 40 years of age. Mean age was 39 for husbands and 36 for wives.

(4) *Parental status.* This datum was reported by 90 percent of the wives and 86 percent of the husbands. Two-thirds of those reporting parental status had no more than three children; the mean number of children was 2.7 for all correspondents who reported this item.

(5) *Length of marriage.* In 1,098 cases, the help-request letter provided information on the length of marriage. In 758 cases, the correspondent explicitly stated how long he had been married. In the remaining 340 cases, estimates of this datum were based on relevant information in the help-request letter. Relevant information included time reference points, indirect references to length of marriage, and other similar information. Approximately 56 percent of the correspondents had been married for less than ten years. The mean length of marriage for both husbands and wives was approximately 12 years.

Revealed Problems

On the basis of a preliminary analysis of the documents, eight categories were developed which subsumed specific problems or "themes" (statements identifying the nature of the problem) expressed in the documents.[11] The revealed problems were then classified as "major" or as "secondary." A major problem was one seemingly regarded by the correspondent as central—the chief cause of the marital unhappiness; each document was coded to reflect but one major problem. Secondary problem themes included any complaints or problems that were disclosed in the letter, apart from the one coded as the major problem. A given document might thus disclose several secondary problems or none. The content analysis developed a total of 30 problem-themes which were grouped in eight categories. Table 1 shows these eight categories of major problems along with the themes which they subsume.[12]

It is apparent from Table 1 that major problems tend to cluster in the two areas of interaction represented by affectional and sexual relations, with problems involving personality relations coming next in order of prominence.[13] Thus, among those persons who perceived themselves as seriously needing professional help, major marital problems connected with the intimate patterns of interaction between mates far outweighed other types. Speculation suggests that these findings reflect a pervasive cultural emphasis on marriage as an emotionally gratifying pair-relationship. Thus, revealed marital problems may

Table 1.
Major Problems Revealed by Husbands and Wives in 1,412 Help-Request Letters

CATEGORY AND RELATED THEMES	HUSBAND	WIFE	TOTAL
Affectional Relations	11.5%	31.0%	27.6%
1. Spouse cold, unaffectionate			
2. Spouse is in love with another			
3. Have no love feelings for spouse			
4. Spouse is not in love with me			
5. Spouse attracted to others, flirts			
6. Excessive, "insane" jealousy			
Sexual Relations	42.1	20.6	24.4
1. Sexual relations "unsatisfactory"			
2. Orgasm inability; frigidity, impotence			
3. Sex deprivation; insufficient coitus			
4. Spouse wants "unnatural" sex relations			
Role Tasks-Responsibilities	0.0	6.0	4.9
1. Disagreement over 'who should do what'			
2. Spouse's failure to meet material needs			
Parental Role Relations	0.0	1.7	1.4
1. Conflict on child discipline			
2. Parent-child conflict			
Intercultural Relations	11.5	11.4	11.4
1. In-law relations troublesome			
2. Religion and religious behavior			
Situational Conditions	4.0	3.4	3.5
1. Financial difficulties, income lack			
2. Physical illness, spouse or self			
Deviant Behavior	7.5	8.7	8.5
1. Heavy drinking, alcoholism of mate			
2. Own heavy drinking or alcoholism			
3. Spouse's "loose" sex behavior			
4. Own illicit sex behavior			
5. Compulsive gambling			
Personality Relations	23.4	17.2	18.3
1. Spouse domineering, selfish			
2. Own "poor" personality, instability			
3. Clash of personalities; incompatible			
4. Spouse's violent temper tantrums			
5. Spouse withdrawn, moody, "neurotic"			
6. Spouse quarrelsome, bickering, nagging			
7. Spouse irresponsible, undependable			
Total	100.0%	100.0%	100.0%
	n = 252	n = 1160	N = 1412

Chi-square $= 91.80$; $P < .001$ (8 categories $\times$ husband-wife status).

increasingly tend to reflect difficulties associated with the attainment of happiness in *interspouse relations* (rather than the attainment of harmony with the socio-cultural context, such as kin, community, religion, etc.). In connection with this speculation on the matter of interspouse happiness, it is interesting to note that problems associated with parental roles ranked lowest in the major problems revealed by the correspondents. Although more than four-fifths of the correspondents reported parental status, less than two percent of the 1,412 revealed major marital problems reflecting this area of interaction. In other research using families not characterized by overt marital problems and help-seeking,[14] parental-role problems were much more frequently revealed.

Sex differences in major problems. A central question in this research concerned possible sex differences in revealed problems; prior research suggested the strong likelihood that such differences would be found in our data. Students of marital interaction have quite commonly assumed that various differences in the subcultural backgrounds of males and females may account in part for differences in the kinds of conflicts and problems typically experienced by husbands and wives. In the present research it was assumed not only that husbands and wives may differ in problem-experiencing, but also that these differential problems would be expressed by persons in the process of seeking help. Presumably, each correspondent was free to impart whatever knowledge he desired about himself and his problems. An implicit question in this research concerned the similarity of sex differentials found in this data to sex differentials revealed by studies using relatively structured questionnaire and interview data. The bulk of our current knowledge about marital relations is derived from data of the latter type.

As Table 1 shows, husbands and wives differ significantly in regard to the kinds of major marital problems revealed in their help-request letters. A salient finding was that husbands and wives differ significantly in their revelation of problems which involve sexual and affectional relations. A significantly larger proportion of husbands than wives revealed problems associated with sexual relations, whereas many more wives than husbands revealed problems associated with affectional relations. This finding converges strongly with theory and empirical evidence on sex differentials stemming from early research by Terman and later studies by Burgess and Wallin.

Table 1 also shows that more wives than husbands revealed major problems associated with role-tasks-responsibilities. This finding seems consistent with the hypothesis that wives may be more prone than husbands to perceive problems associated with the cultural conflict and ambiguity surrounding the female's marital roles.[15] Although there was little reason to expect a particular sex differential in revealed problems involving personality relations, the data show a significantly larger proportion of husbands than wives revealing this type of problem.

Sex differences on specific themes. In addition to comparing husbands and wives on categories of problems (as in Table 1), checks were also made of sex differentials in the revelation of some specific problem-*themes* which seemed likely in view of prior research.[16] A significantly larger proportion of wives than husbands disclosed these themes: (1) "mate's excessive jealousy," (2) "mate is in love with another," (3) "mate wants sex relations too often," (4) "disgust with sexual relations per se," (5) "disagreement over division of labor in the family," (6) "mate's heavy drinking," and (7) "mate's extramarital sex relations." A significantly larger proportion of husbands than wives, as was expected, revealed themes expressing: (1) "unsatisfactory sexual relations with the mate," (2) "sex deprivation or insufficient frequency of marital coitus," and (3) "moodiness or neurotic behavior of the mate." In each of these comparisons, the group differences were significant at a probability level of .05 or below.

Contrary to expectations, husbands and wives as groups did not differ significantly in the proportions revealing the following themes: (1) "mate is cold or too seldom displays affection," (2) "in-law relations are troublesome," (3) "nagging by the mate," and (4) "mate is irresponsible."

Sex differences by social class. Husband-wife differences in the disclosure of four categories of major problems were checked for possible variation by social class of the correspondents. As the data in Table 2 indicate, the direction of husband-wife differences seen earlier (Table 1) persists when the cases are grouped by social class. It is apparent, however, that the sex differentials are more pronounced in cases identified as blue-collar social class. While more than one-fifth of the white-collar husbands disclosed major problems in the affectional relations category, none of the blue-collar husbands indicated this problem type. On the other hand, major problems involving intramarital sexual relations were much more frequently revealed by blue-collar husbands than by their white-collar counterparts. The proportions of white-collar husbands and wives reporting problems which involved personality relations were

TABLE 2.
MAJOR PROBLEMS REVEALED BY HUSBANDS AND WIVES,
ARRANGED BY CATEGORY OF PROBLEM
AND SOCIAL CLASS

MAJOR PROBLEM CATEGORY	SOCIAL CLASS			
	WHITE-COLLAR*		BLUE-COLLAR†	
	Husband	Wife	Husband	Wife
Affectional Relations	23.4%	32.4%	0.0%	28.6%
Sexual Relations	22.7	18.9	61.8	23.8
Role Tasks-Responsibility	0.0	4.0	0.0	9.5
Personality Relations	30.7	20.3	15.4	11.9
Other Major Problems	23.2	24.4	22.8	26.2
Total	100.0%	100.0%	100.0%	100.0%
	(n = 124)	(n = 740)	(n = 128)	(n = 420)

*Chi-square (husband-wife status × problem categories) = 13.79; P < .01.
†Chi-square (husband-wife status × problem categories) = 93.26; P < .001.

appreciably larger than for blue-collar husbands and wives. It may also be noted that, in the white-collar class, sex differences in revelation of personality problems are much more pronounced than in the blue-collar cases.

Variation by length of marriage. Analysis of those letters in which the duration of the marriage had been explictly reported by the correspondent (758) revealed some association between length of marriage and disclosure of problems associated with affectional, sexual, and personality relations. Attention was confined to these categories of problems because of their relatively greater frequency in the documents. The tabulation for this arrangement included each case where either a major or a secondary problem was coded for the categories shown in Table 3. Since the number of cases is rather small and since most of our data pertain to marriages of less than ten years' duration, the findings on this point are quite tentative. However, in terms of an analogous "trend," as shown in Table 3, the analysis has certain implications: (1) For both husband and wife groups, the proportions revealing problems connected with affectional relations tend to increase as length of marriage increases. (2) Revealed problems associated with intramarital sexual relations show considerable decrease over time for husbands; for wives, however, the proportions revealing sexual relations problems are appreciably less than for husbands, but tend to persist in the later years of marriage. (3) For both husbands and wives, problems involving personality relations are revealed by relatively small proportions in the earliest period, but tend to increase with the duration of marriage. This evidence somewhat converges with other research showing changes in critical areas of marital interaction over the duration of marriage.[17] Multiple revelation of problems is also suggested by Table 3. Analysis showed that for both husbands and wives, reports of more than one of these three problems were least frequent in the earliest period and most frequent in marriages of 20 or more years' duration.

Revealed Help-Seeking Behavior

In the analysis of the help-request letters, items illustrative of the correspondent's search for help were recorded. Each letter was, in itself, a component in the help-seeking process; in coding, therefore, certain aspects of each letter were examined (e.g., length, descriptiveness, indications of "urgency," etc.). In addition, each letter was coded for information provided by the correspondent in regard to his relations with sources of help prior to writing the help-request letter. A review of the literature on this topic provided some questions to guide coding and suggested some likely sex differences in help-seeking behavior.[18]

A brief comment seems appropriate in regard to the approximate five-to-one ratio of females to males among the correspondents. Other studies of persons utilizing professional help-sources have shown a similar disproportionate representation of females; the proportion of females to males seems especially high in the initial phases of help-seeking.[19] This sex differential may imply support

238

TABLE 3.
PROPORTION OF HUSBAND AND WIFE GROUPS REVEALING AFFECTIONAL, SEXUAL, AND PERSONALITY RELATIONS PROBLEMS, BY LENGTH OF MARRIAGE

PROBLEM CATEGORY	LENGTH OF MARRIAGE			
	LESS THAN 1 YEAR	1-9 YEARS	10-19 YEARS	20+ YEARS
Affectional Relations*				
Husband	41.7% (5/12)	60.6% (40/66)	61.1% (22/36)	61.9% (13/21)
Wife	36.4% (16/44)	50.2% (152/303)	40.6% (65/160)	48.3% (56/116)
Sexual Relations†				
Husband	50.0% (6/12)	31.8% (21/66)	36.1% (13/36)	14.3% (3/21)
Wife	34.1% (15/44)	28.7% (87/303)	23.1% (37/160)	25.9% (30/116)
Personality Relations‡				
Husband	25.0% (3/12)	48.5% (32/66)	44.4% (16/36)	76.2% (16/21)
Wife	31.8% (14/44)	48.5% (147/303)	50.0% (80/160)	61.2% (71/116)

* Husband: $X^2 = 5.98$, $P < .30$; Wife: $X^2 = 9.04$, $P < .10$.
† Husband: $X^2 = 22.22$, $P < .001$; Wife: $X^2 = 132.63$, $P < .001$.
‡ Husband: $X^2 = 9.20$, $P < .10$; Wife: $X^2 = 11.90$, $P < .02$.
Note: Chi-square values above are for combined tests of proportions indicating the given problems in each of the time segments; degrees of freedom $= 4$ for each Chi-square.

for the hypothesis that wives are relatively more involved in and committed to their marital roles than are husbands; hence, wives may be more highly motivated than husbands to seek professional help as a means of preserving marriage.

Letter-writing as a first step. Analysis showed that the help-request letter represented, for most correspondents, a first step toward contact with a formal helping agency. Only 303 of the correspondents reported that they had sought out some source of help prior to writing a help-request letter. Husbands and wives did not differ significantly in this respect. A related question concerns the prior sources of help which had been explored by these 303 correspondents. Four major sources of help were reported in the following proportions: physicians, 41 percent; clergymen, 19.5 percent; psychiatrists or psychologists, 18.8 percent; and attorneys, 12.2 percent. Help had been sought from miscellaneous others (relatives, friends, astrologists, etc.) by the remaining 8.5 percent. There were no statistically significant differences between husbands and wives in regard to these reported sources of help. A significant social class difference was found in only one instance: proportionately more white-collar than blue-collar correspondents consulted psychiatrists or psychologists.

Sources of information about marriage counseling. In 936 letters, correspondents reported their sources of information concerning the role of AAMC as a referral agency for professional marriage counseling. For both husbands and wives, magazines were by far the most frequently reported source of information about help for a troubled marriage. Approximately 92 percent of each group reported magazines as their source of information. Only two percent of each group had learned of the referral role of AAMC directly from professionals (physicians, clergymen, etc.) in their local community. Other reported sources of information included newspaper articles, lectures, friends, radio or TV programs, and books. Husbands and wives did not differ significantly in their reported sources of information about professional marriage counseling. Neither were any significant differences found when the data were grouped by correspondent's social class.

One implication of this data is that some forms of the mass media may serve significant functions in linking problems and troubled marriages with suitable sources of help. In this connection, most of the prominent women's and family-oriented magazines have, in recent years, carried "case record" articles which deal with marital problems. Such articles are often accompanied by an offer to refer troubled persons to competent counselors. Articles dealing with marital problems (especially "case histories") conceivably afford a means by which a troubled marriage or a specific problem may be identified. "Models" of appropriate help-seeking and problem-solving behavior may also be provided in such materials.[20]

The preceding speculation raises a broad but pertinent question which is not adequately treated in the literature of family research: namely, the impact of culture on the patterns and dynamics of the help-seeking process. The question of how Americans actually do try to solve their marital problems cannot be separated from the related question of how they "ought" to solve them in the light of relevant cultural norms. The role of mass media is probably crucial in the transmission of socially approved models of help-seeking and in providing channels of communication between troubled persons and professional sources of help.

Characteristics of letter content. Since these letters were presumably components in the correspondent's process of help-seeking, content items were coded which seemed illustrative of various aspects of this process. One such item, *urgency*, was coded on the basis of the correspondent's requests for expediency in a reply to his letter. A total of 214 or 15 percent of the correspondents expressed urgency. Husbands and wives were not significantly differentiated on this item, nor were group differences significant when the cases were grouped by social class.

Another relevant content item was *mutuality* or joint appeals for help appearing in the letters. When a correspondent indicated that his spouse was also desirous of pursuing a solution for the marital problem or when the letter was apparently written and/or signed by both spouses, the help-request was classified as *mutual*. Analysis showed relatively little mutuality for either the husbands (14.3 percent) or the wives (14.8 percent), and the husband-wife differences are obviously not significant. An arrangement of the data by social class of the correspondents showed no significant differences by class.

The coding process also provided tabulations on the *length* and *descriptiveness* of the documents. The length of the average help-request letter was 255 words. Our expectation that letters from wives would be somewhat lengthier than those from husbands was not supported by the analysis. An overall Chi-square test (husband-wife status $\times$ letter-length group) did not show group differences significant at the .05 level of probability. A ten-percent sample of the letters was coded to check for possible group differences in verbal descriptiveness. The descriptiveness of each document was ascertained by counting all phrases using adjectives, adverbs, or symbolisms descriptive of self, spouse, or problem. Contrary to expectations, sex differences in verbal descriptiveness were not statistically significant when the descriptive words in each letter were viewed as proportions of the total words in each letter.

Disclosures by the correspondent reflecting an *awareness of economic aspects* of the help-seeking process were also tabulated. With regard to proportions revealing general concern with economic aspects of help-seeking (queries about counseling fees, etc.), there was little difference between husbands and wives (husbands, 13 percent; wives, 16 percent). The data do show, however, that significantly more wives (11.5 percent) than husbands (6.7 percent) stressed a need for economy in the help-seeking or counseling process. A rearrangement of the data by social class of the correspondents showed no differences in these patterns.

Seasonal variation. The analysis revealed some interesting seasonal variation in the writing of help-request letters. A significantly larger proportion of the husbands wrote during relatively colder seasons; 31.4 percent of the husbands' letters were written during January, February, or March. On the other hand, a significantly larger proportion of the wives wrote during relatively warmer seasons; 35 percent of the wives' letters were written during July, August, or September. In passing it may be noted that the question of seasonal and cyclical variation has received attention in various studies.[21]

Information requested. By far the most frequent request from correspondents was for the title of a book or manual which could be read for purposes of solving the marital problem at hand. This kind of request, reflective perhaps of the "do-it-yourself" tendency in American culture, came from 97 percent of the husbands and 98 percent of the wives. There are implications here, perhaps, of a "cook-book" approach to marital problems which embodies the notion of ready-made formulas for the achievement of happiness and the solution of problems. Again the salience of this request may imply a strong tendency toward "self-help" in marital problem-solving, comparable to the phenomena of self-diagnosis and self-treatment in physical illness.

Four other kinds of information, all bearing on intimate aspects of marriage, were requested by the correspondents in the following proportions: (1) information on the control of procreation, 3.6 percent of the husbands and 1.9 percent of the wives; (2) information on techniques of sexual relations, 8.7 percent of the husbands and 2.6 percent of the wives; (3) information on aphrodisia, 13.1 percent of the husbands and 9.0 percent of the wives; (4) information on physiological aspects of marriage, such as sex anatomy, impotence, etc., 17.5 percent of the husbands and 8.9 percent of the wives. In items 2 through 4, the proportion of husbands was significantly larger than of wives; a rearrangement by social class made no difference in these patterns. A few scattered requests for other kinds of specific information were also found in the letters (e.g., legal aid, employment services, etc.).

Revealed Emotional Orientation

Some brief comments on emotional orientation will complete this summary of findings. Emotional orientation was defined in terms of (1) revealed feelings or emotional states which presumably were related to the correspondent's marital problems and (2) reported feelings or anticipations regarding the outcome of help-seeking.

In view of certain sex-role differentials existing in the family system, it was expected that husbands and wives would differ appreciably in revealed emotional orientation.[22] Survey data collected by Gurin show, in this connection, that women report more problems and greater stress in marriage than do husbands. Gurin also found that women to a greater extent than men consciously experience tension and dwell on their problems and that more wives than husbands feel inadequate in their familial roles.[23] Table 4 summarizes the emotional-orientation themes which were developed by the content analysis.

Sex differences in reported negative feelings. A larger proportion of wives than husbands reported feeling that they were degraded by the spouse. Also, wives more often than husbands revealed their feelings of anger and resentment toward the mate. The data further show that many more wives than husbands reported felt experiences of depression, nervous exhaustion, and disillusionment with their marriage. Suicidal feelings were reported by only about two percent of each group. Grouping the correspondents by social class had little effect on the magnitude or direction of differences between husbands and wives with regard to these items. However, in the white-collar class, the husband-wife differential in regard to reports of felt degradation (Item 3, Table 4) was not statistically significant at the .05 level.

Attribution of blame. In 638, or 45 percent of the cases, the correspondent revealed his feelings as to who should be blamed for the marital trouble. The data also show that husbands and wives differ appreciably in their attributions of blame. A much larger proportion of wives than husbands blamed their mate for the marital trouble; also, more husbands than wives attributed blame to themselves. However, it may be noted that the sex difference in self-blaming was not significant for correspondents in the white-collar class. These findings generally seem consistent with prior theory and research.[24] Prominence in self-blame by husbands may be related to the male's greater initiative in certain forms of behavior which are strongly associated with revealed marital problems. Again, assuming a persisting tendency in this culture to portray marital failure in terms of wrongdoer and wronged, it may be that blame would

242

Table 4.

EMOTIONAL ORIENTATION AND EXPERIENCE INDICATED BY HUSBANDS AND WIVES, SHOWN BY SOCIAL CLASS

THEME	SOCIAL CLASS					
	White-Collar			*Blue-Collar*		
	Husband n=124	Wife n=740	(2×2) X²	Husband n=128	Wife n=420	(2×2) X²
1. "I am tired, nervous, depressed because of our trouble."	12.1%	29.2%	15.8*	12.5%	37.6%	28.5*
2. "Life not worth living . . . feel like killing myself."	1.6	2.4	.3	2.3	3.3	.3
3. "I feel degraded. I am treated like dirt."	8.9	15.4	3.7	6.2	24.7	20.7*
4. Angry, resentful toward spouse	6.4	31.1	32.1*	3.9	34.3	45.7*
5. Disillusioned, "disappointed . . . in married life."	8.9	35.1	34.0*	7.0	15.4	6.0*
6. Self-blame for problem	21.8	15.7	2.9	21.9	13.3	5.5*
7. Spouse blamed for problem	25.0	44.8	17.2*	29.7	56.4	28.1*
8. Appeal for reinforcement	4.0	3.6	.04	3.1	4.0	.2
9. Optimism, "believe our problem can be straightened out."	40.3	33.0	2.6	35.9	25.0	5.9*
10. Despairing, "afraid there's no hope."	11.3	16.2	2.0	8.6	21.2	10.4*

*Chi-square significant at .05 level or below.

more likely be attached to the relatively more initiatory, aggressive role of the husband than to the relatively passive role of the wife.

Anticipated outcome of help-seeking. The data show an appreciable difference between husbands and wives in regard to their disclosure of two items which reflect emotional orientation to help-seeking. Husbands more often than wives indicated *optimism* and less often indicated pessimism regarding possibilities for successful solution of their marital problems. Although the overall comparison of proportions of husbands and wives disclosing these two items showed significant group differences, the arrangement by social class shows that most of this difference is traceable to correspondents in the blue-collar social class.

One could speculate that these differences in emotional orientation in regard to problems and the possible outcome of help-seeking stem from integral sex-role differences in marriage. Thus, the centrality of the wife's role probably ensures that she will have more immediate and persisting contact with the everyday dynamics and content of a troubled marriage. These conditions may account, in part, for the sex differential in revealed feelings of despair, depression, degradation, and disappointment.

Appeals for reinforcement. Research on letters to advice columnists has shown that correspondents frequently appeal for validation or reinforcement of their position regarding the nature of their problem and the best solution for it.[25] In the present study, no more than four percent of the correspondents sought this effect in their help-request letters. Also, the difference in proportions of husbands and wives revealing this item was not significant when the cases were grouped by social class. Writing a help-request letter may have served partially to put troublesome factors in a proper perspective and thereby decreased the correspondent's tendency to seek reinforcement.

CONCLUDING COMMENTS

Data presented in this summary of selected findings from a content analysis of help-request letters show that husbands and wives differ significantly in their revelations of marital problems, help-seeking behavior, and emotional orientation. These differential patterns persisted generally when the cases were also arranged by social class of the correspondent. This persistence is perhaps reflective of rather widespread and common patterns of expectation in regard to happiness in marital relations and in regard to acceptable modes of help-seeking. One hypothesis which the present data suggest is that, among seriously troubled spouses, marital unhappiness is mainly defined in terms of unsatisfactory patterns of intimate relations between mates and that these relations are largely affectional and sexual in character. The quality of intimate relations between mates may become increasingly relevant to definitions of marital happiness or unhappiness as the familial group in this society becomes primary in character and less dependent on extended kinship relations.[26]

In regard to sex differentials found in this content analysis, there may be methodological significance in the observation that findings in this study converge remarkably well with evidence developed in prior research using structured data and different methods. In view of the difficulties ordinarily associated with collection of data from seriously troubled marriages, content analysis of verbal materials produced by persons in the process of help-seeking may have considerable potential for contributing to our knowledge of marital problems and conflicts. Also, data of this nature, used in conjunction with evidence developed through a more structured method, may be able to semantically reveal aspects of experience which might not be uncovered by other techniques. Much "natural" data may be available in the form of letters, diaries, legal transcripts, etc., for the student of familial experience who wishes to develop fuller knowledge about the meaning of problems to those who experience them.

NOTES

[1] For example, Bernadette F. Turner, "Common Characteristics Among Persons Seeking Professional Marriage Counseling," *Marriage and Family Living,* 16 (May, 1954), pp. 143–144; Dorothy F. Beck, *Patterns in Use of Family Agency Service,* New York: Family Service Association of America, 1962; Walter Gieber, "The Lovelorn Columnist and Her Social Role," *Journalism Quarterly,* 37 (November, 1960), pp. 499–514; Christine A. Hillman, "An Advice Column's Challenge for Family-Life Education," *Marriage and Family Living,* 16 (February, 1954), pp. 51–54; Gerald Gurin *et al., Americans View Their Mental Health,* New York: Basic Books, 1960, Part II, "Solving Problems of Adjustment."

[2] By "natural" materials we mean such as are produced under the self-motivation of the subject, or voluntary rather than researcher-elicited data. Relevant to use of such material, see Gordon W. Allport, *The Use of Personal Documents in Psychological Science,* New York: Social Science Research Council, 1942.

[3] Gieber, *op. cit.;* and Hillman, *op. cit.;* cf. also Wardell B. Pomeroy, "An Analysis of Questions on Sex," *Psychological Record,* 10 (July, 1960), pp. 191–201.

[4] James E. DeBurger, *Husband-Wife Differences in the Revelation of Marital Problems: A Content Analysis,* unpublished Ph.D. thesis, Indiana University, 1966.

[5] The check on coding reliability followed procedures suggested in Eric F. Gardner and George G. Thompson, *Social Relations and Morale in Small Groups,* New York: Appleton-Century-Crofts, 1956, pp. 194–196.

[6] Ernest W. Burgess and Paul Wallin, *Engagement and Marriage,* Philadelphia: J. B. Lippincott, 1953; Harvey J. Locke, *Predicting Adjustment in Marriage,* New York: Henry Holt and Co., 1951; Lewis M. Terman *et al., Psychological Factors in Marital Happiness,* New York: McGraw-Hill, 1938; Gerald Gurin *et al., op. cit.* Also see Orville Brim *et al.,* "Relations Between Family Problems," *Marriage and Family Living,* 23:3 (1961), pp. 219–226.

[7] Cf. Gieber, *op. cit.,* p. 503; Gurin, *op. cit.,* pp. 303–344; and Turner, *op. cit.,* p. 144.

[8] Modifications were made of a method used by Gieber, *op. cit.;* also see Rowena Wyant and Herta Herzog, "Voting via the Senate Mailbag," *Public Opinion Quarterly,* 5 (Fall, 1941), pp. 359–382.

[9] Gieber, *op. cit.,* p. 503, described 68 percent of his cases as "low" socioeconomic class and 21 percent as "middle" class. Hillman's cases, *op. cit.,* p. 52, were mainly blue-collar status.

[10] U.S. Census Bureau, *Census of Population: 1950,* Vol. 1, Washington, D.C.: U.S. Government Printing Office, pp. 48–65; and same title for 1960, Vol. 1, p. 263.

[11] Bernard Berelson, *Content Analysis,* New York: The Free Press, a division of the Macmillan Co., 1952, pp. 138–140.

[12] A set of detailed tables covering the material summarized in this article and materials not discussed here may be obtained without cost from the author.

[13] In this classification scheme, it was assumed that revealed marital problems tend to reflect unhappiness in basic areas of interaction within marriage. Cf. William J. Goode, "Family Disorganization," in *Contemporary Social Problems,* ed. by Robert K. Merton and Robert A. Nisbet, New York: Harcourt, Brace and World, 1961, p. 431.

[14] Brim, *op. cit.*

[15] Cf. Robert F. Winch, *The Modern Family,* New York: Holt, Rinehart, and Winston, 1963, pp. 412–423.

[16] Cf. Burgess and Wallin, *op. cit.;* Locke, *op. cit.;* Terman *et al., op. cit.*

[17] Some works which focus on or include material bearing on this matter would include: Robert O. Blood and Donald Wolfe, *Husbands and Wives,* New York: The Free Press, a division of the Macmillan Co., 1960; Beck, *op. cit.;* Charles W. Hobart, "Disillusionment in Marriage and Romanticism," *Marriage and Family Living,* 20 (1958), pp. 156–162; James H. S. Bossard and Eleanor Boll, "Marital Unhappiness in the Life Cycle," *Marriage and Family Living,* 17 (1955), pp. 10–14; Peter C. Pineo, "Disenchantment in the Later Years of Marriage," *Marriage and Family Living,* 23 (1961), pp. 3–11; and Vincent D. Mathews and Clement S. Mihanovich, "New Orientations on Marital Maladjustment," *Marriage and Family Living,* 25 (1963), pp. 300–304.

[18] Cf. Gurin, *op. cit.,* pp. 326, 332–370; Turner, *op. cit.*

[19] Gieber, *op. cit.;* Gurin, *op. cit.;* Turner, *op. cit.*

[20] The author is currently engaged in research in this area. Cf. Gieber, *op. cit.*

[21] Cf. Clifford Kirkpatrick and Eugene Kanin, "Male Sex Aggression on a University Campus," *American Sociological Review,* 22 (February, 1957), pp. 52–58. Seasonal variation has received attention in areas of sociological study other than the family. Regarding deviant behavior, see the summary of relevant research in Elmer H. Johnson, *Crime, Correction, and Society,* Homewood, Ill.: Dorsey Press, 1964, pp. 64–69.

[22] Winch, *op. cit.,* pp. 411–417.

[23] Gurin, *op. cit.,* p. xvi.

[24] Gurin, *op. cit.,* p. 131; also cf. E. E. LeMasters, *Modern Courtship and Marriage,* New York: Macmillan Co., 1957, pp. 363–367, regarding subcultural background factors which may be important in differential sex patterns.

[25] Gieber, *op. cit.*

[26] Clifford Kirkpatrick, *The Family: As Process and Institution,* New York, Ronald Press Co., 1963, p. 137.

How Farm Families Cope
with Heart Disease:
A Study of
Problems and Resources

Margaret Jacobson Bubloz and
Robert L. Eichhorn

Participants in alternative life-styles, such as hippie communes and even sexual "swinging" singles, are usually young people and persons in excellent physical health. Pairs within these groups have not yet faced the problems of later years, which often include taking care of each other when serious illness strikes. The marriage contract between equals seldom foresees the possibility that one partner will someday not be able-bodied. But these unhappy situations do occur. If the partners care about each other, one or the other may surrender some precious self-determination, fulfillment, and substantial freedom, modifying his or her life around the physical disabilities of the other. This research addresses the problems and coping strategies that occur when the father of a farm family has a heart attack. The adjustments resulting could as well be applied to any other serious physical illness, accident, or even to alcoholism and mental illness. Often there must be a redivision of labor, and, perhaps, support of the family will be thrown entirely on the healthier spouse. Relationships between spouses and between parents and children will change. The routine of daily living requires extensive rearrangements of both a physical and psychological nature to meet the needs of a sick and convalescent person. A serious illness thus affects the entire family constellation in terms of established roles and relationships, norms and values, images of self, and images of others.

INTRODUCTION

Heart disease today ranks as the major single cause of death in the United States. In 1960 alone, over 600,000 deaths, 39 percent of all those occurring that year, were attributed to it.[1] However, death rates tell only part of the story. In addition to being the leading cause of death, heart disease is the major source of serious illness among the living. The American Heart Association has estimated the number of persons in the United States with some disease of the heart or circulatory system to be around ten million.[2] These people must find ways for living with heart disease.

Diseases vary among themselves, of course, in their duration, symptomatology, threat to life, treatments required, and the images they summon up in the public mind. While there are several different kinds of heart disease, each with its own unique characteristics, they are all alike in some respects. This is especially true for hypertensive and arteriosclerotic heart disease, those that are most prevalent among older people. Heart disease tends to be of long duration, sometimes arrested but never completely cured.[3] The victim of heart disease may experience spells of breathlessness, fatigue, and dizziness, and he may be troubled by insomnia, leg cramps, swelling of the lower limbs, and severe chest pains. Paradoxically, he often exhibits no outward signs of his disease that would alert others to the fact that he is not well. The cardiac's doctor may prescribe a period of hospitalization, medicine, rest, reducing the work load, avoiding emotionally stimulating situations, giving up smoking, changing the kind or amount of food consumed, and reducing responsibilities. Adherence to the medical regimen laid down by the doctor may or may not be rewarded by years of painless, productive activity. Because of the nature of heart disease, its prognosis is necessarily uncertain. This gives rise to the sometimes justified, sometimes unjustified view that heart disease means sudden death.

The life of the cardiac can, thus, be radically altered by the disease he suffers. Life goals may have to be abandoned, as illustrated by the person forced to quit work, thereby giving up income, security, and the sense of personal fulfillment that continued work can give. New means for attaining cherished ambitions may have to be sought. He may be haunted by the fear of death, affecting his own self-conception as well as his relations with others. A shift from dominance to dependence within his own family may be in store for him.

It is apparent from the foregoing that the consequences that flow from being heart diseased are not limited to the cardiac himself. His spouse and his children are affected as well. The research reported in this paper is concerned with the problems heart disease of the husband-father has created for the farm family and the family's means for dealing with these problems.[4]

OBJECTIVES OF THE STUDY

While there has been considerable research on the impact of various crises upon families, few studies have specifically dealt with heart disease.[5] Fewer still have dealt with the problems heart disease presents for farm families. Therefore, while the present authors were materially aided by the findings, hypotheses, and theoretical orientations of preceding authors, this is nonetheless an exploratory study. Specifically, it set out to answer the following questions:

1. What problems are created for the farm family by the husband-father's heart disease?

2. How do farm families cope with heart disease?

3. What factors involved in the family situation influence responses to this crisis?

THEORETICAL CONSIDERATION

Following Lewin,[6] the present authors regarded the behavior of family members that preceded and that followed the onset of the husband-father's heart disease to be the result of the field of forces that impinge upon each person at a given point in time. This field includes the goals toward which each family member strives, the nature of his relations with others, his values, his conception of the disease as well as its character, and the physical and financial resources for coping with the problems which heart disease has created. Responses to heart disease, including changes in household management, changes in work behavior, changes in plans, changes in relations with other family members, and changes in perception of the disease itself will all be viewed as functions of the individual's psychological field.

GROUPS STUDIED AND METHODS USED

A completely adequate use of Lewin's method for the analysis of the family situation would require repeated interviews through time with each family member as well as with significant persons outside the family group. The present study falls short of this ideal. Detailed data were gathered on the changes that the husband-father's heart disease had brought about within the family according to interviews with the wives of 54 farmers diagnosed as having hypertensive or arteriosclerotic heart disease. The 54 farmers themselves, as well as 343 others, were interviewed and medically examined in 1956–57 and again in 1960.[7] This provided an opportunity for comparing husbands' and wives' perceptions of the situation for 54 families as well as affording observations on a larger group of families seen through the eyes of the men alone.

All of the men were engaged in full-time farming in Central Indiana when first contacted in 1955. Sixty-five percent of the husbands of the women interviewed in 1960 had had heart disease for over five years, while just over ten percent had had it for two years or less. Farmers tend to be older than nonfarmers, and cardiacs tend to be older than noncardiacs. Therefore, 35 percent of the husbands of the women interviewed were 65 or over when interviewed in 1960, 36 percent were between 55 and 64, 26 percent were between 45 and 54, and the remainder were under 45 years of age.

Since the intent of the study was to explore family response to the problems of heart disease as fully as possible, an open-ended, semi-structured interview was used in gathering data from the wives.[8] Data from the farmers themselves were secured by means of structured interviews and medical examinations.

MAJOR FINDINGS

The major findings of this study are organized according to such problem areas as financial support; within each area, comments are made regarding what the families did about the problem. Some of the factors constituting resources for coping with illness will be made explicit in the final summary of the paper.[9]

Defining the Seriousness of the Disease

For the majority of families, the occurrence of heart disease was a sudden, unexpected event which constituted a crisis. Most of the women had not noticed a transitional stage from health to illness, and, presumably, this absence of advance warning or preparation contributed to the definition of the situation as critical. In families where a sudden heart attack was the first manifestation, over 70 percent of the women said they were afraid their husbands would die, while fewer than 20 percent in the families where there had been no attack felt this way. Most of the women could not remember whether or not the physician had told them their husband's life was in danger; it appeared that many of them had reached this conclusion themselves or on the basis of conversations with family members or friends. For some, having one's husband hospitalized heightened their fears that he would die.

Later, if there were no outward signs of illness, such as attacks, pains, or slowing down considerably, and if the men did not talk about how they felt, the wives had difficulty in knowing what the husband's condition was. For many of these women, sickness was defined as being sick in bed and/or not being able to do anything. With heart disease, this is not usually the case; as a matter of fact, medical authorities now generally recommend moderate amounts of activity and exercise. Hence, family members have difficulty in deciding how seriously ill the man is.

Within some families, the seriousness with which heart disease was regarded was relative to other family problems. For example, such problems as delinquent behavior of a son and an accidental death of a child made the heart disease recede in importance. One rather common problem was the wife's own health, two-thirds of the women reporting that they had some kind of illness themselves. Most of their illnesses were those which, like heart disease, occur more frequently after age 45, indicating that in many instances the heart disease was not the only health problem in the family.[10] In some families, the wife considered her illness the crucial one, while in others the wife minimized her own condition.

On the whole, just under 60 percent of the women judged the heart disease to be either the most or one of the most serious problems they had had in their married life. For this group, perceiving changes in the husband's personality, having worries related to work and finances, and having to make a relatively large number of changes following the onset of heart disease (or even more following a heart attack) were all factors contributing to the heart disease being defined as the most or one of the most serious problems the family had ever had. In individual families, however, specific factors could also contribute to the disease being judged as serious. These included moving to a new community to take a new job, the wife going to work, and conflicts within the family regarding the farm work and plans for the future.

Problems of Communication

One of the most common problems reported by wives during the period immediately following the first occurrence of the illness was knowing how often to remind their husbands not to overdo. When husbands were told by their doctors to alter their behavior, many wives felt it was their responsibility to see that this advice was followed. For the wives, the initial fears associated with the diagnosis of heart disease made them want their husbands to be especially cautious and careful. However, most wives admitted that their husbands resented being reminded and did not want to be watched. Most of those who had observed the husband's resentment said that they stopped "following him around." Some said that they still worried about it, while others stated that he was able to take care of himself.

It seems reasonable to think that in the early stages of the heart disease, the man may not want to be reminded and given advice, he may not have accepted the fact of the heart disease himself, and being reminded frequently is damaging to his self-concept. To use Beatrice Wright's term, he is "clinging to the normal ideal."[11] Later, however, the man may accept the fact that he must cut down on activity, and in some cases he may become overly protective of himself. A few wives felt that their husbands now were afraid to do some things which the wives thought they could do.

Many wives said that their husbands did not care to talk about their heart disease. Analysis of the husbands' interviews indicated that 52 percent of the men said that they kept heart symptoms to themselves, and nearly three-fourths said that they had no one to talk to about the heart disease.[12] The illness may be a threatening subject and lead to avoidance of communication about it. Of those who did have someone to talk to, the family was most commonly mentioned.

Some of the women indicated that they depended for cues other than words to determine how their husbands were feeling, such as noting that he went to bed at unusual hours or asked the wife to drive. Families have their own "silent language" by which they communicate feelings and motives. If illness is a new and unusual occurrence, it may take time to work out new cues; meanwhile, misunderstandings can occur.

Getting the Work Done

For a variety of reasons, getting the work done presented problems for many families.[13] There was, of course, the immediate problem of keeping the farm going while the farmer was recovering. On the majority of farms in this part of Indiana, the work is done by the farm operator himself, with the assistance of family members and some hired help in peak work seasons. Feeding of livestock, harvesting, and planting cannot be postponed; sometimes there is difficulty in getting help necessary to do the work if there are no family members readily available. Some of the wives recalled that this had been the biggest worry for their husbands.

Three major reasons for adjusting work to heart disease were evident: retiring; husband and/or wife getting a nonfarm job instead of, or in addition to, farming; and continuing to farm at either the same or a reduced level.

Retiring as a course of action was followed primarily by the men over 65. Some had been cutting down their work before the diagnosis of heart disease, and the diagnosis forced a more definite decision.[14] Among the retired for whom income was not a major concern, the meaningful use of time was the main problem. This was a characteristic problem for those who merely reduced the number of hours of work as well as for those who quit completely. Few had acquired new interests and hobbies after the heart disease. The fact that husbands were around the house more was also a problem for some wives. As one woman said, "He always seemed to be underfoot when I was trying to vacuum or clean."

For those who were not yet ready to retire or who felt that they had to keep on working for financial reasons, work posed other problems. For almost all of the men in this group, farming was the only kind of work they had done; most of them had no training for other kinds of work. The majority were middle-aged or older and felt that it would be difficult to go into any other occupation. Twelve of the 54 men, however, did get some kind of job instead of, or in addition to, farming. Selling farm supplies, equipment, or insurance; truck driving; janitor work; operating a small grocery store; or a government inspection job were the kinds of work they found. Getting a job and adjusting to it were problems for some, and several had returned to farming after trying other things. Where the husband's new job meant moving off the farm to a new community, wives had difficulty finding new friends and ways to occupy themselves.

Eight of the wives of the 12 men who got jobs away from home also got jobs for financial reasons. Since they, likewise, had little training for nonfarm jobs, they were typically employed in laundry work, cooking, house cleaning, waitress work, and working in an office or store. The rural areas in which these families lived did not provide many opportunities for training or for work.[15] Most of them had lived in these communities all of their lives, as their families had before them. Uprooting themselves and moving to distant urban areas proved impossible for them.

Where the wife's job required activities or associations with which she was unfamiliar, such as selling and dealing with customers, adjusting to the new work was more difficult than in cases where she could perform tasks in which she felt comfortable, such as cleaning and cooking.

Working wives typically admitted that their husbands did not want them to work away from home, even though they felt they needed the money. Husbands did not mind their working on the farm but resented their getting a job in the community.

Some of the families who continued to farm appeared to have made adjustments relatively easily. In some cases, grown sons were already farming nearby and assumed more of the responsibilities and work load; in other cases, the men changed enterprises, methods, and size of operation but continued to farm. However, in other families, conflicts had arisen between fathers and sons about the farm work and about the sons' plans for the future. It had been traditional that the farm remain in the family and that a son or sons take over the farm, and the father had assumed that this would be the case although the matter had never been explicitly discussed. The onset of the heart disease brought this matter into the open and revealed that the son did not plan to farm. In other cases, where sons did assume responsibilities, it was difficult for fathers to "give up the reins."

Some wives did more farm work after the husband's illness to keep the farm going. This was especially true for younger wives and for those at lower socioeconomic levels. To some, this did not present any particular problem; they said that they were glad to help and believed that their husbands appreciated it. Others, however, felt that their own health had been affected by the extra work; still others felt that it had interfered with their own work and social activities. Those who wanted to help with the work sometimes felt that their efforts were resented and that tact was required not to hurt their husband's feelings.

Money Problems

Financial problems associated with the heart disease were reported by 43 percent of the women. These included both having extra expenses entailed by the illness itself (hospitalization, medication, and hiring extra help)[16] and worry about having enough to live on after cutting down work or quitting.

In many families, the perception of financial problems was relative to goals and standards of living. Often respondents in the highest socioeconomic groups were worried about maintaining their accustomed level of living, while those of lesser means felt they could manage. There were, however, families in which financial resources were very low and in which family members were acutely concerned about the economic future. Farms of respondents varied rather widely in economic class based on gross sales of farm products, ranging from $1,000 to over $40,000. Somewhat more of those in the lowest socioeconomic group reported financial worries than did those in the highest group.

A larger percentage of the women than men reported worrying about financial matters. Only 16 percent of the husbands of the women interviewed admitted that they worried about finances, while 43 percent of the wives said that they did. Perhaps it is less socially acceptable for men to report financial worries, but evidence shows that some of the wives did worry more than their husbands.[17] They were concerned about impending widowhood and having to manage without their husbands.

Problems in the Routine of Daily Living

In most of the families, illness resulted in changes in daily routines and activities. On the surface, these changes—such as kinds of foods prepared, methods of food preparation, times for going to bed and getting up—may seem slight and inconsequential. Since these changes affected long-established patterns of day-to-day behavior, however, making them constituted problems for the wives as well as for their husbands.[18]

With respect to changes in diet, which demands the cooperation of both husband and wife, the women reported a wide range of effort and success. Some had made what, to them, seemed like big changes, such as broiling instead of frying meat and avoiding pastries and cakes, and they felt that this had been one of the main ways in which they had helped their husbands. Others had made attempts to change but had not been successful, while still others admitted that they had not tried to change their usual methods or menus. Such factors as their interest in food preparation, their willingness to experiment, how important they felt diet was to their husband's health, their own needs, and the willingness of other family members to accept changes in food influenced their efforts and success.

Some families made changes in sleeping arrangements, such as moving beds downstairs or getting separate beds for the husband and wife. Others arranged "resting spots" in the living room or kitchen for daytime rests or secured special lounge chairs for the husband.

The husband's illness made it necessary for some wives to change or curtail their own activities in order to stay at home since their husbands did not want to be alone. There were differences in how easily wives accepted this. Where men used their enforced leisure for activities off the farm, wives found themselves going out more.

Shifts in Values and in Personality

In some families, the husband's illness resulted in changes in both the husband's and wife's values. For instance, one woman said, "We learned to do what was most important. Sometimes I leave the dishes go all day and go out with my husband." Others said that the illness had caused them to return to or turn more often to religious help and prayer. Several said that both had learned not to work so hard after the heart disease and to take things more easily. A few of the wives said they had become more accepting of their husband's behavior, even his drinking. A few saw the illness as being the avenue to a larger, fuller life than they had had before; they began to go out more, made new friends, and participated in new activities. These were a small minority, however. The majority were slightly apprehensive about the future, not knowing exactly what stance they should take.

The single most common change reported by the wives (47 percent) was in the husband's personality or characteristic mode of behavior. This change could take many forms: one might become aggressive, argumentative, dependent, egocentric, pessimistic, fearful, or insistent on having things his way. Wives tended to report personality changes more frequently when there had been a heart attack, when the heart disease first occurred at a relatively early age, and when there had been financial problems related to the illness.

Coping with these changes in personality and with the conflicts which sometimes resulted was an especially hard problem for some of the women and one with which very few had received any help.

FAMILY RESOURCES FOR COPING WITH HEART DISEASE: A SUMMARY INTERPRETATION

The success with which a family copes with the problems which heart disease has created for it depends upon its available resources. These resources are to be found within the individuals themselves, within the community, and within the society. Individuals differ in their psychological make-up (their rigidity, intelligence, emotionality); communities differ in their degree of integration; and societies differ in their welfare legislation and the vigor of their economies. But this analysis has shown that perhaps the major resources for coping with the problems of heart disease are to be found within the family itself.

Family Members as Sources for Help

Family members, including the extended family, were named by 65 percent of the wives, either alone or in combination with others, as providing the most help. They were sources for needed labor and for comfort and counsel; they furnished financial aid and other material goods to the family.[19]

Apart from the cardiac himself, the wife figured most importantly in the family's response to its problems. As has already been pointed out, the husband's illness posed particular problems for wives. The adequacy with which they dealt with the emotional, physical, and financial crises that arose varied greatly. Often they were unwell themselves. Many, however, showed great capacity to cope. Some accepted the situation stoically, saying, "Everyone has problems." Others said that although there were difficult times, they had learned to deal with the situation. Some said that there had actually been significant positive benefits, such as distinguishing the important from the trivial, that resulted from grappling with their problems.

Others Who Help

Neighbors, friends, and hired help as well as family members aided in getting the farm work done. This was less the case in 1960, however, than it had been four years earlier. As time went on, more reliance was placed on the family. This may indicate that friends and neighbors can be counted on during the initial stages of the illness but not as a continuing resource. It may also indicate that most farm families cannot afford to have their work done for them.

The wives also reported receiving help from friends, particularly from those who had similar experiences and with whom they could talk over their problems. The doctor alone was named by only three wives as providing the most help, but in combination with someone else, he was named by nine others, making a total of 23 percent. The specific kinds of help received from the doctor included being told that their husband might be hard to get along with, advice on how they could help, and recommendations on diet.

Now, analysis turns from the specific persons who helped the family cope with the problems that heart disease created for them to a different level of abstraction—to the factors in the situation that influenced their ability to cope.

Values

Those farmers who stressed hard work as an end in itself rather than as a means to other ends found it difficult to slow down or to retire. This illustrates how a particular set of values may facilitate or frustrate adjustments to heart disease. The values held by each family member as well as the malleability of these values have to be taken into account. Some wives could not bring themselves to serve lighter meals; large amounts of heavy foods symbolized health, well-being, and security. Children were often unwilling to sacrifice their own plans for the future to allow their ailing father to better attain his goals. Some families, however, were able to rearrange their hierarchy of values in a manner that permitted everyone to attain some satisfactions.

Financial Resources

The actual costs for medical services, though not insignificant, seemed less important than the loss of income which slowing down or quitting would involve. Fear of the future was often rooted in anticipated loss of income. An "adequate income" is a relative thing, however; a reduction of standard of living can be acutely felt at the higher income levels as well as at the lower.

Communication among Family Members

There were so many constraints upon free communication of fears, hopes, and affection within some families that every family member was, in a real sense, isolated. Sometimes husbands wanted to spare their wives worry and, therefore, tried to hide their pains. This seldom worked and only served to increase the wives' concern. Sometimes an absence of free communication stemmed from a feeling on the husbands' part that "nobody cared," and in a few instances they were partially correct, since the other members of the family felt that they demanded too much. Where husbands and wives were able to openly discuss the crisis that confronted them, solutions to their problems were more evident.

Chance Factors

Some farmers had sudden heart attacks; others discovered their disease through routine medical examinations. Some families were beset with problems before the farmer became ill; others were not. Some farmers were ordered by their doctor to radically alter their way of life; others were required to make fewer changes. In some cases, heart disease was discovered during the peak work season; others had more time to prepare.

All of these chance factors, along with values, financial resources, communication patterns, and the availability of others to provide assistance, affect the family's ability to cope with its problems. However, these factors do not act alone but interact in combinations to determine a specific outcome. This can best be illustrated by considering the stage of the life cycle at which the family must deal with the problems of heart disease.

Stage of the Family Life Cycle[20]

The stage of the family life cycle influences the kind of problems which heart disease will create and the resources available for coping with them. If the farmer's heart disease occurs at an "early age," wives may find it easier to help with the farm work, particularly if they are not involved in the care of small children. Children can work more easily at some stages than others, although this would vary with competing activities, plans, and goals of the children. When heart disease occurs in a parent of middle age, children may be making their own life plans and wanting to escape parental authority. This could contribute further to the tensions accompanying illness; in addition, their plans would also have to be considered in work decisions made by the family. If a change in life work seems necessary, it will generally be more easily made by a younger man; it may also be easier for his wife to find a job. They are more likely to have the education and skills other jobs would require. However, older people with grown children may be better prepared financially to retire—a change that could be less traumatic than going into a new line of work.

Since heart disease occurs more commonly after age 45, it is often accompanied by other age-related illnesses in the wife. The problems of reduced income and increased illness and medical expenses are often twin partners of increasing age. At the same time, contacts with neighbors and friends, who may serve as sources of support, tend to be lessened. The use of leisure time is more likely to create problems for older farmers since they tend to be more highly work-oriented than younger farmers.[21]

Summary. In short, the cardiac farmer and his family have problems which flow from the nature of the disease itself, the nature of farming as an occupation, and the social characteristics of a given family. The ability of a farm family

257

to cope with these problems will depend, at least, upon the availability of others to help do the necessary work, age, the presence or absence of other family problems, income (real and perceived), values and their malleability, and patterns of communication within the family. These factors do not act singly but interact to determine a specific outcome, as the analysis by stages of the family life cycle illustrates.

NOTES

[1] In 1960, 1,702,000 persons in the United States died from all causes. Of these, 921,540, or 54 percent of the total, die of diseases of the cardiovascular system. This is comprised of 192,720 (21 percent) deaths from vascular lesions affecting the central nervous system, 659,410 (75 percent) from diseases of the heart, 12,750 (1 percent) from other hypertensive diseases, 36,500 (4 percent) from general arteriosclerosis, and 20,160 (2 percent) from other diseases of the circulatory system. See U.S. Department of Commerce, *Statistical Abstracts of the United States,* 83rd Annual Edition, Washington: U.S. Government Printing Office, 1962, Table No. 70.

[2] The American Heart Association, *The American Heart,* Vol. X, No. 1, 1960.

[3] It is most difficult to generalize about rheumatic heart disease and congenital heart disease since symptoms, prognosis, and treatments depend upon the specific damage done to the heart. Surgical techniques employed in recent years have completely "cured" some cases. However, many of the symptoms of any heart disease can stem from oxygen deficiency.

[4] The Purdue Farm Cardiac Project has as its paramount objective the development of better ways for rehabilitating the farm cardiac. The authors believe that the entire family must be involved if rehabilitation is to be successful.

[5] From the 1930s and 40s, Mirra Komarovsky's study of the consequences of unemployment for the family and Reuben Hill's on the effects of wartime separation are illustrative of research on crises. See Komarovsky, *The Unemployed Man and His Family,* New York: Dryden Press, 1940; and Hill, *Families Under Stress,* New York: Harper, 1949. In more recent years, studies dealing with such problems as the impact of mental illness, alcoholism, and the presence of a brain-damaged child in the family have been increasing. See Marian Yarrow *et al.,* "The Psychological Meaning of Mental Illness in the Family," *Journal of Social Issues,* 11 (No. 4, 1955), pp. 12–24; and Alfred Freedman *et al.,* "Family Adjustment to the Brain Damaged Child," in *A Modern Introduction to the Family,* ed. by Norman Bell and Ezra Vogel, Glencoe, Illinois: The Free Press, 1960.

One early study of the family situations of cardiac patients was reported by Carol H. Cooley in 1937. Student nurses, under her direction, visited the families of 400 cardiacs discharged from the Cook County Hospital in Chicago. She concluded that acceptance of the illness facilitated adjustment, while overprotection frustrated it. See Cooley, "A Review of the Findings on Home Visits to 400 Cardiac Patients," *Hospitals,* 11 (1937), pp. 43–48

Previous studies of the Purdue Farm Cardiac Project have revealed clues to the relationships that exist between the family situation and the farmer's response to his disease. Brewer concluded that family integration, measured by joint family activities and shared decision making with respect to major purchases, was related to less fatalistic attitudes toward heart disease, and would, therefore, result in easier acceptance of existing conditions. See David L. Brewer, *Family Factors in*

Rehabilitation of Heart Patients, M.S. thesis, Purdue University, 1959. Riedel found that the more family and community support given with farm work, the greater was the farmer's compliance with medical advice. See Donald C. Riedel, *Personal Adjustment to Perceived and Medically Established Heart Disease,* Ph.D. dissertation, Purdue University, 1958. Hayes found that men with more highly educated wives were better informed about heart disease than were men with less educated wives, although there was no relationship between the farmer's own educational attainments and his level of information. See John F. Hayes, *The Cardiac Farmer and His Family: A Study of Resources for Meeting the Crisis of Heart Disease,* M.S. thesis, Purdue University, 1960. Goldstein found that farmers who were least likely to discuss major purchases with their wives attached greater value to hard work for its own sake. These high work-oriented farmers, in turn, were less likely to comply with their physician's advice and regarded the recovery from disease as a matter of will power. See Bernice Goldstein, *The Changing Protestant Ethic: Rural Patterns in Health, Work and Leisure,* Ph.D. dissertation, Purdue University, 1959, and an article with the same title, written with Robert L. Eichhorn for the *American Sociological Review,* Vol. 26 (No. 4, 1961), p. 557–565. Ludwig concluded that cardiac farmers were incapable of drastic changes not in accord with their life goals and values. These goals (life itself, farm ownership, acquiring and rearing children, and the realization of an idealized standard of living) obviously involved other members of the family as well as the farmer himself. See Edward G. Ludwig, *Goals, Values, and Rehabilitation: A Case Study of the Goals and Values of Cardiac and Non-Cardiac Farmers and Their Relevance to Rehabilitation,* M.S. thesis, Purdue University, 1961.

All of the previous studies of the Purdue Farm Cardiac Project, including those that have dealt with the family, have collected data from the farmer. The present study differs in that data were collected from the farmers' wives.

[6]Kurt Lewin, *A Dynamic Theory of Personality,* New York: McGraw-Hill, 1935, pp. 66–113, and also Lewin, *Field Theory in Social Science,* New York: Harper, 1951. Lewin's field theory approach was thought to be especially appropriate for the present study's purposes since the researchers wished to relate in some consistent fashion medical, economic, and social factors. Lewin maintained that analysis should begin with the situation as a whole, from which are differentiated the component parts which are then studied in their relations of interdependence.

[7]The interviews with the wives were conducted in late 1960 and early 1961. In 1956–57, 413 men were interviewed and 397 of them medically examined. In 1960, 369 of these men were re-interviewed and 338 given medical examinations. The 54 families reported on here were drawn from the 338 who participated in both phases of the survey.

[8]See Robert K. Merton, *et al., The Focused Interview,* Glencoe, Ill.: The Free Press, 1956.

[9]Two problems exist in presenting the data necessary to document the generalizations that follow. First, there is the limitation of space; hence, the reader can only be referred to Jacobson, *op cit.,* where there will be found further qualitative and quantitative evidence. The second problem is harder to deal with. According to Lewin's "gestaltist" approach, the unique field of forces operating in a given situation determines behavior. Therefore, a correlation between two variables ripped out of context proves very little. However, there is hope for the quantitatively oriented social scientist. The forces that operate in unique situations, as well as the interrelationships among them, are shared by people. Therefore, cardiac farmers may have similar problems and draw upon similar resources. Lewin encourages looking for these. Thus, the reader will find generalizations based upon statistical descriptions of the population, statistical tests of relationships, and clinical judgments about possible relationships between variables. A single case can often be revealing.

[10]The illnesses commonly reported included kidney trouble, gall bladder and colon trouble, "nerves" or "nervous breakdown," heart disease, diabetes, problems related to the menopause, and arthritis.

[11]Beatrice Wright, *Physical Disability—A Psychological Approach,* New York: Harper, 1960.

[12]One-third of the wives did not know whether or not their husbands took medicine for their heart condition. Among the larger survey group, only about a fifth of the men felt that their families withheld information from them. Men who felt that their families withheld information worried more than men who did not feel this way.

[13]The most common recommendation made by doctors to the men with heart disease in the total study group was to give up, cut down, or change their work activities; 90 percent were thus advised in 1956–57. This was also the single most difficult thing for the men to do. Prior research had indicated that many of the men in this group attached high value to work. (See Goldstein, *op. cit.*) This is readily understandable. Not only is it necessary for most men to work to earn a living, but it also satisfies the need for activity and gives one the feeling that he is accomplishing something, that he is a man. The work one does is also the basis for judging status. Having to change or give up work habits to which one has become accustomed after long years can be very difficult.

[14]Andersen found that poor health was a decisive factor in the decision to retire among men in the survey group who had retired after the 1956–57 interviews. See Ronald M. Andersen, *Retirement Decision and Satisfaction: A Study of Cardiac and Non-Cardiac Farmers,* M.S. thesis, Purdue University, 1962.

[15]Age also influenced whether or not nonfarm jobs were secured. All of the men and women among those intensively studied who got nonfarm jobs were under 60, and the majority were under 50. In the entire survey group, more women under than over 50 were working away from home.

[16]Loss of income seemed more significant to these farmers than the actual cost of care.

[17]Forty-five percent of the women who worried about finances said they did not think their husbands worried about this matter.

[18]In 1956, 40 percent of the cardiacs from the total study group were told to change their diet, 27 percent to lose weight, 27 percent to change some personal habit such as smoking, 15 percent to give up responsibilities, 89 percent to alter their work behavior, and 14 percent to change their social activities.

[19]The majority of these families had relatives living nearby and frequently exchanged visits and work with them. It must be remembered that, in the main, these were families living in communities in which their ancestors had been early settlers. Many descendants of the original families lived in the same community or nearby. Perhaps the extended family plays a less vital role for those who have been more mobile geographically. This may also be true for the socially mobile.

[20]The stage of the family life cycle does not completely determine the nature of the problems the family will confront on the resources available to them. For instance, older farmers are not necessarily richer farmers; however, they have often achieved more of their life goals than younger farmers, and a major goal for farmers at all ages is land ownership.

[21]Bernice Goldstein and Robert L. Eichhorn, *op cit.*

Unemployment—Crisis of the Common Man

Ruth Shonle Cavan

Since the 1929 depression rocked the foundations of the family as well as the economy, there has been a paucity of research concern with the problem of unemployment as it affects the family. A renewed interest in poverty alleviation has resulted in growing awareness that many families (especially those of minority status) must cope with chronic long-term or intermittent unemployment. Additionally, the American economy fluctuates in such a way as to leave the middle-class man stranded without a job from time to time. Thus Cavan's article, written in 1950, has current application to an important source of family crises of a large portion of our population. She reviews the research findings available on family interactions and role changes and adjustments during times of unemployment of the husband, and delineates the types of families that do or do not weather financial setbacks. Various types of unemployment and the diversity of their effects are also discussed.

Any period of widespread, prolonged unemployment raises the specter of possible family disorganization and even disintegration. The Great Depression of the 1930's led to a number of studies of family reactions to unemployment and lowered income. These studies can lay the foundation for current studies and even for current methods of alleviation, with some consideration for the differences between the 1930's and the late 1950's.

In order to sharpen our view of the impact of unemployment on family life, this review of the depression studies is organized according to social class, so far as such a classification is possible in studies made before the concept of social class was well defined.[1]

The social classes discussed here are as follows:
1. The lower-lower class family:
   a. with long-term or permanent unemployment,
   b. with regular repetitive unemployment,
   c. usually employed, except in time of personal or economic emergency;
2. The family of the "common man," that is, upper-lower and lower-middle class, regularly employed except in time of great economic emergency;
3. The upper-middle class.

The family of the common man is discussed first, since the traumatic impact of unemployment seems most acute in this social class.

The Common Man, Upper-Lower and Lower-Middle Classes

The conditions imposed by unemployment and lowered income are most significant when seen against a backdrop of what the common man wants, expects, and has partially achieved. One of the chief values of the common man is to be self-supporting at all times, with a backlog of moderate savings. Often the family prides itself on "getting ahead," with a goal of upward mobility, if not for the parents, at least for their children. Wives may work regularly or intermittently and older children work, but the husband is the chief and most steady worker and makes the largest contribution to the family budget. Typically, his status is recognized as the highest in the family. The effort toward upward mobility is chiefly in the acquisition of rather expensive equipment, not always paid for, or in moving into a better neighborhood than the one in which the family originally lived. Culturally and socially, the family may not have established itself in the next higher class. Hence, considerable emphasis is placed on visible material possessions which are symbols of status.

Four depression studies that concentrated on the common man are:[2] Cavan and Ranck, whose study of one hundred Chicago families included sixty-eight of common-man status; Komarovsky, who concentrated on fifty-nine cases; Bakke, *The Unemployed Worker*, based on a number of studies made between 1932 and 1939; and *Citizens Without Work*, by the same author, an eight-year study of twenty-four families suffering prolonged unemployment.

Reaction to Unemployment

A loss of or reduction in employment and hence in income among these families poses a many-sided threat: loss of the symbols of social class status; eventual probable application for relief; disorganized personal reactions; disorganization and rearrangement of roles within the family; downward social mobility.

262

First came the financial adjustment. At least at the beginning of the depression, there was disbelief that the situation was anything except a normal short lay-off. Men therefore were inclined to speak of deserving a short vacation. When no recall came, they sought employment first in their special skill, then in a less specialized and lower paid type of work, finally in any work, and eventually at odd jobs. [Cavan and Ranck, Bakke]. This devaluation of job status was a long-drawn out procedure. For as long as six months, skilled workers held out for the old wages, but by the end of twelve months, 85 percent were willing, although often resentful, to take any kind of job. [Bakke ch. 8]

If other members of the family found work, their employment eased the financial strain, but often produced interpersonal strains.

As unemployment was prolonged, resources (symbols of status) were used with the following order of frequency: credit, small savings, loans, selling or pawning goods, and cashing of insurance policies. [Bakke, ch. 8; Cavan and Ranck, p. 84] Expenses were reduced by having the telephone removed, not taking summer vacations, dropping club memberships, and the like. Some families moved to less expensive living quarters; others moved in with relatives. As long as possible, invisible reductions were made; but eventually it was not possible to conceal the financial condition from neighbors. The final and most difficult financial adjustment was in applying for relief. For these self-supporting and often upwardly mobile families, relief was regarded as a personal disgrace. It was also the end of their hopes for upward mobility and often was preceded by definite downward mobility, partly because personal resources had to be reduced to a very low point before the family would be accepted by most relief agencies.

During this period of declining employment and exhaustion of resources, three types of reaction occurred.

1. Emotional reactions of husband and wife. The period preceding application for relief was a harrowing one as the family resisted the change in self-conception that relief made necessary. Worry, discouragement, and despondency were common emotional reactions. When forced to apply for relief, husband and wife cried at the agency. Definitely neurotic symptoms occurred in a minority of cases, as extreme insomnia, hysterical laughter, burning spots on the body, and suicide threats. However, out of the total of one hundred Chicago cases there were only two suicides, neither attributable solely to the depression. Husband and wife often shared equally in the emotional tension. In some families, one member, often the husband, became more disturbed than the others. A few drank heavily and several had "nervous breakdowns." [Cavan and Ranck, pp. 55–66; Komarovsky, pp. 36 ff., 66 ff.]

2. Changes in roles within the family. Although the husband is the chief earner in the family of the common man, it is accepted that the wife works when necessary, and that older children have an obligation to work part or full time as soon as they reach the legal age for employment. It was less true in the early 1930's than now that the wife works as a matter of choice and not simply from necessity. But even in the 1930's the employment of the

wife was not taken as a threat to the husband's superior status, so long as it was conceded that the wife's employment was temporary.

The unemployment of the husband affected roles in three ways. First, when the husband could not find any work, his role suffered in the eyes of other members of the family. Wives sometimes lost their respect or accused their husbands of not trying to find work. Unless the husband could work out some role in the household (difficult to do), he really had no role to play. [Cavan and Ranck, Komarovsky, various items]

Second, when some members of the family usurped the role of the husband as chief wage earner, interpersonal relationships became strained. Apparently actual reduction in dollars earned was less devastating than change in roles; or, dire poverty was easier to bear than the husband's loss of status to some previously subordinate member. It seems to make little difference what members worked or how much or how little each earned, provided that the husband remained the largest contributor to the family purse. Tension was increased by the custom of children contributing their money to the family through the mother, who then often became the bursar for the family. [Cavan, Komarovsky, Bakke]

Third, when the family finally applied for relief and was accepted as a client, further rearrangement of roles became necessary. The relief worker assumed a role superior to that of the husband. Since the relief worker was usually a woman, and dealt primarily with the wife, the husband now found himself subordinate both to his wife and to the woman relief worker. [Bakke]

3. Change in social class status. In the hierarchy of social class levels, families on relief are relegated to lower-lower class status. Especially for upward mobile families, their descent to lower-lower class was embittering. When these families were forced to move, the search for lower rent sometimes brought many relief families into the same neighborhood. Baake speaks of entire neighborhoods of relief families.

As the depression progressed, certain cushions were devised. One of these was the Works Progress Administration (WPA), established in 1935, which provided work relief. At first, WPA workers were contrasted with persons still on relief; their self-respect increased and their social status was slightly improved. But in time, WPA workers were identified with relief cases and contrasted with persons privately employed. Their status and self-respect then again declined. [Bakke, ch. 12]

Another cushion was unemployment compensation, established in 1938, and by now a customary way to tide over short periods of unemployment. The implications of unemployment compensation are discussed later in this paper.

Readjustment of Family

Emotional disturbance usually continued until the family reached a level, however low, of stability. As soon as the family accepted this level as probably permanent, reorganization began as the family adjusted itself to its new level.

As the depression decreased and various members of the family found work, upward mobility sometimes began again; however, older members of the family often were unable to regain their former personal status, so that the family status might be organized around the older children as the chief earners.

Bakke divides the readjustment process into experimental and permanent. He says that few families remained disorganized for a very long period of time. In experimental readjustment, the husband accepted his lowered status and a new hierarchy of statuses began to develop, with the wife granted the authority to manage finances and each child assigned a status relative to earning capacity. New interests and new plans for children developed, appropriate to the new social class status. The family drew together again with new roles that fitted together into an integrated pattern. Permanent readjustment came when the family stopped comparing the meager present with the more comfortable past, accepted rationalizations for the lowered status, and renewed a full round of family activities although of a different type than formerly.

In other families, the disarrangement of roles and lowering of statuses were less severe and consequently readjustment came more quickly. When the family did not have to make a residential move, loss of social status was less noticeable. Avoidance of relief through reduced expenses or help from relatives saved the family from the greatest humiliation. Activities and goals could be modified without great disorganization. [Cavan and Ranck, ch. 7]

Pre-unemployment Factors

Two studies, Cavan and Ranck, and Komarovsky, emphasized the previous family organization as a factor in the way in which families of the common man reacted to the depression.

Cavan and Ranck used the concept of well organized family, defined as a family with a high degree of unity and reciprocal functioning. Although well and poorly organized familes varied in their reactions to unemployment, in general well organized families fared better than the poorly organized. They suffered emotionally as they approached the relief status, but also attempted to adjust realistically. The family group remained intact and as the lower status was accepted, family goals of a new type evolved. The family group worked together to overcome their problems.

Families disorganized prior to the depression tended to become more disorganized. Previous latent tensions between husband and wife or between parents and children came into the open under the increased tension of unemployment and low income. In a few cases the parents separated, adolescent children ran away from home, or the family broke into several small units. In some of these families, stability increased with the entrance of a relief agency whose worker helped to hold the family together by permitting the members to become dependent upon her. [Cavan and Ranck, ch. 7]

Komarovsky limited her research to a study of the relation between the husband's role as the economic provider of the family and his authority in the family. In forty-five out of fifty-nine cases, all on relief one or more years, the husband did not lose his authority in the family. In these families the authority of the husband was based either on love and respect, or on the traditional semi-patriarchal organization of the common-man family. Unemployment was not interpreted as a reflection on the husband.

When the authority of the husband was based on fear of the husband or was maintained for utilitarian purposes, his unemployment was followed by loss of respect and loss of authority. In some of these families, the wife did not respect her husband prior to the unemployment. When unemployment freed her from economic dependence upon him, the thin veneer of submission cracked. The husbands attempted to force respect from wife and children, psychologically or physically, or selected a few areas of dominance about which they would not yield; some sought compensation in alcohol or religion.

Summary of the Common Man and Unemployment

In general the upper-lower and lower-middle class families suffered greatly from prolonged unemployment which violated deeply revered values of the common man: relief substituted for self-support; transfer of the highest family status from the husband to some previously subordinate member of the family; and downward social mobility. The lengthy period of downgrading to relief status was the most difficult and was marked by severe emotional reactions. Readjustment came with acceptance of the condition of poverty and reorganization of the family in harmony with the reality of the situation. The well organized family with unity of purpose and reciprocal functioning of members in which the husband held his status on the basis of love and respect or tradition weathered the adjustment better than poorly organized families or those in which fear and utilitarian motives were at the basis of the hierarchy of statuses.

THE UPPER-MIDDLE CLASS

The upper-middle class was less affected by the depression than the common man, and very few persons became relief clients.[3] Most upper-middle workers remained in their accustomed positions, sometimes at higher incomes than prior to the depression. The few whose businesses failed or who became unemployed tended to re-establish themselves by their own efforts.

However, one study concentrated on families, primarily upper-middle class, which had suffered a decrease of at least 25 per cent in their income, often accompanied by total or partial unemployment.[4] The reaction of these families was severe but was related chiefly to changes of personal status within the family. With a few exceptions, the families were able to remain in their homes and thus were saved one of the drastic steps in downward social mobility. They also managed to get along without applying for relief.

Angell's main focus was on the effect of reduced income on interpersonal relationships among family members. The two elements of family life found most significant in type of adjustment were integration and adaptability. Angell applied these concepts to the way in which families accepted changes in relative status of family members, especially to lowered status of the husband. The most severe test came when the husband yielded his dominant status to someone else, for example, to the wife who became the chief wage earner. When the husband was able to retain his previous status or modified it only slightly, adjustment was easier. Successful adjustment to modified or markedly changed status called for a change of roles and acceptance of the change by all concerned.

Readjustment of roles without personal or familial disorganization was accomplished most readily by integrated, adaptable families. Unadaptable families, regardless of the degree of integration, experienced personal and/or family disorganization. Unintegrated families with a low degree of adaptability made unpredictable responses.

It was also found that adaptability increased with a non-materialistic philosophy of life, freedom from traditionalism, and responsibleness of the parents.

One may summarize Angell's study of upper-middle class families by saying that adaptability is more important than integration in adjusting to lowered income, but that the unstructured, unintegrated, and unadaptable family tends to increase in disintegration.

THE LOWER-LOWER CLASS FAMILY

Although lower-lower class families experience more unemployment than any other class, they are least affected by it. They may earlier have suffered from it, but in time they tend to accept unemployment as a normal way of life. These families contrast sharply with the unemployment families in the common man class and the upper-middle class.

Long Term or Permanent Unemployment

Permanently unemployed families are relief clients year in and year out, in prosperity as well as in depression; or they have found some unrespectable way to live without working. By the time unemployment is reached, there are usually physical and personality deficiencies, such as disease, vagrancy, petty thievery, alcoholism, unstable emotional reactions, or inability to work with others or to accept authority. Which of these conditions are causes and which effects of unemployment, it seems impossible to say. These deficiencies become a permanent part of the situation and often are used to manipulate relief agencies or the public into giving aid. They become assets rather than disintegrating elements in the family.

These families tend to accept their impoverished status and to stabilize family life at a dependency level. Some members may have been reared in similar families and thus have been socialized into this type of family from birth. Others, however, have slipped downward. With time, some kind of adjustment is made and the family develops rationalizations or a philosophy of life, appropriate family roles, and relationships with the outside world that enable it to function.

In his study, *The Beggar*, Gilmore describes a family in which begging set the mode of life through sixty years and five generations.[5] Beggars not reared in begging families sometimes reach this status after intermittent periods on relief. When all private resources have been exhausted and relief is unavailable or inadequate, these families turn to begging. Soon they have developed a philosophy that they cannot or should not work in ordinary occupations; they refer to begging as work. Even though all members of the family may not beg, the whole family shares the begging philosophy, since the social status of the family is determined by even one begging member. Society places the beggar at one of the lowest social levels, but the beggar himself is protected from feeling debased by his philosophy.

Begging is a family project, which helps to unify the family. Whichever members of the family can make the greatest appeal for sympathy go out to beg, with the family as a whole sharing the proceeds. Parents who thus provide well for their children have family roles of authority and respect.

Studies of families permanently on relief also show how unemployment is accepted as a normal status. The function of the relief agency is important. The longitudinal study of one hundred Chicago families made in 1934-35 by Cavan and Ranck yielded twelve families that had been wholly or partially on relief prior to the depression. In time of high employment, they nevertheless lived in the social world of the permanently unemployed. Many of these families included at least one disorganized person, often the husband, whose disabilities gave justification for the relief status in the eyes of the family. The families held together, having adjusted family roles to the personalities of their members, sometimes in unorthodox ways. Important in the family organization was the relief agency, which often assumed functions typical of a husband. The agency supplied money, sometimes managed the budgeting, helped the family plan, and in general gave stability and security in many areas other than financial.

A third report throws light on mobile unemployed families.[6] When the Atomic Energy Commission established a plant in southern Ohio, many mobile families were drawn into the area for employment. Social services were approached by six mobile families who were not seeking employment, but whose histories showed that their mode of life was constant migration back and forth across the country in battered automobiles, their means of support whatever they could get from relief agencies. The husbands as a rule were very infantile and dependent in personality type; the wives were docile. They wanted to be cared for by the agency. The family units were closely organized and void of conflict. The men maintained their family status through the skill with which they could manipulate the relief workers or community sentiment in their favor. Although the means were unconventional, the husband still held high status as the good provider. As with public begging, the technique of appeal was well developed. The man made the appeal for sympathy, playing up the needs of his family, and ingratiating himself with the relief worker or others in the community who might help him. As a rule, the men were at first success-ful in arousing interest and securing aid. As soon as efforts were made to pro-vide employment, the family quietly disappeared, to turn up later in some other city. As with the dependent families in the Chicago study, already cited, the relief agency tended to assume many of the functions normally held by the husband.

It seems to be possible to conclude from studies of permanently unemployed people that permanent unemployment is not a traumatic, disorganizing ex-perience. It is accepted as the customary way of life. The family devises ways to support itself without work and builds up a supporting philosophy and integrated family roles.

Regular, Repetitive Unemployment

The seasonal worker who follows a yearly routine of alternating periods of employment and unemployment typifies the above category. According to Hathaway's 1934 study of the migratory family, and other fragmentary sources, these families often are not rooted in any community and the standard of living tends to be low.' The families are not, however, disorganized. They have accepted the mobile life and the rotation of employment and unemployment as normal for themselves. Often a regular route is followed year after year and the family knows in advance where it is likely to be throughout the working season. The off-season often finds each family in the same city every year. If the family has not been able to save sufficient money for the off-season, relief is sought. The whole yearly pattern can be foreseen. There is therefore no shock, no crisis, when seasonal unemployment comes; and there is a technique for handling the lack of funds.

The families are organized with the father as head. He makes the arrange-ments for work for the family as a unit. He therefore has authority and respect. Once the family has accepted migrancy as a way of life, the husband fulfills his role if he makes good contacts for work during the working seasons; he is not considered a failure if the family must apply for relief in the off season.

The seasonal working family, like the permanently dependent family, illustrates adjustment to unemployment, the maintenance of roles within the family, and as a consequence little personal or family disorganization as a result of unemployment. Since both types of family tend to be at a bare sub-sistence level with or without relief, there is no question of downward social mobility. These two types of unemployment are cited to illustrate that unem-ployment is not necessarily disorganizing, when it is part of the customary way of life, when roles are integrated, and when the family has developed techniques acceptable to itself for securing maintenance when there is no earned income.

One or More Members Usually Employed

These families are marginal between self-support and dependence on relief agencies—between the common man and the permanently unemployed.

They are usually able to meet their own expenses, but any emergency that either throws the chief wage earner out of work or increases expenses leads the family to some source of temporary help. These temporary lapses from financial self-sufficiency are recognized as emergencies beyond personal control. They do not cause the family to change its conception of itself as self-supporting, nor do family roles change, although one member of the family may temporarily carry out the functions of another member.

A few such families appeared among the one hundred Chicago families studied by Cavan and Ranck. The long-continued unemployment of the depression came as a crisis with which the families could not cope. They could not understand the cause of the depression unemployment, as they had been able to understand previous short periods of distress. They were forced to apply for relief for an indefinite period of time. They were also compelled to change their conception of themselves as self-supporting, and to adjust roles and sometimes class status to conform to their relief status. The reactions of these families were similar to the reactions of common man families who had never been on relief prior to the depression.

CONCLUSIONS

Briefly, one may conclude that the following reactions to prolonged unemployment may be expected:

1. The common man struggles to maintain personal status, family integration, and social class status.

2. The upper-middle class family (when affected at all) struggles to maintain personal roles, especially of the father, within the family.

3. The permanently or seasonally unemployed accept their position as normal, adjust personal statuses and roles, and integrate relief agencies or public donors into the family.

4. Even when family disorganization is marked, the family tends to reorganize once the downward decline in personal and class status reaches a stable point.

5. Characteristics facilitating good adjustment are a well organized family prior to unemployment, adaptability, responsibleness, and a non-materialistic and non-traditional philosophy of life.

Applicability of the 1930 Research
to the 1950 Family

A higher percentage of married women work now than in the early 1930's, a situation that gives more economic security. We assume that the family is more equalitarian in its functioning. Do these two facts, taken together, mean that the unemployed husband could yield the dominant role (which he still retains) more gracefully to his wife than he could in the early 1930's? If so, his emotional disturbance should be less.

The great number of cars, summer homes, electrical household equipment, suburban homes, and college educations that have been bought since World War II suggest increased upward mobility, or at least the collection of material symbols of upward mobility. Many of these are being bought on the installment plan and therefore are insecurely owned. Would prolonged unemployment bring a great downward movement in social class status? Such a movement would increase bitterness and disappointment.

Do families of the common man category have the same aversion to relief that they had in the 1930's? To anything called "relief," probably they have. But the nation-wide forms of relief instituted by the federal government in the 1930's operate under sugar-coated names such as pension, aid, insurance, and compensation. The fact that employees pay into Old Age and Survivor's Insurance has created a widespread idea that they also pay into other forms of aid, such as Old Age Assistance or Pensions and Unemployment Compensation. Actually, they have not done so, but their belief that they have makes it easier for them to apply. The eligibility rules for public assistance programs have been widely publicized and people are urged to apply when eligible; they are not urged to be strong, independent, and self sufficient. Nor does the public agency probe into family relationships or violate the feeling of privacy of the family. When eligibility rules have been met, the applicant receives a check which he may spend as he chooses. It seems probable, therefore, that the unemployed person today accepts Unemployment Compensation as his due and not as charity.

Unemployment Compensation is designed to tide a family or worker over a short period of unemployment. It is much less than the person's wages and it runs for only a few months. If the person becomes re-employed soon, he does not lose social class status and probably family roles are not disturbed. However, if he has no other income, he must reduce expenses and if he has private resources he must dip into them. With long term unemployment, the Unemployment Compensation runs out along with the private resources. At this point, the person is in the same position that the 1930 unemployed person was when he had exhausted his resources; Unemployment Compensation has simply postponed or prolonged the decline to relief status.

It seems probable that the socio-psychological trends and adjustments of the 1930's would be found in the 1950's, but that the conditions under which these trends and adjustments would work themselves out have changed.

271

NOTES

[1] Family life according to social class is discussed in Ruth Shonle Cavan, *The American Family,* New York: Thomas Y. Crowell Company, 1953, Part II.

[2] Ruth Shonle Cavan and Katherine Howland Ranck, *The Family and the Depression,* Chicago: University of Chicago Press, 1938; Mirra Komarovsky, *The Unemployed Man and His Family,* New York: Dryden Press, 1940; E. Wight Bakke, *The Unemployed Worker, A Study of the Task of Making a Living without a Job,* New Haven: Yale University Press, 1940, No. 1; and Bakke, *Citizens without Work,* New Haven: Yale University Press, 1940, No. 2. No. 1 and No. 2 are used in the text to distinguish Bakke's two books.

[3] W. Lloyd Warner and Paul S. Lunt, *Social Life of a Modern Community,* New Haven: Yale University Press, 1941, pp. 277–279; Winona L. Morgan, *The Family Meets the Depression,* Minneapolis: University of Minnesota Press, 1939.

[4] Robert Cooley Angell, *The Family Encounters the Depression,* New York: Charles Scribner's Sons, 1936.

[5] Harlan W. Gilmore, *The Beggar,* Chapel Hill: University of North Carolina Press, 1940, pp. 168–182; Chapter 5 on "Urban Beggardom" also is pertinent to family reactions.

[6] Martha Bushfield Van Valen, "An Approach to Mobile Dependent Families," *Social Casework,* 37 (April, 1956), pp. 180–186.

[7] Studies of migrant workers usually are focused on conditions of work, health problems, and lack of education for the children. Few give very much information on family organization, roles, or reaction to unemployment. Some insight can be gleaned from Marion Hathaway, *The Migratory Worker and Family Life,* Chicago: University of Chicago Press, 1934. *The American Child,* published bi-monthly, November to May, by the National Child Labor Committee, contains numerous articles regarding the handicaps of migratory life for children.

7

The Family as a Locus for Personal Development

When a baby is born, one of the major reactions of doting parents and relatives is to speculate on what kind of person he or she will grow up to be. The hope, of course, is that the child will develop talents and personality characteristics that allow him or her to live a happy, creative, productive life. Socialization at home and in the schools is presumably dedicated to these ends. But after school, and after the grown child has left the family home, what then? Has all that can be done for self-fulfillment occurred in youth, or is this sort of development a never-ending task (including perhaps "undoing" some socialization of the past)? It would seem that the latter is probably closest to the truth. If this is so, then the question becomes: Where and under what conditions can self-fulfillment and development of one's potential continue or be remedied?

Most persons have three possible "sites" for this enterprise—their close relationships with others (such as the family and other long-term arrangements); their jobs or careers; or their spare-time recreation. The best of all possible worlds, of course, is that self-fulfillment would be available to them in all three areas. But in the age of automation, jobs can be deadly dull. Recreation can be costly and dependent on various opportunities not available to financially limited persons. This leaves the family as the most consistently available group or site for self-actualization.

Whether the family operates this way in actuality, however, depends on the role relationships of family members. Each person must be allowed the necessary "room" in which to develop his or her potential. Each person must support the other's need for creativity and give him or her that sense of self-worth through the feeling of being loved that encourages it. As will be seen, this ideal is not always achieved. The roles of family members in traditional families can stunt growth rather than encourage it. The problem becomes one of both planning and balance of the needs of all individuals as well as consideration of the good of the group.

273

Marriage, His and Hers

Jessie Bernard

For years, social scientists have used marital status as a category for analysis, comparing the married with the single and divorced. Implied in many, but not all, of these studies is that marriage means the same and has the same effect on both men and women. Bernard here demonstrates that such is not the case. There are really two marriages in any marital state—his and hers.

    Conventional wisdom has it that men have little to gain and a great deal to lose from marriage. Yet if married men are compared with single men, they are shown to have better physical and mental health and to live longer. Divorced and widowed men remarry at high rates—having tried both ways of living, they apparently prefer the married state. At the same time, the two major drawbacks of marriage for men—sexual limitations and total responsibility for supporting the family—are gradually being replaced with a more permissive moral atmosphere and increasing proportions of married women in the labor force. Marriage should be looking better all the time for men.

    On the other hand, the effect of marriage on women is not so positive. They report more unhappiness and frustration, insecurity, and other negative feelings about marriage than do men. Despite the fact that women live longer than men, they are more likely to have serious mental health problems if married. The fact that never-married women show more happiness and less psychological distress than never-married men would seem to rule out the possibility that it is women's general emotional weakness and not the effects of marriage that accounts for these differences. Traditional sex role characteristics may be bad for women's mental health. The wife is expected to be the accommodating person and to channel her energies not toward her own fulfillment, but toward her husband's. Her temperament must be reoriented to handle his usually less expressive mode. Further, being relegated to housework and nursemaid duties does not aid continued personal development. The evidence seems to point to marriage as socializing women toward development of negative mental health characteristics.

THE HUSBAND'S MARRIAGE

Marriage Has Had a Bad Press Among Men

Despite the insistence of theologians that marriage is a holy estate, divinely instituted, it has had a bad press among men. Writers of the Middle Ages were already inveighing against it, invoking tales of domestic discord to support their complaints that wives were impossible. Not until the middle of the sixteenth century were there books on *The Prayse of All Women* (1541) and *The Defence of Women*. But even then we learn from *The Schole-howse of Women* that women were fastidious, sharp-tongued, quick-tempered, disputatious, fond of double-dealing, and, when married, querulous and gossipy, not willing to mind the house.

Thus, for centuries men have been told—by other men—that marriage is: no bed of roses, a necessary evil, a noose, a desperate thing, a field of battle, a curse, a school of sincere pretense. Robert Louis Stevenson commented on the dread of marriage that men professed. There was an aphorism attributed to Oscar Wilde that marriage was a wonderful institution; every woman should be married, but no man. Another, attributed to H. L. Mencken, is to the effect that since it was to man's interest to avoid marriage as long as possible and to woman's to marry as favorably as possible, the sexes were pursuing diametrically antagonistic ends in this major life concern.

Even today, it is the rare stand-up comedian who omits from his repertoire half a dozen references to the unholy state of matrimony, its fetters, it frustrations. And Russell V. Lee, a physician with forty-four years of clinical experience, tells us, for reasons spelled out below, that, "men really suffer more in marriage than do women"; that "the state is less natural for the male; . . . [that] he contributes more and gets less out of marriage than the female."[1]

Men, in brief, have been railing against marriage for centuries. If marriage were actually as bad for men as it has been painted by them, it would long since have lost any future it may ever have had. In the face of all the attacks against it, the vitality of marriage has been quite stupendous. Men have cursed it, aimed barbed witticisms at it, denigrated it, bemoaned it—and never ceased to want and need it or to profit from it.

The male clichés could hardly have been more wrong. However horrendous the inner picture of the husbands' marriage might be, the measurable evidence against that image is overwhelming. For, contrary to all the charges leveled against it, the husbands' marriage, whether they like it or not (and they do), is awfully good for them.

Marriage Is Good for Men

There are few findings more consistent, less equivocal, more convincing than the sometimes spectacular and always impressive superiority on almost every index—demographic, psychological, or social—of married over never-married men. Despite all the jokes about marriage in which men indulge, all the complaints they lodge against it, it is one of the greatest boons of their sex. Employers, bankers, and insurance companies have long since known this. And whether they know it or not, men need marriage more than women do. As Samuel Johnson said, marriage is, indeed "the best state for man in general; and every man is a worse man in proportion as he is unfit for the married state."

The research evidence is overwhelmingly convincing. . . . Although the physical health of married men is no better than that of never-married men until middle age, their mental health is far better, fewer show serious symptoms of psychological distress, and fewer of them suffer mental health impairments. Married men, Otto Pollak tells us, seem also to be preserved from lives of crime. Blau and Duncan, Melita Odin, and William H. Whyte have shown that marriage is an asset in a man's career, including his earning power. The value of marriage for sheer male survival is itself remarkable. It does, indeed, pay men to be married. "Most men," Paul C. Glick notes, "profit greatly from having a wife to help them take care of their health."

A great sociologist, Emile Durkheim, was one of the first to point out the salvaging effect of marriage on men in connection with a classic study of suicide.[2] He computed what he called a "coefficient of preservation"—the ratio of the suicide rate of the unmarried to that of the married—and found it higher for men than for women. The differential still holds. In the United States, the suicide rate for single men is almost twice as high as for married men, less than one-and-a-half times greater for single than for married women.

Marriage is so demonstrably good for men that when social scientists were asked to come up with a set of social indicators that would tell us how our society was operating, as the economic indicators told us how our economy was operating, one such index proposed by Paul C. Glick as a favorable sign was the proportion of adult males who were married. The statistical underpinning for this rationale was convincing. Compared with never-married men, the lot of married men is a providential one.

. . . and They Know It

The actions of men with respect to marriage speak far louder than words; they speak, in fact, with a deafening roar. Once men have known marriage, they can hardly live without it. Most divorced and widowed men remarry. At every age, the marriage rate for both divorced and widowed men is higher than the rate for single men. Half of all divorced white men who remarry do so within three years after divorce. Indeed, it might not be far-fetched to conclude that the verbal assaults on marriage indulged in by men are a kind of compensatory reaction to their dependence on it.

But Does Marriage Deserve All the Credit?

Statistically speaking, there seems to be no doubt about the value of marriage for men, but a statistical view is not enough. There are selective factors involved that can distort the picture, and hence cannot be ignored. We are never sure how much of the good showing of married men as compared with never-married men is related to the beneficent effects of marriage itself, and how much to the selective processes that weed poor prospects out of marriage in the first place. It should be made clear that, when we speak of selective factors, we include not only conscious choices among both sexes but also the impersonal factors that influence who marries and who does not. A man may be "selected out" of marriage not by any decision on his part but by such factors as residence, occupation, and so on.

Some men do not marry because they do not want to, for whatever reason, and some because no one wants to marry them. In either case, we are faced with the irrepressible, inevitable, and—most researchers concede—insoluble chicken-and-egg, cause-and-effect question. Do the married men look so much better than the never-married because marriage is good for them or because the less good prospects were selected out of the married population in the first place? All the thoughtful researchers who tackle this problem end up by admitting that they cannot solve it. Short of a controlled experiment—unthinkable this side of 1984—we have to pick and choose our way around and through the data. At least two lines of evidence are helpful; one "controls" the selective factor by comparing the married with the widowed, and one by comparing men of the same general status and occupation who have and who have not married.

By comparing the married with the widowed we minimize, though we do not entirely eliminate, the selective factor,[3] for the widowed did once choose marriage or were chosen by someone. Such comparisons give us an indication of the value of marriage by showing what happens to men who are deprived of it by death. They are miserable. They show more than expected frequencies of psychological distress, and their deathrate is high. Men deprived of the benefits of marriage by bereavement show the effects in high mortality rates. That it is the deprivation itself which produces such a result can be seen in the fact that during the first half year after bereavement, one study found an increase of 40 percent in mortality. Five years after bereavement, the survival rate of married or remarried men in a sample of forty-seven men with an average age of seventy-six was higher than that of the never-married, the separated, the unremarried divorced, or the unremarried widowed. And although a fifth of widowed women in another study showed some deterioration of health in the year following bereavement, death resulted twice as often among widowed men as among widowed women. The suicide rate of the widowed man is high, too. In fact, suicide is the third-ranking cause of death among widowed men.[4]

The other, and less macabre, way to minimize the selective factor in measuring the benefits of marriage is to compare men of the same general background who have and who have not married. For one profession, the clergy, this has been done. A spate of studies in Germany, Austria, England, and Wales over a century, comparing the mortality of priests and that of clergy of other denominations does, indeed, as a summary by King and Bailar indicates, show that the married had greater longevity than the unmarried.[5]

Who Is Selected into Marriage? Who Out?

Even if one wants to give due recognition to the selective factor, it is not easy to determine what qualities or types are being strained into or out of marriage. Take health, for example. Because of the higher deathrate among the never-married men, one would expect poor health to characterize the single more than the married. Still, as measured in terms of the absence of chronic conditions or conditions that restrict activity, the never-married seem to show no inferiority to the married, at least in the years seventeen to forty-four, when most men marry.

Yet the higher mortality rates for the unmarried as compared with the married must have some explanation. The man who is not well, Paul Glick suggests, may be withdrawn and therefore not exposed to marriageable women. Or, if he is, he may feel that he cannot add to the stresses of his life by assuming marital responsibilities, or subject a wife to infection. In either case he selects himself out of marriage; he thus remains in the unmarried population and raises its mortality figures. Conversely, Paul Glick continues, it may be the especially ebullient who, whether by temperament or habit, "are prone to take more chances that endanger their lives" who raise the mortality rates of the unmarried.

Quite aside from selective factors related to longevity, one would expect the unmarried to be the "easy riders," the men who cannot tolerate the restrictions of conventionality but seek to satisfy a wide gamut of desires. Veroff and Feld did, indeed, find that the unmarried more than the married felt marriage to be restrictive. It was, however, a more negative kind of reaction than one would expect on the basis of the "easy rider" hypothesis—that is, the single men "seemed to be avoiding the burdens of marriage and . . . the responsibilities to children" involved in marriage. It was, apparently, a passive avoidance of the difficulties of marriage rather than unlimited wants, desires, or aspirations that motivated them. A recessive, constricted, limited orientation rather than an aggressive, expansive one seemed to have selected these men out of marriage.

There are other hints that suggest a recessive rather than an aggressive selectivity at work. Veroff and Feld, for example, found that single men showed less desire than married men to avoid being alone. The National Center for Health Statistics reported inertia and passivity also more common among the single than among the married men.

Antisocial tendencies and greater moral laxness were found by Genevieve Knupfer to be more common among single than among married men, as was also a stressful childhood. All of these must be viewed as selective factors helping to explain the bad showing of the unmarried.

I have given so much attention to the selectivity factor because it is undoubtedly part of the explanation of the superiority married men show over the unmarried, and cannot therefore be ignored in evaluating the impact of marriage. But the weight of the evidence explaining differences by marital status seems to me to be overwhelmingly on the side of the beneficent effects which marriage has on men rather than on the initial superiority of the married men.

Does It Just Seem Longer? Are They Happier?

Survival might not be such a desideratum if a man's married life were miserable. A short and happy life outside of marriage might seem preferable to an infinitely longer one within it. Actually, life is not only longer among the married; it is also happier.[6] Despite all the protestations of men to the contrary, married life makes them happy. . . . In fact, Norman M. Bradburn found that almost twice as many married as never-married men reported themselves as very happy, and, conversely, more than twice as many never-married men as married men reported themselves as not too happy. John Milton was right: "the main benefits of conjugal society . . . are happiness and peace," especially for men. For most husbands' marriage are, in fact, very happy.

It will be noted that only the documentable, research-based evidence of the benefits of marriage have been emphasized here. Every happily married man will be able to add a dozen more. Marriage is more comfortable than bachelorhood; sex is always available; responsibility is a rewarding experience. It is reassuring to have a confidante. And then there is love, friendship, companionship. . . . But the misogynists cited earlier in this chapter can shoot them all down. Marriage hasn't meant all that to *them!* It is difficult, however—indeed, impossible—for them to controvert the hard evidence from mental health, criminality, career success, and sheer survival that is cited here.

• • • •

The Future of the Husband's Marriage

Two major "costs" or grievances of men against marriage have been the sexual restrictiveness it imposes on them and the economic responsibilities it demands of them. The clinician referred to earlier specified among other "agonies" of marriage for men, "the violence that marriage does to the biologically ingrained instinct for promiscuity." And the desire on the part of husbands for extramarital partners has been reported in a wide variety of studies by Burgess and Wallin, Kinsey, Terman, and myself. Another of the clinician's bill of particulars against marriage was that the husband's responsibilities were greater than those of the wife. There seem to be two major ways, then, in which the marriages of husbands could be improved. One would be to relieve them from the responsibility for the entire support of wives and children, and the other would be to make sexual varietism more feasible. Both seem to be in process of realization.

Relief from exclusive responsibility for support of the family is well along the way. The increase in the proportion of wives and mothers who share the provider role has been one of the most outstanding trends in the second half of the twentieth century. Between 1940 and 1950, the Women's Bureau tells us, the proportion of marriages including working wives doubled, and by 1967 it had more than tripled, reaching 34 percent in that year. In a third of all husbands' marriages, in brief, husbands were receiving help in supporting the family, and the proportion was increasing with great rapidity. In marriages where there were school-age children, the proportion of marriages which had help from the wives was as high as 53 percent in income brackets from $3,000 to $5,000. The proportion was less in higher-income families, but even among them it was not negligible; in fact, a considerable proportion of all middle- and upper-middle-class families depend on the wife's contribution to family income for their comfortable, not to say, affluent, style of living. Many would not even be in the upper middle class without the wife's contribution.[7] This "shared-role" pattern will undoubtedly increase in the future. (We add parenthetically here, anticipating fuller discussion later, that the benefits of "shared roles" are not exclusively on the husband's side. Women who work show fewer symptoms of psychological distress.)

With respect to the second grievance of men against marriage, the need for greater sexual freedom, the data are less hard—and, for that reason, quite puzzling. Kinsey and his associates were least satisfied with their data on extramarital relations; such data were most difficult to get. They concluded, therefore, that about 10 to 20 percent more than they had reported (about half of their male respondents) had had extramarital relations. Since data on extramarital relations were so difficult to come by, there is no real bench mark, and a resurvey in our more permissive ambience might be expected only to bring out what was formerly unreported.

Actually, in a study reported in 1970, a generation after Kinsey's work, no increase was discovered. Kinsey had found that among men with high school and at least some college education, the proportion who had had extramarital sexual relations was about 40 percent. And that was precisely the proportion found in a similar sample by *Psychology Today* in 1970.[8]

Whether or not such relations are more frequent, however, the way is being prepared for their growing acceptance, for such a trend toward acceptance is unmistakable. I have shown elsewhere that a conception of marriage which tolerates, if it is not actually sympathetic with, extramarital relations is on its way, and as we shall see, provision for sexual varietism is almost standard in male blueprints for the future. The time is not far off when this desideratum of husbands' marriages may also be achieved.

At the present time, at least, if not in the future, there is no better guarantor of long life, health, and happiness for men than a wife well socialized to perform the "duties of a wife," willing to devote her life to taking care of him, providing, even enforcing, the regularity and security of a well-ordered home. And as the trends just noted become implemented—that is, as the wife shares increasingly the provider role and as there develops greater tolerance for extramarital relations—the pluses of marriage for men will be increased.

•　•　•　•

THE WIFE'S MARRIAGE

Because we are so accustomed to the way in which marriage is structured in our society, it is hard for us to see how different the wife's marriage really is from the husband's, and how much worse. But, in fact, it is. There is a very considerable research literature reaching back over a generation which shows that: more wives than husbands report marital frustration and dissatisfaction; more report negative feelings; more wives than husbands report marital problems; more wives than husbands consider their marriages unhappy, have considered separation or divorce, have regretted their marriages; and fewer report positive companionship. Only about half as many wives (25 percent) as husbands (45 percent) say that there is nothing about their marriage that is not as nice as they would like. And twice as many wives (about a fourth) as husbands (about 12 percent) in a Canadian sample say that they would not remarry the same partner or have doubts about it. Understandably, therefore, more wives than husbands seek marriage counseling; and more wives than husbands initiate divorce proceedings.

In a population of couples undergoing counseling, the wives were found by Emile McMillan to be more

> discontent than the husbands. More of the wives than of the husbands rated themselves as unhappy during the first year of marriage, and also during the next several years. The wives saw the problems as having started sooner and lasting longer.... They saw a greater density of problem areas.... They showed less desire to save their marriage, and gave more negative reasons and fewer positive reasons for saving their marriage.

Even among happily married couples, Harvey J. Locke found, fewer wives than husbands report agreement on such family problems as finances, recreation, religion, affection, friends, sex, inlaws, time together, and life aims and goals; and more report serious marital difficulties. The proportions were not great in most cases, but the proportion of these happily married wives who reported no difficulties at all was considerably lower than the proportion of happily married men who reported none. The wives reported problems in more than twice as many areas as did husbands.

The evidence for the destructive nature of the wife's marriage does not, however, rest on this bill of particulars, impressive as it is. For, despite the dissatisfactions catalogued above, a very large proportion of married women, inconsistently enough, consider themselves and their marriages to be happy, a paradox to be commented on in greater detail below. It is not, therefore, the complaints of wives that demonstrate how bad the wife's marriage is, but rather the poor mental and emotional health of married women as compared not only to married men's but also to unmarried women's.

Husbands and Wives

Although the physical health of married women, as measured by absence of chronic conditions or restricted activity, is as good as, and in the ages beyond sixty-five even better than, that of married men, they suffer far greater mental-health hazards and present a far worse clinical picture. Gurin, Veroff, and Feld, for example, found that more married women that married men have felt that they were about to have a nervous breakdown; more experience psychological and physical anxiety; more have feelings of inadequacy in their marriages and blame themselves for their own lack of general adjustment. Other studies report that more married women than married men show phobic reactions, depression, and passivity; greater than expected frequency of symptoms of psychological distress; and mental-health impairment....

Although marriage protects both marital partners against suicide as compared with single men and women, it protects husbands more than wives. Only about half as many white married as single men commit suicide; almost three-fourths as many married as single women do. And although women in general live longer than men, marriage is relatively better for men than it is for women in terms of sheer survival, quite aside from suicide. That is, the difference in deathrates between married and unmarried women is less than that between married and unmarried men (30 percent as compared to 48 percent).

• • • •

The psychological costs of marriage, in brief, seem to be considerably greater for wives than for husbands and the benefits considerably fewer.

Merely a Sex Difference?

If the mental and emotional health of wives—anxious, depressed, psychologically distressed—is so dismal, perhaps we are dealing with a sex difference quite unrelated to marriage. Perhaps, that is, what we find are not husband-wife but male-female differences. Perhaps the mental and emotional health of wives shows up so poorly simply because they are women? Perhaps it is just the nature of the beast.

This interpretation is one version of the perennial charge against women: it's their own fault. For it has been standard operating procedure among psychiatrists and counselors to place the blame for the psychological symptoms of wives on the women themselves. When or if a woman takes her problems to a psychiatrist, the response of the therapist has all too often taken the form, Robert Stoller reminds us, of convincing her that her misery was self-generated and could be relieved only by learning to come to terms with her position, even though, as Gurin, Veroff, and Feld reported, both husbands and wives believe that the husband is usually the source of problems in the marriage.

It is true that the costs of social change in terms of mental distress may be greater for women than for men. A comparison by Rice and Kepecs of patients in a university medical center in 1958 and in 1969, for example, showed that the young women in 1969 were sicker than those of 1958 had been, whereas the young men were not. But the disparities in mental health we are discussing here are of longer duration than just the last decade.

Even so, does this "it's-merely-a-sex-difference" interpretation really explain the wife's dismal mental and emotional health? This is an answerable question, and the answer is no. For the mental-health picture of wives shows up just as unfavorably when compared with unmarried women. Thus, for example, a study by R. R. Willoughby a generation ago found that married more than unmarried women were troubled by ideas that people were watching them on the street, were fearful of falling when on high places, had their feelings easily hurt, were happy and sad by turns without apparent reason, regretted impulsive statements, cried easily, felt hurt by criticism, sometimes felt miserable, found it hard to make up their minds, sometimes felt grouchy, were burdened by a sense of remorse, worried over possible misfortune, changed interests quickly, were bothered when people watched them perform

282

a task, would cross the street to avoid meeting people, were upset when people crowded ahead of them in line, would rather stand than take a front seat when late, were self-conscious about their appearance, and felt prevented from giving help at the scene of an accident. Moreover, more recent studies tend to confirm such differences. Genevieve Knupfer found that more married than unmarried women tend to be bothered by feelings of depression, unhappy most of the time, disliking their present jobs, sometimes feeling they are about to go to pieces, afraid of death, terrified by windstorms, worried about catching diseases, sometimes thinking of things too bad to talk about, and bothered by pains and ailments in different parts of the body. Overall, more of the wives than of the single women she found to be passive, phobic, and depressed; and although the total number who showed severe neurotic symptoms was small, these were evident in almost three times as many married as single women. And, except in the menopausal decade, more married than single women, Leo Srole found, show mental-health impairment. Many symptoms of psychological distress show up more frequently than expected among married women: nervous breakdowns, nervousness, inertia, insomnia, trembling hands, nightmares, perspiring hands, fainting, headaches, dizziness, and heart palpitations. They show up less frequently than expected among unmarried women[9]. . . .

Related to these findings is Pollak's conclusion that "at least in the culture of Western civilization, the amount of crime committed by married women—independent of age—seems to be higher than the amount of crime committed by single women," suggesting again that something other than sex per se is needed to explain the relatively poor mental and emotional health of married women.

So far, we have held marital status constant and varied sex, as they say in laboratory experiments, and then we have held sex constant and varied marital status. Now again we hold marital status constant and vary sex by comparing single men and women. The sex differences that show up in this "design" are enormous—but quite opposite to those that show up when we compare married men and women. Now it is the women who show up well and the men poorly. Unless one has actually examined the evidence it is hard to realize what a poor showing unmarried men make and what a good showing the unmarried women make. . . .

In Manhattan, for example, about twice as many never-married men as never-married women show mental-health impairments. Single women in this country, Gurin, Veroff, and Feld report, experience "less discomfort than do single men: they report greater happiness, are more active in . . . working through the problems they face, and appear in most ways stronger in meeting the challenges of their positions than men." Single women show far less than expected frequency of symptoms of psychological distress as compared with single men. And, as though further corroboration were necessary, single women suffer far less than single men from neurotic and antisocial tendencies. More single men than single women are depressed and passive. In 1960, about 10 percent of the never-married men thirty-five years of age and over, as compared with only half that proportion of single women thirty years of age and over "resided involuntarily in institutions," and over half were in mental institutions.

• • • •

283

Education, occupation, and income all tell the same story of the relative superiority of unmarried women over unmarried men. At every age level, the average single women surpass the average single men. At the earlier ages, say twenty-five to thirty-four, the single men and women are not very different in education, occupation, or income; the marriageables are still mixed in with the nonmarriageables. But as the marriageable men drop out of the single population, those who are left show up worse and worse as compared with their feminine counterparts, so that twenty years later, at ages forty-five to fifty-four, the gap between them is a veritable chasm. The single women are more educated, have higher average incomes, and are in higher occupations.[10]

When, finally, we vary both marital status and sex, by comparing married men and unmarried women, we find relatively little overall difference so far as mental health is concerned, superiorities and inferiorities tending to cancel out. But the women are spectacularly better off so far as psychological distress symptoms are concerned, suggesting that women start out with an initial advantage which marriage reverses. . . .

All we have done so far is to show that we cannot explain the poor picture of the married woman's mental and emotional health on the basis of sex alone. But dismissing that explanation does not imply that we can explain it exclusively by marriage alone either. There is always that elusive "chicken-and-egg" problem, the selective factor. Do married women show up so poorly as compared to both married men and unmarried women because a certain type of woman prefers to marry? Or because men prefer to marry a certain type of woman?

Before we attempt to answer these questions, though, an interesting difference between the selective process among men and women has to be looked at, for it operates differently in the two sexes and hence produces different results.

The Marriage Gradient

In our society, the husband is assigned a superior status. It helps if he actually *is* somewhat superior in ways—in height, for example, or age or education or occupation—for such superiority, however slight, makes it easier for both partners to conform to the structural imperatives. The girl wants to be able to "look up" to her husband, and he, of course, wants her to. The result is a situation known sociologically as the marriage gradient.

By and large, both men and women tend to marry mates with the same general class and cultural background; there is "homogamy." But within that common background, men tend to marry women slightly below them in such measurable items as age, education, and occupation, and, presumably, in other as yet unmeasurable items as well. The result is that there is no one for the men at the bottom to marry, no one to look up to them. Conversely, there is no one for the women at the top to look up to; there are no men who are superior to them. The result, as shown in figure 1, is that the never-married men (B) tend to be "bottom-of-the-barrel" and the women (A) "cream-of-the-crop."

When we speak of "bottom-of-the-barrel," we have to extend the idea beyond measurable qualities, and recognize that we are talking only about qualities

Figure 1 The Marriage Gradient

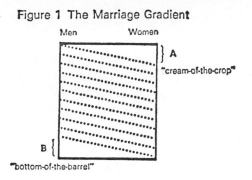

related to marriage. A man might be a poor prospect as a marriage partner but extremely attractive in practically every other way. He might make a pleasant escort. He might be a superb host at parties. He might be a good companion, a good tennis player. He might surpass in all these ways yet lack what Terman and Wallin called "marital aptitude." Suitability for marriage is only one human quality, though admittedly basic in the context of our discussion here.

The marriage gradient is the result of quite abstract sociological processes. But it tells us little about the specific boys and girls, men and women, whose lives are involved in it. For that kind of information we have to turn elsewhere.

What Kinds of Women Are Selected into and out of Marriage?

A generation ago, Raymond R. Willoughby, in a study of the differences between married and unmarried women, raised this very question, and concluded that either "a calm type of woman remains unmarried or . . . marriage has disturbing effects upon women." Evidence for the first of these alternatives shows up at a fairly young age.

Thus, for example, Floyd M. Martinson, a sociologist, studying high school girls in 1955, concluded that in these early years marriage had its strongest appeal to the less mature and less well-adjusted girls. And, of course, once selected into marriage, many of these young women remained in the married population despite the high divorce rate for teen-age marriages. The high school girls who remained single showed better health, better emotional adjustment, greater self-reliance, a greater sense of personal freedom, and fewer withdrawal tendencies. They were also better adjusted to their families. They showed more social aggressiveness, participated in activities more, got better grades, accepted social standards more, and showed fewer antisocial tendencies. "The overall adjustment of the single girls," Martinson concluded, "was decidedly better than that of the married girls."

Girls who marry early tend to drop out of school. And Paul C. Glick has found that marital instability tends to be highest for women who drop out of school, either high school or college. He has posited "certain predisposing factors in the social background and psychological orientation of these persons that affect their persistence in education and also affect their persistence in marriage." The "predisposing factors" tend to be premarital pregnancies.

285

It is not so much the mere fact of dropping out of school that is crucial as the reason for dropping out.

Very few girls are selected out of marriage because they do not want to marry, as in the case of some men. Practically all girls want to marry, want to very badly—too badly, some think. If, therefore, they are selected out of marriage, the reason is likely to lie in the behavior of men. What men select into or out of marriage reflects what men want or do not want in wives.

Especially suggestive in this connection, illustrating what men do not want in wives, is the evidence from a study by Richard Klemer which shows that the never-married women tend to be upwardly mobile; they, more than the married women, had started life in lower socioeconomic levels and pulled themselves up educationally and professionally. The implication is that they must have been "aggressive" and had, more than most women, strong "achievement motivation." Along the same general line is the evidence from the relationship between income and marriage rates. Left to themselves, unpressured, a considerable number of young women might not want to marry, for at every age bracket, the more income a girl or woman has, the lower the rate of marriage, a situation just the reverse of that of men. Similarly, the better her job, the lower the rate of marriage. A good job that pays well is a strong competitor to marriage for many women. . . . And the girl who has the well-paying job may be too achievement-motivated to attract men. For the talents it takes to achieve the best paying jobs—including competitiveness, aggressiveness, drive, and will to succeed—are precisely those not wanted by most men in wives, at least in the years when mates are being selected.

Another kind of woman is also selected out as well, and for quite different qualities. Contrary to the cliché that though men may play around with the freewheeling girl they marry the more conventional one, it is the conventional girl who is less likely to be chosen. That is, fewer unmarried than married women, Knupfer found, have engaged in unconventional heterosexual activities; fewer show antisocial behavior. On the other hand, Klemer reported that more are morally strict. More are conscientious. And, finally, more are scrupulous about family obligations.

What it all adds up to is that, although marriage may have "disturbing" effects on women, some women are more anxious than others to subject themselves to this disturbance, and men are more interested in marrying some types of women than others. The unfavorable mental-health showing of married women may be due at least in part to a perverse preference on the part of men.

We have gone out of our way to pay our respects to the selective factors in explaining the grim mental-health picture of wives precisely because we do not consider them of great importance. For, actually, they have slight weight compared to marriage itself since, sooner or later, practically everyone marries. We are now free, therefore, to explore whatever it might be about marriage itself that could also contribute to an explanation.

•   •   •   •

A Shock Theory of Marriage

A generation ago, I propounded what I then called a shock theory of marriage. In simple form, it stated that marriage introduced such profound discontinuities into the lives of women as to constitute genuine emotional health hazards.

There are some standardized "shocks" that are almost taken for granted. Mirra Komarovsky, for example, has analyzed the conflict the bride experiences between her attachment to her parental family and her attachment to her husband. There is, too, the end of the romantic idealization that terminates the "honeymoon," known in the research literature as "disenchantment." The transition from the always-on-good-behavior presentation of the self during courtship to the daily lack of privacy in marriage, symbolized in the media by hair curlers and the unshaved face, presents its own kind of shock. So also does the change that occurs when the wife ceases to be the catered-to and becomes the caterer-to. These and related discontinuities have to do with redefinition of the self, with the assumption of new role obligations.

Another type of shock, not commonly recognized in the research literature, has to do with a different kind of disenchantment. Girls are reared to accept themselves as naturally dependent, entitled to lean on the greater strength of men; and they enter marriage fully confident that these expectations will be fulfilled. They are therefore shaken when they come to realize that their husbands are not really so strong, so protective, so superior. Like children who come to realize that their parents are not really omniscient or, actually, all that powerful, wives learn with a shock that their husbands are not truly such sturdy oaks. They can no longer take it for granted that their husbands are stronger than they. Like everyone else, they have been fooled by the stereotypes and by the structural imperatives. For some it becomes a full-time career to keep the self-image of husbands intact.

Some of the shocks that marriage may produce have to do with the lowering of status that it brings to women. For, despite all of the clichés about the high status of marriage, it is for women a downward status step. The legal status of wives, for example, is lower not only than that of husbands but also than that of unmarried women. A woman, Diane Schulder reminds us, loses a considerable number of legal rights when she marries. But that is relatively minor compared to other forms of status loss, to be documented presently, as Congreve's Mrs. Millamant in *The Way of the World* so well knew when she spoke of "dwindling" into a wife. Even after she had bargained with Mirabel to preserve at least some of her prerogatives in marriage, she said, "these articles subscribed, if I continue to endure you a little longer, I may by degrees dwindle into a wife." And Mirabel recognized that his status would be enhanced: "Well, have I liberty to offer conditions, that when you are dwindled into a wife I may not be beyond measure enlarged into a husband?"

The Pygmalion Effect

"Dwindling" into a wife takes time. It involves a redefinition of the self and an active reshaping of the personality to conform to the wishes or needs or demands of husbands. Roland G. Tharp, a psychologist, concludes from a summary of the research literature, that wives "conform more to husbands' expectations than husbands do to wives.' " This tendency of wives to shape themselves to conform to their husbands has been documented in recent research in some detail. Among freshman women who were the top 1 percent of their class at Michigan State University, for example, Dorothy Robinson Ross found that those who married lost independence and "impulse expression"; after marriage they became more submissive and conservative. Cheraskin and Ringdorf found that, in emotional state, young married women resembled other young women more than they resembled their husbands, but older wives resembled their husbands more than they resembled other unrelated women. (The authors of this study note laconically that the same kind of marital convergence results in blood-glucose concentration.) The young husbands did not resemble either their wives or the unrelated women; but the older husbands were more like the older unrelated women—as well as more like their wives—than the younger husbands were like the younger unrelated women, suggesting a kind of sexual convergence with age, quite apart from, and in addition to, convergence with marriage.

We do not have to imagine a man enforcing conformity with a whip or clenched fists or even a sculptor lovingly shaping the woman of his dreams to account for the Pygmalion effect. The conditions of marriage itself as now structured lead to this result. Women who are quite able to take care of themselves before marriage may become helpless after fifteen or twenty years of marriage. Genevieve Knupfer describes a woman who had managed a travel agency before marriage, for example, who when widowed at the age of fifty-five had to ask friends how to get a passport. No wonder the self-image of wives becomes more negative with age. No wonder Alice Rossi warns us that "the possibility must be faced . . . that women lose ground in personal development and self-esteem during the early and middle years of adulthood, whereas men gain ground in these respects during the same years." For it is the husband's role—not necessarily his own wishes, desires, or demands—that proves to be the key to the marriage and requires the wife to be more accommodating.

Wives Make More Adjustments

This Pygmalion effect tallies with the finding generally reported that wives make more of the adjustments called for in marriage than do husbands. Understandably so. Because the wife has put so many eggs into the one basket of marriage, to the exclusion of almost every other, she has more at stake in making a go of it. If anything happens to that one basket, she loses everything; she has no fallback position. She tends, therefore, to have to make more of the concessions called for by it. Thus, when a sample of husbands and wives were asked by Burgess and Wallin three to five years after marriage who had made the greater adjustment in marriage, "the preponderance of replies . . . was that the wives had made the greater adjustment." The husband upon marriage maintains his old life routines, with no thought or expectation of changing them to suit his wife's wishes. "Often she submits without voicing a protest," Burgess and Wallin found. "In other cases the wife may put up a contest, although she generally loses." Both wives and husbands in this study agreed that the wives had made the greater adjustment. Sometimes, when the wife concedes that the husband has made more adjustments, he reports himself to be quite unaware of making any; they were probably too trivial for him even to notice.

One of the most poignant adjustments that wives have to make is in the pattern of emotional expression between themselves and their husbands. Almost invariably, they mind the letdown in emotional expression that comes when the husband's job takes more out of him, or the original warmth subsides. Lee Rainwater found in marriages between men and women in the lower-lower classes that wives tended to adopt their husbands' taciturnity and lack of demonstrativeness rather than insist on winning him over to theirs. They settled for a fairly low emotional diet. "I support you, don't I?" is a common reply to the question desperate women sometimes ask, "Do you still love me?" Not a very nutritious one for a starving person. Some women call it dehumanizing.

The psychological and emotional costs of all these adjustments show up in the increasing unhappiness of wives with the passage of time and in their increasingly negative and passive outlook on life. One measure of these costs can be found in the increasing rate of alcoholism with time. Thus, for example, although there is no difference between married and single women in death-rates from cirrhosis of the liver when they are very young, beyond the teens up to the mid-thirties, cirrhosis of the liver is only half as common among married as among single women. Thereafter, however, the difference declines so that, by middle age, the married women have not only caught up with the single women but have even surpassed them. . . . It is not simply a matter of taking over the drinking habits of husbands, for the married women remain more like the single women than like the married men. Something or many things about marriage itself must be involved, the Pygmalion effects being perhaps only one.

Female into Neuter

Some of the changes brought about by marriage are extremely subtle. In sexuality, for example. Women at marriage move from the status of female to that of neuter being. In the East European shtetl this important change was recognized and marked by a rite of passage, the cutting off of a woman's hair; she must not be attractive to other men. Much of the alleged decline in sexual attractiveness of women which is attributed to age is really attributable to the prescriptions for the role of wife. Women who remain active in nonmarital roles often retain their attractiveness far into middle age and even beyond, for modern women are potentially "sexier" than women were in the past. They mature as sexual beings earlier and reach menopause later than in the past, and Kinsey and his associates noted that early sexual maturation was associated with greater sexual activity and longer duration of sexual interest.

In the 1890s, as Henry Seidel Canby remembered it, "women past their twenties, or married, suffered dumbly from an imagination that made them sexless, because they did not know what was wrong and would not have admitted the truth if it had been told to them." Married women were "cinders— agreeable, yes, admirable often, interesting often, yet cinders, . . long emptied of fire—and like cinders they responded." Nor, according to Philip Slater, has the situation changed much since then. Stylistically, he tells us, "it is only young unmarried girls who are allowed to be entirely female. . . . As soon as they are married they are expected to mute their sexuality somewhat, and when they become mothers this neutralization is carried even further." Some women in desperation to validate their own sexuality engage in flirtation or even serious affairs to prove to themselves that they are still sexual beings.

All of these changes brought about by marriage can contribute something to the explanation that we are seeking for the sad picture of the mental health of married women. But there is still another change which may outweigh them. It has to do with the position of the housewife.

• • • •

Occupational Change in Marriage

One of the basic differences in the wife's and the husband's marriages results from this life style—namely, the almost complete change in work that marriage brings in her life but not in his. Until yesterday, and for most women even today, every wife becomes a *house*wife. And this is not always a congenial role. Militant feminists have argued that this occupational change amounts to the same thing as requiring all men upon marriage to give up their jobs and become janitors, whether they like janitor work or not. Regardless of whether this analogy is fair or not, it is true that interest in and aptitude for housework are not as equally distributed among the female population as is the occupation of housework, wherefore a large number of vocational misfits is almost inevitable. For, as it happens, not all women have an interest in or aptitude for the job of housewife—just as, no doubt, there are many men who do and would prefer it to what they are doing.

Thus, for example, despite the powerful engines of socialization which almost from infancy begin to prepare girls for domesticity, only about a third of the girls among high school graduates showed interest in the domestic arts a generation ago, and even fewer—less than a fifth—among college women. The figures would doubtless be less today. These data, taken at their face value, indicate that a fairly large number of women are drawn into housework as an occupation by marriage, in spite of an absence of positive interest in the domestic arts. Coming to terms with domesticity is not the least of the housewife's trauma, however much the sheer drudgery has been alleviated. Housekeeping remains an uncongenial occupation to many women.

"The housewife is a nobody," says Philip Slater, and almost everyone agrees. Her work is menial labor. Even more status-degrading is the unpaid nature of her job. Few deny the economic as well as the sociological importance of housework and homemaking. Housework is part of the great infrastructure on which, as David Riesman has reminded us, the entire superstructure of the economy and the government rests. If women did not supply the services of taking care of the living arrangements of workers, industry would have to do so, as in the case of lumber camps, ships, and the military. But housewives are not in the labor force. They are not paid for the services that they perform.

The low status of the wife's work has ramifications all through her marriage. Since her husband's work is not only higher in status but usually competitive, as hers is not, and he has to meet certain clothing and grooming standards or lose his job, his needs have to be catered to. If there has to be a choice, his new suit is more important than hers. This, quite apart from whatever personal or institutional prestige his work confers, tends to put him in a position of status superiority to the wife.[11]

Housework is a dead-end job; there is no chance of promotion. One cannot grow in it. There is a saying that passes as wit to the effect that Washington is full of talented men and the women they married when they were young. The couple who began their marriage at the same stages of their development find themselves far apart in later years. "Persons who took the initiative in seeking divorce," Nelson Foote has noted, "in explaining their experience, and likewise observers of broken marriages, speak frequently of a mate's having outgrown the other. It is the husband who usually outgrows the wife." Not only does the wife not grow, but the nonspecialized and detailed nature of housework may actually have a deteriorating effect on her mind, as Mary Roberts Coolidge observed long ago, rendering her incapable of prolonged concentration on any single task. No wonder that after hours of passive, often solitary, absorption in television and radio soap operas, she comes to seem dumb as well as dull.

Nelson Foote assesses to the husband some of the responsibility for the deterioration of housewives in his developmental theory of marriage. He points out that

> one's direction of growth as well as the rate of learning is powerfully affected by the responses of those particular others upon whom he inescapably depends for evaluations of his behavior. . . . Husbands are hardly prepared by cultural history [to perform the role of] the most beneficent other in the development of wives for whom the performance of household duties no longer seems to challenge their capacities . . . The commonest picture in American marriages is that in which the husband has no concept whatever of contributing by his manner of speaking and listening to the elaboration of his wife's career, particularly when she has no ostensible professional career. While her constructive achievements with home and children may be honored, her ventures in other directions appear more often to be subject to insensitive disparagement than to insightful and competent facilitation.

● ● ● ●

The occupation of the housewife has other than intellectual effects that can be damaging. As life is now organized in small, private living units, housework is isolating. "The idea of imprisoning each woman alone in a small, self-contained, and architecturally isolating dwelling is a modern invention," Philip Slater reminds us, "dependent upon an advanced technology. In Muslim societies, for example, the wife may be a prisoner, but she is at least not in solitary confinement. In our society the housewife may move about freely, but since she has nowhere in particular to go and is not a part of anything her prison needs no walls. This is in striking contrast to her premarital life, especially if she is a college graduate. In college she was typically embedded in an active group life with constant emotional and intellectual stimulation. College life is in this sense an urban life. Marriage typically eliminates much of this way of life for her, and children deliver the coup de grace. Her only significant relationships tend to be with her husband who, however, is absent most of the day. Most of her social and emotional needs must be satisfied by her children, who are hardly adequate to the task."

Isolation has negative psychological effects on people. It encourages brooding; it leads to erratic judgments, untempered by the leavening effect of contact with others. It renders one more susceptible to psychoses. Melvin Seeman has found that it also heightens one's sense of powerlessness. Anything, therefore, that increases isolation constitutes a hazard, even something as seemingly trivial as the increase in isolation contributed by which story of a building you live on. A study by D. M. Fanning of the families of servicemen in Germany, published in 1967, found, for example, that women living in apartment buildings were more susceptible to psychoneurotic disorders than women who lived in houses, and the higher the apartment the greater the susceptibility. "The incidence of psychoneurotic disorders was nearly three times as high among women living in flats as [it was among] those living in houses, and this [incidence] increased as the height of homes increased. . . . For mothers with preschool children, the confinement within flats provided an added irritant to the monotony and boredom of their lives."

The Housewife Syndrome

That it is being relegated to the role of housewife rather than marriage itself which contributes heavily to the poor mental and emotional health of married women can be demonstrated by comparing housewives, all of whom may be presumed to be married, with working women, three-fifths of whom are also married. Marriage per se is thus at least partially ruled out as an explanation of differences between them. The comparison shows that wives who are rescued from the isolation of the household by outside employment show up very well. They may be neurotic, but, as Sharp and Nye have shown, they are less likely than women who are exclusively housewives to be psychotic. And even the allegation of neuroticism can be challenged. For Sheila Feld tells us that "working mothers are less likely than housewives to complain of pains and ailments in different parts of their body and of not feeling healthy enough to carry out things they would like to do."[12]

But the truly spectacular evidence for the destructive effects of the occupation of housewife on the mental and emotional health of married women is provided by the relative incidence of the symptoms of psychological distress among housewives and working women. In all except one of twelve such symptoms—having felt an impending nervous breakdown—the working women were overwhelmingly better off than the housewives. Far fewer than expected of the working women and more than expected of the housewives, for example, had actually had a nervous breakdown. Fewer than expected of the working women and more than expected of the housewives suffered from nervousness, inertia, insomnia, trembling hands, nightmares, perspiring hands, fainting, headaches, dizziness, and heart palpitations. The housewife syndrome is far from a figment of anyone's imagination.

• • • •

292

Dismissing the housewife syndrome, as some unsympathetic observers do, is like telling a man dying of malnutrition that he's lucky he isn't dying of cancer. Perhaps he is. But this is no reason to dismiss malnutrition because it is slower and less dramatic. The conditions producing both are worthy of attack as epidemiological challenges. In terms of the number of people involved, the housewife syndrome might well be viewed as Public Health Problem Number One.

Comment

I pause here a moment to say that I consider this chapter to be the most important one in the book. And I have been so tediously careful to document the mental and emotional state of health of wives and the possible reasons for it—especially the status denigration that marriage brings—because I believe it important to put the evidence beyond cavil or frivolous disparagement or ridicule. For the woman suffering from the housewife syndrome is not likely to elicit much sympathy; she's sitting pretty, and has no cause for complaint. She annoys us if she even mentions any symptoms of psychological distress. They are not worth anyone's attention. Who but advertisers could take the housewife seriously? And even to the advertisers she seems to be only a laughable idiot.[13] See Table 1.

TABLE 1

SELECTED SYMPTOMS OF PSYCHOLOGICAL DISTRESS AMONG WHITE HOUSEWIVES AND WORKING WOMEN

SYMPTOM	HOUSEWIVES	WORKING WOMEN
Nervous breakdown	+1.16	−2.02
Felt impending nervous breakdown	− .12	+ .81
Nervousness	+1.74	−2.29
Inertia	+2.35	−3.15
Insomnia	+1.27	−2.00
Trembling hands	+ .74	−1.25
Nightmares	+ .68	−1.18
Perspiring hands	+1.28	−2.55
Fainting	+ .82	−2.69
Headaches	+ .84	− .87
Dizziness	+1.41	−1.85
Heart palpitations	+1.38	−1.56

Source: National Center for Health Statistics, *Selected Symptoms of Psychological Distress* (U.S. Department of Health, Education, and Welfare, 1970), Table 17, pp. 30–31.

•　•　•　•

Happiness Is . . . ?

If the wife's marriage is really so pathogenic, why do women marry at all? They marry for a wide variety of reasons. They want emancipation from the parental home, and marriage is one way to achieve it. They want babies, and marriage is the only sanctioned way—as yet—to get babies in our society. In addition, there is the pressure of social expectations, what some radical young women call an "idolatry" of marriage. There are, in fact, few if any better alternatives to marriage for young women in their late teens and early twenties. Most of the alternatives are—or, to date, have seemed to be—too awful. If marriage helps young women to achieve any of these goals and to avoid worse alternatives, their stampede into marriage is understandable.

The problem is not why do young women marry, but why, in the face of all the evidence, do more married than unmarried women report themselves as happy? As, in fact, they do. For it is strange to find wives, such a large proportion of whom are filled with fears and anxieties, so many of whom are depressed, reporting themselves as happy. More of the young than of the old, more of the college-educated than of the less well-educated, and among the college-educated, more of them even than of their husbands. . . .

There are several ways to look at the seeming anomaly involved here. One is that happiness is interpreted in terms of conformity. Wives may, in effect, be judging themselves happy by definition. They are conforming to expectations and are therefore less vulnerable to the strains accompanying nonconformity. The pressures to conform are so great that few young women can resist them. Better, as the radical women put it, dead than unwed. Those who do not marry are made to feel inferior, failures. What's a nice girl like you doing unmarried? The situation may not be as bad as it was in colonial times when sanctions were actually brought against the unmarried, but the opprobrium still remains. Rozanne Brooks, a sociologist, studying the stereotypes of the unmarried, asked her students to describe unmarried women. They did, and the conventional image of a frustrated, repressed, pursed-lipped, unnatural being came through. When asked to describe some specific unmarried woman they knew well, a quite different image came through, one more conformable to the statistical picture drawn above. Escape from being "an old maid" is one definition of happiness.

Such conformity to the norm of marriage does not have to be imposed from the outside. Women have internalized the norms prescribing marriage so completely that the role of wife seems the only acceptable one. And since marriage is set up as the summum bonum of life for women, they interpret their achievement of marriage as happiness, no matter how unhappy the marriage itself may be. They have been told that their happiness depends on marriage, so, even if they are miserable, they *are* married, aren't they? They *must* therefore be happy.

Another way to explain the anomaly of depressed, phobic, and psychologically distressed women reporting themselves as happy may be that they are interpreting happiness in terms of adjustment. Even researchers have confused happiness and adjustment. In their measures of success in marriage, "happiness," "satisfaction," and "adjustment" have received different weights; in all but one, adjustment has received far greater weight than either happiness or satisfaction. If the researchers define success in marriage in terms of adjustment, it is understandable why wives do too. The married woman has adjusted to the demands of marriage; she is reconciled to them. She interprets her reconciliation as happiness, no matter how much she is paying for it in terms of psychological distress.

Orden and Bradburn offer corroboration of such a "calculus." They found that marital happiness, like individual psychological well-being, was a matter of "affect balance." There were both pluses and minuses in the marital relationship, one positive (relating to companionship and sociability) and one negative (relating to tension). The positive contribution made to wives' happiness by companionship and sociability—small as it may be—was apparently great enough to overcome the negative effect of tension. It was not, therefore, anomalous when wives reported more marital stress than husbands but at the same time more overall marital satisfaction also. It was just that they had to pay more than husbands for companionship and sociability.

The Hidden Deformities of Women

Another way to solve the paradox of depressed wives reporting their marriages as happy is to view the socialization process as one which "deforms" them in order to fit them for marriage as now structured. We cut the motivational wings of young women or bind their intellectual feet, all the time reassuring them that it is all for their own good. Otherwise, no one would love them or marry them or take care of them. Or, if anyone did, they would be unhappy and feel caged if they had wings and could not fly, or unbound feet and could not run.

• • • •

Inge K. Broverman and her associates, for example, ask whether a constellation of traits which includes "being more submissive, less independent, less adventurous, more easily influenced, less aggressive, less competitive, more excitable in minor crises, having their feelings more easily hurt, being more emotional, more conceited about their appearance, less objective"—a constellation of traits which a set of clinicians attributed to mature adult women—isn't a strange way of "describing any mature, healthy individual." These researchers conclude that we have a double standard of mental health, one for men and one for women. We incorporate into our standards of mental health for women the defects necessary for successful adjustment in marriage.

We do our socializing of girls so well, in fact, that many wives, perhaps most, not only feel that they are fulfilled by marriage but even hotly resent anyone who raises questions about their marital happiness. They have been so completely shaped for their dependency and passivity that the very threat of changes that would force them to greater independence frightens them. They have successfully come to terms with the conditions of their lives. They do not know any other. They do not know that other patterns of living might yield greater satisfactions, or want to know. Their cage can be open. They will stay put.

Solution to the Paradox

"But what about love? Isn't that what marriage is all about?" the young bride cries. "None of what you say has even included the word!" True, love has been what marriage has been partially if not all about at least since the seventeenth century. Love is, in fact, so important to women that they are willing to pay an exorbitant price for it—even all the costs that marriage exacts.

Women need and want the love and companionship and the mere presence of men in some kind of close relationship. They demonstrate this need by clinging to marriage regardless of the cost. They are willing to pay dearly for it. This fact assures its future.

But the basic question is, does the satisfaction of these needs for love and companionship have to extort such excessive costs? Should young women have to pay so much for them? Should we not try to reduce the costs of marriage to them? Shouldn't it be possible to devise a structure that permits them to eat some of the cake and still have a little left over? . . .

NOTES

[1] As it turned out, Dr. Lee was advocating not less but more marriage. He was sympathetic, that is, to the idea of polygyny.

[2] For an interesting discussion of Durkheim's analysis of divorce as well as of suicide in terms of marital norms, see Barbara G. Cashion, "Durkheim's Concept of Anomie and Its Relationship to Divorce," *Sociology and Social Research* 55 (October 1970): 72–81.

[3] Comparing the married and the widowed does not entirely eliminate the selective factor, because marriage recurs after bereavement as well as in earlier years. Some men— probably the poorest and least desirable—do not remarry, so some kind of selection is operating even here. And since mortality is higher in the less privileged classes, the same factors that led to bereavement lead also to other dysfunctions in the surviving partner.

[4] The same comparison as that made here between the married and the widowed could also be made between the married and the divorced, with essentially the same results. But marriages disrupted by divorce are different from those terminated by death, and the conclusions to be drawn from comparing them with intact marriages are different.

[5] In teaching orders, the mortality rates for priests were not so unfavorable.

[6] There is a strong selective factor here. One study that did not present data by sex showed that the "depression-prone" were less likely to marry, the "depression-resistant" more likely to. See H. J. Gross, "The Depression-Prone and the Depression-Resistant Sibling: A Study of 650 Three-Sibling Families: A Follow-up Note on Marital Status," *British Journal of Psychiatry* 114 (December 1968): 1559. Another study, again without a sex breakdown, corroborated the finding that depressives were less likely than average to marry. This was especially interesting, because in most of the cases the depression had appeared after the age of forty-five—at an age, that is, when practically all who are ever going to marry have already done so. Thus, even before they became ill, the depressives had selected themselves out of the married population. Would marriage have saved them from their depressive illness? See Alistair Munro, "Some Familial and Social Factors in Depressive Illness," *British Journal of Psychiatry* 112 (May 1966): 440.

[7] In families with incomes in the brackets of $7,000 and over, wives' earnings were contributing on the average between a fifth and a fourth of family income. See

Women's Bureau, *1969 Handbook on Women Workers,* p. 35. Wives were contributing 30 percent of family income or more in almost half of the families with incomes of $10,000 to $15,000, and at least a fifth of family income in three-fourths of families with incomes of $15,000 or more (ibid., p. 34).

[8]In another study of a similar but apparently more conservative sample, only 20 percent of the husbands said that they had experienced extramarital relations. See Ralph E. Johnson, "Some Correlates of Extramarital Coitus," *Journal of Marriage and the Family* 32 (August 1970): 451. Lack of opportunity might account for this low figure.

[9]Among women who become ill enough for hospitalization, marriage favors a good readjustment upon release. There is evidence that having a husband, regardless of the nature of the marital relationship, can be therapeutic, especially for women in lower socioeconomic classes.

> . . . even the married patients who had been severely ill . . . were significantly better adjusted than the unmarried patients who had the same degree of illness. . . . The quality of the marital interaction did not necessarily relate to the quality of adjustment. . . . As long as a patient was married, it did not matter whether the marriage was stable and friction-free. . . . It is the [sheer] presence of the husband and not the quality of marital interaction that predicts a good [post-hospital] adjustment (Andrew Ferber, et al., "Current Family Structure, Psychiatric Emergencies, and Patient Fate," *Archives of General Psychiatry* 16 [June 1967]: 659–67).

> Another study of patient adjustment also showed family factors to be favorable, but the sexes were not analyzed separately (Ørnulv Ødegard, "Marriage and Mental Health," *ACTA Psychiatrica et Neurologica Scandinavica,* Supplement No. 80, Report on the 10th Congress of Scandinavian Psychiatrists [Stockholm, 1952]: 153, 160–61.

[10]The income comparisons of unmarried men and women in the text and in table 20 are in terms of averages. But the disabilities under which women perform in the labor force are illustrated by the fact that only 1.9 percent of the single white women who had incomes were in the income bracket of $10,000 and over, as compared with 4 percent of the single men.

[11]Even if a wife is working, a disparity in occupational status between her job and her husband's may make a difference to her. If her occupation is lower in status than her husband's, she is more likely to show symptoms of anxiety (Lawrence J. Sharp and F. Ivan Nye, "Maternal Mental Health," in F. Ivan Nye and Lois Wladis Hoffman, eds., *The Employed Mother in America* [Chicago, Ill.: Rand McNally, 1963]: 309–19). When both are on the same occupational level, as among blue-collar and unskilled workers, the status differential does not exist and the anxiety symptoms do not show up.

[12]Actually, in the earlier age brackets, twenty-five to forty-four, working women averaged more days of restricted activity or bed disability than housekeeping women, though in the later age brackets the reverse was true. (Data from an unpublished table by the National Center for Health Statistics.)

[13]The members of the National Capital Area chapter of the National Organization for Women (NOW) monitored television programs, including advertisements, during the month of April 1971. Viewed through the eyes of these stern, no-nonsense monitors, the enormous pathos of the housewife comes through with a heart-sinking thud: young housewives who have to fortify themselves with pills to get through their day; housewives in a tizzy for fear that neighbors will catch them with their furniture unpolished; housewives cattily comparing the relative whiteness of their laundry; housewives being patronized by smug husbands. . . . Are *these* really the young women we saw in high school and college? Is *this* what they have been reduced to? Mrs. Millamant's "dwindling" was nothing compared to this. It might be mentioned in passing that advertising agencies were not pleased with NOW monitoring.

Some Lethal Aspects
of the Male Role

Sidney Jourard

One might think that men have cornered all the positive aspects of marriage and women were stuck with the negative. However, there are prices to pay for the power that goes with the traditional male role. The fear of appearing "unmanly" deters men from demonstrations of tenderness, sadness, or sympathy. Such necessity to "hold one's emotions in" may be the cause of the higher rates, for men, of ulcers and diseases resulting in hypertension. Further, because of the emphasis of impersonal efficiency in dealings with others, men get less opportunity to experience the joy of a truly empathic relationship than do women. They may even be less in touch with themselves or their own needs, because empathy for others and for self are related. This lack of empathy also reduces their effectiveness as lovers—and makes them more difficult to love. Men base most of their identity not on the human aspects of companionship and interaction, but on culturally defined, stereotyped, masculine identity—which takes its toll of their intrinsic humanity. Thus, the loss of the traditional male role might actually be a humanistic blessing in disguise and a force to equalize the life expectancy of men with that of women.

Men die sooner than women. Health scientists and public health officials have become justly concerned about the sex difference in death age. Biology provides no convincing evidence to prove that female organisms are intrinsically more durable than male ones or that tissues or cells taken from males are less viable than those taken from females. A promising place to look for an explanation of the perplexing sex differential in mortality is in the transactions between men and their environments, especially their interpersonal environments. In principle, there must be ways of behaving among people which prolong a man's life and ensure his fuller functioning, and ways of behaving which

From Sidney Jourard, "Some Lethal Aspects of the Male Role," in *The Transparent Self* (New York: D. Van Nostrand, 1971), pp. 34–41. From *The Transparent Self*, 2nd ed., by Sidney Jourard. © 1971 by Litton Education Publishing, Inc. By permission of D. Van Nostrand Co.

speed a man's progress toward death. What aspects of being a man in American society are related to man's faster rate of dying?

The male role requires man to appear tough, objective, striving, achieving, unsentimental, and emotionally unexpressive. But seeming is not being. If a man *is* tender (behind his *persona*), if he weeps, if he shows weakness, he will probably regard himself as inferior to other men.

Now, from all we can fathom about the *subjective* side of man, men are as capable as women of responding to the play of life's events with a broad range of feelings. Man's potential thoughts, feelings, wishes and fantasies know no bounds, save those set by his biological structure and his personal history. But the male role, and the male's self-structure will not allow man to acknowledge or to disclose the entire breadth and depth of his inner experience to himself or to others. Man seems obliged, rather, to hide much of his real self—the ongoing flow of his spontaneous inner experience—from himself and from others.

MANLINESS AND LOW SELF-DISCLOSURE

Research has shown that men typically reveal less personal information about themselves to others than women. Since men, doubtless, have as much "self," i.e. inner experience, as women, then it follows that men have more secrets from the interpersonal world than women. It follows further that men, seeming to dread being known by others, must be more continually tense (neuromuscular tension) than women. It is as if being manly implies the necessity to wear the neuromuscular "armor" of which Reich wrote with such lucidity. Moreover, if a man has something to hide, it must follow that other people will be a threat to him; they might pry into his secrets, or he may, in an unguarded moment, reveal his true self in its nakedness, thereby exposing his areas of weakness and vulnerability. Naturally, when a person is in hostile territory, he must be continually alert, tense, opaque, and restless. All this implies that trying to seem manly is a kind of work, and work imposes stress and consumes energy. Manliness, then, seems to carry with it a chronic burden of stress and energy expenditure which could be a factor related to man's relatively shorter life-span.

If self-disclosure is an empirical index of openness and if openness is a factor in health and wellness, then research in self-disclosure seems to point to one of the potentially lethal aspects of the male role. Men keep their selves to themselves and impose thereby an added burden of stress beyond that imposed by the exigencies of everyday life. The experience of psychosomatic physicians who undertake psychotherapy with male patients suffering peptic ulcers, essential hypertension, and kindred disorders seems to support this contention. Psychotherapy is the art of promoting self-disclosure and authentic being in patients who withhold their real selves from expression, and clinical experience shows that, when psychotherapy has been effective with psychosomatic patients, the latter change their role-definitions, their self-structures, and their behavior in the direction of greater spontaneity and openness with salutary consequences to their bodies. The time is not far off when it will be possible to demonstrate with adequately controlled experiments the nature and degree of correlation between levels and amounts of self-disclosure and proneness to illness and/or an early death age.

Manliness: the Lack of Insight and Empathy

There is another implication of the fact that men are lower self-disclosers than women, an implication that relates to self-insight. Men, trained by their upbringing to assume the "instrumental role," tend more to relate to other people on an I—It basis than women. They are more adept than women at relating impersonally to others, seeing them as the embodiment of their roles rather than as persons enacting roles. Studies of leadership show that the leaders of the most effective groups maintain an optimum "distance" from their followers, thereby avoiding the distraction of overly intimate personal knowledge of the followers' immediate feelings and needs.

Women (often to the dispair of businesslike men) seem to find it difficult to keep their interpersonal relationships *impersonal;* they sense and respond to the feelings of the *other* person even in a supposedly official transaction, and they respond to their own feelings toward the other person, seeming to forget the original purpose of the impersonal transaction.

Now, one outcome of effective psychotherapy is that the patient becomes increasingly sensitized to the nuances of his own feelings (and those of the therapist) as they ebb and flow in the relationship. The patient becomes more transparent to himself! Coincident with this increase in insight is an increase in empathy with others, an increase in his ability to "imagine the real."

Personal life calls for insight and empathy in men as well as in women. If practice at spontaneous self-disclosure promotes insight and empathy, then perhaps we have here one of the mechanisms by which women become more adept at these aspects of their "expressive" role. Women, trained toward motherhood and a comforting function, engage in and receive more self-disclosure than men. They are more "transparent selves" than men.

Let us now focus upon "insight," in the sense that we have used the term here. If men are trained to ignore their own feelings in order more adequately to pursue the instrumental aspects of manliness, it follows that they will be less sensitive to "all is not well signals" as these arise in themselves. The hypothesis may be proposed that women, more sensitized to their inner experience, will notice their "all is not well signals" sooner and more often than men and change their mode of existence to one more conducive to wellness, e.g., consult a doctor sooner,* or seek bed rest more often than men. Men, by contrast, fail to notice these "all is not well signals" of weaker intensity and do not stop work or take to their beds until the destructive consequences of their manly ways of life have progressed to the point of a "stroke" or a total collapse. It is as if women "amplify" such inner distress signals even when they are dim, while men, as it were, "tune them out" until they become so strong they can no longer be ignored.

Accordingly, manly men, unaccustomed to self-disclosure and characterized by lesser insight and lesser empathy than women, do violence to their own unique needs and persist in modes of behavior which, to be sure, are effective at changing the world, but no less effective in modifying their "essence" from the healthy to the moribund range.

There is an interesting implication of these observations for the training of

---

*I think a survey would show that more women than men consult physicians and psychotherapists.

male psychotherapists. It seems true that an effective psychotherapist of whatever theoretical school is adept at establishing a warm, bilaterally communicative relationship with their patients, one characterized by a refraining from manipulation on the part of the therapist. Effective therapists do not "take over" the patient's problems or "solve" them for the patient. Rather, they seem to "be and to let be." This mode of being is quite alien to the average male. Indeed, it can be discerned among beginning therapists that there is often considerable dread of such passivity because it constitutes a threat to masculine identity. Beginning therapists seem to be most fascinated by "manly," active techniques such as hypnosis, reflection, interpretation, etc.—the kinds which will be difficult for them to master, but which will make them feel they are *doing something* to the patient which will get him well. These techniques, however, leave the self of the therapist hidden behind the mask of his professional role, and have limited effectiveness.

Manliness and Incompetence at Loving

Loving, including self-love, entails knowledge of the unique needs and characteristics of the loved person. To know another person calls for empathy *in situ,* the capacity to "imagine the real," and the ability to "let be," that is, to permit and promote the disclosure of being. The receipt of disclosure from another person obviously must enhance one's factual knowledge about him, and also it must improve one's degree of empathy into him. But data obtained in the systematic study of self-disclosure has shown not only that men disclose less to others than women, but also that, of all the disclosure that does go on among people, *women are the* recipients of more disclosure than men. This fact helps one better to understand why men's concepts of the subjective side of other people—of other men as well as of women and children—are often naïve, crude, or downright inaccurate. In fiction men are often alleged to be mystified by the motives for the behavior of others, motives which a woman observer can understand instantly and apparently intuitively. If this conjecture is true, it should follow that men, in spite of good intentions to promote the happiness and growth of others by loving actions, will often "miss the target." That is, they will want to make the other person happy, but their guesses about the actions requisite to the promotion of this goal will be inappropriate, and their actions will appear awkward or crude.

The obverse of this situation is likewise true. If a man is reluctant to make himself known to another person, even to his spouse—because it is not manly thus to be psychologically naked then it follows that *men will be difficult to love.* That is, it will be difficult for a woman or another man to know the immediate present state of the man's self, and his needs will thereby go unmet. Some men are so skilled at dissembling, at "seeming," that even their wives will not know when they are lonely, anxious, or hungering for affection. And the men, blocked by pride, dare not disclose their despair or need.

The situation extends to the realm of self-love. If true love of self implies behavior which will truly meet one's own needs and promote one's own growth, then men who lack profound insight or clear contact with their real selves will be failures at self-loving. Since they do not know what they feel, want, and need (through long practice at repression), men's "essences" will show the results of self-neglect, or harsh treatment of the self by the self.

It is a fact that suicide, mental illness, and death occur sooner and more often among "men whom nobody knows" (that is, among unmarried men, among "lone wolves") than among men who are loved as individual known persons by other individual known persons. Perhaps loving and being loved enables a man to take his life seriously; it makes his life take on value not only to himself but also to his loved ones, thereby adding to its value for him. Moreover, if a man is open to his loved one, it permits two people—he and his loved one—to examine, react to, diagnose, evaluate, and do something constructive about *his* inner experience and his present condition when these fall into the undesirable range. When a man's self is hidden from everybody else, even from a physician, it seems also to become much hidden even from himself, and it permits disease and death to gnaw into his substance without his clear knowledge. Men who are unknown and/or inadequately loved often fall ill, or even die, as if suddenly and without warning, and it is a shock and a surprise to everyone who hears about it. One wonders why people express surprise when they themselves fall ill, or when someone else falls ill or dies, apparently suddenly. If one had direct access to the person's real self, one would have had many earlier signals that the present way of life was generating illness. Perhaps, then, the "inaccessibility" of man, in addition to hampering his insight and empathy, also handicaps him at self-loving, at loving others, and at being loved. If love is a factor that promotes life, then handicap at love, a male characteristic, seems to be another lethal aspect of the male role.

The Male Role and Dispiritation

Frankl argued that unless a man can see meaning and value in his continuing existence, his morale will deteriorate, his immunity will decrease, and he will sicken more readily, or even commit suicide. Schmale noted that the majority of a sample of patients admitted to a general hospital had suffered some depressing disruption in personal relationships prior to the onset of their symptoms. Extrapolating from many observations and opinions of this sort, I have proposed a theory of inspiration-dispiritation. Broadly paraphrased, this theory holds that, when a man finds hope, meaning, purpose, and value in his existence, he may be said to be "inspirited," and isomorphic brain events weld the organism into its optimal, anti-entropic mode of organization. "Dispiriting" events, perception, beliefs, or modes of life tend to weaken this optimum mode of organization (which at once sustains wellness and mediates the fullest, most effective functioning and behavior), and illness is most likely to flourish then. It is as if the body, when a man is dispirited, suddenly becomes an immensely fertile "garden" in which viruses and germs proliferate like jungle vegetation. In inspirited states, viruses and germs find a man's body a very uncongenial milieu for unbridled growth and multiplication.

The male role provides many opportunities for dispiritation to arise. The best example is provided by the data on aging. It is a well-documented observation that men in our society, following retirement, will frequently disintegrate and die not long after they assume their new life of leisure. It would appear that masculine identity and self-esteem—factors in inspiritation for men—are predicated on a narrow base. If men can see themselves as manly, and life as worthwhile, only so long as they are engaged in gainful employment, or are sexually potent or have enviable social status, then clearly these are tenuous bases upon which to ground their existence. It would seem that women can continue to find meaning and *raisons d'etre* long after men feel useless and unneeded.

8

The Family in Later Portions of the Life Cycle

As advances in medicine create an increasing life span, the need to understand spouse and family interaction in later years becomes imperative. As yet, there is a paucity of data on how married partners in their forties, fifties, and sixties feel about each other, possible retirement from employment, their sexual relations, and about their future lives together when the children are grown and gone, or are presenting them with grandchildren to babysit. Even less is known about the time when one spouse dies and the other is left alone—often to cope with things outside his or her experience.

Somewhat surprisingly, research indicates that many couples are happier after their children are gone than they were during the hectic and self-sacrificing child-bearing and rearing years. They now find they have more time—and sometimes more money—for each other. Others find, when the smoke of child-rearing activities clears, that they are married to strangers with whom they have little in common. How do these very different outcomes develop over the years? Can partners be deflected from a path certain to lead to unhappiness and discontent onto a pattern of interaction that will offer its own rewards in later years of marriage? Related to this is the effect of role expectations in marriage over the years on the players of these roles. If the role inhibited the self-growth of either or both individuals, as discussed in the previous section, partners may find themselves tied to boring, discontented, or depressed persons in later years.

Families in Development at Mid-Stage of the Family Life Cycle*

Catherine S. Chilman*

*For quite some time, almost all research on the family was focused on the part-
ner selection process and on the early years of marriage, when children were young. Little
was known about how partners related to each other and to their adolescent children in
middle age. Chilman's summary of research on the lives of family members at various
points in their life cycle offers some ways of viewing these periods and suggests some research needs. For instance, as the length of life expectancy increases, parents will have
as many years together after their children leave home as they did while raising them.
Additionally, happiness and satisfaction in marriage varies throughout the life cycle.
Interestingly, things improve after the children leave home—and childless marriages are
quite happy, because the intimacy of partners' interaction is unhampered by the presence
of children. The family at midpoint is also a time when all members are in a "dangerous"
or potentially troublesome stage of development. Adolescents are pushing for the freedom
of adult status and parents are moving toward menopause, and—perhaps in desperation
to prove they are still sexually desirable—to extramarital affairs. Women's sex drives
have probably outstripped those of their husbands. Role relationships between all family
members have begun to shift. Mothers and daughters, fathers and sons, are all experiencing personal and relationship crises. None may be truly attuned to the suffering of others.
Grandparents, too, have problems, not the least of which is growing alienation from the
younger generation. The middle-aged parent may be caught between demands from two
generations.*

*Based on a talk originally given at the 1967 Groves Conference.
**United States Department of Health, Education and Welfare.

The development of families at the mid-stage of the family life cycle probably presents a critical period for all three generations that are apt to be involved. This period—when the average couple has been married for about 20 or so years—generally finds a family with adolescent children, husband and wife at middle-age, and grandparents at retirement or post-retirement ages. These stages of individual development are widely regarded as crisis points, yet very little is known about families as families, and the interaction of their members, at this particular period.

A search of the literature for research and theory regarding families at mid-stage in the life-cycle reveals that almost nothing has been published on this subject. This dearth of information creates a knowledge-vacuum which is highly stimulating to the imagination and to a wide-ranging search for related knowledge and ideas. One is forced to proceed rather inductively and intuitively to an examination of this subject to suggest some tentative conclusions derived from this examination and to point up some areas in which research is needed.

FAMILIES AS A UNIVERSAL INSTITUTION

Families, like other phenomena, can be viewed macroscopically or microscopically. Macroscopically, one can speak of "the family" as an institution and consider it as it relates to other social institutions and such factors as the nature of the larger society. This is a familiar approach to the family, most notably developed by a number of sociologists over the past 30 years or more. One aspect of this formulation that has especial relevance to this paper is the concept that "the family" is found universally among all peoples and "the family" universally has the same basic tasks and functions around reproduction: care, support, and socialization of the young; regulation of the sex drive, etc.

FAMILY CYCLES WITHIN CYCLES

From this concept of the universality of the family and its tasks and experiences, I have evolved allied theories based to some extent on the work of Glick (1963), Duvall (1967), Hill & Rodgers (1964), and Rodgers (1962) who have pointed to the universal nature and significance of the family development cycle and the developmental tasks that appear at different stages in this cycle. In the author's observation (considerably affected by Freudian theory) there seems to be a tendency, in human development and most especially in the family experience, to repeat cycles of psychological and biological needs and patterns. "Coming full circle" is a common expression about the human experience. Within families, the cycles of the three generations would seem to interact with each other and to present similar, but slightly different, issues. Thus, the cycle of family development, has cycles within the larger one—or wheels within wheels, as the saying goes.

306

This concept of circularity in family life is related to a larger concept developed out of observations: that all the animate world is circular or at least rounded in nature and that all life is based on cyclical or circular rhythms: seasons, the reproductive cycle, the cycle of birth, and death, time, the "age rings" on a tree, the shape of a cell, the earth, the sun, a raindrop, and a flower, for example.

FAMILY TYPOLOGIES

While families have universal tasks and experiences, tied to larger universals of life, itself, they are also highly various. This variety is primarily induced by the uniqueness of every human being in genetic components (except identical twins) and in environmental experiences. Since a family is a small group made up of unique human beings, it follows that every family is unique. An intensely microscopic view of families reveals endless differences within and between families. Complete recognition of individual and familial uniqueness bars orderly study of, and programming for, families. Thus, while individual characteristics must be kept in mind, families can be viewed typologically as variations on a universal theme. However, both the individual and typological point-of-view lead to the requirement that one think in terms of *families*, not *the family*.

CAUSES OF FAMILY TYPOLOGIES

Families vary for a number of reasons, and these reasons interact with each other in a number of complex and incompletely known ways. Genetic and environmental factors have been mentioned already. Among other important factors are the following: economic, cultural, societal (the nature of the society and its community services), historical (the family's own particular history as well as that of the community), physical (the physical condition and age of family members and physical factors in the environment), structural (in other words, family composition: numbers of family members, their relationship to each other, etc.) and situational (the situation of the family at any given point in time).

FAMILIES AS SMALL GROUPS

Families constitute particularly intimate and intensive small groups in dynamic interaction with each other (Strodtbeck, 1967; Ackerman, 1958; Vogel and Bell, 1960) and with the environment. The whole of the family interaction pattern is greater than the sum of its parts. Many years ago Cooley proposed that the individual personality is a semi-permeable membrane in interaction with environmental forces. Families may also be conceptualized in somewhat the same way—only more so—because each interacts with the environment and this interaction is combined in multitudinous ways within families.

Because families are semi-closed systems interacting within themselves and with the environment, it is imperative to consider both families and the larger environment simultaneously with a discussion of family development at any point in the life-cycle.

FAMILIES AND TIME

The concept of family development has been widely recognized, although not widely researched, especially in reference to families in which the marital pair are between the ages of about 30 to 60 years. Implicit in this concept is the recognition that human beings are at different stages of development at different periods and thus the family functions and tasks change. However, our society is also a fast-changing one. Over the past 20 years, for example, Americans have been faced with tremendous changes which require different functions and tasks of persons at all age levels. Thus, family development takes place within a larger scheme of social, economic, educational, political, and allied developments. Society, like families, has its developmental cycle.

One of the primary issues for human beings is the necessity to maintain a sense of individual identity and, at the same time, a sense of belonging to a group or, as Handel (1967) puts it, a sense of separateness as well as connectedness or, as some psychiatrists state, a sense of personal boundaries without a feeling of alienation. This issue also has been referred to as the conflictive needs of the person for both dependence and independence. Family life, because of its significance to its members, poses this problem to an extreme degree. The same issue is presented, though less poignantly, by the extended family, the larger society, and the world. One can readily imagine the severity of problems that would arise if family members and families themselves were cut off from inter-personal and inter-societal interaction by non-permeable psychological or physical boundaries. Conversely, one can also readily visualize the chaos that would ensue if the inter-familial and societal boundaries were largely or totally dissolved.

FAMILIES AT MID-STAGE

Demographic and related data, largely derived from Glick (1963) make it possible to visualize the "average" family in the late 1960s at mid-stage in the parental marriage. The wife, in this hypothetically average family would be about 40 years old, after 20 years of marriage, and her husband about 42. They would be likely to have three children, with the oldest being a little over age 18 and the youngest about age 12. This family would be on the verge of the so-called "launching stage" (Duvall, 1962). A divorce would probably not have occurred in this family and the couple can anticipate about 25 years more of marriage. In approximately six years, the youngest child probably will have left home (the parents, though only high school graduates themselves, want college for their children). This will mean that they will have almost as many years together without children in the home as they had with children present—a radically different situation than was true for their own parents and even more so for their grandparents.

This same couple is likely to have at least two members of the grandparent generation living (more particularly the grandmothers) and these grandparents are apt to be at retirement age. The grandparents probably live in homes of their own but keep in close contact, through visiting and letter writing, with their children and grandchildren (Sussman, 1967). They may well be foreign-born and/or of rural origins, with an eighth grade education or less.

This "average" family probably lives in an urban or suburban area in a home they are buying and is likely to have a yearly income of about $8,000 (U.S. Census, 1968). The wife is quite apt to work, part-time or seasonally, to supplement the family income and perhaps has been in the labor force, part-time, ever since her youngest child entered school. She plans to work longer hours and more steadily from now on to help finance higher education and other mounting expenses of the children.

Although the two older children are willing to work part-time to help with their own expenses, they find it very difficult to find anything better than low-paying odd jobs. In this family, the oldest is a boy and there is general family concern that he may be drafted for the Army as soon as he finishes high school in June.

The family owns an automobile, radio, television set, an automatic washing machine and dryer, and a number of other electric household appliances; all of these items were bought on time payments. They want many more things than they have and are under constant financial pressure. This pressure will probably escalate in the years immediately ahead, largely because of the cost of higher education.

It will be immediately apparent to the reader that the "average" American family in 1968 is both quite like and quite different from other significantly large groups of families. For instance, the low income Negro families might well be headed by a woman; three generations also might be present in the home; the mother probably would be about 37 years old, not a high school graduate, employed sporadically, if at all. Four or more children, ranging in ages from 3 through 20 years might be in the home and the home would, very likely, consist of a small apartment in a deteriorated urban area (Chilman, 1966).

THE MARRIAGE RELATIONSHIP AT MID-STAGE

Somewhat more information is available that does not pertain to families, as families, but a number of studies of the marriage relationship at different points in time provide useful insights.

Terman's study (1938), now almost 30 years old, revealed that the marital happiness scores of couples reached low points, on the average, after about seven years of marriage and again after about 16 years of marriage. The average scores of both husbands and wives rose after this latter low point to a relative high at about 21 years of marriage—this high peak, however, was considerably lower than the initial euphoria rated for the first few months of the marital state. Whether or not these same trends would be found in respect to marriages today is far from clear—after all, a whole generation has passed since that time and the nature of our society has been radically altered.

Blood and Wolfe's (1960) findings would seem to indicate different trends from those of Terman's, especially in reference to couples with children. Comparing such couples to those without children, they found that the latter marriages appeared to afford higher levels of satisfaction and harmony. Studying only families with children, these investigators concluded that sons and daughters bring considerable adverse pressure to bear on the marital relationship and that this pressure mounts as they become older. After the launching stage, the marriage is likely to improve.

Feldman (1965), in a study of marital communication, also found that children seem to have a negative impact on the marriage in terms of reducing spousal interaction and that, furthermore, the intensity and intimacy of the marital relationship tends to decline over the years.

Dentler and Pineo (1960) and Pineo (1961) in a follow-up study 15 years later of the Burgess and Wallin Sample (1953) of young couples, found that there was a decrease in intimacy and shared activities in marriage over time (in other words, after 15 years of marriage).

Somewhat similar findings are reported by Bossard and Boll (1955) in a 1954 study of 440 married persons whose marital happiness ratings were given by their brothers and sisters. Depth interviews were also held with these siblings regarding factors in marital adjustments of the couples. These couples ranged in age from 20 to 70 years or more. Although percentages of married men and women whose marriages were rated as unhappy varied with age, with the high point for unhappiness occurring in the age of 40 to 50 years for women and 50 to 60 years for men, statistical analyses revealed significant differences at different age levels only for women. Case material suggested the late forties and early fifties as a crisis period for many wives: "their children no longer retain their earlier dependence, their husbands are inadequate as sexual mates, and the menopause casts its passing shadows" (Bossard and Boll, 1955, p. 14).

Various other studies indicate an improvement in the marriage relationship in the post-parental years (i.e., after all the children have left home). While these last-named trends do not apply directly to the period under discussion, they suggest that marriage, at mid-stage, may represent a critical period which becomes less adverse at a later point.

Although these few studies, cited above, do include data on marriage at mid-career, they are not sufficiently extensive (in terms of national samples) or intensive (in terms of analysis of both husbands and wives and the many factors affecting family life, including numbers, ages, and sex of children) to provide a generalization that marital satisfaction declines during the middle years of marriage. If this is indeed a general trend, it probably is not universally true for all couples. Sub-groups of consistently or increasingly satisfied couples might well be found within the larger group. For example, studies of marital happiness indicate that such happiness is most strongly associated with the developmental experiences of husbands and wives in their own families of origin. However, further pursuit of this particular point is beyond the scope of this paper.

Another issue is the differences that are obtained for marriages at different socioeconomic levels, and for the different racial and national groups in different societal settings. For example, both Rainwater (1965) and Komarovsky (1964) have delineated the different (from middle class) orders of intimacy, expectations and satisfactions frequently found between very poor, and working class, husbands and wives. While higher rates of marital unhappiness were generally found for these groups, systematic evidence was not obtained regarding changes in marital happiness over the years.

While the few available studies have noted a downward trend in marital happiness at mid-stage, this is not necessarily synonymous with a decline in satisfaction with family life during the middle years. Although it is only natural that the presence of children would reduce spousal intimacy, for example, this does not mean that the total family constellation necessarily becomes less rewarding. For instance, while Blood and Wolfe's findings suggest that the road to marital harmony is avoidance of parenthood, this should not be expanded, as it might well be, to the concept that life is more satisfying without children. Moreover, marital harmony is not synonymous with a deeply satisfying marriage: the texture of family life, with all its pressures, intimacies, comedies, and tragedies is clearly enhanced through parenthood along with marriage. A rougher trip, to be sure, but it is a more varied and venturesome one. Then, too, the greatest satisfactions in the later marital years seem to be strongly associated with relationships with grandchildren. Such later rewards, quite obviously, are the positive outcomes of earlier and often costly investments.

Another point to be raised as to changes in marital happiness over the life cycle is related to changes that may occur anyway to married and unmarried alike, in association with the many factors that affect individual development. In general, there is a tendency to project onto marriage both positive and negative occurrences that are not necessarily caused by marriage but, rather, are merely concomitant with it.

The family venture probably is stormy for most families at mid-point in the family cycle. One reason that this is likely to be true is that everyone concerned is apt to be at a "dangerous stage" in his or her development.

INDIVIDUAL DEVELOPMENT OF THE THREE GENERATIONS AT MID-STAGE

A full discussion of ages and stages in human development would be far too elaborate for detailed presentation here; rather, a few highlights will be given, drawing on selected research.

Adolescent Development: Selected Features

As students of the family are well aware, adolescence is usually accompanied by considerable stress—at least in our culture (Grinder, 1963). It is experienced somewhat differently by boys than by girls, partly because of differences in culture proscriptions for the sexes, partly because of the different growing-up experiences boys and girls are apt to have in home and community, and partly because of developmental differences, with boys generally being about two years behind girls in physical maturation, yet reportedly, experiencing their sex drives much more acutely and specifically. The preponderance of evidence indicates that, for the most part, adolescence is likely to be more stressful for boys than for girls.

The major social-psychological tasks for adolescents are those of increasing separation from the family and achievement of relative independence from home, balanced, in part, by increasing dependence on the peer group and establishment of a sense of identity in terms of emerging adulthood with all of its demands for occupational, economic, social, psychological, and sexual competency, and for self-direction.

The increasing complexity, impersonality, value-confusion, competitiveness, standardization, and uncertainties of our society seem to be creating additional hazards today for the young person's growth from childhood to adult status. The disruptive effects of swift physical development of the individual are apt to be magnified by the disruptive effects of our explosively changing world.

In terms of physical and mental development, adolescents are on the up-grade of their growth and are moving toward the peak of their "raw" capacities.

For instance, the average adolescent boy or girl experiences a growth spurt from the pre-adolescent years (about age 10 for girls and 12 for boys) on through pubescence. Most girls achieve their maximum height at about age 15 and boys at about age 19. Physical strength, manual dexterity, and reaction time also increase rapidly during this period and reach their height at about age 20 (Miles, 1963), with, of course, boys acquiring far greater strength than girls.

According to Kinsey's findings (1948), the developmental curve of the male sex drive is not too dissimilar from other physical growth curves, with a peak in frequency of sex outlet being found somewhere between age 15 and the early 20s. Kinsey's findings that the female sex drive generally (Kinsey and Gebhard, 1953) emerges more slowly, primarily in response to sex experience, and building up to a peak in the late 20s may no longer be valid. The extensive change in female sex mores during the past 15 or so years, especially in reference to the increase in premarital petting (Reiss, 1967), may have rendered Kinsey's data on women obsolete. It seems quite likely that, with increasing sex equality for males and females and the wide-spread use of such contraceptives as "the pill," the development of the female sex drive may become more and more similar to that of the male.

The same general developmental curve obtains for intellectual growth, as is found for physical growth, although there is not a "growth spurt" in intelligence during the early teens. However, measured intellectual ability, on the average, has been found to reach its peak somewhere between the ages of 18 and 22 (Tyler, 1965). A somewhat similar trend was found, in a 1936 analysis, for many forms of creativity, although the most highly productive years were found to reach their height, on the average, at about age 30 (Lehman, 1963).

Frenkel-Brunswick has termed the adolescent years an expansive period with growing self-determination in independent activities and development of newly acquired, self-chosen personal relationships. This time—preparatory in nature for full maturity, the culmination years which start in the late 20s— is also characterized by extreme physical activity, wanderlust, loneliness, concern with abstract issues, and day-dreaming (Frenkel-Brunswick,1963; Erikson, 1965). Some of these same trends in young males, from about age 15 through 25, are shown in investigations during the 1930s as to shifts in interest patterns over the years. The developmental decade referred to above was found to be characterized by multiple and shifting interests, enjoyment of risk-taking and active sports, gregariousness, and restlessness (Strong, 1931).

Incidentally, an interesting and important side-light here is that, on the average, boys and girls were found to be further apart in their measured interests at age 15 than at any other time during the life span, and the measured interests of 15-year-old boys and middle-aged women, on the average, were found to be strikingly dissimilar. Quite clearly, these findings confirm common observations and probably have strong implications for family dynamics at mid-stage. However, the research quoted, like some of the other studies referred to in this paper, is over 30 years old. With increasingly shared activities of male and female groups, divergence in interest patterns may not be so great as was once the case.

The adolescent stage and the period of early youth are marked, in general, then, by a period of increasing individuality, separateness from family, growing intellectual, creative, physical, and social competency. Partly because of our culture and our complex social structure, it is also a time of stressful searching for personal identity and competence in many areas—sexual, emotional, social, ethical, educational, and occupational fields.

These are apt to be years of intensity: intense pain and pleasure, intense self-doubt and intense self-confidence, intense desire for separation and intense desire for connectedness. Students of human behavior, especially those who have been influenced by psychoanalytic thinking, compare this period to the also stressful emergence from infancy to childhood—the period from age 2, or so, to about 5 when the youngster is also trying to establish his individuality, his separateness, his sex role, his ability to master his environment. The adolescent and young adult may well have the sense of having come full circle to this earlier period which he only dimly remembers; his parents are apt to remember this earlier period far more acutely and to have an even stronger feeling that their son or daughter has, indeed, regressed in many ways to an earlier stage of development. They may have a painful feeling that, as parents, they have succeeded not at all and that the family, as a family, is in an increasingly deteriorating situation.

How this period is experienced by young people and their parents is clearly affected by the cultural context within which it occurs and by the social, economic, educational and occupational opportunities that do—or do not exist— within the environment.

Human Development at Middle Age: Selected Aspects

The common feeling, on the part of middle-aged parents, that the family situation is deteriorating is apt to be enhanced by the developmental changes that are likely to be occurring within the parents, as individuals. For parents, at middle age, are apt to be starting a slow descent from the peak of their capacities, at least in the physical sense and, to some extent, in terms of their mental abilities.

Specialists in the family are well acquainted with Kinsey's findings to the effect that the sex drive and frequency of sex outlet tends to decline with age. According to Kinsey's (1948) figures, married males reach their highest frequency of total sex outlet between the ages of 16 and 20, with a slight steady decline occurring from that time on, so that by age 40 the average frequency of sex outlet is about 2.5 times less than it was 20 years earlier. In the case of women, as already noted, the peak of frequency of sex outlet was found to have occurred in the late 20s. From that point on, there is only a very slight decline up through age 50. Since males have been found to have a far higher level of self-noted and reported sex drive than females at the beginning of the average marriage, it is quite likely that their sex drives may be more similar in perceived frequency during the middle years of the marriage (ages about 40 to 50) than was the case at an earlier period.

However, recent findings, such as in the Masters-Johnson (1966) research indicate that women may have far stronger sex drives than either they or the men previously realized and that they probably have greater orgasm capacity than men. Clinical treatises and popular literature (Reiss, 1967) attest to widespread unrest today, on the part of both men and women, with many men, apparently, feeling threatened and unequal to the sex demands of increasingly liberated women, and many women feeling that they have been frustrated, by men, from achieving their own glorious potential as sexual beings.

Trends such as these seem to have an anxiety producing effect, both on young people and their middle-aged parents. These trends may increase the frequently noted sex-anxiety on the part of both men and women in their middle-aged years, and may be related to the downward trend in marital satisfaction, already noted, for this age. Moreover, with the enormous youth population that is present in American society today (a product of the 1947 to 1958 boom in the birthrate), there is a particularly strong emphasis on sex adequacy and sex expression throughout society.

At this time, middle and upper-class men (and probably women) are more likely to engage in extra-marital affairs, as both Kinsey and popular writers have noted. It is usually assumed that this activity is most closely linked with anxiety over a decline in sexual prowess and fears that one's personal attractiveness is fading.

Other generally moderate physical declines also occur, on the average, at this period. Manual dexterity and reaction time make a sharp downward trend between ages 40 and 50 (Miles, 1963), measured interests show an increasing tendency toward relatively sedentary, non-competitive, less gregarious, more altruistic and intellectual activities (Strong, 1931). Measured intelligence, generally speaking, shows a slight decline, especially in terms of speed and new learnings; there is a marked reduction in sensory and perceptual abilities

(Tyler, 1956). As previously remarked, the highly productive and intensely creative years are likely to belong to the period from the late 20s into the mid-30s.

During the 40s, individuals are beginning to shift from what Charlotte Buhler has called the period of stabilization (from the late 20s to the 40s) to the period of decline (Buhler, 1933) (age 50 to 65), and Erikson (1963) proposes that the central problem of the middle-aged period is one of generativity—reaching out in a giving and supporting attitude towards the larger community as opposed to the tendency toward self-absorption. He assigns the quest for intimacy to the younger years of marriage when family life with young children is more demanding in terms of intense parental involvement.

All of the downward tendencies that have been noted above continue, and generally at a somewhat more rapid pace to age 65 and beyond. The stage after 65 has been called one of retirement by Buhler and gradually increasing disengagement by Cumming and Henry (1960). Erikson (1963) has termed this a period in which the individual must achieve integrity as a total person or else lapse into despair.

In all of the trend data given above, reference has been made to averages. There are wide variations as to the ways in which individuals age. There is some evidence that those who continue to be deeply involved in active participation in various areas of life are less apt to decline in their abilities. For example, those who continue to read and learn appear to be less likely to suffer a loss in measured intelligence.

Actually, research is quite sketchy in reference to the aging process, especially in terms of the middle years of life. Old age and youth both have been studied far more intensively than the period between. Although the trend data quoted show a gradual decline from a peak in the early or late 20s in all areas measured between ages 40 and 65 or older, other more global measures show upward tendencies in some respects. For example, family income is likely to increase well into the 50s (especially for professional and managerial groups) and the participation of wives in the labor force shows a marked upward trend from age 40 and on into the 50s. Moreover, families are likely to experience peak family expenses during the decade from age 40 to 50, but then achieve far greater financial ease after the last child has left home and before the retirement period. It is also likely that, on the average, the adult in his middle years has achieved a far higher level of emotional maturity than is true for the adolescent. He probably has far greater resources of psychological strength to fall back on, because, as an adult he (usually) has had a series of success, as well as failure, experiences. Very likely he has met a number of frustrations and has mustered the strength either to meet them or to accept that they are inevitable. He also is apt to have achieved a certain amount of status in his community and on the job. Although the stresses associated with the middle years may well cause considerable psychological upheaval and regression, this is likely to be temporary and somewhat analogous to the temporary disorganization of the adolescent.

The above description may apply fairly well to those who are full members of our affluent society; evidence is generally lacking, but one can speculate on the probable more severe impact of the middle years on those people who have experienced mainly the failures and rejections associated with acute poverty.

ROLE SHIFTS FOR MIDDLE-AGED PARENTS

There has been little research on the role changes that are likely to occur during the middle years. However, a few studies indicate that this is likely to be a time of occupational restlessness for men and that a number feel, at this time, that they perhaps have chosen the wrong vocational field. For professional and managerial personnel, this is apt to be the "decade of decision"; the period in which significant promotions up the career ladder either occur—or don't. It seems likely that, with the rising expenses connected with adolescent children, many men would feel trapped in their jobs by marriage and parenthood. It is well known that the laborer, at this age, may well find himself obsolete, rated as an old man if he should be forced to look for new employment. Recent radical changes in occupational fields have increased occupational insecurity for many persons in their middle and later years.

Indications that middle-aged and older persons tend not to be so mobile, occupationally, as younger ones may be found in related Census figures for the period March, 1965 to March, 1966. During that year 89 percent of newly married couples changed their residence, with 30 percent moving outside the country. On the other hand, 12 percent of persons over age 35 changed their residence, with only four percent moving outside the county. Moreover, median tenure of the current job increases from about one year for workers 20 to 24 years old to 13 years for those 55 to 64 (USDA, 1967).

Other occupational data show the increasing trend for married women with children to enter the labor force, most especially when these children are in their teens or older. This is especially true for working class (but not very low socio-economic level) women and for those with advanced professional training. Involvement in employment, further education, or community activities are generally recommended these days for women whose children are nearly grown and who feel restless and dissatisfied because they feel they have no full-time function as significant persons. As women take on these extra functions outside the home, they may add many more roles to their lives. Extreme role versatility and capacity to balance competing roles seem to be called for in such a situation.

Different functioning in the parental roles is also required as teenage children become less attached to the family; this requires new role learnings on the part of both father and mother. Adolescent and young adult children are far less physically demanding than younger ones are, but they put heavier pressures on parental psychological reserves. The emotional storms of adolescents; the upheaval in their own, and society's value systems; the educational and vocational crises that they encounter, particularly in today's highly competitive climate; the serious difficulties in which they can become involved: all of these issues deeply affect the parents, as well as the young people (Douvan and Adelson, 1966; Davis, 1968). The whole family can feel quite overwhelmed by them. Perhaps the most difficult aspect of these issues, for parents, is that they are relatively helpless. They can no longer protect their children from the larger society; they can no longer set things right by an outpouring of parental affection and a special treat.

Actually, there is almost no research evidence on the parent-child relationship during this period. The great bulk of research has focused on the younger years. That which does exist for this later stage is generally rather superficial in nature: asking young people, via questionnaires, how they view different aspects of family life. Far more studies are needed in this area.

Moreover, there is a need for more research on how adult socialization occurs and what program strategies might be developed to expedite such socialization (Brim and Wheeler, 1966).

SPECULATIONS ON FAMILY DYNAMICS

Research has not dealt with the dynamics of family life during the middle years of marriage. The foregoing evidence on the generally downward trend in many capacities during the decade of the 40s, contrasted to the upward trend during the adolescent years provides clues to what some of the patterns of family interaction are likely to be. This is especially true when one also considers the social-psychological characteristics of individual development that are likely to be present at these two stages and the role shifts that are apt to occur. Drawing from what research evidence is available, from theory in the behavioral sciences, from observation and meditation, one can speculate on some aspects of what these dynamics may be.

Consider, for instance the basic biological changes in the reproductive and related systems that take place in parents during their middle years. Consider the interaction of these changes with the rising reproductive capacity of their own children and in further interaction with increasing societal emphasis on youthfulness and full sex expression. The middle-aged mother, for instance, is likely to regret, or at least be ambivalent about, her waning, or ended, reproductive capacity. Along with the physiological changes associated with the start (or middle or end) of the menopause, she also may feel disturbed lest she may no longer be sexually attractive as a woman. Her forebodings of increasing decline may be intensified by her awareness that her adolescent daughter (if she has one) is, sexually and reproductively, on the upgrade. Moreover, her daughter, like herself, is likely to be caught in the mood-swings and other psychosomatic phenomena associated with the establishment—or dis-establishment—of the menstrual cycle. Her daughter, like herself, is apt to have fears about her adequacy as a mature, feminine person. In a number of ways, mother and daughter may be at the same, but a somewhat dissimilar, point in reference to the developmental tasks associated with the female side of reproduction, sexual identity, and changing sex roles.

This situation is fraught with both comfort and conflict. There are strong, primitive hidden and unhidden ties of identification between the two. There are the mother-daughter ties of likeness that go back to infancy, through childhood, and early girlhood. There are the ties that have been knotted and frazzled—and partly hidden—that extend from the past to the present, as the two female beings have rivalled each other for the men in the family: the father, the grandfather, and the brothers. There are the two-way stretch ties of the mother's dreams of perfection for her daughter in all ways—in beauty, love, marriage, parenthood, achievement in the outer world: "My daughter who is to have and be all or more than I have ever dreamed for myself, and know now I shall never have or be." And these dreams for the daughter's blissful future are muddied by envy and resentment of the daughter's rise to the years of culmination and the mother's (so it seems) downward descent.

These are the ties, I suggest, that are only dimly acknowledged in most families in our predominant culture. These are the ties of nearly identical anxieties about sexual adequacy and functioning, about forbidden sexual desires and fantasies. For a number of psychological and cultural reasons, mothers and daughters can only partially and elliptically communicate with each other about these matters which they deeply and secretly feel in themselves and in each other. Among these reasons are the increasing need of the daughter to establish her separate identity from the family and, especially, to break her identification with her mother.

There is also the need on the part of both mother and daughter for the mother to stand firm on the established order of a society which calls for self-control, self-confidence, competence and dependability in handling the wife-mother role. While youth needs to rebel against the established order, it needs an established order to rebel against. Daughters experiencing the chaos of their own developing feminine sexuality, want their mothers to demonstrate that this is something that can be handled with competent, calm success and satisfaction. They want their mothers to understand, but not to understand too much. And mothers, on their side, impressed with the need to serve as models to their daughters through the turbulent years, want their daughters to understand their own turbulence and distress—or rather to understand, but not to understand too much. Both want compassion from each other based on a comprehension that must be kept carefully veiled.

Much the same sort of process goes on between father and sons. In some ways it may be less intensely relational and sex-specific because the father-son identification is not likely to be so strong and personal in these days when fathers are out of the home so much of the time. Then, too, changes in the reproductive cycle are not so dramatic for males nor is a man's sense of sexual adequacy so closely tied to physical appearance, as it is in the case of a woman's. On the other hand, adequate virility is generally a source of extreme concern for father and son alike, and it is apt to be spread over a broader range of roles. Thus, both father and son, at the mid-stage of family development, are likely to be caught up in similar anxieties over many areas, such as: physical strength and agility, economic adequacy and, of course, desirability and prowess with women, both within and outside of the family circle.

The son, in his ascendancy to all these spheres of manhood, has not yet reached the plateau of the "years of culmination" and the father has many intimations that he has begun a gradual descent to increasingly waning powers. Thus, father and son, like mother and daughter, are apt to find themselves coming, full circle, simultaneously, to a similar, but different point in human development.

The family dynamics suggested above have been only partly discussed in that, of course, there are the complexities of father-daughter, mother-son, brother-sister, and other sibling relationships, not to mention those with the grandparent generation. This last-named generation must surely be considered for it is very likely to be involved in today's family at mid-stage.

From the view-point of the middle-aged parent, one does indeed, seem to be caught in the middle of three generational cycles: between the increasingly complex, costly and disturbing needs of adolescent children who are bursting with desire for entrance into the adult world and the increasing problems and

318

needs of the grandparents who, generally, are bursting with desire not to leave their full status in the adult world. The middle-aged adult, who may feel that his own status is threatened somewhat by his own developmental stage, is apt to feel further threatened by the competing, but somewhat similar claims of both the older and younger generations.

For the elderly person at retirement stage is also at a critical period. Although research evidence shows that many do make a favorable adjustment to this period there are undeniable threats in our society involved with retirement, increasing loss of physical vigor, the increasing onset of chronic ailments, and relegation to the ranks of "senior citizens." Somewhat as the adolescent and the middle-aged parent, the grandparent, too, is caught up in a new developmental stage which may bring with it self-anxiety and confusion over sex and work identity. For the grandparent, this is the fourth time he has been through a developmental crisis and he brings old skills, as well as old griefs, to it. The elderly person, unlike the adolescent, is apt to be struggling for a sense of connectedness to, rather than separation from, the pivotal parental family. As for the pivotal parents, they are in all likelihood struggling for their own identity as individuals along with maintaining ties with both the younger and older generations.

In terms of family dynamics, each generation is likely to have a different perspective on the familial situation. All of us are simultaneously affected by memories of the past, perceptions of the present, and anticipation of the future. For the adolescent, past memories are relatively few and the present is often viewed as a mere prelude that must be dispensed with as quickly as possible in order to get on to the fantasized enchantment of the future. He looks to his parents and grandparents and rarely sees in them the magic which he is sure must be his if the struggle of growing up is to be worth the effort. Perhaps this is one of the reasons that he tends to write them off as "failures" or, at least, not to be imitated.

The middle-aged parent has a store-house of memories, some of them hidden because they were so painful or so exquisitely tempting. The growth struggles of his own adolescent children may reactivate old pains, fears, joys, failures, hopes and "sins." Such reactivation is confusing, especially when the time has come, quite definitely, for this parent to give up his dreams of enchantment for his own life and to come to terms in accepting what is real both for himself and his children. For he can see, now that they are nearly grown, although they probably cannot, that a magically perfect life will not be theirs anymore than he achieved it for himself. He did not achieve it for himself, nor for his children, although he tried hard on both counts.

So the middle-aged parent is quite likely to be caught with a very clear, and often distressing, view of the present and all of its realities: some positive, some negative but none of them endowed with the imagined splendor that fades slowly as one grows from childhood toward full maturity: the stabilization period, the period of generativity, the time of disenchantment noted by marriage researchers.

Factors such as those just mentioned probably play in to the tendency towards increased marital stress and extra-marital experimentation that is most likely to occur during the middle-years of marriage.

In middle-age, parents can also look squarely at the future that is likely to be theirs as it is embodied in their own aging parents. And by now, they realize that they probably won't be very different themselves, which, all in all, for most of us is really not such a very bad thing, although most of us had planned it otherwise. And parents at middle-age are likely to be stirred by a new empathy for their own parents, as they feel their adolescent children tugging for separation in the way that they themselves once did—and still do when the kinship ties get too strong.

As for the grandparent generation, their future is relatively short, their present somewhat dubious, and their past a long one. They view their children and grandchildren coping with the familiar, universal tasks of living and growing, and moving from one stage to the next, and they feel both the weight and the movement of the cycles as all generations move and interact in the same basic rhythm and direction, around to another rung in the circular manner of all living things.

What Favors Positive Developmental Growth?

But this circular motion—these cycles of development—do not necessarily mean that as human beings, we make no progress. Individual and family development seems to come full circle, it is true, but it is my hypothesis (with acknowledgement to Freud and others in the psychoanalytic tradition as well as to theoreticians of family development such as Duvall and Hill) that people who are developing in a "healthy" manner move in circles, but generally upward, as on a spiral staircase. The generations reach the same point on this staircase, but each generation, at a potentially higher level of human development. Through each cycle of development, new skills are learned and new psychological strengths are developed (if all goes well). Motivations change— again if all goes well—with increasing age, so that "age-appropriate" behavior becomes not only acceptable but desirable. Ideally, when the cycle ends with death, the person has prepared himself by increasing acceptance and pleasure in retirement and disengagement. And, ideally the members of the family that remain are capable of handling this loss and moving on to the next generations that connect the past with the future.

It is also my hypothesis that some stages are more critical and arduous than others. The spiral staircase, used symbolically here, is not uniformly steep in ascent; there are landings, or resting places, as it were. Erikson and others have spoken of the latency stage in the middle years of childhood; a kind of resting and integrating period between the ardors of early childhood and adolescence. Similarly, I suggest, there may be a "latency" stage between about ages 25 and 40 and again between the ages of 50 and 65. During these stages the upheavals associated with critical developmental shifts are—possibly—integrated and accepted so that the individual is ready to move on to the next steep ascent in the developmental spiral.

A point related to the above follows. It seems that many people—perhaps, chiefly those who are imbued with middle class strivings—overly anticipate the tasks that will be theirs in the next developmental stage. They ascribe present feelings and motivations to future demands and fail to take account that these feelings and motivations may well change as they enter the next cycle. For instance, the adolescent is apt to fear that he will not be able to play his heterosexual role in marriage, not being aware that, as he grows and develops, the role of marital partner is likely to come naturally to him—at least fairly much so. Similarly, the 40-year-old man or woman may fear the time when he will be less desireable as a sex partner, not realizing that, in another decade or so he may be less motivated toward a highly active sex life. As we seek to control our lives and the environment, we tend to overlook the age old wisdom expressed so beautifully in Ecclesiastes: "For everything there is a season and a time for everything under the heaven. A time to be born and a time to die. . . ."

On the other hand, human development may not progress so smoothly. For instance, if the individual does not grow successfully from one developmental stage to the next, from adolescence to young adulthood, his circular movement through life may be just that, resembling more the whorls on a snailshell than steps on a circular staircase. A more serious situation exists when the individual regresses in developmental cycles and proceeds backward in movement to early childhood or infancy, as would seem to be the cases in some psychoses. And, from the field of family therapy, there are indications that, in some cases, whole families take part in this lack of forward development or backward movement into psychosis or other severe, regressive illnesses.

What factors are associated with "successful, forward" movement from one developmental level to the next? These factors are only partially and incompletely known, nor is there great clarity about what is meant by "successful development." This has been variously defined by a large number of students of the subject. Rather than enter into the intricacies of this discussion, let us be content here to accept some of the definitions which seem to be both eminently sensible and on which there is considerable agreement. Definitions of "successful development" or "positive mental health" or "good adjustment" generally contain such concepts as: the ability to perceive reality pretty much as it is and act appropriately upon that perception; the capacity to simultaneously satisfy one's self, maintain rewarding personal relationships, and stay within the behavior boundaries set up by society (the separateness-connectedness theme again); the capacity to maximize one's own physical, intellectual, emotional and social potential within a social framework (again the theme); the capacity to adopt age-appropriate and role appropriate behavior and to maintain a number of roles simultaneously.

The application of these concepts to the family and individual development cycles can be seen readily. The complexity that can occur within families harboring different age, sex and role groups can also be seen. The application becomes even more challenging when one visualizes the many typologies of families and familial interaction with the many components of the environment.

NEEDED RESEARCH

Attempts to gain a clearer understanding of what facilitates "healthy" or "successful" human development have been at the core of much child development research, particularly with that large segment that focuses on the parent-child relationship. The relationships between parents and adolescents have been studied very little, as already noted. As for aspects of the parent-child relationship at later points in the family life cycle, no studies exist at all until one arrives at old age and finds research such as that of Streib (1965), Sussman (1955), and Deutcher (1959).

Even fewer studies of the impact of children on the marriage have been carried out, as detailed earlier. And there are but a handful of investigations on marriage development over the life cycle.

Research into the nature of family relationships, and the impact of these relationships on individual development as a total family unit, is scarce indeed, although, in my own view, these are drastically needed. One cannot capture the richness of social-psychological development and functioning unless one studies interpersonal interaction within that group which is the most vital to human behavior: the family. It also follows that one must study many kinds of families in many environments. Studies along these lines are relatively few in number and have been mostly the province of certain anthropologists, psychiatrists, and social psychologists (Hess & Handel, 1959; Lewis, 1959; Friedman, 1967; Rainwater, 1967; Farber, 1964; Ackerman, 1961; Strodtbeck, 1967; Group for the Advancement of Psychiatry, 1954). However, Burgess (1926) saw the importance of such an approach over 40 years ago and Parsons and Bales (1955) also stressed the significance of the processes of family interaction. More recently, the major impetus to the field has been derived from studies of whole families in which severe emotional disturbances, psychosomatic illnesses, or mental illness (most notably schizophrenia) occurred. These studies have given rise to a widespread emphasis on family, as opposed to individual, therapy (Ackerman, 1958).

Whole families have also been studied by anthropologists, especially in reference to arriving at an understanding of the cultural patterns of the very poor, how these patterns grow and of the poverty environment itself, and how these patterns and the situation tend to engulf families and family members in continuing destruction of the human development potential (Lewis, 1958; Rainwater, 1965; Lewis, 1967). Growing attention is also being paid to the impact of poverty and prejudice on the dynamics of Negro family life and the consequences of this triple order interaction for the development of the family and the individuals within it.

While there is widespread awareness of the adverse impact of poverty, prejudice, deprivation, and unemployment on families, such impact has not been studied for families, as whole, interacting family units at different stages in the family life cycle. Considerable disagreement obtains as to (a) whether intervention would help, (b) what kind of intervention is indicated, and (c) at what point in the family life cycle intervention might be most useful. Further basic and program research would also be useful here.

To sum it up, studies of whole families in interaction with the environment are few and far between. What studies do exist focus, almost exclusively on very poor, nonwhite families or on families in which an emotionally disturbed or psychosomatically ill person is present. None of these studies concern themselves with family development or family interaction at different stages in the family cycle. Moreover, almost *no* study exists on family interaction in "healthy, well-adjusted" families. It would seem to be both interesting and worthwhile to select families that appear to fall in this category and to study them in terms of their internal interaction—their "psychosocial interior" as well as in terms of the culture and environment in which they live. Cross-sectional studies of such families at different points in the family life cycle should give considerably more insight and factual evidence than now exist as to what interactional, situational, physical, cultural, economic, socialization, developmental factors, if any, are associated with the healthy development of individuals and families over the life cycle. Isolating crucial factors would be much more possible, of course, if such "healthy" families were compared to "sick" ones.

Such research would, admittedly, be exceptionally difficult. The multiple complexities of such interaction have been revealed, at least in part, by small group research. And family life, as I have tried to indicate, is apt to be infinitely more intense and subtle than that of a small work group. Of course, one would need to select a stratified sample of families from various socio-economic levels and environments. Then, there is another *large* problem. Perhaps there is no such thing as a "healthy family" in which all members might be said to meet the criteria suggested above. One might carefully select such families, only to uncover all sorts of negative coping patterns once the researcher got to know the less public story. Especially, I imagine, if families were studied at the mid-stage of the family development cycle.

The research challenges are many in the field of families and their interaction with each other and with society. There is a need both for basic research and for research which is geared to action programs at all stages of family development. It seems that there is a particularly critical need for both orders of investigation at this particular period of time. For we live in an electronic, computerized, contracepted, air-borne, explosive, achievement-mad, atomic and atomized, psychedelic society. Great integrative and disintegrative forces are at work. Tugs of war go on between violence and compassion, separateness and connectedness, exhilaration and apathy, creativity and rigidity, idealism and cynicism. A period such as this requires great individual and familial stability if equilibrium is to be maintained. There are special tasks and characteristics of our times, but they are variations on the more universal nature of the cycles of the human experience.

REFERENCES

Ackerman, N. W. *The Psychodynamics of Family Life*. New York: Basic Books, 1958.

Ackerman, N. W. *et al. Exploring the Base for Family Therapy*. New York: Family Service Association of America, 1961.

Blood, Robert O. and D. M. Wolfe. *Husbands and Wives: The Dynamics of Married Living*. Glencoe, Ill.: Free Press, 1960.

Bossard, James H. S. and Eleanor S. Boll. "Marital Unhappiness in the Life Cycle." *Marriage and Family Living*, 1955, **17**, 10–14.

Brim, Orville and Stanton Wheeler. *Socialization After Childhood: Two Essays*. New York: John Wiley and Sons, Inc., 1966.

Buhler, Charlotte. *Der Menschliche Lebenslauf als Psychologisches Problem*. Leipzig, 1933.

Burgess, E. W. "The Family as a Unity of Interacting Personalities." *Family*, 1926, **7**, 3–6.

Burgess, Ernest W. and Paul Wallin. *Engagement and Marriage*. New York: Lippincott, 1953.

Chilman, Catherine S. *Growing Up Poor*. U.S. Government Printing Office, 1966.

Cumming, Elaine, *et al.* "Disengagement: A Tentative Theory of Aging." *Sociometry*, 1960, **23**, 23–25.

Davis, Kingsley. "The Sociology of Parent-Youth Conflict." In Marvin B. Sussman (Ed.), *Sourcebook in Marriage and the Family*, (3rd ed.). Boston: Houghton-Mifflin Co., 1968, pp. 378–386.

Dentler, Robert A. and Peter C. Pineo. "Sexual Adjustment, Marital Adjustment and Personal Growth of Husbands." *Marriage and Family Living*, 1960, **22**, 45–48.

Deutcher, Irwin. *Married Life in the Middle Years.* Kansas City, Mo.: Community Studies, 1959.

Douvan, Elizabeth and Joseph Adelson. *The Adolescent Experience.* New York: John Wiley and Sons, Inc., 1966.

Duvall, Evelyn M. *Family Development.* Philadelphia: (Rev. ed.) Lippincott, 1967.

Erikson, Erik. *Childhood and Society.* New York: W. W. Norton and Co. 1963.

Erikson, Erik H. *The Challenge of Youth.* New York: Doubleday and Co., 1965.

Farber, Bernard. *Family Organization and Interaction.* San Francisco: Chandler Pub. Co., 1964.

Feldman, Harold. *Development of the Husband-Wife Relationship.* Ithaca: Cornell University Press, 1965.

Frenkel-Brunswick, Else. "Adjustments and Re-orientations During the Life Span." In Raymond Kuhlen and George Thompson (Eds.), *Psychological Studies of Human Development.* New York: Appleton-Century-Crofts, 1963.

Friedman, Alfred S., *et al. Psychotherapy for the Whole Family,* New York: Springer Pub. Co., Inc., 1967.

Glick, Paul C. "Demographic Analysis of Family Data." In Harold T. Christensen (Ed.), *Handbook of Marriage and the Family.* Chicago: Rand McNally and Co., 1964, pp. 300–334.

Glick, Paul C., *et al.* "Family Formation and Family Composition: Trends In Prospect." In Marvin B. Sussman (Ed.), *Source-book in Marriage and the Family.* (2nd ed.) Boston: Houghton-Mifflin Co., 1963, pp. 30–40.

Grinder, Robert E. *Studies in Adolescence.* New York: The Macmillan Co., 1963.

Group for the Advancement of Psychiatry, *Integration and Conflict in Family Relations.* Topeka, Kans., Government Printing Office, 1954.

Handel, Gerald. *The Psychosocial Interior of the Family.* Chicago: Aldine Publishing Co., 1967.

Hess, R. D. & Gerald Handel. *Family Worlds: A Psychosocial Approach to Family Life.* University of Chicago Press, 1959.

Hill, Reuben & Roy H. Rodgers. "The Developmental Approach." In Harold T. Christensen (Ed.), *Handbook of Marriage and the Family.* Chicago: Rand McNally and Co., 1964, pp. 171–211.

Kinsey, Alfred C., *et al. Sexual Behavior in the Human Male.* Philadelphia: W. B. Saunders Co., 1948.

Kinsey, Alfred C. & Paul H. Gebhard. *Sexual Behavior in the Human Female.* Philadelphia: W. B. Saunders Co., 1953.

Komarovsky, Mirra. *Blue Collar Marriage.* New York: Random House, 1964.

Lehman, Harvey C. "The Creative Years in Science and Literature." In Raymond Kuhlen and George Thompson (Eds.), *Psychological Studies in Human Development.* New York: Appleton-Century-Crofts, 1963.

Lewis, Oscar. *Five Families.* New York: Basic Books, 1958.

Lewis, Oscar. *La Vida.* New York: Random House, 1967.

Masters, William & Virginia Johnson. *Human Sexual Response.* Boston: Little, Brown and Co., 1966.

Miles, Walter L. "Changes in Motor Ability During the Life Span." In Raymond Kuhlen and George Thompson (Eds.), *Psychological Studies of Human Development.* New York: Appleton-Century-Crofts, 1953.

Parsons, T. J. & R. F. Bales. *Family, Socialization and Interaction Process.* Glencoe, Ill.: Free Press, 1955.

Pineo, Peter C. "Disenchantment in the Later Years of Marriage." *Marriage and Family Living,* 1961, **23**, 3–11.

Rainwater, Lee. *Family Design.* Chicago: Aldine Pub. Co., 1965.

Rainwater, Lee. "Crucible of Identity: The Negro Lower Class Family." In Gerald Handel (Ed.), the *Psychosocial Interior of the Family.* Chicago: Aldine Publishing Co., 1967, pp. 362–400.

Maintaining Contact With Sons and Daughters: A Problem of the Elderly

Sheila K. Johnson

It seems sad but true that when children are small they want to spend as much time as possible with their parents. The parents, on the other hand, would like some respite from infant company by socializing with persons in their own age group. Then, just as children come to adulthood and could interest their parents in their company on an equal basis, these sons and daughters lose interest in spending time with their parents. Thus, we have the sociological phenomenon of dwindling interaction between two generations as each changes position in the life cycle. Johnson's study of residents in a retirement trailer park illustrates the truncated nature of some of these parent-child relationships. So confined are visits to "duty" (i.e., holidays) in most cases, that closer contact with children becomes a status symbol for the older parent. Some residents were so alienated from their children that when they became seriously ill or in need of aid while convalescing, they had to turn to understanding neighbors. The development of "surrogate relatives" by those in the trailer court who had no close family ties of their own also emphasizes the need of all humans for close primary group contacts.

It should no longer come as a surprise to anyone that family ties play an important role in the lives of most urban dwellers. Ever since Louis Wirth described "The distinctive features of the urban mode of life . . . as consisting of the substitution of secondary for primary contacts, the weakening of bonds of kinship, and the declining social significance of the family," a host of sociologists have sought to modify if not overturn his assertions. Particularly within the working class it was found that relationships between parents and their grown children—especially mothers and daughters—involved residential proximity, mutual aid, and a great deal of visiting and casual socializing (Young & Will-mott, 1962; Komarovsky, 1962). Such ties exist within white-collar and professional families as well, and although such families tend to live further apart geographically, modern means of communication (particularly the airplane and the telephone) and higher incomes enable their members also to keep in touch and to assist one another in times of need. Among upper middle-class families mutual assistance is more likely to be rendered financially than in terms of personal services such as baby sitting or home nursing, and financial aid is more likely to flow from parents to children than from children to their aging parents, as it often does in the working and lower middle classes. However, neither distance nor urban life seems to have destroyed extended-family obligations and affections.

Even social mobility, while it has an impact on extended-family relationships, seems to be less alienating than was once thought (Litwak, 1960a, 1960b; Adams, 1968). Bert Adams demonstrates, for example, that socially mobile sons tend to draw their parents partly into their new social world and that parental pride in their sons' achievements and feelings of responsibility and gratitude on the part of the sons create strong and affectionate ties between the two generations. Only downwardly mobile children seem often to be alienated from their parents and also from their more successful siblings.

Other studies have shown that while American kinship networks tend to be shallow both vertically and horizontally—that is, acquaintance with one's relatives seldom extends beyond one's parents, grandparents, aunts and uncles, and first cousins—they are unusually adaptable. Thus childless couples or single individuals often compensate for their lack of lineal descendants by maintaining close relationships with their own brothers and sisters and with their siblings' offspring (nieces and nephews). The lengthening of the lifespan and the reduction of the childbearing period have led to an increase in the number of four-generation families, which is also producing interesting role adjustments. For example, some young couples in their 20s are now exchanging services with their grandparents (e.g., driving them to the doctor and the grocery store in return for baby-sitting) that in previous years would have involved their parents. Such adaptations of traditional family patterns accurately reflect the changing needs of various members at the same time that they attest to the continuing strength of the family as a source of mutual affection and aid.

Finally, a number of studies have testified to the important role played by the family in the lives of old people (most notably, Townsend's *The Family Life of Old People*). Even Cumming and Henry (1961), who put forward the theory of disengagement, according to which disengagement from others is a natural process that occurs with aging and that does not necessarily lead to a lowered morale, found that some of their own data tended to dispute their assertions. Thus they argued that disengagement could be broken down into four stages and that morale declined in the intermediate stages (2 and 3) but reached or surpassed the morale of stage 1 (full engagement) once stage 4 (full disengagement) had been achieved. However, their data indicated that "the exceptions to the pattern of decreasing morale in the second and third stages and increasing morale in the fourth stage of disengagement are those men and women who have no siblings or children living in the same geographic area and those women who have both types of kin easily accessible" (Cumming & Henry, 1961: 136). The former had a low morale even in stage 4, and the latter had a high morale even in stages 2 and 3. Thus close family ties have an important bearing on the well-being of elderly people.

It should not come as a surprise, therefore, that among the residents of Idle Haven who had at least one surviving child, 83 percent had a child living in the Bay Area. This included 9 percent who had a grown child living in the same dwelling and 4 percent who had a child living separately but within the same park. Of the 17 percent who did not have a child living in the Bay Area, 5 percent had at least one child living in the northern part of the state (generally no farther than 3 or 4 hours by car from Idle Haven) and another 4 percent had a child in southern California, about 6 to 8 hours by car and less than an hour by plane. . . . The table also reveals a slight tendency for daughters to live closer to their parents than sons. This becomes somewhat more pronounced when one takes into account all of the children of Idle Haven residents: then one finds that whereas 22 percent of all sons live out of the state, only 12 percent of the daughters do so; and that 59 percent of *all* daughters live in the Bay Area as compared with 51 percent of the sons

All of the residents who had a child living in the Bay Area talked on the telephone with him or her at least once a week and some talked to each other daily. If it involved a toll call parents sometimes relied on their children to call them in order not to run up their own phone bill, but one woman who talked every Sunday to her recently divorced daughter in Fresno (about 200 miles away) confessed somewhat ruefully "my telephone bill looks like the national debt!"

• • • •

The mere fact that many older parents have at least one child living nearby does not indicate, of course, who moved closer to whom. It has sometimes been suggested that one reason why older people choose "mobile" homes is that it enables them to follow their geographically mobile children. It should be recalled, however, that 45.5 percent of the households in Idle Haven had either lived all of their lives in the Bay Area or had come there during the 1920s or 1930s. The majority of households had raised their families in the Bay Area and still had one or more children living nearby. For these people the specific choice of Idle Haven as opposed to some other park was often influenced by where a child lived, but the initial decision to move into a mobile home was prompted by other considerations.

Only among the households who came to the Bay Area during the 1960s were there a substantial number who had moved long distances in order to be near their children or another relative. Twelve households—less than 10 percent of the total number of households interviewed but a third of those who had moved during the 1960s—had come to be near a relative.[1] Most of these were recently retired individuals who had been forced to spend their working lives elsewhere—in the coal fields of West Virginia or travelling up and down the West Coast as travelling salesmen—and only retirement had enabled them to join a son or daughter, or a brother or sister, in the Bay Area. Even so, the choice of a mobile home was usually dictated by their low income or by the desire to own something smaller than an entire house, rather than by the anticipation that they would have to move again.

One of the advantages of a mobile-home park for older couples and widows who move away from lifelong friends and neighbors in order to be near their

327

children is that the park serves as a ready-made source of new friends. Thus such uprooted parents do not become wholly dependent on their childen for companionship and entertainment. One couple in Idle Haven who had spent their entire lives prior to their move to the Bay Area in New York City—and who acknowledged that they still wrote long letters every week to old friends there—had nevertheless made numerous new friends in the park and took a very active part in all of the dinners, luncheons, and other occasions.

For most of the residents of Idle Haven the interplay of family and park friends is complex and various. Activities with children or other members of the family are generally assigned a higher priority than park activities. For example, although the park holds a Thanksgiving dinner and a Christmas party, these always precede the actual holidays by about a week because it is assumed that most people want to spend Christmas Day and Thanksgiving Day with their families.[2] Indeed, the park is very quiet on holiday weekends because the older residents are generally visiting relatives and many of the younger, still employed residents are taking advantage of a few days off to go fishing or camping. The sole exceptions to the familistic treatment of holidays are Easter and—surprisingly enough—Mother's and Father's Day. All three of these occasions fall on a Sunday and the park always holds its regular monthly breakfast (usually scheduled for the first Sunday of every month) on these particular holidays. Attendance at each of these three breakfasts includes about a third of the total park population—nearly twice that of the normal monthly breakfast. Among the attractions of the Easter breakfast are the specially flower-decorated tables with vases, made by the park's ceramics class, in the shapes of bunnies, chickens, and Easter eggs. The park's church-goers attend Easter breakfast early and then go on to church, but for many of the residents the breakfast itself seems to represent a sort of semi-religious occasion when they are especially gracious to other park residents, dress up in their best spring outfits, and then perhaps celebrate the rest of the day by going out for a drive or to a movie.

At Mother's and Father's Day breakfasts the atmosphere is less decorous and more jocular. On Mother's Day all the women who are members of the park's association can attend the breakfast for free (usually there is a nominal charge of 65 cents per person) and the men do all the cooking and serving. On Father's Day, of course, this practice is reversed. Occasionally mothers or fathers who are also being feted by their children will bring them (and the grandchildren) to the breakfast. Thus a very young couple of grandparents (in their early 40s) came to the Mother's Day breakfast with their daughter, son-in-law, and two grandchildren; and the grandmother announced that on this particular Mother's Day she was getting them for breakfast and the other grandmother was getting them for dinner. A widow who had been estranged from her daughter for many years and who had only effected some sort of reconciliation the previous year, at her husband's funeral, came to the Mother's Day breakfast proudly showing off a huge orchid that her daughter had sent her. In instances such as these the park celebration serves partly as a public confirmation of family solidarity. But for most elderly residents, whose children are themselves mothers and fathers and who are therefore caught up in family celebrations of their own, the Mother's and Father's Day breakfasts are primarily park celebrations to be enjoyed in the company of one's peers, among whom one can reminisce and take credit for having done one's duty toward society.

There are many other formal and informal occasions when a resident's family and park friends are brought into contact, either directly or indirectly. The guiding principle seems to be that one's family (having "good" children and beautiful or accomplished grandchildren) enhances one's status within the park, and that one's status within the park can be used to enhance one's position vis-à-vis children and grandchildren. With regard to the first alternative, for example, there is always a great deal of gossip and bragging around the recreation hall about one's family. Pictures of a daughter's new house are circulated and a new grandchild, particularly if he lives in the area, is bound to show up at a monthly luncheon where he can be admired by the other grandmothers.[3] The monthly mimeographed park newsletter also contains a great many items about the families of residents. Some typical examples (quoted verbatim except for changed names) are:

> Alma Mark's granddaughter is apparently coming along fine after her last operation. Poor little tyke, she sure has had a rough go of it. She will have to go back for another one too. Keep your fingers crossed for this little one who is fighting so hard to live.

> Any volunteers for sewing on buttons? Well, someone is needed at the Jones residence. Betty Jones's family really believe in propagating the race. Her daughter Suzie presented them with a baby boy named William. Her son, who lives in Fresno, Calif., also presented them with a boy, named John, and her nephew who just recently returned from Vietnam last summer had a baby boy also named Billy. How about that one for the books? Betty has busted all her buttons off. Can't blame her can you?

> Al and Marie Whitsun announced the wedding of another granddaughter on June 18. She graduates from high school and celebrates her 18th birthday and becomes a bride all in 10 days times.

> Grace Mallory is very proud of her daughters and son-in-law. Grace attended three graduations. Ellen from San Francisco State and her husband George from University of California Medical School (he received his Doctor of Pharmacy degree) and Nancy graduating from San Jose State. You can see by this that not all students are rioting. Some really want to go to college to study. I am sure that we of this park join Grace in her pride of her kids.

> Condolences go to Rose O'Riley who just lost her beloved sister. Many of you will remember her sister who was a frequent visitor to the park. That gal sure has really had her share of sorrow.

The use of the park to enhance one's status within the family can be illustrated in a number of ways. Most of the park's functions—such as its monthly breakfasts, dinners, dances, and bingo nights—can be attended by friends and relatives of the residents. They usually involve a small fee for both guests and residents, but for many residents a $1.00-per-person spaghetti feed in the recreation hall is an easy and popular way to entertain their children and grandchildren. At the monthly dances . . . many of the park residents who attend invite friends and relatives who live outside the park and form a "table" by themselves.

329

One of the park's merrier widows once told me that she had fourteen relatives at the most recent dance.

In the summertime the park is also extremely popular with residents' grandchildren because it has a swimming pool. Out of the residents interviewed, only 9 percent said that they themselves used the pool regularly, and another 19 percent had used it once or twice; however, many who never used the pool themselves could be observed sitting beside it watching a grandchild splash about. The recreation hall is also available to residents of the park who want to book it for a private party. Thus a number of wedding receptions for children and grandchildren have taken place there at no extra cost to the family. Others have used the recreation hall for family reunions too large to be held in their own mobile homes, or for their children's baby showers. Perhaps the most spectacular exploitation of the park (and its residents) on behalf of one's own family was a bridal shower given in the recreation hall for the manager's daughter. In addition to a few school friends of the bride-to-be and a few female relatives of the groom, most of the fifty or so ladies who attended were residents of the park. The bride-to-be received an incredible number of gifts—a few of them modest, often handmade, items such as embroidered dishtowels or crocheted potholders, but many of them rather expensive and some of these from residents who lived on welfare checks. A few women in the park who were invited but could not attend nevertheless also sent presents. This event was obviously somewhat unusual in that the manager of the park wielded considerable power over people's lives and few who were invited felt they could afford to antagonize her (myself included).

The members of a park resident's family and other residents in the park interacted and complemented each other in a variety of ways. The first person turned to in times of serious illness was always a relative—usually a child—if available. But neighbors in the park were sometimes the first on the scene in a serious accident or illness, and therefore to call a doctor or an ambulance, and they were also helpful in relieving relatives of the burden of care in prolonged convalescence. For example, a widow who had had a serious operation spent the first two weeks after being released from the hospital at her son's home, but thereafter—although still weak—she returned to the park, where neighbors did her shopping and some of her cooking and cleaning. A neighbor had also looked after her plants and canary while she was away. Another widow broke her leg while coming down her front steps and was driven to the hospital by a neighbor. Thereafter she followed the same pattern as the other widow—first staying with her daughter and then returning to the park, still semi-invalided but under the watchful eye of neighbors and friends.

Some residents were also sensitive to the fact that neighbors or friends of theirs in the park had children who neglected them and tried to compensate for some of this neglect. One widow who was on bad terms with her son and who had broken her shoulder and several ribs in a severe fall had a neighbor (in this case a close friend dating from many years preceding their residence in the park) who brought her a hot dinner every evening for 6 weeks. Other widows who could not drive and whose children seldom visited them or drove them anywhere were often invited along by other women or couples when they went shopping. The manager of the park also occasionally telephoned the children of residents whom she believed were not being looked after properly.

As we noted earlier, 83 percent of the households interviewed who had children had one or more of these children living in the Bay Area and most of these were on extremely good terms with them. However, the few who were estranged from their children, or—more commonly—from one child, seemed to have lost contact completely; there seemed to be no such thing, in Idle Haven, as a strained but civil parent-child relationship. One man who was married for the second time said he had two sons by a previous marriage but he had not seen them for seventeen years and he had no idea where they were living or what sort of jobs they had. Another said one of his wife's sons by a former marriage had "dropped out of sight" 10 years ago. These few cases in which parents and children had totally lost touch always involved severely disrupted families: usually the parent (that is, the resident of Idle Haven) had been divorced and remarried, but occasionally it was the child who had been married several times and had drifted from area to area until the parent no longer knew where he or she lived.

Another occasional cause of estrangement between parents and children was social mobility on the part of the child. There were two virtually identical cases in Idle Haven of widows estranged from their sons: both women were pleasant but uneducated, and both sons had Ph.D.'s and were professors. One woman had not seen her son for 11 years and depended on her four daughters, all of whom lived in the Bay Area and were married to working-class men. The other woman, whose son lived in the Bay Area, saw him occasionally; she largely blamed the son's wife for the fact that she was never invited to their home and that her neighbor in the park had had to look after her when she broke her shoulder.

There were also some residents who were unable to rely on their children because their children were virtually as old—and in some cases in much worse health—as they were. An 82-year-old widow whom I visited one rainy February afternoon told me that she had not left her mobile home or seen a live human being in over a month. Her daughter, in her 60s, who usually came to see her about once a week, had been ill and so they had only talked on the telephone. When I asked this woman how she did her grocery shopping, she proudly led me into the kitchen and showed me a huge upright freezer that her daughter had bought for her sometime before. It was filled not only with frozen vege-tables and meats, but also with frozen bread, fruit juices, and various desserts, so that it seemed possible that this woman could be virtually self-sustaining for about a month, as she claimed she was. What surprised me more, however, was that she seemed not at all disoriented or depressed in her isolated state. Although she had not been expecting me, she was neatly dressed in a house-dress and stockings; and when I asked how she spent her time she showed me a stack of some 80 pillowcases (bought at a January "white sale") that she was in the process of embroidering as gifts for various relatives for their future birthdays, possible weddings, and the following Christmas. Thus, although physically isolated, this woman still felt herself very much a part of an extensive family network.

Of the men and women who were childless, about half were close to one or more of their siblings. One childless divorcée, for example, had moved away from southern California upon her retirement specifically in order to be close to a married sister. This sister, a long-time resident of the Bay Area, had in-cluded her in a number of her own clubs and friendship groups so that the divorcée relied mostly on these new friends and very little upon the people she had met in Idle Haven. Another woman—a childless widow who had married late in life and most of whose family lived in the Bay Area—said that her brothers and sisters and their families kept her so busy that she really "didn't feel like a widow."

Several other men and women who were themselves childless were married to someone who had had children by a previous marriage, and as a consequence they had a good deal of contact with the children and grandchildren of their spouses. Unfortunately, such relationships were generally severed by the death of the spouse whose children they were. One widow who had helped to raise her late husband's two sons had lost all contact with the sons after her husband's death. But whereas stepchild (as well as in-law) ties seem to be easily severed by the death of the connecting relative, sibling ties are not only substituted for ties with children, but they are often extended downward one generation upon the death of a sibling. Thus there were two childless widows and one childless widower in Idle Haven whose closest relative turned out to be a nephew.

One Idle Haven case that illustrates several ways in which relatives were substituted for each other involved an 82-year-old woman who had been widowed at the age of 61. She had subsequently sold her home and lived for about 15 years with her unmarried daughter (her only child, another child having died in infancy), until the daughter had died at the age of 54. She had then gone to live with her widowed older sister, and together these two had moved into Idle Haven—partly because the sister's home had become too ramshackle to repair and partly because the sister could no longer negotiate the steps leading up to the house. Two years after moving into Idle Haven the older sister had died, leaving most of her possessions—including the mobile home—to her son but subject to the sister's use during her lifetime. This son, himself in his 60s, paid the park's rent and utility bills for his aunt and took her grocery shopping every Sunday. He had also sold his mother's car and with the proceeds bought his aunt a splendid color TV set, and he had bought her a new stereo record player when her old one broke down.

In addition to her nephew, however, this elderly widow could also call on friends in the park and on a close neighbor. The friends were a married couple nearly her own age whom she had known for many years and who had been instrumental in getting her and her sister to move into Idle Haven. The husband occasionally ran errands for her during the week—such as going to the bank—which her nephew could not attend to because he was at work then. The husband also did some heavy housecleaning for her, such as washing the windows and—once a year—the outside of the mobile home. She paid him a little for this because he needed the money, but it was also clear that he would not have performed the jobs or accepted the money unless they had been close friends. Similarly there was a neighbor who "looked in" on this widow at least once a day and who did some light housecleaning (vacuuming, dusting, changing the linens) for her once a week, also partly out of friendship and partly for the money. The neighbor was an attractive middle-aged Mexican woman (the only one in the park) who had had no children and who desperately missed her own mother and brothers and sisters in Mexico. The relationship between her and her 82-year-old neighbor was clearly one of mutual benefit: the younger woman had gained a substitute mother and the elderly woman a substitute daughter.

NOTES

[1] There were also two instances where the parental households had moved to the Bay Area first and had been followed by the households of grown children. The children, in both cases, were daughters—in one instance an unmarried daughter and in the other instance a divorced daughter with two children of her own.

[2] But park acquaintances serve as a substitute for those who have no families. In addition to the Thanksgiving dinner for everyone in the park, four childless couples got together on Thanksgiving Day and cooked a turkey in the recreation hall's kitchen and had dinner together.

[3] Another example of status-building within the park occurred one evening while approximately eighty people were gathered in the recreation hall to play bingo. A young man, seated next to a couple who were residents in the park, was announced to the group as "Sergeant ———, the son of Mr. and Mrs. ———, who is just back from Vietnam." He received a huge ovation.

Widowhood Status in the United States: Perspective on a Neglected Aspect of the Family Life-Cycle

Felix M. Berardo

The death of one marriage partner (usually the man) before the other in this country is one crisis in marriage that cannot be "coped with" in the usual meaning of the word. Rather, it must be adjusted to. As Berardo points out, however, little research has been done on what life is like for the survivor, who is usually an elderly widow. The average age of widows, their economic circumstances, their employment possibilities, and their social life are important clues, available through demographic data, to the miniculture in which they find themselves. Even from this limited picture, it can be seen that more attention should be paid the social state in which a woman (or man) finds herself when death strikes down her partner.

Widowhood is rapidly becoming a major phenomenon of American society. National census data indicate that there are close to 11 million widowed persons among our population today, the large majority of whom are women.[1] Over the past several decades the widowed female has, in fact, been outdistancing her male counterpart by a continually widening margin. Whereas the number of widowers has remained relatively constant from 1930 to the present, female survivors have shown a substantial rise during this period. Thus, in 1940 there were twice as many widows as there were widowers. During the following decade widows increased by more than 22 percent while the number of widowers rose by only 7 percent. By 1960 the ratio of widows to widowers had risen to more than 3½ to 1, and throughout the decade has continued to climb to a present ratio of more than 4 to 1. Currently, there are well over eight and three-quarter million widows in the nation, and their total is expected to continue expanding.[2] Widowhood then is emerging as an important area for sociological inquiry because of the growing and extensive population involved. (Unless specified otherwise, the term widowhood as used in this paper will have reference to female survivors and their families only.)

For a variety of reasons, however, widowhood as a topic of study has not engaged the specific interests of sociological investigators to any appreciable extent, although there has been occasional recognition of the need for empirical data regarding their patterns of accommodation. Over a decade ago, for example, Kutner and his associates pointed out that "the effects and sequelae of widowhood have received little attention in empirical research. Widows are coming to represent a sizeable group in American life and there is a growing need for information regarding their pattern of adjustment" (Kutner, *et al.*, 1956, p. 19). In the more recent *Handbook of Social Gerontology* one reviewer particularly notes the lack of references to widowhood in the various publications of that specialized field and related areas, remarking: "It is striking that this inevitable and universal phase of life would be so patently neglected as an area of serious study" (Williams, 1961). In 1965, a sociologist employed with the federal government made a similar observation, stating:

"While much is made of the shock of retirement in gerontological literature, little is made of the shock of bereavement. Both are the common expectation of mankind and each should be studied. But in our society there is a strange silence about death and fear of death that is present with older people" (Kent, 1965, p. 14).

Finally, an informal survey of textbooks currently utilized in marriage and family courses reveals that in many instances the topic of widowhood is given only cursory attention and in still others the subject is not even raised. Such apparent disregard and lack of research concerning this special phase of the family life-cycle appears somewhat anomalous, indeed, in light of the fact that three out of every four wives in the United States survive their husbands.

This paper seeks to call specific attention to this neglected aspect of the family life-cycle. It will attempt to accomplish this goal primarily in two ways: (a) by highlighting the acute and problematic aspects of widowhood status through a concentration on significant sociodemographic indicators which characterize the contemporary condition of the widow and her family, and (b) by critically assessing the interdisciplinary scientific efforts concerning the study of widowhood, with particular emphasis on the sociological research orientation. In the latter connection, this paper represents an argument for a more extensive and systematic development of sociological knowledge concerning the phenomenon of widowhood in the United States and by emphasizing some needed areas of research on the social correlates of widowhood status.

Socio-Demographic Profile on American Widowhood

Widowhood has long been known to entail a variety of social problems at the local level, being related to adult and child dependency, poverty, unemployment, illness, and the more significant facts of family disorganization and of women's insecure industrial status (Phelps, 1938). In order to more fully portray the magnitude of the problem in contemporary society it is necessary to present a concise but somewhat abbreviated demographic profile on American widowhood. In addition to serving as a point of information regarding certain baseline data, the picture to be presented hopefully will also provide proper amplification of the current social conditions surrounding female survivors and will set the stage for exploring the sociological dimensions of their status for both the family and society.

It should be noted at the outset that from a statistical standpoint widowhood is largely a problem of the aged woman. As a result of the impact of advances in medical technology, pervasive health programs, etc., on decreasing mortality prior to midlife, widowhood for the most part has been postponed to the latter stages of the family life-cycle. Around the turn of the twentieth century about 1 in 25 persons was 65 years old or older, as compared to 1 in 11 in the present decade. Since the gains in longevity have been more rapid for females than for males, the growing proportion of elderly women in our population is accentuating the problem of widowhood. Thus, currently more than three-fifths of the widows in the United States are 65 years of age or over (almost another fourth are between 55-64) and "unless the trends in male and female mortality are sharply reversed, the excess of women over men at the upper ages will increase, and our older population will contain a larger proportion of widows" (Sheldon, 1958, p. 93).

Widowhood and Income

Because the majority of widows are aged, their economic circumstances are usually below average. A special survey of widows 55 years of age or older, for example, revealed that almost two-thirds of the husbands left a sum total of assets (including cash, savings, life insurance, property value of the home, and other assets) of less than $10,000 to their families; 44 percent left assets of less than $5,000. Equally significant, the median income of the wives in the year preceding the survey was less than $2,000 (Institute for Life Insurance, 1964). These figures are comparable to some extent with census data on the aged which shows the median income of the widowed as a group to be less than $1,200 per year, in comparison to almost $3,000 for the aged married. The census data also indicate that widows have substantially lower assets than non-widows in all age groups (Epstein and Murray, 1967).

One thing is clear—the available evidence on income levels lends little support to the occasional stereotype of "the wealthy widow," as a statistically prevalent type among our aged population. In this connection, it is frequently stated that women, as a consequence of outliving their husbands, control a great deal of the inherited wealth in the United States. It is said, for example, that they are beneficiaries of 80 percent of all life insurance policies (National Consumer Finance Association, 1963). It is true that as beneficiaries, women in the United States received more than two-thirds of the nearly $5 billion paid in 1965 following the death of a policyholder. Such gross figures, however, can be misleading. In the study cited earlier, for example, almost three-fourths of the husbands owned less than $5,000 in life insurance at the time of their death, and an additional 20 percent owned less than $10,000. Moreover, many of these women have to use what small amounts of insurance their husbands did carry to pay for funeral expenses, medical bills, taxes, mortgages, and so on, leaving them with only small savings on which to survive.

There is no doubt that life insurance has become a principal defense against the insecurity and risk of widowhood in our urban, industrial society with its attendant nuclear family system. It is a concrete form of security which in some instances may help the bereaved family to avoid an embarrassing and reluctant dependence on relatives and/or the state in the case of untimely death. Nevertheless, it has been the experience of investment bankers and the like that few female suvivors are capable of handling the economic responsibilities brought about by the husband's death, inasmuch as they know very little about matters of real estate, titles, mortgage, contracts, stocks, bonds, and matters of property[3] (Schwabacher, 1963).

Widowhood and Employment

Because they frequently encounter serious economic problems soon after their husbands have passed away, many wives find it necessary to seek employment. This is particularly the case where dependent children are involved; approximately 900,000 female survivors carried this responsibility in 1960. Moreover, at that time over half of all widows under age 35 were either employed or else seeking work. At ages 35-54, this proportion rises to nearly two-thirds (Metropolitan Life, 1966).

While women entering widowhood at the older ages are not as likely to have dependent children in the home, they are nevertheless often faced with a similar problem of self-support, since Social Security benefits provide for the minimum necessities only. Moreover, the obstacles to securing employment at this stage of the life-cycle are often rather difficult to overcome. Typically, these women have been absent from the labor market for several years and are, therefore, at a disadvantage with respect to the educational and occupational demands of current employment. In addition, they are frequently confronted with a subtle but pervasive discrimination on the part of the employers who are not in favor of hiring older persons, let alone older women. Since the majority of all widows, but in particular the aged widows, are unemployed, they are unable to support themselves and consequently are partly or wholly dependent on the assistance of children or relatives, and on public or private funds. While the 1965 amendments to the Social Security Act broadened and substantially increased benefits available to widows and their dependent children, their economic circumstances still remain far from satisfactory (Palmore, et al., 1966).

337

Female survivors who have obtained employment are heavily concentrated in the low-paying jobs. Over one-third are private household or other service workers; one-fifth are clerical and kindred workers, and one-seventh are operatives and kindred workers. Less than one-tenth of all widows are engaged in professional or technical occupations. In any event, research indicates that playing a role in the productive economy is predictive of favorable adaptation to widowhood. Kutner, *et al.*, for example, found that an employed widow in later life tends to be better adjusted, that is, to have higher morale, than both a housewife who has never worked and a retired widow (Kutner, *et al.*, 1956). The acts of preparing for work, carrying out one's tasks, and returning home are viewed as being intimately connected to feelings of personal worth, self-esteem, and significance in life. This has led to the suggestion that:

"For widowed women, there is a need for a service that will provide occasional jobs, such as babysitting, service as companions for bedridden persons, and occasional light housekeeping tasks. Many widows have never been in the labor force and have never acquired skills in any other line. These kinds of jobs frequently coincide with their experience as homemakers"[4] (Kutner, *et al.*, 1956, p. 254).

• • • •

Widowhood Mortality and Mental Health

That widowhood presents serious problems of personal adjustment and mental health is rather well established. Empirical research has consistently demonstrated that the widowed typically have higher death rates, a greater incidence of mental disorders, and a higher suicide rate than their married counterparts. More specifically:

The Widowed Die Sooner. Analyses of National Vital Statistics and Census data for the United States reveal that the widowed have a significantly higher mortality rate than married persons of the same age, and that among young widowed people there is a particularly high excess of mortality (Kraus and Lilienfeld, 1959). Additional investigations in this country and abroad have supported these findings. Moreover, recent research by Rees and Lutkins (1967) has provided rather dramatic statistical confirmation of the long-standing hypothesis that a death in the family produces an increased post-bereavement mortality rate among close relatives, with the greatest increase in mortality risk occurring among surviving spouses. At present, little is known of the primary causative agents underlying this association between bereavement and mortality. Homogamy, common affection, point to an unfavorable environment, and loss of care have all been suggested as possible influences. Moreover:

"Personality factors, social isolation, age (old people withstand bereavement better than young), and the nature and magnitude of the loss itself all seem to be important factors. When the bereaved person is supported by a united and affectionate family, when there is something left to live for, when the person has been adequately prepared for the loss, and when it can be fitted into a secure religious or philosophical attitude to life and death there will seldom be much need for professional help. When, however, the bereaved person is left alone in a world which is seen as hostile and insecure, when the future is black and the loss has not been prepared for, help may be needed" (Rees and Lutkins, 1967, p. 3).

Widowhood and Suicide. Durkheim is generally recognized as the first well known sociologist to stress the connection between widowhood and suicide:

"The suicides, occurring at the crisis of widowhood . . . are really due to domestic anomie resulting from the death of husband or wife. A family catastrophe occurs which affects the survivor. He is not adapted to the new situation in which he finds himself and accordingly offers less resistance to suicide" (Durkheim, 1951, p. 259).

Numerous investigations have since demonstrated that within a given age group, the suicide rates of the widowed are consistently higher than the married. A review of these studies indicates that suicide—whether attempted or actual—frequently tends to be preceded by the disruption of significant social interaction and reciprocal role relationships through the loss of a mate (Rushing, 1968). Moreover, these studies further reveal that the death of one or both parents in childhood is common among attempted and actual suicide victims; that the incidence of suicide among such persons when they attain adulthood is much greater than that for comparable groups in the general population.

Widowhood, Social Isolation, and Mental Health. That a high correlation exists between marital status and mental illness has been repeatedly noted in the scientific literature. While considerable professional controversy prevails over identification of the exact sequence of the antecedent-consequent conditions which predispose individuals toward various forms of organic and psychogenic disorders, there is little disagreement with the general hypothesis that "the emotional security and social stability afforded by married life makes for low incidence of mental illness" (Adler, 1953, p. 185). Again, the evidence is quite consistent that the widowed experience a substantially higher rate of mental disorders than the still married, particularly among the older populations.

The association between marital status and mental disorders has been shown to be a function of several intervening factors, including age, socio-economic status, physical condition, and the degree as well as duration of social isolation (Bellin and Hardt, 1958; Lowenthal, 1964, 1965). Problems of social isolation, often accompanied by distressing loneliness, are especially germane to the personal adjustment of aged female survivors, a very high proportion of whom are residing alone as occupants of one-person households. Fried and Stern (1948), for example, found that almost two-thirds of the widowed in their study were dissatisfied with the single state and were lonesome even after 10 years of widowhood. The loss of a husband not only creates many practical problems of living alone, but also produces a social vacuum in the life of the aged widow which is difficult to fill. She may find herself "marooned" in an environment which generally requires paired relationships as a prerequisite to social participation.[5] Consequently, various researchers have found that, compared to married women, widows are more apt to feel economically insecure, unhappy, to suffer from fears of being alone and from loss of self-esteem as women, to exhibit undue anxiety and emotional tensions, and to lack self-confidence. In the case of widows who are still mothers:

"There are the objective problems of limited income and the need to find the time and energy for a job to augment it and still be the kind of mother children need in the circumstances—a mother who can maintain a home, discipline and educate young people, and insure their positive emotional growth. Then there are the countless problems of guilt, fear, frustration and loneliness, ever-present and always threatening" (Ilgenfritz, 1961, p. 41).

To summarize at this point, it can be seen that a rather dismal picture of widowhood status emerges from the brief socio-demographic profile presented in the preceding pages. Clearly, the majority of women survivors generally have had to face a multiplicity of personal and familial adjustment problems while at the same time attempting to establish a satisfactory adaptation to a new and relatively undefined social role. Their economic position is likely to be insecure; more often than not they will need to seek employment, especially if young children are still in the home, and we only have touched on the various difficulties associated with these conditions. Moreover, in comparison to the still married, the widow faces the possibility of an early mortality, and there is a more than average probability that she will develop some mental disorder or even commit suicide.

• • • •

In this paper we have concentrated on the widow in American society. The same type of inquiry, however, needs to be undertaken with respect to the widower, about whom scientific information is even less adequate. Currently, there are well over 2 million widowers in our population, and it can be assumed that the structuring of their adaptation would be different from that of their female counterparts (Berardo, 1967). Unless or until extensive and systematic investigations of widowhood and widowerhood are undertaken and completed, the sociology of isolation will exhibit an unnecessary lag in its development.

NOTES

[1] The national data, of course, reflect the marital status of individuals at the time of the census enumeration only. It should be noted that people in the status of widowhood today may not be in this status tomorrow. Moreover, many currently married persons were once in the widowhood status (U.S. Bureau of the Census, 1967, p. 33).

[2] Three major factors are generally cited to account for the growing excess of widows in the United States, namely: (a) mortality among women is lower than among men and, therefore, larger numbers of women survive to advanced years; (b) wives are typically younger than their husbands and, consequently, even without the sex differences in mortality have a greater probability of outliving their husbands; (c) among the widowed, remarriage rates are considerably lower for women than men. Other major factors which also have an impact on widowhood status are the effects of war casualties, depressions, and disease pandemics (Jacobson, 1959, pp. 24–27).

[3] Actually, the economic dilemma in which widows often find themselves is frequently brought about as a direct result of the failure of husbands to plan their estates and advise their wives. "The truth is that most men leave their affairs in a jumble. This is not because their lives are unduly complicated, but simply because they can't seem to get around to the task of setting up a program for their families that would automatically go into operation upon their death. Death is unpleasant to think about and always seems remote. The tendency is to put the problem off and plan 'to get to it one of these days' " (*Changing Times*, 1961, pp. 9–14). Moreover, many husbands themselves are incapable of making sensible financial decisions and preparations.

[4] A federally sponsored program which dovetails rather nicely with the employment needs of older widows who lack specialized technical skills is the recently initiated Foster Grandparent Project developed by the Office of Economic Opportunity. Under this project, the federal government awards grants of money to the states to be used to employ older people as "foster grandparents" to work with and serve as companions for the mentally retarded, physically handicapped, delinquent, emotionally disturbed, and dependent and neglected children in institutions, day care centers, and homes (*Look*, 1966, pp. 67–71).

[5] Blau has demonstrated that the degree of social isolation among older widows is partially conditioned by the prevalence of similar age-sex peer groupings in the social structure (Blau, 1961).

REFERENCES

Adler, Leta M., "The Relationship of Marital Status to Incidence and Recovery from Mental Illness," *Social Forces,* XXXII (1953), 185–194.

Bellin, Seymour S., and Robert H. Hardt, "Marital Status and Mental Disorders among the Aged," *American Sociological Review,* XXIII (1958), 155–162.

Blau, Zena S., "Structural Constraints on Friendships in Old Age," *American Sociological Review,* XXVI (1961), 429–439.

Durkheim, Emile, *Suicide: A Study in Sociology* (Glencoe: The Free Press, 1951).

Epstein, Lenore A., and Janet H. Murray, *The Aged Population of the United States,* U.S. Department of Health, Education, and Welfare, Social Security Administration, Office of Research and Statistics, Research Report No. 19, U.S. Government Printing Office, Washington, D.C., 1967.

Fried, Edrita G., and Karl Stern, "The Situation of the Aged within the Family," *American Journal of Orthopsychiatry,* XVIII (1948), 31–54.

"How to Help Your Widow," *Changing Times* (November 1961), pp. 9–14.

Ilgenfritz, Marjorie P., "Mothers on Their Own—Widows and Divorcées," *Marriage and Family Living,* XXIII (1961), 38–41.

Institute for Life Insurance, *Some Data on Life Insurance Ownership and Related Characteristics of the Older Population,* 1964 (mimeographed).

Kent, Donald P., *Aging—Fact and Fancy,* U.S. Department of Health, Education, and Welfare, Welfare Administration, Office of Aging, OA No. 224 (Washington, D.C.: U.S. Government Printing Office, 1965).

Kraus, Arthur S., and Abraham M. Lilienfeld, "The Widowed Die Sooner," *Journal of Chronic Diseases,* X (1959), 207.

Kutner, Bernard, D. Fanshel, A. M. Togo, and T. S. Langner, *Five-Hundred over Sixty* (New York: Russell Sage Foundation, 1956).

Lowenthal, Marjorie F., "Social Isolation and Mental Illness in Old Age," *American Sociological Review,* XXIX (1964), 54–70.

Lowenthal, Marjorie F., "Antecedents of Isolation and Mental Illness in Old Age," *Archives of General Psychiatry,* XII (1965), 245–254.

Metropolitan Life Insurance Company, "Widows and Widowhood," *Statistical Bulletin,* XLVII (1966), 3–6.

National Consumer Finance Association, *Finance Facts,* Educational Service Division, Washington, D.C., January, 1963.

Palmore, Erdman, Gertrude L. Stanley, and Robert H. Cormier, *Widows with Children under Social Security,* The 1963 National Survey of Widows with Children under OASDHI. U.S. Department of Health, Education, and Welfare, Social Security Administration, Office of Research and Statistics, Research Report No. 16 (Washington, D.C.: U.S. Government Printing Office, 1966).

Phelps, Harold A., *Contemporary Social Problems* (rev. ed.; New York: Prentice-Hall, 1938), Ch. XV, pp. 516–540.

Rees, W. Dewi, and Sylvia G. Lutkins, "Mortality of Bereavement," *British Medical Journal,* IV (1967), 13–16.

Rushing, William A., "Individual Behavior and Suicide," in Jack P. Gibbs, ed., *Suicide* (New York: Harper and Row, 1968), Ch. 4.

Schwabacher, Albert E., Jr., "The Repository of Wealth," in Seymour M. Farber and Roger H. L. Wilson, eds., *The Potential of Women* (New York: McGraw-Hill, 1963), pp. 241–254.

Sheldon, Henry D., *The Older Population of the United States* (New York: John Wiley and Sons, 1958).

U.S. Bureau of the Census, *Statistical Abstract of the United States: 1967* (88th Edition), Washington, D.C., 1967, p. 33, Table 32, Marital Status of the Population, by Sex: 1890–1966.

Williams, Richard W., "Changing Status, Roles, and Relationships," in Clark Tibbitts, ed., *Handbook of Social Gerontology* (Chicago: University of Chicago Press, 1961), pp. 261–297.

Alone for the First Time in 23 Years: 'I Am in Space, and I Have Nowhere to Land'

Ann M. Kempson

Marriage is really much more than a social relationship. It creates extremely complicated psychological identities, identities the individual often remains unaware of until a terminating crisis occurs. This is because men and women not only relate to each other as husbands and wives, and as parents, but to each other and to friends and acquaintances as a couple, as close companions. Thus, when one member of the couple dies, the survivor is suddenly thrust into a new existential dimension. The special person that he or she was accustomed to being as a result of there being that very close companion no longer exists. The world is suddenly an unfamiliar place. No longer are there those special meanings and mutual experiences that were shared with another at special times. Things, events, and people that were significant before now are insignificant. And perhaps most startling of all, almost all major understandings between the surviving spouse and significant others must be renegotiated because of the changed status from member of a couple to surviving spouse. No relationship remains untouched by the change. Is it any wonder widows and widowers feel disoriented and without social anchorages?

One year ago today, my husband, Norris, died of a heart attack. A physical education teacher and coach, he died in the front office of C. E. Utt Intermediate School in Tustin—the school he loved. He was 49.

I rushed to the school after hearing the news, and stood by helplessly as the paramedics tried to revive him. They had been talking to his doctor at UCLA, and turned the phone over to me. The doctor then spoke the words I knew to

From Ann M. Kempson, "I Am in Space, and I Have Nowhere to Land," *Los Angeles Times*, Part II, p. 7, December 3, 1976. Reprinted by permission of the author.

be true—had known since I had first seen him lying there: Norris was dead. Norris, who was so physical in everything he did, had been defeated by a part of his body that refused to be pushed any longer.

In the beginning, what happened to me—the widow—seemed unimportant, for my grief was, and still is, for a wonderful man who had devoted his life to his family, friends and students. He gave so much . . .

Yet in my despondency I pounded on walls, on my sons' chests, on the ground by his grave. I cried, *No, this cannot be true.* But of course it was true, and as this penetrated my consciousness, I began to realize my own personal dilemma.

For the first time in 23 years I was alone. Not lonely. Alone.

When the misty-eyed bride hears "until death do us part," those are dream words, not real words, not words ever to be reckoned with. They deal with events so far in the future that they never need be thought about at all. In this day of ephemeral marriages, they are words often void of meaning.

In fairy tales, the prince and princess live happily ever after—forever—but what happens to us mortals? What happens after death *does* us part?

Cliches do not help here. People say, "Stay busy" or "Time will heal." What nonsense! Time may heal the wound I have from this relationship being so suddenly severed, but it cannot eradicate the scar of the emptiness.

I had never before realized how couple-oriented our society is. Each television comercial showing a happy couple doing whatever happy couples do—deciding what brand of coffee to buy, discussing toothpaste—became a personal affront to me. Whenever I saw elderly couples, I stared at them, wondering where Norris and I went wrong, how we failed. Growing old with my husband had always been something I looked forward to.

At first I thought the sadness would suffocate me. I wanted to throw it off, to laugh, to have fun again. Now I am getting used to this sadness that permeates every part of me. I accept it.

I have read everything I can find on death, and I have memorized the way a widow should feel at six months, a year, two years. Friends have suggested that if I could make it to these arbitrary anniversaries, I would be all right. But now I know the intensity of my grief may diminish, but never the grief itself.

I had never really thought much about how I looked, but now I study my face in the mirror. The eyes reflect the pain I feel, and I wonder if anyone else notices. I have tried not to burden my friends with this terrible feeling that will not go away, yet it is there, and my eyes tell of its existence.

Before Norris' death, we always had a plan for our future, but now I look into the future and I have no plan. All I see is nothingness.

I have a job that occupies my time. I have three wonderful children who have made this sorrow bearable for me. I have friends who have not deserted me. Nine months ago I went through major surgery without Norris' loving concern. I have been able to cope with being No. 5, No. 7 or No. 11 at a dinner party. I have been able to endure the emotional drain of *our* anniversary, *his* birthday, *my* birthday. I have been able to politely say, "No," to those who persist in asking me if I have started dating yet. I have been able to laugh when, as I leave a party, the hostess apologizes for not having an interesting man there for me.

The thought of returning to the adolescent uncertainty of dating horrifies me. I cringe when I am filling out a form that asks if I am single or married:

The right square in which to put the X is not there. That is the way my life is, a year after.

I am in a different world. I see the same people, do many of the things I did before, but my relationship to everything has changed. I am here, but I am not here. My purpose, my role—they no longer exist. I no longer belong in the same way I did before. I am in space, and I have nowhere to land.

I find comfort in going to the cemetery and talking to the place where he is buried. There my frustrations can surface because, morbid as it may sound, in that small piece of ground lie the remains of someone who cared for me. There, too, I realize I have been one of the lucky ones: I have loved, and been loved.

But now what? My forever and ever did not begin on our wedding date in 1952. Forever began for me on Dec. 3, 1975.

9

Continuing Pressures for Change in the Family

There can be no doubt that the family is constantly under pressure to change. However, these forces appear to be stronger and more varied than ever before. They are also more visible than in times past because both the media and social scientists have highlighted them through attention.

Change in the family can come about in two ways and they are interdependent on one another. The society outside the family can create pressures that family members must face and handle in order to survive. Important among these outside pressures are those created by the economy, by political ideologies, and various other social developments. All of these factors are eventually reflected in the population structure through changes in marriage, divorce, birth, and death rates, which, of course, are reactions to outside conditions. The resulting composition of the population, in turn, again affects these rates, so that a circularity of pressures between the family and population composition can be noted.

Moreover, as discussed earlier, individuals are constantly searching for living arrangements that will bring them pleasure, a sense of accomplishment, and a positive self-identity. Most recently, various groups have pronounced the traditional family as inimical to their long-term happiness and personal development and have united with others to press for changes. The Woman's Liberation Movement and the Gay Liberation Movement are perhaps the best known of these, and in many ways are closely related. Both groups see society as forcing them into limiting roles that are not to their best interests. Although heterosexual women cannot claim to suffer the stigma of gays, both groups have been the victims of job discrimination, infringement on their civil rights, and a feeling of being alienated from their true selves.

Societies have always regulated sexual behavior in some way and people have chafed under the regulations, often covertly skirting them. The so-called sexual revolution grew out of this feeling. Its effect was a diffuse loosening of moral boundaries. In its wake, several groups, braving societal scorn and wrath, have taken more focused stands for sexual freedom and for the end of monogamy. Some have suggested that the traditional nuclear family is outmoded, and call for a restructuring of families of their own making, with members of their own choosing. Many of their approaches to alternative or utopian life are not new. There have been communes that attempted to sponsor and regulate a new and hopefully improved life-style, before hippies tried it. None of these lasted much past one generation, for they were started by youths who apparently lacked both the resources and commitment to see each other and the next generation through all the crises that inevitably occur in living, as discussed earlier. Whether these current forms of the family will survive any longer than earlier experiments cannot be known now. Obviously, an ideology of independence of spirit goes somewhat counter to the commitment and responsibility of taking care of others. Should these alternative approaches to the family become numerous, they will have an impact on the structure of the population because of their low birth rates and high rates of marital or couple dissolution.

A Demographer Looks at American Families*

Paul C. Glick**

Demography is the study of birth rates, marriage and divorce rates, death rates, and immigration rates, and is intimately tied to family life. Although at first it may seem a dull subject—utilizing census statistics to analyze trends—anyone who really becomes involved with the study of population will find it is a fascinating way to understand the interplay of major social forces in human affairs. Marriages, births, length of life, and deaths affect all other aspects of social life and are affected by them. Glick, focusing on marriage rates, age of marriage, and birth rates, demonstrates concomitant social interaction as the United States went from the low birth rates and marriage rates of the Depression to the baby boom following the return of soldiers after World War II. This postwar period also ushered in an ideology of "togetherness," which included early-age marriage. More recently, there has been a decline in the marriage rate and an increase in having first children at an older age. These latter developments may reflect the impact of the Women's Liberation Movement and adherence to social pressure for zero population growth. The new "no fault" divorce will also change termination of marriage, while the proportion of remarriages that follow means an increase in the number of step-children and step-parents living together. The change in sex-role expectations may increase the marriage rate of highly educated women, or it may further depress all marriage rates. A very recent trend—some young women having children at an exceedingly early age—is not discussed, but it will have some important effects on the youthful parents as well as on the lives of the children they produce.

The title of this paper would be more nearly accurate if it had been changed to "A Social Psychologist Turned Demographer Tries to Understand What Is Happening to Marriage and Living Arrangements in the United States Today."

*Burgess Award Address presented at the annual meeting of the National Council on Family Relations in St. Louis, Missouri, on October 25, 1974.
**Paul C. Glick is Senior Demographer, Population Division, Bureau of the Census, Social and Economic Statistics Administration, U.S. Department of Commerce.

I was a social psychology major under Professor Kimball Young (grandson of Brigham Young) at the University of Wisconsin during the mid-1930s when about the only thing that an undergraduate major could find to do after receiving a B.A. degree was to go to graduate school. My greatest ambition had been to do research on attitudes toward various types of social, economic, and religious behavior to learn more about the extent to which people of a given socio-economic level who assert liberal or conservative attitudes in regard to one type of behavior tend to hold similar attitudes in regard to other types of behavior.

But at a critical point in my graduate school career I succumbed to an attractive offer to assist Professor Thomas McCormick on a study of the effects of the depression on Wisconsin's birth rates. This research assistantship carried with it a sure-fire source for a Ph.D. thesis, so I accepted it. And, because of having written the thesis, I was offered a position at the Census Bureau. That is why I left the teaching profession after two years and have been studying U.S. population trends since 1939. During all of these intervening years I have been trying to find out all I could about what relationships exist between marriage, fertility, and living arrangements, on the one hand, and socioeconomic level, on the other. Beyond that, I have tried to trace the changes in these relationships and to offer interpretive comment on what appear to be the changing attitudes that underlie the demographic changes.

In August 1974 the Bureau of the Census conducted a ceremony where the thirty-fifth anniversary of my entry on duty with the Bureau was recognized. Just how long that period of time really is can be appreciated better, perhaps, by noting that a person starting employment at the Bureau in 1974 would have to remain there until the year 2009 to equal my length of service at that honorable, but occasionally criticized, Federal agency.

These last 35 years have encompassed a wide range of changes in the U.S. population picture, and so it has been a most interesting period in which to be observing the American scene. In 1939—when I thought I was starting a 2-or-3-year hitch with the Census Bureau—the country was still in the later stages of the Great Depression. So many people with talent were unemployed that we had a larger choice of enumerators, field supervisors, processors, and professional analysts for the 1940 census than for the 1950, 1960, or 1970 census. As we approached censuses after 1940, we used to joke among ourselves that a stiff recession at hiring time would greatly increase our chances of achieving our constant goal of putting together a first class team to help us produce another first class census.

Recent Changes in Marriage and Fertility

The population picture in the late 1930s was gloomy. Many marriages had been delayed, so that the average age at marriage had risen, and a near-record 9 percent of the women 50 years old had never married. Birth rates had lingered at a low level, even without today's wide variety of means for birth control and without today's high degree of acceptance of a small number of children as a desirable family goal. Lifetime childlessness was edging up toward 20 percent, and many of the children whom some leading demographers thought were merely being postponed were never borne; a speculative interpretation is that many of the women who delayed having those other children reached the point where they liked it better without them than they had thought they would.

Then came World War II, with its extensive dislocations of family life particularly among families with husbands—or would-be husbands—of draft age, extending up to around 40 years of age. Marriage and birth rates remained low, and millions of women—married as well as single—were welcomed into the labor force who would never have gone to work outside the home if the male civilian work force had not shrunk so much.

After World War II, the marriage and divorce rates shot up briefly, fell again sharply, and then subsided gradually (Glick, 1974: chapter III). By the mid-1950s, a relatively familistic period had arrived. Couples were entering marriage at the youngest ages on record, and all but 4 percent of those at the height of the childbearing period eventually married. Moreover, the baby boom that had started with the return of World War II service men reached a plateau in the mid-1950s and did not diminish significantly until after 1960. By that time, the rate of entry into first marriage had already been falling and the divorce rate had resumed its historical upward trend.

By the late 1960s and early 1970s, the familistic style of life seemed to be on the wane again. The marriage rate among single persons under 45 years old was as low as it had been at the end of the Depression. Last year, the average age at marriage was close to a year higher than it had been in the mid-1950s, and the proportion of women who remained single until they were 20 to 24 years old had increased by one-third since 1960 (U.S. Bureau of the Census, 1974). The divorce rate had soared to the high level it had reached soon after the end of World War II, and an estimated one out of every three marriages of women 30 years old had been, or would eventually be, dissolved by divorce (Glick and Norton, 1973; Glick, 1973). The birth rate in 1973 was the lowest in the country's history, 15 per 1,000 population. The total fertility rate in 1973, which shows how many children women would have if they continued having children throughout their childbearing years at the same rate as in 1973, stood at a new low level of 1.9 children per woman. This is just one-half as many as in 1957, when the total fertility rate was 3.8 children per woman.

All of this has happened in the last 35 years, with high or low inflection points (depending on the variable) occurring near the middle of this period. It was an exciting period for a demographer to live through, because it was marked by sharp changes which called for careful measurement and perceptive interpretation. It was a period full of headaches for school administrators who had to adjust plant capacity to student load, as well as for manufacturers and distributors of products for babies or teenagers or any other functional age group because of the widely fluctuating demands by age. And it was a period when ideas were changing about the proper age for marriage, about desired family size, and about how serious it is to disrupt a marriage that does not seem to be viable. As ideas changed in one of these fundamental aspects of family life, other ideas came into question. So, we are now going through a period of change in demographic patterns that undoubtedly reflects basic, underlying attitudes toward conformity with traditional behavior, especially as such conformity comes in conflict with the development of the full potentiality of each member of the family.

Some Implications of Recent Changes

During the 12-month period ending in August 1974, the estimated number of marriages in the United States was about 2,233,000, and the number of divorces was 948,000. For the first time since soon after World War II the marriage total for a 12-month period was significantly smaller (by 68,000) than it had been in the preceding year. However, the divorce total for the 12 months ending in August 1974 had continued to rise (by 56,000) above the level for the preceding 12 months (U.S. Center for Health Statistics, 1974a).

These current figures are the latest available in a growing series which document a slowdown of marriage and a speedup of divorce. Since 1965, the annual number of first marriages has not been keeping pace with the rapid growth in the number of persons in the prime years for first marriage—those who were born soon after World War II. In fact, the number of marriages in recent years would have been even smaller if it had not been for the sharp upturn in remarriages associated with the increase in the number of divorces in this period. According to the latest information available, about four out of every five of those who obtain a divorce will eventually remarry (U.S. Bureau of the Census, 1972a).

From the peak year for births, 1957, to the present the declining birth rate has resulted in part from a decrease in the proportion of children born to women above 30 years of age and has been associated with a decrease in the median age at which women bear their children, from 25 years to 24 years. During this period there has been little change in the interval between marriage and the birth of the first child. At the same time, the proportion of first births that have occurred outside marriage has just about doubled, from 5 percent in the late 1950s to 11 percent in 1971.

When married women today are asked how many children they expect to have in their lifetime, those under 25 years old say they believe they will have just enough for zero population growth (aside from immigration). And answers to this question have been generally consistent over the last few years, with more changes in replies by identical women being in the direction of fewer rather than more children. Although fertility changes during the last 35 years provide ample evidence of the capacity of American couples to change their minds about how many children to have, the general consensus among most demographers is that a repeat of the post-World War II baby boom is most unlikely in the foreseeable future (U.S. Bureau of the Census, 1974a).

Recent Delay in Marriage Among the Young

The average woman at first marriage today is 21 years old. During the approximately 15 years of the post-World War II baby boom, the average woman had been one year younger at marriage, 20 years. Another way of showing the extent of the recent delay in marriage is to point out that a new low level of 28 percent single was registered for women 20 to 24 years of age in 1960; but the corresponding figure for women in their early twenties in 1974 had jumped up by more than one-third to a level of 40 percent single (U.S. Bureau of the Census, 1974b). There is no doubt about it. Young women are now postponing marriage longer than their mothers did in the late 1940s and early 1950s. (Corresponding data for men are not presented because their coverage in censuses and surveys has fluctuated as the size and location of men in the Armed Forces has varied widely since 1940.)

A delay in marriage—identified by an increase in the percent single—has been common to young women (under 25 years old) of all education levels, but census figures show that the increase in singleness was greatest during the 1960's among young women who had not attended college. This finding is probably at least tangentially related to the sharp rise in unwed motherhood among white women during the 1960s; most unwed mothers have never attended college. Young women with a high school education but with no college training continue to be the ones with the smallest percent single. (The situation among older women is different, as will be shown below.)

Why has this delay in marriage occurred among the young? At least a part of the answer lies in the fact that nearly three times as many women were enrolled in college in 1972 as in 1960 (3.5 million versus 1.2 million), and the college enrollment rate has more than doubled for women in their twenties during those 12 years. Another demographic factor was the "marriage squeeze"; during recent years this phenomenon has taken the form of an *excess of young women* of ages when marriage rates are highest, because women born in a given year during the baby boom after World War II reached their most marriageable age range two or three years before men born in the same year (Carter and Glick, 1970). Still other demographic factors include the sharper increase in the employment of women than men and the amazing decline in the birth rate, both of which signaled expanding roles open to women outside the home. Among the less tangible factors has been the revival of the women's movement. In fact, the excess of marriageable women in the last few years may have contributed as much to the development of that movement as the ideology of the movement has contributed to the increase in singleness.

A detailed analysis of recent marriage trends has suggested that it is too early to predict with confidence that the recent increase in singleness among the young will lead to an eventual decline in lifetime marriage. However, just as cohorts of young women who have postponed childbearing for an unusually long time seldom make up for the child deficit as they grow older, so also young people who are delaying marriage may never make up for the marriage deficit later on. They may try alternatives to marriage and like them.

Early Marriage and High Fertility of Those Approaching Middle Age

Women who are now 35 to 44 years old were born during the Depression years of the 1930s. They have been a most interesting group for demographers to study because of their many unique features: they were born when the birth rate was at the lowest level recorded up to that time (total fertility rate averaging about 2.3 children), with only the rates after 1970 being still lower; they set a record for early marriage (average about 20 years) and for high birth rates (total fertility rate peaking at 3.8 in 1957); and now they have in prospect one of the lowest proportions single on record (likely to fall below 4 percent before they end their fifties) and one of the lowest proportions who will remain childless throughout life (10 percent for women regardless of marital status and 6 percent among those who ever marry). They have shared more fully than the preceding generation—and probably more than the following generation—in the process of marrying and replenishing the population.

These women, now 35 to 44 years of age, are featured here and in the discussion of divorce below because of their uniqueness in another respect. They are old enough to have experienced most of their lifetime marriages, childbirths, and divorces, and yet they are young enough to reflect recent changes in family life patterns. Because of the recent developments with regard to the delay in marriage and the fertility decline among those now in their twenties, it would have been tempting to have featured this younger age group. However, this option was not adopted because not enough time would have elapsed after school attendance for those with 4 or more years of college to have essentially established their lifetime levels of marriage and childbearing.

As noted above, the marriage history of women now 35 to 44 has culminated in a record low proportion single for women of that age range (now 5 percent and likely to drop below 4 percent by 1990). But the continuing decline in singleness for women of this age range was not uniformly distributed among the several educational groups. Although the percent single was *rising* most rapidly among *young* college-educated women (those under 25), the percent single was *declining* most rapidly among *older* college-educated women (those 35 to 44). Women college graduates 35 to 44 reduced their excess percent single, as compared with all women in the age group, by a substantial one-fourth during the 1960's. Still, women college graduates with no graduate school training have continued to record a high proportion single, 10 percent in 1960 and 8 percent in 1970; and those with graduate school training recorded a *very* high level of 24 percent single in 1960 but "only" 19 percent single in 1970 (U.S. Bureau of the Census, 1967 and 1972b).

Similar socioeconomic differentials in the decline in singleness were found when the measurement was in terms of occupation and income. For example, the proportion single among women who were professional workers dropped by about one-third from the high level of 19 percent in 1960 to 13 percent in 1970. Moreover, women in the upper income bracket ($7,000 or more in 1960 and $10,000 or more in 1970—about the right difference in income level to adjust for the decreasing value of the dollar) had about a one-fourth decline in the proportion single between 1960 and 1970 (from the very high level of 27 percent to the still quite high level of 21 percent). Thus, in summary, the declines in singleness among the women in these upper socioeconomic groups consisted of tendencies for this aspect of their marital pattern to converge with—to become more like—that of women in the lower socioeconomic groups.

Why did this happen? A partial answer must be the relative *scarcity of women* of optimum age to marry during the mid-1950's, a period of affluence when nearly all men in the upper socioeconomic group were marrying. Thus, all but 2 or 3 percent of the men in 1970 in the upper income bracket had married by early middle age; they had been at the height of their period for first marriage during the late 1940s and the 1950s. Another part of the answer must have

353

been the greatly increasing opportunities for young women to work at attractive jobs outside the home even though they were married—a phenomenon that was far less common only a generation before 1960. It had obviously become far easier for a woman to combine a working career and marriage (Davis, 1972)..

Why have not still more of the women in the upper socioeconomic groups become married? In 1970, fully 1 in every 5 women around 40 years of age with some graduate school education or with an income of $20,000 or more have not married, as compared with only 1 in every 20 women with no college education (U.S. Bureau of the Census, 1972b). Most of these women were submitted to the maximum pressure to marry during the period 10 to 20 years ago. Probably no one would argue with the interpretation that women with graduate school training have far more options for interesting roles to cultivate—including wife, mother, and/or career woman—than those with less education. But, despite the sharp increase in marriage among "fortyish" upper group women, could it be that a significant proportion of men who are also in the upper socioeconomic group still hesitate to marry a woman who expects to be a partner in an *egalitarian* marriage—or a woman who might be a serious competitor for the role of chief breadwinner or "head of the household"? It seems reasonable to expect a substantial further decline in the force of this factor as the impact of the women's movement is felt increasingly among both men and women. The expected direction of change would seem to be a growing acceptance of the situation in which the wife equals or outranks the husband in such matters—without as much of a disturbing effect on the couple's social relationships as it evidently continues to have today.

Divergence and Convergence of Divorce by Social Level

In 1970, the proportion divorced (and not remarried) continued to be lower among men approaching middle age (35 to 44 years old) than among women of comparable age—3.6 percent versus 5.5 percent. This pattern results from the older average age of men at marriage, hence the shorter duration of marriage for the men, and also from the larger proportion of men than women who eventually remarry—about five-sixths versus three-fourths. The difference between men and women in the proportion currently divorced has increased substantially since 1960, when 2.6 percent of the men and 3.8 percent of the women were divorced (and not remarried). This divergence between the sexes may have developed because of several factors including the increasing extent to which divorced women tend to outlive divorced men.

Meanwhile, a "democratizing" development in relation to marriage patterns is reflected in the fact that the proportion divorced among men 35 to 44 years of age has tended to converge since 1960 among the educational, occupational, and income groups. Men in the upper status groups continue to have a below-average proportion divorced (but not remarried), however, the gap was smaller in 1970 than it was in 1960. More specifically, the proportion divorced increased during the 1960s by about three-eighths for all men in the age group but by a considerably larger proportion (about one-half to two-thirds) for men with 4 or more years of college, for professional men, and for men in the top income class for which data are available ($10,000 or more in 1960 and $15,000 or more in 1970).

354

Changes during the 1960s in the proportion divorced among women by social and economic groups were more complex than those for men. For all women 35 to 44, the proportion divorced went up, on the average, by nearly one-half during the 1960's, from 3.8 percent to 5.5 percent. But among women who were professional workers or in the uppermost income level—where the percent divorced among women (unlike men) has been characteristically quite high—the percent divorced rose by a smaller proportion (under one-third) than among other women. (The percent divorced for professional women went up from 6.0 percent in 1960 to 7.8 percent in 1970; and the percent divorced for women in the uppermost income group rose from 11.8 percent to 15.1 percent.) Thus, for these categories of upper group *women*, the percent divorced was tending to converge with that for other women by increasing more *slowly* than the average, while for upper group *men* the percent divorced was tending to converge with that for other men by increasing more *rapidly* than the average.

The pattern is especially complex when changes in the proportion divorced are analyzed for women college graduates 35 to 44 years old. Women who terminated their education with 4 years of college hold the record for the smallest percent divorced (3.0 percent in 1960 and 3.9 percent in 1970). Moreover, they reinforced this position during the 1960's by being the educational group with the *smallest* proportional increase in the percent divorced (three-tenths). By contrast, women 35 to 44 with one or more years of graduate school have had fewer years since marriage in which to obtain a divorce but still hold the record among educational groups for the largest percent divorced (4.8 percent in 1960 and 7.3 percent in 1970). Moreover, they reinforced this position by having the *largest* proportional increase in the percent divorced of all educational groups (over one-half). Thus, both women with 4 years of college and those with 5 or more years of college have tended to diverge from the general level of increase in the proportion divorced but in opposite directions.

Why the Upturn in Divorce?

While the number of couples experiencing divorce has been rising, many other changes have also been occurring. Some of these changes might have actually been expected to cause the divorce rate to *decline*. For example, divorce rates are generally lowest among men in the upper socioeconomic groups, and the proportion of men in the upper education, occupation, and income groups has been increasing; yet the proportion divorced has been rising most in these very same groups. One of the many plausible hypotheses for investigation in this context can be posed in the form of a question: Was a larger proportion of men with "divorce proneness" being drawn into the ranks of upper socioeconomic groups in the two decades after World War II? This was a period when those ranks were being augmented by upwardly mobile persons who were rising from the lower socioeconomic groups; persons in the groups from which they were rising have probably always had the highest rates of marital dissolution.

This hypothesis could be examined by studying the relationship between the direction of intergenerational socioeconomic mobility and rates of marriage and divorce. Men who have been upwardly mobile by a substantial amount (defined as men whose achievement is quite perceptibly above that of their fathers) might be shown to have more initial advantage in the marriage market than their brothers with little or no such upward mobility. However, for many the advantage may not have lasted; these upwardly mobile men might have permitted "excessive achievement orientation" or complications resulting from their change of social level to interfere with the promotion of satisfaction in their marriages. Downwardly mobile persons may tend to have even more difficulty in their marital adjustment. This hypothetical relationship may be tested in the next year or so by the present author and Arthur J. Norton as a by-product of the study of "occupational change in a generation" that is being conducted by David L. Featherman and Robert M. Hauser, of the University of Wisconsin, on the basis of data from a Census Bureau survey in 1973.

Socioeconomic changes during the last decade or two that might have been expected to cause a *rise* in the divorce rate are numerous, but the contribution each has made to this rise cannot be readily demonstrated. Illustrations include the increasing proportion of young wives with small families who have succeeded in translating their higher level of education into jobs that make them financially independent of their husband; an increasing proportion of couples whose income has risen to a level at which they can afford the cost of obtaining a divorce to resolve a marriage that is not viable; the increased availability of free legal aid which may have permitted a large number of impoverished families to obtain a divorce; the war in Vietnam which complicated the transition of millions of young men into marriage or made their adjustment in marriage more difficult than it would have otherwise been.

Other changes that may have contributed in varying degrees to the increase in divorce during the last decade have less of an economic orientation. One cluster of such changes includes a greater social acceptance of divorce as a means for resolving marriage difficulties—in particular, the relaxation of attitudes toward divorce by a growing number of religious denominations; the relatively objective study of marriage and family relationships at the high school and college levels; the movement to increase the degree of equality of the sexes which is making some headway toward easing the social adjustment of persons who are not married; and the reform of divorce laws, in particular, the adoption of no-fault divorce.

No-fault Divorce Laws

An article entitled "Legal Status of Women," prepared at the U.S. Women's Bureau lists 23 States that had adopted "some form" of no-fault divorce by January 1974—16 of them since 1971 (Rosenberg and Mendelsohn, 1974). The 23 states are Alabama, Arizona, California, Colorado, Connecticut, Florida, Georgia, Hawaii, Idaho, Indiana, Iowa, Kentucky, Maine, Michigan, Missouri, Montana, Nebraska, Nevada, New Hampshire, North Dakota, Oregon, Texas, and Washington. A 24th state, Minnesota, passed a no-fault divorce law in the 1974 legislative session. Moreover, the legislators in nearly all other states are in the process of considering how to incorporate this feature into their divorce laws.

Persons who have examined the divorce laws closely have cautioned, however, that the no-fault movement is not really as far along as the advocates of "true" no-fault divorce would like to see. This view was expressed to me in a letter from Lenore J. Weitzman (University of California at Davis) who, together with two colleagues is conducting a Federally sponsored study of "The Impact of Divorce Law Reform on the Process of Marital Dissolution: The California Case" (Weitzman, Kay, and Dixon, 1974). According to their calculations, five states have instituted true no-fault divorce by adopting the provisions of the Uniform Act; nine other states have adopted some other form of no-fault divorce. The states which have merely *added* no-fault divorce to their existing grounds for divorce should really not, according to Dr. Weitzman, be considered no-fault divorce states. Under a "true" no-fault divorce law, a couple may terminate its marriage without any expectation of punitive consequences resulting from the action; the main items to be settled are a reasonable division of joint property and arrangements for the maintenance of the children and the maintenance of one spouse on the basis of need. However, in states where no-fault is only one of several grounds for divorce, one spouse may threaten to consider the other "at fault" but settle for a no-fault divorce in the negotiation for a more favorable settlement. For this reason the number of no-fault divorces in those states may not indicate the true number who obtained divorces without negotiations involving the adversary concept.

Children of Parents Who Have (or Have Not) Been Divorced

Women whose first marriage ended in divorce have been, on the average, about two years younger when they entered marriage than married women of the same age who have not been divorced (U.S. Bureau of the Census, 1973c). However, on the average, about three years elapse between divorce and remarriage. So, if the average divorcee gains a couple of years of married life through early marriage but loses three years of married life through divorce, what is the net effect on her family size? According to 1970 census data for women 35 to 39 years old, the answer varies according to her later marriage experience. First, divorced women 35 to 39 years old who had gone on to marry a man who had not been married before wound up with him and 3.1 children, on the average, or virtually the same number at the census date as that (3.2 children) for couples with both the husband and wife still in their first marriage. Second, those who were still divorced at the census date had borne a smaller number, namely, an average of 2.6 children. And third, among married couples at the census date where both the husband and the wife were divorced after their first marriage, the average number of children was intermediate, 2.9 children ever born (U.S. Bureau of the Census, 1973a).

Another way to show how many children are affected by divorce is to note that 15 percent of all *children under 18 years of age* in 1970 were living with one or both parents who had been divorced after their first or most recent marriage. Some of these children were born after their divorced parent had remarried, but a larger number were living with a stepparent at the census date. Thus, about two-fifths of the children with a previously divorced parent were born after the remarriage and hence were living with their two natural parents; however, the other three-fifths were living with a stepparent. Besides these children of "ever divorced" parents, another 15 percent were not living with both (once-married) natural parents. In other words, these figures imply that only about 70 percent of the children under 18 years of age in 1970 were living with their two natural parents who had been married only once. Among black children the corresponding figure was very low, 45 percent, but that for white children was also low, 73 percent (U.S. Bureau of Census, 1973b).

The proportion of *children of school age* living with both natural parents in their first marriage was even smaller than 70 percent in 1970. Therefore, the remaining more than 30 percent of school children were *not* living with a father and a mother who were in a continuous first marriage. This means that such children are no longer rare. Even though children of separated, divorced, or never-married parents still have many problems today, they at least have far less cause to feel unique or exceptionally deprived than similar children of yesterday. Moreover, because the birth rate has been declining for several years, the *average* number of children involved per divorce has declined since the mid-1960's (to 1.22 in 1970 and 1971); however, the *total* number of children involved in divorce was still rising in 1971, when it was 946,000 (U.S. National Center for Health Statistics, 1974b). In a country where many legal grounds for divorce have been established and used, a large number of children will inevitably be involved in separation and/or divorce. But there is no optimum proportion of children who should be thus involved, any more than there is a fixed optimum proportion of couples who should dissolve their marriage by divorce.

What Is a Reasonable Amount of Lifetime Marriage (or Divorce)?

Saying that there is no fixed optimum proportion of marriages that really should not remain intact leaves much to be said about the current level of divorce and the prospective level over the next decade or two. For one thing it is now very high, in fact the highest in the world, and seems likely to remain that way. In 1972, the most recent date for which many international figures are available, the divorce rate was the highest in the U.S.A., with a rate of 3.72 per 1,000 population. Other countries with high 1972 levels of divorce were the U.S.S.R. with a rate of 2.64 and Hungary with a rate of 2.32. Cuba had a 1971 rate of 3.23 (United Nations, 1973). More recently, the U.S. divorce rate climbed on up to 4.4 per 1,000 population in 1973 and to 4.5 per 1,000 during the 12 months ending in August 1974 (U.S. Center for Health Statistics, 1974a).

In the context of our high divorce rate, some questions worthy of exploration can be raised. How many of the divorces are desired by both parties? On the basis of experience in divorce counseling, Emily Brown, current chairman of the Family Action Section of the National Council on Family Relations, estimates that around 4 out of every 10 of the couples obtaining a divorce include one member who did not want it. But that leaves around 6 out of every 10 who did want it. Did the right couples obtain a divorce? Surely some who did so were ill-advised in this respect, whereas others with far more justification for a divorce were inhibited from obtaining one. And yet the situation may be so complex—when all of the pros and cons are considered—that even the wisest of family counselors must have difficulty in rendering objective judgment about the advisability of continuing or ending the marriages of a large proportion of those who come to them for counseling service.

A certain amount of divorce undoubtedly grows out of the fact that the supply of acceptable marriage partners is very often quite limited, and those who would be most ideal partners never meet, or if they do, they may do so at the wrong time or become unavailable to each other at the optimum time for marriage. In other words, marriage partners are typically joined through a process of chance, often involving compromise, and if the compromise element is substantial, there should be no great surprise if the marriage is eventually dissolved by permanent separation or divorce. In view of the haphazard manner in which the important step of marriage is generally undertaken, and in view of the many frailties of human adults, the surprise may be that the proportion of marriages that last—to a happy (or bitter!) end—is as large as it is.

Men at the top of the socioeconomic scale must have the most advantages in marital selection and in the means for achieving a satisfactory adjustment after marriage. Thus, a potential husband with a promising occupational future no doubt arrived at that enviable position usually—but, of course, not always—because of personal characteristics that should also make him an attractive candidate for marriage. This type of man has the widest choice of women for a potential wife—one with maximum appeal and few "hangups." And if the man's work history materializes into occupational success, his chances of keeping his marriage partner satisfied with their marriage arrangement should be accordingly enhanced—other things being equal. In fact, the statistics demonstrate that the most lasting marriages are contracted by men in the upper socioeconomic levels.

Viewed from the vantage point of the potential wife, the line of reasoning is quite similar in some key respects but has important differences. One similar feature is the great amount of competition they face in their search for men who are attractive candidates for marriage. A dissimilar feature is the somewhat different set of personal characteristics which describe an attractive woman as compared with an attractive man for selection as a marriage partner—under the situation as it has existed for a long time but under a situation that may have already started to make a wide-ranging change.

But if the most attractive men marry the most attractive women, as so often happens, is it any wonder that they turn out to have the highest proportion of continuing marriages? And, by implication, is it any wonder that other persons more often terminate their less-than-ideal matches through separation and divorce? But the situation may not be as bad as it seems, in view of the fact that this discussion relates to a band of persons on or near the diagonal of a distribution showing the marriage appeal of potential husbands cross-classified by the marriage appeal of potential wives.

Thus, a study might be expected to show that, for a given type of men in a given marriage market area, somewhere around the top 20 percent of men in attractiveness might be considered as reasonably acceptable husbands for the top 20 percent or so of women, with (sliding) lower quintiles of men being "acceptables" for corresponding lower quintiles of women. As the lowest 20 percent of potential husbands and wives is approached, those in this group should theoretically be relatively satisfied with their marital partners provided they marry someone within their own range. But are they going to be all that satisfied? And what about those who either by choice or because they lost out in the competition married someone outside their optimal range? It would be logical to expect their marital dissolution rate to be substantial and to account for a disproportionately large share of all divorces. Although dissolution of marriage by divorce is by far the most likely among couples in the lowest economic level, undoubtedly a relatively large proportion of these same couples would still have an above-average divorce rate even if their income levels were augmented considerably.

A key variable in this context is "coping power." Presumably those of upper status have much more of it, on the average, than those who achieve only lower status. Although the development of superior coping mechanisms would ordinarily be expected to result in maintaining a marriage intact, it would also be expected to result from time to time in the firm decision that a marriage is not tolerable and should be dissolved. And yet, the kinds of talent and support that fail to elevate the standing of a person above a low level must tend to leave that person with fewer options within which to achieve satisfactory adjustment either occupationally or maritally. At least the findings for men are generally consistent with this interpretation.

For women, however, the pattern is different, with those who have the most education and the most income being generally less likely to enter marriage or to maintain continuing marriages, on the average, than those with lesser achievement in their educational background and work experience. How long this pattern for women will persist is anyone's guess, but it could last indefinitely among those who genuinely prefer being unmarried. On the other hand, it could change substantially over the next decade or two if modifications of attitudes about what constitute proper sex roles become modernized through appropriate socialization of the younger generation and resocialization of the older generations (Bernard, 1972).

Recent Changes in Living Arrangements

Along with the recent decrease in fertility and increases in separation and divorce have come other developments that have shrunk the typical cluster of persons who live together as a household. Very few married couples live in with relatives as they once did. At the height of the housing shortage after World War II, fully 9 percent of all couples were without their own house or apartment, but now only 1 percent have to—or choose to—double up with others. In the 1940s only 1 in every 10 households was maintained by persons living alone or with a lodger or two, but now 1 in 5 households is of this type, and 1 in every 6 households consists of one person living entirely alone. As an overall measure of the shrinking family size, it is instructive to note that the average household consisted of 5 persons from 1890 to 1910, then 4 persons from 1920 to 1950, and 3 persons since 1960—with the 1974 average dipping fractionally below 3 persons, to 2.97 persons (U.S. Bureau of the Census, 1974b).

This development reflects mainly the longtime decline in fertility, but now more young adults live in apartments away from their parental home or in apartments rather than college dormitories, and more elderly persons are financially able—and evidently prefer—to live apart from their adult children. The most rapid increase in household formation since 1960 has occurred among young adults with no relatives present, but the numerical increase has been much larger among elderly persons living alone. A spectacular 8-fold increase occurred during the 1960's in the number of household heads who were reported as living apart from relatives while sharing their living quarters with an unrelated adult "partner" (roommate or friend) of the opposite sex. One out of every four of these 143,000 "unmarried couples" in 1970 were women who had a male partner "living in." Among older men sharing their living quarters with nonrelatives only, one in every five shared it with a female partner (U.S. Bureau of Census, 1964 and 1973b). These older couples must include a substantial proportion of widowed persons who were living in this manner in order to avoid losing survivor benefits through remarriage.

Another "variant family form" is the commune, a type of living arrangement that has not been adequately quantified on a nationwide basis, partly because many of the communes are not welcome in their neighborhood and would rather not be identified in a census or survey.

The shrinking household size and the growing number of small households consisting of single-parent families, unmarried couples, or persons living entirely alone are evidence that large families are no longer regarded with favor by many persons and that new life styles are being tried by persons who want to learn whether the new ways are more satisfying to them than more conventional patterns. Some of the living arrangements with increasing numbers of adherents are bringing unrelated persons into closer companionship, whereas more of them are providing at least temporary relief from contacts with relatives that were regarded as too close for comfort.

But with four out of every five divorced persons eventually remarrying, the single-parent family has been in large part a temporary arrangement serving as a transition for the parent from one marital partner to another, and between parenthood and stepparenthood. New surveys will be watched for possible evidence that more of those with dissolved marriages will settle down with another unmarried person in a relatively stable union (with or) without a legal "cohabitation contract" that would have to be retracted through a court procedure if the union is to be dissolved later on.

Kin Network Ties and Neighborhood Characteristics

The scattering of adult married and unmarried family members has been accelerated during recent decades through increased migration, which is related to increased amounts of higher education, among many other things. Fewer neighborhoods are now dotted by families of the same surname. Yet a substantial amount of contact is maintained with relatives, even with those who live at a considerable distance. A study under the direction of David M. Heer (on behalf of a committee established by the Family Section of the American Sociological Association) contemplates the collection and analysis of national data on the extent and nature of relationships that keep alive the kin network among persons under 40 years of age and their parents and siblings. The results are expected to quantify variations in types of communication and mutual assistance that are characteristic of "kinpersons" living different distances apart and belonging to different socioeconomic groups. Funds for the support of this project are now being negotiated.

361

As adults move to localities that are beyond commuting distance of their close relatives, they may (or may not) become closely integrated into their new local neighborhoods. Studies are therefore needed to show the adjustment patterns of families in relation to the type of community in which they live. One study along this line is being planned by the present writer and Larry H. Long, also of the Bureau of the Census, on the basis of computer tapes available from the 1970 census. This source permits the analysis of marital and family characteristics in relation to such variables as duration of residence in the neighborhood (census tract or other small area), the ethnic composition of the neighborhood, the educational and income level of the neighborhood, the rate of turnover of population in the neighborhood, and the age and quality of housing in the neighborhood. Funding for this project may be obtained during the next year.

Concluding Remarks

The foregoing review of certain aspects of American marriage and living arrangements included some facts about what has been happening recently to family life in this country and has called attention to some areas where further research is needed. The accompanying interpretative comments were intended to add understanding to the census and vital facts that were presented. That is about as far as a demographer is expected to go in trying to help people do something about "the situation" in which so many American families find themselves today. Surely there is plenty of room for a division of labor between demographers and others who have a contribution to make in this area, including family lawyers, family counselors, socioeconomists, home economists, psychologists, social workers, religious leaders, and journalists.

However, there are undoubtedly some nondemographers who are looking for a cause to promote in this context. My personal opinion is that they might be well-advised to consider some of the following directions in which to exert their efforts:

1. The development of the contents for more practical and effective training at home, in the high schools, and in colleges about how young persons can make a wise selection of their marriage partner and how they can keep their marriage alive and healthy over a long period of time—and about how they can use reasonable criteria to decide whether it is any longer practical to keep their marriage intact (Broderick and Bernard, 1969).

2. Designing a scientifically tested and appealing system for selecting a marriage partner, for bringing together young men and women who would have a much higher probability of establishing an enduring and satisfying marriage than could be expected through the almost universally haphazard system that now exists—at the same time realizing that the rational approach must be supplemented by the strength of emotional appeal (Glick, 1967).

3. Acceptance by the public of the concept of periodic marriage checkups through visits to highly expert marriage counselors (when a sufficient supply becomes available), with these visits occurring in a manner analogous to periodic physical checkups that are voluntarily made, and with the visits considered urgent when a seemingly dangerous marital condition is developing.

4. Continuing modernization of marriage and divorce laws, which would tend to encourage couples to take much more seriously their entry into marriage but not quite so seriously as some couples do the hazards of ending a marriage that is no longer worthy of continuation.

5. Development of child care facilities staffed by highly professional personnel, so that more mothers can feel free to maximize the alternatives available for the use of their time while their children are growing up—provided that careful attention is given in choosing the ways in which the additional free time is used (Campbell, 1973; Low and Spindler, 1968).

6. Finally, programs to increase the appeal of experiencing a good marriage, including the continued collection and dissemination of knowledge about how to cultivate such a marriage—so that more emphasis can be placed on building up the positive side of married life, in a period when so many stimuli that reach the public have the effect of making nonmarriage appear to be much more desirable (Mace and Mace, 1974).

Certainly demographers cannot be counted upon—in their capacity as practicing demographers—to promote such causes as these to improve family relations in the modern world, but they can help to promote such causes indirectly by providing imaginative factual information about the types of circumstances which tend to be associated with enduring marriages and about other types of circumstances that tend to be associated with a substantial amount of seemingly inevitable marital dissolution.

REFERENCES

Bernard, Jessie, 1972, *The Future of Marriage*. New York: World Publishing.

Broderick, Carlfred B., and Jessie Bernard (eds.), 1969, *The Individual, Sex, and Society: A SIECUS Handbook for Teachers and Counselors*. Baltimore: The Johns Hopkins Press.

Campbell, Arthur A., 1973, "Population: The Search for Solutions in the Behavioral Sciences." *American Journal of Obstetrics and Gynecology*, Vol. 116, No.1, pp. 131–152.

Davis, Kingsley, 1972, "The American Family in Relation to Demographic Change" pp. 237–265 in *U.S. Commission on Population Growth and the American Future*, Charles F. Westoff and Robert Parke, Jr. (eds.), Vol. I, *Demographic and Social Aspects of Population Growth*. Washington, D.C.: U.S. Government Printing Office.

Glick, Paul C., 1957, *American Families*. New York: John Wiley & Sons; 1967, "Permanence of Marriage." *Population Index*, Vol. 33, No. 4, pp. 517–526. Presidential Address, Population Association of America, April 1967; 1973, "Dissolution of Marriage by Divorce and Its Demographic Consequences." Pp. 65–79 in Vol. 2 of *International Population Conference*. Liege, Belgium: International Union for the Scientific Study of Population.

Glick, Paul C. (ed.), 1974, *Population of the United States, Trends and Prospects: 1950 to 1990*. U.S. Bureau of the Census, Current Population Reports, Series P-23, No. 49. Washington, D.C.: U.S. Government Printing Office.

Glick, Paul C. and Arthur J. Norton, 1973, "Perspectives on the Recent Upturn in Divorce and Remarriage." *Demography*, Vol. 10, No. 3, pp. 301–314.

Low, Seth and Pearl G. Spindler, 1968, *Child Care Arrangements of Working Mothers in the United States*. U.S. Children's Bureau and U.S. Women's Bureau. Washington, D.C.: U.S. Government Printing Office.

Mace, David and Vera Mace, 1974, *We Can Have Better Marriages*. Nashville, Tenn.: Abingdon Press.

Rosenberg, Beatrice and Ethel Mendelsohn, 1974, "Legal Status of Women," in *Council of State Governments, The Book of States, 1974–75*. Available through U.S. Women's Bureau.

United Nations, 1973, *Demographic Yearbook, 1972*. New York: United Nations.

U.S. Bureau of the Census, 1964, *1960 Census of Population, Vol. II, 4B, Persons by Family Characteristics*. Washington, D.C., U.S. Goverment Printing Office; 1967, *1960 Census of Population, Vol. II, 4C, Marital Status*. Washington, D.C.: U.S. Government Printing Office; 1972a, "Marriage, Divorce, and Remarriage by Year of Birth: June 1971." *Current Population Reports*, Series P-20, No. 239. Washington, D.C.: U.S. Government Printing Office; 1972b, *1970 Census of Population, Vol. II, 4C, Marital Status*. Washington, D.C.: U.S. Government Printing Office; 1973a, *1970 Census of Population, Vol. II, 3A, Women by Number of Children Ever Born*. Washington, D.C.: U.S. Government Printing Office; 1973b, *1970 Census of Population, Vol. II, 4B, Persons by Family Characteristics*. Washington, D.C.: U.S. Government Printing Office; 1973c, *1970 Census of Population, Vol. II, 4D, Age at First Marriage*. Washington, D.C.: U.S. Government Printing Office; 1974a, "Prospects for American Fertility: June 1974." *Current Population Reports*, Series P-20, No. 269. Washington, D.C.: U.S. Government Printing Office; 1974b, "Marital Status and Living Arrangements: March 1974." *Current Population Reports*, Series P-20, No. 271. Washington, D.C.: U.S. Government Printing Office.

U.S. National Center for Health Statistics, 1974a, "Provisional Statistics (Births, Marriages, Divorces and Deaths for August 1974)." *Monthly Vital Statistics Report*, Vol. 23, No. 8. Washington, D.C.: U.S. Government Printing Office; 1974b, "Summary Report, Final Divorce Statistics, 1971." *Monthly Vital Statistics Report*, Vol. 23, No. 8 Supplement 3. Washington, D.C.: U.S. Government Printing Office.

Weitzman, Lenore J., Herma Hill Kay, and Ruth B. Dixon, 1974, "No-Fault Divorce in California: The View of the Legal Community," paper presented at the annual meeting of the American Sociological Association in Montreal, August 25–29.

The Black American Family*

Robert Staples

In the previous reading, Glick looked at the social and demographic history of the United States and made some predictions about the future of the family. However, the primary focus of his discussion was on the majority subgroup in the population—white Americans. Staples here gives a parallel picture of black Americans that has both strong similarities and some startling differences.

Crucial to understanding the black family is its historical beginnings in bondage, often in marriages arranged for breeding purposes. After the Civil War, black families faced extreme economic and social discrimination, the primary target of which was the male. Working in white households, the female often became the major support of the family. The marital life cycle of the black family reveals special traits that are also a reflection of its history and its continued economic subjugation in the United States. Partner seeking among blacks includes premarital intercourse as a continuing and natural occurrence and not as the "new" mass phenomenon it reportedly is with white college students. However, young black people do not live together, and marriage is often not the culmination of the relationship. Like their white counterparts, black men fall in love less deeply than do black women. Finding a compatible male to marry who will treat her with respect is still a problem for the black female. There is a shortage of eligible black men.

Among married blacks, it is assumed the wife will work—the family could not survive economically if she did not. The divorce rate is higher among blacks than whites. Black men have a shorter life expectancy than white men, resulting in a larger proportion of black widows than white. However, because of the strong black kinship system, black women are closer to sons, daughters, and other relatives than those white elderly persons described by Johnson (Reading 27).

Blacks are also aware of the various social "revolutions" in the United States that are discussed in the next section, but their reaction is different from that of whites. Whereas the sexual revolution for whites has the professed goal of the sexual liberation of women, black women have always been sexually permissive. At the same time, middle-class women in the Women's Liberation Movement are attempting to withdraw from the very roles black

---

*This chapter is also to be published concurrently in Dr. Staple's own book, *Introduction to Black Sociology* (New York: McGraw-Hill).

women are trying to attain, that is, dependence on a strong, faithful, providing husband, and an opportunity to devote herself full-time to being a housewife and mother. Far from seeking freedom to do their own thing, or form "families" from collection of compatible strangers, black family members are clinging together to help each other in a hostile world (much as did white frontier families of an earlier era).

As America's largest visible minority, the Black population has been the subject of extensive study by behavioral scientists. Its family life has been of particular concern because of the unique character of this institution due to a history that is uncharacteristic of other ethnic groups. There are four traits of the Black group that distinguish it from many other immigrants to America. These differences are cultural in the sense that (1) Blacks came from a continent with norms and values that were dissimilar to the American way of life, (2) they were composed of many different tribes, each with its own languages, cultures, and traditions, (3) in the beginning, they came without females, and, most importantly, (4) they came in bondage (Billingsley, 1968).

The study of Black family life has, historically, been problem oriented. While the study of white families has been biased toward the middle-class family, the reverse has been true in the investigation of Black family patterns. Until relatively recently, almost all studies of Black family life have concentrated on the lower-income strata of the group, while ignoring middle-class families or even "stable" poor Black families. Moreover, the deviation of Black families from middle-class norms has led to the definition of them as "pathological." Such labels ignore the possibility that while a group's family forms may not fit into the normative model, it may have its own functional organization that meets the needs of that group (Billingsley, 1970).

One purpose of this description of Black family life styles is to demonstrate how it is organized to meet the functional prerequisites of the Black community. Additionally, the forces that Black families encounter, which create the existence of large numbers of "problem" families, must be carefully examined. Out of this systematic analysis of Black-family adaptations may come a new understanding of the Black family in contemporary American society.

HISTORICAL BACKGROUND

The Preslavery Period

There are several historical periods of interest in determining the evaluation of Black family life in America. One era is the precolonial one on the African continent from which the Black American population originated. The basis of African family life was the kinship group, which was bound together by blood ties and the common interest of corporate functions. Within each village, there were elaborate legal codes and court systems that regulated the marital and family behavior of individual members.

The structure and function of the Black family was to radically change under the system of slavery. What did not change, however, was the importance of the family to African peoples in the New World. While the nature of marriage and family patterns was no longer under the control of the kinship group, it nevertheless managed to sustain the individual in the face of the many destructive forces he was to encounter in American society.

The Slave Family

In attempting to get an accurate description of the family life of slaves, one has to sift through a conflicting array of opinions on the subject. Reliable empirical facts are few, and speculation has been rampant in the absence of data. Certain aspects of the slave's family life are undisputed. Slaves were not allowed to enter into binding contractual relationships. Because marriage is basically a legal relationship that imposes obligations on both parties and exacts penalties for their violation, there was no legal basis to any marriage between two individuals in bondage. Slave marriages were regulated at the discretion of the slave master. As a result, some marriages were initiated by slave owners and just as easily dissolved (Stampp, 1956).

Hence, there were numerous cases in which the slave owner ordered slave women to marry men of his choosing after they reached the age of puberty. They preferred a marriage between slaves on the same plantation since the primary reason for slave unions was the breeding of children who would become future slaves. Children born to a slave woman on a different plantation were looked upon by the slave holder as wasting his man's seeds. Yet many slaves who were allowed to get married preferred women from a neighboring plantation. This allowed them to avoid witnessing the many assaults on slave women that occurred. Sometimes the matter was resolved by the sale of one of the parties to the other owner (Blassingame, 1972).

Historians are divided on the question of how many slave families were involuntarily separated from each other by their owners. Despite the slave holder's commitment to maintaining the slave families intact, the intervening events of a slave holder's death, his bankruptcy, or lack of capital made the forcible sale of some slave's spouse or child inevitable. In instances in which the slave master was indifferent to the fate of slave families, he would still keep them together simply to enforce plantation discipline. A married slave who was concerned about his wife and children, it was believed, was less inclined to rebel or escape than would a "single" slave. Whatever their reasoning, the few available records show that slave owners did not separate a majority of the slave couples (Blassingame, 1972).

This does not mean that the slave family had a great deal of stability. While there are examples of some slave families living together for forty years or more, the majority of slave unions were dissolved by personal choice, death, or the sale of one partner by the master. Although individual families may not have remained together for long periods of time, the institution of the family was an important asset in the perilous era of slavery. Despite the prevalent theories about the destruction of the family under slavery, it was one of the most important survival mechanisms for African people held in bondage (Blassingame, 1972).

In the slave quarters, Black families did exist as functioning institutions and as models for others. The slave narratives provide us with some indication of the importance of family relations under slavery. It was in the family that the slave received affection, companionship, love, and empathy with his sufferings under this peculiar institution. Through the family, he learned how to avoid punishment, to cooperate with his fellow slaves, and to retain some semblance of his self-esteem. The socialization of the slave child was another important function for the slave parents. They could cushion the shock of bondage for him, inculcate in him values different from those the masters attempted to teach him, and represent another frame of reference for his self-esteem besides the master (Abzug, 1971).

Much has been written about the elimination of the male's traditional functions under the slave system. It is true that he was often relegated to working in the fields and siring children rather than providing economic maintenance or physical protection for his family. But the father's role was not as significant as presumed (Blassingame, 1972). It was the male slave's inability to protect his wife from the physical and sexual abuse of the master that most pained him. As a matter of survival, few tried as the consequences were often fatal. But it is significant that tales of their intervention occur frequently in the slave narratives. There is one story of a slave who could no longer tolerate the humiliation of his wife's sexual abuse by the master before his eyes. He choked him to death with the knowledge that it meant his death. He said he knew it was death, but it was death, anyhow, so he just killed him (Abzug, 1971:29).

One aspect of Black family life frequently ignored during the slave era is the free Black family. This group, which numbered about half a million, was primarily composed of the descendants of the original Black indentured servants and the mulatto offspring of slave holders. For this minority of Black families, the assimilation and acculturation process was relatively less difficult. They imitated the white world as closely as possible. Because they had opportunities for education, owning property, and skilled occupations, their family life was quite stable. Some of them even owned slaves, although the majority of Black slave holders were former slaves who had purchased their wives or children. It is among this group that the Black middle class was early formed (Frazier, 1932).

After Emancipation

There has been a prevailing notion that the experience of slavery weakened the value of marriage as an institution among Afro-Americans. The slaves, however, married in record numbers when the right for the freedom to marry was created by governmental decree. A legal marriage was a status symbol, and weddings were events of great gaiety. In a careful examination of census data and marriage licenses for the period after 1860, Gutman (1973) found the typical household everywhere was a simple nuclear family headed by an adult male. Further evidence that Black people were successful in forming a biparental family structure are the data that show 90 percent of all Black children were born in wedlock by the year 1917 (Bernard, 1966:3).

The strong family orientation of the recently emancipated slaves has been observed by many students of the Reconstruction era. One newspaper reported a Black group's petition to the state of North Carolina asking for the right "to work with the assurance of good faith and fair treatment, to educate their children, to sanctify the family relation, to reunite scattered families, and to provide for the orphan and infirm" (Abzug, 1971:34). Children were of special value to the freed slaves, whose memories were fresh with the history of their offspring being sold away.

It was during the late nineteenth century that the strong role of women emerged. Males preferred their wives to remain at home, since a working woman was considered a mark of slavery. But during a period described as "the most explicitly racist era of American history" (Miller, 1966), Black men found it very difficult to obtain jobs and, in some instances, found work only as strikebreakers. Thus, the official organ of the African Methodist Episcopal Church exhorted Black families to teach their daughters not to avoid work since many of them would marry men that would not make on the average more than 75 cents a day (Abzug, 1971:39). In 1900, approximately 41 percent of Black women were in the labor force, compared to 16 percent of white women (Logan, 1965).

What was important, then, was not whether the husband or wife worked but the family's will to survive in an era when Blacks were systematically deprived of educational and work opportunities. Despite these obstacles, Black families achieved a level of stability based on role integration. Males shared equally in the rearing of children—women participated in the support of the family. As Nobles (1972) comments, a system in which the family disintegrates due to the loss of one member would be in opposition to the traditional principles of unity that defined the African family. These principles were to be tested during the period of the great Black migration from the rural areas of the South to the cities of the North.

The rise of Black illegitimacy and female-headed households are concomitants of twentieth-century urban ghettos. Drastic increases in these phenomena strongly indicate that the condition of many lower-class Black families is a function of the economic contingencies of industrial America (Anderson, 1971:276). Unlike the European immigrants before them, Blacks were especially disadvantaged by the hard lines of Northern segregation along racial lines. Furthermore, families in cities are more vulnerable to disruptions due to the traumatizing experiences of urbanization, the reduction of family functions, and the loss of extended family supports.

In the transition from Africa to the American continent, there can be no doubt that African culture was not retained in any pure form. Blacks lacked the autonomy to maintain their cultural traditions under the severe pressures to take on American standards of behavior. There are, however, surviving Africanisms that are reflected in Black speech patterns, esthetics, folklore, and religion (Herskovits, 1958). They have preserved aspects of their old culture that have a direct relevance to their new lives. And out of the common experiences they have shared has been forged a new culture that is uniquely Afro-American. The elements of that culture are still to be found in their family life.

THE MODERN BLACK FAMILY

Demographic Characteristics

The majority of Black families adhere to the nuclear-family model. In 1972, approximately two-thirds of Black families had both the husband and wife present. A significantly larger percentage of Black households were headed by a female than in white families. While white families had a woman head in 9 percent of all such families, 30 percent of Black families were headed by a woman. Moreover, this was an increase of 38 percent from the last decade. This large number of female-headed households is mostly a result of socioeconomic forces. As the level of income rises, so does the number of male-headed families. At the upper income level of $15,000 and over, the percentage of male-headed households is comparable to that for white families. If we combine families reconstituted by a second marriage with those never broken, 69 percent of Black children live in families with both a father and mother present (U.S. Bureau of the Census, 1972).

One of the most significant changes in the period 1960–70 was the decline in the Black fertility rate. In 1968, the Black birth rate reached its lowest level in the past 25 years. However, the white birth rate declined even more rapidly (29 percent versus 32 percent), and the total fertility rate of 3.13 children per Black woman is still higher than that of 2.37 for white women. The Black fertility rate is influenced by a number of factors, including regional variations, rural-urban differences, and, most importantly, socioeconomic levels. In 1967 Black women in the South had more children than those who lived in the North, and the birth rate of urban Black women was lower than that of Black women in rural areas. Significantly, middle-class Blacks have the lowest fertility rate of almost every demographic category in America, whereas middle-class Catholics and Mormons have the highest. College-educated Black women actually have a lower birth rate than college-educated white women (Kiser and Frank, 1967; Westoff and Westoff, 1971)

One of the more significant events of the last decade has been the steady decline in the out-of-wedlock births to Black women, while the illegitimacy rate among whites has shown a steady rise. The illegitimacy rate among whites went from 9.2 to 13.2 (per 1,000 unmarried women 15 to 44 years old) between 1960 and 1968, while the rate among Blacks decreased from 98.3 to 86.6 during the same time span (U.S. Bureau of the Census, 1971). Some of this racial difference in the illegitimacy-rate increase can be attributed to the more frequent and effective use of contraceptives and abortions among Black women. One study found that Black women received about 25 per cent of all the legal abortions performed in hospitals nationwide (U.S. Population Council, 1972). However, the white illegitimacy rate has been underreported in the past through unreported abortions, falsification of medical records, and shotgun weddings (Ryan, 1971).

As we reported earlier, about 30 percent of Black families are headed by women. About 60 percent of these families have incomes below the official "poverty" level. This is true despite the fact that 60 percent of the women who are heads of Black households work (most of them full time). Slightly less than

50 percent of them receive welfare assistance (Hill, 1972). These female-headed households include widowed and single women, women whose husbands are in the armed forced or otherwise away from home involuntarily, as well as those apart from their husbands through divorce or separation. The majority of them came about through separation or divorce, while a quarter of them involve widows, and 20 percent were never married (U.S. Bureau of the Census, 1972).

Social Structure

It is generally acknowledged that the Black kinship network is more extensive and cohesive than kinship bonds among the white population. The validity of this assumption is born out by the census data, which show that a larger proportion of Black families take relatives into their households. Billingsley (1968) divides these families into three general categories. They include (1) the "incipient-extended family," composed of a husband and wife who are childless and take in other relatives, (2) the "simple extended family," a married couple with children who have other relatives living with them, and (3) the "attenuated extended family," a household composed of a single, abandoned, legally separated, divorced, or widowed mother or father living with their own children, who takes into the home additional relatives. According to the 1970 Census, the attenuated family is the most common, with 48 percent of families headed by elderly women taking in relatives under 18. The proportion of similar white families is only 10 percent. In the incipient-extended family category, 13 percent of Black couples took in relatives under 18, compared to only 3 percent of white couples (U.S. Bureau of the Census, 1970).

There is some disagreement on the reason for the stronger kinship bonds among Black families. Adams (1970) has suggested that minority status tends to strengthen kin ties because of a need for mutual aid and survival in a hostile environment. Others have attributed it to the individual's general distrust of neighbors and neighborhoods, the prevalence of large female-headed households receiving public assistance, and the high rate of residential mobility that makes long-term friendships difficult (Feagin, 1968; Stromberg, 1967). In opposition to the above theories is the argument by Matthews (1972) and Nobles (1972) that contemporary Black kinship patterns are but a variant of the extended family system found in African societies.

Matthews (1972) advances the proposition that Afro-Americans are relating to their African heritage when they function as members of a corporate group. The individual in the Black community, he says, is always relating to the remainder of the total Black community. In fact, Black togetherness is at the heart of Black social organization. The Black extended family is the functional unit of the Black community. Nobles (1972) has argued that the Black family socializes its members to see no real distinction between his personal self and other members of the family. They are both the same. The individual's identity is always the group's identity, and families function according to this philosophical orientation of the Black community.

With the possible exception of elderly parents, Black families rely more heavily on extended kin than white families. The range of the kin network is extensive and includes parents, siblings, cousins, aunts, uncles, etc. A unique feature of the Black kinship network is the inclusion of nonblood relatives who are referred to and regarded as kinsmen. Among lower-class Black males, for instance, males who are unrelated to one another "go for" brothers and interact on that fraternal basis. Usually, this is a special friendship in which the normal claims, obligations, and loyalties of the kin relationship are operative (Liebow, 1966). These para-kinship ties seem to be a facilitating and validating agent of Black life in America.

One finds no special status or authority associated with roles in the Black family. Contrary to theories about the Black matriarchy and the dominance of women, most research supports the fact that an equalitarian pattern typifies most Black families (Hyman and Reed, 1969; Mack, 1971; Middleton and Putney, 1960). In a succinct summary of authority patterns in the Black family, Hill states: "The husbands in most Black families are actively involved in decision making and the performance of household tasks that are expected of them. And, most wives, while strong, are not dominant matriarchs, but share with their husbands the making of family decisions—even in the low-income Black families" (Hill, 1972:20).

The myth of the Black matriarchy has been reinforced by the failure of many students of Black family life to distinguish between the terms dominant and strong. While Black women have needed to be strong in order for the Black family to survive, she has not necessarily been dominant (Ladner, 1971). In fact, she has not had the resources to impose her authority on many Black males in the society. The husband in most Black families is the primary breadwinner. Even in lower-class Black families, the wife's income is only a small part of the total family income. In 85 percent of low-income Black families, the husband's income is higher than the wife's (Hill, 1972).

Social Class and Style of Life

When it comes to describing social classes and life styles among the Black population, the task is made difficult for a number of reasons. Among them is the fact that social class is an analytical concept that is neither (1) universally accepted in the social sciences, (2) conceived in precisely the same way by all students of social stratification, nor (3) commonly designated by the same label (Hodges, 1964:12–13). This difficulty is magnified when attempting to delineate the Black class structure. Among the difficulties encountered is the massive amount of mobility occurring in the Black class structure, with a fairly large number of upwardly mobile Blacks. Another is the number of middle-class Blacks who want to preserve their cultural traditions and thus adopt values and life styles that are commonly associated with the lower class (Kronus, 1971).

If income and educational levels are used, approximately 30 percent of Black families would be in the middle-class category. The rest would fall in some level of the lower-class stratum, with only a negligible number in the upper-class group. In 1970, about 28 percent of Black families had an income over $10,000. About 38 percent of Black families in the North and West had incomes greater than $10,000. Over 50 percent of Blacks, 25 to 29 years old, had completed high school in 1971. About 20 percent of young Blacks are presently enrolled in college. Most of these Black members of the middle class will have a very recent origin from the lower-class group (U.S. Bureau of the Census, 1972).

But the concept of social class refers to more than a person's educational and income levels. It is measured just as well by cultural values and behavioral patterns, summed up as a class life style. Bernard (1966) divides Black families into two strands: the "acculturated" and "externally adapted." The former term describes those Blacks who have internalized Western norms, the latter, those Blacks who have adapted to these norms superficially. It is this writer's belief that most middle-class Blacks belong in the externally adapted group. Instead of internalizing white values, most new members of the Black middle-class have adopted certain middle-class practices as a strategy for obtaining a decent life.

The paucity of research on middle-class Black families does not provide many data for this assumption (Kronus, 1971). But if one examines the dynamics of middle-class Black behavior, a certain pattern emerges. For example, the sexual behavior of upwardly mobile Black females is more conservative because a premarital pregnancy can mean dropping out of school and ruining one's chances of gaining entrance into the middle class (Ladner, 1971; Staples, 1972). When the middle-class Black female becomes pregnant before marriage, she is more likely to get an abortion than her lower-class counterpart (Gebhard, Pomeroy, Martin, and Christenson, 1958). Middle-class Black families have a significantly lower family size than low-income Black families not because they place less value on children, but because they perceive a very direct link between low income and large families. These class differences in marital and familial behavior among Blacks reflect pragmatic choices, not different values.

Within the lower-class group exists a variety of Black families. One finds a strong belief in hard work and the value of education among them. A recent study revealed that poor Black youth who have grown up in welfare families have a more positive attitude toward the desirability and necessity of work than the children of the white middle class (Goodwin, 1972). In another study, a slightly larger number of Black workers expressed a desire to take a job as a car washer rather than go on welfare even if the pay for the two sources of income was the same (Tausky and Wilson, 1971). A number of studies have documented the strong desire of lower-income Black families to have their children attain a higher educational level than they have (Cosby, 1971; Harris, 1970; Hindelang, 1970). One result of this parental support is that 75 percent of Blacks enrolled in college are from families in which the head had no college education (U.S. Bureau of the Census, 1970).

The Family Life Cycle

Courtship and Marriage. Studies on Black dating and sexual patterns are few and unreliable (Staples, 1971a). As with the research on other aspects of Black family life, the focus has been on problems allegedly resulting from the different dating styles of Afro-Americans. Thus, one rarely finds a study of Black sexuality that does not associate that aspect of Black behavior with the problems of illegitimacy, female-headed households, and welfare dependency. The sexual relationships of Blacks is rarely, if ever, investigated as an element of the normal functioning of Black families. The intricate meaning and emotional dynamics of the Black sexual relationship are seldom captured in most Black family studies (Turner, 1972).

Heterosexual relationships develop at an early age in the communal setting of Black social relationships. Within the Black households exist high life activities of adults in which children participate (Rainwater, 1966). This is a time of feasting, drinking, and dancing. Even very young children are often matched with members of the opposite sex at this time. Males and females learn to interact with one another on the romantic level, usually associated with the post-adolescent stage for whites. Hence, one study of Black students aged 10 to 17 found that half or more of the males and females at all ages claimed to have a boy/girl friend, to have participated in kissing games, and to have been in love (Broderick, 1965).

Within the same sex peer group, Black males and females are socialized into their future pattern of sex-role interaction. Males learn the technique of "rapping," a linguistic pattern designed to convince the female that he is worthy of her interest and as a verbal prelude to more intimate activity. The female acquires the ability to discriminate between men who are with it and how to unmask a weak rap. When the male petitions her for sex, she may accept if interested, or if she has other motivations. Whether she agrees to participate in premarital sexual activity will not be founded on the morality of such behavior but on the practical consequences (pregnancy) that may ensue (Ladner, 1971).

This lack of moral emphasis on sexual behavior will be in opposition to the teachings of her parents. Most Black parents (usually the mother) urge their daughters to remain chaste until an adult—not necessarily until marriage. They are rarely told that premarital coitus is sinful but that sex relations before marriage can result in pregnancy. The Black female's reference group, however, is her peers, and they are more supportive of the philosophy that losing one's virginity is a declaration of maturity, of womanhood. Those who refuse to indulge are often subordinating peer-group approval to their desire for upward mobility. They do not, however, condemn others who decide to participate in premarital sex, even when their decision is to refrain (Ladner, 1971; Rainwater, 1970).

Thus, much dating behavior among Blacks is *ipso facto* sexual behavior (Staples, 1972). In fact, among most Black youth, there is no such thing as the dating pattern found among the white middle class. Young people meet in their neighborhoods and schools and soon begin to go out with one another. Sexual involvement may begin shortly afterward (Rosenberg and Bensman, 1968). In their recent investigation of Black females aged 15 to 19, Zelnik and Kantner (1972) reported that by the age of 19 over 80 percent of their Black subjects had engaged in premarital intercourse. However, while the proportion of comparable white nonvirgins was lower, it was that group that had sex more frequently and with more sexual partners.

While Black women have been socialized to appreciate sexual relationships, it is laden with an emotional meaning for them. Once sex has taken place, the intensity of the emotional relationship begins. As her association with her sexual partner becomes routinized, the emotional aspect is increased, and the male is ultimately expected to limit his close relationships with other women (Ladner, 1971). In the Zelnik and Kantner (1972) study, over 60 percent of their subjects said their relations had been confined to a single partner. Half of the nonvirgins said they intended to marry the male. The Reiss (1964:697) comparison of Black and white premarital sexual standards revealed that although relatively permissive, Blacks are not generally promiscuous. They tend to require affectionate relations as a basis for sexual behavior.

Most Black women desire a stable, enduring relationship—ultimately marriage. This feeling is not always reciprocated by Black males (Broderick, 1965). Many Black men apparently evade the institution altogether, as a fairly large proportion of them (13.8 percent) never marry at all (U.S. Bureau of the Census, 1972). Males, traditionally, have been less oriented toward marriage and the domestic responsibilities it entails. In the case of many Black males, reluctance to marry is reinforced by the unhappy marriages around them and the abundance of women available for companionship in their environment. For the Black female desirous of marriage, these facts of Black life all work to her disadvantage.

When it comes to finding a compatible mate, she faces a number of obstacles. One of the biggest hurdles is the excess number of Black women vis-à-vis Black men. In the age group over 14, there are approximately a million more Black females than males listed by the U.S. Census (1972). Although the number of Black males is higher due to their underenumeration in the census, the number of Black men available to Black women for marriage is actually fewer than the census figures would indicate. This low number of eligible Black males is due to their higher rate of mortality, incarceration, homosexuality, and intermarriage (Staples, 1970; Jackson, 1971). Once all these factors are considered, there may be as many as two million Black females without a male counterpart. This fact is particularly important when the reasons are sought for the large number of female headed households in the Black community. There is simply no way of establishing a monogamous, two-parent household for many Black women within a racially endogamous marriage system.

Still, most Black women maintain an ideal concept of the man they would like to marry. These idealistic standards of mate selection, however, must often be subordinated to the realities they encounter. In the lower-class group, they frequently will settle for a man who will work when he is able to find employment, avoid excessive gambling, drinking and extramarital affairs, provide for the children, and treat her with respect. Even these simple desires cannot be met by lower-class Black husbands who are unable to find work and retreat into psychologically destructive behavior such as alcoholism, physical abuse of their wife, etc. (Drake and Cayton, 1945; Rainwater, 1970).

The middle-class Black woman has a slightly better chance of fulfilling her desires for a compatible mate. She is likely to require economic stability, emotional and sexual satisfaction, and male participation in child rearing. Both Black men and women are in agreement that she will work after marriage. And it has been found that the wife's employment does not pose a threat to the Black male's self-image. Black males are more likely to believe that the wife has a right to a career of her own than white males. The dual employment of both spouses is often necessary to approach the living standards of white couples with only the husband working. It also reflects the partnership of Black men and women that has existed for centuries as part of their African heritage (Axelson, 1970).

Marriage, however, has proved to be a fragile institution for Blacks—even in the middle class. The divorce and separation rate for Blacks as a group is quite high. While marriages are dissolving in record numbers for all racial groups, it has been particularly high for Blacks. In the last decade, the annual divorce rate has risen 75 per cent. In 1971, 20 per cent of ever-married Black women were separated or divorced, compared to 6 per cent of similar white women (U.S. Bureau of the Census, 1972).

The problems of being Black in a racist society have their ramifications in the marriage arena. It seems quite evident that whatever difficulties lower-class Black spouses have in their interpersonal relations are compounded by both the problems of poverty and racism. The middle-class Black marriage is threatened less by poverty than by the shortage of Black males, especially males in the same educational bracket as the women. There are approximately 85 college-educated Black males available for marriage to every 100 Black female college graduates. Many Black college women—especially those who attended Black institutions—remain single (Bayer,1972). Others may marry men with less education, and this type of marriage has a greater statistical probability of ending in divorce (Noble, 1956; Staples, 1973). One result of the male shortage in the Black middle class has been the tendency of women seeking educated, high-status Black professionals to pursue men who are married as fair game. This type of female competition becomes a direct assault on a man's marriage and increases the risk of divorce (Rosnow and Rose, 1972). Such demographic pressures do not pose as great a threat to white marriages.

Another factor decreasing the available supply of educated Black males is the tendency of males in the middle class to date and marry white women, while white males are less involved with Black women (Day, 1972). In the most recent period, there has been a discernible increase in interracial dating and marriage (Porterfield, 1973; Willie and Levy, 1972). Public-opinion polls support the notion that there is a growing tolerance of interracial marriage by both Blacks and whites (Gallup, 1972). The common belief is that most interracial marriages involve a Black male and white female, and some studies document this via an examination of marriage records (Heer, 1966; Monahan, 1970). However, the Bureau of the Census in 1960 reported 51,000 known interracial marriages, and they were about evenly divided between Black men and Black women as the nonwhite spouse. Thus, marrying outside of the race may be a means for Black women to increase their marriage potential.

The growing trend toward interracial marriages has occurred in the midst of a large movement of Black youth toward Black nationalism and separatism. Much of this paradox can be explained by the entrance of many Blacks into previously all-white settings such as the white university in which they meet and associate with whites as equals. Much larger numbers of Blacks and whites date than enter into a marriage. Most Blacks have other Blacks as their first preference for dating and marriage (Goins, 1960). It is estimated that fewer than 5 percent of the Black population are interracially married. Although there are studies showing interracial marriages to be more stable than intra-racial unions (Golden, 1959; Monahan, 1970), one sees indications that the external pressures against such marriages, along with the difficulties of marriage in general, pose a threat to the continued stability of many such unions.

Whereas certain problems exist in Black marriages, high separation and divorce rates are not necessarily a valid measure of the stability and functionality of Black families. What is important is whether they meet their functional obligations. There are many female-headed households, for instance, that socialize their children into successful adult roles. The biggest problem they face is the economic and employment discrimination against women that hinders their ability to sustain a decent life for them and their children (Pressman, 1970). In this endeavor, they frequently have the support of a Black male who may not be the legal husband/father. Schulz (1969) has reported that the lower-class Black male contributes to the welfare of his woman more than is commonly acknowledged and plays an important role as a substitute father to her children.

Childhood and Child Rearing. One of the most popular images of Black women is that of "Mammy," the devoted, affectionate nursemaids of white children who belonged to their slave master or employer. This motherly image of Black women probably has some basis in fact. Motherhood has historically been an important role for Black women, even more meaningful than their role as wives (Bell, 1971). In the colonial period of America, missionaries often observed and reported the unusual devotion of the African mother to her child. The slave mother also developed a deep love for, and impenetrable bond to, her children (Ladner, 1972). It would appear that the bond between the Black mother and her child is deeply rooted in the African heritage and philosophy, which places a special value on children because they represent the continuity of life (Brown and Forde, 1967).

Many studies have conveyed a negative image of the Black mother because she does not conform to middle-class modes of child rearing. Yet Black mothers have fulfilled the function of socializing their children into the multiple roles they must perform in this society. They prepare them to take on not only the appropriate sex and age roles but a racial role as well. Children must be socialized to deal with the realities of white racism, which they will encounter daily. Black females are encouraged to be independent rather than passive individuals because many of them will carry family and economic responsibilities alone (Iscoe, Williams, and Harvey, 1964). Taking on adult responsibilities is something many Black children learn early. They may be given the care of a younger sibling, and some will have to find work while still in the adolescent stage. The strong character structure of Black children was noted by child psychiatrist Robert Coles (1964) as he observed their comportment under the pressures of school integration in the South during a very volatile era.

The Black mother's child-rearing techniques are geared to prepare her children for the kind of existence that is alien to middle-class white youngsters. Moreover, many white middle-class socialization patterns may not be that desirable for the psychological growth of the child. The casual upbringing of Black children may produce a much healthier personality than the status anxieties associated with some rigid middle-class child-rearing practices (Green, 1946). Using threats of the withdrawal of love if the child fails to measure up to the parent's standards is much more common among white parents than Black parents of any class stratum. One result of the Black child's anxiety-free upbringing is a strong closeness to his parents (Nolles, 1972; Scanzoni, 1971).

While Black parents are more likely to use physical, rather than verbal, punishment to enforce child discipline, this technique is often buttressed by the love they express for their children. Moreover, as Billingsley (1969:567) has noted: "Even among the lowest social classes in the Black community, families give the children better care than is generally recognized, and often the care is better than that given by white families in similar social circumstances." One indication of this care is found in the statistics, which show that child neglect and abuse are much more common in white families than in Black families. Black children, for instance, are underrepresented in institutions for dependent and neglected children (U.S. Bureau of the Census, 1960).

The most undesirable aspect of the Black child's socialization is reputed to be the inculcation of a negative self-identity (Rainwater, 1966). A plethora of studies have found that the Black child has a low self-esteem because of his Blackness and the fact that many grow up in homes without a male model. A number of studies are emerging that are in opposition to the theories of low self-esteem among Blacks. McCarthy and Yancey (1971) reviewed the literature on Black self-esteem, found much of it invalid, and concluded that Blacks are less likely to suffer from low self-esteem because they belong to a solitary group that possesses an ideology that explains their lowly position.

In a replication of some of the earlier studies on Black children's drawings, a pair of researchers reported that the current emphasis on Black culture had led to a significant change in the characteristics of those drawings. When Black children were asked to draw features that they most admired and wished were characteristic of themselves, most of their figures resembled other Black people (Dennis, 1968; Fish and Larr, 1971). In another investigation of Black self-esteem, it was discovered that even Black children from a separated or never-married family did not have a lower self-esteem than Black children from other families, and Black children as a group did not have lower self-esteem than white children as a group (Rosenberg and Simmons, 1971).

The Aged. Extensive data on the Black elderly are presently not available. Based on what we presently know, the older Black person is not as likely to live with one of his children as are the white aged. In most cases, the grandmothers are more likely to take children into their own households than to be taken into the household of their kinfolk. About half (48 percent) of elderly Black women have other related children living with them—in contrast to only 10 percent of similar white families (Hill, 1971). This is but one more indication of the strong cohesiveness within Black families as well as the functional importance of the family in the Black community.

Because they live longer than Black men, widowhood comes at an earlier age for Black women. In 1970, over two-thirds of aged Black women were widows in comparison to 54 percent of similar white women. They were also more likely to be widowed than were Black males (32 percent) or white males (17 percent; Jackson, 1972a). Due to a history of gross discrimination against it, the Black aged family only has a median income of $3,222. Of those elderly Blacks living alone, about 75 percent had incomes of less than $2,000 in 1969. One result of this overwhelming poverty is that 26 percent of the elderly wives in Black families continue to work after reaching the age of 65. Only 15 percent of elderly white wives remain in the labor force past that age (Hill, 1971).

The extended kin structure in the Black community manages to buttress the psychological isolation and poverty of the Black aged. Most of them have a significant amount of interaction with their children, especially an older daughter. Where there is no child present or in the vicinity, they can rely on secondary kin, such as siblings, cousins, and even "make-believe" kin (Jackson, 1972b). In return, many Black grandmothers provide in-kind services, such as babysitting. Most aged Black parents desire to live independently of, but in close contact with, their children. Where their socioeconomic conditions permit, the adult children assist their elderly parents (Jackson, 1969).

378

One of the most fluid institutions in American life is the family. Probably in no other sphere of our society have such rapid and profound changes taken place. While the changes are most significant for white Americans, Blacks, too, are influenced to some degree by the same forces. Among the most visible trends are the increase in sexual permissiveness, challenges to the traditional concept of women's role, increases in divorce, and reductions in the fertility rate. Although Blacks are part and parcel of these dynamics, their different history and needs preclude any close convergence of their family lifestyle with that of white families.

There is considerable disagreement over whether a revolution in sexual behavior has occurred. Some argue that only the public acknowledgment of sexual behavior has transpired, which gives the appearance of actual changes in what people are doing sexually. Yet it is impossible to refute the fact that the openness of sexual permissiveness reflects a revolution in attitudes. The most significant change is in the sexual liberation of white women. There are many indications that the double standard of sexual conduct is disappearing or being modified. This change in male attitudes about female sexuality has had little effect on Black female sexuality, for they have rarely been subjected to the same sexual restrictions as white women.

Much of the sexual revolution is caused by challenges to the traditional concept of woman's role in society. White women are demanding equality in employment opportunities, legal rights, shared responsibility for raising children, and to be freed of the liabilities only women face in America. Few Black women are involved in the Women's Liberation Movement because many of its demands seem irrelevant to their needs. They, particularly, cannot relate to the desires of white women to enter the labor force, to cease being viewed as sex objects, or to be freed from child-care responsibilities.

These demands of middle-class white women do not relate to the reality of Black women. They, like many lower-class white women, have always been in the labor force, whether they wanted to or not. Black women have not been depicted as sex objects as much as they have been *used* as sex objects. Motherhood and marriage were two institutions that were denied them in the past. Because they had to work, many were deprived of the time to enjoy their children. Marriage was a luxury many could not afford or the conditions of their lives would not provide. To the many Black women who are heading households, a husband would be a welcome figure.

But many of the methods and goals of the Women's Liberation Movement are of importance to Black women. As a result of women declaring their independence from the domination of men, there will be a greater acceptance of women heading families by themselves. Perhaps the society will then make provisions for eliminating some of the problems incurred by female-headed households, for example, child-care facilities. The demand for equal employment opportunities for women and an income parity for women in the same jobs as men is very important to Black women. It is Black women who are the most victimized by employment and income discrimination against women. They are most likely to be heads of households who will earn the low salaries paid women on the assumption that they do not have families to support.

The shortage of Black males available for marriage may force Black women to rethink the idea of a monogamous marriage that will last forever. There are simply not enough Black males around to permit fulfillment of this desire. Perhaps some convergence of white and Black marital patterns is possible. White women, too, face a shortage of five million males due to the higher infant mortality rate for white males. This discrepancy is not nearly as great for individuals in the young marriageable years.

There is some indication of a homogenization of Black family life styles. This mass family pattern may not be based on the white middle-class nuclear family model. Rather, the increasing nativist sentiments among Black youth may culminate in a family system based on a combination of African and Afro-American cultural systems, which will transcend the class and regional variations that now exist. While white Americans are questioning whether the family as an institution can survive, Blacks may decide that it must become stronger and more relevant to their lives. As the Black youth of America, the group most imbued with the spirit of Black nationalism, becomes the majority of the Black population, this process of Africanizing the Black family may be accelerated. Whether this occurs or not will depend on whether the forces of racial integration and movement into the middle-class strata lead Blacks in the direction of assimilation and acculturation or in the development of an Afro-American identity.

Internal Adaptations

The changes in the interior of the Black family, while ideologically in the direction of pan-Africanism, are statistically in the direction of assimilation and acculturation. Examples of this phenomena are seen in the diffusion of Blacks into predominantly white suburbs, the increase in interracial dating and marriage, higher incidences of suicide and mental illness, and a decline in the extended family pattern. But these patterns reflect the variation in the Black community. What is surprising is that, given the pace of racial integration in American society, more Blacks have not become assimilated into the majority population's mode of behavior. The integration of the school systems, desegregation of suburbia, and greater access to knowledge of majority cultural norms through the mass media have provided opportunities for Black acculturation without precedent.

Instead, we find Blacks demanding separate facilities and organizations on white university campuses. Those Blacks who moved to the suburbs continue their social lives in the inner cities. While the extended family may not exist together in the same household, its functions of providing emotional solidarity and other kinds of assistance are still carried out. Moreover, the concept of the extended family is broadened to include all members of the Black community. These are among some of the internal adaptations made by the Black community to prevent the trend of racial integration from diluting their cultural unity.

In contrast to the demands of white women for emancipation from the passive role ascribed to the female gender, Black women are discussing adopting the subordinate position of African women. Their contention is that the roles of men and women are different, not unequal. In some of the Black nationalist organizations, the women are placed in auxiliary groups, while the men take leadership roles. Much of this behavior is a reaction to the history of Black life in this country when Black women had the leadership of the family thrust upon them. Black men were not allowed to fulfill the ascribed male-role functions. Hence, in some circles, it is now believed that Black women should step back and let Black men emerge as the leader of the family and the race.

Another most important adaptation under consideration is the adoption of polygamy as the Black marriage system. The assumption here is that there are not enough Black males to go around and that the sharing of husbands could stabilize Black marriages and provide certain legal benefits to women now deprived of them. At least two Black nationalist organizations are on record as advocating polygamy for the Black population. The actual number of Black polygamous marriages is infinitesimal. Since such marriages are illegal in this country, no legal benefits can accrue to the second wife. Moreover, in African society, the practice of polygamy is closely related to the economic system, and people are socialized to accept it.

Problems and Prospects

The problems Black people face are essentially the same as for the past century. Those problems are not related to family stability but to the socioeconomic conditions that tear families asunder. In general, the problems are poverty and racism. While the past decade has produced a decline in racial segregation and white stereotypes of Black inferiority, Blacks are still singled out for discriminatory treatment in every sphere of American life. Moreover, while whites are in agreement about the racial discrimination Blacks are subjected to, any national effort to further remedy these racist practices has a low priority among white Americans.

A low socioeconomic status continues to plague many Black families. Whereas some Blacks have achieved a higher standard of living as a result of the civil rights movement, large numbers of Blacks continue to live below the poverty level. A disproportionate number of these Blacks will be female heads of families. They will have more responsibilities and less income than any other group in American society. Yet no effective programs are being proposed to meet the needs of a third of all Black families. The persistence of employment and salary discrimination against women will continue to handicap Black women in their struggle to maintain a decent life for their families.

However, poverty is not the only reason for the high breakup rate of Black marriages. The increase in the Black divorce rate in recent years is due to sociopsychological factors as well. A primary cause is the independence of Black women. Marital stability among whites in the past was based on the subordinate status of women. Once white women were emancipated from the economic domination of men, their divorce rate increased radically. More Black women have been independent—economically and psychologically—for a much longer period of time. There is nothing inherently wrong with the equality of sex roles in the family, but when men are socialized to expect unchallenged leadership in family affairs, conflict is an inevitable result.

The increased rate of interracial marriages will continue because more

381

Blacks and whites will meet as peers. Some Black men will marry white women because the society's standards of beauty are still white. More Black women will marry white men because the latter can provide them with a greater amount of economic security and because some have become disenchanted with Black men. Whatever the reason, these marriages will face many obstacles. In an era of unabated white racism and Black nationalism, many interracial couples will become outcasts in both Black and white communities.

It is difficult to project the future of Black families because there are several parallel trends occurring at the same time. Many Blacks are entering the middle class as a result of higher education and increased opportunities. At the same time the future is dim for those Blacks in the underclass. The forces of automation and cybernation are rendering obsolete the labor of unskilled Black men, who are in danger of becoming a permanent army of the unemployed. The status of Black women is in a state of flux. Some welcome the forthcoming liberation from male control, while others urge a regeneration of Black male leadership. Easier and cheaper access to contraceptives and abortions may mean a considerable decline in the Black fertility rate. Simultaneously, some Blacks express concern with the implications of genocide in Black family limitation. Whatever the future of Black families, it is time to put to rest all the theories about Black family instability and give recognition to the crucial role of this institution in the Black struggle for survival.

REFERENCES

Abzug, Robert H. 1971. "The Black Family During Reconstruction." In Nathan Huggins (ed.): *Key Issues in the Afro-American Experience.* New York: Harcourt, Brace and Jovanovich, pp. 26–39.

Adams, Bert N. 1970. "Isolation, Function and Beyond: American Kinship in the 1960's." *Journal of Marriage and the Family* 32 (November):575–98.

Anderson, Charles H. 1971. *Towards a New Sociology.* Homewood, Illinois: Dorsey Press.

Axelson, Leland J. 1970. "The Working Wife: Differences in Perception among Negro and White Males." *Journal of Marriage and the Family* 32 (August):457–64.

Bayer, Alal E. 1972. "College Impact on Marriage." *Journal of Marriage and the Family* 34 (November):600–10.

Bell, Robert. 1971. "The Relative Importance of Mother and Wife Roles among Negro Lower-Class Women." In Robert Staples (ed.): *The Black Family: Essays and Studies.* Belmont: Wadsworth, pp. 248–56.

Bernard, Jessie. 1966. *Marriage and Family Among Negroes.* Englewood Cliffs, N.J.: Prentice-Hall.

Billingsley, Andrew. 1968. *Black Families in White America.* Englewood Cliffs, N.J.: Prentice-Hall.

———. 1969. "Family Functioning in Low-Income Black Community." *Social Casework* 50 (December):563–72.

———. 1970. "Black Families and White Social Science." *Journal of Social Issues* 26 (November):127–42.

Blassingame, John. 1972. *The Slave Community.* New York: Oxford.

Broderick, Carlfred. 1965. "Social Heterosexual Development among Urban Negroes and Whites." *Journal of Marriage and the Family* 27 (May):200–203.

Brown, A. R. Radcliffe, and Darryl Forde. 1967. *African Systems of Kinship and Marriage.* New York: Oxford University Press.

Carter, Lewis F. 1968. "Racial Caste Hypogamy: A Sociological Myth." *Phylon* 29 (Winter): 349–52.

Coles, Robert. 1964. "Children and Racial Demonstrations." *The American Scholar* 34 (Winter):349–92.

Cosby, Arthur. 1971. "Black-White Differences in Aspirations among Deep South High School Students." *Journal of Negro Education* 40 (Winter):17–21.

Day, Beth. 1972. *Sexual Life Between Blacks and Whites.* New York: World.

Dennis, Wayne. 1968. "Racial Change in Negro Drawings." *Journal of Psychology* 69 (July): 129–30.

Drake, St. Clair, and Horace Cayton. 1945. *Black Metropolis.* Chicago: University of Chicago Press.

Feagin, Joe R. 1968. "The Kinship Ties of Negro Urbanites." *Social Science Quarterly* 49 (December):660–65.

Fish, Jeanne, and Charlotte Larr. 1971. *A Decade of Change in Drawings by Black Children.* Unpublished manuscript.

Franklin, John Hope. 1967. *From Slavery to Freedom.* New York: Knopf.

Frazier, E. Franklin. 1932. *The Free Negro Family.* Nashville, Tenn.: Fisk University Press.

———. 1939. *The Negro Family in the United States.* Chicago: University of Chicago Press.

———. 1962. *Black Bourgeoisie.* New York: Collier Books.

Gallup, George. 1972. "Growing Tolerance Found Regarding Interracial, Interfaith Marriages." *New York Times* (November 19).

Gebhard, Paul, Wardell Pomeroy, Clyde Martin, and Cornelia Christenson. 1958. *Pregnancy, Birth, and Abortion.* New York: Harper and Brothers.

Goins, Alvin. 1960. "Ethnic and Class Preferences Among College Negroes." *Journal of Negro Education* 29 (Spring):128–33.

Golden, Joseph. 1959. "Facilitating Factors in Negro-White Intermarriage." *Phylon* 20 (Fall):273–84.

Goodwin, Leonard. 1972. *Do the Poor Want to Work: A Socio-Psychological Study of Work Orientations.* Washington, D.C.: The Brookings Institution.

Green, Arnold. 1946. "The Middle-Class Male Child and Neurosis." *American Sociological Review* 11 (February):31–41.

Gutman, Herbert. 1976. *The Negro Family.* New York: Pantheon.

Hall, Gwendolyn Midlo. 1970. "The Myth of Benevolent Spanish Slave Law." *Negro Digest* 19 (February):31–38.

Harris, Edward E. 1970. "Personal and Parental Influences in College Attendance: Some Negro-White Differences." *Journal of Negro Education* 39 (Fall):305–13.

Hays, William, and Charles Mindel. 1972. "Extended Kinship Relations in Black and White Families." *Journal of Marriage and the Family* 35 (February):51–57.

Heer, David. 1966. "Negro-White Marriage in the United States." *Journal of Marriage and the Family* 28 (August):262–73.

Herskovits, Melville. 1958. *The Myth of the Negro Past.* Boston: Beacon Press.

Hill, Robert. 1971. "A Profile of the Black Aged." *The Los Angeles Sentinel* (October 7), A14.

———. 1972. *The Strengths of Black Families.* New York: Emerson-Hall.

Hindelang, Michael. 1970. "Educational and Occupational Aspirations among Working Class Negro, Mexican-American and White Elementary School Children." *Journal of Negro Education* 39 (Fall):351–53.

Hobson, Sheila. 1971. "The Black Family; Together in Every Sense." *Tuesday* 6 (April): 12–14, 28–32.

Hodges, Harold. 1964. *Social Stratification.* Cambridge, Mass.: Schenkman.

Hyman, Herbert, and John S. Reed. 1969. "Black Matriarchy Reconsidered: Evidence from Secondary Analysis of Sample Surveys." *Public Opinion Quarterly* 33 (Fall): 346–54.

Iscoe, Ira, Martha Williams, and Jerry Harvey. 1964. "Age, Intelligence and Sex as Variables in the Conformity Behavior of Negro and White Children." *Child Development* 35 (March-December):451–60.

Jackson, Jacquelyn. 1969. "Negro Aged Parents and Adult Children: Their Affective Relationships." *Varia* 2 (Spring):1–14.

———. 1971. "But Where Are the Men?" *The Black Scholar* 3 (December):30–41.

———. 1972a. "Marital Life Among Older Black Couples." *The Family Coordinator* 21 (January):21–28.

———. 1972b. "Comparative Life Styles and Family and Friend Relationships among Older Black Women." *The Family Coordinator* 21 (October):477–86.

Kiser, Clyde and Myrna Frank. 1967. "Factors Associated with the Low Fertility of Non-White Women of College Attainment." *Milbank Memorial Fund Quarterly* (October):425–29.

Klein, Herbert. 1967. *Slavery in the Americas.* Chicago: University of Chicago.

Kronus, Sidney J. 1971. *The Black Middle Class.* Columbus, Ohio: Merrill.

Ladner, Joyce. 1971. *Tomorrow's Tomorrow: The Black Women.* Garden City, N.Y.: Doubleday.

———. 1972. "The Legacy of Black Womanhood." *Tuesday* 7 (April):4–5, 18–20.

Liebow, Elliot. 1966. *Tally's Corner.* Boston: Little, Brown.

Logan, Rayford. 1965. *The Betrayal of the Negro.* New York: Collier.

Mack, Delores. 1971. "Where the Black Matriarchy Theorists Went Wrong." *Psychology Today* 4 (January):24.

Matthews, Basil. 1972. *Black Perspective, Black Family and Black Community.* A paper delivered to the annual Philosophy Conference, Baltimore, Md.

McCarthy, John, and William Yancey. 1971. "Uncle Tom and Mr. Charlie: Metaphysical Pathos in the Study of Racism and Personal Disorganization." *American Journal of Sociology* 76 (November):648–762.

Middleton, Russell, and Snell Putney. 1960. "Dominance in Decisions in the Family: Race and Class Differences." *American Journal of Sociology* 29 (May):605–609.

Miller, Elizabeth. 1966. *The Negro in America: A Bibliography.* Cambridge, Mass.; Harvard University Press.

Monahan, Thomas. 1970. "Are Interracial Marriages Really Less Stable?" *Social Forces* 48 (June):461–73.

Moynihan, Daniel Patrick. 1965. "Employment, Income, and the Ordeal of the Negro Family." *Daedalus* 94 (Fall):745–70.

Murray, Albert. 1970. *The Omni-Americans.* New York: Outerbridge and Diensterey.

Noble, Jeanne. 1956. *The Negro Woman College Graduate.* New York: Columbia University Press.

Nobles, Wade. 1974. *African Root and American Fruit: The Black Family. Journal of Social and Behavioral Sciences* 20 (Spring):52–64.

Nolle, David. 1972. "Changes in Black Sons and Daughters: A Panel Analysis of Black Adolescent's Orientation toward Their Parents." *Journal of Marriage and the Family* 34 (August):443–47.

Podell, Lawrence. 1970. *Families on Welfare in New York City.* New York: The Center for the Study of Urban Problems, pp. 38–39.

Porterfield, Ernest. 1973. "Mixed Marriage." *Psychology Today* 6 (January):71–78.

Pressman, Sonia. 1970. "Job Discrimination and the Black Woman." *The Crisis* (March): 103–108.

Purcell, Theodore and Gerald Cavanaugh. 1972. *Blacks in the Industrial World.* New York: The Free Press.

Rainwater, Lee. 1966. "The Crucible of Identity: The Lower-Class Negro Family." *Daedalus* 95 (Winter):258–264.

———. 1970. *Behind Ghetto Walls: Negro Families in a Federal Slum.* Chicago: Aldine.

Reiss, Ira L. 1964. "Premarital Sexual Permissiveness among Negroes and Whites." *American Sociological Review* 29 (October):688–98.

Rosenberg, Bernard, and Joseph Bensman. 1968. "Sexual Patterns in Three Ethnic Sub-cultures of an American Underclass." *Annals of the American Academy of Political and Social Science* 376 (March):61–75.

Rosenberg, Morris, and Roberta Simmons. 1971. *Black and White Self-Esteem: The Urban School Child*. Washington, D.C.: American Sociological Association.

Rosnow, Irving, and K. Daniel Rose. 1972. "Divorce among Doctors." *Journal of Marriage and the Family* 34 (November):587–99.

Ryan, William. 171. "Savage Discovery: The Moynihan Report." In Robert Staples (ed.): *The Black Family: Essays and Studies*. Belmont: Wadsworth, pp. 58–65.

Scanzoni, John. 1971. *The Black Family in Modern Society*. Boston: Allyn and Bacon.

Schulz, David. 1969. "Variations in the Father Role in Complete Families of the Negro Lower Class." *Social Science Quarterly* 49 (December):651–59.

Siegel, Paul M. 1965. "On the Cost of Being Negro." *Sociological Inquiry* 35 (Winter):52–55.

Stampp, Kenneth. 1956. *The Peculiar Institution*. New York: Vintage.

Staples, Robert. 1970. "The Myth of the Black Matriarchy." *The Black Scholar* 1 (January-February):9–16.

———. 1971a. "Towards a Sociology of the Black Family." *Journal of Marriage and the Family* 33 (February):19–38.

——— (ed.). 1971b. *The Black Family: Essays and Studies*. Belmont: Wadsworth.

———. 1972. "The Sexuality of Black Women." *Sexual Behavior* 2 (June):4–15.

———. 1973. *The Black Woman in America*. Chicago: Nelson-Hall.

———. 1974. "The Black Family Revisited: A Review and a Preview." *Journal of Social and Behavioral Sciences* 20 (Spring):65–78.

Stone, Robert, and P. T Schlamp. 1966. *Family Life Styles Below the Poverty Line*. A report to the State Social Welfare Board from the Institute for Social Science Research, San Francisco State College.

Stromberg, Jerome. 1967. *Kinship and Friendship among Lower-Class Negro Families*. A paper presented to the annual meeting of the Society for the Study of Social Problems. San Francisco, Calif.

Tannenbaum, Frank. 1947. *Slave and Citizen*. New York: Knopf.

Tausky, Curt, and William J. Wilson. 1971. "Work Attachment among Black Men." *Phylon* 32 (Spring):23–30.

Turner, Clarence Rollo. 1972. "Some Theoretical and Conceptual Considerations for Black Family Studies." *Black Lines* 2 (Winter):13–28.

U.S. Bureau of the Census. 1960. *Inmates of Institutions*. P.C. (2), 3A.

———. 1970. "School Enrollment: October, 1970." *Current Population Reports: Population Characteristics Series* p. 20, no. 222.

———. 1971. "Fertility Indicators: 1970." *Current Population Reports*, Special Studies, Series p-23, no. 36. Washington, D.C.: U.S. Government Printing Office.

———. 1972. "The Social and Economic Status of the Black Population in the United States." *Current Population Reports*, Series p-23, no. 42. Washington, D.C.: U.S. Government Printing Office.

U.S. Population Council. 1972. *Report on Abortions by Age and Race*. Washington, D.C.

Westoff, Charles, and Leslie Westoff. 1971. *From Now to Zero*. Boston: Little, Brown.

Willie, Charles, and Joan Levy. 1972. "Black Is Lonely." *Psychology Today* 6 (March):50–52.

Yancey, William. 1972. "Going Down Home: Family Structure and the Urban Trap." *Social Science Quarterly* 52 (March):893–906.

Zelnik, Melvin, and John Kantner. 1972. *Sexuality, Contraception, and Pregnancy among Young Unwed Females in the United States*. A paper prepared for The Commission on Population Growth and the American Future (July).

Lesbian Socialization and Identity

Nancy E. Cunningham

If traditionally minded Americans see sexual license as a threat to marriage and the family, it can be understood why they have historically been horrified by homosexuality and pronounced it a "perversion." No children are produced from such unions and sexual contact is, of anatomical necessity, quite different than that of the heterosexual relationship. In their fear of homosexuality, "straight" Americans also see "gays" as different and/ or dangerous, not only in sexual orientation, but in every way. As a result, the civil rights of homosexuals have been severely infringed in the name of morality, and they are often forced to hide their sexual persuasion from the world. Clearly, this treatment has alienated them from their own sexual identity. The Gay Liberation Movement is gradually changing this. Inasmuch as homosexuals and lesbians are a minority, it is of sociological interest to discover how they acquire a positive self-identity in an atmosphere that up to recently has been quite repressive. What is the socialization process of gay persons? What problems result when one develops attitudes and traits that run counter to those of the majority, and that are almost never encouraged by such major socializers as parents? Cunningham's study of lesbian women tackles this important issue in this more enlightened time. She found that lesbian women were attracted early in life to other females, while at the same time finding themselves impatient with the limitations of the traditional female role. Aware of societal expectations, many of these women tried to suppress their true sexual interests, and dated men. This only increased their feeling of isolation. Those women who have "come out of the closet" with the advent of Gay Liberation report two important results: an end to the use of stereotyped roles (i.e., the "butch" and the "femme") that are copies of traditional sex roles, and the development of a positive and strong self-identity.

Importance of the Study[1]

Individuals who do not conform to socially established and expected forms of behavior are labeled non-conformists and are stigmatized. A majority of these individuals internalize the negative label assigned to them and establish a variant self identity.

Homosexuals and lesbians have been no exception to this general pattern of internalization and acceptance of a negative label. However, a new and rather unique phenomenon has been developing in recent years among members of the homophile community. Gay men and women are beginning to resist and fight the negative labels society attempts to place upon them. Gays no longer appear resigned to the fate of being viewed as outsiders and labeled as variants by the dominant culture. Gay people are working to cast off the negative labels applied to them and establish positive identities as homosexuals and lesbians.

This recent change in attitudes and behavior patterns is significant and deserves extensive examination. It is quite possible that this attempt by homosexuals to resist societal labels, while establishing and maintaining their identities, will carry over to other stigmatized groups. This may result in a re-ordering of society's perception of variance as well as the stigmatized individual's own perception of self.

The subject of homosexuality has remained taboo in American society for quite some time. Male homosexuality is beginning to be discussed more openly now, particularly in the social science literature. However, lesbianism seems to be suffering from somewhat of a cultural lag. Most of the limited amount of research, previously conducted, concerning lesbians was in the form of case studies.

The focus of inquiry in this study is directed toward two aspects of the lesbian's identity formation. The first is the socialization process a lesbian experiences, including social conditioning, isolation and stereotypes; the second involves gay women's reaction to their lesbian identity, their feelings of present identity and the possibility of changing their sexual identity.

Through a description of the socialization process lesbians are exposed to, the negative sanctions and labels applied to their behavior become evident. A presentation of the lesbian's personal feelings of identity will illustrate the positive self identity the women in this study established in spite of the negative societal attitudes directed against their chosen life-style.

Methodology

The data for this study was obtained through qualitative, in-depth interviews with lesbians on the east and west coasts. The sample for this study was drawn from lesbians in San Francisco, New York City, Long Island, Boston, Cambridge, Massachusetts and central New Jersey. The initial source of contact for respondents in San Francisco and Boston was Daughters of Bilitis (D.O.B.), a national lesbian organization, and Women's Centers in Cambridge, Massachusetts, New York City and Princeton, New Jersey. Several interviews were obtained from women who work in the organizations' offices, and from other members of the organizations. Interviews and referrals were also received from personal acquaintances of the author.

A stratified or random sampling technique was not used to obtain respondents. The nature of the population studied is such that these sampling methods would be very difficult if not impossible. The so-called "snowball" method was employed in obtaining respondents, but as the interviewees were drawn from several different sources the scope of the sample was varied.

It is not claimed that a representative sample of the lesbian population was obtained—the primary reasons for this being the limited number of women interviewed and the sampling method employed. However, the sample chosen contained respondents who had a wide range of personal and social characteristics.

Various religious affiliations, vocational and economic positions were represented, and the range of educational backgrounds extends from a high school education through completion of a doctoral program. Forty-seven gay women were interviewed for this study. Two of the interviewees were Black and the remainder of the respondents were Caucasian. The respondents received the interview schedule directly from the researcher, and the study was conducted over a six month period.

SOCIALIZATION

Lesbianism has been viewed as "abnormal" and is stigmatized by a majority of people in our society. There are legal and social sanctions against such behavior, and the ideology surrounding these negative sanctions is effectively instilled through the socialization process. This socialization process entails the acceptance or internalization of the norms and values proscribed by the dominant culture. In terms of human sexuality, the prevailing norms and value systems expressed are clearly heterosexual, i.e., only male–female sexual relationships are sanctioned.

Social Conditioning

In exploring the area of homosexuality two distinguishing characteristics become apparent: 1) homosexuality is almost universally stigmatized, and 2) no one is socialized within it or towards it as a child. Men and women have what Sidney Abbot and Barbara Love (1972) term social contracts with society. The contract for a female child specifies the role of wife and mother.

As children women are all taught their appropriate female roles, and any deviation from the established heterosexual role models in our society is frowned upon and viewed in a negative context. Lesbians obviously fall short of internalizing the ideal female role model and thus deviate from the norm. John Kitsuse (1973) describes this situation:

> Homosexual roles and behaviors are conceived to be "inappropriate" to the individual's ascribed sex status and thus theoretically they're defined as deviant (p. 17).

388

For some women however, the narrow boundaries of the traditional female role have made heterosexuality unappealing, and the independence and self-determination of lesbians appears much more attractive. As a child, this decision is generally not a conscious denial of heterosexuality, but rather a vague dissatisfaction with the stringent female role requirements. One respondent expressed these feelings in the following way:

I feel like it's the restrictions of the female role, even though you can't verbalize that, you know you have to get out of that. You just can't be that passive little submissive woman. (42)

And another:

I think being a lesbian means rejecting a whole set of roles and rules of behavior. I think that's what I did as a kid, and I think that's what's probably behind most decisions for women to become homosexuals. That they can't stand the kind of roles that are imposed on us. (20)

Awareness of female role restriction at a young age is unusual. A more frequent response to early heterosexual socialization is general compliance. It is difficult to measure the exact dimensions of this form of heterosexual indoctrination, or to determine how deeply the taboos against homosexuality are instilled in each individual. Some women learn at an early age that feelings for other women are inappropriate. One respondent experienced an extreme negative reaction to verbalizing her interest in another woman when she was eight:

And the next year when I went back to camp, she wasn't there, and I asked another counselor who was there where she was and what she was doing. And she said to me, "what's the matter, do you have the hots for her or something?" And I thought that was just the most disgusting thing to say, you know, and I felt so ashamed. I didn't know how to deal with that, so I just never mentioned it again. (17)

Strong emotional attachments for other members of the same sex are not always seen in a negative context. Childhood crushes on other women are often tolerated and viewed as just a phase that young girls go through.

And I also knew it was natural to go through stages when you had crushes on people of your own sex. So I didn't get terribly upset about it. (18)

Societal tolerance for this form of childhood behavior, and the later intolerance of adult homosexual behavior, is filled with ambiguities, and often results in confusion and problems for many gay women. Socialization into heterosexual roles is so thorough and ingrained that even after having sexual relations with other women some women still do not comprehend their real sexual identity. As one interviewee states:

> I don't think I ever put myself together with queer, homosexual or lesbian. I never identified myself clearly as a woman who wanted to be with women. I defined myself as being heterosexual, even though I had crushes on women. (7)

And another:

> I met the second girl when I was 24. I never considered myself a lesbian before. It just happened that I met a woman at the time, it could have been a man. l didn't consider myself a lesbian. (14)

A fine line exists between having crushes on other women, which is acceptable to a degree, and being considered or labeled a lesbian. Some women go for years trying to convince themselves, while engaging in homosexual activities, that they are not lesbians simply to avoid having to confront the label with all of its negative and degrading connotations.

> That relationship lasted about three and a half to four years. No, I don't think I identified myself as a lesbian. It was never talked about. It was hidden. I guess when I read about it in textbooks, and so on, I knew it was me, but I think I was resisting, you know, the label. (12)

The process of denying one's lesbianism to avoid internal or external stigmatization is complex and involves a great deal of rationalization for some women. However, there are also many women who do not, for one reason or another, experience this denial system. While many lesbians initially attempt to deny their sexual orientation because of societal attitudes, other gay women feel heterosexuals should be more aware and attuned to lesbianism.

> In the straight world I'm very conscious of my sexuality. "Out there" people assume you're straight, and I'm not. I feel different. They're not relating to me and my needs. They're relating to their expectations. The conflict is outside me. (29)

Dr. C. A. Tripp, in Bettie Wysor's book, *The Lesbian Myth* (1974), comments on his feelings toward homosexuality and social conditioning:

> As a matter of fact, overt homosexual contacts are so frequent before and shortly after puberty that the question is not how the homosexual conditioning develops, but why it doesn't develop even more often than it does. The general answer, of course, is that various social pressures and expectations work toward the development of heterosexual standards and tastes, and

toward the eradication of any and all behavior which appears contrary to this mainstream. (p. 154)

Throughout the socialization process no alternatives to the prevailing heterosexual life-style are presented. The option of engaging in homosexual relationships is never suggested, and if the subject should come up at all it is quickly dismissed as being abnormal or "sick." No flexibility is allowed in one's sexual behavior; no choices are available.

> I was a male-identified woman, to use that term. I always felt very uncomfortable with it, but I never knew the alternatives to it. Like I ended up getting married when I was a junior in college. And I knew I didn't want to, but I didn't see what else to do, you know. (42)

There can be no doubt that everyone in our society is socialized toward a heterosexual life, and this is regarded by the majority as the only acceptable and truly rewarding path to follow.

> All aspects of society treat gay people as a separate class, as the "other." And the rules they have for dealing with us are based on the assumption that our lives are inferior, second rate, and not as fulfilling as heterosexual life. (27)

Heterosexuality is an institution in our society which is supported and perpetuated by nearly every other major institution in our culture. We are all heterosexually conditioned through the church, the schools, mass media and the family.

> Before I met my first girlfriend I didn't think it was feasible for two women to love each other. And my mother made a comment like that. She said, "But why do you want to go out with women? You'll never find true love or happiness the way you will with a man." (36)

The socialization process begins in infancy and continues in one form or another throughout one's life. For the women who are able to resist or overcome the strict heterosexual social conditioning and establish a lesbian identity, the next problem they must face is simply finding other lesbians.

Isolation

The concept and actual feelings of isolation in the gay world exist in varying degrees. A few of the older lesbians interviewed indicated that they had no knowledge of what lesbianism was until their late teens or early twenties. Several of the younger women expressed some knowledge of lesbianism earlier in their lives and realized they had strong feelings toward other women. However, they could not locate other women with similar interests, and often did not even know where to begin the search.

Within the past six or seven years lesbianism and homosexuality have come to the forefront as social issues. Through the efforts of the Gay Liberation Front and related groups advocating gay rights, homosexuality is somewhat publicized and people are beginning to discuss the subject more openly. However, before the mid sixties the topic was usually discussed only behind closed doors, if at all.

I never heard the word homosexual or lesbian, or even saw it written before I went to college. You must remember I came from a very small town and was very sheltered. I had never even heard any aspersions cast about people. (12)

Self isolation is yet another reaction to societal pressure and attitudes, and results from fear of exposure of one's gay identity. Many lesbians remain in the "closet" for years to protect themselves from legal and social sanctions against their behavior.

We tried really hard, but the world and all our fears conspired to—it just demanded too much. It's really exhausting to try and live this way. It's always having to watch what you say, and remembering who you're with, and wondering what's on other people's minds. Wondering who you can trust and who you can't; it's not easy. (18)

A great many women choose to remain "closeted" about their lesbian life-styles in order to avoid discrimination and harassment incurred from others if their lesbianism were known. This is not a free choice, only the lesser of two equally oppressive evils.

If women want to go out and say they're lesbians that's O.K., but I'm not going to. I've had enough problems. Why do you think I left East Germany? You have to lie in order to survive. You have to change as the world changes, and make choices as to what is more important—to hide your homosexuality or to survive. (9)

I feel crazy that homosexuality is against the law; that we're discriminated against in jobs, that people are fired for that. That I can't say what I want to say all of the time. We had a real argument about who's free and who's not free, and there's no way I'm pretending I'm free. You know, I'm not. (16)

The magnitude of heterosexually dominated socialization patterns again comes into play, perhaps a bit more subtly, in the form of homosexual isolation. The approach of not openly discussing homosexuality is suppressive in several ways. It succeeded in keeping many gay women isolated from other lesbians, at least initially. Forty-two percent of the sample indicated that they knew of no existing gay community at the time they were coming to grips with their own identities. Many women confessed that they believed they were the only individuals in the world who had strong emotional feelings for other women. This "closed mouth" technique did not deter women from becoming lesbians. It only served to make the coming out process more difficult and painful.

> I dated mostly because of pressure from my peers. I couldn't relate to men before. This was before I realized there was a lesbian community . . . I was Catholic and read bad things about it and I kept it hidden. I thought I was the only one in the world with these feelings. I didn't know others existed who had similar feelings. (4)

As a consequence of this lack of information, a real sense of an overground community has not been allowed to develop in the past, and much frustration and anger has resulted. (There has always been an underground gay community—the trick is finding it.)

> We really don't have any meeting place. We don't have very much. We're not given the opportunity to have very much. A place the size of New York City, I mean, it's outrageous! No wonder women don't want to come out. Where do you come out—where do you go? To the corner with a little banner? It's very, very oppressive. (18)

Social oppression is an effective political measure employed to keep minority groups from organizing and gaining power or influence within a society. Minorities have typically included racial, ethnic and religious groups. However, there can be no doubt that homosexuals form a rather large minority group as well. It is often difficult to identify a homosexual from physical appearance alone, and thus, many gay women and men remain in the closet to avoid blatant discrimination. Once their sexual identity is exposed, however, they will be subjected to all forms of social, political and economic oppression. The gay women interviewed in this study are very much aware of the situation they must face if their lesbianism were known:

> I'm definitely oppressed by my lesbianism when I let my lesbianism be exposed. I'm limited by certain social factors, no question about it. I definitely do not have the option to live openly with social approval. The minute I expose any area of my lesbianism I'm going to get clobbered in every respect. (36)

A feeling of helplessness often prevails because lesbians have little or no control over the outside forces which stigmatize them. They place the responsibility for many of their actions on the oppressive attitudes and behavior of the larger society. It is the individuals who make and enforce the rules against homosexual behavior who are at fault. Viewed from this perspective, stigmatized or variant behavior is not seen as the quality of an act or the person performing the act, but rather is a product or result of the application of rules backed by institutionalized social power.

Howard Becker (1963) refers to rule makers, or those who define an act or class of individuals as variant, as moral entrepreneurs. He distinguishes between two types of moral entrepreneurs, the rule creators, who are generally of the upper class and possess power, and the rule enforcers, who are the agents of social control, or the police. The rule makers label something as evil and go to great lengths to destroy or weaken it. Their primary interest is with the ends rather than the means, and they employ professionals to draw up legislation against the act or persons. As new rules are created, new agencies or officials are established to enforce the rules. In this way rules, laws or labels are frequently forced upon people against their will and without their consent, by the persons in power.

Any sexual act between persons of the same gender is illegal in all but a few states in this country. Although very few women have ever been arrested for lesbian activities, the fact that their very existence is illegal often produces psychological and emotional strain.

> Well, first of all it's against the law. I mean if you want to get very practical about it. And I'm not used to letting anyone get anything on me. And it can be used against you in a very, very damaging way. And that's a very frightening thing. (18)

As a result of the negative labels imposed upon lesbians by the moral entrepreneurs, many gay women isolate themselves from the straight world by remaining secretive about their sexual orientation. They also frequently isolate themselves from other lesbians who are more open about their sexuality for fear of exposure by identification.[2]

> I came out publicly in 1970, but I had been a lesbian for twenty years. Before that I was completely closeted. The psychological repression, you know, it's hard for me to condense 19 or 20 years into just a sentence or two. It was tremendous. What I did to myself in that context I cannot describe. I psychologically repressed my anger, my emotions, my feelings. I was always so frightened that someone would find out. I played a hell of a good heterosexual game. (12)

Particularly for older women who have been gay for many years, a realization that much of their lives had been spent or wasted, hiding and covering up their feelings and actions is quite demoralizing. They lived in ". . . voluntary psychological imprisonment for a crime never committed." (Abbott and Love, 1972:160) In retrospect it becomes apparent that external social forces were responsible for their destructive behavior.

> Just a lot of really good horror stories that make me want to say, no, I never felt my lesbianism was sick or my love for other women was sick, but

the pressures put upon us to make us keep quiet about that drove us to distraction and drove us into isolation. And into throat cutting and into the most inhuman of relationships. I just get really angry about that and I don't think it was our fault. It really, honest to God, wasn't. (36)

The majority of gay women see the necessity of "closetedness" and forced isolation as repressive and psychologically damaging understandably so, as one of the primary motivating forces behind negative societal labeling is the prospect of eradicating, or at least limiting, homosexual behavior by presenting it as an undesirable alternative life style.

Some lesbians, however, are not convinced that isolation from the dominant heterosexual culture is necessarily a bad thing. These women rationalize that it is often more advantageous and rewarding to live their lives outside the mainstream of society.

I think to be really honest about it, there are times that I think I'm very aware of the isolation, of the non-acceptance. One of the fears I had before I came out was that I would be cut off. And what actually happened was completely the opposite. It was good to get cut off from the mainstream of society, and I felt like the possibilities really opened up. (20)

Whether social isolation is seen as positive or negative by the lesbians who experience it, it is nevertheless a method used by the forces in power to discourage women from adopting a lesbian identity.

A third technique utilized to further dissuade women from becoming lesbians is stereotyping. Stereotyping is an integral part of the socialization process.

Stereotypes

Stereotyping is very prevalent in American culture. Individuals develop rigid, standardized images of a particular group and categorize all of its members together, not allowing for, or taking into account individual distinguishing characteristics or qualities. This procedure operates for all types of groups, not simply or necessarily only stigmatized groups.

American society has been quite effective in establishing and perpetuating myths, in the form of undesirable homosexual stereotypes, as another apparent method of reinforcing the negative attitudes towards lesbianism and homosexuality. Barry Dank (1974) discusses this process in his work on homosexual identity.

It is to be expected that societal stereotypes of homosexuals have historically been firmly believed in because of the social invisibility of homosexuals and the societal taboos which only allow homosexuality to be presented in a negative context in the mass media. Probably one of the major functions of such stereotyping and silence has been to prevent homosexually oriented individuals from coming out. (p. 16)

Lesbians have typically been stereotyped as masculine women possessing few feminine qualities. This was the only model available for a gay woman to identify with, and it caused many problems and anxieties for women who could not fit the "butch" role. Some women denied that they were lesbians for a long while, because they could not conform to this masculine model. Once they realized that being a lesbian does not mean wearing boots and men's trousers, it became a bit easier for them to accept their own gay identities. The following quotes express some of the stereotypes the women in this study had of homosexuals.

I hadn't met any gay women. I had this idea that lesbians were either macho women who wanted to be men, or they were decadent femmes who were addicted to opium and lived in Paris. (5)

I thought homosexuals were these strange creatures like Stephen in *The Well of Loneliness* who dressed up like a man and fell in love with a very feminine woman. And since I couldn't identify with Stephen whatsoever, and since I was never a very feminine woman, it didn't have anything to do with my life. (38)

What one would term the "old school" lesbians, or older gay women who came out fifteen or twenty years ago, the stereotypical lesbian was in many ways a reality. These women frequently internalized and acted out societal stereotypes and expected role patterns for lack of a more viable model.

And with my sisters, my women friends who were also gay, we did, it was unfortunate, but we were into all the heavy heterosexual game playing with butches and femmes and stealing people's lovers. And doing the whole old gay trip in ways I don't even like to remember . . . I knew even then that somehow I didn't want those roles and some of my friends knew too, but we didn't know how to escape them. That was the only model that we had. (12)

Heterosexuality, or male-female relationships, is the ideal in our society. This type of union is necessary in very practical terms to perpetuate the human race. Every individual, be they homosexual, bisexual or heterosexual by definition, came from or was produced by a male and female sexual relationship. Persons are conditioned to think in terms of male-female role models. Therefore, it is not surprising that the concept of lesbianism was often presented in a dichotomized fashion, with gay women being viewed as very masculine at one end of the spectrum and extremely feminine at the other.

It was presented to me as the role playing thing. I can't remember, I'm sure it was my mother more than my father. Lesbians were women who wanted to be men with other women. There was never the feeling of two feminine beings together, always one wanting to be masculine. (14)

For a woman who was trying to grapple with her own sexual identity the stereotypical lesbian model presented to her was not very encouraging or helpful. It is difficult enough to suffer through the "adolescent identity crisis," but with the added dimension of possibly having to identify with the attributes of the opposite sex, the process becomes nearly impossible. Some of the problems and anxieties resulting from attempting to identify with these stereotypes are expressed by the following women:

> I knew at that age that there were male homosexuals and females, but at that time I just thought that men were feminine types and women wore men's clothing. So at that time it was very upsetting to think I was that type who wore men's clothes and such. (15)

> And the reason I don't like people using the word lesbian is because of what that conjures up in the normal imagination. Because that represents me no better than a lumberjack does, and that's the reason I don't like classifications. Because I'm not comfortable with them, obviously. (18)

The presentation of a negative "butch" stereotype as a role model can be even more distressing for a woman who is not, by social definition, extremely feminine in appearance.

> I didn't like the term. I mean, the term is very negative to me. I didn't know what it was. I didn't have any role models. I didn't have any good role models, you know. The only lesbians I've ever run across were in James Baldwin's books, and who wants to be like that? And my physical presence puts me in a role of being a butch, and I'm not. So for me to accept, for me to call myself a lesbian, to call myself a dyke, would be to accept the butch role. (34)

Many women do not admit their feelings of attraction towards other women to themselves or to others for quite some time, for fear of having to conform to society's rather rigidly defined lesbian stereotypes. Carol Warren (1974) expresses a similar opinion:

> The lack of positive imagery, and the corresponding absence of homosexual role models for the young, may be one reason for the typically long period of time between the first homosexual experience or feeling and the self-identification as gay. (p. 147)

The following quote exemplifies how one woman's fears about having to conform to negative stereotypes delayed her coming out process:

> I had all the stereotypes. I thought you were either very masculine or very feminine. It was frightening to think you had to be one or the other. I grew

up in the military and met many WACs. I thought that was what it meant to be a lesbian. When I found out it wasn't true it shed a whole new light on things. If I knew I could be myself I'd probably have come out a long time ago. (8)

The socialization process, entailing adoption of the prevailing norms and values of the dominant culture, is essential in the establishment of self-identity. How others perceive our actions and behavior patterns is gleaned through interaction with members of our society. The development of one's self-identity, and subsequently the direction of one's actions, is greatly influenced by positive or negative reinforcement from our socializers. Employing the techniques of rigid heterosexual social conditioning, isolation and megative stereotyping, "society" has been effective in applying a negative label to lesbians.

Given this negative presentation of lesbians in our society, it is difficult to understand how any gay woman could endure the devaluation and develop a positive self identity. Two factors come into play here which are instrumental in overcoming the negative stereotypes—education and community support.

The realization that lesbians are not freaks or women in drag, i.e., male impersonators, occurs most frequently with actual face-to-face association with gay women. Carol Warren in her book, *Identity and Community in the Gay World* (1974) terms this new awareness the conversion effect.

The conversion effect starts with what's been called the "phenomenological shock" of encountering a stigmatized group and finding that they appear "normal" and aren't distinguished by bizarre physical markings or extra-ordinary appearance and behavior. (p. 156)

Contact with other gay women is perhaps one of the most expedient methods for overcoming hesitations and fears in associating and identifying oneself with the lesbian community. One woman in this study expressed her feelings about her fears in the following manner:

There were a lot of women's dances going on in New York City at that time, and scared as I was, I finally got myself to go. Just seeing other women that were lesbians and that didn't look like freaks, you know, that just looked like they could have gone to high school with you, and if you passed them on the street you wouldn't know they were lesbians. Realizing that there was a peer group that seemed as normal as I thought I was. That made me able to use the word, and hear other people use it. (45)

Within the past few years several well known individuals have taken it upon themselves to come out publicly. Elaine Noble, politician, and Kate Millett, academician, are but two examples of noted women who have announced their homosexuality. The act of others' publicly coming out is important in providing positive meaning and support to individuals establishing or coming to terms with their gay identity.

The second factor relating to the transition from fears and anxieties aroused by negative lesbian stereotypes to feelings of confidence in adopting a positive lesbian identity, is support from the gay community. The Women's Movement plays a large part in providing strength and unity for the lesbian community. Women are now beginning to realize their importance and capabilities, and are openly providing encouragement and support for their sisters.

> The Women's Movement has made it easier. It's made it easier for me to come out, anyhow, in that I could dissolve my marriage and know that if all hell broke loose and I were thrown out, and my children were taken away from me, and all those things, there was someplace I could go. Someone would be there to help me out of my mess. (37)

As Blumstein and Schwartz (1975) state, an appropriate ideological environment may in some cases serve as a support for sexual experimentation. The Women's Movement has certainly been instrumental in providing this environment, as the following quote illustrates:

> I'm conscious of my privilege. I feel like it's a—I'm almost embarrassed, it was so easy for me. I feel bad for a lot of women who were gay before the Women's Movement. I'm certainly one of the ones that was totally privileged by the Women's Movement existing. It was comfortable, it was easy, I was accepted. I had a peer group. I had support, constant support. (16)

FEELINGS OF PRESENT IDENTITY

One would probably expect that given the prevailing social attitudes stigmatizing homosexuality, lesbians would have ambiguous or mixed feelings about the fact that they have developed a gay identity. Contrarily, the findings of this study indicate a strong positive attitude regarding the adoption of a lesbian identity in nearly one hundred percent of the cases. However, a few of the respondents expressed negative as well as positive feelings about their lesbianism. Their reactions include a sense of relief and happiness at finally establishing a positive identity, feelings of amazement in overcoming the heterosexual socialization process, and a greater understanding of themselves and other women.

Several women expressed a feeling of normality in their convictions.

> I have no question about my sexuality anymore. I don't struggle with it. It's a natural part of me rather than something I have spent time thinking about. (7)

Other researchers have not always found such positive reactions from their interviewees. Charlotte Wolff, a psychologist, in her book, *Love Between Women*

(1971), reports a quite different response from the gay women she interviewed. When asked why they choose to live their lives as lesbians, the overwhelming response was that they had no choice, it happened that way. They sadly expressed the inevitability of their lesbian life-styles.

A great contrast was found in this study as a number of respondents expressed a great joy and satisfaction with themselves after realizing their gay identities.

> I feel really positive about it. I think about that every now and then, and I think that that's one major decision I've made in my life that I've never regretted. Like I've always felt very positive about it, and really felt it's a great source of energy to me. It's really what I want for my life. And I'm glad that I was able to make that commitment at the point that I did. (21)

> I don't feel that I compromise. I don't feel like I'm less than I am or different than I am. I feel comfortable and I feel happy and stimulated. I love it. I mean, I sort of get up in the morning and embrace it. (16)

Probably, most individuals conceive of homosexuals in strictly sexual terms, i.e., that means they sleep with someone of their own sex. However, awareness and acceptance of a lesbian identity is likely to encompass much more than just positive feelings about sexual relations with other women. Self identification as a lesbian may influence every aspect of one's life. It may affect their daily interactions with other people on a very basic level, as well as influencing how they view the world in general.

> It's a natural, comfortable thing for me. There was never any separation from that marriage, from that affinity with lesbianism, with loving women. This love for women is never going to diminish. It's the prime thing in my life, it's my model, my value concept. (36)

Positive feelings about loving other women often result from strong feelings of self love. If a woman feels good about herself as a woman, it is easier to transfer these emotions to others like herself. Homosexual women are therefore both subject and object to each other at the same time.

The concept of "narcissism," or self love, in gay relationships has been a controversial issue among researchers in the field of homosexuality. C. A. Tripp (1975) does not believe that some elements of narcissism can exist in homosexual women and men.

> Notions to the effect that the homosexual is looking for some narcissistic reflection of his own image are as mythical as was Narcissus himself. (p. 98)

Contrary to Tripp's opinion, several women in this study expressed self love as the primary force behind their love for other women.

> They're positive feelings. Sometimes I feel it's sort of a miracle. Since this is such a woman hating society, it amazes me that there are so many women

400

who still love each other . . . It's evident that everyone is trained to be heterosexual, so a lot of women are that way because that's how they were brought
up. For me, my love for women comes from my love for myself. It's just the
sameness of both being the same sex; of both being women. (10)

Although all of the women interviewed expressed positive feelings of self
identity, a few admitted that there were negative aspects to their chosen identities as well. The negative feelings are a direct result of the oppressive societal
attitudes which have forced many lesbians to hide their true sexual identity.

> I have very good feelings about being a lesbian, except for the fact that I
> have to be a closet lesbian. (40)

> Oh sure, lots of negative feelings. Sure. Of course, obviously I have more
> positive than negative. The negative feelings are that the thing that is most
> important to you can be used against you by society, with its good house-
> keeping stamp of approval. That really bothers me. It's wrong, it shouldn't
> be, but it is. And somehow I have to live, to fit in there someplace, and of
> course that leaves me to absorb the strain. (18)

Other women felt a disadvantage of adopting a lesbian life-style was the fact
that they must be self-supporting for the rest of their lives.

> Well, I expect that I'll always consider myself a lesbian. I don't have any
> intentions of getting married. It scares me in some ways, because I know it
> means being alone, in terms of supporting myself. (45)

Awareness and acceptance of a lesbian identity provided some women with
increased insight into themselves and others. They believed that only through
loving other women could they begin to overcome some of the weaknesses
within themselves, and begin to establish a firm and positive identity as a
woman.

> I was happy that I had the courage of my conviction, so to speak. So I
> felt terrific, in fact, I felt like I had stumbled upon this secret source of
> strength. And I really believed that that's where it's at for women. You do
> reclaim yourself when you identify with women in a way you never can if
> you're with a man. (11)

CHANGING SEXUAL IDENTITY

Although many lesbians are satisfied and happy with their present sexual
identity, there remains the possibility that they may desire to change their
sexual orientation. It would obviously be easier to slide along with the main-

stream of society, protected in a cloak of heterosexuality. Again, the results of the study do not support this. The entire sample expressed negative reactions to the idea of changing their sexual identity at the present time.

C. A. Tripp (1975), in his review of surveys conducted over the past several years arrived at the same results. He found that ninety to ninety-six percent of the homosexuals questioned would not choose to change their sexual identity, even if they could do so by merely "pushing a button."

Some of the women interviewed in this study experienced initial doubts about their sexual orientation and questioned the validity of their decision, but did not wish to reverse it.

> Not really. At one time I thought it would be easier to be straight, but I never really wanted to be straight, so I dropped that idea. (15)

> When I first became aware of my feelings I tried to label myself a bi-sexual and screwed around with men. It was not a conscious attempt to change, just to deny. I've never made a conscious attempt to change around. I doubt I ever will. (5)

For gay women who have developed a feminist consciousness the prospect of returning to heterosexual relationships is likely to be quite unappealing. Relating to other women allows them greater independence and freedom to be themselves. These women have found the inequality that may result in male-female relationships to be restrictive and oppressive.

> I will say absolutely that I'll never change back, because I know enough about the bad trips that can happen. I'm enough of a feminist to know that I can't play the games that have to be played in a straight life. The most liberal men that I know still have ego problems. And I'm just not interested in a relationship that isn't equal. It's too much of a burden on me. (37)

Gay women often view the adoption of a lesbian identity as a conscious choice, a decision they made to which they are committed. These women experienced both heterosexual and homosexual relationships and declared a preference for one over the other.

> I don't think I'll change my lesbian identity. I'm happy the way I am. I made a choice a long time ago and I've continued to make that choice, and I see no reason to change. (1)

> No, I'm not a martyr. I know what I like and I can get it, so why shouldn't I want it? (9)

Often external social pressures exist which advocate resumption of a heterosexual life-style for a woman who has engaged in homosexual activities. Families, friends and the society at large frequently suggest that a gay woman will find a "better life" with a man. Many women, despite this opposition, still believe that a gay life-style is best for them.

> I don't see any reason for wanting to change. I don't feel like I'm missing anything, or that there's anything wrong with me, or that I'm any kind of a second class person. I don't consider my life second best, or that I need to do anything to change it. (29)

A real problem in labeling individuals as heterosexual or homosexual is that it often implies a rigid, irreversible pattern of behavior. A majority of the women in this study had heterosexual relationships prior to their lesbian involvements, and they made a choice as to which they prefer. Many individuals, including some social scientists, overlook this possible flexibility in sexual relationships.

Evelyn Hooker (1966) in her research on homosexuality indicates that gay women and men are fixed in their sexual orientation and have little possibility for change.

> In any case, it is a fate over which they have no control and in which they have no choice. It follows as a consequence that the possibility of changing to a heterosexual pattern is thought to be extremely limited. (Gagnon & Simon, 1967:183)

One fact that Hooker has overlooked is that most homosexual women have had heterosexual relationships prior to becoming involved in homosexual unions. This pattern in itself indicates a choice, or a change in one's sexual identity. In addition, some of the women in this study stated that although they are satisfied with homosexual relations at this point in their lives, they are flexible enough to allow the possibility of re-entering a heterosexual relationship at some future date.

The total sample in this study stated no desire to resume a heterosexual lifestyle at the present time; however, several of the women indicated they could not foresee what might happen in the future.

> I have no idea. I think not, but then who knows, you know? If you'd asked me four years ago if I'd ever be a lesbian, I would have said no, are you crazy? So, who knows? (2)

However, just as there are many heterosexual women who have strong feelings about their sexual identity, many gay women are extremely dogmatic in their convictions about their life-styles.

> My God no! Why? Incredible! Absolutely not, I wouldn't do it for the world. That would be very foolish. That would be like cutting out a vital organ. (12)

No, never. Because I've always been happy with it. I've had my ups and downs like anyone in a relationship, but my relationships have been very good. I wouldn't want in the world to change. (14)

DISCUSSION AND CONCLUSION

The labels and sanctions against homosexual behavior become blatantly evident through a description of the socialization process in our society. Ideal heterosexual role models have been established and everyone is expected to conform to these molds. As Abbott and Love (1972) state:

Perhaps the greatest social crime a homosexual commits is the rejection of sex-role stereotypes. (p. 167)

If they do not conform they are stigmatized by the larger society.

The topic of lesbianism had not been openly discussed as a social issue until recently. The result of this suppression has been a feeling of social isolation among lesbians, and a sense of community has not been permitted to develop in the past.

The typical portrayal of lesbians as masculine or butch serves initially as a deterrent to women who are attempting to identify themselves as lesbians. They are torn between having to adopt the traditional female role on the one hand, which they clearly do not identity with, or choosing to assume the stereotypical lesbian butch role on the other, which can be equally dissatisfying. Society generally presents a negative and distorted view of lesbians through the mere process of identifying them as stigmatized individuals, as well as through the perpetuation of myths and stereotypes.

Lesbians have been portrayed in stereotypical roles not only by the larger society, which is generally mis-informed and uneducated on the whole issue of lesbianism, but by individuals who have some knowledge of the lesbian community as well. Carol Warren (1974), in her book on gay identity, speaks of lesbians who socialize with the gay men in her study in the following manner:

The gay women are most often those who do not fit into the lesbian community; they may be professional in occupation, prefer more traditionally "feminine" dress, than the norm in the lesbian community, or prefer the company of men (p. 81).

Generalizations such as these based on scant evidence only serve to reinforce the myths and negative stereotypes of lesbians. Over half of the respondents in this study are either presently involved in professional occupations or are in training for professional careers. The responses of the lesbians in the above section on stereotypes illustrates that they prefer being themselves and not having to dress or act in a masculine fashion. And few of the women expressed a desire to totally segregate themselves from male society.

The findings of this study support the hypothesis that people generally have a negative and distorted view of lesbians through the mere process of identifying them as deviant and undesirable individuals, as well as through the perpetuation of myths and stereotypes.

The phenomena, discussed in the introduction to this study, involving a recent attempt by lesbians to cast off the negative "baggage" they have had to travel with for years, and develop a positive and assured gay identity, is remarkable. This changing philosophy and ideology of self worth and esteem is clearly evident in the interviewees' responses concerning their feelings of present identity, and the reactions to the possibility of changing their sexual orientation. Nearly one hundred percent of the sample expressed positive feelings about their present sexual identities, and the total sample revealed no desire to change their sexual identity and resume a heterosexual life-style at the present time.

The data presented in this study illustrates that the gay women interviewed possess a positive self identity, despite negative attitudes towards their behavior. A possible explanation for these findings is the support and strength provided by the Women's Movement in recent years. The feminist movement has had a great impact on changing women's ideas about sexuality in general, and has been instrumental in somewhat reducing the stigma attached to lesbian relationships. The Movement offers support and encouragement to women to develop their full potential in all areas of life, thus increasing women's nonsexual positive feelings towards one another as well. The existence of a large support group advocating love among women has provided reinforcement and made it possible for many lesbians to develop an assured self image.

With the recent and growing interest focused on women, both gay and straight, in the past few years, it is becoming increasingly important to represent an accurate picture of lesbian life. This study is a beginning attempt to fill the void presently existing in the sociological literature regarding lesbians. The focus of this paper has concentrated only on the socialization process and feelings of self identity gay women possess. Further research is required to investigate the continuing life-style of lesbians after they have recognized their affiliation with the gay community. There is also a vital need to explore the developmental process and resulting life-style of lesbians who do not establish positive self identities, but who rather internalize the socially induced negative aspects of their behavior. Virtually no work has been done on the issues of class, race and religion and lesbianism. A lower class black lesbian has vastly different life experiences than does an upper class white lesbian. These areas certainly need to be studied by sociologists. Additional information might also be gathered on the recently changing social conditions and climate which have created, to a degree, the growing popularity and interest in lesbianism as a social issue.

NOTES

[1]The author will use the terms stigmatized or variant to describe the behavior of non-conforming individuals. The term deviant will be employed only when directly quoting another's work.

[2]For further information on stigmatization and fear of exposure see, *Identity and Community in the Gay World,* Carol Warren, New York, 1974: pp. 146–147.

REFERENCES

Abbott, Sidney, and Barbara Love, 1972, *Sappho Was a Right-On Woman.* New York: Stein and Day.

Becker, Howard S., 1963, *Outsiders.* New York: Free Press.

Blumstein, Philip W., and Pepper Schwartz, 1975, *Report on Bisexuality in Women.* Seattle: University of Washington.

Dank, Barry M., 1974, "Symbolic Interactionism and the Homosexual Identity." Paper presented at the 69th meeting of the American Sociological Association, Montreal.

Hooker, Evelyn, 1967, "The Homosexual Community." Pp. 167–84 in John H. Gagnon and William Simon (eds.), *Sexual Deviance.* New York: Harper and Row.

Kitsuse, John I., 1973, "Societal Reactions to Deviant Behavior." Pp. 16–25 in Earl Rubington and Martin S. Weinberg (eds.) Deviance: The Interactionist Perspective. New York: Macmillan.

Tripp, C.A., 1975, *The Homosexual Matrix.* New York: McGraw-Hill.

Warren, Carol A. B., 1974, *Identity and Community in the Gay World.* New York: Wiley.

Wolff, Charlotte, 1971, *Love Between Women.* New York: Harper and Row.

Wysor, Bettie, 1974, *The Lesbian Myth.* New York: Random House.

The Affair

Morton Hunt

In a country where monogamy is the law and the general expectation, extramarital affairs are most often covert. However, the range of types of illicit relationships is as broad as or broader than that discussed by Cuber and Harroff's typology of marriage types (Reading 14). A major ingredient in extramarital affairs is the emotional ambivalence they cause. Guilt and joy, frustration and happiness, can all play havoc with the emotions of married individuals involved in affairs. Security and boredom, love and longing, can soothe and plague those who are not. Beyond the emotional turmoil of participants is the possible reaction of the spouse, close family members, and friends—often feared enough to deter a person from entering an extramarital liaison in the first place. How do these intense illicit dyadic relationships begin? Here is one of the great mysteries of social life, yet to be understood by either sociologists or psychologists. What, exactly, makes two people have empathic responses to each other? How does each convey this feeling to the other? Why does this mutual phenomenon happen with some and not with others? What makes it so satisfying that persons are willing to risk their honor, their fortunes, the regard of their families, and their very futures when these extramarital opportunities develop? What happens to affairs over the years when participants would like to devote more (or less) time to them than the other participant (or the spouses of each) would like? The sociological problem is not only that of overt and covert norms, but finding a balance in the distribution of time and attention to all those persons who become someone's "significant other."

INTRODUCTION

Described on the following pages are the major types of extramarital affair in contemporary America, as I learned about them from people I interviewed, or to whom I sent questionnaires. Every significant deed, speech and emotion recorded here is drawn from real life; I have, however, hidden the identities

From Morton Hunt, "The Affair," *Ladies Home Journal,* (September 1969) pp. 141–153 and (October 1969) pp. 159–168. Copyright © 1969 by Morton Hunt. Reprinted by permission.

of the persons involved by altering their names and external characteristics. I have not tried to be encyclopedic; the emphasis is on the patterns of behavior of the white middle class, drawn from five principal sources:

1. Ninety-one tape-recorded interviews with men and women in all parts of the country, nearly all of whom had had, or were still having, extramarital affairs. The rest were "wronged" mates, or unmarried lovers of the married persons having affairs;

2. Some diaries kept by interviewees, letters exchanged by extramarital lovers, and tape-recorded comments by friends of the principals, ex-mates, ministers, doctors and others;

3. Interviews and correspondence with psychologists, psychiatrists, sociologists, marriage counselors and other persons with special knowledge of the subject;

4. Three hundred and sixty completed replies to a questionnaire designed and administered for me by a social-science research team at an Eastern university;

5. Previously published data and findings of other persons.

• • • •

DEFINING AN AFFAIR

The question—what is an extramarital affair in present-day America?—is difficult to answer. Although in other times and places the extramarital affair might have had one dominating pattern and one generally agreed-upon meaning—a proof of *machismo* in one society, the expression of idealistic love in another, and so on—in our own society there are several kinds of extramarital affair, each with its own reasons for being.

On one day last winter, for instance, the following scenes all took place in the United States within a few hours of one another:

In a supermarket in Denver, a man in his early forties and a somewhat younger woman stop their carts side by side and pretend to study the products on the shelves while talking to each other softly. They talk about his work as a building contractor, her children—she has three—and her efforts to get back to part-time work as an interior designer. They have been lovers for three years. In her marriage she has never known anything like the total absorption in each other that she knows with him; he, in his marriage and three previous affairs, was never passionate and truly loving as he has been with her. Her father is a minister, and she could not think of scandalizing him by divorce; the contractor has held off seeking his own divorce until she gets hers. They spend one afternoon a week together at the apartment of a bachelor friend of his, and sometimes they manage a summer evening at another friend's mountain lodge not far away. Nearly every day they talk on the phone while her children are in school, and two or three times a week they arrange to see each other for a few minutes in the supermarket, the library, or a large bookstore, in order to hold hands, to look at each other, to talk about everyday things. The frozen surface of their marriages is all sham, but beneath it, unseen, their love flows on and is the reality of their lives.

In a Cleveland hotel a well-tailored man of 35 looks through a small address book and dials a number. "Julie, honey!" he says in radiant tones, and waits for a surprised, happy reply. A look of puzzlement comes over his face. "Why, sweetheart," he says, "it's Ellis. I wrote you I'd be here this week. . . . Do I gather you can't talk freely now? Can I ask questions and you just say yes or no? Good. You've got someone else there—another traveling friend. No? You haven't gone and got married? You *have*? . . . Hey, darling, that's wonderful! Congratulations! . . . OK, I'll cut out now before I get you in trouble. So long—and good luck." He hangs up and curses softly. Three strikes and out—not one working contact left in Cleveland, and four days to kill here. He adjusts his tie, and heads off for a downtown bar to look for a replacement. A manufacturer's representative, he covers a six-state area, spending about a quarter of his time at home with his wife and the other three-quarters on the road with, as he tells his male friends, "my thirty other wives." Each woman sees him once every couple of months, and finds him an enthusiastic lover. His real wife gets little from him except complaints about her housekeeping, and their love-making is perfunctory and swift. Now and then she accuses him of being interested in some other woman, but he laughs at her, or flies into a righteous rage. She once studied his address book, but found no women's names; it never occurred to her that he uses a code, and that over 100 names in the book, accumulated through the years, represent women he has had affairs with in their decade of marriage.

A station wagon parks in front of a shabby rooming house in Camden, N.J.; a young woman, plain-featured but voluptuous of figure, gets out, hurries inside, and knocks on a door. A husky, black-haired man, his shirt open halfway to the waist, lets her in and locks the door; smiling, but without a word, he takes her coat off and draws her into his embrace. Thereafter their conversation consists chiefly of monosyllabic sounds, laughter and appreciative murmurs. As she is leaving, it occurs to her that in nearly two hours she has exchanged only a few words with him. Driving home, she thinks about this with mingled shame and pride; she, the wife of a college professor, has discovered in herself the capacity—and an addict's craving—for simple, animal sex. Joe, a long-distance truck driver with a wife and three children 600 miles away, gets to town once every 10 days or so and spends a couple of hours with her in wild, wordless coupling; but she can't imagine spending a whole day or even a weekend with him. What would they say to each other, what would they do?

In the evening, a man and a woman in their early thirties, sit in a car parked by a beach near Bridgeport, Conn. They whisper endearments and cover each other's faces with kisses. They speak of their longing for each other, their feelings of loyalty toward their families, their surprise at being in this situation. In the three months since they fell in love, this is all that has happened between them, except in imagination. He was raised a Congregationalist in Connecticut, she a Catholic in Boston, both in staid and moralistic homes. Although each suffers spells of excruciating desire for the other, they remain immobilized by fear, guilt and the thought that thus far they have done nothing "wrong." At least, so it was until recently; but three times during the last month he was unable to make love to his wife when he tried to. Deeply alarmed, he went to his doctor for a check-up and a long talk, and learned that he was physically healthy but suffering the effects of psychological infidelity.

The foregoing examples give some idea how wide a range of meaning and experience the term "extramarital affair" covers in American life. I asked my questionnaire respondents, for instance, about this situation: "A married person has sexual relations with someone picked up in a bar." Did that constitute an extramarital affair? Half the men and women who had never been unfaithful thought it did, but only about a third of the unfaithful agreed. Differences in definition also appear between the sexes: Apparently, women are more apt to define an "affair" as a relationship involving depth of feeling; they would regard quick, spontaneous extramarital sex as "cheating," "running around," or "stepping out."

Such ambiguities in defining infidelity may account in part for the lack of expert consensus on the frequency of extramarital affairs in America. But at least there is some sound statistical information on extramarital sexual activity in the United States whether or not one would call all of it "affairs." It is to be found in the first and second volumes written by Alfred Kinsey and his associates, of the Institute for Sex Research at Indiana University. Despite the limitations of Kinsey's methodology and sampling procedures—his sample, critics have said, is overweighted with the too-willing-to-talk—these reports do say how many men and women in a very large sample have had sexual relations outside their marriages. As the authors wrote, in their celebrated estimate, "It is probably safe to suggest that about half of all the married males have intercourse with women other than their wives at some time while they are married." For women, the cumulative incidence of extramarital experience was calculated at about one in four; it is possible that the true figures might be still higher, due to cover-up.

These are the best figures available. But since *Sexual Behavior in the Human Male* was published in 1948, and *Sexual Behavior in the Human Female* in 1953, I returned to the same source to ask what the figures might be today. Dr. Paul Gebhard, successor to Kinsey and present director of the Institute, said that he and his staff feel there has been a continuation of previous trends. To quote Dr. Gebhard: "If I were to make an educated guess as to the cumulative incidence figures for 1968, they'd be about 60 percent for males and 35 to 40 percent for females. This is change, but not revolution. The idea that there has been a sexual revolution in the past decade or two comes from the fact that we have become so rapidly permissive about what you can say and print."

Despite the change in what can be said and printed, the dominant sexual code in the United States disapproves of premarital sex and condemns common-law marriage, illegitimacy, abortion, sexual variations and deviations of most sorts, and, of course, adultery. In actual fact, a vast underground of good middle-class citizens overtly accept the code but secretly disregard various parts of it, while a small avant-garde openly defies it.

There are widespread indications of this schism between code and reality. Adultery is still a punishable offense in the criminal codes of 45 of the 50 states; maximum penalties range from a $10 fine in Maryland to a five-year jail term, plus substantial fines, in Maine, Vermont, South Dakota and Oklahoma—yet these laws are almost never enforced.

A large majority of the respondents to my own questionnaire said they always or usually disapprove of adultery; those who had had affairs themselves were somewhat more tolerant, although even in this group over half were disapproving.

This is what the disjunction between code and reality looks like, when one penetrates the façade:

In a well-to-do suburb of Philadelphia, a somewhat over-dressed woman of 38 speaks of some facts she has learned about life since her separation from her husband: "The first couple of months after my husband and I broke up, about ten of his friends rang up and wanted to take me to dinner, or openly told me what they were after. It shook me up. Since then I've noticed things I never used to—I've seen Frank's car parked at a motel in the afternoon, and Joe Goodbody's car a half block from Lynn's house one night when Lynn's husband was out of town. I lived in the middle of this for years and never knew what was going on: it was all a lie around me."

In Washington D.C., a 44-year-old woman recounts the dozen trivial affairs and two deep ones she has had during her happy marriage to a man she has never thought of leaving, and who is unaware of her infidelity: "When I compare my life to the lives of women I know who haven't had affairs, I feel I'm happier than most of them, and my marriage is better than most of theirs. Not that I would urge anyone else to do the same thing. I don't even approve of affairs, on the whole—most people can't handle them and still have a good, solid marriage. But I can, and I don't regret a single one."

AMBIVALENCE AND THE AFFAIR

The American ambivalence about the extramarital affair is the result not only of the clash between code and reality but also of a mixed cultural heritage that brings us not only the rigid Judeo-Christian condemnation of extramarital relationships, but a contrary tradition as well. Greek, Roman, Teutonic and Celtic strains were stirred into the mix long ago.

In the Northern European Puritan-bourgeois tradition, marriage came to be viewed romantically as the only human relationship in which sex, love and parenthood were socially and morally acceptable. Any outside involvement was seen as evil. For people who hold this view, affairs produce guilt and conflict, and must be kept secret. In contrast is the pagan-courtly tradition, found mostly in Southern European countries and throughout France. Marriage remained a practical, functional arrangement having to do with property, chil-

411

dren and creature comforts. It included sex, of course, but romantic involvement was sought in extramarital love affairs.

Our cultural heritage is thus schizoid. It offers us an approved model of
marriage that, for all its values, is suited to the needs of only some—perhaps a
minority—of us; simultaneously it offers us a deviant, disapproved model that,
for all its disadvantages, is suited to the needs of the rest of us, perhaps even
a majority. We now live longer and marry earlier than formerly, but to love
only one person emotionally and sexually over a 40- or 50-year span, and to
keep that love intense and physically gratifying all that time is very difficult
for most people, if not impossible. Many authorities have come to doubt our
cultural belief that the majority of men and women are happiest when monogamous and faithful; it may be that many of those who do remain faithful to a
single partner throughout life pay dearly in frustration, resentment of their
mates and desiccation of their emotions.

The disapproved model seems better suited to the emotional capacities and
requirements of many people, particularly men; it offers renewal, excitement
and the continuance of experiences of personal rediscovery; it is an answer
to the boredom of life-long monogamy. But again, those who choose this alternative may have to pay for it: infidelity conflicts with the home-based habits of
middle-class society, it is socially and professionally hazardous, it may be psychologically traumatic to one's self, wife and children, especially if discovered.

It is the very essence of the human condition that we want many things that
cannot all be had at the same time. Life continually requires us to choose
between alternatives, each of which offers us something but costs us something.
The grasshopper played and sang, but died young of cold and hunger; the
ant got through the winter nicely, but never knew the meaning of joy.

Man's thoughts, even more than his actions, belie the notion that he is by
nature a monogamous animal. For nearly all husbands and wives, even the
well-mated, the righteous and the hard-working, sooner or later find themselves not only desiring extramarital relationships but also committing infidelities in their minds. To people who are suffering severe sexual frustration or
deprivation of love in marriage, such fantasies may represent the first break-
someday to be able to leave advertising.

Neal has long been proud of his departures from orthodoxy: raised a Presby-
well, but conservatively, has neatly parted straight blond hair, and a square,
open face. But we are misled by his looks. He is a sensitive and gifted man, a
poet *manqué* who became an advertising writer in a small New York agency.
In his spare time he sweats over poems of contemporary despair and hopes
someday to be able to leave advertising.

Neal has long been proud of his departures from orthodoxy: raised a Preby-
terian, he became an agnostic in college; reared in a Long Island suburb and
educated at Yale, he has for years been a left-liberal Democrat. But six years ago
he was dismayed by the onset of another deviation. In a diary that he began in
April, 1966, and kept locked in a desk, he talks to himself about it:

*When did it all start? Not the first time I kissed Mary, not the first time I desired her,
not the first time I saw her. It started three years ago, when Those Thoughts sprouted
overnight, like a wet-weather plague of brown mushrooms on the green lawn of my
mind. That was the first betrayal in ten years of marriage; that was when it began.*

As a rather shy and inhibited youth, he had fallen in love with Laurie

VanZandt while he was a junior at Yale, and never again gone near another woman. But suddenly and unexpectedly, after years of marriage, there came the first of the daydreams of other women. The first episode was unforgettable. He had had dinner with two clients and Jack Gillespie, an account executive, and Gillespie's date, Norah. She looked girlish and fragile, buoyant and yet secretive. Gorham kept glancing at her, and thought she looked back at him with some obscure message in her eyes. *That night I lay in bed and was unfaithful to Laurie, in my thoughts, even while she was snuggled up against me. I never realized that Laurie and I had been drifting into trouble for years, and that this was the fever symptom.*

Most husbands and wives occasionally envision themselves in scenes of sex or romance with people other than their mates. A hundred thousand priests, psychotherapists and marriage counselors could be witness to this statement, for they hear the evidence every day. Neal Gorham's fantasies are only one type; others range from the brief and fragmentary to the extended and detailed, from the purely sexual to the wholly romantic; some are occasional, others regular, some are built around imaginary ideal lovers, others around real persons.

The dominant code in our society so strongly condemns adultery, even in imagination, that many fantasizers have guilt feelings about their imaginary affairs. A common way of dealing with such guilt is to consciously focus on and exaggerate the discontents in the marriage. But it is true, all the same, that the more a person daydreams, the more likely it is that he has good grounds for doing so: In my interviews I found extramarital fantasies far more frequent among the sexually deprived and emotionally insecure husbands and wives than among the merely bored.

Besides the marital discontents that give rise to fantasies, there is a more general cause, affecting even those whose marriages are satisfactory: We grow slowly tired of the things we have, even though they first delighted and fulfilled us, and want other things that will delight and fulfill us in the original way. *Will there be no more than this?* We are by nature polygamous, by upbringing monogamous, and therefore perennially at war with ourselves. And this is why so many of the married—even the happily married—sometimes dream of other loves, allaying through make-believe the harassing desire to know another and more exquisite love while there is yet time.

Edwin Gottesman (as I shall call him) exemplifies the point. A businessman in Washington, D.C., Gottesman lives with his wife and two children in a handsome 10-room colonial house, complete with swimming pool, on two acres of wooded land in Bethesda, Md. At 40, he is a shrewd promoter whose special skills include the ability to find land suitable for supermarket or shopping-center development, and to pull together syndicates of investors. He has a small potbelly, his flesh is pale and formless, as though he had never played an outdoor game in his life, and his faded brown hair has begun to thin. For all that, there is an intensity and manliness about him that can be compelling. Of his marriage to Betsy Weiss, whom he met in college, he says: "I can't say we were ever wildly in love. We went together a long while and felt good about each other, so we got married. It wasn't earth-shaking . . ."

Like the courtship, the marriage was comfortable and companionable. What with two children, a lovely home and his absorption in business, their life together was good. Although they seldom quarreled, they treated each other more like old chums than man and woman. Edwin, though seemingly in love with business, hungered for something else, and hardly knew what it was.

Once in a while Gottesman wanted to seize Betsy and embrace her passionately, but he felt he would look absurd; she would probably pat him on the cheek, and ask what had come over him. Yet she seldom refused him when he wanted her, and for years Gottesman thought that his sex life and his marriage were about as good as anyone could hope for even if they fell short of his dreams.

Then his real-estate transactions began to bring him into frequent contact with a group of six investors and developers in Philadelphia. Gottesman was astonished to find that all of them, although married, had occasional pick-up affairs while away in the city or long-term affairs going on with steady "girl friends." At first he was shocked; eventually he became jealous and inflamed.

"I couldn't help wanting what they seemed to have—secret meetings with beautiful women, really uninhibited sex, the feeling of being daring and young and successful with women. Betsy was a wonderful wife, but our marriage was very much like a good business partnership. I began to feel that I was missing something important."

Setting out on a business trip, he would start thinking that this time something might happen. He would meet a beautiful woman, some incident would give him reason to speak to her and after a little talk she would sense that inside this thick waisted, balding businessman there was a passionate and hungry soul. "I wanted to imagine all of it in detail," he says, "but somehow I could never picture the sexual part. I could only daydream the preliminaries."

•   •   •   •

Nearly all married men and at least a majority of married women are conscious of extramarital desires from time to time. The general view of psychologists and psychiatrists, especially those of Freudian orientation, is that healthy control of one's extramarital desires is based on full awareness of those desires, plus a realistic appraisal of all that is involved in gratifying them: the risk of harm to one's mate and to one's children, public disgrace, and all the rest.

For most people, this is too demanding a method of control; if they do exercise inner control, it is usually in the easier form of unthinking obedience to the dictates of conscience, and of fear of their own overpowering guilt feelings. Nearly all observers agree, however, that the inner controls have lost much of their power in recent years, whether implanted by religious belief, by parents, or by culture. The result is overt disapproval of infidelity combined with surreptitious fascination by it. The internal controls still exist, but for a growing number of people they are no longer effective deterrents.

What does hold many people back are the external controls—the penalties that others stand ready to impose on the discovered violator of the code. One person, in particular—the spouse—is as effective an enforcer of fidelity as ever. Many men and women who would like to have extramarital experiences are deterred by their fear of what their mates would do to them if they found out.

The wronged husband or wife can demand all sorts of reparations, including divorce. Even if the marriage is not a happy one, divorce is a dismal prospect: The break-up of the home and the division of property, the separation from one's children (in the man's case), the disruption of friendships and familiar patterns of daily life, the disgrace one suffers in the eyes of friends, and the harsh financial terms the adulterer may have to agree to—all these continue to act as powerful restraints of extramarital behavior.

Other external controls, however, have lost a good deal of their effectiveness in the past generation. The law does not prosecute the adulterer, nor are business, the church and society nearly as likely to punish him severely as they once were. He still runs some risk of blighting his career prospects, of being ostracized by friends and acquaintances, but penalties of this sort are most likely to be applied in small communities, where many feel a social obligation to show disapproval even if they feel none. This may explain why, in my questionnaire sample, only a tenth of the people living in towns of under 5,000 population said they had had affairs, as compared to a quarter of those who lived in cities of 500,000 or more.

• • • •

Among the people I interviewed, many who had sought relief from unhappy marriage in extramarital affairs had been divorced and made successful second marriages—without benefit of therapy. Yet these people often spoke of their first marriages in tones identical with those of the neurotic complainants. One cannot, therefore, call all such complaints and all such infidelity neurotic. Indeed, I get the impression that quite a few people who ascribe their infidelities to unhappy marriage or disagreeable mates do so because such complaints come closest to being acceptable to friends and confidants.

Sexual deprivation or frustration, though often a part of the unhappy-marriage syndrome, is also mentioned many times as the only reason the individual ventured outside of marriage. The analytically oriented therapist or marriage counselor takes this complaint, too, to be a symptom of neurosis in the very person who makes it; again, he asks the questions: Why did he or she choose an unresponsive mate? What did he or she do that destroyed the mate's responsive capacity?

Many of those whose justification for infidelity is sexual frustration neither made a neurotic choice of mate nor created the frustrating situation; they simply chose marriage partners before they were experienced enough to know what they were getting, or without any testing of the sexual relationship.

"I was a virgin when I married seven years ago, a good little convent girl, and I didn't know a *thing*. After we married, I believed everything he told me— that once a month was about normal, that it shouldn't take long, and that most women didn't have orgasms. I was the most frustrated bundle of nerves you ever heard of, and I didn't even know what my trouble was, until I happened to look at a marriage manual in the library and began to discover what it was all about. And then I couldn't *stand* my own frustration."

Nearly half of the men and women I interviewed indicated that the need for self-esteem was a major motivation behind their infidelity. Some of their statements could be interpreted as the complaints of neurotics, but others seem more like the expressions of people struggling to keep or recapture emotional health. An example:

"As a teen-age boy I was very shy and never tried to make out with girls.

415

Then I went and married a girl who had no more experience than I—and who couldn't have an orgasm except when I stimulated her manually. That does a lot for a man's confidence and good opinion of himself, doesn't it?"

Among my interviewees, well over half of the men admitted that one kind of boredom or another was the major reason for their first affairs; so did an even larger number of women, almost two-thirds of whom blamed the emotional boredom of marriage. (Among those who had had more than one affair, the figures were even higher.) They said things like this:

"For all those years, my wife never refused me. But she never *relished* it, she never said appreciative things, she never saw the silliness there can be in it or the beauty, either. That's the way it was in the rest of our life, too—everything cut and dried, no excitement, no playfulness. It slowly got to where I felt I had to experience something else, or I'd be taking it out on her."

"His family was warm, stable and traditional, and this appealed to me, because my parents had been divorced. But, although I liked the security of marriage to him, I gradually became terribly restless. He's solid and good, but very *flat* in his emotions. He's the only man I've ever wanted to be married to, but after a while things got so stagnant that I couldn't endure it."

Finally, there are a number of middle-class Americans whose inner controls are so weak as to be virtually nonexistent, and who, given suitable opportunities, will be unfaithful without powerful needs. A few of these people could be classified as having personality disorders or developmental defects, but far more of them are psychologically normal. These people are neither unfaithful out of neurotic motives nor out of frustrations and deprivations within marriage; they are simply polygamous persons in a monogamous culture.

Preliminaries to an Affair

Fiction and fantasy often use the meeting with the fascinating stranger as the prelude to the first affair, but in actual fact the first affair is more likely to involve a partner close at hand and well known. One-third of my questionnaire respondents and interviewees had their first—or only—affairs with persons who had been close friends before becoming their lovers, and another quarter to a third with acquaintances. The experience of Neal Gorham is a case in point.

In the fall of 1965, Gorham's firm lost the hotel advertising account that had provided over half his work. This was a serious loss for a small agency, but by January there was a new account in the shop—a large book publisher—and Neal was assigned to it as account executive and writer. The work threw him into almost daily contact with the company's advertising manager, Mary Buchanan. He wrote in his diary:

First met her with her boss, Calvin Prestwick, sales manager: he stolid, aging; she freckled and red-haired, gamine, young; he impervious to humor, she playful, nimble-witted. I was startled to learn that she is his wife; wondered how happy she was with him.

This first conference dealt with the advertising campaign for the spring list. Time was short, and Neal suggested prolonged meetings, including evenings if necessary. Prestwick agreed, but said he was about to leave on a three-week business trip—anyway, Mary handled advertising.

The second session—or was it the third? Mary and I decided to continue into the evening; over to Danny's Hideaway for dinner; we still talked business, but all around us were dating couples, and when I ordered Martinis, I felt as if we, too, were on a date. By the end of dinner our talk had drifted far from book advertising. Mary said softly, "You're quite a sensuous person, aren't you?" A thumping in my chest, my face growing hot. . . . Dangerous business? No; I love Laurie; would never be capable of cheating; no danger . . .

But he had not let himself see how things had changed in his marriage to Laurie, one-time beauty and bit-part actress now beginning to fade; disillusioned with the theater long ago, but now resentful of Neal because she "gave it up for his sake"; once interested in everything he did, now bored by his advertising writing and faintly patronizing about his poetry; once eager to join their bodies at night, now unwilling or at best apathetic. To all of which Neal had adapted himself in one way or another: by his absorption in eight-year-old Robin and six-year-old Billy; by escaping to books or the typewriter for long hours in the study over the garage. He had not let himself see how vulnerable he was; but—

It was the next evening that Mary touched me and spoke that fateful sentence. We had gone back to her office after dinner to work on the juvenile list; the building was chilly, and she suggested we work in her Tudor City apartment, five blocks away, where all was warm and quiet—her husband on the road and stepson Freddy away at prep school. Worked in her dinette, papers spread all over, hands often close. Phoned home; while I was dialing, she, passing by to freshen my drink, touched my neck, for an instant and said, "It's good to have you here." Stab of desire in me. Later, having finished our work, we talked about ourselves for an hour, and I realized that with her I felt unaccountably manly, witty and brilliant. As I was leaving, she looked at me oddly and said, "I'm afraid this is beginning to bother me," and swiftly closed the door between us.

Mary Buchanan: 5 feet 5 and 118 pounds, slim-waisted, small and firm of bosom, trim of ankle; bright brown eyes and lopsided grin in round, lightly freckled face. Thirty-four when Neal met her; A.B., Barnard, 1952; raised a Catholic, still attends mass on holidays, although barred from sacraments because of her marital history: married at 22, divorced at 26; then married her boss, Calvin Prestwick, three and a half years before meeting Neal Gorham.

"I went with Cal for a year before we got married, and the last few months of that year I all but lived with him and his son, Freddy (Cal had insisted on custody as the price of giving his first wife a divorce). I was great with Freddy, and Cal could see me as a good mother, while I saw Cal as a kindly, strong, fatherly lover—just what I wanted, after four years of marriage to an emotional adolescent. After Cal and I got married, he promoted me to advertising manager. We were never the same after that. I was so much better at the book business than he that it was embarrassing; it seemed to him that I was always cutting him down. I found out he wasn't a big strong Daddy at all, but a weak, petulant boy, wanting me to take charge of everything—but angry when I did so. A year or so of warfare, and then truce. Our sexual relationship withered away because my sexual feelings for him faded out, and he hardly ever demanded it. Other than that we got along well enough, and at work I tried hard not to outshine him when anyone was looking.

"Then along came Neal Gorham. He was the first man I'd ever met who bested me intellectually without even trying, and did it lightly and amiably; it made me feel weak inside. He didn't have any idea how appealing he was.

I was astonished to find myself sexually stirred when we worked together. I didn't want an affair, but the feeling kept growing and I couldn't ignore it. I could read him like a book—passionate but inhibited, burning to have me, but scared to make a move. I knew he never would unless I cued him. One night, after some verbal skirmishing, I said on impulse as he was going out the door, 'This is starting to bother me' and shut the door on him fast—but not before I saw the look on his face and knew that I had pushed the right button."

The seemingly innocent persons who have temptation thrust upon them by fate are thus usually not so innocent after all; they have conspired in their own seduction. Even in their first infidelities, many people—perhaps a majority—do not wait passively for temptation to overtake them; they actively cultivate the possible temptations around them, or deliberately seek out special situations that they know will give them the chance to play an active part. Yet even in a relatively unambiguous and safe situation, the neophyte may not clearly recognize his own intention; he may refuse to acknowledge his purpose in pursuing a temptation. Such was the case with Edwin Gottesman.

In the fall of 1965, Gottesman had to visit Philadelphia frequently to promote a suburban shopping center. Late one October afternoon he visited a real estate agent named Hartman, in Upper Darby. In the outer office was a secretary, who told Gottesman he was expected and could go right in. Gottesman told Hartman that he was moving too slowly. Hartman apologized, blaming the weather, his rheumatism and the secretary outside, Jennifer Scott, who was inept but whom he hesitated to fire. Depressed by the recent break-up of her engagement, Hartman said, and deeply in debt for an operation, she had been talking of committing suicide. Gottesman was shocked; he swung around and looked through the glass panel at the girl. She was tall and slender—almost skinny—and had black, shoulder-length hair, loose-hanging and rather untidy. She seemed to be in her early twenties, but sat round-shouldered, as if dejected.

Gottesman and Hartman discussed their business for nearly an hour, then decided to have dinner while finishing up the details. As they emerged from the office, Jennifer Scott was putting on her coat. Gottesman thought she looked lonely, and impulsively invited her to join them.

"At the time I thought of her as a charity case—or let's say I *thought* that's how I thought of her. But at dinner I got to talking about my house and my children and my art collection; I could see that she was impressed, and I played up to her. When I phoned Hartman the next morning, she recognized my voice and was warm and friendly. It made me feel very set up. I talked to Hartman, and as soon as he hung up I dialed back and asked Jennifer to dinner."

She accepted eagerly and agreed to meet Gottesman at a restaurant on Walnut Street. Waiting for her at the bar, he felt excited and a trifle wicked. He glanced at himself in the mirror, thinking that, freshly shaved and in a custom-tailored suit, he wasn't bad-looking after all. Their conversation was a trifle awkward at first, but then they fell into a game of telling each other how dreadful their childhoods had been, each trying to top the other, until they went off into a gale of laughter.

Evidently, she had had a number of involvements with men, though Gottesman couldn't tell how many had included sex. "But I wasn't particularly concerned. She made me feel younger and more interesting than I had ever felt in my life. And even romantic—one night we were walking in the falling snow,

418

in Rittenhouse Square, and she took my hand and put our two hands in my coat pocket; I felt marvelous, I felt *handsome*. That night she waited at the front door of her apartment for me to kiss her good-night, and from then on I always did. But I never got any hint of anything more, and I was afraid to try."

After three months he was offered an important role in a syndicate created to buy a large piece of land in Puerto Rico and build a hotel on it; he decided to spend a three-day weekend there working on the deal. While telling Jennifer about it, he asked her on the spur of the moment whether she'd go with him; she said that she'd love it, and affectionately took his hand and kissed it. Gottesman's heart began pounding, and he fumbled for the top button of her blouse, but she whispered "Let's wait till we get there. It'll be so much more special."

Though Gottesman acted deliberately in continuing to expose himself to temptation, his doing so might never have taken place but for the accident of meeting someone, outside his normal social circles, who appealed to him. But some people consciously go out hunting for temptation. One favorite place in which to look for it is in the cocktail lounge. A recent study by two sociologists report that over 70 percent of the men in one high-caliber cocktail lounge in a West Coast city were married, successful, stable persons looking for a little excitement and sexual variety. The women in the lounge, all unmarried, were seeking companionable, casual sexual liaisons with married, sophisticated men.

When the novice first enters such a setting, he is apt to feel uncomfortable; he isn't sure just how to talk or act, cannot tell whether the women he sees around him are decent or are "hookers," does not know how he looks to them. He may be so unsure of himself that he goes time and again without asking any of the women for dates. He comforts himself by thinking that he is virtuous or choosy. But when the balance tips, and he does make a date, he promptly discards his old self-appraisal and thinks of himself as either daring or charming.

．　．　．　．

BUILDING TO A DECISION

Neal Gorham, too, sensed the danger to his formerly total marriage, and hesitated on the brink; Mary Buchanan, though she had touched things off, had twice sought to have such a marriage, twice failed, and therefore belatedly felt alarm, fearing that an affair would shatter her patchwork relationship with her husband Cal.

The morning after she had said to Neal, "This is beginning to bother me," all he could think of was her parting words, and his fantasies.

Phoned Mary from the office, spilling out warm words—and astonished to hear her begin to cry. She: "I shouldn't have said that last night. I knew what I was doing, and it was wrong. I have no right to endanger my marriage and yours. We mustn't see each other alone." I replied with a torrent of words, pleading, reassuring, adoring. Had no idea I could be like that. Said we mustn't run away from it; we must at least meet for lunch and be open and honest about our feelings, even if we agreed to do nothing more.

She agreed, and at lunch her pinched look slowly yielded; after a while they were holding hands under the table, telling each other how careful they would be not to let this affect their marriages. She said she thought they ought not

419

to sleep together, at least not until they could handle their feelings; he, looking Spartan but feeling unexpectedly relieved, agreed.

They met the following night for dinner, radiant and happy, deceived by their truce into thinking themselves safe. Neal said firmly that they were going to her apartment; he knew what they had agreed, but they had to be in each other's arms for a little while. In her apartment they sat on the couch and kissed, self-consciously and awkwardly at first, but soon eagerly and fervently. They went no further that night. For the next few days they lived with thoughts of each other, often drifting through the hours somnambulant and remote. They spoke on the phone in hushed tones and bought little presents for each other.

Three days later they met again. In her apartment, holding her close, he caressed her; at first she asked him in a whisper not to, but then sighed and yielded to her feelings. Fully dressed, they lay on the sofa in each other's arms for an hour, close and yet making no effort to be closer.

Mary: "For a while, we behaved like two kids, quaking with desire. Neal would have gone further if I'd said the word, but I kept reminding him and myself that we might not be able to control our feelings. But the last night before Cal was due home, we were in bed and I was clinging to him and thinking how good it was to feel so much desire and to know I wasn't really frigid, and all at once I said to myself, 'I don't care. It's bound to be worth it, and I'm only going to have one life.' So I said, 'Take me'. And in a moment there we were. For about five seconds it was wonderful and then, in an instant, I dried up. It hurt me so that I couldn't bear to have him move—I had no desire left, just despair and disgust with myself and rage at my Catholic conscience. But Neal was marvelous; he said we'd be lovers in the full sense sooner or later, and there was no hurry."

How long does it take most husbands and wives, in their first affairs, to proceed from the beginning to the consummation? I know of no statistics other than those I gathered in my questionnaire; the sample is small, but the results are at least suggestive.

In their first (or only) affairs, just over one-fifth of the men had intercourse within one day of beginning the relationship, and one-seventh did so within the first week. Another seventh took between a week and a month, and about one-third, probably experiencing conflicts similar to those we have just observed, took somewhere between one and six months. The rest—just under a third—took anywhere from half a year to several years.

Long-delayed consummation usually involves one or more of these factors: little or no premarital experience; no previous extramarital relationships; strong inhibitions due to religion or familial influences; marriage that is or once was romantic and involved. Half the men I interviewed did not have their first affairs until they had been married at least six years, and a quarter of the men did not begin until after ten years. Women did not delay quite so long; those who became unfaithful tended to do so while they still had their youthful looks.

According to cultural mythology, these same people—conscience-directed, romantic, faithful—first fall deeply in love, then are overcome by urgent physical desire, and so break the marriage vow; according to the cynic, they first feel the physical pull, then convince themselves that they are deeply in love and, having thus ennobled the urge, commit the deed. In all likelihood, most cases fall between these extremes; in people of this type, sexual arousal and caring tend to go together; one creates the other, the other increases the first.

From the outset, both Neal and Mary had felt not only liking for each other but also a concomitant sexual pull. But each of them anticipated the consummation of their love with apprehension, knowing that it would produce major emotional upheavals. One night Neal had driven home in an intoxicated mood, frustrated and yet in high-strung good humor. Laurie was sitting up in bed and reading, and to his own surprise he was glad to see her—he wanted company. She made a pot of hot chocolate and brought it into the bedroom, but before settling down with him to drink it, she went into the bathroom and reappeared with her hair down and smelling faintly of a light cologne. Neal noticed, understood, and felt both excitement and guilt. *Could never have believed it of myself—straight from the arms of my love, and instantly, gladly, unfaithful with my wife! Never hesitated, but rejoiced in the chance. Had a most unoriginal thought: Perhaps a man need not love only one woman and in only one way. Perhaps I could love both, each in a special way; perhaps that was the simple, obvious and overlooked answer.*

Mary, too, had a few difficult days, and for comparable reasons. "Cal came home from his three-week trip and I made a special effort to be friendly, but I couldn't bear the thought of his making love to me. I pleaded a migraine the first night; he didn't say much, but he looked hurt. All I wanted to think about was Neal, and how much I wanted to make love to him completely.

"On Friday morning of that week, at the beginning of the mid-year school vacation, Neal called, very excited. Laurie had suddenly decided to take the children to visit their grandparents in Virginia for a week. Neal said she'd be leaving early Saturday morning, and I should come up by noon. I said, 'What can I tell Cal? And won't your neighbors see me come? And where . . . I mean . . . Neal!—in your own house? Your own bedroom?' I said he should give me some time, and he said, in a frosty tone, 'Take all the time you want,' and hung up.

"That night I phoned Neal at his home. If Laurie had answered, I would have hung up, but Neal took the call. I said, 'If you still want me, I'll be there tomorrow.' He seemed stunned, but then he said, 'Yes, of course I want you, you know how much I want you'."

The next day Mary drove to a gas station and called Neal; Laurie and the children had already left, and he was in a fever of impatience. He gave her instructions, and told her to pull right into his garage; the house was reasonably isolated on its own grounds, but it would be best to have her car out of sight.

After one drink in front of the fire they were kissing each other feverishly. He took her by the hand and led her into the bedroom, where they fell into each other's arms. There was no trouble this time; Mary was intensely excited and responsive.

Neal wrote in his diary: *I might have lived and died, never knowing a woman could be like that in response to me. Her face was wet with tears, she was showering kisses on me. I myself cried out. I said I had never known, never suspected, how it could be; she told me I was a superb lover, had brought her back to life.*

• • • •

People like Neal and Mary approach extramarital sex filled with longing, but harassed by guilt. Because they could rationalize their guilt out of sight, the experience was deeply satisfying. But for many others who cannot resolve their conflicts the first experience may be distressing. The immediate emotional effects of the first extramarital sexual experience are usually mixed. A very few people have only positive reactions to what they have just done, and a few others feel only negative ones; the great majority, however, experience both positive and negative feelings, either intermingled or in alternation. A third of my questionnaire respondents frankly admitted that they felt pride as a result of their first affair, and most said it made them feel happier, younger, or more self-confident. The testimony of my interviewees is emphatic on these points.

"I'd been horribly discouraged about myself; if my husband didn't want me, I wasn't worth wanting. But this made everything look different. I could win a man after all—I was fine."

"I proved to myself that even as a man of forty-five I could still attract a new love, and it gave me a great psychological lift."

"She appreciated me, she valued me, she would do anything I asked. This made me feel like a man again for the first time in many years."

"That first experience made me feel I was something special, a woman worth paying attention to, worth trying to win."

For a large number of people, the increased sense of worth and the heightened self-esteem is linked to specific discoveries about their sexual capacities.

"For years and years my wife would say, 'I don't feel like it tonight,' and when she did agree to it, she hardly ever got worked up. She would tell me that I didn't excite her; it wasn't her fault. Yet here I was with another woman, and my voice, my hands, even the way I smelled, all seemed extremely exciting to her. I was amazed at the intensity of her reactions. I felt ten feet tall."

Women are less prone to react so strongly; nevertheless, some of them speak like this about the sexual awakening that a first affair can produce:

"I was twenty-seven and had never responded all the way. Then this man burst into my life—he was a client of my husband's—and put on a real campaign. He was a playboy and a gambler, and nobody I would ever let myself love, but he excited me. When we finally went to bed, he was very different from my husband—sensuous and ferocious, but at the same time free and natural. I got so wound up it was as if I were losing control and sliding, or being carried away on a current of some kind. And then—it was happening, it *happened!* I started laughing and crying, crying and laughing. I kept thinking, *I'm complete, I'm a normal woman after all.*"

For other people, the ego-reward of the first extramarital act is largely the result of seeing one's self in a romantic role. This is what happened to Edwin Gottesman. He insists that his marriage to Betsy has always been happy; but Jennifer, though inferior to Betsy in intelligence, education and looks, could get Edwin to act in an impulsive, carefree way he had never thought himself capable of. He looked askance at her bare and dirty feet and her heavy eye makeup, he was shocked by her brink-of-disaster finances and her irresponsibility—and found it all irresistible.

His trip to Puerto Rico with her involved deceptions such as he never thought he could carry off. Jennifer, in a holiday mood, was enraptured by the luxury of flying first-class, and by the news that they would be guests on a yacht chartered by Sol, one of the principals in the real-estate deal. To Edwin and Jennifer, the yacht was an exotic pleasure palace. There were four luxuriously furnished staterooms, each with its own bathroom, and a crew of four. After changing into sports clothes, they joined Sol and his girl-of-the-month on deck. Lights twinkled across the dark harbor, and a faint sound of native music floated through the air. Edwin, lying back in a deck chair, the rum punch making his head a little light, his girl, eye-catching in snug pants and deep-cut blouse, was almost overcome by the wonder of it all, by the spectacle of a handsomer, younger and wittier Edwin enjoying a life he had never imagined possible.

After dinner they had a brandy on deck and said their good-nights. What came next seemed right and natural to Edwin. "It wasn't physically overwhelming—just a good time. Afterward we had a couple of drinks and kidded each other about whose fault it was that we had been so slow to go to bed with each other. We did it again, later on. She wasn't nearly as good as Betsy, but it made me feel marvelous anyhow; I was delighted by the *idea* of what I was doing more than by the thing itself."

From my interviews and from indications in other sources I estimate that a quarter to a half of the newly unfaithful feel no intensification of fear or guilt after their initial extramarital experience. Peggy Farrell, who had 30 or 40 extramarital affairs in a seven-year period, enjoyed them all, and found them a continual source of renewal, a sense of worth and repeated proof of her appeal. She remembers her first infidelity this way:

"It was different, it was someone else. I was happy; I thought, 'Peggy, my lass, you've got a reason to feel good when you wake up each morning.'" She smiled. "I suppose that sounds sick—being pleased with myself because I had just managed to cheat on my husband. But that's the way it was."

But others have an abrupt increase of fear or guilt or both. Some, after the mists of passion have cleared, perceive certain unconsidered risks in what they have just done:

"I didn't feel any aftereffects until a couple days later when the phone rang, and my wife answered it and seemed very much puzzled by what the other person was saying. From what I overheard, I could guess it was the girl I had made out with two days earlier. I had told her I was single; I had said I lived with my folks, because I thought that was safe. But she looked up the last name in the phone book and was trying to find me. For the next couple of weeks, I would practically jump out of the chair every time the phone rang. I swore that if I got by with this one I'd never lie to a girl again, or at least I'd do a better job of it."

Any one of a number of things may give rise to such attacks of fear: the arrival in the mail of hard-to-explain promotion literature from a motel just outside the city; the appearance of a tiny rash or vague sensation of discomfort somewhere in the private parts; a delay in the onset of the month's menstrual flow.

Many others suffer physical or emotional ailments caused by conscious or unconscious guilt: these include insomnia, hysterical crying, inability to concentrate, compulsive hand-washing and general depression. In some people the morning-after syndrome leads to a precipitous flight from the adulterous relationship. Even when the experience of extramarital love has been liberating,

423

guilt feelings may create a sense of impending doom—a fantasy of punishment created by the unconscious.

The yacht on which Edwin Gottesman and Jennifer Scott were staying had a telephone plugged into a line on the dock. In the midst of that first marvelous evening on board, Edwin felt that he ought to call home to see if everything was all right. In the morning he phoned from the main saloon while Jennifer was still asleep. Betsy sounded querulous and even suspicious (or so he thought): she asked how things were going, and he fumbled his way through lies about the business deal. When he hung up, he felt even more uneasy. That evening, he, Sol and the two girls were to dine ashore and go to a native nightclub. Before dinner they went to their cabins to dress, and after he and Jennifer had showered, he took her to bed. Then the steward tapped on the door and said there was a call from Bethesda coming through for him in five minutes. Gottesman got an instant headache. He pulled on some clothes and hurried to the main saloon. It was Betsy, of course; she apologized for sounding cranky that morning, said she was feeling unaccountably weepy, and wondered if he had to be away another two whole days.

"I got a very strange feeling that I'd better get home fast or something terrible was going to happen. But what? A fire? Sickness? An automobile accident? My father having a stroke? I could hardly eat dinner. I was a lump at the nightclub, and I slept miserably that night. In the morning I told Sol I would have to work out the rest of the contract details back in Washington, because I had to get back at once. I was leaving within the hour, and had already made a plane reservation. I lied to Jennifer, telling her there was only one available seat on the plane, and she'd have to fly back the next night on her original reservation. Jennifer was disgusted with me. I gave her money for cabs and other expenses, and got out of there. I didn't think she'd ever want to see me again, and I didn't care. I just wanted to get home."

Gottesman did not recognize that guilt feelings had caused his rout; it felt to him like anxiety at having left his family alone and helpless while he was far away, enjoying himself. But, in fact, his conscience was threatening him with punishment for having violated his moral code; he merely projected the punishment outside himself onto persons he held dear. If his relationship to Jennifer had been openly competitive with his relationship to Betsy, he might have been consciously aware of his guilt feelings, but this was not yet the case.

To Neal Gorham, however, it was clear very early in his affair with Mary Buchanan that his feelings for her imperiled his marriage to Laurie; when he suffered morning-after symptoms, he was clearly aware that guilt was causing them. The attack of guilt came about a week after the ecstatic day of consummation. During that week he and Mary talked on the phone every day, but scheduled no business meetings, thinking it safer at this point not to see each other with people present. Mary managed, however, to spend most of one afternoon with him in a hotel room and a whole evening with him in Darien (she told Cal she was having a reunion dinner with two college classmates in Scarsdale). Both meetings were rapturous; not even the *mise-en-scène* of a small hotel room, in the afternoon, could spoil their mood.

Friday night he was alone at home. Laurie phoned to say she'd be leaving Virginia early Sunday morning. She wanted to know if he felt all right; she said he sounded weary or depressed. He protested his perfect health, but realized that he had been cool in his manner.

It was the first alarming indication of something happening to my feelings for Laurie. Poured long drink, reminding myself how much I loved her. Got to thinking about her long drive home, the rainy weather, the sleep-inducing Jersey Turnpike. . . . What would happen to me if she had an accident in which the children escaped unhurt but she died? Almost wept thinking of it; but, of course, it would permit Mary and me—God! Was the whole fantasy a death-wish against Laurie? Unquestionably; I couldn't deny it.

He drank too much, went weaving to bed, and leaped up in cold-sober alarm five minutes later, remembering that he had forgotten to inspect the house for bobby pins, lipstick marked cigarette butts and other clues.

Mary had a similar attack. She started to feel lousy about deceiving Cal, because now the affair was real and had a future that had to be bad for Cal. "I made up lies in order to meet Neal those next two times, but I found I didn't like myself in the role of liar and cheat. Also, I could see that Cal was puzzled, but afraid to challenge me, and I knew that over the past several years I had made him afraid; I can be tough and bitchy, and he had become weaker and more timid than he was when I first met him.

"What bothered me most of all was the realization that although I was hiding the affair from Cal, I was hoping he'd figure it out from the way I was acting and do something rash—throw things, hit me, walk out on me. I didn't want to be responsible for breaking up the marriage; I wanted *him* to be."

*   *   *   *

Emerging Patterns
of Innovative
Behavior in Marriage*

*James W. Ramey***

In previous readings, some of the flaws in traditional marriage and family and the problems it can cause, have been discussed. Alternative approaches to partner formation are being tried by persons of varied ages and social classes some of which have been successful while some have not. Ramey reports on research among these innovators. Sex relations is often a focal point of new family forms but concomitant interests include creating joint living arrangements offering as much freedom as possible for self-actualization plus warm companionship. Ramey first defines various innovative approaches to what he terms pair-bonding. *Then he points out that these forms may be arrayed along two continuna—depth of commitment (how responsive to and responsible for the partner each is), and complexity of the relationship (how deeply involved are the persons with each other). There is some evidence that people move gradually from little involvement and complexity (as might be found in swinging) to more involvement and more complicated relationships (as in group marriage and some communes). The key word to the success of some of these forms appears to be* commitment, *especially in communes. Ramey also suggests that equalitarian relations are more closely related to innovative forms of pair-bonding than to the traditional male-dominant form of marriage. It is theorized that this is because equalitarian relationships are more likely to encourage an atmosphere where each person is able to fulfill his or her complete potential and be an interesting companion as well. Yet the paradox of equality is that it reduces individual freedom to some extent, as each participant must give up something of his living plan to honor the wishes of the other. This is why the most long-lasting communes carefully screen their members—not unlike persons entering traditional marriages in Eastern cultures!*

*Revised version of a paper presented at the Groves Conference on Marriage and the Family, San Juan, Puerto Rico, May 1971. An abbreviated version of this paper appeared in the *Journal of Sex Research,* Vol. 8, No. 1, under the title "Emerging Patterns of Behavior in Marriage: Deviations or Innovations?"

**James W. Ramey, Ed.D., is Director of the Center for the Study of Innovative Life Styles, Box 426, New York City, New York 10956.

The mass media are replete with sensational stories of free loving, swinging, communes, and group marriages; usually implying ruptured standards, moral decay, and threats to the institution of marriage. Moralists point with alarm to one out of four marriages ending in divorce, freely circulating swinger ad magazines, campus orgies, and flourishing communes. Here is their proof that the minions of hell are fast taking over. Fortunately there is another, more positive, explanation for these phenomena. Viewed in the context of diffusion of innovation, we are witnessing the realignment of traditional marital relationship patterns rather than deviations from the norm. As Beigel (1969) indicated, this is a supportive development aimed at reforming monogamous marriage.

Diffusion of innovation refers to the process of change and the generally accepted means of determining which of many possible changes is actually taking place. It has been found that no matter how long a particular practice has been accepted by small groups, such changes do not move into the main stream of society until approximately seven to ten percent of the population adopt them (Pemberton, 1936). Once this level of saturation is reached, general acceptance rapidly follows, so that within a few years the vast majority of people can be expected to accept ideas or activities that may have been the norm for a small percentage of the population for decades. As an example of this kind of change, some women were smoking more than a generation ago, but it was not until World War II that this activity was accepted generally as proper behavior. When acceptance did come, it happened almost overnight—in just less than a decade (Ramey, 1963).

This paper presents a paradigm, or model, for research in the area of evolutionary sexual behavior in marriage. This model serves three purposes. First, it provides a basis for systematic classification of current research on alternative sexual life styles for pair-bonded couples, particularly free love, swinging, communal living, and group marriage. Some of this research will be examined and analysis of this material will be organized in respect to the paradigm. A more critical look will be taken at current research findings and gaps in present research knowledge identified. Second, the paradigm is designed to foster further inquiry, to suggest fruitful lines of endeavor for new research. It should not be conceived as a complete theory of evolutionary marital sexual behavior, but is offered merely as a proposal that ultimately may lead to the development of a useful theory. Third, the model provides marriage partners with a cogent way of conceptualizing their relationship, and hence affords them a guide for analyzing their pair-bond behavior, and evaluating their own degree of commitment and effectiveness as partners in a union of equals.

Before introducing our definitions of the behaviors with which this paper is concerned, the scope of the inquiry will be defined, the point of view from which it is being undertaken, and the limits imposed upon it. Initially an attempt is being made to link together, as part of a composite whole, several types of marital behavior generally considered to be deviant. Reasons will be presented for believing that these behaviors are in fact evolutionary, stemming from two basic changes in our society; the shift toward a "temporary systems" society, and the shift toward regarding women as people with equal rights, privileges and responsibilities, rather than as chattel. We do this as a means of clarifying the growing number of contradictory statements, many of which claim to be based on actual participant-observer experience, with regard to swinging, group marriage, and communes. We hope and believe this approach will help to focus research in the field on the gaps and overlaps that would seem to have the highest payoff potential in increasing our understanding of what is happening. We do not propose to critique and/or relate all of the previous research in the field. It would seem much more important to sketch in the broad picture as we see it, leaving more detailed analysis to later efforts. We hope the sketch will prove sufficiently interesting to tempt others to do likewise.

It seems appropriate to begin with several definitions.

Free love is open-ended sexual seeking and consummating without legal or other commitments of any kind.

Swinging generally involves two or more pair-bonded couples who mutually decide to switch sexual partners or engage in group sex. Singles may be included either through temporary coupling with another individual specifically for the purpose of swinging or as a part of a triadic or larger group sexual experience.

Intimate friendship is an otherwise traditional friendship in which sexual intimacy is considered appropriate behavior.

When individuals agree to make life commitments as members of one particular group, rather than through many different groups, they may constitute a commune. The number of common commitments will vary from commune to commune, the critical number having been reached at the point at which the group sees itself as a commune rather than at some absolute number.

In a group marriage each of three or more participants is pair-bonded with at least two others.

The term pair-bond is used to reduce ambiguity. A pair-bond is a reciprocal primary relationship involving sexual intimacy. A pair-bonded couple see themselves as mates. This is not necessarily the case in a primary relationship which can be one-sided and need not include sexual intimacy. The term pair-bond is preferred rather than married couple for another reason—not all pair-bonded couples are married.

Four basic definitions deal with a range of behavior that is increasingly complex. They are interrelated and often sequential. They stem from the human propensity to become involved in ever more complex relationships, a propensity based on the fact that humans are problem-solving organisms. Today's world is increasingly inundated with evidence that this is so—that man seeks to increase the complexity of his interactions. Toffler (1970) has added a new word to our lexicon—future shock. Yet somehow one of the age-old institutions, marriage, has resisted this trend. Why should this be?

There appear to be two interrelated causes. First is the existence of male dominance in society, with all that it implies. Unequals tend not to form complex relationships. Second, in the past, and indeed in many subcultures and in much of the lower-middle and working class levels of society today, two married persons in a stable and permanent social context need to seek little from each other. Psychological needs are filled in a variety of ways through kin, neighbors, and friendship. Husband and wife literally live in two different worlds. As Bott (1957) pointed out:

Couples in close-knit relational networks maintained a rigid division of labor, were deeply involved in external bonds, and placed little emphasis on shared interests, joint recreation, or a satisfying sexual relationship. Couples in loose-knit networks, on the other hand, show little division of labor, emphasize marital togetherness, and are highly self-concious about child-rearing techniques. The transition from working class to middle-class status and from urban villager to suburban environment tends to bring about a loosening of relational networks and is therefore usually associated with an increase in the intensity and intimacy of the marital bond, and a decrease in marital role differentiation.

Marriage did not change much, over the ages, until the pair-bond was composed of peers. As long as the woman was considered chattel, the relationship was not one of equality. Such terms as "doing wifely duty," "marriage rights," and "exclusivity," literally meant, and for most people still mean, that the pair-bond is male dominate. Little wonder, then, that marriage has so long resisted the universal human urge to intensify the complexity of relationships. Komarovsky (1962) and Babchuck and Bates (1963) have strongly supported the thesis that both husband and wife maintain close relationships with same-sex peers and that the marital relationship tends to be male dominated in both blue-collar (Komarovsky) and lower-middle-class couples (Babchuck and Bates).

It is possible to point to attempts by some, at various times and places, to free marriage to some degree from the restraint of male domination and by thus proclaiming equality of the sexes, to permit the emergence of alternatives to exclusivity in marriage. These efforts always failed or were tolerated only in certain special, small, restricted and segregated groups, because in the larger society women were not yet peers. Bird (1970) shows how, in a patriarchal society, conditions at a physical or economic frontier may, of necessity, produce equality of the sexes, but as soon as the period of consolidation and stability is reached, it becomes a mark of status to keep an idle woman. The emergence of free love in conjunction with revolutionary movements is noted time and again, only to see the return of male-dominated pair-bond exclusivity as soon as the revolution succeeds or fails. Indeed, free love can be considered a revolutionary tool, for it quickly sets apart and isolates the in-group from family and friends, both symbolically and literally.

In this context it is important to understand that "revolutionaries" or dissidents can be political, social, religious, economic, cultural, or a combination of these. Often the combination is called utopian, hippie, or anarchistic without regard to the actual goals or beliefs involved. A few of these people are regarded as "the lunatic fringe" and are tolerated by the larger society because they are amusing and sometimes even productive, especially the cultural radicals such as musicians, artists, or theatrical types. Others have been less tolerated, typically driven out or underground, and often persecuted, no matter what the stripe of their dissident bent. The survival factor in such groups appears to be strong patriarchal and/or religious orientation and considerable structure. Almost invariably they have eased away from sexual experimentation in favor of exclusive male-dominated marriage bonds. This happens in spite of the fact that in theory, at least, any alternative to pair-bond exclusivity could be practiced in a closed group, provided the group was willing to accept joint child-rearing and nurturing responsibility.

Nevertheless, until the society as a whole began to accept the right of the female to be a peer, such excursions into marriage alternatives could only fail. A woman who is dependent on her husband must grant his requests, including the demand for sexual exclusivity, even though she may know that he is not practicing the same exclusivity. If she has no skills to sell, no viable means of support without him, she can hardly demur. An economically emancipated wife is in a much better position to insist on equality because she is self-sufficient, a factor that may also increase her social self-sufficiency. Thus the stage is set for pair-bonding between equal partners, each able to sustain a life outside marriage, so that both enter into a relationship voluntarily on the assumption that the anticipated benefits will be greater than would be available in a non-pair-bonded state. Furthermore, survival of the marriage depends on each continuing to place a higher value on maintaining the pair-bond than on reverting to their previous state. In other words, a continuing relationship depends on each continuing to extend to the other the privileges of "open marriage" in the O'Neill (1972) sense. Osofsky (1971) has characterized this as a form of parity or androgyny where each partner has an equal number of options for roles outside the marriage. Consensual sexual activity outside the pair-bond would be among these options but should not be construed as a determinant characteristic of a pair-bond. The final touch to this new equal status in the pair-bond is female control over conception, for the first time in history. Pregnancy is no longer a viable threat to the female. The advent of the pill has removed the last major physical weapon in the male arsenal.

In the 1950s trends toward increased geographic and career mobility and toward greater social and economic freedom for women began to come together for the emergence of the new life styles in marriage. Academic, professional, and managerial people became increasingly mobile, leading William H. Whyte, Jr. (1956) to write *The Organization Man* and Russell Lynes (1953) to coin the term Upper Bohemian to describe these people. The United States Bureau of the Census pointed out that 20 percent of the population moved to a new location, outside the county in which they had been living, and much of this movement was accounted for by the aforementioned academic, professional, and managerial groups. Riesman, Glazer, and Denny (1955) pointed out that this is an "other directed" society and identified these same types of individuals as typifying the new breed which must be capable of self-restraint while recognizing that groups vary in what is considered desirable and undesirable behavior. As Slater (1968) tells us, they saw the other directed individual as one who must be acutely sensitive and responsive to group norms while recognizing the essential arbitrariness, particularity, and limited relevance of all moral imperatives. Pity the inner directed conformist, therefore, the throwback who was programmed from birth to display a limited range of responses in all situations, regardless of environmental variation, which, while possibly heroic, is excessively simpleminded.

As Slater develops the temporary systems theme, following in the footsteps of Bott, Komarovsky, and others cited earlier, he says:

> Spouses are now asked to be lovers, friends, mutual therapists, in a society which is forcing the marriage bond to become the closest, deepest, most important, and putatively most enduring relationship of one's life. Paradoxi-

430

cally, then, it is increasingly likely to fall short of the emotional demands placed upon it and be dissolved.

The end point of Slater's argument is that people can and must press toward the full exploitation of their talents, since in a truly temporary society, everyone would have to be a generalist, able to step into any role in the group to which he belongs at the moment. This is in marked contrast to the present situation in which the upper bohemians tend to specialize in certain roles (which is one of the reasons they are mobile) both on the job and in social situations. Consequently, each time they move to a new geographic location they must search for groups that need their roles.

It is these several reasons that have caused some of the results in the sexual area of shifting from ritualistically determined marriages based on rights to self-determined ones based on privilege. Highly mobile pair-bonds who are here today and moved tomorrow cannot depend on formal or ritual structure because they are perpetually in a time-bind. They must turn to each other and evolve a much more complex relationship to replace kin, neighbor, and friendship relational structure that is no longer available on a long-term basis. They must also develop means of getting informally "plugged-in" quickly whenever they move. When Lynes coined the upper bohemian label, it was for the purpose of describing just such informal networks, although he did not describe their sexual overtones. It is interesting to find Farson (1969) and Stoller (1970) advocating various forms of intimate networks as a means of dealing with the interpersonal intimacy impoverishment of the isolated nuclear family. It is rather surprising that recognition of the existence of such systems has been so late in coming.

The temporary systems strata is the group in which women are most likely to be treated as peers. This group is augmented by others with sufficient education and exposure to ideas to be strongly influenced by current trends (Gagnon and Simon, 1968; McLuhan and Leonard, 1967; O'Neill and O'Neill, 1970; Ramey, 1972; and Smith and Smith, 1970). Already many of the college age young people have the same attitudes toward peer relationships in the pair bond that exist among some of the better educated upper-middle-class members of the depression generation. A surprising number of people in the general population seem to believe that, indeed, it is the young people who should be blamed for giving birth to the idea that men and women are equals!

The current forays into sexual alternatives to monogamy are seen as attempts to build a more complex network of intimate relationships that can absorb some of the impact of the new-found complexity of the pair-bond by short circuiting the process of developing ancillary relationships in the usual ritualistic manner. It is believed that this occurs for two reasons: (1) because there is not time to go through a long process of finding a group that needs the roles the couple can fill, and (2) because using sexual intimacy as an entry role guarantees the couple that, other things being equal, they can fill the role. Particularly if such ties are to take up the slack of the unavailable kin-neighbor-friendship relational systems, as well as relieve some of the pressure on the newly complex pair-bond interaction, they must begin on a much deeper, more intimate basis than the ties they replace. Both time and emotional press will allow nothing short of this. The relationship must cut through the ritual layers quickly in order to be of any help, and indeed, as Brecher (1969) indicates, the entire courting sequence is often telescoped from several weeks or months to as little as an hour. What better way to insure that this will happen than to attempt to relate in a taboo area? Everyone has had the discouraging experience of pursuing a friendship for many months, only to discover suddenly an emotional block to further progress toward meaningful interaction, which was not apparent when the relationship first began. Usually there is no means of discovering what the other person's taboos will be until one comes up against them. While the assumption that those without sexual taboos will have a minimum of other taboos to intensive interaction on the "gut" level is not a valid one, it seems to hold up well for many people in many situations, perhaps because sexual inhibitions are among the deepest rooted.

Entry into free love or swinging relationships typically takes place from this set of circumstances. A less typical set will be described later. Entry into communes and group marriage sometimes takes place without going through either of these stages, but more typically proceeds from them, especially among the 30 and over age group (Ramey, 1972).

Given the societal conditions that have made it necessary for couples living in a "temporary systems" world to find new ways to function as a couple that are more complex than have been necessary in the past, and given also that women are more likely to be peers at such a societal level than formerly, it does not follow that all couples in this situation will react by becoming involved in one of the alternative life styles under discussion. But these conditions do foster such behavior on the part of some people, and for them it will be a more successful adaptation than for those whose pair-bond is not relationship of peers. It is evident that this behavior is also emulated by others who are neither in the temporary systems strata nor peers in the pair-bond, as well as by a few who may be part of the working-class (Ramey, 1972; Smith and Smith, 1970; Symonds, 1970; Bartell, 1970).

THE MODEL

Much of the confusion in discussions of swinging, communes, and group marriage relates to the difference between committed and uncommitted relationships. For heuristic purposes, this embraces Kanter's (1968) three types of commitment: cathectic, or, commitment to the individual; cognitive, which involves weighing the value of continuing in a group or leaving it; and evaluative, which involves belief in the perceived moral rightness of group ideology.

The following hypotheses are proposed:

1) Non-consensual adultery and swinging are "free love" activites which involve no commitment or minimal commitment.

2) Intimate friendship, evolutionary communes, and group marriage involve considerable individual commitment, and in the case of the communes and group marriage, commitment to the group as well.

3) Swinging may constitute a transitional step between minimal individual commitment and growth of such commitment between spouses.

4) Once husband and wife have begun to experience the joy and satisfaction

of individual growth through joint dialogue and commitment, they may find their new found responsiveness to one another so satisfying that they drop out of swinging.

5) As the marriage takes on more and more aspects of a peer relationship, the couple may consensually agree to increase the complexity of their relationship through the development of intimate friendships with other individuals or couples, through which the sense of commitment to the individual is extended to these significant others.

6) A significant portion (apparently about 50 percent, Ramey 1972) of the couples who become candidates for evolutionary communes or group marriage come from among those who have developed intimate friendships.

7) Group marriage, which combines commitment to the group with multiple pair-bonding among the members of the group, is the most complex form of marriage.

8) These various marriage alternatives can be placed on a continuum that ranges from dyadic marriage with minimal commitment (in which there may be nonconsensual adultery), to swinging, to peer marriage, to intimate friendship, to evolutionary commune, to group marriage.

In general, by commitment we mean a relationship involving dialogue, trust, and responsibility. Within the pair-bond, we accept Kanter's definition of cathectic commitment, i.e., "willingness to accept unlimited liability for."

Neither of these profiles concerns intelligence, income level, or formal education, although it is unusual to find the committed person lacking money or education unless he has deliberately chosen to renounce them. Extreme pictures have been drawn in order to sharpen the contrast. Some people have insight in some areas and not in others, but it is nevertheless possible to clearly distinguish between those who seek to relate to others and those who do not find it possible to do so. This differentiation is necessary to comprehension of the diffusion process to be described, but it should be emphasized that these are normal, average people. Although their religious commitment tends to be low, they range politically from radical to conservative, are better educated than most of the population, and are of high socioeconomic status, so that they hardly fit popular conceptions of deviant individuals. (Smith and Smith, 1971) In fact, one recently completed study employed the MMPI and found the subjects "disgustingly normal" (Twitchell, 1970, as reported by Smith and Smith, 1971).

Figure 1 indicates the relationship between the degree of complexity of the commitment individuals are willing to make and the type of pair-bond relationship one is likely to find them enjoying. The figure reads in one direction only, i.e., not all individuals with deep and complex levels of commitment will necessarily join a group marriage, but individuals in a group marriage can be expected to have such a commitment within their relationship. The pair-bond involving peers is deliberately indicated to be at a level above the zero point on this figure.

The first thing that is apparent from Figure 2 is that free love activities such as affairs, adultery, or swinging are treated differently from intimate friendship, evolutionary communes, or group marriage. Free love is an uncommitted activity (open-ended sexual seeking and consummating without legal or other commitment of any kind) that is widespread among both single and married individuals. It may occur between the marriage partners within some marriages,

FIGURE 1.

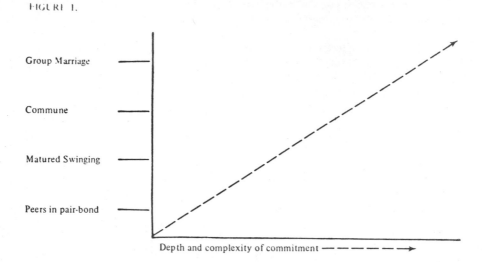

and is the type of activity which Bell and Silvan (1970) refer to as: "activity which usually involves guilt and dishonesty and often does not include any notion of fun and recreation." It is easy to understand that people caught up in the stereotype of high drama, jealousy, and tragic romance as part of their cultural expectation about a one-sided relationship outside the pair-bond would not only not have fun, but would neither invest nor receive enough pleasure from the relationship to make it a joyous exchange rather than a contest-chase, tragic loss, or terrible trap.

There is a crossover between the free love and committed levels through swinging. Most uncommitted couples never manage to get beyond the two stages of swinging, since their activity remains strictly on a free love basis, even though it involves joint activity. Such a couple may decide to legitimize individual nonconsensual activity by becoming jointly involved in swinging. The reverse is also possible.

It is possible, though unlikely, that an uncommitted couple may become temporarily involved in intimate friendship, group marriage, or a commune. Intimate Friendship, which will be more fully defined later, can be distinguished from free love swinging in terms of Martin Buber's (1955) distinction between collectivity and community:

Collectivity is not a binding but a bundling together: individuals packed together, armed and equipped in common, with only as much life from person to person as will enflame the marching step. But community . . . is the being no longer side by side but with one another of a multitude of persons. And this multitude, though it also moves toward one goal, yet experiences everywhere a turning to, a dynamic facing of, the other, a flowing from I to thou . . . collectivity is based on an organized atrophy of personal existence, community on its increase and confirmation in life lived toward one another.

If such involvement results in the removal of blocks to the ability to develop and sustain complex relationships, well and good. In many instances, however, such attempts are indeed temporary and may be disastrous for the intimate friendship group, commune, or group marriage involved. There is a great deal of evidence to support this contention (Kanter, 1970; Nordhoff, 1961). Many reports of communes and group marriages that have not succeeded indicate that the group was unable to deal with uncommitted people who had not been recognized as unable to deal with complex relationships before they were accepted into the group. It is usually easy for the intimate friendship group to simply drop the couple (Palson, 1970; Breedlove, 1964).

Some uncommitted couples manage to grow sufficiently to graduate to either intimate friendship or consensual individual sexual activity that is based on more than simple sex. While this does not seem to be the case for most of the uncommitted, the potential is always present, and it is not unreasonable to con-

FIGURE 2.

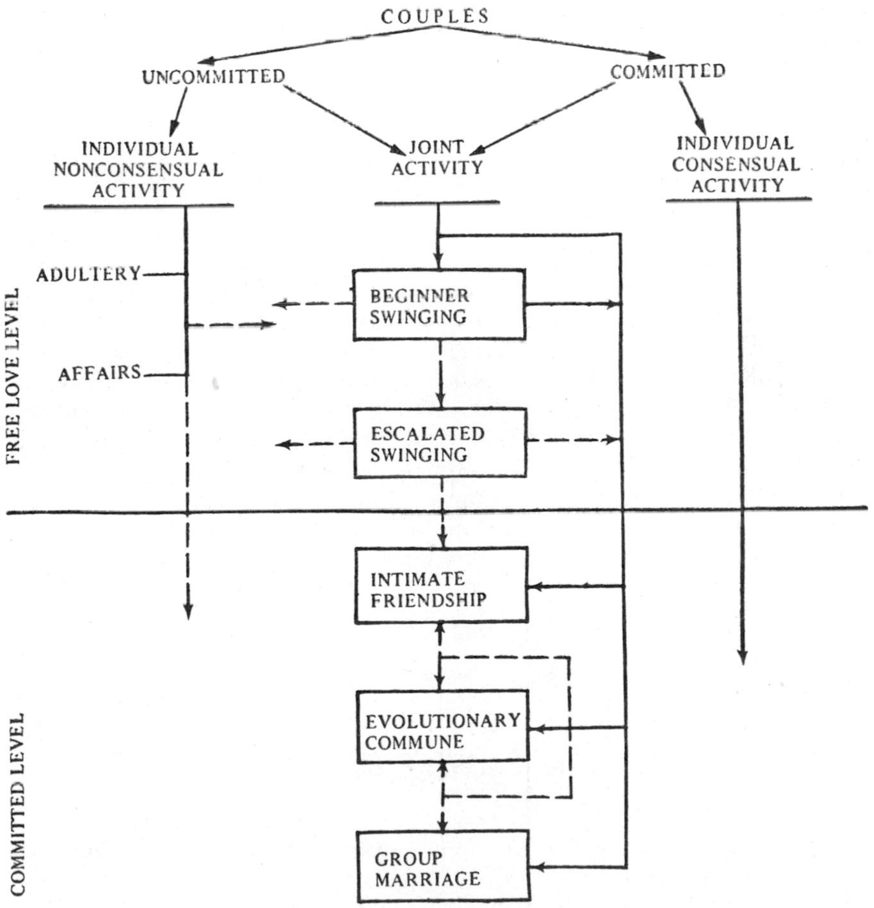

jecture that, given time, greater numbers will move into the ranks of the committed. Considering the degree to which this has occurred over the past two decades, it may not take as long as expected. While most of these people continue to operate at the free love level, many seem to be progressing from individual excursions outside the pair-bond to joint swinging. Even if they never move to a more complex relationship than this, they will have taken a significant and rewarding step toward ability to relate in their marriage, for the one spontaneous response interviewers frequently hear is the vast improvement experienced in ability to talk to one another, not only about sexual matters, but in general (Brecher, 1969; Denfield and Gordon, 1970; O'Neill and O'Neill, 1970; Palson, 1970; Smith and Smith, 1970).

Turning to the "committed" side of Figure 2, one finds that in a union of equals, both persons are free to explore, on a consensual basis, any and all forms of complex relationship that seem interesting. In the O'Neills' terms (1972), this activity can be termed open marriage. Those who practice open marriage often develop intimate friendships. Some couples begin moving toward more complex experiences in this manner and progress to making multiple life commitments through the same group (generally identified as a commune) or to the most complex type of marital commitment—establishing more than one pair-bond simultaneously (group marriage). Other couples skip the intimate friendship stage and move directly into the communal or group marriage stage. How many will ultimately be satisfied to relate at which level is not known.

Since there are so many new recruits swelling the ranks of swingers, communalists, and group marriages, and there is also constant turnover of those who are interested but uncommitted who find such activity too threatening once they have tried it, it is difficult to assess the degree of diffusion as well as the level of complexity at which most people ultimately establish relational system homeostasis. One cannot guess how long the process will take for the average couple.

Sometimes one or more group marriages can be found in a commune. Members of communes and group marriages almost always feel free to swing or engage in individual sexual activity outside the group with complete acceptance of such activity by the group. Also, while many committed couples enter swinging activity at the intimate friendship stage via personal introduction by friends who are already intimate, some go through the beginner stage first, especially if they live in a new neighborhood or a socially limiting situation that forces them to use surreptitious means, such as a blind ad in a swinging magazine, to gain entry into the swinging scene. A few of these people might pass through the escalated stage.

SWINGING

Swinging was defined at the beginning of this paper as:

Generally involving two or more pair-bonded couples who mutually decide to switch sexual partners or engage in group sex. Singles may be included either through temporary coupling with another individual specifically for the purpose of swinging or as part of a triadic or larger group sexual experience.

To say that swinging generally involves two or more pair-bonded couples may seem inexact. Actually, swinging may involve adding only one person of either sex to the pair-bond. Some couples find it easier to relate to one person than to two. Some find it easier to locate one person who is compatible with both than to find another couple in which both the male and the female are compatible with both husband and wife. Singles are thus involved in swinging directly. It is surprising that this point has been disputed by some reporters on the swinging scene (Breedlove, 1964) especially since many acknowledge that it is the swinging singles who sometimes give the total swinging scene a bad name. Palson (1970) points out that:

> To singles, swinging looks more like a long time of sexual encounters with no attempt to form the "proper" kind of personal union, whereas married couples, secure in their own union, can experience friendly sex with others, knowing that they have achieved a permanence with one mate as morality ordains, and that sex with others can actually enhance this relationship.

Many researchers have interviewed threesomes (Smith and Smith, 1970; O'Neill and O'Neill, 1970) and it would appear that more stable threesome relationships exist than any other type. The author recently analyzed ads in four major swinger magazines and found that the second most looked for situation, whether the advertiser was a couple, a single male, or a single female, was "couples or single females desired." The third ranked desire was for "couples or singles, male or female." Bartell (1971) reports similar results.

The implied threat to the pair-bond of accepting a single into a sexual union, even temporarily, obviously is a problem for the committed couple. More couples swing with single women than with single men. In a male dominate pair-bond, the male has little to gain from swinging with a single male along with the threat of direct competition in the swinging situation with his wife, unless he happens to enjoy sexual contacts with other men. Even in the latter case, he would be unlikely to expose such inclinations to his wife. Such activity would be more likely to occur if the couple regarded themselves as equals, free to explore all kinds of multiple sexual relationships.

Some people, especially therapists, have characterized swinging as a male dominated activity that serves largely to actualize male fantasies. The recent report of the President's Commission on Obscenity and Pornography (1970) suggests that women are just as likely to have such fantasies, as did Masters and Johnson (1966). It has often been pointed out that men are most likely to suggest swinging, but less often remarked that men are also most likely to suggest getting out of swinging. This seems to occur because swinging is a great "equalizer" which appears to promote female independence due to the markedly different capacity of the female for prolonged sexual involvement and the new found sense of self-worth that many wives find in swinging. This is one of the reasons that many couples re-evaluate their own pair-bonding relationship as a result of their involvement in swinging.

Our definition emphasized that swinging does not necessarily involve mate switching. It simply may involve participation in group sex, as defined by the O'Neills (1969). Some swingers who will not swing with a single are quite willing to involve singles in group sex, as at a party. Singles may also form temporary couples for the purpose of swinging with those couples who will not swing with a single alone or because the single is a married person whose mate refuses to swing.

Symonds' (1970) definition of swinging suggests that this is an activity involving strangers. Brecher (1969) has pointed out, however, as have others, that the same sort of courtship occurs in swinging that occurs between two people on a conventional date, but that this courtship is more likely to be truncated than among the unmarried.

Swinging has been separated into a beginner and escalated stage, both of which are uncommitted in nature, and are linked to intimate friendship, to which many swingers graduate.

Couples becomee involved in swinging for many reasons. They want to make out, they seek an alternative to clandestine individual adventures outside the pair-bond, they see other people doing it, or one partner, usually the husband, forces the other into it, often to assuage guilt or to "save the marriage." They make an issue of swinging without any emotional involvement, at least at the beginning. "It is just a sex thing."

The committed couple, by contrast, becomes involved in intimate friendship because they wish to expand their already joyous relationship by joint investment in other people at the sociosexual level, in responsive, responsible relationships. In either case, the societal pressures outlined earlier, will have contributed greatly to developing the climate in which such activity can be expected to flourish.

Many committed couples grow into intimate friendship naturally with friends of long standing. Others are introduced into intimate friendships by mutual friends, where the person-to-person interaction is more important than the genital-to-genital interaction and the object is to form relationships that may include sexual involvement as one part of a much larger and more complex level of interaction. The complexity depends on the people involved. Some find that developing a close union with one or a few couples is sufficient to meet their needs. Others form looser bonds with a greater number of people. The nature of the involvement varies much the same way as the involvement between mates in a pair-bond.

How does one become a swinger? An essential ingredient is to see one's self as a swinger. Many people who switch partners occasionally do not consider themselves swingers, although others might say they are. Some, who do not actually swing, like to believe they are swingers although they would not be so classified by others. Many "would be" swingers try it once and decide it is not for them. Little is known about this group because it is hard to identify. No one can even say how large it is. While it may be relatively unimportant, there are those who are keenly interested because they are concerned about just how many swingers there are in the population. The percentage varies with the definition of swinger, not to mention the other difficulties with establishing it. In terms of the diffusion of innovation, however, it is of interest to know whether current saturation is nearing the critical eight to ten percent level at which one would look for rather rapid and overwhelming acceptance of swinging by the society.

Once the decision is made to try swinging, one must find the swingers. Many non-swingers think swinging is a made up fantasy created by journalists and others with something to sell. Many swingers are convinced that the whole world swings! If the potential swinger does not have swingers among his friends that he knows about, he may attempt to seduce friends to try it. This can be risky business, especially in the eyes of the neophyte, who may turn next to public entry points. Apparently only about five percent are forced to do this (Breedlove and Breedlove, 1964), although Bartell claims it is the most used method. A number of public swinging institutions have parallels in the "singles" world, such as swinging bars, socials, magazines, personal columns in underground papers, and the Sexual Freedom League. The uncommitted seem much more likely to use these public entry points than the committed, who find it much easier to relate to others in a meaningful way.

The second swinging stage, called "escalated swinging," is avoided by most swingers. Those who get there may do so because they made a poor decision. It may take some time for the uncommitted couple to arrive at this decision. She may begin to feel like a prostitute. He may become impotent. Having sex with people with whom one does not relate gets stale pretty quickly, for most people.

Some people drop out at this point, deciding that swinging is not for them after all. Others realize that they must invest in people if swinging is to continue to have meaning for them. These people may graduate to intimate friendship. The sharing of intimacy not only has been working on them as a couple, it has also given them a bridge to other people. A few make the third choice—they escalate. They restore potency by upping the ante, experimenting with more and more "way out" behavior. Ultimately this path must form a closed loop for such escalation cannot be continued indefinitely. Eventually they must drop out or begin to relate to people as people and not as sex objects.

Swingers do not appear to handle their swinging relationships on a different basis than other friendships. On the contrary, it would appear that most swinging couples simply add swinging to the list of criteria they use for selecting friends, just as the "sailing crowd" and the "mah jong" group choose most of their friends from among those who share this common interest. Reports that swingers compartmentalize swinging apart from the otherwise ordinary lives appear to confuse the common tendency of some swingers to hide swinging from their business associates or others in "straight society" with having two "social worlds." Time constraints alone would argue against this. As Paul Goodman said in a recent interview (1971):

> In the instances where I have been able to make a contact I have almost invariably found a friend and in many of these cases these friendships have gone on for 30 or 40 years. Even though they rapidly become non-sexual relationships . . . St. Thomas Aquinas has pointed out the chief use of human sexuality, aside from procreation, is getting to know another person—in other words, you don't love somebody and then have sex with them. You have sex with them and then love them.

439

Many couples indicate that they were quite active when they began swinging, but tapered off as soon as they found people with whom they shared the same norms and standards that they had previously used to select friends. The decision to largely confine their circle of friends to those people, they explain, is because relationships with these people are more honest and open on all levels and not just in relation to swinging. In a significant number of these relationships there is only occasional swinging, or no longer any swinging, and it is not unusual to find that these couples are no longer actively looking for new swinging partners.

No one knows, at this juncture, how many of the uncommitted get beyond the free-love levels we have been discussing. So many newcomers are joining the scene that the issue is quite confused. It may be some time before we can say with any assurance how many of the uncommitted are able ultimately to relate to others well enough to be graduated to the "intimate friendship" classification.

Symonds (1970) classified swingers as either recreational or utopian, whereas Bartell (1969) claimed that the chief characteristic of all couples in his sample was their inherent normality. We believe Symonds may have failed to differentiate between those beginners who constitute the extremist fringe at the lower edge of the spectrum and those swingers who are in academic, professional, and managerial strata and tend to exhibit more of the attributes of her utopians than of her recreationals (Brecher, 1969; Ramey, 1972; O'Neill and O'Neill, 1970). Also there is the possibility that she failed to distinguish between this group and the beginners who are still overwhelmed with the idea of swinging, and even more with relating to people on a more complex level. Most swingers exhibit *some* of the attributes she identifies with recreationals, while few, if any, exhibit all of her utopian attributes and none of the recreational. This may be especially important in California, where knowledge of swinging has permeated many layers of society that are not usually involved in complex pair-bond relationships.

An important distinguishing characteristic of the intimate friendship, commune, or group marriage is the open problem-solving and relating they favor. Carl Rogers said in 1951 that people resist experience which might force them to change through denial or distortion of symbolization. Thus the uncommitted swinger must either drop out or ritualize the swinging experience. Recognizing this, those who wish to help the uncommitted bridge the gap must relax the situation and reduce the threat. As Rogers went on to say:

> The structure and organization of self appears to become more rigid under threat; to relax its boundaries when completely free of threat. Experience which is perceived as inconsistent with the self can only be assimilated if the current organization of self is relaxed and expanded to include it.

The committed appear to recognize this. Their striking emphasis on openness, sensitivity to feelings, and acceptance of differences is not uncharacteristic of some other in-groups where there is a marked perceived difference between the in-group peers and "other" (Ramey 1958).

Observers of the swinging scene have been consistently impressed by the degree to which swingers accept people as they are, allowing them to express their feelings and attitudes freely and non-judgmentally, and operating in a generally democratic manner, treating males and females as peers (Brecher, 1969; Lewis, 1969; Kanter, 1970). The basic rule seems to be responsiveness to the other person's needs and desires; the next most basic: "do your own thing." It is this atmosphere of permissiveness and understanding that provides a situation free of threat in which the beginners can work out their own internal frame of reference and reach responsible interpretations and insights. The resulting self-acceptance generally leads to observable improvement in the individual's interpersonal relations. This fits Roger's thesis well. It also facilitates graduating from swinging to intimate friendship.

COMMUNES

Many people seem to equate commune and intentional community without realizing that a commune is only one of many different types of intentional community. A commune is an expression of the desire to make the dyadic pair-bond a subset of one, rather than many mediating groups between it and the society at large. Most people make life commitments through a number of groups: work groups, play groups, special interest groups, hobby groups, health groups, religious groups, economic groups, social groups, political groups, cultural groups; in fact, as Alexis de Tocqueville is alleged to have said, every time four or five Americans get together they form a new group. The critical point is that most persons do not make a large percentage of their commitments through one single group. Marks (1969) has defined commune in terms of:

Joint or common ownership and function and specfically sharing dining and sleeping quarters.

This definition seems more restrictive than necessary. Huxley (1937) claimed that:

All effective communities are founded upon the principle of unlimited liability. In small groups composed of members personally acquainted with one another, unlimited liability provides a liberal education in responsibility, loyalty, and consideration . . . individual members should possess nothing and everything—nothing as individuals and everything as joint owners of communally held property and communally produced income. Property and income should not be so large as to become ends in themselves, not so small that the entire energies of the community have to be directed to procuring tomorrow's dinner.
At all times and in all places communities have been formed for the purpose of making it possible for their members to live more nearly in accord with the currently accepted religious ideals than could be done "in the world." Such communities have devoted a considerable proportion of their time and

energy to study, to the performance of ceremonial acts of devotion and, in some cases at any rate, to the practice of "spiritual exercises."

From . . . the salient characteristics of past communities we can see what future communities ought to be and do. We see that they should be composed of carefully selected individuals, united in a common belief and by fidelity to a shared ideal. We see that property and income should be held in common and that every member should assume unlimited liability for all other members. We see the disciplinary arrangements may be of various kinds, but that the most educative form of organization is the democratic. We see that it is advisable for communities to undertake practical work in addition to study, devotion and spiritual exercises; and that this practical work should be of a kind which other social agencies, public or private, are either unable or unwilling to perform.

Definitions of commune are difficult to find, but many of the elements are in this lengthy quote from Huxley. In order to encompass all of the groups that claim to be communes today, however, it is necessary to devise a less restrictive definition, such as the one at the beginning of this paper:

When individuals agree to make life commitments as members of one particular group rather than through many different groups they may constitute a commune. The number of common elements will vary from commune to commune, the critical number having been reached at the point at which the group sees itself as a commune rather than at some absolute number.

Although some communes do share dining and/or sleeping quarters and some espouse joint ownership, income, and function, this is not the case for all communes. Quite a few communes have separate quarters, either in a jointly owned apartment building or in separate houses, for example. The type and range of common commitments is such that "being a commune" is almost a state of mind. Some groups, which have many more of the kinds of commitments in common usually associated with communes, call themselves co-ops.

Which of the many life commitments are most commonly met through a commune? Creating goods and services, worshiping in a specific manner, merchandising, purchasing, property ownership and management, farming, travel, educating and rearing children in a specific manner, study, friendship, and social or political action are some of the common attributes of communes. The world has always functioned through interest groups. The most common of these through the ages has been the tribe and its components, the families. One of the most often cited reasons for the current upsurge of interest in communes is the desire to return to an extended family or tribal grouping. Indeed, many communes refer to themselves not by name, but simply as "the family."

It is not by accident that the successful communes, i.e., those that have survived, have not been extended families but have instead been groups with a strong unifying and motivating drive and a strong leader. In many cases this unifying factor has been religious. Currently, in addition to the religious drive, there is a substantial number of successful communes built around the desire to optimize coping capacity in a quasi-capitalistic society; i.e., these are people

442

who establish a commune in order to do better that which they are already doing well.

There are three major varieties of communes and one trial variety. They can be classified as the religious communes which have existed in America since 1680, if not earlier; the utopian communes, and the new breed of evolutionary communes mentioned above. What distinguishes this latter group is that they are not about to drop out of or attempt to change the existing society. They simply seek to increase their ability to work effectively within the system. The fourth type of commune is the student commune, which will be handled in a separate section because of its two unique characteristics—it is temporary and it is a learning situation.

Religious communes have enjoyed the highest survival rate among all United States communes, probably due to their strong patriarchal, highly structured, and fervently goal-directed orientation. Although some have loosened up a bit over the years, others have survived with little change. The most successful group, the Hutterites, have grown from three original colonies in 1874 to over 170 colonies today, each averaging about 150 members. Most of these groups are in the provinces of Alberta, Saskatchewan, and Manitoba, Canada, but approximately 50 colonies are scattered through South Dakota and Montana. A religious group of more recent origin, the Bruderhof, came from Germany to the United States in the 1950s, by way of England and Paraguay because of persecution that began in the 1930s. Already the original settlement in Rifton, New York, has spawned two other groups, one in Connecticut and the other in Pennsylvania. Religious communes are not the concern of this paper but for those who wish to pursue the subject, see Carden, 1969; Hostetler, 1968; Krippner and Fersh, 1970; Nordhoff, 1961; Kanter, 1970; and Redekop, 1969.

The utopian communes have suffered unreasonably at the hands of the press. Many are unjustifiably called "hippie communes" while others actually fit this designation. The most successful of these new "drop out" groups are highly structured, centering around the leadership of strong charismatic individuals, or deliberately submerging leadership in a consensual format that seeks to elevate all group members to the level of "generalist." Some groups have strong political overtones, either in the revolutionary sense or in terms of complete withdrawal from society. These are the back-to-the-land, organic food, vegetarian, hand-labor groups who typically seek to become completely self-sustaining without recourse to the rest of society. Still other groups are "do your own thing—when the spirit moves you" groups. Some of these are heavily involved in the drug culture. Most utopian groups espouse the values of rural living although few of them are found in the country.

Just as the religious communes cluster at the highly structured end of a continuum, so do many of the utopian communes cluster at the unstructured end of the continuum, but the failure rate is extremely high among these groups. Other utopian groups can be found at points on the continuum, and many of them seem to be slowly migrating toward the more highly structured end. All of the utopian groups located in the country labor under the handicap of high visibility, which makes survival especially difficult in the light of sensational headlines in the mass media. A significant recent development among the utopians is the emergence of collectives of communes. There are at least a dozen of these collectives already and more are being set up all the time. Free Vermont, for example, is a collective of sixteen communes which already sponsors

443

a number of joint projects, such as a children's commune, a traveling medical test service, and a peak-load work-sharing system. The Powelton Village Association of Communes in Philadelphia, which includes 30 communes, operates a flourishing food purchasing co-op, a baby-sitting service, and a "free garage" for fixing communal automobiles at cost. They are now considering alternative ways of dealing with banks and insurance companies, and setting up a car pool. As in the case of religious communes, the focus of this paper is elsewhere and the reader is directed, for further information, to Collier, 1969; Houriet, 1969; Hine, 1953; Kriyanada, 1969; *Modern Utopian,* all issues; Kanter, 1970; and Spiro, 1963.

The new breed among communes, those the author calls evolutionary communes, are the least known. They are springing up across metropolitan areas without fanfare, going out of their way to avoid publicity in most cases, realizing that if they attract attention they will be diverted from their goals. There is particular concern about evolutionary communes here because they appear to be the most attractive to those academic, professional, and managerial people who make up the temporary systems strata, assuming they elect to continue working within the present society. Those who do not choose to do so can be expected to go in the direction of the utopian commune rather than the religious commune in almost every case. For this reason, many of the things said about evolutionary communes will also apply to some of the more highly structured utopian communes.

UTOPIAN COMMUNE	EVOLUTIONARY COMMUNE	RELIGIOUS COMMUNE
Drop out orientation	High achievers	Highly structured
Do your own thing	Highly mobile	Authoritarian leader
Loosely organized	Straight jobs	Work ethic
Usually subsidized	Upper middle class	Usually self-sustaining
Youth oriented	Opinion leaders	Withdrawn from society
Sometimes revolutionary	Most over 30	Family oriented
Usually short-lived	Many post-children	

While there may be those who are enamored with the back-to-the-land movement, most evolutionary communalists have no intention of abandoning either their careers or their middle-class comforts. The basis for establishing such a commune is the desire of a group of committed people to cope with our present-day society in a more successful manner than they can manage as couples or individuals. This coping can take many forms, depending on the particular group. The desire to provide better schooling for their children, to pool resources for investment, shelter, purchasing, and to provide access to luxuries otherwise unavailable are among the reasons for this movement. One group may be especially concerned about providing the buffer of group security against extended unemployment so that members can be free to stay in a particular geographic area without suffering career setbacks because they refuse to move physically in order to move up the career ladder. Few couples have sufficient resources of their own to take a chance on waiting, perhaps for several months, until an appropriate job can be found in the same city. A related concern in many groups is the desire to provide educational opportunities for group members or their children that are beyond the resources of a single couple.

The most basic reason for becoming involved in an evolutionary commune, however, is the desire to expand the complexity of interrelationships beyond the possibilities inherent in the pair-bond itself. In the widest sense, the key term is propinquity, for communal living makes possible a person-to-person intimacy on both sexual and non-sexual levels that goes far beyond even the most closely knit intimate friendship group. It simply is not possible to sustain the same level of interaction among intimate friends that one has in the pair-bond unless members of the group are in close proximity to one another much of the time. The level of interaction falls short of multiple pair-bonds (in most cases), however. While group marriages have been found in communes, most communalists are not yet ready to go so far as to consider themselves married to several people at once. The size of most communes argues against such intimacy, if the "readiness state" of the members does not, for evolutionary communes range in size from ten to 130 individuals.

As mentioned earlier, man is a problem-solving organism, happiest when he is solving problems of an ever-increasing degree of complexity. It is at the level of commune or group marriage that one most often hears couples speak about the joy of interrelating on a more complex basis. They speak with excitement and animation about personal growth in the shared context of a group larger than two, which seems to provide a different and more stimulating "critical mass" for personal development, often in directions the couple do not share in common and therefore cannot develop on their own.

An overriding external factor that may contribute to the predisposition of many people toward more complex interrelationships is the current swing of family life to its lowest common denominator—the barely viable nuclear family. Leaving aside the political and economic forces that have promoted this move, the lack of viability remains sadly evident, since the "norm" of working father, housekeeping mother, and children actually exists in less than fifty percent of American families. The vast majority of Americans have had personal experience with the sense of aloneness that comes with growing up in or being a marriage partner in a nuclear family that must cope alone with the vicissitudes of life. Many know the burden of life in a nuclear family that proved not to be viable, and became "less than the norm"—a single-parent family or a two-working-parent family. Childless couples or couples with grown children also experience great difficulty when problems threaten the viability of the family. The extended family is "remembered" as a less vulnerable life style for the family because the larger size of the group made it more viable. Communes and group marriages are seen as a way of moving back toward that more viable group size and doing so, moreover, with *chosen* individuals.

Before discussing evolutionary communes further, two important points about communes in general must be made: first, with respect to how they get established, and second, with regard to how they handle sexual intimacy.

Some communes are started with almost no preplanning or attention to the basic questions that should be answered in order to avoid almost certain failure. This is the case especially with so called "hippie communes," where the word of the day is "Action! Let it all hang loose and it will all come together." This kind of simple faith in miracles is pathetically common and the communes that begin this way are almost certainly doomed to failure. Others engage in

445

talk marathons that may go on for months, without ever discussing the basic questions that must be resolved, or without resolving them. Again, the end result is usually failure. The religious commune groups usually seem to avoid this problem because they are typically led by a strong man who makes all the decisions and will not brook dissension and because they are united in religious fervor, i.e., the strong leader is expressing God's will. The evolutionary communes are most likely to have approached the decision to establish a commune by establishing a consensual process for working through structure and process as the first step in moving from being "talkers" to becoming "doers" (Ramey, 1967).

Five distinct types of sexual intimacy prevail in communes, some of which are so destructive that, everything else being equal, the commune is still very likely to fail because of the sexual structure. One of these patterns is celibacy. A commune that practices celibacy can last only one generation unless it is able to attract enough recruits to replace those who die. The Shakers were one such group that did not succeed. Exclusive monogamy is another sexual stance; in most religious communes exclusive monogamy is practiced with extreme prohibitions against the transgressor, who may even be expelled from the group. Free love is sometimes the sexual mode of the commune, but this is less often the case than is generally imagined. Free love groups seem to be very short lived; probably a group that is uncommitted sexually is uncommitted in general and thus unable to sustain the level of cooperation necessary to the survival of a commune. A few communes claim to practice free love on a committed basis, i.e., the group consists of "brothers and sisters" who are all one family and the family takes responsibility jointly for child rearing and nurturing. Since they practice free love only within the group, albeit without pair-bonding, they are enjoying the best of two worlds. Their responsibility is to the group, not to the individual, but they are not a group marriage because no one is pair-bonded. The author knows of at least one such group that has survived for more than two years and appears to be getting stronger. It is too early to speculate about the long-range effects, however, even though one is strongly tempted to draw parallels with the early days of the kibbutzim, many of which began this way.

The most generally practiced intimacy pattern is intimate friendship, especially in the evolutionary commune but also in many utopian communes. Group marriages can sometimes be found in a commune, usually involving three to six individuals out of the total population. A commune that involves both group marriage and intimate friendship is not likely to break up over sexual problems. On the other hand, a commune that includes both exclusive monogamy and any kind of sex outside the pair-bond is a good candidate for trouble (*The Modern Utopian*, all issues). Combinations of exclusive monogamy and free love, exclusive monogamy and group marriage, or celibacy and free love are very unlikely to occur. Swinging or group marriage and celibacy in the same group would seem an unlikely combination, but not necessarily a fatal one, although such combinations would seem to lower the survival factor. The combination of either intimate friendship or group marriage with free love is unlikely, but if it did occur, survival of the group would probably depend either on weeding out the uncommitted or helping them work out their inability to relate to others on a responsible level. Examples of the problems discussed in this paragraph are most numerous in *The Modern Utopian*, Vol. 1, Nos. 1–6; Vol. 2, Nos. 1–6;

Vol. 3, Nos. 1–3; and Vol. 4, Nos. 1–4, which contain many articles about the life and death of communes, written by participants.

The evolutionary commune appears to be a comparatively recent development on the commune scene. It is clearly distinguishable from the utopian commune because its members are not reacting against the system. They come together out of the desire to do better that which they are already doing well. In an economic sense, the lesson of the co-op movement is not lost on these people. But in general, especially if they have already explored the possibilities inherent in intimate friendships, they are aware that there is a tremendous exhilaration in pushing the limits of interaction potential. They know that involvement at higher levels of complexity is more demanding on the individual than staying within the limits of the pair-bond. Also they are aware that it is more rewarding, the degree of pleasure equalling the amount of investment in these relationships. As mentioned earlier, the committed pair-bond does not necessarily go through the transitional or experimental stage of intimate friendship along the route to the more complex communal or group marriage situation. Some couples develop friendships to a degree of interaction that transcends the usual taboos on "gut level" dialogue and makes possible direct exploration of the possibilities inherent in communal sharing of life commitments. This paper has concentrated on the swinging stage of this development because at this time, more people seem to be at this stage of growing into more complex interrelationships than are possible within the exclusive framework of the pair-bond.

GROUP MARRIAGE

Group marriage involves an even greater degree of complexity of interaction than communal living. The Constantines (1971) have defined this type of union admirably. They state:

> A multilateral marriage is one in which three or more people each consider themselves to have a primary relationship with at least two other individuals in the group.

The definition at the beginning of this paper is a restatement of the Constantines' definition which simplifies and clarifies the nature of the relationship.:

> In a group marriage each of the three or more participants is pair-bonded with at least two others.

The term "pair-bond" is more explicit than primary relationship for the reason stated earlier, i.e., pair-bonded individuals are mates.

Group marriage may involve a couple and a single, two couples, two couples and a single, three couples, or three couples and a single. As far as is known to the author, no group marriage consisting of more than seven individuals has been verified as existing, and the likelihood that such a group might exist is doubtful. The addition of one individual greatly increases the number of possible pair-bonds in the group. In a triad, each individual has twice as many pair-bonds as in a dyad. Six pair-bonds are possible in a group of four people, ten are possible in a group of five, fifteen are possible in a group of six, and 21 pair-bonds are possible in a group of seven people. The odds against developing all possible pair-bonds rises rapidly with additional group members, yet a fully developed group marriage would presumably be one in which all possible pair-bonds did in fact exist. Thus adding an eighth person would add seven more possible pair-bonds, for a total of 28. Triads and two-couple group marriages are the most popular types.

The suggestion was made that triads and pentads (Ramey, 1972) should prove more stable than tetrads or hexads because they start out with odd numbers, and indeed, the Constantines have found more triads than any other size group, half of which involved two males and half involved two females. The argument is based on the somewhat negative assumption that couples may decide to form a group marriage on the basis of much less initial "talking-through" than would be likely with odd size groups. This assumption is based on personal knowledge of several group marriages that were started on very short notice and lasted only a few weeks or months. In fact, one of these, involving three couples, began on the basis of three weeks of discussion among couples who were hitherto strangers! One would expect a great amount of soul-searching among three or five people before they entered into a group marriage. Of course one would hope most couples would investigate thoroughly, but with the basic pair-bond relationship to fall back on, this might not occur.

Implicit in any serious discussion of group marriage is an examination of reactions to same-sex pair-bonds. Same-sex pair-bonds are most common among females in group marriages. The Constantines have found same-sex bonds between males both less frequent and much more critical to the success of the marriage. The author also knows of other instances in which incipient development of a male-male relationship broke up the marriage. It would seem relatively safe to say that a group marriage in which everyone is ambisexual will have higher survival potential, all other things being equal, than one involving one or more monosexual individuals.

For some people the idea of being married to two or more individuals at once is overwhelming. But establishing a dyadic marriage involves a "growing together," not a spontaneous happening. The same is true for a group marriage which begins with a set of potentials that are developed fully only over time. To begin, all that is necessary is the assurance that everyone in the group can sustain multiple pair-bonding. This is why the definition specifies that each individual in the group have at least two pair-bonds before the group can be called a group marriage. Many groups that first appear to be group marriages do not meet this qualification, especially in the case of threesomes, in which two people are pair-bonded with the same person, usually of the opposite sex, but not with each other. There are many such relationships and a number of people are led to believe that the number of group marriages in existence is much greater than it really is because they assume these relationships to be group marriages. As a matter of fact, upon confirming such relationships, it would appear that there may be one hundred threesomes for each triad. Such a union might be considered an intermediate step between dyadic marriage and group marriage, but it is clearly two dyadic marriages with one common partner rather than a group marriage.

The complexity of interaction that must be faced upon establishing a commune or group marriage is greater than that faced upon moving from pair-bond exclusivity to intimate friendship. The situation is further complicated by the fact that each group must work out its own ground rules. Premarital courting at the dyadic level occurs within an understood structure that is already well defined by society. Each couple makes major and minor decisions in terms of already internalized givens and expectations about marriage, and what is appropriate and permissible within the framework of marriage. Since society has not proscribed norms, standards, and activities for group marriages or communes, a great deal more preplanning and exploration must be undertaken to work through expectations and structure behavior than is the case upon entering into dyadic marriage.

A representative list of the types of problems that must be dealt with will quickly indicate the magnitude of the task. The following list is not definitive, nor are the decision areas listed in order of importance, since there are matters that each group will have to decide for itself:

Decision-making procedures, group goals, ground rules, "no-no's," intra- and extra-groups sexual relationships, privacy, division of labor, role relationships, careers, relationship with outsiders, degree of visibility, legal jeopardy, dissolution of the group, personal responsibilities outside the group (such as parent support), urban or rural setting, type of shelter, geographic location, children, child-rearing practices, taxes, pooling assets, income, legal structure, education, trial period, etc.

Many decisions can be put off until after the group embarks upon their new adventure, but most of those listed above must be worked out in the planning stage.

Age appears to be a prominent earmark of success in both communes and group marriages. The complexities to be faced are such that personal hang-ups, pair-bond hang-ups, and career hang-ups should have been solved before a couple takes this step, since a tremendous investment of time, effort, and emotional energy will be required to achieve success in the new undertaking. It follows that one would expect to find people over 30 most often involved in a successful group, and indeed, this is the case. In fact, the Constantines have not found a group marriage with participants under this age level still extant, while there is knowledge of only one tetrad in which one individual is 28 and another is 25 and the group is still extant.

The two areas of concern that are most frequently discussed in group marriage, money and the division of labor, are the least worrisome in actual practice. Developing a viable decision-making pattern is much more involved, because consensus takes an inordinate amount of time, and until the group develops the degree of trust necessary to be comfortable with differentiation of function and concomitant delegation of routine decision-making, there will necessarily be many hours spent in deciding as a group. Once sufficient trust has developed to assign functional responsibility, the group will have to consider only major or policy decisions, just as in a dyadic marriage or any other organization. Although a set of ground rules will probably be established initially, they will become less and less important as the marriage develops informal norms, standards, and activities. It has been suggested that a rough measure of the current stability of a group marriage is the degree to which they persist in clinging to the formal rules and contracts set up at the beginning of the marriage.

A trial period of some sort is essential to the success of dyadic marriage, in the eyes of many people. This is an even more important factor in working through the developmental stages of a group marriage, and of a commune as well. This can become a problem if it is not handled on a reasonable basis. A recent advertisement in the *Village Voice* placed by a group of would-be communalists led to the interesting discovery, upon talking to the initiators, that they wished to start the commune with ten couples and that a prerequisite to beginning would be for all the individuals in the group to live with each other for one week in pairs first. A quick count reveals that 190 pairs are involved here, so that for 19 weeks every individual would be separated from his own mate while living with all the others. Yet these people were surprised when the impracticality of this plan was pointed out to them. It had not occurred to them that they were talking about a 19-week project! Nevertheless, however it is arranged, some kind of physical sharing is an important step in the planning stage. Many people handle this trial stage by planning a joint vacation or renting a summer house together. Others may join one of the communal work brigades that are becoming an important part of the utopian rural commune scene. This mechanism not only provides the work brigade with a taste of working together as a communal group but also provides existing farm communes with essential seasonal labor.

It is important to remember that a group marriage is a "hot house" situation, which generates intense pressure on all its members to grow. In such a situation relaxation, quiet time, and personal privacy assume much greater importance than in the dyad. Also, the group marriage should not lose sight of the need to have fun together. The old saw, "the group that plays together stays together" is not far wrong—remembering that pleasure and happiness are major goals of any kind of marriage.

Visibility is a special problem for both communes and group marriages, but particularly for the latter, since in most states, group marriage is not legal. Especially if there are children involved, the marriage is vulnerable to attack on the basis of "contributing to the delinquency of minors" if not on the basis of fornication, adultery, immoral conduct, or operating a bawdy house. How will the group handle interaction with relatives, friends, neighbors, tradesmen, and the like? Will visitors or tourists be allowed, and on what basis? Will the group maintain secrecy about its existence, and how much secrecy? Location will affect the answers to these questions. Rural locations have high visibility; so rural groups must be particularly careful to build bridges to the neighborhood. For example, Franklin Commune in Vermont was "hassled" by all kinds of official and unofficial groups for the first six months of its existence. They assumed that the work ethic of Vermont farmers was best for establishing peaceful coexistence with the community and they devoted much of their energy to this end, which corresponded with their desire to make the farm self-sustaining. Soon these efforts began to pay off. In their second summer they brought in 2700 bales of hay, plus 1300 bales for their neighbors, which they did out of neighborliness and not for pay. This is only one example of their effort to be good neighbors. It is not surprising that they have earned the respect and admiration of their community, which is now willing to "go to bat" for *them* when the need arises.

Groups with children in public school have higher visibility than those with no children in school but there seems to be no pattern of problems associated with this factor. Teachers and other children tend to see and hear what they expect to see and hear rather than the reality (Ramey, 1968).

Perhaps the most deep-rooted difference that can develop in a group marriage regards child rearing. Deciding about parentage is easy, and agreement on having children and on what to do about the children if the marriage breaks up can be settled beforehand. Groups that start with babies or no children find it much easier to work out a joint child-rearing agreement than those who come into the marriage with older children. Not only must the parents work out a mutually agreeable program that is also agreeable to the non-parents, there is also the problem of compatibility and adjustment among the children themselves. Finally, there is the incipient problem, which many swingers avoid, that of deciding how developing children should fit into the sexual interrelationship of the marriage.

Uncommitted swingers almost universally hide their swinging activities from their children (how successfully is a matter of question), whereas many individuals involved in intimate friendships are as open with their children about their inter-family relationships as they are about all other aspects of life. Some of the successful communes (Oneida, for example) initiated the children into full sexual participation in the life of the commune at puberty. This is such a taboo area today that there is little or no data about current practices. Some swinging groups include unmarried teenagers and/or married children and their spouses. The author has heard of at least one group involving a three-generation swinging family. How widespread such practices might be is unknown, since only very recently has it been discussed. The author has knowledge of one group marriage that consisted of a widow, her son and daughter, and their spouses. This group broke up over an incipient sexual relationship between the two males because one was unable to handle the possible implication that he would be deemed homosexual if he allowed the union to develop.

The types of problems we have raised as examples of issues facing a group marriage have had to do largely with the group maintenance aspects of marriage. There is also "goal directedness" to be dealt with. Goals have not been discussed at length here because it is believed that those people who undertake to add a more complex dimension to marriage are not in basic conflict with the goals of marriage as generally espoused by today's society. Offered, therefore, is the following definition of the kinds of behavior desired of members of the intimate friendship group, evolutionary commune, or group marriage:

> Desired behavior, as evidenced in intimate friendship, evolutionary commune, or group marriage member, is behavior that permits and promotes the growth of the group in a shared direction. Growth of the member can be measured in terms of the degree and value of his active participation and demonstration of his capacity to cooperatively assist the group to successful achievement of its goals. Group achievement of goals must be measured by society.

451

Student communes were mentioned earlier in this paper, but not discussed. Whether students call their shared living quarters a crash-pad, a co-op, a nest, a commune, or simply a shared apartment, all these loosely organized coed living arrangements have one thing in common. They are temporary. They afford students an opportunity to experiment with a number of living modes, of varying complexity, with the tacit understanding that they are not making permanent commitments. Under these circumstances, free love, serial monogamy, and group sex can be fully explored without the pressure of value judgments with respect to "success." Casual nudity, brother-sister type non-sexual intimacy, and celibacy all find acceptance in such a setting. Changes in the personnel of the group often lead to dramatic shifts in sexual practices, and the pill makes all of this investigation safe, within a loving, sharing, nonjudgmental setting that permits much freer expression and exploration of relationship potentials than is easily possible in the more structured adult society.

Although this is almost always uncommitted behavior, with respect to the individual, it is most decidedly committed behavior with respect to the group search for a satisfying life style, in terms of equality of the sexes and critical examination of accepted societal marriage standards. These young people can be counted on to form pair-bonds based on equality. With their trial experience in more complex relationships they can be expected to swell the ranks of intimate friendships, evolutionary communes, and group marriages, assuming they decide to cast their lot with existing society and work within existing social structures. This, in turn, should have a major impact on restructuring marriage in the direction of societal sanction of intimate friendship, communes, and group marriage.

REFERENCES

Babchuck, Nicholas and Alan P. Bates. "The Primary Relations of Middle Class Couples: A Study in Male Dominance." *American Sociological Review*, 1963, **28**, 377–84.

Bartell, Gilbert D. Personal conversation reported by Edward M. Brecher in *The Sex Researchers*. Boston: Little, Brown, 1969.

Bartell, Gilbert D. "Group Sex Among the Mid-Americans." *Journal of Sex Research*, 1970, **6**, 113–130.

Bartell, Gilbert D. *Group Sex*. New York: Wyden, 1971.

Beigel, Hugo. "In Defense of Mate Swapping." *Rational Living*, 1969, **4**, 15–16.

Bell, Robert R. and Lillian Silvan. "Swinging: The Sexual Exchange of Marriage Partners." Mimeo. Read at annual meeting, Society for the Study of Social Problems, Washington, D.C. 1970.

Bird, Caroline. *Born Female: The High Cost of Keeping Women Down*. New York: Pocket Books, 1970.

Bott, Elizabeth. *Family and Social Network*. London: Tavistock, 1957.

Brecher, Edward M. *The Sex Researchers*. Boston: Little, Brown, 1969.

Breedlove, William and Jerrye Breedlove. *Swap Clubs*. Los Angeles: Sherbourne Press, 1964.

Buber, Martin. *Between Man and Man*. Boston: Beacon Press, 1955.

Carden, Maren L. *Oneida: Utopian Community to Modern Corporation*. Baltimore: Johns Hopkins, 1969.

Collier, James L. "Communes: Togetherness Sixties Style." *True*, February, 1969.

Constantine, Larry L. and Joan M. Constantine. "Where Is Marriage Going?" *The Futurist* (Spring), 1970a.

Constantine, Larry L. and Joan M. Constantine. "How to Make a Group Marriage." *The Modern Utopian*, 4 (Summer), 1970b.

Constantine, Larry L. and Joan M. Constantine. "Report on Ongoing Research in Group Marriage." Presentation to January meeting, Society for the Scientific Study of Sex, New York, 1971.

Denfeld, Duane and Michael Gordon. "The Sociology of Mate Swapping: Or, the Family that Swings Together Clings Together." *Journal of Sex Research*, 1970, 6, 85–100.

Farson, Richard Evans. *The Future of the Family*. New York: Family Service Association of America, 1969.

Gagnon, John H. and William Simon. *The Sexual Scene*. New York: Aldine, 1970.

Goodman, Paul. Interview with Paul Goodman, *Psychology Today*, 1971, 5, 96.

Heinlein, Robert. *Stranger in a Strange Land*. New York: Avon, 1967.

Hine, Robert V. *California's Utopian Colonies*. San Marino, California: Huntington Library, 1953.

Hostetler, John A. *Amish Society*. Baltimore: Johns Hopkins Press, 1968.

Houriet, Robert. "Life and Death of a Commune Called Oz." *New York Times Magazine*, February 16, 1969.

Huxley, Aldous. *Ends and Means*. Westport, Connecticut: Greenwood, 1937.

Kanter, Rosabeth M. "Communes." *Psychology Today*, 1970, 4, 53–78.

Kanter, Rosabeth M. "Commitment and Social Organization: A Study of Commitment Mechanisms in Utopian Communities." *American Sociological Review*, 1968, 33.

Komarovsky, Mirra. *Blue-Collar Marriage*. New York: Random House, 1962.

Krippner, Stanley and Donald Fersh. "Mystic Communes." *The Modern Utopian*, 1970, 4 (Spring), 4–9. (Research report on 18 hip religious communes supported by Society for Comparative Philosophy)

Kriyananda. *Cooperative Communities*. San Francisco: Ananda Publications, 1969.

Lewis, Richard W. "The Swingers." *Playboy*, 1969, 16, 149–228.

Lynes, Russell. *A Surfeit of Honey*. New York: Harpers, 1953.

Marks, Paul J. *A New Community*. San Diego: Youth Resources, 1969

Masters, William H., and Virginia E. Johnson. *Human Sexual Response*. Boston: Little, Brown and Company, 1966.

McLuhan, Marshall, and George B. Leonard. "The Future of Sex." *Look*, 1967, 31 (July 25).

The Modern Utopian.
       1967 Vol. 1, Nos. 1–6
       1968 Vol. 2, Nos. 1–6
       1969 Vol. 3, Nos. 1–3
       1970 Vol. 4, Nos. 1–4

Nordhoff, Charles. *The Communistic Societies of the United States*. New York: Hillary House, 1961.

O'Neill, George C. and Nena O'Neill. 1969 Personal communication to the author.

O'Neill, George C. and Nena O'Neill. "Patterns in Group Sexual Activity." *Journal of Sex Research* 1960, 6 (May), 101–112.

O'Neill, Nena and George C. O'Neill. *Open Marriage*, New York: Evans, 1972.

Osofsky, Howard and Joy Osofsky. "Androgyny as a Life Style." *Family Coordinator*, 1972, 21.

Palson, Chuck and Rebecca Markle Palson. *Swinging: The Minimizing of Jealousy*. Mimeo. Philadelphia 1970, 20.

Pemberton, H. Earl. "The Curve of Culture." *American Sociological Review*. 1936, 1, 547–556.

President's Commission on Obscenity and Pornography. *The Illustrated Presidential Report of the Commission on Obscenity and Pornography*. San Diego: Greenleaf Classics, 1970.

Ramey, James W. "The Relationship of Peer Group Rating to Certain Individual Perceptions of Personality." *Journal of Experimental Education* 1958, **27.**

Ramey, James W. "Diffusion of a New Technological Innovation." *Health Sciences TV Bulletin* (O. S.) 1968, **4,** 2–3.

Ramey, James W. "Conflict Resolution Through Videotape Simulation." Paper presented at annual meeting, American Psychiatric Association, Detroit, May 1967.

Ramey, James W. "Teaching Medical Students by Videotape Simulation." *Journal of Medical Education* 1968, **48** (January), 55–59.

Ramey, James W. "Group Marriage, Communes, and the Upper Middle Class." (in preparation) 1972.

Redekop, Calvin W. *The Old Colony Mennonites*. Baltimore: Johns Hopkins Press, 1969.

Riesman, David, Nathan Glazer, and Reuel Denney. *The Lonely Crowd*. Garden City, New York: Doubleday, 1955.

Rimmer, Robert H. *The Harrad Experiment*. New York: Bantam, 1967.

Rimmer, Robert H. *Proposition 31*. New York: Signet, 1968.

Rogers, Carl. *Client Centered Therapy*. New York: Houghton Mifflin, 1951.

Rossi, Peter H., W. Eugene Groves, and David Grafstein. *Life Styles and Campus Communities*. Baltimore: Johns Hopkins Press, 1971.

Scheflen, Albert E. "Quasi-Courtship Behavior in Psychotherapy." Monograph. William Alanson White Psychiatric Foundation 28, 1965.

Slater, Philip E. "Some Social Consequences of Temporary Systems." In W. G. Bennis and Philip E. Slater. *The Temporary Society*. New York: Harper and Row, 1968.

Smith, James R. and Lynn G. Smith. "Consenting Adults: An Exploratory Study of the Sexual Freedom Movement." (to be published by Little, Brown in 1971) as discussed with Edward M. Brecher, *The Sex Researchers*. Boston: Little, Brown, 1969.

Smith, James R. and Lynn G. Smith. "Co-Marital Sex and the Sexual Freedom Movement." *Journal of Sex Research* 1970, **6,** 131–142.

Spiro, Melford. *Kibbutz, Venture in Utopia*. New York: Schocken Books, 1963.

Symonds, Carolyn. "The Utopian Aspects of Sexual Mate Swapping." Mimeo. Paper delivered at the annual meeting, Society for the Study of Social Problems, Washington, D. C., September, 1970.

Stoller, Frederick H. "The Intimate Network of Families as a New Structure." In Herbert Otto (Ed.). *The Family in Search of a Future*. New York: Appleton-Century-Crofts, 1970.

Toffler, Alvin. *Future Shock*. New York: Random House, 1970.

Twitchell, Jon. Unpublished research, as reported by Lynn G. Smith, "Co-Marital Sex: The Incorporation of Extra Marital Sex into the Marriage Relationship," paper delivered at 61st annual meeting, American Psychopathological Association, New York, February, 1971.

U. S. News and World Report. "How the Four-day Workweek Is Catching On." March 8, 1971.

Whyte, William H. Jr. *The Organization Man*. New York: Simon and Schuster, 1956.

10

Societal Reactions and Policy Intervention to Changing Family Forms

---

It seems obvious to proponents of more open marriages that in an age when family forms seem to be moving toward abolition of traditional sex role relationships and long-term commitment to partners, society itself will be forced to change to fit the new needs of citizens who refuse to continue to live in more conventional ways. In many cases, discriminatory legislation must be repealed and replaced with laws that regard persons as equal individuals without concern for sex or family form. Also important will be the development or modification of existing human service delivery systems in order that they take into account the needs of persons who no longer can turn to their families for aid, or who, because of their unique family forms, have developed some special types of needs for themselves or their dependents. This is obviously a pioneering area, both in terms of actual policy development and research. As to how the desired legislative or policy changes will affect the individual, the family, or the society, little is yet known. The next decade should be both exciting and problematic as these policy matters are tried, tested, and developed. Many unintended consequences may result. The pressures to change the family may lead society to some of the most profound restructuring it has ever experienced.

Social Policy to Liberate Marriage, the Institution of the Family, and Family Life

Constantina Safilios-Rothschild

Safilios-Rothschild is concerned about equalizing the civil rights of women with those of men, singles and divorced with marrieds, parents with childless couples, homosexuals with heterosexuals, illegitimate children with legitimate, and elderly with the young and middle-aged adult. Put into effect, her proposals would change the entire fabric of traditional legal systems and social expectations; many of the types of discrimination under which people now suffer would be expected to disappear. Despite the development of alternative life-styles, which the author urges be given open acceptance, her major concern is for reform within the traditional nuclear, monogamous family, which will probably continue to be the predominant way in which marital partners live. Its participants can be liberated from traditional sex roles, however, so that husbands and wives can become their own persons rather than living the stereotyped role expectations of society. To make her proposals a reality, Safilios-Rothschild calls for, among other things, passage of the Equal Rights Amendment, drastic revision of standard marriage and family textbooks, as well as more realistic, nonstereotyped media presentations of men, women, and families, plus the extensive use of marriage contracts.

SOCIAL POLICY TO LIBERATE WOMEN AND MEN FROM COMPULSIVE MARRIAGE AND PARENTHOOD

The ongoing process of women's and men's liberation is not compatible with traditional, compulsive marriage and parenthood. Women and men have increasingly more options, including those of remaining single or childless. From

From Constantina Safilios-Rothschild, *Women and Social Policy,* © 1974, pp. 96–120. Adapted by permission of Prentice-Hall, Inc., Englewood Cliffs, New Jersey.

among them they can choose the one that seems to be most palatable and best suited to their personalities, needs, and life styles. The obligations to marry as soon as possible (and to quickly remarry after divorce) and to have children in order to be accorded a certificate of "normalcy" by society and peer groups drastically limit people's freedom to explore and adopt whatever marital or familial style they find most appropriate. Up to now the married status in the United States automatically included one in societal living as a full-fledged member, while single people, especially past a certain age, have been considered unstable, immature, and overall suspect. Many jobs were not formally or informally open to single adults; social circles tended to be closed to them; the American tax system up to 1971 discriminated against them; they could not adopt children; and they were reacted to as a class of people possessing a definite set of undesirable psychological characteristics. Due to the extremely potent social pressure placed upon single people, up to very recently most of them succumbed so that the few who did resist were often in fact "deviant," thus fulfilling the predictions.

There are, however, indications that since the middle 60s there has been a significant increase in the percentage of single people in the United States, especially among people between twenty-five to thirty-five years old; this is due mainly to marriage postponement. There is also some research evidence that in the late 60s and early 70s a considerable number of college students and young adults have been living together in a variety of arrangements and styles, without the legal sanction of marriage, and for varying lengths of time. Actually it seems that, among college students, living together is becoming widely practiced and almost "natural." A recent study showed that 34 percent of junior and senior women and 60 percent of graduate students had experienced cohabitation at least once. These living-together arrangements seem to substitute for early college-age marriages, to provide valuable training for marriage (Macklin, 1972), and to postpone marriage for some years. These trial relationships and living-together arrangements provide them with the opportunity to balance privacy, autonomy, independence, and freedom with social and affective closeness and exclusivity, discovering which combination in what context makes them happiest and most comfortable (Macklin, 1972).

But despite these ongoing changes in the American society, marital status and gender are still very important characteristics of individuals; they determine several aspects of their lives as well as the lives of their offspring. For example, in the United States a married professional woman pays more taxes than a single woman with the same income simply because she is married, especially if her earnings approach those of her husband or are above $10,000. The difference is around $500–1,000 as the wife's income moves from $14,000–16,000 to $18,000–20,000. The implication seems to be that working married women are particularly "deviant" and are penalized by the current tax system when they are successful professionals or business-women competing with men at the high levels! In these cases not only the wives but their husbands are also penalized. These husbands most often file separately (in order to avoid higher bracket taxation) and must pay more tax than single men at the same income level because they are married to "deviant" women. Furthermore, until 1971 married women could benefit from tax deductions for child care only when their income was close to subsistence level, and only divorced mothers could claim such deductions, regardless of income (Bader Ginsburg, 1971). The 1972 tax rules permit adequate deductions when the joint gross income of the couple is under $18,000 and some deductions over this level. While these new tax rules represent an improvement over past rules, they still leave much to be desired since married women going to school, working part-time and going to college, or just working part-time are not permitted any deductions for child care expenses. And finally, a child is still considered illegitimate if his parents were not married when he was born (rather than when he was conceived), and has, therefore, very different social and legal status than a child born in wedlock. Furthermore, a married woman cannot in most states legally establish residence in another city or state than her husband, and so may suffer serious occupational penalties.

• • • •

In order to end all existing legal discrimination on the basis of marital status, a close examination of societal law is necessary. In all aspects the law should treat women and men as independent, legally equal individuals, regardless of their marital status. With such a legal basis, many of the present inequities that, depending upon the individual's sex, sometimes benefit married people and sometimes benefit single people could be rather easily corrected. Only through legal equality can people begin to choose freely the life style that is the most suitable and appropriate for them, rather than selecting the least penalizing option.

Only, for example, when some of the important attractions of marriage for many women cease to exist, such as financial security for the rest of their lives regardless of the outcome of the marriage, will they be able to evaluate their wish to marry more clearly. Only then, will women (and men) be able to refrain from marrying, unless they find some intrinsic value in marriage besides sexual attraction. If a woman knew that her husband's money was primarily his, and that in case of divorce it would still be his, many opportunistic, short-lived marriages would not take place. The individualization of the spouses' income and property throughout marriage and after the dissolution of marriage might be quite instrumental in improving the quality of marital relationships, especially in the elimination of marriages for money. In addition, many divorce complications would be eliminated. More people could divorce without bitterness, and could remain friends.

If women and men knew that children born outside wedlock would not be legally stigmatized and penalized, they might, in many cases, decide against marriage. Tying parenthood to marriage may have contributed more than any other factor to the compulsive marriage habits of Americans, who often marry because they want to have children or because of a premarital pregnancy. Some family studies have shown that women and men seem to be strongly attached to their children even when they are not affectively attached to their spouses, and are disillusioned in their marriage (Cuber and Harroff, 1966). Thus it could well be that the possibility of having one or more children without marriage would free women and men to enjoy parenthood without the entire marriage package, and would help render marriage a more voluntary decision.

At this point, it is interesting to note that in Sweden up to now unmarried (but not married) fathers were discriminated against in separation from the women they were living with, in that they could almost never be granted custody of their children. There a different legal standard was applied to unmarried and married fathers and mothers in the case of divorce. Custody of children was granted according to the best interests of the child rather than automatically to the mother, but only in the case of married couples (*Abstract of Protocol on Justice Department*, 1969). In the United States there is no such legal double standard. All fathers, whether married or unmarried when their children are born, and while they are growing up, cannot live with their children unless they are also living together with the children's mothers, either in marriage or in some living-together arrangement. The only exception is the proven moral or mental unfitness of the mother.

• • • •

Near the center of many American cities small clusters of modern apartment houses have developed that often attract divorced and single men and women who live alone or with other members of the same or opposite sex in a variety of cohabitation styles. These apartment houses are usually located near services, facilities, and a small shopping area; they have swimming pools, tennis courts, child care facilities, and large rooms to rent for parties and receptions. This type of apartment house should multiply, not only in large cities but also in smaller cities and towns. They should be appropriately modified after joint teams of architects, sociologists, and psychologists, who have studied housing arrangements, recreational facilities, common spaces, and other facilitating mechanisms, recommend what conditions encourage and stimulate meaningful interaction between the residents, and what situations encourage the breakdown of social and psychological isolation and loneliness.

Communities, townships, and neighborhoods (for example, the cluster of six to seven apartment houses in the same area) could devise and organize different activities and structures to facilitate the social integration of residents, regardless of sex, marital status, or age. After all, it must not be forgotten that one of the very potent justifications for marriage and parenthood has been to avoid loneliness in old age. The creation, therefore, of a social integration option for older unmarried, widowed, or divorced women and men takes on additional crucial importance. Apartment houses could have a policy of admitting a minimum quota of older persons, especially the unmarried (possibly 20 percent of all residents), and using them in the child care facilities as well as, whenever possible, in other community projects. Older people should always be invited to and encouraged to actively participate in all common recreational gatherings, parties, and other get-togethers. Effective mixing of the generations at the social and affective levels would have a significant impact on people's fears of loneliness and isolation in old age, a presently dreadful reality (not always alleviated by marriage or parenthood). And it would provide older people with some attractive alternatives. The option for true affective, social, and residential integration (regardless of marital status) would tend to be greatly facilitated by changes in occupancy rules that would permit a group of people of different ages and sexes to live together as friends and companions with various affective and sexual commitments. This would mean that leases or ownership of apartments would have to be written to a group of unrelated persons (rather than to a family head) who make a commitment to co-lease or co-own the apartment.

459

Here it must be mentioned that old people in Southern European and Middle Eastern cities like Rome, Athens, or Beirut, in which different generations intermingle socially at dinners, parties, excursions, and other gatherings, enjoy tremendously and are stimulated from these interactions with younger people. Because up to now old people in the United States have been socially isolated and cut off from normal interactions with younger people, they *appear* to prefer interacting with their peers. This preference is actually the result of awkward, uncomfortable interactions with younger people, even their own children, and their inability to go beyond "fictional acceptance." Everyone is "nice" and polite to old people but very few can accept them on an equal basis with everybody else and relate to them individually rather than categorically as "old." Opening the avenues for social interaction and friendships between the old and the young could provide the old, single or married, with enjoyable alternatives to interaction only with their peers or loneliness. New images of the old projected by mass media which portray middle-aged and older women and men as vital, fun-loving people with a sense of humor, relativity, experience, and sound judgment who can be great friends to younger people might also be helpful in breaking through "fictional acceptance."

Societal Acceptance of Childlessness

Liberation for both women and men from compulsive parenthood is another area where new societal attitudes must be encouraged. Some demographers have supported the thesis that when women do in fact have alternative sources of identity that gratify them or give them status, they will cease to opt (not only once but repeatedly) for motherhood as a source of "instant identity" (Blake Davis, 1970). Others have pointed out that it is very true that childbearing and childrearing are the *only* sources of creativity and achievement for women within the confines of the traditional "feminine" role (Wladis Hoffman and Wyatt, 1960). Thus the liberation of women in terms of employment and occupational careers might help women opt for motherhood as a privilege rather than as a duty or as the only possible choice. Liberation from compulsive motherhood will only take place if women become psychologically liberated from "femininity" hangups, and if their occupational options can provide them with considerable rewards and satisfaction.

When women hold demanding, important, responsible, or "masculine"-stereotyped jobs, they will not feel that they have to prove their "femininity" by having several children, as it has been true up to now (Poloma, 1972; Fortney, 1972). The implications of satisfying, rewarding occupations for women's fertililty will become clear-cut and very significant. Free of "femininity" constraints, women's fertility will be influenced by the degree of their commitment to work, that is, by the meaning work has for them; the importance they attach to it in comparison to other activities and commitments; the degree to which they invest time, energy, and emotional involvement in it; and the satisfactions and sense of identity they derive from work. Only in the case of psychologically liberated women, living in a liberated society that provides them with satisfying work options, will the working role become a significantly competitive alternative to motherhood.

460

Furthermore, liberation from compulsive parenthood cannot be achieved for all women and men in the absence of implementation of a broader range of pertinent social policy. First, of course, until a variety of 100 percent safe contraceptives that can be used by all women and men have been developed, different types of "corrective" mechanisms and techniques must be easily available at low cost to all women and men. At present the only type of almost 100 percent safe contraceptive available, the oral pill, cannot be used by all women because of health complications, side effects, as well as fears about potential long-range related problems. Thus a considerable number of women of childbearing age cannot use the oral pill; but even among those who use it some conceptions do occur because of a variety of mistakes in using the pill.

Similarly, women using some kind of an intrauterine device are seldom perfectly protected. Anatomical peculiarities and local inflammations and infections often dictate temporary or permanent removal and other complications. A potentially considerable number of "unwanted" pregnancies must therefore be controlled if women are to be able to choose to become parents. And there is no safe contraceptive that can be used by men. It seems, then, that until a range of safe contraceptives for women and men are developed (so that everyone can find one type that she [he] can use), abortion, on the one hand, and vasectomy, on the other, must be available on demand. Expenses must be covered by all available health schemes, or be free to low-income women who are not covered by health insurance. The repeal of all antiabortion laws by the Supreme Court of the United States on January 22, 1973, represents a landmark in significant social change. The model is now there for other nations to follow.

Much, however, remains to be done in the United States before abortions become accessible to women at all income levels. As things now stand, the cost of an abortion ($250–350) and not covered by health insurance schemes is forbidding to low-income women. Thus the change is not spectacular since upper-middle- and upper-class women have always been able to secure abortions, regardless of the type of prevailing abortion law, by traveling to another country (or more recently to another state within the U.S.) with "liberal" abortion laws, or by paying the exorbitant fees of the few physicians who were willing to perform the operation.[1] The present changes in the American law make abortion widely accessible (but not cheap) to middle-class women but not to low-income women for whom it is still problematic.

It is interesting to note that Russian and most Eastern European women definitely have the right to determine the fate of their own bodies and their reproductive lives. Abortion is granted on demand—in Russia without any explanations or council approval, in the Eastern European countries after relatively easily obtainable bureaucratic approval (Barker, 1972; David, 1970). They are therefore able to effectively opt for childlessness, or for one child, and to accurately control the timing of their childbearing so that it interferes minimally with their other life plans. Liberation in this area is not, however, related to liberation in family life and husband-wife interaction. Russian women, however, can divorce very easily and painlessly when their marriage does not involve children (Barker, 1972).

Men, on the other hand, must also be able to control the outcome of their reproductive behavior—independently of the women involved. There can be a variety of situations and circumstances in which the man does not want a child as the outcome of sexual relations but the woman does. Both are motivated by different sets of wishes, values, and needs. Up to now the man could never implement his preference with a great degree of certainty, and in such disagreements he most often fathered a child. In the current absence, then, of safe contraceptives for men, vasectomy should be readily available to men, and be covered by all health insurance schemes (or free of cost for low-income men), so that they can father only as many children as they want. An important condition, however, for safeguarding the individual rights of women and men (and the privacy of relationships between them) would be granting an abortion or a vasectomy on demand, regardless of marital status and without the consent of anyone else.

• • • •

Current research has shown that spouses in childless marriages are much happier with their marriages than are those who became parents, even when couples married for the same length of time are compared. There is evidence too that the birth of children decreases spouses' satisfaction and happiness with their marriage and their ability to be close and affectionate companions and lovers, especially when their relationship before children had been very close and companionate (Feldman, 1964 and 1969; Rollins and Feldman, 1970). Such findings, however, are not usually integrated in family textbooks because they "go against the grain" and are not compatible with the flowery rhetoric of the guaranteed-instant-motherhood-happiness.

• • • •

Dissemination of findings by a variety of mass media and "experts" would help to break down negative images and beliefs. Television programs in which childless and one-child couples discuss the advantages ensuing from having taken these options could be shown. Childless couples could be presented in movies and soap operas as happy "normal" couples living full, satisfactory lives, who have developed close, warm, vital companionate relationships, and who have no remorse about their decision. The portrayal of the childless couple's old age is of particular importance. Older childless people must escape the label of loneliness and despair, the probability of which they share equally with those who have children. They must be portrayed as happy people who still enjoy the company of each other very much and who are surrounded by friends of all ages. One-child families should be similarly presented. The child should be shown to have a "normal," happy childhood, with the same "normal" experiences as children in larger families.

• • • •

THE MEANING OF THE LIBERATION OF THE INSTITUTION OF THE FAMILY AND FAMILY LIFE

Since it may be less self-evident than in other areas, the meaning of liberation in the context of the family and family life must be carefully elucidated. The institution of the family in its traditional form has come under heavy attack and drastic criticism for restricting and distorting the lives and potential of adults and children, especially of women of all ages (Cooper, 1971; Laing and Esterton, 1971). Hence one goal of liberation is to allow all family members to develop their potential and individual personalities and to find the most satisfactory arrangements and combinations for their needs, rather than to achieve an "ideal," standardized family life model.

• • • •

Liberation of Familial Structure and Organization

A basic, common, and influential assumption made up to now has been that there is *only one* ideal family life model. This model, referred to as the nuclear family, is composed of the father, the mother (married before or during their early twenties), and their three children. The father is a successful breadwinner, and the wife is a devoted mother, housekeeper, and wife. Their happy and love-filled marriage will last throughout life (that is, on the average, about fifty years). This has been the ideal image against which people have had to measure their marriage and its success. Very few deviations were allowed for differences in values, beliefs, and needs. Every woman and man had to fit into the narrow definition of family or face social ostracism, if not more serious occupational sanctions, regardless of her (his) idiosyncratic needs, inclinations, wishes, values, and beliefs. Familial behavior in the past represents a most striking example of boundless conformity. Childless marriages were not even considered families. Extended, one-parent, and dual-career families represented "deviant" types of family constellations. And several women and men and children living together without any legal ties and under a variety of social, affective, and sexual ties and combinations represented Sodom and Gomorrah.

Conformity to one model of "good" family life has been restricting and suffocating. One restriction has been the lack of many marital and familial options, such as remaining single, marrying late, not having children, having children in late twenties, limiting family size to one child, living with compatible and beloved close relatives or friends attached to the nuclear family, maintaining dual-career families, or living in a variety of arrangements with other couples or individuals of both sexes or with one or more members of the same sex. Such options did not exist—even theoretically. Women and men could not even imagine the potential advantages of alternatives, let alone choose them. Women and men were only free to do what they wanted as long as what they wanted fell within the ideal model of "good" family life.

In addition, the economic and social vulnerability of women has discouraged (and is still discouraging) most women from considering family life styles which do not provide them with financial security and legal safeguards. As long as women are not economically and socially liberated, they will not be able to opt for flexible, often short-lived family life styles, perhaps without security, even when such family life styles become more socially acceptable. And unless women become psychologically liberated from "femininity" stereotypes, they will not be able to consider or to opt for singlehood, childlessness, or homosexual relations without feelings of total failure and self-depreciation. Liberation, then, of family

463

structure and organization in this sense entails creation of a society where women and men may opt for different types of family life styles (some of them marital and others nonmarital), and often for several different family life styles at different stages of their lives.

A second serious structural restriction results from some of the so-called ground rules of marriage. According to them, spouses must be the exclusive sources of sexual and affective satisfaction for each other throughout the fifty years of marriage. Even close friendships with members of the opposite sex have been taboo, they might involve potentially threatening intellectual and emotional involvements. One could actually question the extent to which binding and meaningful friendships even with members of the same sex have been tolerated in the past, if these ties involved sets of specific reciprocal commitments beyond ordinary social, recreational exchanges. The range of permitted relationships with other persons than the spouse has been narrow and constricted, and the relationships shallow and superficial.

Furthermore, even the nature of the husband-wife relationship has been by definition restricted, and has not allowed for a real exchange of feelings and the mutual interinfluence that leads to the self-discovery and growth of two individual personalities. Instead, husbands and wives were supposed to blend their personalities—or more accurately the wife was. She was not supposed to have a distinct personality when she married, and was to be shaped and molded according to her husband's values, attitudes, and beliefs to become a mirror image of him (Safilios-Rothschild, 1972a). Also, husbands and wifes were not supposed to have serious disagreements and quarrels, but were instead to want to please each other; to spend most of their free time in each other's company; and to love, cherish, and never try to manipulate each other.

Thus spouses could not have a variety of deep and meaningful relationships with any other person but each other, and even the relationship between them was restricted and made artificial by the proscriptions for expressing feelings (especially negative feelings). The prevailing prescriptions dictated behavior according to sex-stereotyped norms.

Of course, the existence of all the taboos, prescriptions, and proscriptions included in the ground rules of marriage does not mean that spouses have followed them consistently. On the contrary, proscriptions have been honored mostly in being violated. Such breaches have often been functional in making many marriages tolerable and livable for a considerably longer time. They very often have provided the necessary breathing spells for restricted lives and relationships which have bound spouses in marriage. Furthermore, the existence of frequent violations rather clearly indicates that the traditional ground rules regulating the marital relationship tend to be oppressive to and incompatible with the needs of most people. But the fact still remains that people commit infractions of the marital ground rules, even when they do so to be able to have a better relationship with their spouses or to stay in the marriage. Unfaithful spouses, for example, know all the time that, at least according to the rules, they have deviated, and many feel quite guilty over their deviance (Cuber and Harroff, 1965). It seems that this rule-breaking is an area in which behavior has altered before the corresponding attitudes have changed to the same extent. But there is considerable evidence that attitudes are also changing quite drastically and at quite a rapid pace (Cuber and Harroff, 1965; Johnson, 1970;

Mulligan, 1969; Bartell, 1971). It then remains to change the rules and structures so that behavioral options considered "deviant" up to now can become institutionalized, and thus become socially acceptable and stigma-free.

What would these changes entail and what are the facilitating strategies? Legal changes that would treat all men and women equally, regardless of their marital status, nature and mode of cohabitation, and private life style, could considerably diminish a certain degree of social stigma that is still attached to some life styles and living arrangements, such as swinging couples, group marriages, or homosexual couples. Two conditions must change: First, people must be able to create the model of "family life" that suits them the best, as long as all the involved adults consent and are willing to live in such a "family." Second, the particular model of "family life" that one chooses and the involved sexual patterns and arrangements must not in any way reflect on this person's character, or competence.

Legal safeguards should be established so that people living any type of life style are not discriminated against in terms of taxation, housing, occupational opportunities and promotions, active political participation, or legal treatment in case of any type of violation or offense. Also, in order for the lack of discrimination on the basis of marital status and living arrangements to become institutionalized, a new constitutional amendment might be necessary to guarantee the equality of people under the law, regardless of their marital or familial status. Of course, much more resistance is expected to be shown here on the part of many different conservative groups, but it may be important that recommendations be already moving in this direction, if the change is to take place sometime in the not-too-distant future.

• • • •

LIBERATION OF FAMILIAL ROLES AND FAMILY DYNAMICS

This restrictive element of family life is much more closely and directly related to traditional sex stereotypes concerning appropriate roles and behavior for women and men. Women and men, under the influence of prevailing sex stereotypes, have been prevented from playing certain roles and engaging in some behavioral repertories which would earn them the label of "deviance." Of course, in many instances socialization had been so effective that many of these "deviant" behaviors and roles held little appeal, and their unavailability created little discontent in the minds of wives and husbands. But even in cases of most effective socialization, there were at least some sex inappropriate behaviors and role elements that were attractive, or that were actually engaged in, with various ensuing guilt, discomfort, or stigmatization.

It seems, for example, that even in the past only working- and lower-class black and white American (and other Western) fathers restricted their role strictly to the breadwinning function, while many college-educated fathers played, with different degrees of intensity, a variety of affective-expressive roles. Working- and lower-class men in the United States and other Western societies bound by rigid concepts of masculinity cannot openly express love and affection for their children, since such behavior would represent a "flaw" in their tough, inscrutable, and unconquerable facade. College-educated men, however, seem to be more liberated in this area, since they consider expression of love and affection as a very important component of the parental role (Safilios-Rothschild and Georgiopoulos, 1970). In India, however, even middle-class fathers have been reported to be inhibited in establishing a warm and affectionate relationship with their children, but can do so with their grandchildren later on when they are viewed as "asexual" and the sex-related norms no longer apply to them (Gore, 1961; Ross, 1962; Narain, 1969).

But even when American men have been liberated enough to want to be good friends with their children, to interact with them, and to show them love and affection, the mothers have often successfully kept them in a marginal position in their attempt to safeguard the primary importance of the mother-child relationship, a relationship crucial to justifying their existence, indispensability, and identity (Lopata, 1971; Safilios-Rothschild, 1972a). And the mothers' behavior was motivated by their wish to avoid further restriction of the meaningful life options that were available through prevailing sex stereotypes. Of course, it must be noted here that the few studies in which mothers and fathers were separately interviewed report that fathers perceive that they play a much more active and affectively supportive role than their wives are willing to attribute to them (Safilios-Rothschild, 1969). But even so their reported involvement (affectively and time-wise) is most probably greatly influenced by their stereotyped version of the male role in society and the family (Miller, 1972).

The prevailing sex differentiation in marital roles based on sex stereotypes further restricts married women's and men's behavior in that some options cannot be even theoretically considered. Since, for example, the main role of husbands has been the "instrumental" breadwinning role, the option not to work could not be considered as a possibility, even for a short period of time. In addition, the options to work part-time or to work at a less prestigious or less well-paying job in order to have more time to spend with and enjoy their families have also not existed for men. Because the family's social status and standard of living depend upon men, some occupational options that would give them more time and flexibility to enjoy life have not been possible.

And since the main sex-stereotyped roles of women have been those of "housekeeper" and "mother," with the mother role further specified as a twenty-four-hour-a-day job (especially when children are very young), the option to have a continuous career has been unavailable to married women. Consequently, women could not hold important, responsible, prestigious jobs. They could generally only engage in unimportant, low-prestige, low-paid, meaningless, routine work. Thus, women were for the greater part of their lives forced to derive all satisfaction from their marital and familial roles and interactions, a condition that rendered them much more dissatisfied with their marriages and their lives than men (Bernard, 1972), and seemingly contributed to their depressed feelings in middle-age (Bart 1970a and b and 1973). In fact all available research evidence reviewed by Bernard indicates that the married status (versus singlehood) is much more favorable to men's happiness and mental health than to women's (1972). Women can be further frustrated and disappointed by marriage since they have been socialized to have very low aspirations for personal achievement and to achieve vicariously through the successes of their husbands, sons, and to a lesser extent, their brothers (Tangri, 1969; Brinbaum, 1971; Veroff and Feld, 1970; Wladis Hoffman, 1972).

As for men, the option to be "househusband" and father has never existed. And the desire for these options could not be voiced, since it would represent an extreme "deviance" and would tend to be treated as an indication of serious mental disturbance.

● ● ● ●

In addition to exclusion from the above-discussed options for one of the spouses on the basis of sex stereotypes, wives' and husbands' behavior has, on the basis of the same stereotypes, been restricted in many important areas of family dynamics. One very basic type of behavioral restriction running through all aspects of family dynamics is that men must always take initiative, play the most active role, and dominate interaction, while women must follow in a passive, submissive, and supportive role (Polk and Stein, 1972). Any deviation from this pattern has up to now been considered (by sociologists and the spouses themselves) unsatisfactory for both spouses, or even pathological. For example, a Detroit study showed that whenever decision-making was reported to be dominated by women, the same women reported low marital satisfaction. This finding was duly interpreted by the researchers to mean that women who are dominant in familial decision-making have become dominant not by choice but by default, because their husbands were passive and incapable of making decisions and undertaking responsibilities. Therefore, since these women had to "step into the shoes" of their husbands, who did not behave according to the "masculine" norms, they were unhappy with their marriage (Blood and Wolfe, 1960).

● ● ● ●

Finally, the existing sex stereotypes influence the behavior of spouses, and particularly that of husbands, in two important areas of family dynamics: communication and empathy. Thus husbands who feel bound by masculinity norms (as seems to be the case for most working-, lower- and even lower-middle-class American and other Western men) do not feel that they can talk to their wives about anything beyond simple information (Komarovsky, 1967). They cannot express their feelings, their worries, their anxieties, their insecurities, their weaknesses, and fears to their wives because they would lose their "cool" and their rational, brave, tough facade. It would also be more difficult to dominate wives who knew their secrets, their failings, and their anxieties. Communication with wives is kept at a minimal, informative, superficial level, while true communication, whenever (very rarely) it occurs, is only with other men who can "better understand" them and not use the communicated content to manipulate them to undermine their dominant role.

Of course, it must be noted that there are important cross-cultural differences in the extent to which stereotyped masculinity allows depth of communication in feelings, doubts, fears, and emotions with other men. Mediterranean, Middle Eastern, and Latin men tend, much more than American or Western

European men, to communicate inner feelings, anxieties, and emotions to close male friends than to their wives.

However, sometimes these "masculine" husbands from different cultures have "poured out their souls" to their mistresses or prostitute girlfriends, possibly because they were in a different category from the "good" women they married. This differential treatment could be also explained by the fact that they were not afraid to lose their dominant position in this relationship, since by its nature they had the "upper-hand"; that is, they could always sever it. But it may also indicate that men felt the need to have intimate communication with a woman, and they felt freer to do so in a secret, prohibited relationship.

Because of these attitudes, two different worlds were created: the women's world and the men's world. The men's world included the husband and his male friends and confidantes (and eventually his growing sons), and the women's world included the wife, her female relatives, a few female friends and confidantes, and eventually her growing daughters (Komarovsky, 1967). The overlap between the two worlds was minimal and superficial—or solely sexual. The model of separate communication and companionship outlets represents an extreme, but with certain "face-saving" modifications, it holds true even for a considerable number of higher-status and better-educated families.

Another important area of family dynamics in which behavior has been effectively regimented by the prevailing sex stereotypes has been in empathy between spouses. Husbands, due to their "masculine" nature, are not expected to understand the feelings and desires of their wives. Wives, on the contrary, are endowed with "feminine" intuition and are supposed to understand their husbands, even guessing their feelings and desires in order to satisfy them. Husbands do not feel that they have to make any particular effort to understand their wives' feelings, needs, and desires, or to accurately assess how well they satisfy these needs and desires, simply because they are men and can unilaterally expect this type of understanding and empathy without significant reciprocity (Komarovsky, 1967). In many circles, in which the prevailing sex-stereotypes have been quite influential, husbands who were understanding of and sensitive and empathic to their wives' feelings, needs, and desires were often ridiculed as weak, henpecked, and not too "masculine." They were viewed in such negative terms because the implication was that they did not occupy the superior position provided by their maleness, but behaved instead "like women," trying to understand and please their wives instead of dominating them. Thus, men often did not in fact have the option to play socioemotional, expressive roles; they had to restrict themselves to stereotyped "masculine" behavior.

Husbands have had to be powerful and to dominate their wives and children in order to be respected. Even when they were actually unable to dominate or make all decisions, their wives and children had to take all kinds of precautions and use a variety of strategies in order to "save their face." There could never be open admission that somebody else had, in fact, decided or imposed his (her) opinion. Husbands were always to have at least the illusion of power whenever they were unable to have the family power in their hands. This pretense was necessary and functional as long as sex stereotypes influenced familial behavior. Women and men had to pretend in order to maintain the appearance of "normalcy" within the family, the level of marital satisfaction, and the mental health of all family members.

Men also had to manage the family's budget and make all important financial decisions because they are "masculine," even when they performed badly and their wives could have functioned in a much more competent manner. Women, on the other hand, were forbidden to openly assume and exert power. They could only play the power game "underground" by means of "sneaky," "feminine" influence techniques that were hardly satisfactory to their egos since they could never receive and enjoy credit for any victory (Safilios-Rothschild, 1973). In this way both husbands and wives could not use their skills, talents, and inclinations in making the decisions for which they were best suited. The best person did not win in the family power game. Instead, both husbands' and wives' behavior had to be restricted by sex-stereotyped notions of appropriate behavior.

Strategies to Liberate Family Structure and Dynamics

The previous discussion of the meaning of liberation in family structure and dynamics indicates that much of it is closely related to the psychological and social liberation of wives and husbands. During the transitional period, however, and until women and men become quite liberated, some additional, specific strategies would be quite helpful.

A very crucial strategy focuses upon all experts that are in some way related to the family (marriage and family counselors, family life educators, family sociologists, clincial psychologists, psychiatrists, as well as social workers). All such experts who are often called in to help family members in critical moments, or who intervene in family situations without invitation, or who study families and establish norms and models have to be resocialized and helped to become liberated from their own sex-stereotypic notions of familial behavior and modes of interaction. Liberated family counselors, consulting psychologists, and psychiatrists would learn not to try to mend family crises by helping spouses "accept" their sex-stereotyped niche, behavior, and roles. Instead they would help them to express themselves freely within the familial setting, according to their particular needs, talents, wishes, and inclinations, in order to be able to accept each other as independent, valid, and integral personalities. They would try, for example, to help husbands overcome their masculinity "hangups" and feel comfortable, relaxed, and pleased in a wife-dominated relationship, instead of trying to suppress the wife's domination inclinations, needs, and talents as "deviant," undesirable, disturbed behavior. And they would aid wives who wished to assume power to do so without guilt or threat to their femininity. They would try to find ways to help spouses discover what behavioral options would be best suited to each of them, and would try to aid them in increasing the degree of satisfaction they derive from their marriage, as well as from their lives. They would not exclude any option as deviant or inappropriate for a woman or a man, and would not compare the different types of marital relationships to a monolithic "ideal" family model.

But how can such liberation of the family counselors and advisors be achieved? Again, eventually very few strategies will be needed; their training should liberate them. But until all basic textbooks are rewritten, enough liberated research has accumulated, and basic theories have been reconceptualized from a sex-stereotype-free viewpoint, transitional strategies are necessary. The National Institute of Mental Health and other governmental as well as private funding agencies and foundations should establish funding for programs aimed at exactly this type of liberation. Special intensive workshops could be funded throughout the nation for different types of family counselors, psychologists, psychiatrists, and social workers. These workshops, designed and conducted by liberated social scientists and clinicians, would concentrate on different techniques of consciousness-raising and would present problematic cases to be discussed and handled by the participants under the critical evaluation of the instructors. Mental hospitals, state and city psychiatric clinics, welfare units, as well as departments of psychiatry, psychology, and sociology, schools of social work, and family counseling training institutes and centers, could be required to send their staff and students to these workshops as an integral part of their training and specialization.

• • • •

In addition, family textbooks at all levels, particularly those at the high school and undergraduate college level, desperately need "liberation." Those widely used at present are thoroughly permeated by sex stereotypes and are clearly insulting to women. Here the large number of women teaching assistants, part-time teachers, instructors, and assistant professors who teach large undergraduate family courses have considerable consumer power in their hands. By complaining and putting pressure on the publishers of these sexist textbooks, they can "convince" them to contract with liberated women and men family sociologists to write family textbooks. Similarly, students can exert considerable pressure on nonliberated instructors to use liberated textbooks by refusing to read sexist family texts or to register for courses given by professors who assign such materials.

In addition to a new constitutional amendment guaranteeing equality regardless of marital status and family style, in order to provide marital relationships with flexibility and to assure the actualization and social acceptance of all types of "familial" arrangements, two specific social policies are necessary. First, individual marital contracts mutually agreed-upon by those entering a marital relationship must be legalized. This mutually agreed-upon individual marital contract would have to be discussed and deposited with a lawyer, as is presently done with wills, and would be legally binding upon the counter-signing individuals, unless changed by mutual consent. It could include much more than agreements concerning responsibilities toward children, wages to be paid to the spouse(s) undertaking housekeeping activities, type of division of labor, ownership and use of money, property ownership, or contractual duration of marriage. It could contain the ground rules regulating the relationship, as well as the built-in mechanisms for changes, adjustments, and renegotiations. In this way marrying individuals would feel reassured that their relationship was "legally protected," a desirable feeling for some women and men, without any loss of flexibility and power of self-determination. Individuals entering a marital relationship could in fact largely determine their familial lives and the type of relationship they would have with all due legal approval.

• • • •

470

Passage of the Equal Rights Amendment would, of course, require some significant changes in the present family law that would eliminate inequalities in the marriage relationship based upon gender. Thus, women would be able to keep their maiden name, to establish another domicile, if they wished, to manage community property and to establish credit. Furthermore, men would no longer be held legally responsible for financial support; women would be equally responsible. And women would no longer be held legally responsible for providing housekeeping and sexual services to their husbands; men would be just as accountable legally for provision of the same services. The amendment would make many features of liberated persons' marriage contracts more legally binding, although in many cases litigation would be necessary to establish new legal rulings and precedents. Several lawyers have voiced the opinion that the financial contractual arrangements between spouses have a better chance of standing up in court than contractual arrangements affecting personal aspects of the marriage. Probably the most difficult financial agreement to receive legal validation would be the contractual arrangement for providing payment for household services, but even this may have a chance after the Equal Rights Amendment is passed and implemented in the courts (Edmiston, 1972).[2]

• • • •

NOTES

[1]Actually higher income women even in "liberal" nations like Sweden can afford to travel to Poland to have an abortion when their demand for a legal abortion is rejected.

[2]It must be noted, however, that the cost of the services rendered by wives is quite high. In 1972 a British management consultant firm evaluated that a mother of two working overtime for 85 hours per week should be paid by her husband a salary of $192.40 a week ("British Wives Found Worth $192.40 a Week").

11

Summing Up—What Form for the Family of the Future?

Current relationships among men, women, and their children are in turmoil, beset by many pressures. The very process of attempting summation, however, aids us in analyzing the conflicting themes and/or contributing ideologies that have developed in this decade. One thread that runs through many of the readings is that of the increased emphasis on individual self-interest and self-fulfillment. Of course, this ethos runs counter to the traditional family expectation of commitment and responsibility to others, often at the expense of self, which increases dissonance within the family. Another and related theme is that of the desirability of individual freedom from the burdens or restrictions each family member may seek to place upon the other. Attempts to actualize this freedom has resulted in many experimental family forms. However, this very emphasis on reduction of responsibility to others has its antithesis in the need for increased social service aid in areas in which the family was traditionally the effective provider. Obviously, the acceptance of government help is neither individualistic nor independent. However, it is more impersonal than the family, which may be the key to this change. On the other hand, many innovations in family living may indeed aid in fulfilling the current and long-term goals of members. Women's liberation should eventually provide men with more interesting wives and sex partners over the years and women with more personal integrity and satisfaction in life. Relationships between parents and children may be more enjoyable for all concerned when traditional sex role expectations are dropped.

The final discussions presented in this book are drawn from contemporary popular periodicals, inasmuch as social scientists have not produced a definitive survey on the current state of marriage and the family. Each article offers a different perspective on the current state of marriage. Neither should be taken as the final word, but rather as provocative straws in the wind—catalysts for future research. Looked at together, the material in these readings offer both challenge and hope. The challenge lies in that it should be possible to retain some of the traditional strengths of the family to help its own members, as lauded by Novak. The hope is that, at the same time, we can rid ourselves of the less healthy and less helpful aspects of family life. Sullivan's survey report suggests such mediation is indeed being managed by today's young couples. Ideally, this synthesis should result in a family that functions as a haven of security, love, encouragement, and joyous commitment to the development of *all* members. Such an environment would be a happy place for all persons of all ages. Only time will tell if this ideal is possible. One thing seems almost certain, however. People only bother to tinker with the things they think are worth saving. Constant experimentation with family form down through time is indicative of its viability and importance to human welfare. In one form or another, then, the family as an important institution will survive.

The Family Out of Favor

Michael Novak

People who put personal freedom and fulfillment ahead of security and commitment to family appear to be on the increase. According to Novak, they are ignoring the dictum that a good family makes day-to-day life much more satisfactory and fulfilling. Rather than being the enemy of personal development, marriage can be its source and the most fruitful setting. The family gives persons needed roles and a purpose for being. It establishes a unit within which people can easily identify and provides a social mechanism to help overcome identity problems. Novak suggests that the current fear of marriage and family living is the fear of possible failure in spouse relationships or child socialization. On the other hand, these very pitfalls in the family situation can be seen as opportunities for learning. Participation in the institution of marriage may help us remedy our inadequacies and give us an opportunity to work toward improvement. Overcoming marital crises may force us to be the kind of persons we should want to be. Novak reaffirms the importance of the many functions the family performs for its members. He calls for recognition that it is the family—not the state—that is best for socializing new members, looking after the multitudinal minutiae of member needs, and providing emotional security. The family is also the most efficient and least psyche-damaging institution to create political, economic, and educational opportunities for its members. When all members work together to help each other, no other institution functions as successfully as a cradle of survival for infants, youngsters, adolescents, adults, and the elderly.

The courage to marry and raise children presupposes a willingness (presently unfashionable) to grow up

Recently a friend of mine told me the following anecdote. At lunch in a restaurant, he had mentioned that he and his wife intended to have a second child soon. His listener registered the words, stood, and reached out his hand with unmistakable fervor: "You are making a political statement. Congratulations!"

We live in lucky times. So many, so varied, and so aggressive are the anti-family sentiments in our society that brave souls may now have (for the first time in centuries) the pleasure of discovering for themselves the importance of the family. Choosing to have a family used to be uninteresting. It is, today, an act of intelligence and courage. To love family life, to see in family life the most potent moral, intellectual, and political cell in the body politic is to be marked today as a heretic.

Orthodoxy is usually enforced by an economic system. Our own system, postindustrial capitalism, plays an ambivalent role with respect to the family. On the one hand, capitalism demands hard work, competition, sacrifice, saving, and rational decision-making. On the other, it stresses liberty and encourages hedonism.

Now the great corporations (as well as the universities, the political professions, the foundations, the great newspapers and publishing empires, and the film industry) diminish the moral and economic importance of the family. They demand travel and frequent change of residence. Teasing the heart with glittering entertainment and gratifying the demands of ambition, they dissolve attachments and loyalties. Husbands and wives live in isolation from each other. Children of the upwardly mobile are almost as abandoned, emotionally, as the children of the ghetto. The lives of husbands, wives, and children do not mesh, are not engaged, seem merely thrown together. There is enough money. There is too much emotional space. It is easier to leave town than to pretend that one's lives truly matter to each other. (I remember the tenth anniversary party of a foreign office of a major newsmagazine; none of its members was married to his spouse of ten years before). At an advanced stage capitalism imparts enormous centrifugal forces to the souls of those who have most internalized its values; and these forces shear marriages and families apart.

To insist, in the face of such forces, that marriage and family still express our highest moral ideals, is to awaken hostility and opposition. For many, marriage has been a bitter disappointment. They long to be free of it and also of the guilt they feel, a residual guilt which they have put to sleep and do not want awakened. They loathe marriage. They celebrate its demise. Each sign of weakness in the institution exonerates them of personal failure.

Urban industrial life is not designed to assist families. Expressways divide neighborhoods and parishes. Small family bakeries, cheese shops, and candy stores are boarded up. Social engineers plan for sewers, power lines, access roads, but not for the cultural ecology which allows families of different histories and structures to flower and prosper. The workplace is not designed with family needs in mind; neither are working hours.

Yet, clearly, the family is the seedbed of economic skills, money habits, attitudes toward work, and the arts of financial independence. The family is a stronger agency of educational success than the school. The family is a stronger teacher of the religious imagination than the church. Political and social planning in a wise social order begin with the axiom *What strengthens the family strengthens society*. Highly paid, mobile, and restless professionals may disdain the family (having been nurtured by its strengths), but those whom other agencies desert have only one institution in which to find essential nourishment.

The role of a father, a mother, and of children with respect to them, is the absolutely critical center of social force. Even when poverty and disorientation strike, as over the generations they so often do, it is family strength that most defends individuals against alienation, lassitude, or despair. The world around the family is fundamentally unjust. The state and its agents, and the economic system and its agencies, are never fully to be trusted. One could not trust them in Eastern Europe, in Sicily, or in Ireland—and one cannot trust them here. One unforgettable law has been learned painfully through all the oppressions, disasters, and injustices of the last thousand years: *if things go well with the family, life is worth living; when the family falters, life falls apart.*

UNFASHIONABLE FAMILIES

These words, I know, go against the conventional grain. In America, we seem to look to the state for every form of social assistance. Immigrant Jews and Catholics have for fifty years supported progressive legislation in favor of federal social programs: for minimum wage, Social Security, Medicare, civil rights. Yet dignity, for most immigrant peoples, resides first of all in family strength. Along with Southern blacks, Appalachians, Latins, and Indians, most immigrants to America are family people. Indeed, virtually all Americans, outside our professional classes, are family people.

There are, perhaps, radical psychological differences between people who center human life in atomic individuals—in "Do your thing," or "Live your own life," et cetera—and people who center human life in their families. There may be in this world two kinds of people: "individual people" and "family people." Our intellectual class, it seems, celebrates the former constantly, denigrates the latter.

Understandably, to have become a professional means, often enough, to have broken free from the family of one's birth. (How many wounds suffered there!) To have become successful, often enough, leads to the hubris of thinking one can live, now, in paradise, emotionally unfettered, free as the will to power is free.

There are many different traditions, styles, patterns, and emotional laws in different ethnic and regional cultures in America. The Jewish family is not quite like the Italian family; the families of the Scotch-Irish of Appalachia have emotional ties different from those of families from Eastern Europe. The communal families of the South Slavs are not like those of the Japanese. There is not *one* family pattern in America; there are many. All are alike in this, however: they provide such civilization as exists in these United States with its fundamental infusion of nurture, grace, and hope, and they suffer under the attacks of both the media and the economic system. Half the families of the nation have an annual income under $12,500; 90 percent have an income under $22,000. How can a family earning, say, $11,000 a year (too much for scholarship assistance) send three children to college? or care for its elderly?

As for the media, outrageous myths blow breezily about. Everyone says that divorces are multiplying. They are. But the figures hide as much as they reveal. Some 66 percent of all husbands and wives stick together until death do them part. In addition, the death that "parts" a marriage comes far later now than it did in any previous era. Faithful spouses stay together for a longer span of years than ever. For centuries, the average age of death was, for a female, say, thirty-two, and, for a male, thirty-eight. That so many modern marriages carry a far longer span of years with a certain grace is an unprecented tribute to the institution.

Finally, agressive sentiments against marriage are usually expressed today in the name of "freedom," "openness," "play," or "serious commitment to a career." Marriage is pictured as a form of imprisonment, oppression, boredom, and chafing hindrance. Not all these accusations are wrong; but the superstition surrounding them is. Marriage *is* an assault upon the lonely, atomic ego. Marriage is a threat to the solitary individual. Marriage does impose grueling, humbling, baffling, and frustrating responsibilities. Yet if one supposes that precisely such things are the preconditions for all true liberation, marriage is not the enemy of moal development in adults. Quite the opposite.

In our society, of course, there is no need to become an adult. One may remain—one is exhorted daily to remain—a child forever. It is difficult to have acquired a good education, a professional job, and a good salary, without meeting within one's circle of associates not a few adult children. In medieval paintings, children look like miniature adults. In tableaux from life today, adults appear as wrinkled adolescents.

THE SOLITARY SELF

Before one can speak intelligently of marriage, one must discuss the superstition that blocks our vision. We lack the courage nowadays to live by creeds, or to state our doctrines clearly (even to ourselves). Our highest moral principle is flexibility. Guided by sentiments we are embarrassed to put into words, we support them not by argument but by their trendiness.

The central idea of our foggy way of life, however, seems unambiguous enough. It is that life is solitary and brief, and that its aim is self-fulfillment. Next come beliefs in establishing the imperium of the self. Total mastery over one's surroundings, control over the disposition of one's time—these are necessary conditions for self-fulfillment. ("Stand not in my way.") Autonomy we understand to mean protection of our inner kingdom— protection around the self from intrusions of chance, irrationality, necessity, and other persons. ("My self, my castle.") In such a vision of the self, marriage is merely an alliance. It entails as minimal an abridgment of inner privacy as one partner or the other may allow. Children are not a welcome responsibility, for to have children is, plainly, to cease being a child oneself.

For the modern temper, great dreads here arise. Sanity, we think, consists in centering upon the only self one has. Surrender self-control, surrender happiness. And so we keep the other out. We then maintain our belief in our unselfishness by laboring for "humanity"—for women, the oppressed, the Third World, or some other needy group. The solitary self needs distant collectivities to witness to its altruism. It has a passionate need to love humankind. It cannot give itself to a spouse or children.

There is another secret to this aggressive sentiment, dominated as it is by the image of enlightenment. Ask, "Enlightenment from what?" and the family appears: carrier of tradition, habit, prejudice, confinement, darkness. In this view, the seeds of reaction and repression, implanted by the family of one's birth, are ready to sprout as soon as one sets up a family of one's own.

THE GREAT ESCAPE

Theories of liberation, of course, deserve to be studied in the light of flesh, absurdity, and tragedy. There is a pervasive tendency in Western thought, possibly the most profound cultural undercurrent in 3,000 years (compared to it, C. S. Lewis said, the Reformation was a ripple on the ocean), in which liberation is imagined as a breaking of the bonds of finiteness. Salvation comes as liberty of spirit. "Don't fence me in!" The Fall results from commitments that "tie one down," that are not subject to one's own controlling will. One tries to live as angels once were believed to live—soaring, free, unencumbered.

The jading of everyday, the routines of weekdays and weekends, the endless round of humble constraints, are, in this view, the enemies of human liberty.

In democratic and pragmatic societies, the dream of the solitary spirit often transfers itself into a moral assault upon institutions, traditions, loyalties, conventions. The truly moral person is a "free thinker" who treats every stage of life as a cocoon from which a lovely moth struggles to escape the habits of a caterpillar. This fuzzy sentiment names each successive breakaway "growth" and "development." It describes the cumulative process as "liberation."

There is, of course, a rival moral tradition. I do not mean the conventional variant, which holds that fidelity to institutions, laws, conventions, and loyalties is sufficient. The more compelling alternative—call it "realist"—differs from the romantic undercurrent by associating liberation with the concrete toils of involvement with family and/or familial communities. The romantic undercurrent takes as the unit of analysis the atomic individual. The realist alternative takes as the unit of analysis the family. To put it mythologically, "individual people" seek happiness through concentration upon themselves, although perhaps for the sake of service to others. Most television cops, detectives, cowboys, and doctors are of this tribe. The "family people" define themselves through belonging to others: spouse, children, parents, siblings, nieces, cousins, and the rest. For the family people, to be human is to be, so to speak, molecular. I am not solely I. I am husband, father, son, brother, uncle, cousin; I am a family network. Not solitary. On television both *All in the Family* and *Good Times* have as a premise the molecular identity of each character. The dramatic unit is the family.

There is, beyond the simplicities of half-hour television, a gritty realism in family life. Outside the family, we choose our own friends, like-minded folk whose intellectual and cultural passions resemble ours. Inside the family, however, divergent passions, intellections, and frustrations slam and batter us. Families today bring together professions, occupations, social classes, and some-

478

times regional, ethnic, or religious differences. Family life may remain in the United States the last stronghold of genuine cosmopolitanism and harsh, truthful differences.

So much of modern life may be conceived as an effort to make ourselves pure spirits. Our meals are as rationalized and unsensual as mind can make them. We write and speak about sexual activity as though its most crucial element were fantasy. We describe sex as though it were a stage performance, in which the rest of life is as little as possible involved. In the modern era, the abstract has grown in power. Flesh, humble and humbling, has come to be despised.

So it is no surprise that in our age many resistant sentiments should war against marriage and family. Marriage and family are tribute paid to earth, to the tides, cycles, and needs of the body and of bodily persons; to the angularity and difficulties of the individual psyche; to the dirty diapers, dirty dishes, and endless noise and confusion of the household. It is the entire symbolic function of marriage and family to remind us that we come from dust and will return to dust, that we are part of the net of earth and sky, inspirited animals at play for our brief moment on this planet, keeping alive our race. The point of marriage and family is to make us realistic. For it is one of the secrets of the human spirit that we long *not* to be of earth, not to be bound by death, routine, and the drag of our bodies. We long to be other than we are.

A generation ago, the "escape from freedom" was described in terms almost the reverse of those required today. In those days, as writers like Erich Fromm rightly worried, many persons were afraid of risks and responsibilities; many sought shelter in various fixed arrangements: in collectivism, in religion, in family. But dangers to freedom change with the generations. In our own time, the flight most loved is flight from flesh. The restraints Fromm worried about have proven, under the pressures of suburbs, automobiles, jet planes, television, and corporate mobility, all too fragile. Today the atomic individual is as free as a bird. The threat to human liberation today is that the flesh, the embodied psyche, earthy roots, bodily loyalties, will be dismissed with contempt.

The consequence of this freedom is likely to be self-destruction. Whoever nourishes spirit alone must end by the ultimate denial of the flesh. A flaming burst of destruction and death is the image that fascinates us (as in *The Towering Inferno*), that most expresses our drift of soul. For fear of the flesh is fear of death. A love for the concrete and humble gestures of the flesh meant, even in the concentration camps, spiritual survival.

A return to the true conditions of our own humanity will entail a return, on the part at least of a dedicated few, to the disciplines and terrors of marriage and family. Many will resist these disciplines mightily. (Not all, of course, are called to marriage. The single life can have its own disciplines, and celibacy its own terrors. What counts is the governing cultural model. The commitment of "the family people" to the demands of our humanity provides a context within which singleness and even celibacy have a stabilizing strength; and the freedom and dedication of the single, in turn, nourish the family.)

People say of marriage that it is boring, when what they mean is that it terrifies them: too many and too deep are its searing revelations, its angers, its rages, its hates, and its loves. They say of marriage that it is deadening, when what they mean is that it drives us beyond adolescent fantasies and romantic dreams.

They say of children that they are piranhas, eels, brats, snots, when what they mean is that the importance of parents with respect to the future of their children is now known with greater clarity and exactitude than ever before.

Marriage, like every other serious use of one's freedom, is an enormous risk, and one's likelihood of failure is rather high. No tame project, marriage. The raising of children, now that so few die in childbirth or infancy, and now that fate takes so little responsibility out of the hands of affluent and well-educated parents, brings each of us breathtaking vistas of our inadequacy. Fear of freedom—more exactly, fear of taking the consequences—adds enormously to the tide of evasion. The armies of the night find eager recruits.

It is almost impossible to write honestly of marriage and family. Who would like the whole world to know the secret failures known to one's spouse and one's children? We already hate ourselves too much. Given our affluence and our education, we are without excuses. We are obliged by our own vague sentiments of progress and enlightenment to be better spouses, better parents, than our ancestors—than our own parents, or theirs. Suppose we are not? We know we are not. Having contempt for ourselves, we want desperately to blame the institution which places our inadequacy in the brilliant glare of interrogation.

Still, just as marrying and having children have today the force of public political and moral statements, it is necessary to take one's private stand. Being married and having children has impressed on my mind certain lessons, for whose learning I cannot help being grateful. Most are lessons of difficulty and duress. Most of what I am forced to learn about myself is not pleasant.

The quantity of sheer impenetrable selfishness in the human breast (in *my* breast) is a never-failing source of wonderment. I do not want to be disturbed, challenged, troubled. Huge regions of myself belong only to me. Getting used to thinking of life as bicentered, even multicentered, is a struggle of which I had no suspicion when I lived alone. Seeing myself through the unblinking eyes of an intimate, intelligent other, an honest spouse, is humiliating beyond anticipation. Maintaining a familial steadiness whatever the state of my own emotions is a standard by which I stand daily condemned. A rational man, acting as I act? Trying to act fairly to children, each of whom is temperamentally different from myself and from each other, each of whom is at a different stage of perception and aspiration, is far more baffling than anything Harvard prepared me for. (Oh, for the unselfconscious box on the ears used so freely by my ancestors!)

My dignity as a human being depends perhaps more on what sort of husband and parent I am, than on any professional work I am called upon to do. My bonds to them hold me back (and my wife even more) from many sorts of opportunities. And yet these do not feel like bonds. They are, I know, my liberation. They force me to be a different sort of human being, in a way in which I want and need to be forced.

Nothing, in any case, is more poignant and private than one's sense of failing as a father. When my own sense of identity was that of a son, I expected great perfection from my father. Now that I am a father, I have undergone a psychic shift. Blame upon institutions, upon authorities, upon those who carry responsibilities, now seems to me so cheap. Those who fail in their responsibilities have a new claim upon my sympathies. I know the taste of uncertainty. To be a father rather than a son is to learn the inevitability of failure.

It would be a lie, however, to write only of the difficulties of marriage and family, and not of the beauty. The joys are known. The more a man and a woman are in love, the more they imitate the life of husband and wife; long, sweet affairs are the tribute romances pay to matrimony. Quiet pleasures and perceptions flow: the movement of new life within a woman's belly; the total dependence of life upon the generosity and wisdom of its parents; the sense that these poor muscles, nerves, and cells of one's own flesh have recreated a message to the future, carried in relays generation after generation, carried since the dim beginnings. There may not be a "great chain of being." But parents do forge a link in the humble chain of human beings, encircling heirs to ancestors. To hold a new child in one's hands, only ounces heavy, and to feel its helplessness, is to know responsibilities sweet and awesome, to walk within a circle of magic as primitive as humans knew in caves.

But it is not the private pleasures of family life that most need emphasis today. Those who love family life do not begrudge the price paid for their adulthood. What needs elucidation is the political significance of the family. A people whose marriages and families are weak can have no solid institutions.

In intellectual terms, no theme is so neglected in American life and thought. The definition if issues given both by our conservatives and by our liberals is magnetized by two poles only: "the state" and "the individual." Both leave the family out. Emphasis on the family appears to conservatives a constraint upon the state, and to liberals a constraint upon the individual. Our remarkable humanitarianism holds that attention to family weaknesses will stigmatize those who suffer. No concept in the heavens of theory is as ill-starred. Turning toward the family, our minds freeze in their turning.

The time to break taboos in our minds must surely come. Every avenue of research today leads to the family. Do we study educational achievement? nutrition? the development of stable and creative personalities? resistance to delinquency and violence? favorable economic attitudes and skills? unemployment? sex-role identification? political affiliation? intellectual and artistic aspiration? religious seriousness? relations to authority and to dissent? In all these instances, family life is fundamental. A nation's social policies, taken as a whole, are most accurately and profoundly to be engaged by their impact upon the families that make up that nation.

There are three critical points in American political life today at which a more profound consideration of the politics of the family is closer to the essence than in any previous era: among white ethnics (some 70 million); among blacks (some 22 million); and among upper-class "opinion leaders" of all races (perhaps 10 million).

The meaning of Left and Right has, in recent years, come to be defined according to the tastes, interests, and prejudices of the upper 10 percent of the American population, that (roughly) 10 percent that has a four-year college education, an annual income over $20,000; and professional standing, so as to be paid monthly (not weekly), to possess travel privileges and expense accounts, and a considerable degree of control over the conditions of their work. Thus, Left and Right are now defined by culture rather than by economics, by attitudinal issues salient to those whose economic needs are well beyond the level of survival. The governing language of upper-class attitudes, therefore, distorts the true political struggle. The competition between the left and right wings of the upper 10 percent is interesting and important. It hardly begins to touch the restlessness of the bottom 90 percent.

In this context, the true political leanings and energies of "the white ethnics" are consistently misperceived. Richard Hamilton, in *Restraining Myths*, for instance, describes related gross distortions in the conventional wisdom. Suffice it to say that white ethnic voters, traditionally more Democratic than the national average and now more independent, are economic progressives. But in matters touching the family, they are fiercely traditional. The bulwark of conservatism in America is the white Anglo-Saxon Protestant—68 percent for Nixon in 1972; 16 percent for Wallace in 1968 (compared to 7.7 percent of the Catholic vote). Slavic-Americans gave George McGovern 53 percent of their vote in 1972 (down from 80 percent for Lyndon Johnson, and 65 percent for Hubert Humphrey). The white ethnics are becoming increasingly impatient with both Republicans (their traditional opponents) and Democrats (their former allies). Neglect of the politics of the family is the central issue. It is on this issue that "a new majority" will—or will not—be built.

For a thousand years, the family was the one institution the peoples of Eastern and Southern Europe, the Irish, and others could trust. The family constitutes their political, economic, and educational strength. The public schools of the United States failing them, they reached into their families and created an astonishingly successful system of parochial schools. Hardly literate, poor, and diffident peoples, they achieved something of an educational miracle. Economically, the Jews, the Greeks, the Lebanese established one another in as many small businesses as they could open. The Italians, the Poles, the Slovaks, the Croatians gave each other economic help amounting to two or three thousands of dollars a year per family. Cousin Joe did the electrical work; Pete fixed cars; Emil helped paint the house; aunts and uncles and grandparents canned foods, minded the children; fathers in their spare time built playrooms, boats, and other luxuries in the basements of row houses.

The family network was also a political force in precinct, ward, or district. People of the upper classes could pass on to their children advantages of inheritance, admission to exclusive schools, and high-level contacts. Children of the immigrants also made their families the primary networks of economic and political strength. Kinship is a primary reality in many unions and in all urban political "machines." Mothers and fathers instructed their children simultaneously, "Don't trust anybody," and "The family will never let you down."

In contemporary conditions, of course, these old family methods and styles have atrophied. There is no way of going back to the past. (Not everything about the past, in any case, was attractive.) Education media help children to become sophisticated about everything but the essentials: love, fidelity, child-rearing, mutual help, care for parents and the elderly. Almost everything about mobile, impersonal, distancing life in the United States—tax policies, real-estate policies, the demands of the corporations, and even the demands of modern political forms—makes it difficult for families that feel ancient moral obligations to care for their aged, their mentally disturbed, their retarded, their needy.

It is difficult to believe that the state is a better instrument for satisfying such human needs than the family. If parents do not keep after the children to do their schoolwork, can the large, consolidated school educate? Some have great faith in state services: in orphanages, child-care centers, schools, job-training programs, and nursing homes. Some want the state to become one large centralized family. Such faith taxes credulity. Much of the popular resistance to federal child care arises from distrust of social workers and childhood engineers who would be agents of state power. Families need help in child care, but many distrust the state and the social-work establishment.

Almost everything about both "liberal" and "conservative" economic thought neglects, ignores, or injures family networks. It is not benign neglect. Millions of dollars are spent on the creation of a larger and larger state apparatus. Resources are systematically taken from the family. Is this an accident? One by one, all centers of resistance to the state are being crushed, including the strongest, family. The trend does not augur well for our liberties.

An economic order that would make the family the basic unit of social policy would touch every citizen at the nerve center of daily life. No known form of social organization weds affect to efficiency in so powerful a way. The family is the primary teacher of moral development. In the struggles and conflicts of marital life, husbands and wives learn the realism and adult practicalities of love. Through the love, stability, discipline, and laughter of parents and siblings, children learn that reality accepts them, welcomes them, invites their willingness to take risks. The family nourishes "basic trust." From this spring creativity, psychic energy, social dynamism. If infants are injured here, not all the institutions of society can put them back together. Familial arts that took generations to acquire can be lost in a single generation, can disappear for centuries. If the quality of family life deteriorates, there is no "quality of life." Again, emphasis on family life is politically important because it can unite people of diverse religious, ethnic, regional, and racial traditions. Families differ in their structures, needs and traditional inclinations; but they share many basic economic and political necessities.

A politics based on the social unit of the family would have a revolutionary impact on the sterile debate between Democrats and Republicans, and between libertarians and socialists. To strengthen the family through legislative reform is, indeed, a social intervention, but one which creates a counterpoise to the state. It is the forgotten lever of social change.

In particular, a fresh approach here promises unparalleled gains for blacks. "The repair of the black condition in America disproportionately depends upon the succor of strong families," Eleanor Holmes Norton told the Urban League in Atlanta last year. "We must make marriage and family life unabashedly a tool for improving all our lives." The stunting of black progress in America, she held, was done most effectively through tearing asunder the black family both in slavery and by discrimination. No institution, she observed, had so nourished blacks in the darkness of slavery; none had helped them to joy, laughter, and affirmation through the bitter days, as had the family. No institution is so beloved in black consciousness. None is more at the heart of social hope. "Were it not for law-enforced slavery and discrimination," she said, "our families would have thrived like most others and our time in America would have waxed into prosperity as for all other immigrant groups." She told the assembly, in sorrow, that the percentage of black households headed by women increased to 35 percent in 1975. (By the age of sixteen, two-thirds of all black children have spent some years without a father. In 1973 46 percent of all black children were born outside of wedlock.) The psychological and economic penalties, she argued, are immense. She called for a resurgence of the love and loyalty that had carried blacks in America through the centuries.

Such a call instantly makes possible alliance between the white and black working class. The families of both are in trouble; the difference in degree does not remove the similarity in root and remedy. Our media exalt the flashy, the hedonistic, the individualistic; they dwell upon the destructive orbits of the doomed: James Bond and Patty Hearst. Destruction, hustling, and defiance—one side of the Black Panthers—is picked up; the feeding of children and the nourishing of families receives no public praise. Love between a husband and wife, discipline in children, virtues of work, effort, risk, and application—these now visibly embarrass, as pornography once did. Yet these are the substance of working-class morality. They are the base of all advantage.

A Choice for Survival

Why does the preferred liberal solution for the sufferings of blacks look to every avenue of approach—school buses, affirmative action, welfare—except the family? Could it be that the family is too truly at the center, and is the one thing that liberals themselves cannot supply? That the family is the one social standing place for independence?

Economic and educational disciplines are learned only in the home and, if not there, hardly at all. Discipline in black families has been traditionally severe, very like that in white working-class families. Survival has depended on family discipline. Working-class people, white and black, cannot count on having their way; most of the time they have to be docile, agreeable, and efficient. Otherwise, they are fired. They cannot quit their jobs too often; otherwise their employment record shows instability. Blacks as well as whites survive by such rules, as long as authority in the home is strong. From here, some find the base for their mobility, up and out. Without a guiding hand, however, the temptations to work a little, quit, enjoy oneself, then work a little, are too much encouraged by one's peers on the street. *Either* the home, *or* the street: This is the moral choice. Liberals too seldom think about the economic values of strong family life; they neglect their own source of strength, and legislate for others what would never have worked for themselves.

Consider the figures for unemployment for teen-agers. The figure frequently given for blacks in New York is 40 percent. The huge number of female-run households among blacks correlates with the unemployment rates. The rough discipline of Slavic, Italian, and Irish fathers regarding the employment of their sons is an economic advantage. One of the requirements for obtaining and holding a job, especially at the unskilled level, where jobs abound, is a willingness to accept patriarchal discipline. Many young black males find such disciplines both unfamiliar and intolerable. Many will not take available jobs; many others quit.

Consider, as well, the educational preparation of black children as they leave their homes, before they enter school. Among successful blacks, patterns are like those among whites. Parents watch over their children. Books and papers are available in the home. Where the parents take education seriously, there is high probability that children will. Where the parents do not, schools cannot reasonably be expected to reach the psyches of the young. Why, then, do we habitually try to help schools, but not families? For both blacks and whites of the working class and all the more for the still more needy "underclass," the provision of books and newspapers to the home, and sessions to assist parents in teaching their children, might be more profitable than efforts in the school.

In a word, a politics aimed at strengthening families, white and black, would be a politics of unity rather than of division. It would also have higher prospect of success. The chief obstacle in its execution is the mysterious contempt liberals unthinkingly manifest toward their own greatest source of advantage.

As Jean-Paul Sartre has taught us, it is bad faith to plead "to each his own," to permit intellectual laissez-faire. Actions speak louder than shrugs of the shoulder. To marry, to have children, is to make a political statement hostile to what passes as "liberation" today. It is a statement of flesh, intelligence, and courage. It draws its strength from nature, from tradition, and from the future. Apart from millions of decisions by couples of realistic love, to bring forth children they will nourish, teach, and launch against the void, the human race has no future—no wisdom, no advance, no community, no grace.

Only the emptiness of solitary space, the dance of death.

It is the destiny of flesh and blood to be familial.

The Marriage Boom: A Nationwide Report

Ellen Sullivan

Despite the doomsaying of the past few years that the traditional marriage and family forms are passing out of existence, there is more currently equally strong evidence that some legal and binding form of marriage is on the resurgence. The family may again be undergoing the full cycle, from traditional to radical, and back again. Goode, in the opening article, suggests this is the usual course of this hardy social institution. However, some important modifications, vestiges of the recent area of experimentation, may become a permanent part of the partner relationship.

People are first living together, then marrying eventually as a pledge of increased devotion to each other. Some experts have noted that people are finding the freedom of various types of "open" marriages difficult to cope with and less rewarding than they had originally expected. Partners seem to want again the enduring and dependable relationship that they feel is enhanced by the marital state. Even the responsibilities of parenthood may regain their positive status despite the constrictions they bring to the partnership. The major emphasis today is on a deep relationship rather than romantic love, close friendship rather than sex-role stereotypes. Many young people seem once again willing to risk the marriage bond in the hope it can help them capture the personal happiness they sought so intensely in the turbulent sixties and early seventies.

Ellen Sullivan is a former staff correspondent in the Rome bureau of "Newsweek" magazine. She lives in New York and is currently a free-lance writer. This article was researched and produced with the assistance of Lanie Jones, who is currently a researcher and reporter at WNET Public Television in New York City.

Four years ago Mary Klemensky and Herschel Hicks, of New Milford, Connecticut, were remarkably like many other liberated Americans in their early 20s. As college students in the late 1960s they had joined the youthful rebellion against society. And in 1971, a few months after they met at a peace vigil protesting the war in Vietnam, they affirmed their rebelliousness by beginning to live together, defying the institution of marriage. Today Mary, a 28-year-old grammar-school teacher in New Milford, and Herschel, 29, who supervises retarded boys in a state hospital, are still typical of many liberated young Americans—they are married. On February 5, 1973, after living together for a year and a half, Mary and Herschel recited the traditional wedding vows. They were married by a Congregationalist minister and celebrated afterward with a simple supper reception in their apartment. When it was over, their friends tossed rice at the newly married couple.

"We got married to make permanent all the things we meant to each other," explains Mary. "Marriage is so much more than simply living together. We just needed to be married."

The need to be married—the ageless yearning of one woman and one man to pledge themselves to each other for life in a lawful relationship—is reasserting itself everywhere in the United States. Many may fear that the institution of marriage is withering away, but it is not. It is flourishing.

Marriage certainly did go through a rocky decade in the 1960s, as the U.S. Census showed. During those ten years the number of American men and women who lived together without being married jumped from 34,000 in 1960 to 286,000 in 1970, and it is popularly supposed that the statistics will climb again when the census is taken in 1980. But Redbook believes that this will not happen. In fact, since the early 1970s the editors have perceived a vigorous trend back to marriage, and we have been carefully watching this turnabout.

For documentation, Redbook has conducted a three-month-long scrutiny of the status of marriage in the United States today. We have completed 384 in-depth interviews with a cross section of men and women in 43 cities and towns to ascertain exactly what Americans think about marriage, and what they are doing about it.

Beyond that, Redbook has put questions to 239 of the country's leading experts in the field. We have spoken to marriage counselors, clergymen, psychologists and psychiatrists, seeking their opinions and the benefit of their experience to find out who is marrying, why they are marrying and whether our experts expect these marriages to succeed.

This report is the result of our investigation, and the findings are startling. Among them: Thousands of couples—of all ages, races, religions and social and economic strata—who a few years ago scorned the idea of marriage are marrying today legally and with ritual. And although it is expressed in myriad ways, they all are marrying for a single reason: commitment.

Commitment is the key to it all. As Barbara and Artie Prosser, of Topeka, Kansas, express it, after having been married for a year and a half and living together for two years before that: "We needed something that would add to our relationship. We had to be married." In Jackson, Mississippi, Janna and Billy Avalon recall their decision to make a permanent commitment after living together for almost a year: "We were ready to take another step." And Eunice and James Palmer, a Black couple in Atlanta who had lived together before marrying, declare that marriage is "just a more satisfying way to live."

487

Is Open Marriage a Dead End?

Even experienced marriage counselors are amazed to discover the renewed impulse to marry. The Reverend Cecil Williams, of San Francisco's ultraliberal Glide Memorial United Methodist Church, declares: "I'm so used to people not wanting to get married, objecting to marriage. People are finding now that they do want to get married, and frankly, I hadn't expected that." In Honolulu, from her vantage point as a long-time family-court referee, Naomi Campbell analyzes the phenomenon this way: "Young people who experiment with trial marriages are realizing that there is no substitute for a stable relationship between a man and a woman. That means marriage—with a certificate."

It also means that "open marriage," with extramarital sexual freedom, as well as mate swapping and communal marriages, are fast becoming passé. "A year or two ago people got excited about open marriage, but it didn't work. They couldn't handle it," says Sandra Badtke, director of the Cambridge House marriage-counseling center in Milwaukee. In Jackson, Mississippi, clinical psychologist James Baugh finds that among couples who openly agree to have affairs, "it never works out. They end up in my office." Even among the radicals in Berkeley, California, where, it is widely believed, free sex and communal marriages are still in vogue, many are planning to be married or are already married.

The Importance of Being Equal

Although people indeed are returning to marriage, many are viewing marriage itself in a way that is strikingly different from the stereotyped man-as-bread-winner, woman-as-housewife, roles of previous decades. They are consciously choosing marriage as their option; moreover, they are marrying at a mature age, as two honest and equal individuals within a partnership, melding independence with companionship. (Joyce and David Swafford, of Topeka, describe their married relationship: "We need the security of each other and the independence to be ourselves.") The majority believe that each partner should have a career, and that the wife should take time from her career building to bear and raise children. A few do not want to disrupt their way of life with children, but most would like to have one or two. And a great number believe that if both husband and wife work, they should share bills, housework and child care.

The single most important catalyst in this new view of marriage is the Women's Liberation Movement. Dr. Stuart Shapiro, a physician and a director of Boston's Cambridgeport Problem Center, where he is in touch with hundreds of couples, says flatly, "The Women's Movement is the biggest impetus for change in the marital structure. Women are seeing themselves as other than slaves in the home. They are entering the job market, and their careers are enabling them to bring more to their marriages. And as more men share in household tasks, they will bring more to marriage too."

Other marriage experts, however, are disturbed by some aspects of this new outlook on marriage. Rabbi Herbert M. Baumgard, of Miami's Temple Beth Am, is distressed to find "an increasing number of couples who are more concerned about their life-style than with perpetuating the family." In Nashville, Tennessee, Frank Neiswender, who has counseled married couples for more than 25 years, worries that, because of the Women's Movement, "the role of the woman has been changed, leaving her confused and unsure of her goal in life." And Dr. Joseph Trainer, a professor at the University of Oregon's medical school, sees men who are devastated because they feel that the Movement is making some women sexually overaggressive. "The old complaint was that the wife wasn't an adequate sex partner," he explains. "Now the reverse is true, and this is pretty tough on the men."

Nevertheless, most counselors and therapists agree that, on balance, the trend is good. Psychologist Dr. Virginia Pendergrass, a Miami leader of the National Organization for Women, believes that because of the Women's Movement "people are much more thoughtful about their reasons for getting married. The major change I see is that a woman really makes a choice now. She gets married because she wants to, not because it is the only expectation she has."

SEARCH FOR A BEST FRIEND

This exercising of the option to choose marriage thoughtfully is sweeping high schools and college campuses, manifesting itself in the increasing numbers of women who are postponing wedlock. In fact, more than 60 percent of all American women who marry now are 20 or older—a phenomenon that is growing every year, according to the Census Bureau. Largely because of the Women's Movement, "the old pressure on women to get married fast is dead," asserts University of Wisconsin guidance counselor Sally Durwald. "In high school, 'going steady' is out. Women are waking up to the alternatives." But she emphasizes that most plan to marry and to combine having families with careers.

Still other experts perceive that the Movement is generating a deeper honesty between men and women. "A lot of young people are discussing freely problems that their parents were afraid to bring up," says a Milwaukee psychologist. And the Reverend Keith Tonkel, a Methodist minister in Jackson, Mississippi, finds that men and women "are looking for more in marriage now. They're looking for a best friend."

But not all segments of the nation have felt equally the impact of the Women's Movement. In the South, as one Jackson sociologist puts it, "most girls are still terribly involved in being wives and mothers" and don't plan careers, although big Southern cities are feeling the influence of the Movement. Rural areas in many parts of the country appear barely touched by the trend toward postponing marriage. Mrs. Carolyn Collamore, society editor of the Newberg, Oregon, *Graphic,* a weekly newspaper, sees "too many" after-high-school marriages, "many more than there should be. But there aren't many interesting jobs here for young girls. And when there are only 8,000 people, what else is there besides marriage?"

Among Blacks the effect of the Women's Movement is also uneven. Overall, the Movement "has not had the same influence on Blacks as it has on the white community," notes the Reverend Matthew Gottschalk, a Catholic priest whose Milwaukee parish is about half white and half Black. But Dr. John Reid, the Black chairman of Atlanta University's sociology department, believes that because many Black women are able now to get a better education and better jobs, they too are being affected by the Movement, and are staying in the job market a long time before starting a family.

Dr. Ann Ashmore Poussaint, a Black psychologist in the Boston area, points out that working outside the home is nothing new for Black women, because traditionally they have been compelled to help support their families. But now, she says, "the Women's Movement has influenced Black women too. Younger Black women are beginning to say, 'Hey, if a man isn't meeting my needs for support, what's it all about, anyway? I can earn my own living. . . . I've had to.'" But in Milwaukee, Juanita Kelly, 31, a Black library clerk married to a detention supervisor in the city's Children's Court, says disdainfully: "Women's Liberation is for white women. Black women work because they have to. If I didn't have to work, I certainly wouldn't."

Despite such demurs, many foresee sound and enduring relationships, largely because of the Women's Movement, for those who are postponing marriage, marrying with plans for careers for both husband and wife, striving for a more honest relationship and sharing family tasks.

"DECIDEDLY UNCOOL"

Who is marrying whom these days? The vast majority of young men and women still are choosing mates from their own race and economic and social strata, but one fact leaps out of the statistics: The rate of interracial marriages is climbing fast. Dr. Robert Staples, a University of California sociologist who has done extensive analyses of interracial marriages, believes these marriages are multiplying primarily "because of racial integration in the work force and colleges, where people come together as equals and without parental influence." But he notes that interracial marriages have a far higher disaster rate than noninterracial marriages, and that those that are headed for the rocks end in divorce courts after an average of only three years.

Between Blacks and whites it is increasing numbers of Black men who are marrying white women, rather than white men who are marrying Black women. In the South both Blacks and whites frown on Black-white couples; elsewhere, disapproval is abating in white communities. With the rise of Black awareness, however, many Blacks nationwide are vehemently rejecting Black-white marriage. "The kids, especially, regard it as decidedly uncool," notes a Black professor of education.

Americans of Asian descent are marrying outside their race too. More than one fourth of all citizens of Chinese ancestry who are marrying now are marrying non-Asians. The proportion rises sharply to 50 percent among those of Japanese parentage. This is a radical change from the beginning of the 1960s, "when such marriages among Asian families in the United States were taboo," points out a sociologist of Japanese background. "Then the rate was only about fifteen percent." Similarly, in the Southwest, Americans of Mexican descent are marrying non-Mexican Americans with increasing acceptance by their neighbors. As Kay Torrez, the non-Mexican wife of a Mexican American in Phoenix, Arizona, describes the trend: "When we married, thirty years ago, everyone stared at us. Today no one thinks about it."

American Indians also are marrying outside their race. About 37 percent nationwide have non-Indian spouses, but some tribes—the Navajos, for example—remain adamantly opposed to interracial marriage. "Heck," exclaims a non-Indian woman who is an honorary member of the tribe in Arizona, "the Navajos don't even approve of marriage with other tribes!"

White interracial marriages are certainly accelerating in some areas of the country, interfaith marriages are fast outpacing them; they are skyrocketing everywhere. Jews are increasingly marrying non-Jews; about 32 percent of all Jews who married last year took non-Jewish spouses (compared with only 17.4 percent a decade ago). And Catholics are marrying Protestants at about the same rate.

It appears that the less a person cares about his or her religion, the more apt he or she is to marry outside it. "If, for example, a nonpracticing Catholic marries a nonpracticing Protestant," explains Dr. Alexander Taylor, head of the Peterson-Guedel Family Center, in Los Angeles, "the religious issue doesn't mean anything at the time. But problems erupt about which religion the children will be raised in. Ultimately you've got to make a decision about your kids."

On the other hand, if one or both partners in an interfaith marriage feel strongly about religion, the marriage is often headed for trouble. Father Kenneth Whitney, the executive director of Arizona's Episcopal Counseling Ministry, finds "more problems between strong Fundamentalists and strong Episcopalians, for instance, than between nonpracticing Catholics and nonpracticing Jews."

Lovelier the Second Time Around

Curiously, among the most compelling evidence of Americans' faith in the institution of marriage is the growing rate at which divorced people are remarrying. Today four out of every five divorced men and women will marry again. In fact, the current reappraisal of marriage accounts for many divorces—but that may not be a calamity in every case. As a family social worker in Tennessee sees it, "Women know now that they can work and live independently. They're no longer going to stay married and be miserable."

On the other hand, the reassessment of marriage also is bringing deeper fulfillment to many first-married couples and to people who remarry after divorce. Joy Marcus, San Francisco Bay-area psychotherapist, has discovered: "People now are interested in having more-meaningful relationships. They're getting it together more than they did a few years ago."

Even at the sunset end of the age spectrum, more widowed senior citizens are marrying than ever before, and more widows would like to marry but can't find new mates. "There are more older women than men," Dr. Paul Popenoe, founder of the American Institute of Family Relations, explains ruefully. "And a lot of those men want younger brides."

Among the elderly who do find love the second time around, Uncle Sam often thwarts a trip to the altar because Federal regulations would take away their separate Social Security checks and hand back a combined income hacked by as much as 40 percent. As a result, many law-abiding older citizens are forced to live together without being married. Nevertheless most retirees—like sprightly Benjamin Forbes, 101, of Lakeland, Florida, who recently married Mary Klee, 82, and jetted off on his fourth honeymoon—brave the financial hardship and reaffirm their affinity for marriage.

And the Bride Wore Shoes

Among young couples the trend in weddings is back to traditional—but simple. And there is a return to taking traditional wedding vows in front of clergymen, a ritual that many couples feel emphasizes their commitment to each other. Bizarre ceremonies are virtually a thing of the past, or, as one society-page editor puts it: "I haven't seen a barefoot bride in quite a while." One bride in Phoenix, who wore a white bridal dress and invited 150 to the wedding and reception, recalls with amazement, "Believe me, I never imagined I'd do anything like that. I always thought we would just stand in a field of flowers, say a few words to each other and that would be it." In Boston the city's leading society columnist, Rose Walsh, has made the pronouncement that: "This year the traditional is back. The bride is wearing her mother's wedding veil."

The bride also is wearing a white wedding gown, but "a lot of those dresses have to be let out because the brides are pregnant," an Arizona fashion consultant confides. The dress is also apt to be a simple one, as in Honolulu, where brides are opting for $40 white muumuus instead of lace and ruffles. In most of the South, however, expensive wedding gowns are still in favor. "It seems as though there are two things people simply won't scrimp on," one bridal-shop owner reports jubilantly. "One is a wedding dress; the other is a casket."

In the South generally, extravagant weddings with a platoon of bridesmaids and ushers remain an exception to the trend toward simplicity in other parts of the nation. "It blows my mind to see the money that's spent on weddings around here," says the Reverend Dr. Webb Howard, of Miami's Plymouth Congregational Church. Many Blacks, too, prefer big weddings, often with flower girls, ring bearers and lavish receptions. A few Black brides and bridegrooms are wearing simple African dashikis, but the luxurious wedding prevails in the Black community.

Generally bridal couples are making the celebration that follows the ceremony less elaborate. "We're doing a lot of small receptions for twenty-five to seventy-five guests," one wedding specialist notes. "People are spending much less money and doing simpler things."

A Name is a Name is a Name

Although it's back to tradition in wedding rituals, one decidedly untraditional development is the marriage contract. These documents, clearly define each partner's role, and perhaps specify that either the wife will be paid for housework or that the husband and wife will share equally in household tasks and child raising. Although there has been a great deal of talk about marraige contracts, almost no couples are writing them, and Redbook did not find any wives being paid to keep house.

In Detroit, for example, not a single couple interviewed had written a contract or even considered doing so. And as a young woman in Phoenix explained, "We decided that if we had to write a contract, it would mean we couldn't trust each other to keep our word and we had no business marrying." The experts are not unanimous in their opinions, however. Although one marriage counselor believes contracts are a "passing fad," another has found that those dealing with such practical problems as bill paying sometimes can bolster faltering marriages.

A different legal twist to the reassessment of marriage—one that emphasizes a couple's independence within their partnership—is the spreading practice among women of retaining their own last names after they marry. Surprisingly, there is no law in any state except Hawaii that stipulates a woman must take her husband's name at marriage. It is merely a custom. A few women are not adopting their husband's name at all, but many more are retaining their maiden name on drivers' licenses and checking accounts.

In a substantial number of recent marriages both partners are adopting the husband's and wife's last names as their common last name. For example, in New York, when the name-sharing trend began there about three years ago, economist Alice Tepper married John Marlin, who is also an economist; she became Alice Tepper Marlin and he became John Tepper Marlin. "We both wanted to keep our own names; yet we wanted to bestow something on each other," Alice explains. It was her husband who proposed that the two share their last names because, he says, "many women experience a closer union and identity with their husbands when they take their spouse's name. I wanted to do the same thing—in reverse."

An Old Story—With a New Ending

How is it all working out—getting married and staying married under 1975 guidelines, often with both partners working and sharing housework? And what of the important decisions that must be made about having children and raising them?

Today, two years after they were married, Mary and Herschel Hicks, of New Milford, seem content, even radiant. "Being married has helped us to work out so many problems," Mary asserts. "I don't know if we could have done it if we were just living together." In New York, Ellen and Matt Mallow feel their marriage is "symbolic of our emotional maturity, our adulthood and our commitment to each other." And in Boston Dr. Ann Ashmore Poussaint declares, "Being married is fun!"

With 43 percent of American wives working—most out of economic necessity but many because they want a career—housework is becoming an increasingly shared enterprise. As Dr. John W. Hudson, president of the American Association of Marriage and Family Counselors, says, "Many couples today don't divide household chores according to sexual stereotypes; they divide them according to competence. You see a lot of women mowing lawns now, and a lot of men scrubbing toilets." For couples like Mike and Marie Rohde, both busy reporters for the Milwaukee *Journal,* shared housework means minimal housework. "I do most of the cooking," Marie explains. "It ranges from peanut butter sandwiches to Hamburger Helper. And if the floor doesn't get washed—well, tough. We've decided that our priorities lie elsewhere."

Complete reversal of traditional roles is rare. Redbook found no husbands who intend to keep house and take care of children permanently while their wives work. Most, like Stan Williford, of Los Angeles, are willing to pitch in and divide household chores before and after children arrive. But Stan protests, "I'm no househusband. In fact, I'd probably be pretty upset if that kind of duty fell altogether on me."

Ward Shaw, of Jackson, Mississippi, is a temporary househusband. He takes care of his seven-year-old son, Leam, and manages to take a few graduate classes while his wife Susan, a social worker, supports the family. The only thing that jars him about the arrangement is hearing himself say to Leam when the boy pesters him for a treat, "Wait until your mother gets home!"

Another aspect of role reversal—the husband's quitting his job if his wife's career takes her to another city—is being talked about but it isn't being widely practiced. Some couples admit that if they had to make such a decision, it could cause a marital crisis, while others, like the Rohdes, "just try not to think about it."

As for having children, the overwhelming majority of young couples look forward to raising a family. A nationwide poll of American women conducted recently by the Roper Organization emphasized this determination: "Only one in 100 women suggests childless marriage." The same poll found that 45 percent want two children and 46 percent "favor three or more children." These findings were borne out in Redbook's interviews with couples of childbearing age. Exceptions are Jean and Bill Zehrung, 20 and 24, of New Milford, who were married in October, 1972. They declare: "We don't want any children, ever. We both plan careers."

But most couples plan instead to postpone having the children they want until they are established financially or professionally. In Honolulu, for instance, Nancy and Mike Kim explain, "As soon as we have traveled a bit and are financially set, then we'll have children—probably not more than two." In Newberg, Oregon, Shelley and Steve Cadd plan "at least two children" when Steve has finished college.

In Atlanta a young Black couple, Joan and Fred Miller, give a poignant explanation of why they want children. "Marriage is a chance to build something, and I don't think you have lived or contributed anything to the world until you have children," declares Joan. "You have the joy of seeing someone you created." Her husband adds: "My parents created me and I want to create a person too, and do my best to shape a worthwhile life."

Among Blacks who have achieved middle-class status, "the way they're looking at marriage is changing also," observes Wallene Dodson, a Black sociologist at Atlanta University. "They're looking for quality of involvement now, as well as stability." Dr. Poussaint concurs. "Our parents and grandparents married without expectation of happiness," she explains. "A woman looked for a man who would take care of her and be a father to her children, and in some ways those values were sounder.

"Happiness then was survival, making it in a white man's world," she continues. "But there's a whole new level of demand among Blacks now that involves something called 'Meet my needs.' It's a heavy demand to ask someone to make you happy."

Success: What Are the Odds?

As the nation enters the second half of the 1970s the experts examining the status of marriage in the United States predict that it has a robust future indeed. Boston feminist China Altman prophesies: "Marriage is a bedrock institution that America is going to maintain as far into the future as anyone can foresee," and a family counselor in Nashville insists that the family "will remain the basic unit of American society." The Roper poll finds that among American women, their "extreme reluctance to dispense with marriage and children . . . underscores the fact that the quest for careers and redefined roles in marriage does not indicate rejection of family life."

The president of the American Association of Marriage and Family Counselors, Dr. John Hudson, says: "People have been mourning the death of marriage for ten years, but there is nothing to substantiate that view." In Phoenix, psychologist Susan K. Palmer asserts: "People want the security and permanence of marriage. Everyone I see envisions himself or herself as being married at some point." And Los Angeles marriage counselor Dr. Alexander Taylor declares, "Marriage is very much in style, and it's going to stay in style."

In Nashville, family counselor Betty Neiswender sums it up after long reflection: "Our nation has been going through a troubled and painful time of transition in re-examining the institution of marriage. But when this period is over most marriages will be stronger and more enduring."

5-10
87-90 91-92
160-176 278-303